Every Day, Everywhere

Every Day, Everywhere

GLOBAL PERSPECTIVES ON POPULAR CULTURE

Stuart Hirschberg
Rutgers, The State University of New Jersey

Terry Hirschberg

Boston   Burr Ridge, IL   Dubuque, IA   Madison, WI   New York
San Francisco   St. Louis   Bangkok   Bogotá   Caracas   Kuala Lumpur
Lisbon   London   Madrid   Mexico City   Milan   Montreal   New Delhi
Santiago   Seoul   Singapore   Sydney   Taipei   Toronto

McGraw-Hill Higher Education

A Division of The **McGraw-Hill** Companies

4 5 6 7 8 9 0 FGR/FGR 0 9 8 7 6 5 4 3 2

Library of Congress Cataloging-in-Publication Data
    Hirschberg, Stuart.
      Every day, everywhere : global perspectives on popular culture / Stuart Hirschberg,
    Terry Hirschberg.
        p. cm.
      Includes index.
      ISBN 0-7674-1170-6
        1. Culture—Study and teaching. 2. Popular culture—Study and teaching. I. Hirschberg,
    Terry. II. Title.

    HM621 .H57 2001
    306′.071—dc21

                                                                              2001041052

Sponsoring editor, Renée Deljon; production editor, April Wells-Hayes; manuscript editor, Beverley J. DeWitt; design manager, Susan Breitbard; text and cover designer, Linda M. Robertson; art editor, Emma Ghiselli; illustrator, Gerald Bustamante; photo editor, Brian Pecko; manufacturing manager, Rich DeVitto. The text was set in 10.5/13 Jansen by Thompson Type and printed on 45# New Era Matte by Quebecor World Fairfield.

www.mhhe.com

Alavidha
Our darling cousin
Mandy Reichman
(1979–2001)
You left us much too soon

Preface

Every Day, Everywhere is a popular or common (that is, everyday) culture reader with a twist. Like its predecessors, it is rooted in the pedagogical belief that composition students do their best work when they are reading, thinking, talking, and writing about topics they're most familiar with and knowledgeable about. Unlike other popular culture readers, though, *Every Day, Everywhere* includes selections that represent global as well as American perspectives. These additional perspectives provide unique analytical writing opportunities for students, whose backgrounds are increasingly diverse, whether they are American born, immigrants to America, or temporary international residents. First and foremost, *Every Day, Everywhere*'s global perspectives provide all students with a very accessible means of recognizing the signs of their own and others' cultures. That means of easy cultural recognition is comparison and contrast, which almost automatically prompts the critical thinking that cultural analysis requires so students can successfully connect cultural signs to the cultural meanings they carry.

At the heart of this book are seventy-five reading selections and almost as many visuals, representing diverse genres, time periods, disciplines, and rhetorical aims, as well as diverse cultural perspectives. Prepublication reviewers loved the texts *Every Day, Everywhere* presents, saying that the selections would definitely engage their students, provoke critical thought, and engender interesting analytical essays. The book's selections are presented within the framework of eight familiar aspects of everyday life: food, clothing, gender roles, language, "otherness," entertainment, sports, and consumerism. Preceding and supporting these thematic chapters is a substantial but entirely student-friendly introduction to the book that includes brief introductions to culture, popular culture in particular, and cultural analysis. A full chapter of composition instruction (Chapter 1, "Critical Thinking, Reading, and Writing") follows the introduction and further supports students' work in the thematic chapters. This chapter includes sample student cultural analyses as well as a guide to analyzing visual texts, including Web pages.

OVERVIEW OF THE TEXT'S THEMATIC CHAPTERS

Chapter 2, "Food for Thought," is the first of the book's eight thematic chapters; it looks at how cultural meanings can be found in the food preferences and practices of different groups. In this chapter, students analyze topics such as the phenomenon of fast food, the significance of ethnic foods, and reasons for food-related taboos.

Chapter 3, "Cross (Cultural) Dressing," explores the meanings of various styles of clothing, both historically and in contrasting contemporary cultural contexts. Student writing in this chapter draws on sources that explore, among other topics, the meanings of the sari in India, the kimono in Japan, and the veil in Middle Eastern countries.

Chapter 4, "Gender (Mis) Representation," examines gender roles and how they shape expectations of what it means to be male or female in different cultures. In this chapter, students explore, among other topics, popular images of masculinity and femininity, the part played by race or ethnicity in concepts of gender, and how identity is shaped by gender-based restrictions.

In Chapter 5, "Language Matters," students explore language, discovering that something as seemingly self-evident as conversing is subtly conditioned by hidden cultural expectations. An analysis of the way e-mail is reshaping our everyday speech and another analysis focused on how dialect acts as a filter for the way we perceive people are among the selections included in this chapter.

Chapter 6, "Otherness," focuses on how cultures construct the "other." The readings reveal how ideas about normalcy and disability, health and disease, and "in-groups" and "out-groups" vary from culture to culture, often serving hidden cultural agendas, as well as how media depictions of the "other" and social rituals constrain those who are considered "other."

In Chapter 7, "That's Entertainment," students discover that the kinds of amusements a society prefers can reflect underlying cultural forces, and they have the chance to explore how performers serve as cultural icons, in addition to how well served American ethnic communities are by American films' representations of them.

Chapter 8, "It's All in the Game," offers some unusual perspectives on sports and games and the ideologies behind them. Students' writing in this chapter draws on multiple sources to examine the competitive ethic in American sports, how ethnicity shapes the public's perception of athletes, and the role sports play in defining national identity.

Finally, Chapter 9, "Worldly Goods," looks at the pervasive role of consumerism in U.S. culture and the methods advertisers use to sell their products. The readings examine why we buy what we do and how our possessions function in our lives. Students are asked to consider the agendas underlying America's consumer culture and to compare those agendas with the different values other societies place on material possessions.

OVERVIEW OF THE TEXT'S APPARATUS

The thematic chapters include elements designed to help students read and write critically about selections:

- Chapter-opening quotes comment on each chapter's theme.
- Chapter introductions discuss individual themes and the written and visual selections that follow.
- "Connecting the Texts" questions appear at the end of each chapter and ask students to work with one or more of the readings in the chapter.
- "Writing about [food, clothing, language, etc.]" questions, which give students a chance to write essays that could be included among the selections they've read in a given chapter, also appear at the end of each thematic chapter.

Each selection is also accompanied by several elements:

- Headnotes precede each selection and provide context for students' reading; they include information about the authors, dates, and places of original publication.
- A "Thinking Critically" question also precedes each selection to help focus students' reading.
- "Engaging the Text" questions follow each selection and prompt students to think, discuss, and write about specific sections or ideas found in the selection.
- "Exploring Your Cultural Perspective" questions also follow each selection and invite students to compare and contrast the subjects and themes of the selection with those of their own or another culture.

Finally, one type of apparatus appears at the back of the book:

- "Writing across Themes" provides essay suggestions for working with selections from more than one chapter and making connections across themes.

Individually and together, this book's questions and assignments encourage students to think critically about cultural signs—including the cultural ideas and beliefs they signify—that are discussed and analyzed in each reading. The readings and apparatus likewise encourage students to identify and analyze (in personal, expository, and argumentative essays) the myriad additional signs of culture that surround them or inform their actions and identity every day.

SUMMARY OF *EVERY DAY, EVERYWHERE*'S FEATURES

- **Seventy-five reading selections that place American popular culture in a global context.**
- **Eight high-interest, accessible themes**—Food for Thought, Cross (Cultural) Dressing, Gender (Mis) Representation, Language Matters, Otherness, That's Entertainment, It's All in the Game, and Worldly Goods.
- **A student-friendly introduction that explains the book's approach and models its analytic method.**
- **A full chapter of rhetorical instruction.** Chapter One, "Critical Thinking, Reading, and Writing," provides concise but useful instruction covering critical reading, thinking, writing, and analyzing images. It also includes sections on working with sources, boxed guides for easy reference, and numerous student models (sample annotations, a sample single-source essay, and a sample multiple-sources essay).
- **Selections representing diverse genres, time periods, disciplines, and rhetorical aims,** as well as diverse cultural perspectives. Short stories, poems, song lyrics, and a novel excerpt are interspersed among the articles and essays that represent such disciplines as ethnic studies, film studies, history, media studies, culture studies, women's studies, political science, psychology, and anthropology. The collection includes some expressive and humorous pieces as well as expository and argumentative selections.
- **Rich apparatus.** A general introduction; chapter-opening quotes and introductions; headnotes and "Thinking Critically" prompts preceding each selection; "Engaging the Text" and "Exploring Your Cultural Perspective" questions following each selection; "Connecting the Texts" and "Writing about [the chapter's topic]" questions concluding each chapter; and "Writing across Themes: Essay Suggestions" concluding the book.

- **Abundant visual texts.** Each chapter includes an average of four to six thematically related visual texts (which are incorporated into selections' accompanying apparatus).
- **An appendix, "Documenting Sources in MLA Style"; a glossary;** and alternate **tables of contents by rhetorical strategy and academic discipline.**

ANCILLARIES TO ACCOMPANY *EVERY DAY, EVERYWHERE*

- **An Instructor's Resource Manual** (written by the text's authors)
- **A custom Web site.** Organized to follow the book's chapters, this large site provides extensive links to sites whose content complements the selections in the text, as well as numerous general writing and researching resources.
- *Researching and Writing across the Disciplines,* **Second Edition** (Adams/Keene)
- *The Mayfield Quick View Guide to the Internet for Students of English, Version 2.0* (Campbell Koella/Keene)

We hope you'll take a few minutes to review the book's table of contents, which includes brief descriptions of each selection and offers a good preview of what lies ahead. We also hope you will browse among the actual chapters, sampling the selections themselves and their instructional apparatus.

ACKNOWLEDGMENTS

We are thankful to those who reviewed the manuscript and who made such constructive suggestions: Claudia Barnett, Middle Tennessee State University; Roy Bird, University of Alaska–Fairbanks; Mary M. Chavarria, Los Angeles Pierce College; Gina Claywell, Murray State University; Diane R. Crotty, University of Wisconsin–Oshkosh; Kevin Davis, East Central Oklahoma University; Michael Day, Northern Illinois University; Kathy Evertz, University of Wyoming; John Jebb, University of Delaware; Joe M. Lostracco, Austin Community College; Janice Norton, Arizona State University; Larry Silverman, Seattle Central Community College; Gordon Thomas, University of Idaho; and Mark Wollaeger, Vanderbilt University. Thanks go as well to Fred T. Courtright for obtaining the permissions.

We are grateful to the crew at Mayfield Publishing Company, to our editor, Renée Deljon, for her titanic efforts, and to our developmental editors, Rick Roehrich and Barbara Armentrout. We especially thank manuscript editor Beverley DeWitt, and most of all, April Wells-Hayes for being such a wonderful production editor of *Every Day, Everywhere*. Finally, much appreciation goes to our liaison to the youth of America, Arnold Calderón, and to our other friends at the Arthur Murray Studio for their encouragement.

Contents

6   *Otherness*   *366*

Analyzing Everyday Life

It is the way of barbarians to think of the customs of their tribe as the laws of nature.

—GEORGE BERNARD SHAW (1856–1950)

"The customs of their tribe"—what is Shaw referring to? We think he's referring to the cultures of different groups. His reference to barbarians aside, Shaw's statement about culture is clear and, we think, true. That is, cultures are many and varied; not one of them is "natural," or "according to nature." Instead, all cultures are created by humans and perpetuated by groups of people, their descendants, and others who join the group. Experts in many fields have studied the phenomenon of culture and have come to a variety of different conclusions about it. All generally agree that cultures are perpetuated unconsciously—so much so that it's possible for us to mistake what is specific to our own culture as something "natural," some sort of universal human norm.

So culture is to humans as water is to fish: we live in our native culture unaware of it until we're taken, one way or another, out of it. That is, we don't notice what's distinctive about our own culture until we encounter another one, whether by reading a book or a magazine article, logging on to a Web site, seeing a movie, talking with an international visitor or an immigrant, traveling or moving to another country, or some other way. (Sometimes, when a country is as big as the United States, all we have to do to experience cultural differences is travel to another region of our own country, or even another part of our city or community.) However it is that we encounter another culture, when we do we not only learn how things are done elsewhere but also gain a fresh perspective on our own beliefs and behaviors.

Such awareness, insight, and understanding are coming to be basic expectations of educated people, as global travel, commerce, and communication continue to shrink our world and make us all world citizens. Expanding our cultural knowledge not only raises us above the level of Shaw's "barbarians" but also gives us advantages in our personal, school, and work lives, whether it helps us understand a classmate or colleague from another country, gracefully navigate an intercultural situation, or transact an international business deal.

The readings in *Every Day, Everywhere: Global Perspectives on Popular Culture* offer opportunities for this kind of exploration and discovery. By focusing on universal aspects of everyday human life (such as clothing, food, fads, gender roles, and entertainment), the readings help bring into view the values, traditions, customs, and beliefs that govern people's behavior in different places around the world. As you read the selections and work with the questions that precede and follow them, you will find yourself learning things about other cultures as well as noticing things about American culture (or your native culture, if you or your family is from another part of the world) that may previously have been outside your awareness. The questions and writing topics will focus your attention and sharpen your critical reading, thinking, and writing skills, helping you to use the readings to their full benefit. Together, the readings, questions, and writing topics will challenge you to reflect on the differences and similarities you find; to examine your beliefs, your assumptions, and even your prejudices; to deepen and broaden your understanding of the world; and to grow as a thinker and a writer.

SEEING CULTURE, READING CULTURAL SIGNS

Let's come down to basics for a minute: What exactly is **culture**? Most broadly, the term refers to the patterns of living that are learned and shared by a social group and passed down from one generation to the next. Culture includes language; knowledge; beliefs; customs; traditions; and all the social, economic, and political forms that human beings have developed to survive in their environment. (In contrast, other animal species have survived, through evolution, by developing inheritable physical traits.) From birth onward, we learn the ways of our group or society and come to understand, at a subconscious level, the symbolic meaning of everything that our senses encounter and that we experience and do. To put it another way, our culture provides us with models or structures of understanding and interaction that guide our perceptions and define our particular version of reality, all of which we share with other members of our society or group.

Cultural anthropologist Clifford Geertz describes the phenomena of culture as "the ensemble of stories we tell ourselves about ourselves" (412). These "stories" (that is, our structures of understanding and interaction) are embodied in the formal and informal behaviors and rituals that govern everything we do, from what we wear and eat to how we interact with strangers on a bus to how we elect a president. The stories contain the "scripts" that we unconsciously rely on to live comfortably within our society, guiding us as we enact our cultural values and assumptions, just as actors rely on scripts to enact the words, intention, and vision of an author or a playwright.

In his book *Beyond Culture*, scholar Edward T. Hall describes these scripts as "deep cultural undercurrents [that] structure life in subtle but highly consistent ways that are not consciously formulated. Like the invisible jet streams that determine the course of a storm, these hidden currents shape our lives" (12). And here we return to the crucial point that, for the most part, culture is lived and perpetuated *unconsciously*. That it is perpetuated unconsciously is one of the primary challenges we face when we want to analyze or interpret some aspect of a culture: to see it, we have to look, and look hard. The question, then, is how do we "see" culture, given how predominantly unconscious and inescapable cultural stories and scripts are? How do we identify an aspect of culture and make its underlying values and assumptions visible?

One way to see culture (or *read* its underlying meaning) is to look for an aspect, or a **sign,** of culture. A **cultural sign** is anything that, when analyzed, reveals something meaningful about a culture, something about its assumptions, values, beliefs, or struggles. Just about everything is a cultural sign: objects, artifacts, events, images, sounds, gestures, actions, words, people. Like ordinary street signs, cultural signs are abundant; they surround us. Unlike street signs, though, cultural signs require critical awareness on our part—deliberate vigilance and a willingness to try to penetrate surfaces—to yield, or expose, their underlying meanings.

When we discover and read a cultural sign, we gain access to the otherwise invisible stories and scripts of a culture. The signs we notice first, as suggested earlier, are often those belonging to another culture; they provide the comparative framework within which we can then see and read the signs of our own culture. As an example, let's consider beautiful teeth and their meaning in U.S. culture.

When Croatian journalist Slavenka Drakulić was in the United States, she was struck by the sight of well-cared-for teeth everywhere she turned—on television, in movies, in magazine ads, on billboards. She noted too how much money Americans were willing to spend on electric toothbrushes, toothpaste, bleaching, capping, and expensive orthodontic braces. She writes: "As we all know, beautiful teeth are used to advertise beer, hair shampoo, cars, anything. Indeed, they are an indispensable feature of any American advertisement" (127).

In Croatia (at the time, part of communist Yugoslavia), having good teeth was not a priority, Drakulić explains; in fact, undue attention to one's personal appearance was considered selfish and decadent. Status was determined instead by political factors, particularly affiliation with the Communist Party. After the demise of communism, however, priorities changed. People began to get their teeth fixed, even before buying a new carpet—something that previously would have been unthinkable.

Drakulić claims that in the United States, good teeth "stand not only as a symbol for good looks and good health, but for something else as well": they are a sign that one is taking personal responsibility for one's life, a praiseworthy attitude in a culture that values individual effort (126). When communism failed and Croatians began replacing communal values with more individualistic ones, they started paying more attention to their personal appearance. Drakulić concludes that bad teeth are the result not only "of bad dentists and bad food, but also of a specific culture of thinking, of not seeing yourself as an individual" (134). In other words, beautiful, straight, white teeth can be seen as a cultural sign pointing to underlying beliefs about the importance of the individual and of individual responsibility. This kind of analysis and connection making is at the center of "reading" cultural signs.

The differing value placed on beautiful teeth in the United States and Croatia also illustrates the cultural relativity of signs—that is, the fact that the same sign can have different meanings in different cultures—as well as the "constructed" nature of cultures and their signs, the fact that values and beliefs are historically and collectively invented by human groups, not given to us by nature. The concept of "personal space"—proximity in conversation—which varies widely from one culture to the next, is another example of cultural relativity. In the United States, approaching someone more closely than two to four feet for social interactions is considered an intrusion. In many Middle Eastern cultures, however, people stand much closer to each other for conversation; the typical zone for social interaction is what Americans reserve for intimacy, about twelve to eighteen inches. Finding themselves nose to nose with strangers, many Americans experience great discomfort. What someone considers comfortable proximity in conversation, then, depends on (is relative to) his or her cultural background.

Public behavior is another cultural sign subject to wide variation, or relativity. In the United States, it is considered normal for heterosexual couples (though not same-sex couples) to hold hands, touch, hug, and even kiss in public. In India, kissing is considered so intimate that female film stars refuse to kiss on screen. In the Dominican Republic, public displays of affection are a ticketable offense. As another example, it is considered crude and even insulting in many countries, including Morocco and Thailand, to sit with your legs crossed so that the bottom of your shoe faces outward. Such a posture is not insulting in American culture.

What meanings do these different signs point to? What deeper cultural logic, values, or assumptions are embodied in concepts of personal space and social interaction, of gesture and posture? These are the questions the student of culture must investigate, and they are the questions addressed in *Every Day, Everywhere.* By comparing a variety of cultures—that is, through **cross-cultural analysis**—we seek to discover, examine, and interpret (in other words, to read or analyze) cultural signs, thereby heightening our awareness and critical understanding of the world as it exists today.

DISTINGUISHING "POPULAR" CULTURE FROM OTHER SUBTYPES OF CULTURE

Although the term *culture* most broadly refers to all the learned living patterns of a social group, there are also other, more specialized uses of the term. As our subtitle suggests, most of the chapter themes and reading selections in *Every Day, Everywhere* are about aspects of **popular** ("pop") **culture.** Sometimes referred to as "common" or "mass" culture, pop culture is probably best understood as the material goods, activities, and forms of communication that are part of most people's everyday lives: music, food, movies, sports, Web sites, ads, books, magazines, TV shows, videos, sports, clothes, and so on.

Maybe you have heard someone or something referred to as "an icon of popular culture." A pop culture **icon** is typically someone, some group, or something that has attracted huge audiences (or customers) and come to symbolize a historic moment, a social impulse, or a common attitude or feeling shared by a large segment of the population. Selena, the Beatles, Snoopy, the Macy's Thanksgiving Day Parade, McDonald's, Mickey Mouse, *ET, Star Wars,* Prince, James Brown, baseball caps, the Super Bowl, Elvis, Madonna, Marilyn Monroe, *The Simpsons*—all are pop culture icons. Icons achieve their status because of their ability to connect with a large group of people at a particular time. Additionally, icons endure over time, whereas **trends** or **fads** (Razor scooters, Swatch watches, platform shoes, leather clothing, the Back Street Boys) are, by definition, temporary, enduring only until they are displaced and replaced by the next "big thing." Icons and trends are mainstays of popular culture—readily available cultural signs worth "reading."

Popular culture occupies a central place within a society's **dominant,** or mainstream, **culture.** In the United States, the mainstream culture is generally understood to be white (of European descent), middle class, heterosexual, and married with children. Numerous subcultures, however, exist within any given dominant culture. **Subcultures** are ethnic, regional, economic, and social groups that "exhibit characteristic patterns of behavior sufficient to distinguish [them] within a [dominant] culture or society" ("Subculture," def. 2). Within the United States, for example, numerous subcultures are visible, whether they're legal or illegal, accepted or rejected: geek and nerd; hip-hop; punk; rave; skateboard; vampire or goth (all of the groups just listed are referred to collectively as part of "youth culture"); drug; Mafia; biker (motorcycle); senior; Young Urban Professional (Yuppy); Gen X; gay, lesbian, bisexual, transgendered (GLBT); Far-Right; Liberal; blue-collar; rural; soccer mom; and on and on. Some subcultures are considered *deviant* (they *deviate*—depart from—a society's **norms**). The term is problematic, however, because members of groups singled out as "deviant" usually don't label themselves as such, believing, instead, that their behaviors are or should be considered perfectly normal (that is, within the norm).

As you may have noticed, there can be some overlap between popular culture and subcultures. Identification with or participation in one or the other is usually a matter of degree and personal preference. Skateboarding, for instance, is both part of popular culture and a subculture. When does it stop being one and start being the other? When the person who gets caught up in the popularity of skateboarding (the trend) begins to dress the part (the long, baggy shorts, the suede shoes, the backwards baseball cap), identify her- or himself as a "skateboarder," socialize almost exclusively with others who consider themselves skateboarders, read skateboarding magazines (whether in print or online), and maybe even go to skateboard events or competitions, then that person has moved from participating in a popular cultural activity to being a member of the subculture of skateboarders.

Pop culture is most easily distinguished from **high culture,** the refined creative products of a people, their highest artistic and intellectual expressions. High culture includes creative works whose value is considered to have stood the test of time, such as the sculpture of Michelangelo or the music of Mozart. High culture tends to attract the attention of a smaller group of people (such as opera or jazz lovers) than popular culture, in part because it is generally less accessible (for various reasons, such as cost, perceived or assumed exclusivity, or specialized locations).

In contrast, popular culture, as we've mentioned, is by definition readily available—it is literally all around us. Because the themes presented in *Every Day, Everywhere* reflect aspects of everyday life that are common to all cultures, you will find subjects with which you are already familiar and about which you have significant knowledge. The reading selections—essays and articles, short fiction, and poetry—questions, and writing topics presented in each chapter will make good use of your expertise in popular culture and challenge you to apply that expertise in new and perhaps surprising ways.

AN OVERVIEW OF THE BOOK'S ORGANIZATION, THEMES, AND ASSIGNMENTS

The opening chapter of *Every Day, Everywhere*, "Critical Thinking, Reading, and Writing," offers instruction in the skills and strategies you will need to do the kind of cultural analysis the text's readings and activities call for. It also contains samples of cultural analyses done by other students.

Chapter 2, "Food for Thought," is the first of the book's eight thematic chapters; it looks at how cultural meanings can be found in the food preferences and practices of different groups. In this chapter you will analyze and interpret such topics as the phenomenon of fast food, the significance of ethnic foods, and reasons for food-related taboos.

Chapter 3, "Cross (Cultural) Dressing," explores the meanings of various styles of clothing, both historically and in contrasting contemporary cultural contexts. Your writing in this chapter will draw on sources that explore the meaning of the sari in India, the kimono in Japan, and the veil in Middle Eastern countries.

Chapter 4, "Gender (Mis)Representation," examines gender roles and how they shape expectations of what it means to be male or female in different cultures. Your writing in this chapter will explore popular images of masculinity and femininity, the part played by race or ethnicity in concepts of gender, and how identity is shaped by gender restrictions in some cultures.

In Chapter 5, "Language Matters," you may be surprised to discover that something as seemingly self-evident as conversing is subtly conditioned by hidden cultural expectations. Your writing in this chapter may include a personal narrative about how e-mail is reshaping your everyday speech, an analysis of how dialect acts as a filter for the way we perceive people, and a synthesis from multiple sources on how language determines identity.

Chapter 6, "Otherness," focuses on how cultures construct the "other." The readings reveal how ideas about normalcy and disability, health and disease, and "in-groups" and "out-groups" vary from culture to culture and often serve hidden cultural agendas. Your writing will investigate such topics as depictions of the other by the media and social rituals that constrain the other in some cultures.

In Chapter 7, "That's Entertainment!" you will discover that the kinds of amusements a society prefers can reflect underlying cultural forces. Some of the texts you will analyze (and may even argue with) explore how performers serve as cultural icons and whether the Asian community is well served by American films.

Chapter 8, "It's All in the Game," offers some unusual perspectives on sports and games and the ideologies concealed behind them. Your writing in this chapter will draw on multiple sources to examine the competitive ethic in American sports, how ethnicity shapes the public's perception of athletes, and the role sports play in defining national identity.

Finally, Chapter 9, "Worldly Goods," looks at the pervasive role of consumerism in U.S. culture and the methods advertisers use to sell their products. The readings examine why we buy what we do and how our possessions function in our lives. In your writing, you will be asked to consider the agendas underlying our consumer culture and compare them with the different values other societies place on material possessions.

The thematic chapters include several elements designed to help you read and write about the selections critically. Each chapter opens with a quote that comments, in one way or another, on the theme at hand, whether food, clothes, language, or any of the other chapter themes. A discussion of the theme and an introduction to the reading selections in the chapter follow.

Each selection is also accompanied by several elements. Preceding the selection you will find a headnote providing context for the selection, including information about the author and the date and place of original publication, as well as comments to direct your reading, called "Thinking Critically." Following the selection are two different types of questions. "Engaging the Text" questions prompt you to think, discuss, and write about specific sections or ideas found in the selection. "Exploring Your Cultural Perspective" questions invite you to compare and contrast the subjects and themes of the selection with those of your own or another culture.

At the end of each chapter are "Connecting the Texts" questions, which ask you to work with one or more of the readings in the chapter, and "Writing about . . ." questions, which give you a chance to write an essay that could itself be included in the chapter. Finally, at the back of the book, "Writing across Themes: Essay Suggestions" provides guidance for working with selections from more than one chapter and making connections across themes.

Individually and together, then, the questions and assignments encourage you to think critically about the cultural signs—and the cultural ideas and beliefs they signify—that are described in each reading. Your job is to identify and evaluate each author's underlying assumptions, relationship to his or her audience, writing strategies and use of evidence, and cultural analysis. You will have the opportunity to develop and polish your own writing in several different forms: personal narrative, expository writing (writing that explains), persuasive writing (writing that argues a point of view), and writing that relies on analysis and research.

We hope you find the selections in *Every Day, Everywhere* stimulating and challenging, and we hope you enjoy working with them to develop your reading, thinking, writing, and speaking skills. The analytical work you do here will stand you in good stead as you continue in your academic career. In addition, if you allow the global perspectives on culture that are at the heart of this text to inform your attitudes and actions, they will help you make your way as a citizen of the world in the twenty-first century. At the very least, you will not be tempted to think of the "customs of your tribe"—your native culture—as the laws of nature!

Works Cited

Drakulić, Slavenka. *Cafe Europa: Life after Communism.* New York: Norton, 1997.

Geertz, Clifford. *The Interpretation of Cultures.* New York: Basic Books, 1973.

Hall, Edward T. *Beyond Culture.* Garden City, NY: Anchor Books, 1977.

"Subculture." *Merriam Webster's Collegiate Dictionary.* 10th ed. 1996.

CHAPTER ONE

Critical Thinking, Reading, and Writing

Critical thinking and the closely related skills of critical reading and writing form the basis for being a successful student. Each skill depends on the others because much of what you write in college (and in your career) is based on your response to what others have written. In the humanities you may be asked to analyze and defend interpretations of literary texts and to write research papers and book reviews. In the social sciences you may be required to write field reports and case studies as well as research papers. In the sciences you will most often be asked to analyze and write up the data from laboratory experiments and review specialized literature in a subfield. The presentation format varies from discipline to discipline, but the essential skills of critical thinking, reading, and writing remain constant. Let's look at each skill more closely.

CRITICAL THINKING

Have you heard this bit of news (or something almost like it) or maybe received it in an e-mail?

> KFC has been a part of our American traditions for many years. Many people, day in and day out, eat at KFC religiously. Do they really know what they are eating? During a recent study of KFC done at the University of New Hampshire, they found some very upsetting facts.
>
> First of all, has anybody noticed that just recently, the company has changed their name? Kentucky Fried Chicken has become KFC. Does anybody know why? We thought the real reason was because of the "FRIED" food issue. It's not. The reason why they call it KFC is because they cannot use the word *chicken* anymore. Why? KFC does not use real

chickens. They actually use genetically manipulated organisms. These so called "chickens" are kept alive by tubes inserted into their bodies to pump blood and nutrients throughout their structure. They have no beaks, no feathers, and no feet. Their bone structure is dramatically shrunk to get more meat out of them. This is great for KFC because they do not have to pay so much for their production costs. There is no more plucking of the feathers or the removal of the beaks and feet.

   The government has told them to change all of their menus so they do not say *chicken* anywhere. If you look closely you will notice this. Listen to their commercials, I guarantee you will not see or hear the word *chicken*. (Heimbaugh)

Is this story true? Well, no. It's what is known as an urban legend (UL), a piece of gossip that has taken on a life of its own. This one seems to have started circulating by e-mail and word-of-mouth in late 1999. According to the frequently asked questions (FAQ) of an urban legend newsgroup (alt.folklore. urban), an urban legend

1. appears mysteriously and spreads spontaneously in varying forms;
2. contains elements of humor or horror (the horror often "punishes" someone who flouts society's conventions);
3. makes good storytelling;
4. does *not* have to be false, although most are. ULs often have a basis in fact, but it's their life after-the-fact (particularly in reference to the second and third points) that gives them particular interest. (van der Linden and Chan)

The KFC story seems to fit these four criteria: (1) the source was anonymous, and the story was spread by word-of-mouth and e-mail; (2) those mutant chickens are definitely an "element of horror"; (3) it is certainly a good story; and (4) if we apply a little critical thinking (and detective work on the Internet and at the library), we can discover that most of the claims made in this story are false. For example,

- the University of New Hampshire has never done a study of KFC (it has even put up a Web page, called "Kentucky Fried Chicken Hoax," to that effect <http://www.unh.edu/BoilerPlate/kfc.html>);
- Kentucky Fried Chicken changed its name to KFC in 1991, when it started selling barbecued, grilled, and roasted chicken dishes (Keegan);
- KFC does use the word *chicken* on its menus (just check out its Web site <http://www.kfc.com> or <http://www.kentuckyfriedchicken.com>).

And then, of course, there's the common-sense question of whether it would really be possible or economical to bioengineer beakless, featherless, footless, and nearly boneless chickens and keep hundreds of thousands of them alive on life-support systems. If there is any remote basis in fact for this urban legend, it might be the current concerns about experiments with genetic engineering of food products and about the safety of food at fast-food chains. (For more urban legends, see About.com's <http://urbanlegends.about.com/science/urbanlegends/mbody.htm>, the San Fernando Valley Folklore Society's <http://www.snopes2.com>, and the AFU and Urban Legends Archive <http://www.urbanlegends.com>.)

Critical Thinking about the World of Texts

As we saw with the mutant chicken story, critical thinking is the process of asking questions, forming and supporting opinions, evaluating evidence, and placing issues in a broader context. The ability to think critically can help you sift through the ever-growing amount of information designed to influence what you think, believe, and buy: the Web pages and the e-mails, the newspaper and magazine articles, the television shows, the billboards, advertising everywhere, the gossip you hear, and even the styles people are wearing and the ways they behave. All of these things are **texts** that can be **read,** or critically analyzed and interpreted.

Critical thinking is basically a two-part process: (1) analyzing a text, or carefully examining its components, and then (2) drawing some conclusions. It often starts when something strikes you as not quite believable. That's how critical thinking about an urban legend like KFC's mutant chickens gets started. You analyze, or take apart, the claims (such as the claim of a research study by the University of New Hampshire) and examine them. Then you put together the results of your examination and assess them. In the case of the story about KFC's mutant chickens, the claims don't hold up. The story isn't likely to be true.

You can use critical thinking to explore and to learn—whether it's about mutant chickens or the job market. You can also use critical thinking to solve problems—such as whether you can afford to buy a newer car or which courses next term would best further your career goals. First, you analyze the problem, or identify its separate elements. In the case of buying a car, you might note how much of a down payment you can make, how much you can afford to spend each month to pay back a car loan, and what kind of cars would be in your budget range. Then you evaluate those elements and see what solutions you come up with. For example, you might discover that the cars you can afford wouldn't be much of an improvement over what you have now, or you might discover that if you saved some extra money for six months, you could afford a used car without having to take out a loan. When you get to the point of shopping for a car and sorting out the claims about various models, you can apply the skill of critical reading, which we discuss next.

CRITICAL READING

Critical reading means systematically analyzing and responding to what you read. This process includes

- considering what you already know about the topic,
- identifying the main ideas in the text,
- locating the evidence that supports these ideas, and most importantly,
- evaluating how well the author presents them.

In addition, you must question discrepancies between what you read and what you already know or believe. Critical reading can make you aware of your own preconceptions, expectations, and biases and sometimes can cause you to change your views when the evidence warrants it.

The Process of Reading Actively and Analytically

When you read critically, you need to read selections a second and even a third time to look beyond the immediately observable features (such as the topic and the length) and gain a deeper understanding of the subordinate (or supporting) but related ideas and the underlying organization of the piece. The process of critical reading has three parts: gaining an overview of the text, reading it, and then rereading and actively analyzing it. As you read, you can annotate the text, and you can record your observations in a reading journal. Both techniques are described later in this chapter.

Critical reading requires you to enter into a "conversation" with the author—that is, a **dialogue** between yourself and the text. As in a real conversation, you are free to pose questions, ask for clarification of a point, or start your own line of reasoning in response to what you have read. You can agree or disagree, defend your point of view, and even argue as long as you interact with the text.

Critical reading also requires you to evaluate the relative strengths and weaknesses of the author's presentation and to distinguish facts from opinions. Facts (such as the repair records of various models of cars) can be verified by reference to reliable sources, whereas opinions (such as "it's a girl [or guy] car") require a well-supported argument to be persuasive. Critical reading sometimes also involves comparing what one writer says with the observations and claims of other writers.

Gain an Overview

An overview of the text will help you identify the topic and assess what you might learn from the piece before you start reading through it. You can get an overview by reading

- the title,
- any internal headings, and
- the opening and closing paragraphs.

In addition, some articles in the sciences and social sciences are preceded by abstracts that summarize the entire piece, and readings in anthologies are sometimes preceded by headnotes that include facts about the author or the selection. After you have identified the topic and the scope of the article, ask yourself what you already know about the subject (for example, standardized procedures at McDonald's restaurants) as a way of creating a frame of reference from which to understand the selection.

Read the Text for Basic Meaning and Organization

After you have considered all these elements, read the text to understand its literal meaning and to identify its **thesis** (that is, the central or controlling idea). Look for the sequence of ideas and the internal organization. Pay attention to your reactions, and note any questions you have. As you identify the various elements, also note them in the margin (see the sample annotated essay, pp. 19–24) or in a reading journal.

The organization of a piece of writing usually reflects its purpose. For example, if its purpose is to suggest how a problem might be resolved, you might reasonably expect the writer to describe the problem, explore its possible causes, and propose a solution. Or if the purpose is to persuade the audience that a particular thesis or opinion is valid, the piece is likely to use a series of examples based on research, observation, or personal experience. Other kinds of organizational strategies include chronological or spatial descriptions, comparison and contrast of two things, and process explanations.

Reread the Text, and Analyze the Rhetorical Situation

After you have read the text once to understand its literal meaning and basic structure, read it a second time to analyze how it develops and supports the central idea. Consider its **rhetorical situation** (the context for its writing) by assessing the following elements:

1. *The author.* What are the author's credentials for writing about the subject? Are they based on personal experience or professional expertise? What is the author's **attitude**—that is, his or her emotional stance— toward the topic? What is the **tone** of the piece; that is, what sense do you get of the writer's personality and his or her attitude toward the subject? How are word choice and sentence structure used to convey this tone?

2. *The audience.* Who was the original **audience**—the intended readers or viewers—for the piece? What kind of language does the author use? Is it formal? informal? technical? What **assumptions** (beliefs) does the author expect the audience to share? What level of education or previous knowledge about the subject does the author assume the audience has?

3. *The purpose.* What does the writer hope to accomplish—that is, what is the writer's **purpose**? Is he or she writing to explain something, to convey information, to persuade an audience, to express feelings, or to entertain? Most writing has more than one purpose, but one usually predominates. For example, in the sample annotated essay that follows, Judith Ortiz Cofer is explaining the various myths about Latinas, but she does so by expressing her feelings about her experiences with those myths.

4. *The occasion.* What prompted the writer to create this piece—that is, what was the **occasion** for its writing? What was happening at the time the piece was written? Where did it originally appear? For example, was it first published in an academic journal or in a popular magazine? (For a selection in an anthology, you can often find this information in the headnote or in the list of permissions, usually in the back of the book.)

5. *The topic.* What do you, the reader, know about the **topic**—that is, the subject of the piece? What opinions do you already have about it? What assumptions are you making about it, especially if it is an unfamiliar topic? Do you expect to be bored or interested? Do you expect that you will understand the essay easily or that you will have to work at it?

How to Analyze an Argument

Some pieces of writing specifically attempt to change the readers' thinking or to get them to take a new course of action. The basic structure of an **argument** is (1) the statement of an opinion and (2) the presentation of one or more reasons to support that opinion. (Note that here the word *argument* does not mean a quarrel but rather an attempt to prove a point through reasoning.) To analyze an argument, you must consider not only the elements of the rhetorical situation listed above but also how the argument anticipates readers' reactions and what kinds of support it uses.

Does the Argument Acknowledge Other Points of View?

Arguments are more persuasive when they try to take into account readers' prior knowledge, beliefs, and values and their probable reactions to the argument. Sometimes writers try to establish common ground with readers, presenting the argument in the spirit of a mutual search for the best information to support the claim. Sometimes they try to anticipate readers' objections by objectively summarizing their positions while pointing out weaknesses in the opposing viewpoints. Writers who seek to identify the likely causes or probable consequences of something should be sure to consider alternative explanations. If the argument suggests a course of action, it should be objective about other solutions to the problem.

Does the Argument Use Appeals of Logos, Ethos, and Pathos?

The most persuasive arguments appeal to the "whole person"—to the intellect, the conscience, and the emotions. They use various combinations of logical appeals, ethical appeals, and emotional appeals to win over the audience. Scientific arguments (such as those scientists make in behalf of their research findings) use predominantly logical appeals, whereas advertisements (which are a kind of argument) often use predominantly emotional appeals.

Logos, or an appeal to logic, is based on sound evidence and reasoning. The next main section of this chapter, "Critical Writing," discusses the reliability of sources of evidence (pp. 26–49). Examples of some common logical fallacies, or unsound reasoning, are listed in "Is the Chain of Reasoning Sound?" which follows. Sometimes the chain of reasoning in an argument is explicitly stated, but at other times, unstated assumptions link that chain, and readers will need to fill those gaps.

Ethos, or an appeal based on the writer's (or spokesperson's) expertise or reputation, is the reason why Steve Young is hired to advertise Toyotas or Tiger Woods to advertise Nike sports gear. Acknowledgment of opposing views, as discussed in the preceding section, is also about ethos. In addition, value judgments (that something is good or bad according to a specified standard) should be supported with clearly defined ethical or moral criteria.

The third type of appeal, **pathos,** is an appeal to the emotions. For example, an article supporting the installation of a stoplight at a busy intersection or the cleanup of a toxic dump near a school would be likely to start with the story of someone who was injured at the intersection or someone whose health was endangered by toxic fumes from the dump. Pathos is also used frequently in advertisements. If pathos is the only type of appeal an argument uses, however, it is a faulty argument.

Is the Chain of Reasoning Sound?

In addition to analyzing the kinds of appeals in an argument, you need to consider the soundness of the reasoning. Among the dozens of different kinds of logical fallacies, here are some of the most common:

- *Ad hominem* (Latin for "to the man") fallacies attack a person rather than address the issues. For example, a common comment about some of the candidates during the 2000 Presidential primaries and campaign was "I'm not voting for him because he's too boring and stiff." Many political cartoons are also based on ad hominen fallacies.

- *Begging the question* means that part of the conclusion is already assumed to be true and does not need to be proved. An example is businessman Ivan Boesky's advice to a graduating class: "Greed is all right. . . . Greed is healthy. You can be greedy and still feel good about yourself."

- An *either-or* fallacy assumes that there are only two solutions or alternatives to a problem. An example is Kurt Cobain's line from "Stay Away" (1991): "I'd rather be dead than cool."

- A *false analogy* is based on the assumption that two things that are similar in one way must be similar in many ways. This fallacy is one of the reasons why producers make so many sequels of hit movies and spin-offs of popular TV shows in the hope that they will be as successful as the original movie or TV show.

- A *false cause* fallacy (also known as *post hoc, ergo propter hoc*) is a mistaken assumption that when one event happens after another, the earlier event must have caused the later one. An example is the assumption that, given a choice, little girls will play with dolls and little boys will play with trucks because those preferences are in their genes. This fallacy also characterizes many superstitions.

- A *hasty* (or *sweeping*) *generalization* is a conclusion based on too little evidence. For example, if you know one accountant who is boring and conclude that all accountants are boring, you are making a hasty (or sweeping) generalization.

- A *non sequitur* is a statement that does not logically follow from a preceding one. An example is Black Panther H. Rap Brown's assertion at a 1967 press conference: "I say violence is necessary. It is as American as apple pie."

- A *red herring* is irrelevant evidence intended to divert attention from the real issue at hand. An example is commentator Rush Limbaugh's response to news that dolphins may be almost as intelligent as humans: "Could somebody please show me one hospital built by a dolphin? Could somebody show me one highway built by a dolphin? Could someone show me one automobile invented by a dolphin?"

- A *slippery slope* is the false assumption that if one event is allowed to happen, a series of ever more undesirable events will follow. For example, in1901 Henry T. Fink, writing in *The Independent*, forecast dire consequences if women were given the vote: "Woman's participation in political life . . . would involve the domestic calamity of a deserted home and the loss of the womanly qualities for which refined men adore women and marry them."

Tools for Critical Reading

As you read and reread a text to grasp its meaning and to understand its rhetorical context, you should make notes about what you discover and any questions you have. Those notes can go right on the pages of the text, or they can go in a reading journal. Later, you can draw on them when you write a paper about the text.

Text Annotations

Annotations create a dialogue between you and the writer. By asking questions and making observations about meaning and structure in the margins, you can better understand what you are reading. There are as many styles of annotating as there are readers; you will develop your own after some practice. In the meantime, here are some suggestions for annotating a text:

- Write your responses to the author's ideas in the margin. Use the margin to create a conversation with the author. Ask questions. Agree or disagree with points the author makes.
- Identify central ideas expressed in the title, the headings (if there are any), and the introductory and concluding paragraphs.
- When you locate the thesis (the central claim or assertion that the text develops), underline it. If the thesis is not stated in so many words, compose an explicit version and write it at the top or bottom of the first or last page (see the sample annotated essay that follows for an example). Sometimes writers place the thesis in the first paragraph to help readers perceive the relationship between the supporting evidence and this main idea. At other times, in essays that are exploring an idea rather than arguing a point, the thesis may not become clear until the end of the piece.
- Identify examples, statistics, quotations from authorities, comparisons, visual features (such as charts, graphs, and tables), and other evidence that supports or clarifies the primary assertions.
- Look up unfamiliar words, and write their definitions in the margin.

- Note transitional words and phrases that show relationships between ideas. These **transitions** may express chronological relationships (*now, when, before, after*) or causal relationships (*because, therefore*), or they may signal additional information (*furthermore, moreover*) or qualifying information (*although, however*).

You can see how this process works in the sample annotation of Judith Ortiz Cofer's essay "The Myth of the Latin Woman" that follows.

Sample Annotated Essay

JUDITH ORTIZ COFER

The Myth of the Latin Woman: I Just Met a Girl Named María

> What is "the myth"? Is it defined?

On a bus trip to London from Oxford University where I was earning some graduate credits one summer, a young man, obviously fresh from a pub, spotted me and as if struck by inspiration went down on his knees in the aisle. With both hands over his heart he broke into an Irish tenor's rendition of "María" from *West Side Story*. My politely amused fellow passengers gave his <u>lovely</u> voice the round of <u>gentle</u> applause it deserved. Though I was not quite as amused, I managed my version of an English smile: no show of teeth, no extreme contortions of the facial muscles—I was at this time of my life practicing reserve and cool. Oh, that British control, how I coveted it. But María had followed me to London, reminding me of a prime fact of my life: <u>you can leave the Island, master the English language, and travel as far as you can, but if you are a Latina, especially one like me who so obviously belongs to Rita Moreno's gene pool, the Island travels with you.</u>

> Example supporting thesis

> Sarcasm?

> Thesis?

1

This is sometimes a very good thing—it may win you that extra minute of someone's attention. But with some people, the same things can make *you* an island—not so much a tropical paradise as an Alcatraz, a place nobody wants to visit. As a Puerto Rican girl growing up in the United States and wanting like most children to "belong," I resented <u>the stereotype that my Hispanic appearance called forth from many people I met.</u>

> Metaphor with two contrasting meanings

> Part of thesis?

Our family lived in a large urban center in New Jersey during the sixties, where life was designed as a (microcosm) of my parents' (casas) on the island. We spoke in Spanish, we ate Puerto Rican food bought at the (bodega,) and we practiced strict Catholicism complete with Saturday confession and Sunday mass at a church where our parents were accommodated into a one-hour Spanish mass slot, performed by a Chinese priest trained as a missionary for Latin America.

> = miniature model of something

> = houses

> = grocery store

As a girl I was kept under strict surveillance, since virtue and modesty were, by cultural equation, the same as family honor. As a teenager I was instructed on how to behave as a proper señorita. But it was a conflicting message girls got, since the Puerto Rican mothers also encouraged their daughters to look and act like women and to dress in clothes our Anglo friends and their mothers found too "mature" for our age. It was, and is, cultural, yet I often felt humiliated when I appeared at an American friend's party wearing a dress more suitable to a semiformal than to a playroom birthday celebration. At Puerto Rican festivities, neither the music nor the colors we wore could be too loud. I still experience a vague sense of letdown when I'm invited to a "party" and it turns out to be a marathon conversation in hushed tones rather than a fiesta with salsa, laughter, and dancing—the kind of celebration I remember from my childhood.

5   I remember Career Day in our high school, when teachers told us to come dressed as if for a job interview. It quickly became obvious that to the barrio girls, "dressing up" sometimes meant wearing ornate jewelry and clothing that would be more appropriate (by mainstream standards) for the company Christmas party than as daily office attire. That morning I had agonized in front of my closet, trying to figure out what a "career girl" would wear because, essentially, except for Marlo Thomas on TV, I had no models on which to base my decision. I knew how to dress for school: at the Catholic school I attended we all wore uniforms; I knew how to dress for Sunday mass, and I knew what dresses to wear for parties at my relatives' homes. Though I do not recall the precise details of my Career Day outfit, it must have been a composite of the above choices. But I remember a comment my friend (an Italian-American) made in later years that coalesced my impressions of that day. She said that at the business school she was attending the Puerto Rican girls always stood out for wearing "everything at once." She meant, of course, too much jewelry, too many accessories. On that day at school, we were simply made the negative models by the nuns who were themselves not credible fashion experts to any of us. But it was painfully obvious to me that to the others, in their tailored skirts and silk blouses, we must have seemed "hopeless" and "vulgar." Though I now know that most adolescents feel out of step much of the time, I also know that for the Puerto Rican girls of my generation that sense was intensified. The way our teachers and classmates looked at us that day in school was just a taste of the culture clash that awaited us in the real world, where prospective employers and men on the street would often misinterpret our tight skirts and jingling bracelets as a come-on.

Margin notes:

What's the author's attitude to these contrasts?

= young woman

= Puerto Rican neighborhood

Mainstream = positive models

Puerto Rican women = negative models for Anglo students

"Text" of Puerto Rican style misunderstood by Anglos

Personal experience with stereotype

Why weren't teachers models?

A universal experience— so true!

Mixed cultural signals have perpetuated certain stereotypes—for example, that of the Hispanic woman as the "Hot Tamale" or sexual firebrand. It is a one-dimensional view that the media have found easy to promote. In their special vocabulary, advertisers have designated "sizzling" and "smoldering" as the adjectives of choice for describing not only the foods but also the women of Latin America. From conversations in my house I recall hearing about the harassment that Puerto Rican women endured in factories where the "boss men" talked to them as if sexual innuendo was all they understood and, worse, often gave them the choice of submitting to advances or being fired.

It is custom, however, not chromosomes, that leads us to choose scarlet over pale pink. As young girls, we were influenced in our decisions about clothes and colors by the women—older sisters and mothers who had grown up on a tropical island where the natural environment was a riot of primary colors, where showing your skin was one way to keep cool as well as to look sexy. Most important of all, on the island, women perhaps felt freer to dress and move more provocatively, since, in most cases, they were protected by the traditions, mores, and laws of a Spanish/Catholic system of morality and machismo whose main rule was: *You may look at my sister, but if you touch her I will kill you.* The extended family and church structure could provide a young woman with a circle of safety in her small pueblo on the island; if a man "wronged" a girl, everyone would close in to save her family honor.

This is what I have gleaned from my discussions as an adult with older Puerto Rican women. They have told me about dressing in their best party clothes on Saturday nights and going to the town's plaza to promenade with their girlfriends in front of the boys they liked. The males were thus given an opportunity to admire the women and to express their admiration in the form of *piropos:* erotically charged street poems they composed on the spot. I have been subjected to a few piropos while visiting the Island, and they can be outrageous, although custom dictates that they must never cross into obscenity. This ritual, as I understand it, also entails a show of studied indifference on the woman's part; if she is "decent," she must not acknowledge the man's impassioned words. So I do understand how things can be lost in translation. When a Puerto Rican girl dressed in her idea of what is attractive meets a man from the mainstream culture who has been trained to react to certain types of clothing as a sexual signal, a clash is likely to take place. The line I first heard based on the aspect of the myth happened when the boy who took me to my first formal dance leaned over to plant a sloppy overeager kiss painfully on my mouth, and when I didn't respond with sufficient passion said in a

---

Marginal notes:

Examples of other myths of Latinas used by media

= culture, not biology

Puerto Rican women = positive models for Puerto Rican girls

Compare to "tropical paradise" in para. 2

Contrast "small pueblo" to "large urban center in New Jersey" in para. 3 and men on the street at end of para. 5

= village

Reason why she knows about life on the island

A more specific way to describe thesis?

Compare to "English smile" in para. 1

Was she angry? embarrassed?

Personal experience supporting thesis

resentful tone: "I thought you Latin girls were supposed to mature early"—my first instance of being thought of as a fruit or vegetable—I was supposed to *ripen*, not just grow into womanhood like other girls.

Stereotype makes "other" different from mainstream

It is surprising to some of my professional friends that some people, including those who should know better, still put others "in their place." Though rarer, these incidents are still commonplace in my life. It happened to me most recently during a stay at a very classy metropolitan hotel favored by young professional couples for their weddings. Late one evening after the theater, as I walked toward my room with my colleague (a woman with whom I was coordinating an arts program), a middle-aged man in a tuxedo, a young girl in satin and lace on his arm, stepped directly into our path. With his champagne glass extended toward me, he exclaimed, "Evita!"

Personal experience supporting thesis

10

Why did girl say this?

Popular song of the '50s

Why did girl want Cofer to laugh?

Good way to express what a stereotype is

Our way blocked, my companion and I listened as the man half-recited, half-bellowed "Don't Cry for Me, Argentina." When he finished, the young girl said: "How about a round of applause for my daddy?" We complied, hoping this would bring the silly spectacle to a close. I was becoming aware that our little group was attracting the attention of the other guests. "Daddy" must have perceived this too, and he once more barred the way as we tried to walk past him. He began to shout-sing a ditty to the tune of "La Bamba"—except the lyrics were about a girl named María whose exploits all rhymed with her name and gonorrhea. The girl kept saying "Oh, Daddy" and looking at me with pleading eyes. She wanted me to laugh along with the others. My companion and I stood silently waiting for the man to end his offensive song. When he finished, I looked not at him but at his daughter. I advised her calmly never to ask her father what he had done in the army. Then I walked between them and to my room. My friend complimented me on my cool handling of the situation. I confessed to her that I really had wanted to push the jerk into the swimming pool. I knew that this same man—probably a corporate executive, well educated, even worldly by most standards—would not have been likely to regale a white woman with a dirty song in public. He would perhaps have checked his impulse by assuming that she could be somebody's wife or mother, or at least *somebody* who might take offense. But to him, I was just an Evita or a María: merely a character in his cartoon-populated universe.

Musical and movie about wife of former Argentinian president

What did she mean by this?

Is this true? Or would he be obnoxious to any woman?

Because of my education and my proficiency with the English language, I have acquired many mechanisms for dealing with the anger I experience. This was not true for my parents, nor is it true for the many Latin women working at menial jobs who must put up with stereotypes about our ethnic group such as: "They make

Para. 13 is example of one mechanism

good domestics." This is another facet of the <u>myth of the Latin woman</u> in the United States. Its origin is simple to deduce. Work as domestics, waitressing, and factory jobs are all that's available to women with little English and few skills. The myth of the Hispanic menial has been sustained by the same media phenomenon that made "Mammy" from *Gone with the Wind* America's idea of the black woman for generations; María, the housemaid or counter girl, is now indelibly etched into the national psyche. The big and the little screens have presented us with the picture of the funny Hispanic maid, mispronouncing words and cooking up a spicy storm in a shiny California kitchen.

This media-engendered image of the Latina in the United States has been documented by feminist Hispanic scholars, who claim that such portrayals are partially responsible for the denial of opportunities for upward mobility among Latinas in the professions. I have a Chicana friend working on a Ph.D. in philosophy at a major university. She says her doctor still shakes his head in puzzled amazement at all the "big words" she uses. Since I do not wear my diplomas around my neck for all to see, I too have on occasion been sent to that "kitchen," where some think I obviously belong.

One such incident that has stayed with me, though I recognize it as a minor offense, happened on the day of my first public poetry reading. It took place in Miami in a boat-restaurant where we were having lunch before the event. I was nervous and excited as I walked in with my notebook in my hand. An older woman motioned me to her table. Thinking (foolish me) that she wanted me to autograph a copy of my brand new slender volume of verse, I went over. She ordered a cup of coffee from me, assuming that I was the waitress. Easy enough to mistake my poems for menus, I suppose. I know that it wasn't an intentional act of cruelty, yet of all the good things that happened that day, I remember that scene most clearly, because it reminded me of <u>what I had to overcome before anyone would take me seriously.</u> In retrospect I understand that my anger gave my reading fire, that I have almost always taken doubts in my abilities as a challenge—and that the result is, most times, a feeling of satisfaction at having won a convert when I see the cold, appraising eyes warm to my words, the body language change, the smile that indicates that I have opened some avenue for communication. That day I read to that woman and her lowered eyes told me that she was embarrassed at her little faux pas, and when I willed her to look up at me, it was my victory, and she graciously allowed me to punish her with my full attention. We shook hands at the end of the reading, and I never saw her again. She has probably forgotten the whole thing but maybe not.

Margin annotations:

This is the title

Stereotype of Latinas compared to black women

Role of media again

Scholarly research to support thesis

Sounds angry

Personal experience that supports thesis

Consequence of the myth

Interesting choice of words

Why doesn't she give any examples of harsher forms of prejudice?

Yet I am one of the lucky ones. My parents made it possible for me to acquire a stronger footing in the mainstream culture by giving me the chance at an education. And books and art have saved me from the harsher forms of ethnic and racial prejudice that many of my Hispanic (compañeras) have had to endure. I travel a lot   *= women friends* around the United States, reading from my books of poetry and my novel, and the reception I most often receive is one of positive interest by people who want to know more about my culture. There are, however, thousands of Latinas without the privilege of an education or the entrée into society that I have. For them life is a struggle against the misconceptions perpetuated by the myth of   *Thesis?* the Latina as whore, domestic, or criminal. We cannot change this

Call for change

by legislating the way people look at us. The transformation, as I see it, has to occur at a much more individual level. My personal goal in my public life is to try to replace the old pervasive stereotypes and myths about Latinas with a much more interesting set of realities. Every time I give a reading, I hope the stories I tell, the dreams and fears I examine in my work, can achieve some uni-   *Goal = to overcome stereotype through art* versal truth which will get my audience past the particulars of my skin color, my accent, or my clothes.

15

I once wrote a poem in which I called us Latinas "God's brown daughters." This poem is really a prayer of sorts, offered upward, but also, through the human-to-human channel of art, outward. It is a prayer for communication, and for respect. In it,   *Is poem example of her goal in para. 14?* Latin women pray "in Spanish to an Anglo God / with a Jewish heritage," and they are "fervently hoping / that if not omnipotent, / at least He be bilingual."

Thesis: Women who appear Latina because of their skin color, accent, or clothes have to struggle "against the misconceptions perpetuated by the myth of the Latina as whore, domestic, or criminal."

Reading Journals

In addition to annotating the text, you can jot down your thoughts, questions, and impressions in a reading journal. For example, you could use your journal to list the facets of the myth of the Latin woman described in Judith Ortiz Cofer's essay. You can also use your journal to record short summaries of pieces you read (for hints, see the box "Writing a Summary"). A reading journal can serve as a storehouse from which to draw for your own writing. In fact, some instructors may require you to hand in your reading journal with your drafts and final paper.

If a reading journal is part of the required work for your class, the instructor may specify particular topics for the entries. If not, here are some suggestions for journal entries about reading selections:

- Take notes during the class discussion. Afterward, respond to a comment by your instructor or another student.

WRITING A SUMMARY

A summary condenses the original source, restating its main ideas and distinguishing them from the supporting details. You can summarize at any time, but it is most effective to do it after a full and careful reading.

To summarize an essay, compose a sentence or two that expresses the essential idea of each paragraph or of each group of related paragraphs in your own words. Your annotations and underlining of topic sentences, main ideas, and supporting evidence (as part of the process of critical reading) will help you follow the author's line of thought. Next, whittle down this list by eliminating repetitive ideas. Then formulate a clear statement that objectively expresses the main idea in the article. Begin your summary with this statement, and combine your notes so that the summary flows together and reads easily.

Summaries are by definition brief and should accurately reflect the central ideas of the text in as few words as possible. Try not to interject your own opinions or critical evaluations into the summary. The test of a good summary is whether someone who has not read the original text can get an accurate idea of its content.

Notice that, in the following example of a summary, the first sentence contains the author's name, title of the work, and main point of the text.

Sample Summary

> In "The Myth of the Latin Woman: I Just Met a Girl Named María," Judith Ortiz Cofer relates how, although she is highly educated and is an acclaimed writer, she is still treated according to the stereotypes of Latinas. Cofer, who is Puerto Rican, describes how her Hispanic appearance provokes inappropriate responses from people who should know better and would never treat a white woman as a "hot tamale" or assume she was a menial worker. She attributes these misunderstandings between cultures to the different codes that govern behavior and clothing in Puerto Rico and on the U.S. mainland and to media stereotyping of minorities.

- Write about a question you had while you were reading the text. Explain the reasons for your questions, and discuss whether a rereading of the text answered it.

- Write about why you agree or disagree with a point the author made.

- Explain why you can or can't identify with a particular character or situation in the reading selection.

- Write a letter to the author asking questions or making comments about the work.

- Copy a phrase or a sentence from the reading selection that seemed particularly memorable or particularly puzzling, and discuss your response to it.

CRITICAL WRITING

Critical writing is based on critical thinking and critical reading. You have to ask questions, analyze one or more sources about a topic, and draw conclusions. In college, critical-writing assignments usually entail analyzing a single source or analyzing and then synthesizing two or more sources.

In an analytical essay (the kind you will write for the "Engaging the Text" exercises at the end of each reading), you evaluate the text according to a set of standards, which may be general (such as use of evidence, clarity of presentation, absence of **bias,** or preconceived opinion) or specific to a particular field of study or discipline (such as history, economics, political science, women's studies, anthropology, biology). When you write an analytical essay, you move beyond your personal reactions and base your writing on the information you have gained from a critical reading of the source. Once you have identified the thesis, supporting points, types of evidence, chain of reasoning, overall organization, and style, you are ready to begin to form conclusions about the text. An analytical essay can address such topics as

1. the organization (the order in which ideas, topics, and issues are discussed),
2. the style (sentence structure, word choice, use of figurative language),
3. the author's attitude toward the topic (the tone adopted), and
4. the validity and **objectivity** (lack of bias) of the evidence and supporting materials.

An essay based on two or more sources (the kind you will write for the "Connecting the Texts" exercises at the end of each chapter) needs to consider some additional questions such as these:

1. Does one reading or source reinforce or contradict another?
2. Do the readings represent entirely different points of view without opposing each other?
3. What additional insight might a third source or even a fourth add to the analysis?

Preliminary Questions about the Rhetorical Situation

To spend your time more efficiently on a writing project, no matter what kind it is, you need to start by thinking about its **context,** or the rhetorical situation (which we explored from the reader's perspective in the discussion of critical reading).

1. What is the assigned topic, if there is one? What is the assigned length? How much time do you have to complete the paper?

2. What do you already know about the topic? What more do you need to find out? What sources might you use?

3. Who is the audience? In college courses, it may be the instructor, other students, or an unspecified general audience. How much does the audience know about your topic? How much background information will you need to provide? For example, if not everyone in your audience has read the source you are analyzing, you may have to describe it in more detail than if everyone is familiar with it.

4. What is your purpose? The most basic purposes of writing are to convey information (expository writing), to argue for the acceptance of an idea or interpretation (persuasive writing), or to express personal feelings or to entertain (expressive writing). Many of the selections in this book combine all three purposes, but most of your writing for college classes will be expository or persuasive—or a combination of the two.

The Process of Writing Critically

Writing critically requires planning, organizing, rethinking, reorganizing (sometimes), and polishing. It is very different from zipping off a quick e-mail—and the result is very different too. We will consider the four parts of the process—prewriting and planning, drafting, revision, and proofreading—one by one, but you may need to return to some parts more than once. For example, as you draft your paper, you might discover that you have taken on too big a topic, so you need to revisit your invention strategies and see how you can narrow the topic. Or as you are revising, you might see that your introductory paragraph no longer works, so you need to redraft it. After we describe the four basic elements of the critical-writing process, we will discuss how to use sources for critical writing.

Prewriting and Planning

Prewriting is a little like batting practice before stepping up to the plate. It is the process of finding your thesis and exploring how best to support it.

Invention Strategies   Invention, or prewriting, strategies help you discover ideas and explore them in an informal way. (These strategies can also help you at any point in the writing process when you feel you have run into a dead end.) We describe three of the most common strategies here: freewriting, the five

W's, and mapping (or clustering). These strategies are more than simple lists of ideas; they can help you discover connections between ideas.

Freewriting   Freewriting is setting down whatever occurs to you on a topic within a few minutes. There are no restrictions on what you can or cannot put down. Don't worry about using complete sentences, and don't worry about spelling, punctuation, or grammar. Write without stopping to edit or correct. You will find you are more creative when you simply free-associate without stopping to censor, evaluate, or edit your thoughts.

As an example, here is a student's freewriting based on Neil Postman and Steve Powers' essay "TV News as Entertainment," which appears in Chapter 7, "That's Entertainment!":

> Why is there so much trash on television, including the news? Gruesome scenes of destruction and violence and intrusion into people's private lives.
>
> Ratings govern what gets on the air. People want to be entertained, not informed.
>
> TV needs exciting visual images and special effects and not many words.
>
> Compare current news broadcasts and talk shows to those of earlier times.

The Five W's   Write down your topic, and then ask yourself the questions that journalists often use to find out about a subject:

1. *Who* is involved?
2. *What* is it?
3. *Where* did it happen?
4. *When* did it happen?
5. *Why* did it happen?

Although these questions are not useful for every topic, they can sometimes reveal new information or a new perspective.

Mapping   Mapping (also called clustering) is a prewriting strategy that allows you to visually perceive the relationship between ideas. Begin by writing the word or phrase that represents the starting point (as the phrase "current news broadcasts" does in Figure 1.1) in the center of the page and drawing a circle around it. Jot down related ideas, topics, or details around this main idea, and connect them to the main idea and to one another with lines to represent the

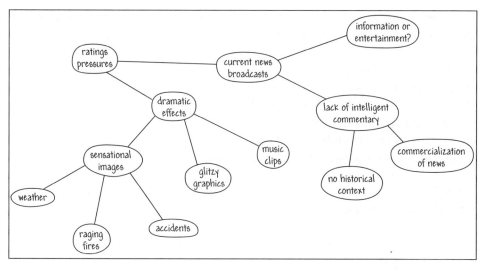

FIGURE 1.1

relationships between them. When you group ideas in this way, you discover a map, or cluster, of ideas and patterns that will help you decide which ideas are central and which are subordinate. This strategy can help you narrow your topic and see details and examples that you can use to support your thesis.

In the map shown in Figure 1.1, the student began with the subject of "current news broadcasts" and discovered the more specific topic of how "dramatic effects" are used on news shows to capture viewers' attention.

Identifying Your Thesis   As you explore and narrow your topic with invention strategies such as those just described, you may also discover a thesis for your paper (although you may decide to alter it as you continue writing). In an analytical essay, a thesis is a sentence or two that identifies the paper's topic and the author's opinion about it or approach to it; the thesis can also indicate the author's purpose and establish the tone. It may take several tries to come up with a workable thesis, but once it is formulated, you can use it as a way to test the relevance and effectiveness of the evidence and the conclusion.

The thesis is a type of contract or promise; it tells readers what to expect. For example, consider this thesis statement that a student composed for a rough draft of her paper about the reading that was annotated earlier in this chapter:

> In "The Myth of the Latin Woman: I Just Met a Girl Named María," Judith Ortiz Cofer refutes the "María" stereotype by creating an impression of herself as an articulate and accomplished Latina.

This example of a trial thesis (which may be revised as the paper takes shape) contains the title of the original essay, the author's name, and the student's main or primary assertion, stated as a single sentence. This thesis obligates the student to

1. define the "María" stereotype and explain why Cofer finds it demeaning,
2. show specifically how Cofer creates "an impression of herself as an articulate and accomplished Latina," and
3. show how Cofer uses stylistic techniques to persuade her audience.

Each of these three ideas can then be developed in paragraphs or sections of the paper. You can create an informal outline to explore the insights expressed in your thesis. An informal outline can help you identify the key ideas you will develop in each section and the kind of evidence that will support these ideas.

An analytical essay does not have to take apart every single aspect of the original essay. You need to be selective and discuss only those elements that support your thesis, or main assertion. After formulating a thesis that expresses your evaluation of the text, you need to be able to refer to specific passages in the text to support your thesis. You do this by summarizing, paraphrasing, and quoting these passages as evidence to illustrate and support your judgment. (We will describe these techniques shortly, in the section "Providing Evidence from Sources.")

Drafting

The process of writing more than one draft is at the heart of what writers do. It is how they explore, develop, and refine the ideas they generate during prewriting and planning.

The main purpose of your first draft is to get all your ideas down on paper. To start your first draft, review your purpose, your audience, and your topic; look through your reading journal and your annotations; and think about what your thesis might be. Then begin writing as quickly as you can, without worrying about diction or spelling (which are concerns for the revision and proofreading stages). You don't necessarily have to write the paragraphs in order; if some paragraphs or ideas come more readily than others, write those first and come back to the others later. A draft is not carved in stone and can be changed many times.

While you read through your first draft, try to see how it might look to a reader. If you didn't already know what you meant, would you be able to understand your ideas from the words on the page? (A peer review of your writing at this point can be helpful.) If some of the ideas are not clear, would a change in the order of presentation make them clearer? Which of the ideas needs additional explanation or more supporting evidence?

In your next draft you can try out different organizational arrangements and, if necessary, use invention strategies to think of additional supporting evidence. It can also be helpful to review each paragraph (or section) of the draft to see whether it supports your thesis. You might discover that information you assumed was essential is in fact extraneous, or you might see discarded ideas in a new light.

Writing the Introduction   Sometimes writers find it helpful to compose the introduction first, informing readers in a straightforward way of the topic and the thesis the paper will cover. But at other times the introduction just isn't evident when they begin to write, so they proceed to subsequent paragraphs and return to the introduction later, when they have a clearer idea of the focus of the paper.

Introductions can take many forms other than a straightforward statement of the issue. They can include

- a provocative question that challenges readers to reexamine their beliefs on a subject,
- a dramatic or amusing story or anecdote,
- a relevant quotation,
- a brief overview about the historical context,
- a striking statistic,
- a brief description of both sides of a debate, or
- a description of a central person, place, or event.

In all of these cases, the introductory paragraph should either include or relate to your thesis. Persuasive essays (ones that are arguing for a particular point) often include the thesis at the start. In contrast, analytical essays (ones that are exploring a question) may lead up to the thesis in the concluding paragraphs.

Developing and Organizing the Body of the Essay   The organizational choices open to you when you write the middle portion, or body, of your essay depend on the best way to support your thesis. For example, if the thesis reads, "Office computers are being used in ways that infringe on the privacy of employees," then the middle portion of the essay might demonstrate how new software can monitor various aspects of employees' behavior (including productivity, contents of their files, e-mail, and Internet surfing). In this case, the body of the essay would demonstrate the causal relationship (the impact of office computers on privacy) implied in the thesis.

Different strategies, or methods of development, are particularly suited to different purposes. These organizational patterns (traditionally referred to as rhetorical modes) include illustration (or exemplification), description, definition, classification/division, comparison and contrast, causal analysis, and narration.

When you use **illustration,** or **exemplification,** you provide one or more examples that document or substantiate the idea you wish to clarify. Well-chosen examples are useful for showing the nature and character of a whole group through individual cases. One instance can represent many others in the same category. Exemplification is especially useful as a technique for explaining abstract concepts. Examples drawn from personal experience can help support an asser-tion, although several examples are more effective in supporting a generalization. In "The Social Sense" (Chapter 2), for instance, Diane Ackerman gives exam-ples from four geographically and historically diverse cultures to support her claim that every culture uses some foods symbolically or ritualistically. And Con-stance Classen, in "The Odour of the Other" (Chapter 6), uses examples from tribal and industrial societies as well as literature to support her argument that people ascribe different characteristic odors to different races and social groups.

Descriptions are powerful because they can evoke an image in readers' minds and create an emotional response. Effective descriptions use specific lan-guage, carefully chosen details, and an orderly sequence. For an example, see Lennard Davis's opening paragraph in "Visualizing the Disabled Body" (Chap-ter 6); after this description of a mutilated woman missing several limbs, he then reveals that he is talking about the famous statue of Venus de Milo, which is considered the epitome of classical female beauty. Objects and places can be described spatially (top to bottom, right to left, near to far). Events, such as the search for the perfect meal in William Maxwell's "The Pilgrimage" (Chapter 2), can be described chronologically from start to finish.

Definition is a useful method for specifying the basic nature of any phe-nomenon, idea, or condition. A definition can be a sentence that gives the exact meaning of a word or key term (to eliminate ambiguity), or it might extend several paragraphs or even become a complete essay. For example, the defini-tions of the words *marked* and *unmarked* are central to Deborah Tannen's essay exploring gender differences, "There Is No Unmarked Woman" (Chapter 3).

Writers use **classification** to sort or group ideas, issues, topics, themes, and arguments into categories based on one or more criteria. In an effective classi-fication, a writer identifies significant features in a systematic way, divides phe-nomena into at least two different classes on the basis of these criteria, and pre-sents the results in a logical and consistent manner. For example, in "Thinking in Pictures" (Chapter 5), Temple Grandin uses this technique to help readers understand autistic people's visual style of thinking; first, she explains how they process different kinds of words (nouns, prepositions, and verbs) and then dif-ferent kinds of texts.

Comparison and contrast are useful techniques for helping audiences understand basic differences and for pointing out unsuspected similarities or dif-ferences between two or more subjects. In "Hygiene and Repression" (Chapter 2), for example, Octavio Paz builds his argument around contrasts between North American and Third World cuisines and attitudes toward work, sex, hygiene, and race; and Germaine Greer in "One Man's Mutilation Is Another Man's Beautification" (Chapter 3) compares and contrasts what Western and tribal cultures mean by various hairstyles and body adornments and alterations. Comparative essays may be arranged in one of two ways. In the subject-by-subject method, the writer first discusses all the relevant features of one subject (such as the characterization, setting, costumes, and plot of a movie) and then retraces the same points as they apply to a second subject (such as another movie). The second method of organization is point by point, which alternates between the features of the two subjects (by comparing, for example, the characterizations of two movies, then their settings, then their costumes, and then their plots).

Causal analysis is a technique often used in persuasive essays. Its purpose is to determine whether a cause-and-effect relationship exists. As Neil Postman and Steve Powers do in "TV News as Entertainment" (Chapter 7), writers may work backward from the effect to seek the cause or chain of causes that could have produced the observed effect, or they may explore potential effects from a known cause. Causal analysis can go off track, however, when a writer confuses sequence with causation, creating a false cause (or *post hoc*) fallacy, which was discussed along with other fallacies in "How to Analyze an Argument" earlier in this chapter.

Narration is the recounting of events to entertain or to persuade. A narrative can be brief, such as the various anecdotes Judith Ortiz Cofer recounts in her story earlier in this chapter. Or an entire essay can be in the form of a narrative. In "The Kelly Bag as Icon" (Chapter 3), for example, Dodie Kazanjian presents the history of the prestigious handbag within the framework of a narrative about her attempts to buy one. Effective narration usually focuses on a single action. Narratives can entertain or amuse, or they can dramatize an idea or event that is important to the writer.

Writing the Conclusion   The conclusion brings together all the lines of reasoning developed in the body of the essay. Your readers should feel that you fulfilled the obligation you incurred when you presented your thesis. You can achieve this sense of closure in several ways, including

- summarizing the points made in the paper as they relate to the thesis,
- referring to points presented in the opening paragraph or introduction,
- challenging the reader to think further about the issue, or
- providing a personal response.

Revision

Although revision is often discussed as something you do after writing your essay, it is actually part of the continuous editing process that goes on as you write your paper. Each time you change a word to clarify a sentence or change the order of supporting statements to make your essay more coherent or pursue a promising idea that may have not been apparent when you began writing, you are revising your essay.

The novelist James Michener once observed, "I never thought of myself as a good writer. Anyone who wants reassurance of that should read one of my first drafts. But I'm one of the world's great revisers." Transforming a rough draft into a final draft entails testing everything you have written—every section and paragraph—to see whether it relates to the central idea expressed in your thesis. Revising consists of editing or eliminating everything that does not develop, illustrate, clarify, explain, or substantiate your thesis.

Try to see your paper as a reader would, that is, as someone who did not know in advance the ideas you wanted to present. Reading your essay aloud can help you see what you actually wrote—rather than what you intended to write. You may hear inconsistencies in grammatical structure or usage, and you may spot repetitive words or phrases that escaped your notice while you were concentrating on writing.

Another helpful strategy to improve the quality of your paper during the revision process is to ask for the reactions of others—your friends, teacher, and classmates. To get the most out of peer review, don't take any criticisms personally. You are not your paper. You will often find that other people's suggestions are quite helpful in pinpointing problems for you to solve. Many campuses have writing centers or tutoring services that provide reviewers.

Reconsidering the Whole   Here are some questions for you or your reviewer to use in assessing the overall structure of the paper:

1. Does the paper's introduction capture the reader's interest and introduce the thesis? The beginnings of most rough drafts can usually be easily revised to produce a stronger paper.

2. At what points might the reader need more examples to clarify an idea? Which assumptions need to be supported with more evidence? Have you taken into account how someone who holds an opposing view might regard your analysis? What new information could you add to be more persuasive?

3. Are the issues raised in the best possible order? Would some other arrangement more effectively communicate the relationships implicit in the thesis? Let your thesis guide you to the best sequence to follow.

4. Do transitions effectively signal connections between paragraphs and ideas? You might need to write sentences to guide your readers smoothly from one idea or section to the next.

Reconsidering Paragraphs   Once you are satisfied with the overall organization of your ideas, consider what might be clarified within paragraphs.

- Does each paragraph have a topic sentence that is related to the paper's thesis?
- Do other sentences in the paragraph explain the idea in the topic sentence or present evidence to support it?
- If the sentences were in a different order, would the explanation be clearer?
- Are there assertions that need to be supported by examples or quotations?
- Are there any short paragraphs that can be consolidated under a more general idea?
- Are there very long paragraphs that can be divided?

Reconsidering Sentences   After you are satisfied with the overall organization of your paper and the coherence of the paragraphs, it is time to turn your attention to matters of grammar, usage, punctuation, and style. Just as every paragraph must help develop the paper's thesis, so every sentence within a paragraph must support, illustrate, or clarify the paragraph's topic sentence, and every word in a sentence must contribute to the thought expressed by that sentence.

Look for verbs in the passive voice that might be recast in the active voice. Find the verb, ask who is the doer of the action, and rewrite the sentence in the basic subject-verb-object pattern. For example, revising the passive verb in the sentence "Personal experiences are used by Cofer as evidence to support her thesis" conveys the idea more directly and concisely: "Cofer uses examples drawn from her personal experiences to support her thesis."

Consider how you might improve your choice of words. Choose words that express your ideas clearly, simply, and concretely. Be on the lookout for the following:

- mixed **metaphors,** such as "the hand that rocks the cradle has kicked the bucket" and "don't pull the wool out from under me";
- abstract **jargon,** or specialized language used in a particular field as a quick way of communicating information (if technical terms are necessary, define them the first time you use them);
- **clichés,** hackneyed expressions, and trite phrases, such as "put your two cents in," "cool as a cucumber," "safe and sound," "fair and square," or "adding fuel to the fire"; and
- roundabout phrases whose idea could be expressed in a single word, such as *although* for *in spite of the fact that, because* for *due to the fact that, if* for *in the event that, after* for *at the conclusion of, now* for *at this point in time.*

⊕ REVISING AND EDITING WITH A COMPUTER

Revising with a computer offers several advantages. You can create multiple drafts and try out different configurations. You can easily move sentences and paragraphs by cutting and pasting. Some computer programs also provide outline tools and spell checkers that can help you edit and proofread your paper.
  But there are several cautions to remember when you revise with a computer:

- Although useful, spell-checking programs cannot detect an error if the unintended word is a correctly spelled word (for example, *to* for *too* or *two*, *these* for *there*, or *peace* for *piece*).

- Print out a version of each draft before you revise it just in case you accidentally delete some material (and be sure to create a backup file at the end of each session at the computer).

- When you move text within a file, make sure that you have moved everything in the passage to its new location.

- Work done on a computer looks far more polished than its handwritten equivalent and can therefore delude you into thinking it is a final draft when it is still a work in progress.

Revising the Title   As you read through your rough draft, you may think of a different title that would better reflect a change in emphasis in your paper or more accurately express the idea in the thesis. Titles are a concise means of focusing the reader's attention on the main idea of the essay. For example, Juliet B. Schor's title "The Culture of Consumerism" (in Chapter 9) leads readers to anticipate an argument characterizing a society obsessed with buying things. Another strong title is "The Real Vampire" (by Paul Barber in Chapter 6), which should make readers curious.

  Computers can be both a boon and a challenge as tools in the process of revision. For some tips on using them to advantage, see the box "Revising and Editing with a Computer."

Proofreading

Proofreading means focusing on spelling, punctuation, repeated words, spacing, margins, and anything else that would impair the look of the final paper. Most people find it easier and more accurate to proofread on paper than onscreen, and many people also find it helpful to proofread aloud.

  If you habitually misspell certain words, make a list of them and consult it when you proofread. Do not rely on your computer's spell-checking program to catch all spelling errors because it cannot tell when you have typed the wrong word, such as "a" for "as" or "won" for "own."

Make sure you have properly documented the source of every quotation, paraphrase, and summary. Compare your in-text citations with your list of works cited, and compare that list with your record of the sources to make sure you did not change any words or punctuation.

Check the formatting of your paper. Most English instructors require papers to be formatted in Modern Language Association (MLA) style, but teachers in other classes may require American Psychological Association (APA) style or *Chicago Manual of Style* (*CMS*) style. Here, however, are some universal formatting points to check during proofreading:

- one-inch margins on the top, bottom, and sides of each page
- page number and running head on each page (you can use the "header" function for this)
- half an inch indention of the first line of each paragraph
- double-spaced text in a standard 12-point font (do not put an extra double space between paragraphs)
- works cited (or references) on a separate page at the end of the paper (for citation guidelines in MLA style, see the Appendix, "Documenting Sources in MLA Style")
- your name, the title of the paper, the name of your school or the course, and the date on the title page (if one is required by your instructor) or on the first page of the essay

Working with Sources

For some papers, you may need to do research to provide additional information or to strengthen an argument. You can look for this information in the library's books and periodicals, on the Internet, or even do interviews or conduct a survey, depending on your topic. Whatever kinds of sources you use, however, you need to think critically about them and make sure that they are relevant and reliable. Skim your potential sources and ask these questions to decide if they will be useful:

- What qualifies the author as an expert on the subject? Is the author likely to have a particular bias?
- If your topic requires the latest news, is your source current or out of date? For a paper on the Human Genome Project, for example, a ten-year-old source would probably not be helpful.
- What is the audience for the source? What level of knowledge is assumed of them? Is the information more detailed or technical than you need?
- What kind of evidence does the author use? Is it sufficient? Is it credible?

🌐 TIPS FOR EVALUATING ELECTRONIC SOURCES

The ease with which anyone can create a Web page and post information on it requires you to carefully evaluate the pages you intend to use as sources. When you look at a Web page's address—its uniform resource locator, or URL—check to see whether it contains a tilde (~), which indicates that the site is a personal page. Without knowing the purpose of the Web page (to entertain, to sell a product or service, to provide information, to promote a cause), you might find it difficult to gauge the objectivity and reliability of the information it contains. Therefore, you must evaluate the extent to which your source is

- authoritative (what are the author's credentials?),
- unbiased (is the purpose to get you to buy or believe something?),
- timely (when was the content posted?), and
- relevant (can the information be verified by other sources?).

The domain name (the letters between the double slash and the first single slash) can provide a clue about the nature of the source. Common abbreviations include *.com* for commercial; *.edu* for educational; *.gov* for governmental; *.mil* for the military; *.net* for some Internet service providers; and *.org* for organizational. You can often find the sponsor or the creator of the Web page by going to the home page of the Web site; if there is not a link to the home page, try deleting the last part of the URL (for example, if the URL is <http://www.mundanebehavior.org/issues/v1n1/caesar.htm>, you would go to <http://www.mundanebehavior.org/>). In addition, most reliable Web pages have links that provide information about the creator or the document or at least give the e-mail address of the creator or Webmaster.

If you use sources from the Internet, you must be especially careful to verify their validity (see the box "Tips for Evaluating Electronic Sources"). Remember first of all, though, that a great deal of valuable information is not available on the Web. The Web only contains information that has been converted to digital format. Many important scholarly journals are not available online. Moreover, online journals and some major newspapers, such as the *New York Times,* often provide only abridged versions of the full printed text of the most recent edition; many periodical publishers charge a fee to access older editions.

Providing Evidence from Sources
After formulating a thesis, you need to support it with evidence. You can provide this evidence by paraphrasing or by quoting relevant passages.

Paraphrases   Paraphrasing is the restatement of an author's ideas in your own words. Unlike summaries, which aim to be concise, paraphrases attempt to convey the complexity of the original text and are often similar in length to it. Paraphrasing is something of an art because it involves re-presenting in your own words the meaning of a passage written by someone else.

First of all, your paraphrase must be different enough from the original so that it does not lead you to commit plagiarism, or to use someone else's words as if they were your own. For example, here is a sentence from Octavio Paz's "Hygiene and Repression" (Chapter 2):

> The prestige of science in American public opinion is such that even political disputes frequently take on the form of scientific polemics.

The following paraphrase would be too close to Paz's original sentence and would constitute plagiarism if Paz were not given credit for the thought:

> The status of science in American public opinion is so great that even political debates are often patterned after scientific debates.

Not only do you need to make the paraphrase sufficiently different from the text, but you must also make sure that you do not project your own biases into the paraphrase. For example, here is a paraphrase that misses Paz's skeptical tone and meaning:

> The wonders of science compel such admiration that even nonscientific political discussions benefit from its objectivity.

Here is a more faithful paraphrase of Paz's sentence:

> Americans hold science in such high regard that their disagreements over public policy issues are expressed as if they were debates over scientific controversies.

A thesaurus can sometimes prove useful when you are paraphrasing, but you must check the dictionary definition of the synonym you intend to use in case there is a subtle difference in meaning. For example, if you substitute the word *aroma* for the word *odor,* you might create a positive **connotation** (an associative meaning) that is not in the original.

Quotations   Quotations are useful when you wish to support, illustrate, or document important points by citing the opinion of experts or authorities who either support or challenge your position. Direct quotations are preferable to paraphrases when the original passage is especially important, vivid, or memorable. Quotations let your readers hear the author's voice. Be careful, though, not to overuse quotations; your paper needs to be primarily in your own words. It should not be simply a patchwork of stitched-together quotations.

Brief quotations (no more than four lines) are normally run into the text and enclosed in double quotation marks (" "). Include the author's name with the quotation, either in your text (as in the following example) or in a parenthetical reference, as shown in the Appendix, "Documenting Sources in MLA Style" (at the end of the book). Parenthetical citations for page numbers follow the closing quotation marks but precede the punctuation mark at the end of the sentence:

> As Cofer writes, "It is custom, however, not chromosomes, that leads us to choose scarlet over pale pink" (134).

Longer quotations (more than four lines) are separated from the text, indented one inch from the left margin and reproduced without quotation marks. These block quotations are introduced with a colon (:) if they follow a grammatically complete introductory clause. Parenthetical citations of page numbers follow the quotation's final mark of punctuation. Use longer quotations for complex or especially vivid passages, but don't use too many. Here is an example of a long quotation:

> In her essay "The Myth of the Latin Woman: I Just Met a Girl Named María," Judith Ortiz Cofer analyzes the role culture plays in stereotyping and concludes:
>
> > It is custom, however, not chromosomes, that leads us to choose scarlet over pale pink. As young girls, it was our mothers who influenced our decisions about clothes and colors—mothers who had grown up on a tropical island where the natural environment was a riot of primary colors, where showing your skin was one way to keep cool as well as to look sexy. (134)

If you quote more than one paragraph, the first line of the second and subsequent paragraphs should be indented an additional one-quarter inch or three typewriter spaces.

Quotations must be accurate. If you need to omit part of a passage to integrate it into your text, you must replace the omitted segment with an ellipsis mark, or three spaced periods inside square brackets [. . .]. Here is an example of the use of an ellipsis mark:

> As Cofer says, "It is custom, [. . .] not chromosomes, that
> leads us to choose scarlet over pale pink."

The ellipsis [. . .] indicates that a word or words have been omitted.

When you add words to a quotation to clarify it, use square brackets ([ ]) around the words you have added. Here is an example of brackets used to show the translation of a foreign word:

> Cofer says, "Our life was designed by my parents as a
> microcosm of their *casas* [homes] on the island."

When you wish to emphasize a word or phrase in a quotation, you may italicize or underline it, but you must indicate that you have done so by adding the phrase "emphasis added" in parentheses after the closing quotation mark. Here is an example:

> Cofer says that "it is *custom,* however, not chromosomes,
> that leads us to choose scarlet over pale pink" (emphasis
> added).

Whenever you quote, summarize, or paraphrase material from a source, you must identify the source. If you do not, you are committing plagiarism, that is, appropriating the language and ideas of another person and representing them as your own. Source documentation also shows readers the scope of your research and enables them to refer to the original materials if they wish. The Appendix, "Documenting Sources in MLA Style," provides detailed guidelines for styling in-text citations and lists of works cited.

Writing from a Single Source: Sample Essay

As you read through the following essay, which analyzes Judith Ortiz Cofer's essay presented earlier in this chapter, note how quotations, paraphrases, and summaries are used as evidence of the thesis statement. Note also its organization into a discussion of the content of Cofer's essay and then of its style.

The title refers to the thesis statement.

Refuting the Latina Stereotype

In the musical *West Side Story,* the beautiful and innocent María, newly arrived from Puerto Rico, falls tragically in love with the leader of an Anglo gang. The play is filled with memorable songs, but the characters, including María and her friend, the Puerto Rican "spitfire" Anita, are familiar

The introduction gives the background for Cofer's title.

Thesis
statement
stereotypes of Latinas. In "The Myth of the Latin Woman: I Just Met a Girl Named María," Judith Ortiz Cofer refutes these stereotypes by contrasting them with the realities of her life as an articulate and accomplished individual.

A Puerto Rican writer of some renown, Cofer is offended when strangers make unwarranted assumptions about her. She confesses that since childhood she has been troubled by these cross-cultural misperceptions:

> You can leave the Island, master the English language, and travel as far as you can, but if you are a Latina, especially one like me who so obviously belongs to Rita Moreno's gene pool, the Island travels with you.

Quotations
for four lines
are indented
one inch.

Cofer uses personal experiences to show how she has learned to cope with these misperceptions about her. As a Puerto Rican growing up in the United States, she was caught between her parents' Puerto Rican culture and the values of her Anglo schoolmates. When Cofer was young, Puerto Rican mothers encouraged their daughters to dress and act like women. So on her high school's Career Day, she and her Puerto Rican friends wore their mothers' flashy jewelry and clothing, which her teachers and Anglo classmates, who were attired in tailored skirts and silk blouses, ridiculed.

Paragraph
answers an
alternative
viewpoint.
Some people might disagree with Cofer's blaming cross-cultural misunderstandings and feel that she was old enough and had lived on the mainland long enough to know what clothes were appropriate. But Cofer was raised in a Puerto Rican community in New Jersey and had never been out in the world. Given her background, it was natural for her to interpret the meaning of "dressing up" in an entirely different way than her Anglo classmates and teachers. She explains that "it is custom, [. . .] not chromosomes, that leads us to choose scarlet over pale pink."

Bracketed
ellipsis mark
shows omis-
sion of word
or words
from source.

Years later, when Cofer was in graduate school at Oxford, she was unexpectedly treated as a Latina stereotype. On a bus trip to London, a drunken young passenger knelt before her and serenaded her with "María" from *West Side Story;* imagine a total stranger coming up and singing, "María—I just kissed a girl named María/And suddenly I found how wonderful a sound can be." Although her fellow passengers were "politely amused," Cofer struggled to hide her anger with her version of "an English smile"—a response that recalls the "studied indifference" of the young women subjected to off-color *piropos* on Saturday nights in the plaza of her mother's village in Puerto Rico.

In addition to the assumption that Latinas are sexually available, there is a second damaging aspect of the stereotype: that all Latinas are uneducated, socially inferior, and suited only for menial work. Cofer likens the stereotype of the funny Hispanic maid "cooking up a spicy storm in a shiny California kitchen" to the "Mammy" stereotype of black women, which allows them to be treated in ways that would be unthinkable if they were white.

Transitional sentence signals two-part structure of discussion of stereotype.

As an example, Cofer describes an event that happened before her first public poetry reading. Upon arriving at the restaurant, Cofer was called over to a table by an older woman. Nervous and excited, Cofer walked over, expecting to autograph a copy of her newly published volume of poems. However, when she reached the table, the woman, who had assumed that she was the waitress, ordered a cup of coffee. Cofer expresses her anger with irony: "Easy enough to mistake my poems for menus, I suppose."

Transitional sentence signals switch from discussion of content to analysis of style.

The language and the organization of the essay are carefully crafted, demonstrating that Cofer is indeed an accomplished and articulate writer. In the introductory paragraphs, she uses two contrasting metaphors of an island to express what it feels like to be stereotyped. In the first paragraph, "the Island" is Puerto Rico, the vividly colored "tropical paradise" that is the homeland of her parents. But in the second paragraph the island becomes gray and barren, "an Alcatraz, a place nobody wants to visit"—a metaphor for her feeling of isolation in mainland Anglo culture.

Cofer's essay has a loosely chronological structure— a series of episodes that trace the development of her reactions to cultural stereotyping from childhood to adulthood. As a child, Cofer felt humiliated and "out of step" when she was dressed "wrong" for a birthday party or a Career Day.

To help the reader understand the difference between Puerto Rican and Anglo customs, Cofer inserts into the chronological series her mother's description of Saturday nights on the town plaza when she was young. There, the flirtations between boys and girls had clear boundaries, and the fundamental rule, says Cofer, was "You may look at my sister, but if you touch her I will kill you." To illustrate the lack of such boundaries on the mainland, Cofer describes her date's mistaken assumptions and unwanted kiss at her first formal dance.

As she gained more experience and more confidence as well as professional success, Cofer's reaction changed to anger at disrespectful behavior that diminished her as a person. When she was accosted in a hotel lobby by a tuxedoed guest singing an off-color version of "La Bamba," she waited in silence until he was finished and then insulted him indirectly but sharply by cautioning his daughter never to ask him what he had done in the army. Later Cofer told her friend that she had really wanted "to push the jerk into the swimming pool."

In the last episode of the essay, when she was mistaken for a waitress rather than a poet, Cofer also responded with anger, gazing intently at the offending woman throughout her poetry reading—a tactic that Cofer describes as "punish[ing] her with my full attention."

Cofer's adolescent feelings of embarrassment have changed into regarding stereotyped assumptions as challenges to open some avenue for "communication." Her goal, she says, is to use her art "to try to replace the old pervasive stereotype [. . .] with a much more interesting set of realities."

Cofer concludes her essay with an example of
that art: lines from a poem about Latinas that she calls
"a prayer for communication, and for respect." Her
Latin women praying "in Spanish to an Anglo God/

**Conclusion
refers back
to thesis
statement.**

with a Jewish heritage/[. . .] fervently hoping/that if not
omnipotent,/at least He be bilingual" are one of the
realities behind the stereotype of María.

Writing from Multiple Sources: Sample Essay

Many of the writing assignments you will be asked to do in your college courses
will require you to read, evaluate, and discuss multiple readings, essays, or selections on the same topic. You may also be asked to do outside research drawing
on library sources, the Internet, and your own observations. These assignments require analyzing two or more sources and formulating your own thesis
based on them.

The following sample assignment (based on readings in Chapter 7, "That's
Entertainment!") requires you to synthesize information from two sources and
to do some direct observation to formulate your argument:

Compare the essays "TV News as Entertainment" by Neil Postman and
Steve Powers and "Freak Parade" by Charles Oliver. View a couple of
news broadcasts and daytime talk shows, and locate relevant Web sites. In
a short essay, state your views on the authors' positions and information
you have gathered from your media research.

As you would when writing an essay based on a single reading, you begin
by carefully reading, annotating, and evaluating each of the selections and identifying the topic you wish to discuss in your essay. You then focus specifically
on what the sources have to say on selected aspects of the topic (in this case,
the issue of sensationalism on television news and talk shows). Then you can
formulate a thesis that synthesizes what the sources say and your position on
the issue. In the following sample essay, the thesis makes a value judgment:

Sensationalism on TV news broadcasts and
daytime talk shows has increasingly come to
define what the American public views as
normal.

Assignments of this type might also ask you to draw on books, scholarly
journal articles, lectures, and class discussions. (Note that the following paper
uses MLA style to cite these additional sources.) This particular assignment
asks the student to incorporate personal observations of TV news shows.

Sensationalism on American TV Feeds
Our Addiction to Entertainment

Television was created to provide entertainment and to give people news about important events. Now, however, our desire to be constantly entertained has transformed traditional news broadcasts and talk shows. In the past, newscasts offered detailed information. Today, they offer quick, flashy stories that require little thought. Once-informative talk shows have deteriorated into sleazy shows catering to the lowest common denominator of their audiences. Sensationalism on TV news broadcasts and daytime talk shows has increasingly come to define what the American public views as normal.

Thesis
statement

Years ago, newscasts offered viewers articulate explanations of important events. Today's superficial coverage fails to delve very deeply into any story, no matter how significant it may be. The desire to capture the attention of ever-younger audiences has become the driving force in TV programming. As Dave Berkman, a professor of mass communication, wrote in the *Shepherd Express Metro,*

> Since serious journalistic enterprise seldom attracts a large audience or readership, especially among those youthful viewers advertisers value most, most serious journalism has become increasingly rare. (3)

Producers seem to have concluded that words alone could not hold an audience and began to include more and more images. In fact, as media commentators Neil Postman and Steve Powers have observed, "All the words uttered in an hour of news coverage could be printed on one page of a newspaper. And the world cannot be understood in one page" (104).

Page number
of source
follows final
punctuation
in indented
quotation.

Page number
of source
precedes final
punctuation
in run-in
quotation.

The images that news programs use to entertain their viewers often seem to be dominated by scenes of violent activity. Neil Postman and Steve Powers speculate that "violence and dynamic destruction find their way onto television so often" because the medium of television favors images that change rather than ones that are static (106). However, the damaging effects of so many violent scenes on viewers cannot be overestimated. According to the American Psychological Association (APA), "The average American child views 8,000 murders and 100,000 other acts of violence before finishing elementary school" (Broder). The negative effects of viewing so much media violence include increased fear of becoming a victim of violence, desensitization to violence, and greater likelihood of behaving violently (APA Public Policy Office).

Additional sources provide more evidence for argument.

Pictures on newscasts may capture our attention, but they cannot convey full understanding of an event because they "speak only in particularities" (Postman and Powers 104). Images can even be misleading. For example, the local New York Channel 4 news broadcast on December 12, 1999, opened with the report of a plane crash in the Poconos. However, the footage shown was not of that crash but of one a month earlier in Hasbrouck Heights, New Jersey; it had been the subject of a news broadcast then (accompanied by the exact same picture). Other than the fact that one of the planes had been flying toward Teterboro Airport and the other had departed from it, no connection existed between the two flights. By showing pictures of an unrelated incident, the Channel 4 news created the erroneous impression that there was a connection between the two crashes.

Personal observation is used as evidence.

The need to capture the attention of viewers who, by now, have come to expect sensational visual effects results in newscasts filled with incessantly moving pictures and superimposed graphics. For example, during the traffic report on New York Channel 4, the background scene consists of an illuminated New York skyline with streams of moving cars. Throughout the weather forecast, computer-simulated weather systems and other distracting graphics have become more important than the information. As Dave Berkman has noted, "Meaningless weather details fascinate [. . .] local newscast viewers" (3).

During news broadcasts, the rate at which pictures change (every six to eight seconds on the average) actually dictates the amount of air time a story receives. Music also plays an important role in creating a dramatic atmosphere. Almost all broadcasts begin with impressive "arena-like" music. The tone and volume of this music "suggests important events are about to unfold" (Postman and Powers 108). When the music begins, the names of the newscasters are triumphantly announced as if they were gladiators entering an arena. The buildup to this proclamation is accompanied by the constant movement of people in the background, typing, answering ringing phones, and scurrying around as if something very important were taking place. These carefully engineered distractions are meant to signify to viewers that they are about to receive vital information.

The decline in the quality of news programs is paralleled by a similar decline in talk shows. Today, like the freak shows in carnivals of old, talk shows "cater to the dark side of man's need for spectacle by allowing people to escape temporarily from their dull everyday lives into a world that [is] dark, sleazy, and seemingly dangerous" (Oliver 52). Except for some talk shows, such as those of Rosie O'Donnell and Oprah Winfrey, that attract viewers with celebrities, not freaks, and feature interesting guests and meaningful topics, the fringe element has taken center stage. The purpose of such programming seems to be to attract viewers who can then wallow in sympathy while secretly feeling superior to the people they are watching. Commentator Charles Oliver calls this trend "emotional voyeurism" (52).

Carnivals also used "hoochie coochie dancers" to attract crowds (Oliver 52). Today's version of these dancers are strippers of both genders, young and old, who appear as guests on talk shows. Other shows present supposedly normal people with bizarre sexual lifestyles. Sexual story lines on these shows are so common that producers really have to work hard to come up with new angles. One such twist was the "I Married a Horse" episode on the *Jerry Springer* show. It featured interviews with "three guests who regularly engage in bestiality," including someone who married a horse (Strode). Although the episode was eventually withdrawn nationally because of its offensive nature, it did air in a few markets.

Conclusion challenges reader to think further about the issue.

    Imagine for a moment how people from other cultures might view these shows. What would such tastelessness, lack of compassion, and declining morality suggest about our society? Do we so desire to be entertained at any cost that the typical fare of successful television talk shows— sex, lies, humiliation, and betrayal—has now become the norm, even on the evening news?

Works Cited list begins on a new page.

For more examples of MLA style for works cited, see the Appendix.

Works Cited

APA Public Policy Office. *Is Youth Violence Just Another Fact of Life?* 16 May 2000. American Psychological Association. 17 Nov. 2000 <http://www.apa.org/ppo/violence.html#epidemic>.

Berkman, Dave. "Media Musings." *Shepherd Express Metro: Milwaukee's Weekly Newspaper* 20.45 (1999): 3. 17 Nov. 2000 <http://www.shepherd-express.com/mediamusings.html>.

Broder, Sharon. *Fighting Media Violence! 2000.* The Learning Network. 17 Nov. 2000 <http://familyeducation.com/article/0,1120,22-2376,00.html>.

Oliver, Charles. "Freak Parade." *Reason* April 1995: 52+.

Postman, Neil, and Steve Powers. *How to Watch TV News.* New York: Penguin, 1992.

Strode, Tom. *Springer Show Pulls Program on Bestiality.* 27 May 1998. The Ethics and Religious Liberty Commission of the Southern Baptist Convention. 17 Nov. 2000 <http://www.erlc.com/Culture/TV/Articles/springer_show_pulls_program.htm>.

ANALYZING VISUAL TEXTS

Just as you can read verbal texts critically, you can also read visual texts. You encounter hundreds of them every day on television; in films; on the Internet; in newspapers, magazines, and textbooks; and on the street. Some, like magazine ads, billboards, CD covers, store windows, and photographs, are purely visual images. Others, such as Web pages, films, and ads on TV, combine sound and movement with images. All of these visual texts have been artfully constructed to convey precise meanings and to influence your behavior. All of them can be analyzed by looking at how they use the elements of rhetoric and of design.

Visuals Are Rhetorical

In the discussions of critical reading and critical writing, we looked at the elements of the rhetorical situation. We can use these elements to analyze visual texts too.

The Audience
Who is the intended audience? Children? Teenagers? Young professionals? Parents? Senior citizens? Men? Women? What knowledge, beliefs, and attitudes do they have in common? If you compare the ads on different kinds of TV shows—Oprah, Monday Night Football, and Saturday morning cartoons, for example—you'll see different kinds of products being advertised and different kinds of appeals used in the ads.

The Purpose
The three basic purposes of texts are to explain or inform, to persuade, and to entertain. As with written texts, visual texts may express a combination of these purposes, but one usually predominates. News photographs are primarily intended to inform an audience—to show them an event or a person. Ads, obviously, are intended to persuade. Most films and TV shows are meant to entertain.

The Topic
How does the image illustrate the topic? Does a CD cover show a picture of the band, or does it show an image evoking some kind of emotion or theme? Does an ad focus on the product (as most car ads do), or does it use images to enhance the product's image (such as sportswear ads that focus on athletes or oil company ads that showcase the company's environmental efforts)?

The Occasion
Is an ad part of a campaign to introduce a new product? Is the store window organized to promote the new line of fall clothes? Is the billboard part of a political campaign? Is the public sculpture intended to commemorate a famous event or person?

The Artist or Creator
The artist or creator decides what image will be most effective for the purpose, the audience, the occasion, and the topic. For example, Maya Lin's design

for the memorial to U.S. troops who had died during the Vietnam War was an immense, curved black marble wall with the names of all the dead carved into it. At the time Lin's design was chosen, it was controversial: there were many who wanted a more traditional memorial showing figures of uniformed soldiers.

Elements of Design

The artist or creator uses principles of design to create particular moods and messages. The appeal can be based on logos (sound proof), ethos (reliability), or pathos (emotion, including humor), or some combination of the three. Art departments teach whole courses on the principles of design. What we provide here is a bare-bones introduction to the five basic elements: balance, proportion, movement, contrast, and unity. These elements determine how we scan a visual image and what we notice first.

Balance
Balance is how the elements of a design relate to each other—in terms of size, color, and shape—along a horizontal or a vertical axis. Balance is about symmetry or asymmetry. A symmetrical design is formal and static. For an example, see the L. L. Bean ad in Figure 1.2 (page 52); the right and left sides of the ad mirror each other. The effect is one of tradition and reliability; L. L. Bean's clothes are classic. In contrast, an asymmetrical design is informal and dynamic.

Proportion
Proportion is the relative size of the elements in a design. Elements that are bigger or more colorful are noticed first. For example, look at the images in this chapter and be aware of what your eye takes in first, second, and so on. The design creates an agenda that influences the importance you attribute to each of its elements.

Movement
In this context we are focusing on movement within a single image, not the movement from image to image in film or in a hypertext. In this sense, movement is the ways in which elements in a composition lead our eyes to scan for information. The eye usually goes first to the upper left corner of an image— that is the way we read a written page. However, the size and arrangement of the elements can make us scan differently.

In two-dimensional images, the direction of lines can also indicate movement or the absence of it. Horizontal and vertical lines can imply stability, whereas diagonal lines or zigzags imply movement. Many ads for cars, especially those that emphasize performance, show the car at a diagonal, as does the Toyota Sequoia ad in Figure 1.3 (page 53).

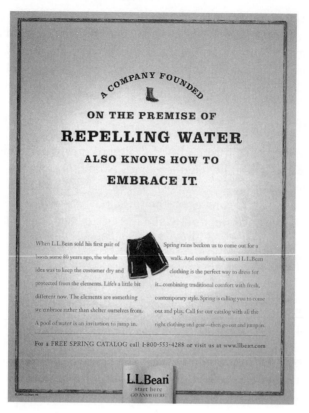

FIGURE 1.2

Contrast

Visual elements also gain meaning from contrast of size, shape, and color. In the Toyota Sequoia ad, contrast is achieved by the sharp focus on the car and the haziness of the mountains behind it and by the size of the car in relation to the obviously high mountains behind it.

Unity

Unity is the way all the elements work together to produce a feeling of completeness. Most ads function this way. In contrast are some commercial Web pages that carry ads and other elements to sidetrack you and persuade you to click on a link that will carry you somewhere you did not intend to go. This kind of fragmentation can even be the goal of the artist or creator.

Multimedia Texts and Hypertext

In addition to the five basic design elements, multimedia texts, such as films and the Internet, have additional elements that the artist or creator can manip-

FIGURE 1.3

ulate. These include movement, sound, and rhythm, or pacing. (For more on online design, see the box "Analyzing a Web Site.")

Movement

In addition to the elements of movement used in a single two-dimensional image, editors of multimedia texts, especially films and increasingly some video games, have other tools at their disposal to show the passage of time between two scenes or the linkage of two scenes (Berger, 97). They can use "wipes" to replace one image with another and create a sharp break with the earlier image. With "dissolves," one image gradually fades into another, suggesting the passage of a good deal of time. With "fade-outs," the image gradually fades to black, and with "fade-ins," the image gradually appears from an empty screen. In "flip-frames," the image appears to flip into a new sequence. "Cuts" stop a sequence to show a new image; they can create the sensation that a number of things are going on at once. With a "defocus shot," one scene ends by moving out of focus as a new scene moves into clear focus, linking the two scenes.

Camera movement can also affect the rhythm and our reactions to scenes (Berger, 104–05). With a "pan," the camera travels across a person, an object,

---

⊕ ANALYZING A WEB SITE

Aside from analyzing a Web site to evaluate its credibility as a potential source for a research-based paper (see the box on page 38, "Tips for Evaluating Electronic Sources"), you might choose or be assigned the task of analyzing a Web site as a class project. Or you might want to analyze your own Web site, whether it's one you've already created or one you're in the process of creating, to ensure the quality and effectiveness of its design and function. With improvements in software, more and more people can create their own Web sites—ones with a lot of bells and whistles, but the interactive nature of the medium requires some special design considerations, especially ease of use and a correspondence between form and content (Schultz). Regardless of a site's intended purpose (see "Visuals Are Rhetorical" on pages 50–51), if you're analyzing it, you'll need to keep the following design considerations in mind:

- Because the medium is primarily visual (rather than verbal), some designers are tempted to use more graphics and plug-ins than they need to simply because they want to use all the new technology they can. But too much can distract from the main message. The search engine Google <http://www.google.com> gained quick popularity because of its simplicity. Its uncluttered home page promises a search engine and only that. It downloads quickly and provides search results quickly.

- Motion or animation should be used only when it enhances the content. A good example is Honda's Web site for the current model year <http://www.honda2002.com>, which lets potential buyers customize the color and other aspects of their model on-screen. Another good example is the Web site of the Fine Arts Museum of San Francisco <http://www.thinker.org>, which lets users zoom in on parts of artworks in its extensive online collection.

- A Web site should not use such a complicated design that it will require a lot of memory and load time, unless its audience is only those with very powerful Internet access.

---

or a scene. With a "roll," the camera flips an image, causing disorientation. In a "truck," the camera moves horizontally in front of a scene. To move toward or away from a scene, the camera (and its support) moves closer or farther in a "dolly-in" or a "dolly-out." An arc is a semicircular movement around a scene.

Sound

Film directors use spoken dialogue and voice-overs to let us know what characters are thinking and what is happening in what we are seeing. They also may add sound effects—such as thunder or footsteps or gunshots—to enhance a scene (pay close attention the next time you see a horror film). For the same reason, they use music. Music can cue us to expect a light, sunny love scene or impend-

- Links to other Web sites should give credibility to the site; they should be reputable and useful links. The humanities Web site Voice of the Shuttle <http://www.ucsb.edu> is a good example of a site with useful links. And the links should be live. Dead links are a sign that the page is not being actively maintained and updated.

- A good Web site should have a consistent layout, with links to the home page and the top of the page on every page.

- A good Web site should have an organization that is not too complex. Ideally, users shouldn't have to click more than three times to find what they are looking for.

- Some designers use frames for complex sites, with a navigational index on the left side. This can be a solution for making navigation easier, but some Internet users dislike frames because they may increase download time, they decrease the size of the linked page, and they make going back to the previous Web site more difficult because it can't be accomplished by a simple click of the mouse.

- A professional Web site uses colors and font types and sizes consistently on all pages to give the site unity. Moreover, the font types and the colors are appropriate to the subject matter.

- A Web site should use plug-ins that are available to a large number of users. Users shouldn't have to take the time to download some obscure plug-in that is not on their computer, unless the intended audience is computer experts.

- Grammar and spelling errors are a signal to question the Web site creator's credibility.

ing doom. As the sound capabilities of computers become more sophisticated, designers of computer graphics are adding more sound to their productions.

Pacing

Both movies and commercials often pace the action to move quickly. Commercials on television need to fit into their allotted thirty seconds or less. They need to use the shorthand of referring to symbols and icons that their intended audience will already recognize. They don't have time to establish a context, and the actors in them will probably use exaggerated facial expressions and gestures so that their reactions don't have to be explained. Video games may use the same techniques. Similarly, action films depend on a lot of quick cuts to move the action along and on a lot of broad acting (perhaps enhanced by musical cues) to help the action along—think of Batman and his villains.

Works Cited

Berger, Arthur Asa. *Seeing Is Believing*. Mountain View, CA: Mayfield, 1998.

Boesky, Ivan F. Commencement address, 18 May 1986, School of Business Administration, University of California, Berkeley.

Heimbaugh, Jason R. "KFC Mutant Chickens." *AFU and Urban Legends Archive*. 14 Aug. 2000. 1 Mar. 2001 <http://www.urbanlegends.com/ulz/kfc.html>.

Keegan, Peter O. "KFC Shuns 'Fried' Image with New Name." *Nation's Restaurant News* 25 Feb. 1991: 1–2.

Schultz, Heidi. *The Elements of Electronic Communication*. Needham Heights, MA: Allyn and Bacon, 2000.

van der Linden, Peter, and Terry Chan. *The alt.folklore.urban FAQ*. 1 Mar. 2001 <http://www.urbanlegends.com/afu.faq/intro.html>.

CHAPTER 2

Food for Thought

If you're going to America, bring your own food.
—FRAN LEBOWITZ (b. 1951, U.S. journalist), *Social Studies*

All cultures differentiate themselves through their attitude toward food. People around the world have evolved specific food preferences and practices that are as uniquely adapted to their particular cultures as are the languages they speak and the clothes they wear. Specific foods—such as pasta for Italians, curry for South Asians, and pierogi for Poles—serve as a focus for ethnic identity. Business, religion, social class, and national identity influence, in overt or subtle ways, our attitude toward the food we eat.

FOOD AS SOCIAL BOND

The sharing of food creates a bond between people that is at the root of human society: by "breaking bread" together, we confirm our ties to each other. In almost all countries, the offering of food is a central feature of hospitality. An invitation to eat in someone's home is commonly understood as a sign of friendship. In many cultures, the quality of the meal reflects the guest's status.

Taking food together at certain times of the year is an important feature of social relationships. Feasts and ritual celebrations commemorate times we wish to remember. As a sign of abundance, such meals play a central role in banquets, festivals, holidays, and special occasions such as weddings. We honor people at a special feast or dinner. In the past, truces between warring parties were often celebrated with feasts, and treaty signings are often followed by festive banquets. In some societies, food is offered to ghosts and spirits. On November 2 (the "day of the dead"), for example, Mexicans honor the deceased with sugar skulls, marzipan skeletons, and other treats that they leave at gravesites decorated with candles, photographs, and statues of the saints.

Over the past century, the shift from an agricultural to an urban society has been reflected in dramatic changes in America's eating habits. Today we get together far less often to share meals than we did in the past. In "What's Cooking? Eating in America," Bill Bryson traces the advent and rise of restaurants as social institutions and explores the proliferation of fast-food franchises as replacements for the home-cooked meal. One example of this trend is McDonald's. In "Rituals at McDonald's," Conrad P. Kottak speculates that this international business conglomerate creates a unique image of hominess that may even provide a kind of spiritual comfort. Kottak's point, ironically, may be worth considering: has Old McDonald's farm been resurrected under McDonald's golden arches?

FOOD PREFERENCES AND CUSTOMS

The acquisition of food is a primary human activity. Consider the effort the people of the world invest in hunting, growing, transporting, storing, and preparing food. Although we need food to live, we consume it in ways that reflect cultural values that vary from society to society. In fact, culture may strongly influence what we consider to taste good and even the customs that govern the way we eat. For example, eating raw fish (sushi) once was limited to Japanese culture but has become a sign of culinary sophistication in the West.

The extent to which culture determines what is considered good to eat might explain why insects provide ten percent of the quality protein consumed worldwide. By contrast, in the United States, for example, most people would never consider consuming insects as a source of protein.

We can see the influence of culture on food preferences in other countries as well. For example, the Masai of Tanzania and Kenya revere cattle as a symbol of wealth and drink cow's blood to connect them with (what for them is) the source of life. Although Hindus also hold the cow to be sacred, they do not use cattle for food. Protests greeted the opening of a McDonald's franchise in India, until the restaurant changed it's fare from hamburgers to the "Maharajah Mac," made from lamb. The cultural clout of McDonald's as a symbol of the West makes it a hit with residents of cities from Moscow to Bejing to London. In fact, McDonald's earns half of it's total receipts, now in the tens of billions, from overseas sales—a testimony to the successful marketing of the American lifestyle throughout the world.

The kinds of food a culture prefers can tell us a great deal about that society. For example, in ancient Rome (as Diane Ackerman tells us in "The Social

Sense"), a feast might have included a calf stuffed with a pig that was, in turn, stuffed with a lamb, which contained a chicken, inside of which was a rabbit stuffed with a dormouse. This culinary practice might suggest to some that the ancient Romans were decadent and turned their banquets into spectacles. Today most Americans would consider the Scottish national dish haggis strange. Haggis is made of the heart and liver of a sheep or calf, minced with suet and oatmeal, highly seasoned, and boiled in the stomach of the animal.

Although most societies find cannibalism abhorrent, in the past, the Maori of New Zealand, tribal peoples in the Solomon Islands, and ancient Fijians ate human flesh during public feasts. The Aztecs not only engaged in ritual sacrifice but also cooked the flesh of the victims (whose hearts had been torn out) in a chili pepper sauce and then served it to the elect with bowls of maize. This ritual (carried out with elaborate costumes and special utensils) horrified the Spanish invaders, whose culture prohibited the eating of human flesh.

The food practices of many societies are governed by bans, or **taboos** (the Maori word *tapu* is the origin of "taboo"), and customs dictated by religion. For example, Islamic dietary laws (called *halal*) based on the Koran prohibit pork and alcohol. Muslims must also fast from sunrise to sunset during Ramadan, the ninth month of the Islamic lunar calender. Orthodox Jews follow the laws of kashruth (keeping kosher), which dictate which foods are clean and fit to eat and which are prohibited. Pork and shellfish are forbidden, meat must be ritually slaughtered, and milk products and meat must not be mixed.

Hindus and most Buddhists are vegetarians and adhere to the concept of ahimsa, or nonviolence. Jains extend the creed of ahimsa and avoid blood-colored foods, such as tomatoes, and root vegetables, whose harvesting may have caused the death of insects. Mormons prohibit all stimulants, including alcohol, coffee, and tea, as do Seventh Day Adventists, who also strongly discourage the eating of shellfish and pork.

The meanings various religions have attached to specific foods (like pork) offer an instructive example of how food taboos are created. Dinitia Smith in "Did a Barnyard Schism Lead to a Religious One?" argues that the abstention of Jews from pork and the consumption of pork by Christians was one important means by which these religions distinguished themselves from each other. Later, followers of Mohammed may have banned the consumption of wine (which played such a central role in Christian ritual) as a way to mark their difference from other major proselytizing religions in the Middle East.

Aside from religious taboos, ecology and culture can determine which foods are valued. For example, bats (whose meat is banned in many European nations) cooked in underground pits are popular in Africa, Asia, Australia, and the South Pacific. The extent to which cultural codes govern food preferences can be inferred from a recently proposed law in California designed to prohibit people from eating animals traditionally viewed as pets. This law was labeled as racist because in the view of many it was clearly intended to keep certain ethnic groups from eating dogs. Yet in many Asian countries, cats and dogs are considered desirable to eat. In fact, in Korea, dog is the fourth most consumed meat and is thought to give strength and vitality.

Besides religion, ecology, and culture, food choices clearly reflect underlying values, philosophies, and social attitudes. For example, in our society, in which food is so abundant, why do millions of young women starve to be thin? For some Americans, a juicy steak dinner is the quintessential meal. Yet scientists tell us that, compared with other primates, many humans may overconsume meat as part of their diet. In many societies, people remain healthy although their diets include no meat. To what extent do attitudes toward meat eating reflect cultural values of aggression and domination over the environment and other species? Beef may be king in the United States because it represents the triumph of civilization over nature and taps into the blood-based symbolism that contributes to the mystique of eating animal flesh. Chicken, pork, and lamb do not enjoy the same status.

Vegetarians, by contrast, reject the slaughter of animals for food and instead eat grains, fruits, and vegetables that can be consumed without harm to the environment. Vegetarianism has gained popularity in the West as more and more consumers have become concerned about the impact on the environment of large-scale meat production. Far from believing that meat is indispensable to strength and good health, vegetarians seem to have conquered the mythic belief in the regenerative power of blood.

Although vegetarianism, organic foods, and herbal medicines are now widely accepted, Americans are still firmly committed to producing food by means of technology. However, genetically engineered foods (including corn, wheat, milk, and soybeans) have begun to attract the attention of Americans. In Europe, consumers have coined the term "Frankenfood" for these genetically engineered products and demand that they be clearly labeled. Europeans are used to buying fresh food every day and are therefore more attuned to the problems that might ensue from this new technology.

DINING RITUALS

The influence of culture has always determined dining rituals. The introduction of metal implements to replace eating with one's hands or using chopsticks is a good illustration. In "Fingers," Margaret Visser shows how the elaborate protocols that govern the use of knives, forks, and spoons speak volumes about the societies in which this practice became the norm.

In *The Empire of Signs* (1982), French literary critic and theorist Roland Barthes compared the Westerner ("armed with pikes and knives") to a predator.

By contrast, Barthes saw the use of chopsticks in Chinese and Japanese societies as more natural ("there is something maternal, the same precisely measured care taken in moving a child [. . .] the instrument never pierces, cuts or slits, never wounds but only selects, turns, shifts. For the chopsticks [. . .] never violate the foodstuff"). In "Chopsticks," Guanlong Cao provides an appreciative analysis of these implements in which he takes us back to his student days in Shanghai, where a handmade pair of chopsticks was cherished and could even become a romantic gift that boys gave to girls.

FOOD AS SYMBOL

Octavio Paz in "Hygiene and Repression" contends that Americans are Puritans at heart—rejecting strong spices and, by implication, anything foreign. Paz contrasts the cuisines of traditional cultures (such as Mexico and India) with American food, with its emphasis on what is good for you rather than what tastes good.

Garrett Hongo, in his poem "Who among You Knows the Essence of Garlic?" begins with the same assumption—that mainstream American society is indifferent, for the most part, to the sensuous qualities of ethnic foods. Hongo challenges his readers to appreciate the diversity of immigrant cultures through their unique dishes. This situation may be evolving: even high school cafeterias throughout the country are adding ethnic foods (everything from Indian-style chicken curry to Jamaican jerk pork and fried plantains, to beef teriyaki, to Greek gyros, and Middle Eastern yogurt sauces) as the tapestry of the student population becomes more **multicultural**—that is, as it includes youth from many cultures with non-European roots.

Even politics plays a role in constructing the social meaning of food. For example, in Slavenka Drakulić's "Pizza in Warsaw, Torte in Prague," which is based on her experiences in Eastern Europe under communism, scarcities of certain foods began to symbolize the failure of the political system to provide for its citizens' needs. The way food can come to embody social aspirations is the theme of William Maxwell's ironic story about an American couple in France obsessed with finding the same delicacies sampled by their friends. These two works provide complementary perspectives on how two different societies designate certain foods as luxuries whose consumption raises social status.

The selections in this chapter illustrate how the meaning food acquires reflects the trends, interests, and values of particular societies. The writers reveal how we read meanings into food and then consume those meanings along with that food.

BILL BRYSON
What's Cooking? Eating in America

Have home-cooked meals become a thing of the past? What does the instant gratification offered by junk foods and fast foods tell us about our society? In this essay, from *Made in American: An Informal History of the English Language in the United States* (1994), Bill Bryson provides a fascinating historical perspective on the catch-as-catch-can eating habits we now accept as normal. Because he lived in England for many years before returning to the United States, Bryson brings a fresh perspective to American culture in works such as *A Walk in the Woods* (1998) and *I'm a Stranger Here Myself* (1999).

Thinking Critically
As you read, consider how Bryson puts fast food in a historical context.

As America became increasingly urbanized, people more and more took to eating their main meal in the evening. To fill the void between breakfast and dinner, a new and essentially American phenomenon arose: lunch. The words *lunch* and *luncheon* (often spelled *luncheon, lunchen, lunchion,* or *lunching*) have been around in English since the late 1500s. Originally they signified lumps of food— "a lunchen of cheese"—and may have come from the Spanish *lonja,* a slice of ham. The word was long considered a deplorable vulgarism, suitable only to the servants' hall. In America, however, "lunch" became respectable, and as it dawned on opportunistic restauranteurs that each day millions of office workers required something quick, simple, and cheap, a wealth of new facilities sprang up to answer the demand. In short order Americans got *diners* (1872), *lunch counters* (1873), *self-service restaurants* (1885), *cafeterias* (1890s), *automats* (1902), and *short-order restaurants* (1905).

The process began in 1872 in Providence, Rhode Island, when one Walter Scott loaded a wagon with sandwiches, boiled eggs, and other simple fare and parked outside the offices of the *Providence Journal.* Since all the restaurants in town closed at 8 p.m., he had no competition and his business thrived. Soon wagons began appearing all over. By the time Scott retired forty-five years later he had fifty competitors in Providence alone. They were called *lunch wagons,* which was a little odd, since lunch was one thing they didn't serve. A few, seeking greater accuracy, called themselves *night lunch wagons* or *night cafés.* When residents complained about having food sold outside their houses, cities everywhere enacted ordinances banning the wagons. So lunch wagon proprietors hit on the idea of moving their wagons to vacant lots, taking off the wheels, and calling them restaurants, since restaurants were immune from the restrictions. By the 1920s, several companies were mass-producing shiny, purpose-built restaurants known everywhere as *diners.* From a business point of view, diners were an appealing proposition. They were cheap to buy and maintain. You could set them up in hours on any level piece of ground, and if trade didn't materialize you loaded them onto a flatbed truck and moved them elsewhere. A single diner in a good location could turn a profit of $12,000 a year—a lot of money in the 1920s. One of the more enduring myths of American eating is that diners were built out of old railway dining cars. Hardly any were. They were just made to look that way.

The first place known to be called a *cafeteria*—though the proprietor spelled it *cafetiria*—was opened in Chicago in the early 1890s. The word came from Cuban Spanish and as late as 1925 was still often pronounced in the Spanish style, with the accent on the penultimate syllable. Cafeterias proved so popular that they spawned a huge, if mercifully short-lived, vogue for words of similar form: *washeteria, groceteria, caketeria, drugeteria, bobateria* (a place where hair was bobbed), *beauteria, chocolateria, shaveteria, smoketeria, hardware-ateria, garmenteria, furnitureteria*—even *casketeria* for a funeral home and the somewhat redundant *restauranteria.*

The *automat*—a cafeteria where food was collected from behind little windows after depositing the requisite change in a slot in each—was not an American invention but a Swedish one. In fact, they had been common in Sweden for half a century before two entrepreneurs named Horn and Hardardt opened one in Philadelphia in 1902 and started a small lucrative empire.

Luncheonette (sometimes modified to *lunchette*) entered American English   5 in about 1920 and in its turn helped to popularize a fashion for words with *-ette* endings: *kitchenette, dinette, usherette, roomette, bachelorette, drum majorette,* even *parkette* for a meter maid and *realtyette* for a female real estate agent.

The waitresses and *hash slingers* (an Americanism dating from 1868) who worked in these establishments evolved a vast, arcane, and cloyingly jocular lingo for the food they served and the clients who ate it. By the1920s if you wanted to work behind a lunch counter you needed to know that *Noah's boy* was a slice of ham (since Ham was one of Noah's sons) and that *burn one* or *grease spot* designated a hamburger. *He'll take a chance* or *clean the kitchen* meant an order of hash, *Adam and Eve on a raft* was two poached eggs on toast, *cat's eyes* was a tapioca pudding, *bird seed* was cereal, *whistleberries* were baked beans, and *dough well done with cow to cover* was the somewhat labored way of calling for an order of toast and butter. Food that had been waiting too long was said to be *growing a beard*. Many of these shorthand terms have since entered the mainsteam, notably *BLT* for a bacon, lettuce, and tomato sandwich, *over easy* and *sunny side up* in respect of eggs, and *hold* as in "hold the mayo."

Eating out—usually quickly, cheaply, and greasily—became a habit for urban workers and a big business for the providers. Between 1910 and 1925 the number of restaurants in America rose by 40 percent. A hungry New Yorker in 1925 could choose among seventeen thousand restaurants, double the number that had existed a decade before. Even drugstores got in on the act. By the early 1920s, the average drugstore, it was estimated, did 60 percent of its business at the soda fountain. They had become, in effect, restaurants that also sold pharmaceutical supplies.

As the American diet grew livelier, it inevitably sparked alarm among those who believed that sensual pleasures were necessarily degenerate. There arose, in the second half of the nineteenth century, mighty bands of men and women who believed with a kind of religious fervor that the consumption of the wrong foods would lead to the breakdown of the nation's moral fiber. One man went so far as to form a Society for the Suppression of Eating, which would appear to be taking matters about as far as they will go. Others were only slightly more accommodating to the need for sustenance. Typical of the breed was the Reverend Sylvester Graham, who connected insanity with eating ketchup and mustard, and believed that the consumption of meat would result in the sort of hormonal boisterousness that leads men to take advantage of pliant women. Many believed him—so many indeed that by mid-century the nation was not only following his cheerless recipes, but many thousands of people were living in Graham boardinghouses, where his dietary precepts were imposed with rigor. His one lasting contribution to the American stomach was the graham cracker. Then there was Horace Fletcher, who gave the world the notion that each bite of food should be chewed thirty-two times. Though he had no standing as a nutritionist—he was an importer by trade—that didn't stop him from disseminating his theories in a phenomenally successful book, *The ABC of Nutrition*, published in 1903.

But the zenith of America's long obsessive coupling of food with moral rectitude came with a Seventh-Day Adventist doctor named John Harvey Kellogg who in 1876 took over the failing Western Health Reform Institute in Battle Creek, Michigan, renamed it the Medical and Surgical Sanitarium (though everyone soon knew it as the Battle Creek Sanitarium or simply the Kellogg), and introduced a regime of treatments that was as bizarre as it was popular. Possibly the two were not unconnected.

10   Patients who were underweight were confined to their beds with sandbags on their abdomens and forced to eat up to twenty-six meals a day. They were not permitted any physical exertion. Even their teeth were brushed by an attendant lest they needlessly expend a calorie. The hypertensive were required to

eat grapes and nothing else—up to fourteen pounds of them daily. Others with less easily discernible maladies were confined to wheelchairs for months on end and fed experimental foods such as gluten wafers and "a Bulgarian milk preparation known as yogurt." Kellogg himself was singular in his habits. It was his practice to dictate long tracts on the evils of meat-eating and mastur-bation (the one evidently led to the other) while seated on the toilet or while riding his bicycle in circles around the lawn. Despite—or very possibly because of—these peculiarities, Kellogg's "Temple of Health" thrived and grew into a substantial complex with such classy amenities as elevators, room service, and a palm house with its own orchestra. Among its devoted and well-heeled patrons were Teddy Roosevelt and John D. Rockefeller.

Throughout much of his life, Kellogg nurtured a quiet obsession with invent-ing a flaked breakfast cereal. One night the process came to him in a dream. He hastened to the kitchen in his nightshirt, boiled some wheat, rolled it out into strips, and baked it in the oven. It was not only tasty but sufficiently un-usual to be unquestionably good for you. Dr. Kellogg's patients simply couldn't get enough of it. One of these patients was a young man named C. W. Post, who spent nine months at the sanitarium sitting listlessly and needlessly in a wheelchair before abruptly embracing Christian Science and fleeing. One thing Post took away with him was a profound respect for the commercial possibili-ties of Dr. Kellogg's cereal. Unable to get a license from Kellogg, he decided to make his own, and in a breathtakingly short time became one of America's wealthiest men. Among Post's inventions were *Grape-Nuts* (a curious name, since it contained neither grapes nor nuts) and *Post Toasties*, or *Elijah's Manna* as it was known until 1908.

As it dawned on people that breakfast cereals were awfully easy to make, innu-merable imitators sprang up. By the turn of the century at least forty-four compa-nies in Battle Creek were churning out breakfast cereals with names like *Grip Nuts, Hello-Billo, Malt-Ho, Flake-Ho, Korn Kure, Tryabita, Tryachewa, Oatsina, Food of Eden,* and *Orange Meat* (which, like Grape-Nuts contained neither of the speci-fied ingredients). Without exception these products were sold as health foods.[*] Each packet of Grape-Nuts contained an illustrated leaflet, *The Road to Wellville,* explaining how a daily dose of the enclosed toasted wheat-and-barley granules would restore depleted brain and nerve cells and build strong red blood. For a short but deliriously exciting time, fortunes were there for the taking. A Method-ist preacher named D. D. Martin cooked up some healthful goop on the kitchen stove, dubbed it *Per-Fo,* and immediately sold the formula for $100,000. Curi-ously almost the only person in Battle Creek unable to capitalize on Kellogg's invention was Kellogg himself. Not until 1907, when he at last brought to market his cornflakes, did he begin to get the credit and wealth his invention merited.

---

[*]Compared with later cereals they certainly were. Kellogg's Sugar Smacks, introduced in 1953, were 56 percent sugar.

Preoccupation with health-enhancing qualities became a theme for all manner of foods. Moxie, known for its soft drinks, was founded in 1885 as the Moxie Nerve Food Company of Boston, and Dr. Pepper, founded in the same year, was so called not because the name was catchy but because it sounded sternly healthful. For a time, it seemed that no food product could hope to sell unless it dealt vigorously with a range of human frailties. Quaker Oats claimed to curb nervousness and constipation. Fleischmann's Yeast not only soothed frayed nerves and loosed the bowels, but also dealt vigorously with indigestion, skin disorders, tooth decay, obesity, and a vague but ominous-sounding disorder called "fallen stomach." Fleischmann's kept up these sweeping claims—occasionally added to them—until ordered to desist by the Federal Trade Commission in 1938 on the grounds that there wasn't a shred of evidence to support any of them.

Against such a background it is little wonder that Americans turned with a certain enthusiasm to junk food. The term *junk food* didn't enter the American vocabulary until 1973, but the concept was there long before, and it began with one of the great breakthroughs in food history: the development of a form of edible solid chocolate.

15   Though a New World food (the Mayas and Aztecs so prized it that they used cocoa beans as money), chocolate took a long time to become a central part of the American diet. Not until just before the Revolution did it become known in colonial America, and then only as a drink. At first chocolate was so exotic that it was spelled and pronounced in a variety of ways—*chockolatta, chuchaletto, chocolate, chockolatto*—before finally settling in the late eighteenth century into something close to the original Nuahtl Indian word, *xocólatl*. Chocolate came from the cacao tree, which somehow became transliterated into English as *cocoa* (pronounced at first with three syllables: "co-co-a"). The chocolate bar was invented in England in the 1840s and milk chocolate in Switzerland some thirty years later, but neither became popular in America until Milton Snavely Hershey gave the world the nickel Hershey bar in 1903. (The price would stay a nickel for the next sixty-seven years, but only at a certain palpable cost to the bar's dimensions. Just in the quarter century following World War II, the bar shrank a dozen times, until by 1970, when it was beginning to look perilously like a chocolate credit card, the bar was reinvigorated in size and the price raised accordingly.)

As is so often the case with American entrepreneurs, Milton Hershey was an unlikely success. His formal education ended with the fourth grade and he spent decades as a struggling small-time candy maker before suddenly and unexpectedly striking it rich in middle age with caramels, a new sensation that swept the country in the late nineteenth century.

In 1900, he sold his caramel business for $1 million—this at a time when $10 was a good weekly wage—and turned his attentions to the still fairly novel process of making milk chocolate. This new venture was such a huge and instantaneous success that within three years he was able to embark on building his own model community, complete with streets named Chocolate Avenue and Cocoa Avenue, near his birthplace of Derry Church in central Pennsylvania. Among the names Hershey considered for the new town were *Ulikit, Chococoa City,* and *Qualitytells,* but eventually he decided on *Hersheykoko.* For reasons lost to history, the postal authorities refused to countenance the name and he was forced to settle on the more mundane, but unquestionably apt, name *Hershey.* As well as the world's largest chocolate factory, the town of Hershey boasted several parks, a boating lake, a museum, a zoo, a professional ice hockey team, and the usual complement of banks, stores, and offices, all owned by Mr. Hershey.

Hershey ran the town as a private fiefdom. He prowled the streets looking for malingering municipal workers, whom he would instantly dismiss, and personally supervised (with presumed keenness) the censoring of movies at the local bijou. But he also engaged in many charitable works, notably the building of one of the world's largest orphanages for boys (and boys alone; orphan girls would have to look elsewhere) and endowing it with most of his fortune, some $66 million (today worth $1.7 billion).

The first true candy bar—that is, one containing ingredients additional to chocolate—was the Squirrel Brand peanut bar. Introduced in 1905, it sold well, but was quickly overtaken by the innovation of 1912, the *Goo Goo Cluster.* But the golden age of candy bars was the 1920s. Several classics made their debut in that busy decade—the *Oh Henry!* and *Baby Ruth* bars in 1920, the *Milky Way* and *Butterfingers* in 1923, *Mr. Goodbar* in 1925, *Snickers* in 1930. The Baby Ruth was originally called the *Kandy Kake,* but in 1920 the Curtiss Candy Company changed the name. The company steadfastly maintained that change had nothing to do with the baseball hero Babe Ruth—who just happened to be the hottest thing in baseball in 1920—but rather was in honor of the daughter of president Grover Cleveland. This bonny infant had indeed captured America's heart and gained the affectionate sobriquet Baby Ruth, but that had been more than twenty years earlier. By 1920 she had been dead for sixteen years, and thus would not appear to have been an obvious candidate for gustatory immortalization. Still, if the Curtiss story is to be believed, Baby Ruth was no odder a designation for a candy bar than *Oh Henry!*—said to be named for the fresh-faced youth whose droll quips to the girls at the George Williamson candy factory in Chicago provoked the constant cry, "Oh, Henry!"

Among the many hundreds of other candy bars loosed on a willing nation   20
during the decade were *Big Dearos, Fat Emmas,* the *Milk Nut Loaf,* and the intriguing *Vegetable Sandwich.* Made of chocolate-covered vegetables, it was sold with the solemn assurance that "it will not constipate." As might have been predicted, constipation was not a compelling preoccupation among America's children and the Vegetable Sandwich soon disappeared from the scene. Equally improbable was the *Chicken Dinner* candy bar, so called because it was supposed

to engender the feeling of well-being provided by a steaming roast chicken dinner. Though few people were able to make the leap of imagination necessary to equate a 5-cent chocolate peanut roll with a well-balanced meal, the Chicken Dinner sold well and survived into the 1960s. Curiously, none of these products were known as *candy bars*. The term is not recorded in print until 1943.

The 1920s saw the birth of many other well-loved snack foods, including such perennial mainstays of the American diet as the *Good Humor* bar in 1920, the *Eskimo Pie* a year later, *Popsicles* in 1924, *Milk Duds* in 1926, *Hostess Cakes* in 1926 (with *Twinkies* to follow in 1930), and *Dubble Bubble Gum* in 1928. This last was invented by Frank H. Fleer, whose earlier bubble gum, *Blibber-Blubber*, was something of a failure—it tended to dissolve in the mouth but to stick tenaciously to everything else, including Junior's face, when popped—but who had made a fortune with an earlier invention, *Chiclets*. But the runaway success of the decade was the Eskimo Pie (originally called the *I-Scream-Bar* by its inventor, a high school teacher and part-time ice cream salesman in Onawa, Iowa). So immensely popular was the Eskimo Pie that within three months of its introduction more than a million bars a day were being sold and the price of cocoa beans on the open market had leaped 50 percent in response.

But all of these paled in comparison with a dietary behemoth that emerged from the shadows in the 1920s and took its place at the top of the table. I refer of course to the hamburger. No one knows where the first hamburger was made. The presumption has always been that it came to America from Hamburg, Germany, in the same way that the frankfurter came from Frankfort and baloney came from Bologna. But this overlooks the niggling consideration that Hamburg has never had any tradition of serving such a dish. Considering its central role in the American diet, the evidence as to when the hamburger first appeared and why it was so called is vexingly uncertain, though there is no shortage of claimants for the title. Among the more insistent, if not necessarily most likely, contenders have been the towns of Seymour, Wisconsin, and Hamburg, New York, both of which claim to have been the birthplace of the hamburger in 1885. Seymour attributes the invention to one Charles Nagreen and unequivocally advertises itself as the "Home of the Hamburger," though its supporters tend to grow quiet when asked to explain on what basis Nagreen chose to commemorate a distant German city. More plausible, on the face of it, would appear to be the claim of Hamburg, New York, whose proponents believe that it was the inspired creation of the brothers Frank and Charles Menches, who developed it at the Erie County Fair in 1885.

Unfortunately for both claims, the etymological evidence suggests an earlier birth for the name, if not the dish. There is some evidence to suggest that it may have appeared as *Hamburg steak* on a Delmonico's menu as early as 1836 or 1837. The first undisputed sighting has been traced to the *Boston Journal* of February 16, 1884, which wrote in passing. "We take a chicken and boil it. When it is cold we cut it up as they do meat to make a Hamburg steak." As so often happens with first citations, the context makes it clear that by this time the dish was already well known. Unfortunately, it also indicates that it was a different dish from the one that we know today, involving as it did beef cut up rather than ground, and eaten cold. What is certain is that *Hamburg steak* was widely called *hamburger steak* by 1889 (the first reference was in a newspaper in Walla Walla, Washington, suggesting that by this time it was eaten nationwide). The term in turn was generally being shortened to *hamburger* by 1901, by which time it had come to signify a patty of ground beef fried on a grill.

But it was still not a sandwich. It was, rather, a lump of ground beef served bare and eaten with a knife and fork. Who first had the idea of serving it in a bun is unknown and essentially unprovable, though once again there is no shortage of claimants. One such is Louis' Lunch of New Haven, Connecticut, which claims to have invented the true article in 1900, though some purists dismiss Louis' on the grounds that it served its burgers (indeed still does) on toasted bread rather than buns. Kaelin's Restaurant in Louisville, meanwhile, claims to have concocted and named the first cheeseburger in 1934, and I've no doubt that there are many other places around the country making similar heartfelt assertions. In any case, we can safely say that by about 1910 the object that we now know and venerate as the hamburger was widely consumed and universally known by that name. Even so, it had yet to fully establish itself in the hearts, and stomachs, of Americans.

In its early years the hamburger was often regarded by short-order cooks 25 as a convenient way of passing off old or doubtful meat, and by its consumers, in consequence, as an item to be approached with caution. Not until 1921, with the rise of two entrepreneurs in Wichita, Kansas, did the hamburger begin to take its first vigorous strides towards respectability. The men in question were a former insurance executive named E. W. "Billy" Ingram and a short-order cook named Walter A. Anderson, and their brilliant stroke was to offer the world decent hamburgers using fresh meat. Not much fresh meat, mind you. Their steam-fried hamburgers cost a nickel and weren't much larger. Ingram and Anderson managed to squeeze eighteen hamburgers from a pound of ground beef, significantly less than one ounce each. Nonetheless, people were soon flocking to their tiny cubicle, built of rock-faced concrete shaped vaguely, and a little preposterously, in the image of a castle. They called it White Castle because, they explained, *white* symbolized purity and cleanliness, and *castle* suggested permanence and stability.

Anderson and Ingram hit on three novelties that sealed their success and have been the hallmarks of fast-food service ever since. They offered a limited menu, which promoted quick service and allowed them to concentrate on what they were good at; they kept their premises spotless, which encouraged confidence in their hygienic integrity; and they employed a distinctive, eye-catching design for the building, which made it instantly recognizable from blocks away. Soon there were White Castles all over the country and a following throng of eager imitators—White Tower, White Diamond, Royal Castle, and White

Crest—some of which are said to survive yet. The age of fast food was upon us, though no one would know it as such for another thirty years. *Fast food* first appeared in 1954 (as an adjective it had appeared three years earlier). *Takeout food* was even slower to arrive; its first recorded appearance was not until 1962.

Engaging the Text

1. What does the appearance of the restaurant as a social institution signify about the change in eating habits of Americans between 1827 and 1870? What social factors explain why the luncheonette, cafeteria, and diner became increasingly important?

2. How was the creation of ready-to-eat breakfast cereals intended to offset the deteriorating moral fiber and changing values of the country? What role did Dr. Kellogg and Reverend Sylvester Graham play? Are their values, as expressed in food, still relevant? What form do they take? If you are near Battle Creek, Michigan, you might visit Kellogg's Cereal City USA, a $22 million interactive museum devoted to corn flakes, which opened in 1998. If you are not nearby, you can go to <http://kelloggscerealcityusa.org>.

3. How is Bryson's analysis structured to emphasize the cause-and-effect relationships of trends and fads in America's food preferences in the past century? Evaluate the evidence Bryson offers to support his analysis. Can you cite some of the transitions he provides to help readers see the logical connections between the assertions he makes?

Exploring Your Cultural Perspective

1. Why, in your opinion, are outlandish eating contests so popular? What does their popularity imply about America's attitude toward the conspicuous production and consumption of food? Are the same needs met by creating food as spectacle (for example, a fifty-foot pizza)? *The Guinness Book of Records* (2000) is a good source for authenticated examples of food on an unsurpassed scale: a two-ton pumpkin; the biggest strawberry shortcake, measuring 827 feet and using 3,995 pounds of strawberries. If you could be listed in this book for a food-related exploit, what would it be? In a short essay, speculate on how food consumed or displayed in these unique ways takes on a significance it does not have in its everyday context. For example, in a noncontest setting, someone who ate ten hot dogs in two minutes would be avoided, not applauded.

2. In what way does the cartoon by Cathy Guisewite in Figure 2.1 offer a tongue-in-cheek comment on the evolution of American cooking habits that Bill Bryson describes? How does the picture from *Consumer Reports* in Figure 2.2 support Bryson's analysis?

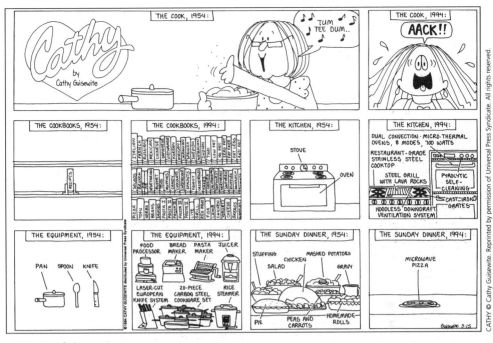

FIGURE 2.1

FIGURE 2.2

CONRAD P. KOTTAK
Rituals at McDonald's

The success of McDonald's (where, by some estimates, seven percent of all restaurant meals in the United States are eaten) has made the hamburger a symbol of American culture throughout the world. But what exactly does this venerable institution tell us about ourselves? In "Rituals at McDonald's," the cultural anthropologist Conrad P. Kottak examines how McDonald's utilizes mass production, speed, and standardization to create the commercial equivalent of a religious experience under its golden arches. This classic essay first appeared in Kottak's book *Anthropology: The Study of Human Diversity* (1978). Kottak has also written *Prime Time Society* (1990), an account of television as a social force; *Mirror for Humanity: A Concise Introduction to Cultural Anthropology* (1999); with Kathryn A. Kozaitis, *On Being Different: Diversity and Multiculturalism in the North American Mainstream* (1999); and *Cultural Anthropology* (2000).

Thinking Critically
Kottak examines the McDonald's experience as a set of unique cultural rituals. Why is McDonald's perceived as being a distinctly American icon?

The world is blessed each day, on the average, with the opening of a new McDonald's restaurant. They now number more than 4,000 and dot not only the United States but also such countries as Mexico, Japan, Australia, England, France, Germany, and Sweden. The expansion of this international web of franchises and company-owned outlets has been fast and efficient; a little more than twenty years ago McDonald's was limited to a single restaurant in San Bernardino, California. Now, the number of McDonald's outlets has far outstripped the total number of fast-food chains operative in the United States thirty years ago.

McDonald's sales reached $1.3 billion in 1972, propelling it past Kentucky Fried Chicken as the world's largest fast-food chain. It has kept this position ever since. Annual sales now exceed $3 billion. McDonald's is the nation's leading buyer of processed potatoes and fish. Three hundred thousand cattle die each year as McDonald's customers down another three billion burgers. A 1974 advertising budget of $60 million easily made the chain one of the country's top advertisers. Ronald McDonald, our best-known purveyor of hamburgers, French fries, and milk shakes, rivals Santa Claus and Mickey Mouse as our children's most familiar fantasy character.

How does an anthropologist, accustomed to explaining the life styles of diverse cultures, interpret these peculiar developments and attractions that influence the daily life of so many Americans? Have factors other than low cost, taste, fast service, and cleanliness—all of which are approximated by other chains—contributed to McDonald's success? Could it be that in consuming McDonald's products and propaganda, Americans are not just eating and watching television but are experiencing something comparable in some respects to a religious ritual? A brief consideration of the nature of ritual may answer the latter question.

Several key features distinguish ritual from other behavior, according to anthropologist Roy Rappaport. Foremost are formal ritual events—stylized, repetitive, and stereotyped. They occur in special places, at regular times, and include liturgical orders—set sequences of words and actions laid down by someone other than the current performer.

Rituals also convey information about participants and their cultural traditions. Performed year after year, generation after generation, they translate enduring messages, values, and sentiments into observable action. Although some participants may be more strongly committed than others to the beliefs on which rituals are based, all people who take part in joint public acts signal their acceptance of an order that transcends their status as individuals.

In the view of some anthropologists, including Rappoport himself, such secular institutions as McDonald's are not comparable to rituals. They argue that rituals involve special emotions, nonutilitarian intentions, and supernatural entities that are not characteristic of Americans' participation in McDonald's. But other anthropologists define ritual more broadly. Writing about football in contemporary America, William Arens (*see* "The Great American Football Ritual") points out that behavior can simultaneously have sacred as well as secular aspects. Thus, on one level, football can be interpreted simply as a sport, while on another, it can be viewed as a public ritual.

While McDonald's is definitely a mundane, secular institution—just a place to eat—it also assumes some of the attributes of a sacred place. And in the context of comparative religion, why should this be surprising? The French sociologist Emile Durkheim long ago pointed out that some societies worship the ridiculous as well as the sublime. The distinction between the two does not depend on the intrinsic qualities of the sacred symbol. Durkheim found that Australian aborigines often worshipped such humble and nonimposing creatures as ducks, frogs, rabbits, and grubs—animals whose inherent qualities hardly could have been the origin of the religious sentiment they inspired. If frogs and grubs can be elevated to a sacred level, why not McDonald's?

I frequently eat lunch—and, occasionally, breakfast and dinner—at McDonald's. More than a year ago, I began to notice (and have subsequently observed more carefully) certain ritual behavior at these fast-food restaurants. Although for natives, McDonald's seems to be just a place to eat, careful observation of what goes on in any outlet in this country reveals an astonishing degree of formality and behavioral uniformity on the part of both staff and customers. Particularly impressive is the relative invariance in act and utterance that has developed in the absence of a distinct theological doctrine. Rather, the ritual aspect of McDonald's rests on twentieth-century technology—particularly automobiles, television, work locales, and the one-hour lunch.

The changes in technology and work organization that have contributed to the chain's growth in the United States are now taking place in other countries. Only in a country such as France, which has an established and culturally enshrined cuisine that hamburgers and fish fillets cannot hope to displace, is McDonald's expansion likely to be retarded. Why has McDonald's been so much more successful than other businesses, than the United States Army, and even than many religious institutions in producing behavioral invariance?

10   Remarkably, even Americans traveling abroad in countries noted for their distinctive food usually visit the local McDonald's outlet. This odd behavior is probably caused by the same factors that urge us to make yet another trip to a McDonald's here. Wherever a McDonald's may be located, it is a home away from home. At any outlet, Americans know how to behave, what to expect, what they will eat, and what they will pay. If one has been unfortunate enough to have partaken of the often indigestible pap dished out by any turnpike restaurant monopoly, the sight of a pair of McDonald's golden arches may justify a detour off the highway, even if the penalty is an extra toll.

In Paris, where the French have not been especially renowned for making tourists feel at home, McDonald's offers sanctuary. It is, after all, an American institution, where Americans, who are programmed by years of prior experience to salivate at the sight of the glorious hamburger, can feel completely at home. Americans in Paris can temporarily reverse roles with their hosts; if they cannot act like the French, neither can the French be expected to act in a culturally appropriate manner at McDonald's. Away from home, McDonald's, like a familiar church, offers not just hamburgers but comfort, security, and reassurance.

An American's devotion to McDonald's rests in part on uniformities associated with almost all McDonald's: setting, architecture, food, ambience, acts, and utterances. The golden arches, for example, serve as a familiar and almost universal landmark, absent only in those areas where zoning laws prohibit garish signs. At a McDonald's near the University of Michigan campus in Ann Arbor, a small, decorous sign—golden arches encircled in wrought iron—identifies the establishment. Despite the absence of the towering arches, this McDonald's, where I have conducted much of my fieldwork, does not suffer as a ritual setting. The restaurant, a contemporary brick structure that has been nominated for a prize in architectural design, is best known for its stained-glass windows, which incorporate golden arches as their focal point. On bright days, sunlight floods in on waiting customers through a skylight that recalls the clerestory of a Gothic cathedral. In the case of this McDonald's, the effect is to equate traditional religious symbols and golden arches. And in the view of the natives I have interviewed, the message is clear.

When Americans go to a McDonald's restaurant, they perform an ordinary, secular, biological act—they eat, usually lunch. Yet immediately upon entering, we can tell from our surroundings that we are in a sequestered place, somehow apart from the messiness of the world outside. Except for such anomalies as the Ann Arbor campus outlet, the town house McDonald's in New York City, and the special theme McDonald's of such cities as San Francisco, Saint Paul, and Dallas, the restaurants rely on their arches, dull brown brick, plate-glass sides, and mansard roofs to create a setting as familiar as home. In some of the larger outlets, murals depicting "McDonaldland" fantasy characters, sports, outdoor activities, and landscapes surround plastic seats and tables. In this familiar setting, we do not have to consider the experience. We know what we will see, say, eat, and pay.

Behind the counter, McDonald's employees are differentiated into such categories as male staff, female staff, and managers. While costumes vary slightly from outlet to outlet and region to region, such apparel as McDonald's hats, ties, and shirts, along with dark pants and shining black shoes, are standard.

The food is also standard, again with only minor regional variations. (Some restaurants are selected to test such new menu items as "McChicken" or different milk shake flavors.) Most menus, however, from the rolling hills of Georgia to the snowy plains of Minnesota, offer the same items. The prices are also the same and the menu is usually located in the same place in every restaurant. *15*

Utterances across each spotless counter are standardized. Not only are customers limited in what they can choose but also in what they can say. Each item on the menu has its appropriate McDonald's designation: "quarter pounder with cheese" or "filet-O-fish" or "large fries." The customer who asks, "What's a Big Mac?" is as out of place as a southern Baptist at a Roman Catholic Mass.

At a McDonald's that I frequent, the phrases uttered by the salespeople are just as standard as those of the customers. If I ask for a quarter pounder, the ritual response is "Will that be with cheese, sir?" If I do not order French fries, the agent automatically incants, "Will there be any fries today, sir?" And when

I pick up my order, the agent conventionally says, "Have a nice day, sir," followed by, "Come in again."

Nonverbal behavior of McDonald's agents is also programmed. Prior to opening the spigot of the drink machine, they fill paper cups with ice exactly to the bottom of the golden arches that decorate them. As customers request food, agents look back to see if desired item is available. If not, they reply, "That'll be a few minutes, sir (or ma'am)," after which the order of the next customer is taken.

McDonald's lore of appropriate verbal and nonverbal behavior is even taught at the "seminary," Hamburger University, located in Elk Grove Village, Illinois, near Chicago's O'Hare airport. Managers who attend choose either a two-week basic "operator's course" or an eleven-day "advanced operator's course." With a 360-page *Operations Manual* as their bible, students learn about food, equipment, and management techniques—delving into such esoteric subjects as buns, shortening, and carbonization. Filled with the spirit of McDonald's, graduates take home such degrees as bachelor or master of hamburgerology to display in their outlets. Their job is to spread the word—the secret success formula they have learned—among assistant managers and crew in their restaurants.

20   The total McDonald's ambiance invites comparison with sacred places. The chain stresses clean living and reaffirms those traditional American values that transcend McDonald's itself. Max Boas and Steve Chain, biographers of McDonald's board chairman, Ray Kroc, report that after the hundredth McDonald's opened in 1959, Kroc leased a plane to survey likely sites for the chain's expansion. McDonald's would invade the suburbs by locating its outlets near traffic intersections, shopping centers, and churches. Steeples figured prominently in Kroc's plan. He believed that suburban churchgoers would be preprogrammed consumers of the McDonald's formula—quality, service, and cleanliness.

McDonald's restaurants, nestled beneath their transcendent arches and the American flag, would enclose immaculate restrooms and floors, counters and stainless steel kitchens. Agents would sparkle, radiating health and warmth. Although to a lesser extent than a decade ago, management scrutinizes employee's hair length, height, nails, teeth, and complexions. Long hair, bad breath, stained teeth, and pimples are anathema. Food containers also defy pollution; they are used only once. (In New York City, the fast-food chain Chock Full O' Nuts foreshadowed this theme long ago and took it one step further by assuring customers that our food was never touched by human hands.)

Like participation in rituals, there are times when eating at McDonald's is not appropriate. A meal at McDonald's is usually confined to ordinary, everyday life. Although the restaurants are open virtually every day of the year, most Americans do not go there on Thanksgiving, Easter, Passover, or other religious and quasi-religious days. Our culture reserves holidays for family and friends. Although Americans neglect McDonald's on holidays, the chain reminds us through television that it still endures, that it will welcome us back once our holiday is over.

The television presence of McDonald's is particularly obvious on holidays, whether it be through the McDonald's All-American Marching Band (two clean-cut high school students from each state) in a nationally televised Thanksgiving Day parade or through sponsorship of sports and family entertainment programs.

Although such chains as Burger King, Burger Chef, and Arby's compete with McDonald's for fast-food business, none rivals McDonald's success. The explanation reflects not just quality, service, cleanliness, and value but, more importantly, McDonald's advertising, which skillfully appeals to different audiences. Saturday morning television, for example, includes a steady dose of cartoons and other children's shows sponsored by McDonald's. The commercials feature several McDonaldland fantasy characters, headed by the clown Ronald McDonald, and often stress the enduring aspects of McDonald's. In one, Ronald has a time machine that enables him to introduce hamburgers to the remote past and distant future. Anyone who noticed the shot of the McDonald's restaurant in the Woody Allen film *Sleeper*, which takes place 200 years hence, will be aware that the message of McDonald's as eternal has gotten across. Other children's commercials gently portray the conflict between good (Ronald) and evil (Hamburglar). McDonaldland's bloblike Grimace is hooked on milk shakes, and Hamburglar's addiction to simple burgers regularly culminates in his confinement to a "patty wagon," as Ronald and Big Mac restore and preserve the social order.

Pictures of McDonaldland appear on cookie boxes and, from time to time, ₂₅ on durable plastic cups that are given away with the purchase of a large soft drink. According to Boas and Chain, a McDonaldland amusement park, comparable in scale to Disneyland, is planned for Las Vegas. Even more obvious are children's chances to meet Ronald McDonald and other McDonaldland characters in the flesh. Actors portraying Ronald scatter their visits, usually on Saturdays, among McDonald's outlets throughout the country. A Ronald can even be rented for a birthday party or for Halloween trick or treating.

McDonald's adult advertising has a different, but equally effective, theme. In 1976, a fresh-faced, sincere young woman invited the viewer to try breakfast—a new meal at McDonald's—in a familiar setting. In still other commercials, healthy, clean-living Americans gambol on ski slopes or in mountain pastures. The single theme running throughout all the adult commercials is personalism. McDonald's, the commercials tell us, is not just a fast-food restaurant. It is a warm, friendly place where you will be graciously welcomed. Here, you will feel at home with your family, and your children will not get into trouble. The word *you* is emphasized—"You deserve a break today"; "You, you're the one"; "We do it all for you." McDonald's commercials say that you are not simply a face in the crowd. At McDonald's, you can find respite from a hectic and impersonal society—the break you deserve.

Early in 1977, after a brief flirtation with commercials that harped on the financial and gustatory benefits of eating at McDonald's, the chain introduced one of its more cautious incentives—the "Big Mac attack." Like other extraordinary and irresistible food cravings, which people in many cultures attribute to demons or other spirits, a Big Mac attack could strike anyone at any time. In one commercial, passengers on a jet forced the pilot to land at the nearest McDonald's. In others, a Big Mac attack had the power to give life to an inanimate object, such as a suit of armor, or restore a mummy to life.

McDonald's advertising typically de-emphasizes the fact that the chain is, after all, a profit-making organization. By stressing its program of community projects, some commercials present McDonald's as a charitable organization. During the Bicentennial year, commercials reported that McDonald's was giving 1,776 trees to every state in the union. Brochures at outlets echo the television message that, through McDonald's, one can sponsor a carnival to aid victims of muscular dystrophy. In 1976 and 1977 McDonald's managers in Ann Arbor persuaded police officers armed with metal detectors to station themselves at restaurants during Halloween to check candy and fruit for hidden pins and razor blades. Free coffee was offered to parents. In 1976, McDonald's sponsored a radio series documenting the contributions Blacks have made to American history.

McDonald's also sponsored such family television entertainment as the film *The Sound of Music*, complete with a prefatory, sermonlike address by Ray Kroc. Commercials during the film showed Ronald McDonald picking up after litterbugs and continued with the theme, "We do it all for you." Other commercials told us that McDonald's supports and works to maintain the values of American family life—and went so far as to suggest a means of strengthening what most Americans conceive to be the weakest link in the nuclear family, that of father-child. "Take a father to lunch," kids were told.

30   Participation in McDonald's rituals involves temporary subordination of individual differences in a social and cultural collectivity. By eating at McDonald's, not only do we communicate that we are hungry, enjoy hamburgers, and have inexpensive tastes but also that we are willing to adhere to a value system and a series of behaviors dictated by an exterior entity. In a land of tremendous ethnic, social, economic, and religious diversity, we proclaim that we share something with millions of other Americans.

Sociologists, cultural anthropologists, and others have shown that social ties based on kinship, marriage, and community are growing weaker in the contemporary United States. Fewer and fewer people participate in traditional organized religions. By joining sects, cults, and therapy sessions, Americans seek many of the securities that formal religion gave to our ancestors. The increasing cultural, rather than just economic, significance of McDonald's, football, and similar institutions is intimately linked to these changes.

As industrial society shunts people around, church allegiance declines as a unifying moral force. Other institutions are also taking over the functions of formal religions. At the same time, traditionally organized religions—Protestantism, Catholicism, and Judaism—are reorganizing themselves along business lines. With such changes, the gap between the symbolic meaning of traditional religions and the realities of modern life widens. Because of this, some sociologists have argued that the study of modern religion must merge with the study of mass culture and mass communication.

In this context, McDonald's has become one of the many new and powerful elements of American culture that provide common expectations, experience, and behavior—overriding region, class, formal religious affiliation, political sentiments, gender, age, ethnic group, sexual preference, and urban, suburban, or rural residence. By incorporating—wittingly or unwittingly—many of the ritual and symbolic aspects of religion, McDonald's has carved its own important niche in a changing society in which automobiles are ubiquitous and where television sets outnumber toilets.

Engaging the Text

1. Kottak suggests that McDonald's is taking over the function of formal religion as church allegiance declines in America ("By incorporating [. . .] many of the ritual and symbolic aspects of religion, McDonald's has carved its own important niche in a changing society [. . .]," paragraph 33). In what ways does Kottak's analysis of the ritualistic aspects of eating at McDonald's support his thesis? Do you find his argument credible or far-fetched? Explain your reasons.

2. What aspects of its corporate image does McDonald's wish to emphasize through the character Ronald McDonald and by sponsoring the Ronald McDonald House? If these services overlap those traditionally provided by churches, will the public be more likely to consider McDonald's as altruistic? Or is the Ronald McDonald House a cynical marketing ploy? Explain your answer in a short essay.

3. Did Kottak's article change your perceptions of the behind-the-scenes construction of folksiness by a huge modern conglomerate? Why is it significant that selections must be called by their exact names and servers always close transactions with "Have a nice day"?

FIGURE 2.3

Exploring Your Cultural Perspective

1. If you are a fast-food aficionado, draw on your own knowledge and experience to describe the unique appeal of your favorite fast-food franchise. Describe the rituals, if any, that contribute to its identity. How often do you go there? Do you always order the same thing? Explain how this particular franchise uses architecture, advertising, employees' uniforms, menu items, and other features to create its distinctive image.

2. A number of themes in popular culture intersect in the McDonald's franchise, as discussed by Kottak. Address two of the issues listed below, drawing on Kottak's observations, your own analysis of McDonald's significance in American culture, and the story conveyed by the pictures in Figures 2.3 (taken in 1955) and 2.4. The official McDonald's Web site at <http://www.mcdonalds.com> gives information on McDonald's restaurants in the 120 countries in which they operate. Issues might include:

   a. the marketing of McDonald's as an oasis of predictability in a controlled environment

   b. the decline of the family meal and how hominess is commercially constructed

   c. similarities between McDonald's and Disney World in terms of the worlds they create for their customers

FIGURE 2.4

d. the Americanization of other cultures

e. the significance of elaborate fast-food packaging and the ethics of a throw-away culture

f. the destruction of tropical forests in Central and South America to raise cattle to produce cheap beef for export

DIANE ACKERMAN
The Social Sense

Although we might not realize that what we like to eat is culturally determined, Diane Ackerman shows us this is indeed the case by revealing the incredible variations in what different cultures have considered to be tasty or repulsive through the ages. "The Social Sense" is drawn from *A Natural History of the Senses* (1990), which later became the PBS television series *Mystery of the Senses*. Ackerman, an accomplished poet and essayist, has also written *The Rarest of the Rare* (1995); *A Slender Thread* (1996); a collection of poems, *I Praise My Destroyer* (1998); and *Deep Play* (1999), and *Cultivating Delight: A Natural History of My Garden* (2001).

Thinking Critically
As you read, evaluate whether Ackerman makes a persuasive case that culture determines what foods we prefer.

The other senses may be enjoyed in all their beauty when one is alone, but taste is largely social. Humans rarely choose to dine in solitude, and food has a powerful social component. The Bantu feel that exchanging food makes a contract between two people who then have a "clanship of porridge." We usually eat with our families, so it's easy to see how "breaking bread" together would symbolically link an outsider to a family group. Throughout the world, the stratagems of business take place over meals; weddings end with a feast; friends reunite at celebratory dinners; children herald their birthdays with ice cream and cake; religious ceremonies offer food in fear, homage, and sacrifice; wayfarers are welcomed with a meal. As Brillat-Savarin says, "every . . . sociability . . . can be found assembled around the same table: love, friendship, business, speculation, power, importunity, patronage, ambition, intrigue . . ." If an event is meant to matter emotionally, symbolically, or mystically, food will be close at hand to sanctify and bind it. Every culture uses food as a sign of approval or commemoration, and some foods are even credited with supernatural powers, others eaten symbolically, still others eaten ritualistically, with ill fortune befalling dullards or skeptics who forget the recipe or get the order of events wrong. Jews attending a Seder eat a horseradish dish to symbolize the tears shed by their ancestors when they were slaves in Egypt. Malays celebrate important events with rice, the inspirational center of their lives. Catholics and Anglicans take a communion of wine and wafer. The ancient Egyptians thought onions symbolized the many-layered universe, and swore oaths on an onion as we might on a Bible. Most cultures embellish eating with fancy plates and glasses, accompany it with parties, music, dinner theater, open-air barbecues, or other forms of revelry. Taste is an intimate sense. We can't taste things at a distance. And how we taste things, as well as the exact makeup of our saliva, may be as individual as our fingerprints.

Food gods have ruled the hearts and lives of many people. Hopi Indians, who revere corn, eat blue corn for strength, but all Americans might be worshiping corn if they knew how much of their daily lives depended on it. Margaret Visser, in *Much Depends on Dinner*, gives us a fine history of corn and its uses: livestock and poultry eat corn; the liquid in canned foods contain corn; corn is used in most paper products, plastics, and adhesives; candy, ice cream, and other goodies contain corn syrup; dehydrated and instant foods contain cornstarch; many familiar objects are made from corn products, brooms and corncob pipes to name only two. For the Hopis, eating corn is itself a form of reverence. I'm holding in my hand a beautifully carved Hopi corn kachina doll made from cottonwood; it represents one of the many spiritual essences of their world. Its cob-shaped body is painted ocher, yellow, black, and white, with dozens of squares drawn in a cross-section-of-a-kernel design, and abstract green leaves spearing up from below. The face has a long, black, rootlike nose, rectangular black eyes, a black ruff made of rabbit fur, white string corn-silk-like ears, brown bird-feather bangs, and two green, yellow, and ocher striped horns topped by rawhide tassels. A fine, soulful kachina, the ancient god Maïs stares back at me, tastefully imagined.

Throughout history, and in many cultures, *taste* has always had a double meaning. The word comes from the Middle English *tasten*, to examine by touch, test, or sample, and continues back to the Latin *taxare*, to touch sharply. So a taste was always a trial or test. People who have taste are those who have appraised life in an intensely personal way and found some of it sublime, the rest of it lacking. Something in bad taste tends to be obscene or vulgar. And we defer to professional critics of wine, food, art, and so forth, whom we trust to taste things for us because we think their taste more refined or educated than ours. A companion is "one who eats bread with another," and people sharing food as a gesture of peace or hospitality like to sit around and chew the fat.

The first thing we taste is milk from our mother's breast,[1] accompanied by love and affection, stroking, a sense of security, warmth, and well-being, our first intense feelings of pleasure. Later on she will feed us solid food from her hands, or even chew food first and press it into our mouths, partially digested. Such powerful associations do not fade easily, as if at all. We say "food" as if it were a simple thing, an absolute like rock or rain to take for granted. But it is a big source of pleasure in most lives, a complex realm of satisfaction both physiological and emotional, much of which involves memories of childhood. Food must taste good, must reward us, or we would not stoke the furnace in each of our cells. We must eat to live, as we must breathe. But breathing is involuntary, finding food is not; it takes energy and planning, so it must tantalize us out of our natural torpor. It must decoy us out of bed in the morning and prompt us to put on constricting clothes, go to work, and perform tasks we may not enjoy for eight hours a day, five days a week, just to "earn our daily bread," or be "worth our salt," if you like, where the word *salary* comes from. And, because we are omnivores, many tastes must appeal to us, so that we'll try new foods. As children grow, they meet regularly throughout the day—at mealtimes—to hear grown-up talk, ask questions, learn about customs, language, and the world. If language didn't arise at mealtimes, it certainly evolved and became more fluent there, as it did during group hunts.

5   We tend to see our distant past through a reverse telescope that compresses it: a short time as hunter-gatherers, a long time as "civilized" people. But civilization is a recent stage of human life, and, for all we know, it may not be any great achievement. It may not even be the final stage. We have been alive on this planet as recognizable humans for about two million years, and for all but the last two or three thousand we've been hunter-gatherers. We may sing in choirs and park our rages behind a desk, but we patrol the world with many of a hunter-gatherer's drives, motives, and skills. These aren't knowable truths. Should an alien civilization ever contact us, the greatest gift they could give us would be a set of home movies: films of our species at each stage in our evolution. Consciousness, the great poem of matter, seems so unlikely, so impossible, and yet here we are with our loneliness and our giant dreams. Speaking into the perforations of a telephone receiver as if through the screen of a confessional, we do sometimes share our emotions with a friend, but usually this is too disembodied, too much like yelling into the wind. We prefer to talk *in person*, as if we could temporarily slide into their feelings. Our friend first offers us food, drink. It is a symbolic act, a gesture that says: *This food will nourish your body as I will nourish your soul.* In hard times, or in the wild, it also says *I will endanger my own life by parting with some of what I must consume to survive.* Those

---

[1]This special milk, called colostrum, is rich in antibodies, the record of the mother's epidemiologic experience.

desperate times may be ancient history, but the part of us forged in such trials accepts the token drink and piece of cheese and is grateful.

FOOD AND SEX

What would the flutterings of courtship be without a meal? As the deliciously sensuous and ribald tavern scene in Fielding's *Tom Jones* reminds us, a meal can be the perfect arena for foreplay. Why is food so sexy? Why does a woman refer to a handsome man as a real dish? Or a French girl call her lover *mon petit chou* (my little cabbage)? Or an American man call his girlfriend cookie? Or a British man describe a sexy woman as a bit of crumpet (a flat, toasted griddle-cake well lubricated with butter)? Or a tart? Sexual hunger and physical hunger have always been allies. Rapacious needs, they have coaxed and driven us through famine and war, to bloodshed and serenity, since our earliest days.

Looked at in the right light, any food might be thought aphrodisiac. Phallic-shaped foods such as carrots, leeks, cucumbers, pickles, sea cucumbers (which become tumescent when soaked), eels, bananas, and asparagus have all been prized as aphrodisiacs at one time or another, as were oysters and figs because they reminded people of female genitalia; caviar because it was a female's eggs; rhinoceros horn, hyena eyes, hippopotamus snout, alligator tail, camel hump, swan genitals, dove brains, and goose tongues, on the principle that anything so rare and exotic must have magical powers; prunes (which were offered free in Elizabethan brothels); peaches (because of their callipygous rumps?); tomatoes, called "love apples," and thought to be Eve's temptation in the Garden of Eden; onions and potatoes, which look testicular, as well as "prairie oysters," the cooked testicles of a bull; and mandrake root, which looks like a man's thighs and penis. Spanish fly, the preferred aphrodisiac of the Marquis de Sade, with which he laced the bonbons he fed prostitutes and friends, is made by crushing a southern European beetle. It contains a gastrointestinal irritant and also produces a better blood flow, the combination of which brings on a powerful erection of either the penis or the clitoris, but also damages the kidneys; it can even be fatal. Musk, chocolate, and truffles also have been considered aphrodisiac and, for all we know, they might well be. But, as sages have long said, the sexiest part of the body and the best aphrodisiac in the world is the imagination.

Primitive peoples saw creation as a process both personal and universal, the earth's yielding food, humans (often molded from clay or dust) burgeoning with children. Rain falls from the sky and impregnates the ground, which brings forth fruit and grain from the tawny flesh of the earth—an earth whose mountains look like reclining women, and whose springs spurt like healthy men. Fertility rituals, if elaborate and frenzied enough, could encourage Nature's bounty. Cooks baked meats and breads in the shape of genitals, especially penises, and male and female statues with their sexual organs exaggerated presided over orgiastic festivities where sacred couples copulated in public. A mythic Gaia poured milk from her breasts and they became galaxies. The ancient Venus figures with global breasts, swollen bellies, and huge buttocks and thighs symbolized the female life-force, mother to crops and humans. The earth itself was a goddess, curvy and ripe, radiant with fertility, aspill with riches. People have thought the Venus figures imaginative exaggerations, but women of that time may indeed have resembled them, all breasts, belly, and rump. When pregnant, they would have bulged into quite an array of shapes.

Food is created by the sex of plants or of animals; and we find it sexy. When we eat an apple or peach, we are eating the fruit's placenta. But, even if that weren't so, and we didn't subconsciously associate food with sex, we would still find it sexy for strictly physical reasons. We use the mouth for many things—to talk and kiss, as well as to eat. The lips, tongue, and genitals all have the same neural receptors, called Krause's end bulbs, which make them ultrasensitive, highly charged. There's a similarity of response.

10   A man and woman sit across from one another in a dimly lit restaurant. A small bouquet of red-and-white spider lilies sweetens the air with the cinnamon-like tingle. A waiter passes with a plate of rabbit sausage in molé sauce. At the next table, a blueberry soufflé oozes scent. Oysters on the half shell, arranged on a large platter of shaved ice, one by one polish the woman's tongue with silken saltiness. A fennel-scented steam rises from thick crabcakes on the man's plate. Small loaves of fresh bread breathe sweetly. Their hands brush as they both reach for the bread. He stares into her eyes, as if filling them with molten lead. They both know where this delicious prelude will lead. *"I'm so hungry,"* she whispers.

THE OMNIVORE'S PICNIC

You have been invited to dinner at the home of extraterrestrials, and asked to bring friends. Being considerate hosts, they first inquire if you have any dietary allergies or prohibitions, and then what sort of food would taste good to you. What do humans eat? they ask. Images cascade through your mind, a cornucopia of plants, animals, minerals, liquids, and solids, in a vast array of cuisines. The Masai enjoy drinking cow's blood. Orientals eat stir-fried puppy. Germans eat rancid cabbage (sauerkraut), Americans eat decaying cucumbers (pickles), Italians eat whole deep-fried songbirds, Vietnamese eat fermented fish dosed with chili peppers, Japanese and others eat fungus (mushrooms), French eat garlic-soaked snails. Upper-class Aztecs ate roasted dog (a hairless variety named *xquintli*, which is still bred in Mexico). Chinese of the Chou dynasty liked rats, which they called "household deer,"[2] and many people still do eat rodents, as well as grasshoppers, snakes, flightless birds, kangaroos, lobsters, snails, and bats. Unlike most other animals, which fill a small yet ample niche in the large web of life on earth, humans are omnivorous. The Earth offers perhaps 20,000 edible plants alone. A poor season for eucalyptus will wipe out a population of koala bears, which have no other food source. But human beings are Nature's great ad libbers and revisers. Diversity is our delight. In a time of drought, we can ankle off to a new locale, or break open a cactus, or dig a well. When plagues of locusts destroy our crops, we can forage on wild plants and roots. If our herds die, we find protein in insects, beans, and nuts. Not that being an omnivore is easy. A koala bear doesn't have to worry about whether or not its next mouthful will be toxic. In fact, eucalyptus is highly poisonous, but a koala has an elaborately protective gut, so it just eats eucalyptus, exactly as its parents did. Cows graze without fear on grass and grain. But omnivores are anxious eaters. They must continually test new foods to see if they're palatable and nutritious, running the risk of inadvertently poisoning themselves. They must take chances on new flavors, and, doing so, they frequently acquire a taste for something offbeat that, though nutritious, isn't the sort of thing that might normally appeal to them—chili peppers (which Columbus introduced to Europe), tobacco, alcohol, coffee, artichokes, or mustard, for instance. When we were hunter-gatherers, we ate a great variety of foods. Some of us still do, but more often we add spices to what we know, or find at hand, *for variety,* as we like to say. Monotony isn't our code. It's safe, in some ways, but in others it's more dangerous. Most of us prefer our foods cooked to the steaminess of freshly killed prey. We don't have ultrasharp carnivore's teeth, but we don't need them. We've created sharp tools. We do have incisor teeth for slicing fruits, and molars for crushing seeds and nuts, as well as canines for ripping flesh. At times, we eat nasturtiums and pea pods and even the effluvia from the mammary glands of cows, churned until it curdles, or frozen into a solid and attached to pieces of wood.

Our hosts propose a picnic, since their backyard is a meadow lit by two suns, and they welcome us and our friends. Our Japanese friend chooses the appetizer: sushi, including shrimp still alive and wriggling. Our French friend suggests a baguette, or better still croissants, which have an unlikely history, which he insists on telling everyone: To celebrate Austria's victory against the invading Ottoman Turks, bakers created pastry in the shape of the crescent on

---

[2]It was the food-obsessed Chinese who started the first serious restaurants during the time of the T'ang dynasty (A.D. 618–907). By the time the Sung dynasty replaced the T'ang, they were all-purpose buildings, with many private dining rooms, where one went for food, sex, and barroom gab.

the Turkish flag, so that the Viennese could devour their enemies at the table as they had on the battlefield. Croissants soon spread to France and, during the 1920s, traveled with other French ways to the United States. Our Amazonian friend chooses the main course—nuptial kings and queens of leafcutter ants, which taste like walnut butter, followed by roasted turtle and sweet-fleshed piranha. Our German friend insists that we include some spaetzle and a loaf of darkest pumpernickel bread, which gets its name from the verb *pumpern*, "to break wind," and *Nickel*, "the devil," because it was thought to be so hard to digest that even the devil would fart if he ate it. Our Tasaday friend wants some natek, a startchy paste his people make from the insides of caryota palm trees. The English cousin asks for a small platter of potted ox tongues, very aged blue cheese, and, for dessert, trifle—whipped cream and slivered almonds on top of a jam-and-custard pudding thick with sherry-soaked ladyfingers.

To finish our picnic lunch, our Turkish friend proposes coffee in the Turkish style—using a mortar and pestle to break up the beans, rather than milling them. To be helpful, he prepares it for us all, pouring boiling water over coffee grounds through a silver sieve into a pot. He brings this to a light boil, pours it through the sieve again, and offers us some of the clearest, brightest coffee we've ever tasted. According to legend, he explains, coffee was discovered by a ninth-century shepherd, who one day realized that his goats were becoming agitated whenever they browsed on the berries of certain bushes. For four hundred years, people thought only to chew the berries. Raw coffee doesn't brew into anything special, but in the thirteenth century someone decided to roast the berries, which releases the pungent oil and the mossy-bitter aroma now so familiar to us. Our Indian friend passes round cubes of sugar, which we are instructed to let melt on the tongue as we sip our coffee, and our minds roam back to the first recorded instance of sugar, in the Atharvaveda, a sacred Hindu text from 800 B.C., which describes a royal crown made of glittering sugar crystals. Then he circulates a small dish of coriander seeds, and we pinch a few in our fingers, set them on our tongues, and feel our mouths freshen from the aromatic tang. A perfect picnic. We thank our hosts for laying on such a splendid feast, and invite them to our house for dinner next. "What do jujubarians eat?" we ask.

OF CANNIBALISM AND SACRED COWS

Even though grass soup was the main food in the Russian gulags, according to Solzhenitsyn's *One Day in the Life of Ivan Denisovich*, humans don't prefer wood, or leaves, or grass—the cellulose is impossible to digest. We also can't manage well eating excrement, although some animals adore it, or chalk or petroleum.

On the other hand, cultural taboos make us spurn many foods that are wholesome and nourishing. Jews don't eat pork, Hindus don't eat beef, and Americans in general won't eat dog, rat, horse, grasshopper, grubs, or many other palatable foods prized by peoples elsewhere in the world. Anthropologist Claude Lévi-Strauss found that primitive tribes designated foods "good to think" or "bad to think." Necessity, the mother of invention, fathers many codes of conduct. Consider the "sacred cow," an idea so shocking it has passed into our vocabulary as a thing, event, or person considered sacrosanct. Though India has a population of around 700 million and a constant need for protein, over two hundred million cattle are allowed to roam the streets as deities while many people go hungry. The cow plays a central role in Hinduism. As Marvin Harris explains in *The Sacred Cow and the Abominable Pig*:

> Cow protection and cow worship also symbolize the protection and adoration of human motherhood. I have a collection of colorful Indian pin-up calendars depicting jewel-bedecked cows with swollen udders and the faces of beautiful human madonnas. Hindu cow worshippers say: "The cow is our mother. She gives us milk and butter. Her male calves till the land and give us food." To critics who oppose the custom of feeding cows that are too old to have calves and give milk, Hindus reply: "Will you then send your mother to a slaughter house when she gets old?"

Not only is the cow sacred in India, even the dust in its hoofprints is sacred. And, according to Hindu theology, 330 million gods live inside each cow. There are many reasons why this national tantalism has come about; one factor may be that an overcrowded land such as India can't support the raising of livestock for food, a system that is extremely inefficient. When people eat animals that have been fed grains, "nine out of ten calories and four out of five grams of protein are lost for human consumption." The animal uses up most of the nutrients. So vegetarianism may have evolved as a remedy, and been ritualized through religion. "I feel confident that the rise of Buddhism was related to mass suffering and environmental depletions," Harris writes, "because several similar nonkilling religions . . . arose in India at the same time." Including Jainism, whose priests not only tend stray cats and dogs, but keep a separate room in their shelters just for insects. When they walk down the street, an assistant walks ahead of them to brush away any insects lest they get stepped on, and they wear gauze masks so they don't accidentally inhale a wayward midge or other insect.

One taboo stands out as the most fantastic and forbidden. "What's eating *15* you?" a man may ask an annoyed friend. Even though his friend just got fired by a tyrannical boss with a mind as small as a noose, he would never think to say *"Who's* eating you?" The idea of cannibalism is so far from our ordinary lives that we can safely use the euphemism *eat* in a sexual context, say, and no one will think we mean literally consume. But omnivores can eat anything, even each other,[3] and human flesh is one of the finest sources of protein. Primitive peoples all over the world have indulged in cannibalism, always ritualistically, but sometimes as a key source of protein missing from their diets. For many it's a question of headhunting, displaying the enemy's head with much magic and flourish; and then, so as not to be wasteful, eating the body. In Britain's Iron Age, the Celts consumed large quantities of human flesh. Some American Indian tribes tortured and ate their captives, and the details (reported by Christian missionaries who observed the rites) are hair-raising. During one four-night celebration in 1487, the Aztecs were reported to have sacrificed about eighty thousand prisoners, whose flesh was shared with the gods, but mainly eaten by a huge meat-hungry population. In *The Power of Myth*, the late Joseph Campbell, a wise observer of the beliefs and customs of many cultures, tells of a New Guinea cannibalism ritual that "enacts the planting-society myth of death, resurrection and *cannibalistic* consumption." The tribe enters a sacred field, where they chant and beat drums for four or five days, and break all the rules by engaging in a sexual orgy. In this rite of manhood, young boys are introduced to sex for the first time:

> There is a great shed of enormous logs supported by two uprights. A young woman comes in ornamented as a deity, and she is brought to lie down in this place beneath the great roof. The boys, six or so, with the drums going and chanting going, one after another, have their first experience of intercourse with the girl. And when the last boy is with her in a full embrace, the supports are withdrawn, the logs drop, and the couple is killed. There is the union of male and female . . . as they were in the beginning. . . . There is the union of begetting and death. They are both the same thing.
>
> Then the couple is pulled out and roasted and eaten that very evening. The ritual is the repetition of the original act of the killing of a god followed by the coming of food from the dead savior.

When the explorer Dr. Livingstone died in Africa, his organs were apparently eaten by two of his native followers as a way to absorb his strength and courage. Taking communion in the Catholic Church enacts a symbolic eating of the body and blood of Christ. Some forms of cannibalism were more bloodthirsty than others. According to Philippa Pullar, Druid priests "attempted divination by stabbing a man above his midriff, foretelling the future by the convulsions of his limbs and the pouring of his blood. . . . Then . . . they devoured him." Cannibalism doesn't horrify us because we find human life sacred, but because our social taboos happen to forbid it, or, as Harris says: "the real conun-

---

[3]In German, humans eat (*essen*), but animals devour or feed (*Fressen*). Cannibals are called *Menschenfresser*—humans who become animals when they eat.

drum is why we who live in a society which is constantly perfecting the art of mass-producing human bodies on the battlefield find humans good to kill but bad to eat."[4]

THE UTIMATE DINNER PARTY

Romans adored the voluptuous feel of food: the sting of pepper, the pleasure-pain of sweet-and-sour dishes, the smoldery sexiness of curries, the piquancy of delicate and rare animals, whose exotic lives they could contemplate as they devoured them, sauces that reminded them of the smells and tastes of love-making. It was a time of fabulous, fattening wealth and dangerous, killing poverty. The poor served the wealthy, and could be beaten for a careless word, destroyed for amusement. Among the wealthy, boredom visited like an impossible in-law, whom they devoted most of their lives to entertaining. Orgies and dinner parties were the main diversions, and the Romans amused themselves with the lavishness of a people completely untainted by annoying notions of guilt. In their culture, pleasure glistened as a good in itself, a positive achievement, nothing to repent. Epicurus spoke for a whole society when he asked:

> Is man then meant to spurn the gifts of Nature? Has he been born but to pluck the bitterest fruits? For whom do those flowers grow, that the gods make flourish at mere mortals' feet? . . . It is a way of pleasing Providence to give ourselves up to the various delights which she suggests to us; our very needs spring from her laws, and our desires from her inspirations.

Fighting the enemy, boredom, Romans staged all-night dinner parties and vied with one another in the creation of unusual and ingenious dishes. At one dinner a host served progressively smaller members of the food chain stuffed inside each another: Inside a calf, there was a pig, inside the pig a lamb, inside the lamb a chicken, inside the chicken a rabbit, inside the rabbit a dormouse, and so on. Another host served a variety of dishes that looked different but were all made from the same ingredient. Theme parties were popular, and might include a sort of treasure hunt, where guests who located the peacock brains on flamingo tongues received a prize. Mechanical devices might lower

---

[4]For an excellent discussion of cannibalism, and the nutritional fiats that have prompted it in a variety of cultures (Aztecs, Fijians, New Guineans, American Indians, and many others), including truly horrible and graphic accounts by eyewitnesses, see Harris's chapter on "People Eating." Marvin Harris, *The Sacred Cow and the Abominable Pig: Riddles of Food and Culture* (New York: Simon and Schuster/Touchstone Books, 1987).

acrobats from the ceiling along with the next course, or send in a plate of lam-
prey milt on an eel-shaped trolley. Slaves brought garlands of flowers to drape
over the diners, and rubbed their bodies with perfumed ungents to relax them.
The floor might be knee-deep in rose petals. Course after course would appear,
some with peppery sauces to spark the taste buds, others in velvety sauces to
soothe them. Slaves blew exotic scents through pipes into the room, and sprinkled the diners with heavy, musky animal perfumes like civet and ambergris.
Sometimes the food itself squirted saffron or rose water or some other delicacy
into the diner's face, or birds flew out of it, or it turned out to be inedible
(because it was pure gold). The Romans were devotees of what the German call
Schadenfreude, taking exquisite pleasure in the misfortune of someone else. They
loved to surround themselves with midgets, and handicapped and deformed
people, who were made to perform sexually or caberet-style at the parties.
Caligula used to have gladiators get right up to the dinner table to fight, splashing the diners with blood and gore. Not all Romans were sadists, but numbers
of the wealthy class and many of the emperors were, and they could own, torture, maltreat, or murder their slaves as much as they wished. At least one high-
society Roman is recorded to have fattened his eels on the flesh of his slaves.
Small wonder Christianity arose as a slave-class movement, emphasizing self-
denial, restraint, the poor inheriting the earth, a rich and free life after death,
and the ultmate punishment of the luxury-loving rich in the eternal tortures of
hell. As Philippa Pullar observes in *Consuming Passions*, it was from this "class-
conciousness and a pride in poverty and simplicity the hatred of the body was
born. . . . All agreeable sensations were damned, all harmonies of taste and
smell, sound, sight and feel, the candidate for heaven must resist them all. Pleasure was synonymous with guilt, it was synonymous with Hell. . . . 'Let your
companions be women pale and thin with fasting,' instructed Jerome." Or, as
Gibbon put it, "every sensation that is offensive to man was thought acceptable to God." So the denial of the senses became part of a Christian creed of
salvation. The Shakers would later create their stark wooden benches, chairs,
and simple boxes in such a mood, but what would they make now of the volup-
tuousness with which people enjoy Shaker pieces, not as a simple necessity but
extravagantly, as art, as an expensive excess bought for the foyer or country
house? The word "vicarious" hinges on "vicar," God's consul in the outlands,
who lived like an island in life's racy current, delicate, exempt, and unflappable,
while babies grew out of wedlock and bulls died, crops shriveled up like pokers
or were flooded, and local duennas held musicales for vicar, matrons, and spicy
young women (riper than the saintliest mettle could bear). No wonder they
lived vicariously, giving pause, giving aid, and, sometimes, giving in to the embo-
lisms, dietary manias, and sin. Puritanism denounced spices as too sexually
arousing; then the Quakers entered the scene, making all luxury taboo, and
soon enough there were revolts against these revolts. Food has always been

associated with cycles of sexuality, moral abandon, moral restraint, and a return to sexuality once again—but no one did so with as much flagrant gusto as the ancient Romans.

Quite possibly the Roman empire fell because of lead poisoning, which can cause miscarriages, infertility, a host of illnesses, and insanity. Lead suffused the Romans' lives—not only did their water pipes, cooking pots, and jars contain it, but also their cosmetics. But before it did poison them, they staged some of the wildest and most extravagant dinner parties ever known, where people dined lying down, two, three, or more to a couch. While saucy Roman poets like Catullus wrote rigorously sexy poems about affairs with either sex, Ovid wrote charming ones about his robust love of women, how they tormented his soul, and about the roller coaster of flirtation he observed at dinner parties. "Offered a sexless heaven," he wrote, "I'd say *no thank you*, women are such sweet hell." In one of his poems, he cautions his mistress that, since they've both been invited to the same dinner, he's bound to see her there with her husband. *Don't let him kiss you on the neck*, Ovid tells her, *it will drive me crazy*.

Engaging the Text

1. According to Ackerman, why does food play such an influential role in establishing and confirming group ties ("Humans rarely choose to dine in solitude, and food has a powerful social component," para. 1)? For example, how do rituals involving corn illustrate the way food and religious values are interconnected for the Hopi Indians?

2. How effectively does Ackerman use sources from different fields of study (such as history, physiology, and mythology) to illustrate her thesis? Does she sensationalize her subject, and if so, for what purpose? Why does she include details of the Roman banquets? Does Ackerman's approach intrigue you, or does it not appeal to you?

3. Ackerman draws inferences about the values of Roman society from the Romans' ingenious and decadent banquets. How strong do you find Ackerman's case that early Christian attitudes toward food were a reaction to everything Roman culture represented? Evaluate her argument.

Exploring Your Cultural Perspective

1. With several classmates, analyze what each of these innovations (see pages 94 and 95) suggests about the social history of food: canned food (Figure 2.5), the globalization of Coca-Cola (Figure 2.6), gourmet coffee and the coffee bar (Figure 2.7), and truth-in-labeling laws (Figure 2.8).

FIGURE 2.5

FIGURE 2.6

FIGURE 2.7

FIGURE 2.8

FIGURE 2.9

2. Ackerman says that customs and taboos determine what people in different
   cultures consider good to eat. What does the photograph in Figure 2.9 of a
   Cantonese food market in China say about the different values North Americans and the Chinese attach to certain animals? Do you agree with Ackerman that what tastes good is simply a result of cultural conditioning, or is it
   a property of the food itself? What role do you think cultural conditioning
   plays? Explain your reasons in a paragraph or two, and supply your own
   examples.

DINITIA SMITH

Did a Barnyard Schism Lead to a Religious One?

Dinitia Smith's accomplishments include a screenplay, *Refugio, They Named You Wrong* (1991); a novel, *Remember This* (1989); and stories for *Hudson Review* and *Cosmopolitan*. In this article (which originally appeared in the *New York Times* in 1998), Smith delves into the reasons why the pig has evoked such disparate responses from Christians, Jews, and Muslims through the ages. Reactions to the eating of pork clearly transcend issues of biology or hygiene and have come to define and symbolize the crucial differences between these religions.

Thinking Critically

Food has served as a vehicle for expressing boundaries, distinctions, and divisions between people throughout history. As you read, evaluate whether Smith's analysis credibly explains how food taboos function as a way for one religion to distinguish itself from another.

Throughout history, the pig has been an animal with a deeply fraught significance for Christians and Jews as well as Muslims. Why, for example, are Jews forbidden to eat pig meat at the same time Christians happily serve up ham for Easter?

The answer may involve more than simply the biblical prohibition against Jews eating pork. If you understand the pig's symbolism, you can understand the complex and often tortured relationship between Jews and Christians, says the French cultural anthropologist, Claudine Fabre-Vassas. In her book "The Singular Beast: Jews, Christians and the Pig" (Columbia University Press, 1997), Ms. Fabre-Vassas depicts the pig not only as a beloved figure in medieval and modern Christian households, prized as both a pet in peasant cultures and a source of delicious food, but also as a symbol of a hated figure, the Jew, of the very group that scorns it as unclean. Ms. Fabre-Vassas argues that the cultural tension between those who did and those who did not eat pork helps set the stage for a murderous anti-Semitism.

The Jewish interdiction against the pig is first mentioned in the Old Testament. In Leviticus 11:27, God forbids Moses and his followers to eat swine "because it parts the hoof but does not chew the cud." Furthermore, the prohibition goes, "Of their flesh you shall not eat, and their carcasses you shall not touch; they are unclean to you." That message is later reinforced in Deuteronomy. Muslims, who follow Muslim law, inherited the prohibition.

Over the years, various explanations have been offered for the Old Testament commandment. The 12th-century rabbi Moses Maimonides, court physician to the Muslim sultan and warrior Saladin, said the prohibition against eating pig meat was for health reasons as it had a "bad and damaging effect" upon the body.

5   Beginning in the 19th century, scholars offered a different explanation. In "The Golden Bough," Sir James Frazer wrote that pig meat was forbidden because it had originally been an animal used for sacrifice. "All so-called unclean animals were originally sacred," Sir James wrote. "The reason for not eating them is that many were originally divine."

The British anthropologist Mary Douglas, in her 1966 book "Purity and Danger: An Analysis of Concepts of Pollution and Taboo," explains the prohibition as a problem of taxonomy: the pig did not fit conveniently into the Israelites' definitions of what a domestic animal should be (the cloven hooves, the failure to chew their cud like cows). Animals like pigs that cross over definitions, Ms. Douglas argues, that crawl instead of walk or swarm instead of fly, defied the tribal need to create an intellectual ordering of the world. Disorder of any kind, Ms. Douglas writes, provided a frightening glimpse into the chaos inherent in the universe.

Later, another anthropologist, Marvin Harris, gave a decidedly utilitarian explanation for the taboo against pork, arguing in his 1974 book "Cows, Pigs, Wars and Witches: The Riddles of Culture" that the prohibition was a response to the realities of nomadic life in the arid stretches of Palestine.

Mr. Harris points out that the pig does indeed wallow in its own filth, and eat its own feces, but usually only under conditions of severe drought. Cows and sheep will also eat their own feces under extremely dry conditions, he adds.

But pigs require larger amounts of moisture than cows or sheep, he says, and are therefore difficult to raise in hot, dry climates: it was easier, in the end, to forbid people to eat something that they might long for. "Better then, to interdict the consumption of pork entirely," Mr. Harris writes, "and to concentrate on raising goats, sheep and cattle. Pigs tasted good, but it was too expensive to feed them and keep them cool."

10   Whatever the reason, the prohibition against eating pig meat became an identifying feature, a defining characteristic of Jewishness. And that, says Alan Dundes, professor of anthropology and folklore at the University of California, Berkeley, is precisely the reason that Christians not only eat pork, but even

celebrate it by eating it on holidays. "You distinguish yourself by not doing what others do," Mr. Dundes writes.

It was in the early Christian period, in the first century, that the great divide opened up between those who ate pork and those who didn't. Early Christians, then simply a sect among the Jews, were faced with the problem of distinguishing themselves. They did not circumcise their children. And they ate pork, the very animal that their fellow Jews avoid. What's more, where Jews, under biblical command, drained the blood of meat before they ate it, Christians symbolically drank the blood of Christ, and ate His body through the sacrament of the Eucharist.

"It is in the most intimate things, the things people sometimes take for granted that people define themselves," said Gilliar Feeley-Harnik, a professor of anthropology at Johns Hopkins University and the author of "The Lord's Table: The Meaning of Food in Early Judaism and Christianity" (Smithsonian Institution Press, 1994). "There is virtually no religion that we know of that doesn't define itself with food."

It is a tragic irony, Ms. Fabre-Vassas writes in her book, that as anti-Semitism took on its shape in medieval Europe, the pig—and his blood—became a symbol for a Jew himself.

Taking her cue from the French anthropologist Claude Lévi-Strauss, Ms. Fabre-Vassas studied the culinary habits of southern France, and the way in which the pig began to be associated with the Jew in the anti-Semitic imaginings of peasant culture, and by implication the rest of Europe. Ms. Fabre-Vassas shows how the pig became the food of choice for many Christian religious feasts. "In my research in the mountains," she said recently, through a translator, "I realized that the pig was the most important animal in the village culinary tradition. A whole ceremony is attached to its death and cooking. It unites members of the community around a party." Ms. Fabre-Vassas studied methods of breeding pigs, feeding them, circumcising them, detecting disease in them and slaughtering them, up until the 20th century.

But according to Ms. Fabre-Vassas, Christians were faced with the prob-   *15* lem. They had defined themselves as being "not-Jews," in other words pig eaters and, symbolically, blood drinkers. Yet at the same time, Christians acknowledge the Hebrew Bible, the Old Testament, as part of their Scripture. Ms. Fabre-Vassas writes that Christians were faced with the spiritual problem of how to separate themselves from their Jewish heritage while acknowledging their common Old Testament roots.

Therefore, she writes, rituals grew up around the pig that drew on both traditions. For instance, frequently the blood was drained from the pig before it was cooked and eaten, as Jewish law decrees in the eating of all meats.

Above all, Christians had to explain away the Jewish prohibition against eating the pig, a central tenet of Old Testament Law. "The duality of the pig's image is fascinating," she said, "It is seen as evil, wild, diabolical on one side, and on the other it is a symbol of the wealth and pride in the house." More than any other barnyard animal, pigs were adaptable as household pets, often living in close proximity to children. There had to be justification for the eventual killing of these pets for meat, she said. It was amid these seemingly insoluble problems that the pig began to be seen as a symbol for Jews.

In the anti-Semitic lore that sprang up, it was said that Christ had turned Jewish children into pigs to show His power, and that Jews didn't eat pigs because they were their own children. Another result of these crude imaginings was the explanation that Jews actually originated from pigs, that they didn't eat pig meat because it would be like eating themselves. "Since they deprived them-selves of this meat," Ms. Fabre-Vassas wrote, "they were constantly seeking the closest human substitute, the flesh and blood of Christian children." Myths like these spread through the folklore of Poland and Ukraine, areas that were to become the killing grounds of the Holocaust.

Ms. Fabre-Vassas's book includes illustrations of anti-Semitic woodcuts that show Jews suckling pigs. Later, during the 1930's, it was vicious, primitive images like these that found their way into the anti-Semitic writings of Julius Streicher's newspaper Stürmer, which has been called the mass circulation gazette of genocide.

20   Through a complex, subrational process, Ms. Fabre-Vassas writes, it was as if a tragic variation of the old folkloric belief had taken place: in the end, Jews had become what they did not eat.

Engaging the Text

1. Which of the various theories advanced by researchers that Smith cites to explain religious prohibitions against the eating of pork seem the most plau-sible? Why? Why does the eating of pork lend itself so well to the distinc-tion one religion makes between itself and others? Could any other food have served this function as effectively? Why or why not?

2. How did the pig serve as a means for expressing anti-Semitism in medieval Europe? To what extent does the pig still serve as a vehicle for antipathies between Jews and Christians today?

3. In what ways did Smith's analysis help you understand how divisions between religious groups originate and can be perpetuated by an arbitrary symbol like a pig?

Exploring Your Cultural Perspective

1. How have interpretations of religious texts served as a foundation for food-related taboos in a religion (for example, Judaism, Hinduism, Buddhism,

Islam, Jainism)? For instance, Jewish food laws specify that warm-blooded animals must be ritually slaughtered and that dairy and meat products must not be mixed. In a short paper, discuss one such case, emphasizing what is considered clean and unclean. Two good information sources are Mary Douglas's "Deciphering a Meal" (1971) in *Myth, Symbol, and Culture*, edited by Clifford Geertz, and the Web site on World Food Habits created by Illinois State University at <http://www.ilstu.edu/class/anth273-foodways/foodbib.html>.

2. As a research project, investigate the symbolism of pigs in ancient cultures and modern adaptations of these themes by the media. Wilson Bryan Key in *Media Sexploitation* (1976) analyzes the subliminal use by William Friedkin of the sound of pigs squealing to evoke terror in his film *The Exorcist*. Key tells us that "pigs were also substituted for human victims during religious sacrifices. A black pig has often been symbolic in Christian art of the devil and satan [. . .] In Celtic mythology pigs were even portrayed as returning to life after being eaten (111)." Rent *The Exorcist*, and see if you can discern the subliminal use of pig squeals with visual images in ways that connect to the archetypal significance of pigs and religions. Drawing on your observations, Dinitia Smith's analysis, and other sources you might find, write an essay that addresses the mythological roots and modern use of the pig as a symbol.

MARGARET VISSER

Fingers

Margaret Visser's historical survey of eating habits in different cultures suggests that the shift to eating with utensils, rather than with our hands, is a relatively recent development. Visser, who taught classics at York University in Toronto, discusses the evolution of table manners in this piece. Her research reveals that the introduction of knives, forks, and spoons fundamentally altered our attitudes toward food. The system of etiquette viewed as normal in fact varies enormously from culture to culture, especially on the question of whether it is proper to eat with one's fingers. Visser is the author of *Much Depends on Dinner* (1990), *The Way We Are* (1997), and *The Geometry of Love: Space, Time, Mystery, and Meaning in an Ordinary Church* (2001). Her books have been translated into French, German, and Portuguese. She appears frequently on radio and television and has lectured extensively in Canada, the United States, Europe, and Australia. Most recently, Visser has written and presented a six-part series on everyday life in six European cities for BBC Radio Four. "Fingers" is from *The Rituals of Dinner* (1991), which won the International Association of Culinary Professionals Award for Literary Food Writing.

Thinking Critically

What function do good table manners serve? How does the broad range of examples Visser presents support her analysis? If it were socially acceptable, would you prefer eating with your fingers rather than with utensils? What foods do you eat with your fingers?

One of the more spectacular triumphs of human "culture" over "nature" is our own determination when eating to avoid touching food with anything but metal implements. Our self-satisfaction with this marvellous instance of artificiality, however, should not lead us to assume that people who habitually eat with their hands are any less determined than we are to behave "properly"; for they too overlay "animal" instincts with manners, and indulge in both the constraints and the ornamentations which characterize polite behaviour. Forks, like handkerchiefs, look dangerously grubby objects to many people encountering them for the first time. To people who eat with their fingers, hands seem cleaner, warmer, more agile than cutlery. Hands are silent, sensitive to texture and temperature, and graceful—provided, of course, that they have been properly trained.

Washing, as we have already remarked, tends to be ostentatious and frequent among polite eaters with their hands. Ancient Romans, like the modern Japanese, preferred to bath all over before dinner. The etiquette of hand-washing in the Middle Ages was very strict. During the washing ritual, precedence was observed as it was in the seating of diners at the table; the bows, genuflections, and ceremonial flourishes of the ewerers or hand-washers were carefully prescribed. It was often thought disgusting, as it is in India today, to dip one's hands into the basin of water: a servant had to pour scented water *over* the hands so that it was used only once. (The modern North American preference for showers over baths is similar.) In modern Egypt, the basin is sometimes provided with a perforated cover so that the dirty water disappears at once from view. Hand-washing rules always insist that one must not splash or swish the water; be careful to leave some dry towel for a person washing next; and above all touch as little as possible between washing and beginning to eat. If an Abbasid (ninth-century Arab) guest scratched his head or stroked his beard after washing, everyone present would wait before beginning to eat, so that he could wash again. An Abbasid, like a modern Egyptian, host would wash first, so that guests need not look as though they were anxious to start the meal; alternatively, washing was done outside, and the meal began directly after the seating, usually when the guest of honour stretched his hand to take the first morsel.

Desert Arabs go outside the tent, both before and after the meal, to perform ablutions by rubbing their hands with sand; they often prefer to perform this ritual before washing, even when there is plenty of water available. It is thought very rude to perform one's final washing before everyone else has finished eating; it would be the equivalent of our leaving the table while the meal is in progress. The corollary of this is that people who eat with their hands usually try to finish the meal together, since it is uncomfortable, for one thing, to sit for long when one has finished eating, holding out one greasy hand. Where family eating is done from a shared pot, there are rules about leaving some food over for the children, who eat more slowly than adults do. A great deal of attention, forethought, and control is required in order to finish a meal together, or at a moment agreed on in advance; it is a manoeuvre few of us have been trained to perform.

A monstrously greedy Greco-Roman banqueter is said to have accustomed his hands to grasping hot things by plunging them into hot water at the baths; he also habitually gargled with hot water, to accustom his mouth to high temperatures. He would then bribe the cook to serve the meal straight from the stove, so that he could grab as much food as possible and eat it while it was still hot—before anyone else could touch it. The story reminds us that eating food while it is hot is a habit both culture-specific and modern; a taste for it has developed in us, a taste which is dependent both on technology and on the little brothers of technology, the knife, fork, and spoon. People who eat their food with their hands usually eat it warm rather than steaming, and they grow up preferring it that way. (It is often said that one of the cultural barriers that divide "developed" from "developing" peoples is this matter of preference in the temperature at which food is eaten.) Where hot drinks are served, on the other hand (an example is the Arab coffee-drinking habit at mealtimes), people tend to like them very hot, as a contrast, and because the cups or glasses, together with the saucers under them, protect their hands.

5   Delicacy and adroitness of gesture are drummed into people who eat with their hands, from childhood. It might be considered polite, for example, to scoop food up, or it could be imperative to grasp each morsel from above. Politeness works by abjuring whole ranges of behaviour which the body could easily encompass—indeed, very often the easier movement is precisely what is out of bounds. It was once the mark of the utmost refinement in our own culture to deny oneself the use of the fourth and fifth fingers when eating: the thumb and first two fingers alone were allowed. Bones—provided they were small ones—could be taken up, but held between thumb and forefinger only. We hear of especially sophisticated people who used certain fingers only for one dish, so that they had other fingers, still unsticky and ungreasy, held in reserve for taking food or sauce from a different platter. This form of constraint was possible only if the food was carefully prepared so that no tugging was necessary: the meat must be extremely tender, cut up, or hashed and pressed into small cakes. None but the rich and those with plenty of servants were likely to manage such delicacy; it followed that only they could be truly "refined."

Distancing the fourth and fifth fingers from the operation of taking food can be performed by lifting them up, elegantly curled; the constraint has forced them to serve merely as ornament. A hand used in this manner becomes a dramatic expression of the economy of politeness. When a modern tea-drinker is laughed at for holding her cup-handle in three fingers, lifting the two unused digits in the air, we think it is because we find her ridiculously pretentious. What we really mean is that she is conservative to the point that her model of social success is completely out of date, and the constraints and ornaments with which she clothes her behaviour are now inappropriate—which is another way of saying that, although she is trying very hard to be correct, she succeeds merely in being improper. Modern constraints and ornaments are, quite simply, different. We should remember that snobbery has usually delighted in scorning what is passé.

Left hands are very commonly disqualified from touching food at dinner. The *Li Chi* tells us that ancient Chinese children were trained from infancy never to use their left hands when eating. Ancient Greeks and Romans leaned on their left elbows when reclining at meals, effectively withdrawing their left hands from use. You *had* to lean on the left elbow even if you were left-handed: if you did not, you ruined the configuration of the party by facing the wrong way. The same problem confronted, even more vitally, an ancient Greek hoplite soldier. He formed part of a phalanx of shields, all which had to be held on left arms so that they could overlap; fighting was done with swords grasped in the right. A shield on the right arm would have created a gap in the closed phalanx. It must have been very difficult to be left-handed in the ancient world.

Abbasid Arabs used to hold bread in their left hands because this was the part of the meal not shared from a common dish, and even strict modern Middle Eastern manners permit the use of the left for operations such as peeling fruits; the main thing is not to take from a communal dish with the left, and to avoid bringing the left hand to the mouth. The left hand is traditionally discouraged at table because it is the non-sacred hand, reserved for profane and polluting actions from which the right hand abstains. One example of these tasks is washing after excretion. Now it is invariably important for human beings both culturally and for health reasons to understand that food is one thing and excrement another: the fact that they are "the same thing," that is, different phases of the same process, merely makes it imperative that we should keep the distinction clear, and continually demonstrate to others that we are mindful of it.

Eating together is a potent expression of community. Food is sacred, and must also be pure, clean, and undefiled. It crosses the threshold of the mouth, enters, and either feeds or infects the individual who consumes it: anything presented to us as edible which is perceived as impure in any sense immediately revolts us. Homage is paid to the purity of what we eat, and precaution taken to preserve it, in many different ways: we have already considered washing, white cloths and napkins, dish covers, poison-tastings, prayers, and paper wrappings, and we shall see many more of these. In our culture, lavatories (literally, "wash places"—only euphemisms are permissible for this particular piece of furniture) are kept discreetly closeted, either alone or in a bathroom; a "washroom" or a "toilet" (literally, a "place where there is a towel") is nearly unthinkable without a door for shutting other people out. The lavatory bowl is covered (sometimes the cover is covered as well), usually white, wastefully water-flushed (people even like to tint this water an emphatically artificial blue), and hedged about with special paper rolls and hand-washings.

Our fascination when we learn that people exist who will not touch food *10* with their left hands is rather interesting. It begins with our conviction that "civilized" people (ourselves, of course) should eat with knives and forks in the first place—that is, try not to handle food at all. We do not like the reason left hands are most often said to be banned among certain "foreigners," fastening as we do upon one reason when it is only one from a whole category of "profane" actions, because our taboo about washrooms is so strong that we cannot bear to be reminded of excretion—which we are, by the prohibition. In other words, our taboo is even stronger than theirs. Moreover, left hands have in fact an "unclean" connotation in our own culture.

"Right," after all, means "correct" or "okay" in English. "Sinister" originally meant "left." In French, a just man is *droit*, meaning both "right" and "straight," while *gauche* ("left") describes one who lacks social assurance, as well as dexterity and adroitness (both of which literally mean "right-handedness"). We raise right hands to take oaths and extend them to shake hands: left-handed people just have to fall in with this. In fact, left-handed people, like left-handed ancient Greeks, have always been regarded as an awkward, wayward minority, to the point where left-handed children have been forced, against their best interests, to use their right hands rather than their left. When sets of opposites (curved and straight, down and up, dark and light, cold and hot, and so forth) are set out, our own cultural system invariably makes "left" go with down, dark, round, cold—and female. Males are straight, up, light, hot—and right. Our metal eating implements free us from denying the left hand—but most of us are right-handed anyway, and knives (quintessentially "male" weapons, by the way) are held in right hands. And as well shall see, North Americans still perfer not only to cut with the right, but to bring food to their mouths with the right hand as well.

Eating with the help of both hands at once is very often frowned upon. The Bedouin diner is not permitted to gnaw meat from the bone: he must tear it away and into morsels using only the right hand, and not raise the hand from the dish in order to do so. Sometimes right-handed eaters confronted with a large piece of meat, a chicken, for instance, will share the task of pulling it apart, each of two guests using his right hand and exercising deft coordination; no attention should be drawn to this operation by any movement resembling a wrench or a jerk. Even on formal occasions our own manners permit us, occasionally, to use our fingers—when eating asparagus for example (this is an early twentieth-century dispensation), or radishes, or apricots. But all of these are taken to the mouth with one hand only. We are still advised that corn kernels should be cut off the cobs in the kitchen, or that corn should, better still, be avoided altogether unless the meal is a very intimate affair. One reason why this vegetable has never become quite respectable is that corn cobs demand to be held in two hands. (More important reasons are of course that teeth come too obviously into play when eating them, and cheeks and chins are apt to get greasy.) When we chew, we should also be careful to fill only one cheek—not too full, to be sure. Two hands and two cheeks both signify indecent enthusiasm; cramming either hands or mouth is invariably rude.

People whose custom it is to eat with their hands make a further rule: Never take up and prepare a new morsel while you are still chewing. When left hands are allowed as well as right, it is quite dreadful to be feeding one's mouth with one hand while the other is groping in the dish for more. (We are far more lax than they on this point: we are permitted to use the knives and forks in our hands, and chew at the same time.)

Engaging the Text

1. What kinds of rules and constraints characterize proper behavior in those cultures in which people habitually eat with their hands? Evaluate the advantages and disadvantages of eating with one's hands.

2. How does eating with one's hands instead of with utensils influence the size of portions, the manner in which food is served, timing, temperature of the food, sensuous dimensions of eating, dexterity required, avoidance of contamination, and cooperation between diners? Compare the traditional manner of eating with the hands with the historically newer use of utensils.

3. In what ways has the reliance on utensils placed greater emphasis on bodily control? How has this emphasis enforced distinctions between social classes?

Exploring Your Cultural Perspective

1. What is the significance of the use of china, metal cutlery, real glasses, and salt and pepper shakers, as well as the way meals are served, in first-class cabins on airplanes? How are these trappings connected with the social class of the passengers?

2. What table manners were you taught while you were growing up? What might be their cultural or hygienic purposes? Have eating habits become more casual? If so, what does this relaxing of table manners and etiquette in North America tell us about ourselves?

GUANLONG CAO

Chopsticks

Guanlong Cao (Kuan-lung Ts'ao) was raised in Shanghai, China. Under communist rule, his family lost their possessions, and all six were forced to live in a small attic over a button factory. Cao describes his life from the 1950s through the 1970s in his award-winning book *The Attic: Memoirs of a Chinese Landlord's Son*, translated by Cao and Nancy Moskin (1996); this selection is a chapter in that book. Cao emigrated to the United States in 1987 and, at forty-two, graduated from Middlebury College; he later received an MA in fine arts from Tufts University. His artwork includes sculpture, photographs, and paintings. In "Chopsticks," Cao describes the obsession of students at the automotive school he attended with making their own chopsticks from stolen bamboo. In a situation in which food was rationed, devoting so much time and care to making chopsticks had special significance.

Thinking Critically

*Do you use chopsticks? How does your attitude toward food change when you use them? Observe how Cao uses **irony**—the use of words to express the opposite of their actual meaning—while at the same time recounting the hard life the students endured.*

I always think chopsticks are an invention unique to Asian culture. Its historical and cognitive significance is no less than that of the Great Wall, the compass, gunpowder, and paper.

The greatest wisdom appears to be foolishness. Complexity ultimately ends in simplicity. Maybe it is because chopsticks are so simple that, just as air's weight was long ignored and white light was mislabeled as colorless, in thousands of years no one has ever scientifically or conscientiously researched them. A sensitive probe for examining the characteristics of Asian culture has been ignored. In my four years at the automotive school, I witnessed and experienced a splendid chopsticks civilization. I record it here for the benefit of future researchers.

In those days almost every male student carried an elongated pouch hanging from his belt. It was fashioned from canvas, leather, or leatherette. Like a warrior's dagger, it dangled all day from the student's waist.

Female students didn't wear belts, so the slim bags usually hung from a cord around their necks. Their materials were more delicate: nylon, silk, or linen. Embroidery was often added as an embellishment.

Within these bags were chopsticks. 5

Because the rationed food offered insufficient calories, oxygen-intensive activities were not encouraged. Chess, card games, and calligraphy were the officially recommended pastimes. But the most popular activity was making chopsticks.

The number of students at the school increased each year, and new dormitories were constantly being built. Owing to limited funds, the dormitory roofs were constructed out of tar paper, straw, and bamboo. That bamboo became the primary source of chopstick lumber.

The selection of material was critical. Segments close to the plant's roots were too short. The meat between the skin and hollow core of the segments close to the top was too thin. A bamboo tree about one inch thick provided only a few middle segments that could be used to make quality chopsticks.

The bamboo poles were covered with a tarp and stored on the construction site. In the evenings, taking advantage of the absence of the construction workers, we started looting.

If only a few trees were missing, nobody would have noticed. But when an 10 idea becomes a fad, things can easily get out of hand. There were hundreds of students. A newly delivered pile of bamboo would be half gone the morning after an all-out moonlit operation.

The superintendent of the construction site was furious and demanded that the student dormitories be searched. We got scared and threw our booty out the windows. The superintendent called a meeting of the school leaders to deal with the problem. He arrived with both arms laden with cut segments of bamboo. With a crash, he slammed the sticks down on the meeting table. The leaders, gathered around the table, looked like diners at an exotic feast.

The next day, a large notice was posted listing the price of the transgression: one bamboo tree = one big demerit. But the punishment was never really put into effect. After the immediate storm passed, the bamboo continued to go missing, but not in the same flagrant quantities.

After a bamboo segment was split open, it had to be dried in the shade for about a week. Experienced students put their bamboo strips on the mosquito netting over their beds. Their rising body heat helped evaporate the moisture.

Although the bamboo's skin is hard, it must be stripped away. If left on, the different densities of the inner and outer materials cause the chopsticks to warp. The best part comes from the quarter inch of meat just inside the skin. There the texture is even and dense, and the split will go precisely where the knife directs it.

15   The student-made chopsticks usually had a round cross-section. Round chopsticks require little skill to make. Wrap sandpaper around the strip of bamboo and sand for an hour or two, and a round cross-section is the result.

Only experts dared to make square cross-sectioned chopsticks. To make the four sided straight and symmetrical from tail to tip required real expertise. Sandpaper could not be used, because it would wear away the sharp edges you were trying to create.

To begin the procedure, you have to soak a fine-grained brick in water for a couple of days, and then grind it flat on a concrete floor. Laying the roughed-out chopstick on the brick, with one finger applying pressure to the tail and another to the top, you slowly ground the stick on the brick. Water was dripped on the brick to ensure fine grinding. Only by this painstaking process could chopsticks be formed with clear edges and smooth surfaces.

A boy student unprecedently produced a pair of five-sided chopsticks, which created a sensation on campus. The boy dedicated his efforts to a girl on whom he had a crush. Unfortunately, his gift was spurned and, desolate, he broke the chopsticks in front of his peers. This became the classic tragedy of the school year.

In addition to varying cross-sections, the top two or three inches were another place to show off your skill. The usual decoration was a few carved lines with inlaid color. Some students borrowed techniques from seal carving and sculpted miniature cats, turtles, and dragons out of the upper portions of the sticks. One student, who was good at calligraphy, carved two lines of a Song dynasty poem on his chopsticks:

"Vinegar fish from the West Lake," read one of them.
"Cinnamon meat from East Hill," read the other.

20   He cherished the chopsticks as sacred objects, not intended for daily use. He employed them only on special occasions or festival days when excitement rippled through the student body:

"Today we are going to eat meat!"

Only then would he take his chopsticks from his trunk. Applying a thin layer of beeswax, he would polish them for at least ten minutes with a piece of suede. Then they were ready to be brought into the dining room.

Following the epochal five-sided masterpiece, chopsticks became a popular gift for boys to give to girls. If the girl liked the boy, she would accept his present and later give a gift to her admirer—a sleeve for chopsticks. The painstaking needlework expressed her sentimental attachment. We had never heard about Freud, but with our raw wisdom we subconsciously felt that there was some symbolic meaning, which could hardly be expressed in words, in this exchange, in the coming and going of the chopsticks and the sleeves. But school regulations clearly stated:

NO DATING ON CAMPUS

I think the regulation was well supported by science. Dating belonged to the category of oxygen-intensive activities. Before you could open your mouth, your heart started jumping and your cheeks were burning, clearly indicating a rapid consumption of valuable calories.

Engaging the Text

1. Cao mentions that food at the automotive school was not plentiful and having meat was a special event. What is the relationship between the scarcity of food and the fact that the students spent so much time and effort making their own chopsticks?

2. What picture do you get of the relationship between the students and the authorities? What is Cao's attitude toward the authorities? How does Cao's use of irony and language convey his feelings about these experiences?

3. Cao describes how the chopstick-making enterprise took over student life at the school. What did it mean to them individually and as a group? What campuswide activities or projects have galvanized the student population at your school?

Exploring Your Cultural Perspective

1. What are some of the differences between eating in a Chinese restaurant and a more traditional American restaurant? Research some of the ways in which authentic Chinese meals (as opposed to Americanized Chinese meals) differ from Western meals. Write a short essay exploring the cultural implications of the different table manners and social relationships among the diners in the two settings.

2. Cutting up food so that it can be cooked quickly (and eaten with chopsticks) is much more fuel efficient than is the Western custom of roasting or broiling large slabs of meat or boiling vegetables for long periods of time. Discuss these contrasts in food preparation in terms of the utensils employed and the attitudes toward food that are implicit to them.

OCTAVIO PAZ
Hygiene and Repression

Octavio Paz (1914–1998), an unequalled observer of Mexican society, served as a diplomat in France and Japan and as Mexico's ambassador to India. His many volumes of poetry include *Sun Stone* (1958) and *The Monkey Grammarian* (1981). In 1990, Paz was awarded the Nobel Prize for literature. Paz's essays, especially *The Labyrinth of Solitude* (1961), redefined the concept of Latin American culture. "Hygiene and Repression," translated by Helen R. Lane (1987), originally appeared in *Convergences: Essays on Art and Literature.* This selection offers insight into the Puritan roots of North American attitudes toward what is perceived as being foreign in food.

Thinking Critically

Consider whether one can draw reliable inferences about a culture from its preferences in food, as Paz does.

Traditional American cooking is a cuisine without mystery: simple, nourishing, scantily seasoned foods. No tricks: a carrot is a homely, honest carrot, a potato is not ashamed of its humble condition, and a steak is a big bloody hunk of meat. This is transubstantiation[1] of the democratic virtues of the Founding Fathers: a plain meal, one dish following another like the sensible, unaffected sentences of a virtuous discourse. Like the conversation among those at table, the relation between substances and flavors is direct: sauces that mask tastes, garnishes that entice the eye, condiments that confuse the taste buds are taboo. The separation of one food from another is analogous to the reserve that characterizes the relations between sexes, races, and classes. In our countries food is communion, not only between those together at table but between ingredients; Yankee food, impregnated with Puritanism, is based on exclusions. The maniacal preoccupation with the purity and origin of food products has its counterpart in racism and exclusivism. The American contradiction—a democratic universalism based on ethnic, cultural, religious, and sexual exclusions— is reflected in its cuisine. In this culinary tradition our fondness for dark, passionate stews such as moles, for thick and sumptuous red, green, and yellow sauces, would be scandalous, as would be the choice place at our table of *huit-lacoche*, which not only is made from diseased young maize but is black in color. Likewise our love for hot peppers, ranging from parakeet green to ecclesiastical purple, and for ears of Indian corn, their grains varying from golden yellow to midnight blue. Colors as violent as their tastes. Americans adore fresh, delicate colors and flavors. Their cuisine is like watercolor painting or pastels.

American cooking shuns spices as it shuns the devil, but it wallows in slews of cream and butter. Orgies of sugar. Complementary opposites: the almost apostolic simplicity and soberness of lunch, in stark contrast to the suspiciously innocent, pregenital pleasures of ice cream and milkshakes. Two poles: the glass of milk and the glass of whiskey. The first affirms the primacy of home and mother. The virtues of the glass of milk are twofold: It is a wholesome food and it takes us back to childhood. . . . As for whiskey and gin, they are drinks for loners and introverts. For Fourier,[2] Gastrosophy was the science of combining not only foods but guests at table: Matching the variety of dishes is the variety of persons sharing the meal. Wines, spirits, and liqueurs are the complement of a meal, hence their object is to stimulate the relations and unions consolidated round a table. Unlike wine, pulque, champagne, beer, and vodka, neither whiskey nor gin accompanies meals. Nor are they apéritifs or digestifs.[3] They are drinks that accentuate uncommunicativeness and unsociability. In a gastrosophic age they would not enjoy much of a reputation. The universal favor accorded them reveals the situation of our societies, ever wavering between promiscuous association and solitude.

Ambiguity and ambivalence are resources unknown to American cooking. Here, as in so many other things, it is the diametrical opposite of the extremely delicate French cuisine, based on nuances, variations, and modulations—transitions from one substance to another, from one flavor to another. In a sort of profane Eucharist, even a glass of water is transfigured into an erotic chalice:

> Ta lèvre contre le cristal
> Gorgée à gorgée y compose
> Le souvenir pourpre et vital
> De la moins éphémère rose.[4]

It is the contrary as well of Mexican and Hindu cuisine, whose secret is a shock of tastes: cool and piquant, salt and sweet, hot and tart, pungent and delicate. Desire is the active agent, the secret producer of changes, whether it be the transition from one flavor to another or the contrast between several. In gastronomy as in the erotic, it's desire that sets substances, bodies, and sensations in motion; this is the power that rules their conjunction, commingling, and transmutation. A reasonable cuisine, in which each substance is what it is and in which both variations and contrasts are avoided, is a cuisine that has excluded desire.

Pleasure is a notion (a sensation) absent from traditional Yankee cuisine. Not pleasure but health, not correspondence between savors but the satisfaction of a need—these are its two values. One is physical and the other moral; both are associated with the idea of the body as work. Work in turn is a concept at once economic and spiritual: production and redemption. We are condemned to labor, and food restores the body after the pain and punishment of work It is a real *reparation*, in both the physical and the moral sense. Through work the body pays its debt; by earning its physical sustenance, it also earns its spiritual recompense. Work redeems us and the sign of this redemption is food. An active sign in the spiritual economy of humanity, food restores the health of body and soul. If what we eat gives us physical and spiritual health, the exclusion of spices for moral and hygienic reasons is justified: They are the signs of desire, and they are difficult to digest.

5   Health is the condition of two activities of the body, work and sports. In the first, the body is an agent that produces and at the same time redeems; in the second, the sign changes: Sports are a wasteful expenditure of energy. This is a contradiction in appearance only, since what we have here in reality is a system of communicating vessels. Sports are a physical expenditure that is precisely the contrary of what happens in sexual pleasure, since sports in the end become productive—an expenditure that produces health. Work in turn is an expenditure of energy that produces goods and thereby transforms biological life into social, economic, and moral life. There is, moreover, another connection between work and sports: Both take place within a context of rivalry; both are competition and emulation. . . . Sports possess the rigor and gravity of work, and work possesses the gratuity and levity of sports. The play element of work is one of the few features of American society that might have earned Fourier's praise, though doubtless he would have been horrified at the commercialization of sports. The preeminence of work and sports, activities necessarily excluding sexual pleasure, has the same significance as the exclusion of spices in cuisine. If gastronomy and eroticism are unions and conjunctions of substances and tastes or of bodies and sensations, it is evident that neither has been a central preoccupation of American society—as ideas and social values, I repeat, not as more or less secret realities. In American tradition the body is not a source of pleasure but of health and work, in the material and the moral sense.

The cult of health manifests itself as an "ethic of hygiene." I use the word *ethic* because its prescriptions are at once physiological and moral. A despotic ethic: sexuality, work, sports, and even cuisine are its domains. Again, there is a dual concept: Hygiene governs both the corporeal and the moral life. Following the precepts of hygiene means obeying not only rules concerning physiology but also ethical principles: temperance, moderation, reserve. The morality of separation gives rise to the rules of hygiene, just as the aesthetics of fusion inspires the combinations of gastronomy and erotics. In India I frequently witnessed the obsession of Americans with hygiene. Their dread of contagion seemed to know no bounds; anything and everything might be laden with germs: food, drink, objects, people, the very air. These preoccupations are the precise counterpart of the ritual preoccupations of Brahmans fearing contact with certain foods and impure things, not to mention people belonging to a caste different from their own. Many will say that the concerns of the American are justified, whereas those of the Brahman are superstitions. Everything depends on the point of view: For the Brahman the bacteria that the American fears are illusory, while the moral stains produced by contact with alien people are real. These stains are stigmas that isolate him: No member of his caste would dare touch him until he had performed long and complicated rites of purification. The fear of social isolation is no less intense than that of an illness. The hygienic taboo of the American and the ritual taboo of the Brahman have a common basis: the concern for purity. This basis is religious even though, in the case of hygiene, it is masked by the authority of science.

In the last analysis, the cult of hygiene is merely another expression of the principle underlying attitudes toward sports, work, cuisine, sex, and races. The other name of purity is separation. Although hygiene is a social morality based explicitly on science, its unconscious root is religious. Nonetheless, the form in which it expresses itself, and the justifications for it, are rational. In American society, unlike in ours, science from the very beginning has occupied a privileged place in the system of beliefs and values. The quarrel between faith and reason never took on the intensity that it assumed among Hispanic peoples. Ever since their birth as a nation, Americans have been modern; for them it is natural to believe in science, whereas for us this belief implies a negation of our past. The prestige of science in American public opinion is such that even political disputes frequently take on the form of scientific polemics. . . . Two recent examples are the racial question and the feminist movement: Are intellectual differences between races and sexes genetic in origin or a historico-cultural phenomenon?

The universality of science (or what passes for science) justifies the development and imposition of collective patterns or normality. Obviating[5] the necessity for direct coercion, the overlapping of science and Puritan morality permits the imposition of rules that condemn peculiarities, exceptions, and deviations in a manner no less categorical and implacable than religious anathemas. Against the excommunications of science, the individual has neither the religious recourse of abjuration nor the legal one of *habeas corpus*.[6] Although they masquerade as hygiene and science, these patterns of normality have the same function in the realm of eroticism as "healthful" cuisine in the sphere of gastronomy: the extirpation or the separation of what is alien, different, ambiguous, impure. One and the same condemnation applies to blacks, Chicanos, sodomites, and spices.

Notes

1. The changing of one substance into another; in the Eucharist of the Roman Catholic Church the conversion of the whole substance of the bread and wine into the body and blood of Christ. —Ed.
2. Charles Fourier (1772–1837), French socialist and writer. —Ed.
3. A small drink of liquor taken to stimulate the appetite before a meal or at the end of a meal to aid digestion. —Ed.
4. Your lip against the glass/Draught by draught therein creates/The deep persisting crimson memory/Of the last fleeting rose. —Stephane Mallarme, "Verre d'Eau" ("Glass of Water"). —Ed
5. To prevent or eliminate by effective measures. —Ed.
6. Latin for "we have the body": a legal protection that prevents a person from being imprisoned without being formally charged with a crime. —Ed.

Engaging the Text

1. Paz discerns a Puritan emphasis on achieving virtue by exclusion in all aspects of North American life; he calls this an "ethic of hygiene." In what ways does this Puritanism underlie American attitudes toward food, sexuality, work, and sports? Is Paz's assessment fair? Why or why not? Can one form reliable inferences about a society based on its food preferences, as Paz does? Why or why not?

2. Paz identifies "ambiguity and ambivalence" as characteristic of French cuisine and the "shock" of contrasting tastes as a feature of Mexican and Hindu cuisines. In Paz's view, why is it significant that both are missing from the traditional North American cooking? What does the exclusion of spices signify, according to Paz?

3. In Paz's view, how does the North American obsession with hygiene express itself in attitudes toward race? What kinds of things are being "repressed" in North American culture?

Exploring Your Cultural Perspective

1. Based on your experience, is North America less hygiene obsessed and intolerant now than when Paz wrote this essay in 1971? Explain your answer.

2. In an essay, identify the kinds of foods that you, your family, and your friends eat most of the time. Describe the national origins of these dishes, and discuss whether they contradict Paz's observations about North American food preferences.

GARRETT HONGO

Who among You Knows the Essence of Garlic?

Garrett Hongo's poetry springs from his Japanese and Hawaiian background and his experiences growing up in southern California. He has received numerous awards for his poetry, including the Pushcart Prize and the Wesleyan University Press Poetry Competition Award. Collections of his works include *The River of Heaven* (1988) and *Volcano: A Memoir of Hawaii* (1995). In the poem reprinted here, Hongo challenges the reader to enter the labyrinth of sensations evoked by foods from his Asian culture.

Thinking Critically

Have you ever noticed unfamiliar fruits and vegetables in supermarkets or in open-air food stalls. Have you tried any of them? Why or why not? As you read Hongo's poem, notice the sensuous **metaphors**—*figures of speech that imply a comparison between two different things—he uses to communicate unfamiliar tastes and flavors.*

Can your foreigner's nose smell mullets
roasting in a glaze of brown bean paste
and sprinkled with novas of sea salt?

Can you hear my grandmother
chant the mushroom's sutra?   5

Can you hear the papayas crying
as they bleed in porcelain plates?

I'm telling you that the bamboo
slips the long pliant shoots
of its myriad soft tongues   10
into your mouth that is full of oranges.

I'm saying that the silver waterfalls
of bean threads will burst in hot oil
and stain your lips like zinc.

15 The marbled skin of the blue mackerel
    works good for men. The purple oils
    from its flesh perfume the tongues of women.

    If you swallow them whole, the rice cakes
    soaking in a broth of coconut milk and brown sugar
20 will never leave the bottom of your stomach.

    Flukes of giant black mushrooms
    leap from their murky tubs
    and strangle the toes of young carrots.

    Broiling chickens ooze grease,
25 yellow tears of fat collect
    and spatter in the smoking pot.

    Soft ripe pears, blushing
    on the kitchen window sill,
    kneel like a plump women
30 taking a long luxurious shampoo,
    and invite you to bite their hips.

    Why not grab basketfuls of steaming noodles,
    lush and slick as the hair of a fine lady,
    and sqeeze?

35 The shrimps, big as Portuguese thumbs,
    stew among cut guavas, red onions,
    ginger root, and rosemary in lemon juice,
    the palm oil bubbling to the top,
    breaking through layers and layers
40 of shredded coconut and sliced cashews.

    Who among you knows the essence
    of garlic and black lotus root,
    of red and green peppers sizzling
    among squads of oysters in the skillet,
45 of crushed ginger, fresh green onions,
    and pale-blue rice wine simmering
    in the stomach of a big red fish?

Engaging the Text

1. How do the complex descriptive effects of the poem depend on transposing
   sense impressions—that is, on appealing to one sense in terms of another?
   Where can you see this operating? Why is this stylistic method effective in
   getting Hongo's point across?

"Food as metaphor for love? Again?"

FIGURE 2.10

2. What kinds of associations do the sensuous qualities of certain ethnic foods trigger in the speaker's mind? In what sense does the unfamiliar cuisine stand for the richness and diversity of an immigrant culture that is largely unknown to mainstream society?

3. In what ways does the speaker's tone shift over the course of the poem? How is this tactic designed to encourage the reader to accept the speaker's claims?

Exploring Your Cultural Perspective

1. What is the first "foreign" food you ever ate? Describe the circumstances in which you encountered it, your reactions to it, and the place, if any, it has come to occupy in your diet. Describe a dish from your own ethnic heritage using metaphors that suggest not only its taste but also the qualities that connect it to that particular culture.

2. What is your favorite comfort food—that is, a food that makes you feel better when you eat it? What associations do you have with this food? What factors make certain foods trigger emotions like those evoked in the Edward Koren cartoon in Figure 2.10. What is Koren's attitude toward this phenomenon?

SLAVENKA DRAKULIĆ
Pizza in Warsaw, Torte in Prague

Slavenka Drakulić is a prominent Croatian journalist and novelist. Her thoughtful observations on life in Eastern Europe under communism and after its fall in 1991 were featured in the magazine *Danas*, published in Zagreb. She is a regular contributor to the *Nation*, the *New Republic*, and the *New York Times Magazine*. Her novel *Holograms of Fear* (1992) received the Independent Foreign Fiction Award. Drakulić's nonfiction, including *The Balkan Express: Fragments from the Other Side of War* (1993) and *Cafe Europa: Life after Communism* (1996), has been translated into eleven languages. Drakulić's latest work is *S.: A Novel about the Balkans* (2000), translated by Marko Ivić. This essay on food and politics first appeared in *How We Survived Communism and Even Laughed* (1992).

Thinking Critically

The next time you are in a supermarket, look at all the choices you have, and imagine what it would be like to live in a society where even basic foods were in short supply. As you read this essay, think about whether food is ultimately more important then political **ideology.**

We were hungry, so I said "Let's have a pizza!" in the way you would think of it in, say, New York, or any West European city—meaning "Let's go to a fast-food place and grab something to eat." Jolanta, a small, blond, Polish translator of English, looked at me thoughtfully, as if I were confronting her with quite a serious task. "There are only two such places," she said in an apologetic tone of voice. Instantly, I was overwhelmed by the guilt of taking pizza in Poland for granted. "Drop it," I said. But she insisted on this pizza place. "You must see it," she said. "It's so different from the other restaurants in Warsaw."

We were lucky because we were admitted without reservations. This is a privately owned restaurant, one of the very few. We were also lucky because we could afford a pizza and beer here, which cost as much as dinner in a fancy hotel. The restaurant was a small, cozy place, with just two wooden tables and a few high stools at the bar—you couldn't squeeze more than twenty people in, even if you wanted to.

It was raining outside, a cold winter afternoon in Warsaw. Once inside, everything was different: two waiters dressed in impeccable white shirts, with bow ties and red aprons, a bowl of fresh tropical fruit on the bar, linen napkins and the smell of pizza baked in a real charcoal-fired oven. Jolanta and I were listening to disco music, eating pizza, and drinking Tuborg beer from long elegant glasses. Perhaps this is what you pay for, the feeling that you are somewhere else, in a different Warsaw, in a dreamland where there is everything—pizza, fruit juice, thick grilled steaks, salads—and the everyday life of shortages and poverty can't seep in, at least, for the moment.

Yet to understand just how different this place is, one has to see a "normal" coffee shop, such as the one in the modernistic building of concrete and glass that we visited the same day. Inside neon lights flicker, casting a ghostly light on the aluminum tables and chairs covered with plastic. This place looks more like a bus terminal than like a *kawiarnia*. It's almost empty and the air is thick with cigarette smoke. A bleached blond waitress slowly approaches us with a very limited menu: tea, some alcoholic beverages, Coke, coffee. "With milk?" I ask.

"No milk," she shakes her head.   5

"Then, can I get a fruit juice perhaps?" I say, in the hopes of drinking just one in a Polish state-owned restaurant.

"No juice." She shakes her head impatiently (at this point, of course, there is no "sophisticated" question about the kind of juice one would perhaps prefer). I give up and get a cup of coffee. It's too sweet. Jolanta is drinking Coke, because there is Coke everywhere—in the middle of Warsaw as, I believe, in the middle of the desert. There may be neither milk nor water, but there is sure to be a bottle of Coke around. Nobody seems to mind the paradox that even though fruit grows throughout Poland, there is no fruit juice yet Coke is everywhere. But here Coke, like everything coming from America, is more of a symbol than a beverage.

To be reduced to having Coke and pizza offered not only as fancy food, but, what's more, as the idea of choice, strikes me as a form of imperialism, possibly only where there is really very little choice. Just across the street from the private restaurant, where Jolanta parked her tiny Polski Fiat, is a grocery store. It is closed in the afternoon, so says a handwritten note on the door. Through the dusty shop window we can see the half-empty shelves, with a few cans of beans, pasta, rice, cabbage, vinegar. A friend, a Yugoslav living in Warsaw, told me that some years ago vinegar and mustard were almost all you could find in the stores. At another point, my friend noticed that shelves were stocked with prune compote. One might easily conclude that this is what Poles probably like the best or why else would it be in stores in such quantities? But the reason was just the opposite: Prune compote was what they had, not what they liked. However, the word "like" is not the best way to explain the food situation (or any situation) in Poland. Looking at a shop window where onions and garlic are two of the very few items on display, what meaning could the word "like" possibly have?

Slowly, one realizes that not only is this a different reality, but that words have a different meaning here, too. It makes you understand that the word "like" implies not only choice but refinement, even indulgence, *savoir-vivre*—in fact, a whole different attitude toward food. It certainly doesn't imply that you stuff yourself with whatever you find at the farmer's market or in a grocery that day. Instead, it suggests a certain experience, a knowledge, a possibility of comparing quality and taste. Right after the overthrow of the Ceausescu government in Romania in December 1989, I read a report in the newspaper about life in Bucharest. There was a story about a man who ate the first banana in his life. He was an older man, a worker, and he said to a reporter shyly that he ate a whole banana, together with the skin, because he didn't know that he had to peel it. At first, I was moved by the isolation this man was forced to live in, by the fact that he never read or even heard what to do with a banana. But then something else caught my attention: *"It tasted good,"* he said. I can imagine this man, holding a sweet-smelling, ripe banana in his hand, curious and excited by it, as by a forbidden fruit. He holds it for a moment, then bites. It tastes strange but "good." It must have been good, even together with a bitter, tough skin, because it was something unachievable, an object of desire. It was not a banana that he was eating, but the promise, the hope of the future. So, he liked it no matter what its taste.

10   One of the things one is constantly reminded of in these parts is not to be thoughtless with food. I remember my mother telling me that I had to eat everything in front of me, because to throw away food would be a sin. Perhaps she had God on her mind, perhaps not. She experienced World War II and ever since, like most of the people in Eastern Europe, she behaves as if it never ended. Maybe this is why they are never really surprised that even forty years afterwards there is a lack of sugar, oil, coffee, or flour. To be heedless—to behave as if you are somewhere else, where everything is easy to get—is a sin not against God, but against people. Here you have to think of food, because it has entirely diverse social meanings. To bring a cake for dessert when you are invited for a dinner—a common gesture in another, more affluent country—means you invested a great deal of energy to find it if you didn't make it yourself. And even if you did, finding eggs, milk, sugar, and butter took time and energy. That makes it precious in a very different way from if you had bought it in the pastry shop next door.

When Jaroslav picked me up at Prague airport, I wanted to buy a torte before we went to his house for dinner. It was seven o'clock in the evening and shops were already closed. Czechs work until five or six, which doesn't leave much time to shop. "The old government didn't like people walking in the streets. It might cause them trouble," said Jaroslav, half joking. "Besides, there isn't much to buy anyway." My desire to buy a torte after six o'clock appeared to be quite an extravagance, and it was clear that one couldn't make a habit of bringing a cake for dessert. In the Slavia Café there were no pastries at all, not to mention a torte. The best confectioner in Prague was closed, and in the Hotel Zlatá Husa restaurant a waitress repeated "Torte?" after us as if we were in the wrong place. Then she shook her head. With every new place, my desire to buy a torte diminished. Perhaps it is not that there are no tortes—it's just hard to find them at that hour. At the end, we went to the only shop open until eight-thirty and bought ice cream. There were three kinds and Jaroslav picked vanilla, which is what his boys like the best.

On another occasion, in the Bulgarian capital Sofia, Evelina is preparing a party. I am helping her in the small kitchen of the decaying apartment that she shares with a student friend, because as an assistant professor at the university, she cannot afford to rent an apartment alone. I peel potatoes, perhaps six pounds of them. She will make a potato salad with onions. Then she will bake the rest of them in the oven and serve them with . . . actually nothing. She calls it "a hundred-ways potato party"—sometimes humor is the only way to overcome depression. There are also four eggs for an omelet and two cans of sardines (imported from Yugoslavia), plus vodka and wine, and that's it, for the eight people she has invited.

We sit around her table: a Bulgarian theater director who lives in exile in Germany, three of Evelina's colleagues from the university, a historian friend and her husband, and the two of us. We eat potatoes with potatoes, drink vodka, discuss the first issue of the opposition paper *Demokratia*, the round-table talks between the Union of Democratic Forces and the communist government, and calculate how many votes the opposition will get in the forthcoming free elections—the first. Nobody seems to mind that there is no more food on the table—at least not as long as a passionate political discussion is going on. "*This is our food*," says Evelina. "We are used to swallowing politics with our meals. For breakfast you eat elections, a parliament discussion comes for lunch, and at dinner you laugh at the evening news or get mad at the lies that the Communist Party is trying to sell, in spite of everything." Perhaps these people can live almost without food—either because it's too expensive or because there is nothing to buy, or both—without books and information, but not without politics.

One might think that this is happening only now, when they have the first real chance to change something. Not so. This intimacy with political issues was a part of everyday life whether on the level of hatred, or mistrust, or gossip, or just plain resignation during Todor Živkov's communist government. In a totalitarian society, one *has* to relate to the power directly; there is no escape.

Therefore, politics never becomes abstract. It remains a palpable, brutal force directing every aspect of our lives, from what we eat to how we live and where we work. Like a disease, a plague, an epidemic, it doesn't spare anybody. Paradoxically, this is precisely how a totalitarian state produces its enemies: politicized citizens. The "velvet revolution" is the product not only of high politics, but of the consciousness of ordinary citizens, infected by politics.

15   Before you get here, you tend to forget newspaper pictures of people standing in line in front of shops. You think they serve as proof in the ideological battle, the proof that communism is failing. Or you take them as mere pictures, not reality. But once here, you cannot escape the *feeling* of shortages, even if you are not standing in line, even if you don't see them. In Prague, where people line up only for fruit, there was enough of all necessities, except for oranges or lemons, which were considered a "luxury." It is hard to predict what will be considered a luxury item because this depends on planning, production, and shortages. One time it might be fruit, as in Prague, or milk, as in Sofia. People get used to less and less of everything. In Albania, the monthly ration for a whole family is two pounds of meat, two pounds of cheese, ten pounds of flour, less than half a pound each of coffee and butter. Everywhere, the bottom line is bread. It means safety—because the lack of bread is where real fear begins. Whenever I read a headline "No Bread" in the newspaper, I see a small, dark, almost empty bakery on Vladimir Zaimov Boulevard in Sofia, and I myself, even without reason, experience a genuine fear. It makes my bread unreal, too, and I feel as if I should grab it and eat it while it lasts.

Every mother in Bulgaria can point to where communism failed. From the failures of the planned economy (and the consequent lack of food, milk), to the lack of apartments, child-care facilities, clothes, disposable diapers, or toilet paper. The banality of everyday life is where it has really failed, rather than on the level of ideology. In another kitchen in Sofia, Ana, Katarine and I sit. Her one-year-old daughter is trying to grab our cups from the table. She looks healthy. "She is fine now," says Ana, "but you should have seen her six months ago. There was no formula to buy and normal milk you can hardly get as it is. At one point our shops started to sell Humana, imported powdered milk from the dollar shops, because its shelf life was over. I didn't have a choice. I had to feed my baby with that milk, and she got very, very sick. By allowing this milk to be sold, our own government poisoned babies. It was even on TV; they had to put it on because so many babies in Sofia got sick. We are the Third World here."

If communism didn't fail on bread or milk, it certainly failed on strawberries. When I flew to Warsaw from West Berlin, I bought cosmetics, oranges, chocolates, Nescafé, as a present for my friend Zofia—as if I were going home. I also bought a small basket of strawberries. I knew that by now she could buy oranges or even Nescafé from street vendors at a good price—but not strawberries. I bought them also because I remembered when we were together in

New York for the first time, back in the eighties, and we went shopping. In a downtown Manhattan supermarket, we stood in front of a fruit counter and just stared. It was full of fruits we didn't know the names of—or if we did, like the man with the banana in Bucharest, we didn't know how they would taste. But this sight was not a miracle; we somehow expected it. What came as a real surprise was fresh strawberries, even though it was December and decorated Christmas trees were in the windows already. In Poland or Yugoslavia, you could see strawberries only in spring. We would buy them for children or when we were visiting a sick relative, so expensive were they. And here, all of a sudden— strawberries. At that moment, they represented all the difference between the world we lived in and this one, so strange and uncomfortably rich. It was not so much that you could see them in the middle of the winter, but because you could afford them. When I handed her the strawberries in Warsaw, Zofia said: "How wonderful! I'll save them for my son." The fact that she used the word "save" told me everything: that almost ten years after we saw each other in New York, after the victory of Solidarity, and private initiatives in the economy, there are still no strawberries and perhaps there won't be for another ten years. She was closer to me then, that evening, in the apartment where she lives with her sick, elderly, mother (because there is nobody else to take care of her and to put your parent in a state-run institution would be more than cruelty, it would be a crime). Both of them took just one strawberry each, then put the rest in the refrigerator "for Grzegorz." This is how we tell our kids we love them, because food is love, if you don't have it, or if you have to wait in lines, get what you can, and then prepare a decent meal. Maybe this is why the chicken soup, cabbage stew, and mashed potatoes that evening tasted so good.

All this stays with me forever. When I come to New York and go shopping at Grace Balducci's Marketplace on Third Avenue and 71st Street, I think of Zofia, my mother, my friend Jasmina who loves Swiss chocolates, my daughter's desire for Brooklyn chewing gum, and my own hungry self, still confused by the thirty kinds of cheese displayed in front of me. In an article in *Literaturnaya Gazeta* May 1989 the Soviet poet Yevgenii Yevtushenko tells of a *kolkhoz* woman who fainted in an East Berlin shop, just because she saw twenty kinds of sausages. When she came back to her senses, she repeated in despair: "Why, but why?" How well I understand her question—but knowing the answer doesn't really help.

Engaging the Text

1. Which episodes reveal how living under a communist regime makes ordinary foods take on extraordinary meanings?

2. How does Drakulić's effort to buy a torte to bring for dessert give the gift a different meaning from what it would have in the West?

3. What is the point of the story of the woman who fainted when she saw twenty kinds of sausages? To what extent does Drakulić's essay change your perspective on the common foods so readily available to most North Americans?

Exploring Your Cultural Perspective

1. In what ways is being poor in the United States equivalent to living in Eastern Europe as described by Drakulić? Use Drakulić's essay as a jumping-off point to explore the relationship between food choices and class-related expectations in North American culture.

2. Visit a warehouse store that sells food in bulk at wholesale prices and also visit a typical supermarket. Take notes on the prices of identical items, displays, checkout procedures, architectural scale, size of shopping carts, background music, the customers (how they are dressed, their demeanor), and other features that define the experience of shopping in one place as opposed to the other. What makes shopping in one store a qualitatively different kind of experience than shopping in the other?

WILLIAM MAXWELL
The Pilgrimage

While traveling in France, two U.S. tourists go to desperate lengths to obtain specific dishes recommended by their friends back home. In "The Pilgrimage" from *Over the River and Other Stories* (1953), William Maxwell takes the reader along with Ellen and Ray on their quest to attain sophistication and social acceptance. This thought-provoking story asks why certain foods have come to represent refinement and upper-class values. Maxwell (1909–2000) was a prolific writer whose works include *Billie Byer and Other Stories* (1992) and *All the Days and Nights: The Collected Stories of William Maxwell* (1995).

Thinking Critically
As you read Maxwell's story, pay particular attention to his tone. Does he sympathize with or make fun of Ray and Ellen's predicament?

In a rented Renault, with exactly as much luggage as the back seat would hold, Ray and Ellen Ormsby were making a little tour of France. It had so far included Vézelay, the mountain villages of Auvergne, the roses and Roman ruins of Provence, and the gorges of the Tarn. They were now on their way back to Paris by a route that was neither the most direct nor particularly scenic, and that had been chosen with one thing in mind—dinner at the Hôtel du Domino in Périgueux. The Richardsons, who were close friends of the Ormsbys in America, had insisted that they go there. "The best dinner I ever had in my entire life," Jerry Richardson had said. "Every course was something with truffles." "And the dessert," Anne Richardson had said, "was little balls of various kinds of ice cream in a beautiful basket of spun sugar with a spun-sugar bow." Putting the two statements together, Ray Ormsby had persisted in thinking that the ice cream also had truffles in it, and Ellen had given up trying to correct this impression.

At seven o'clock, they were still sixty-five kilometres from Périgueux, on a winding back-country road, and beginning to get hungry. The landscape was gilded with the evening light. Ray was driving. Ellen read aloud to him from the "Guide Gastronomique de la France" the paragraph on the Hôtel du Domino:

"Bel et confortable établissement à la renommée bien assise et que Mme. Lasgrezas dirige avec beaucoup de bonheur. Grâce à un maître queux qualifié, vous y ferez un repas de grande classe qui vous sera servi dans une élégante salle à manger ou dans un délicieux jardin d' été. . . ."[1]

As they drove through village after village, they saw, in addition to the usual painted Cinzano and Rasurel signs, announcements of the *spécialité*[2] of the restaurant of this or that Hôtel des Sports or de la Poste or du Lion d'Or—always with truffles. In Montignac, there were so many of these signs that Ellen said anxiously, "Do you think we ought to eat *here*?"

"No," Ray said. "Périgueux is the place. It's the capital of Périgord, and so it's bound to have the best food.

5   Outside Thenon, they had a flat tire—the seventh in eight days of driving—and the casing of the spare tire was in such bad condition that Ray was afraid to drive on until the inner tube had been repaired and the regular tire put back on. It was five minutes of nine when they drove up before the Hôtel du Domino, and they were famished. Ray went inside and found that the hotel had accommodations for them. The car was driven into the hotel garage and emptied of its formidable luggage, and the Ormsbys were shown up to their third-floor room, which might have been in any plain hotel anywhere in France. "What I'd really like is a roast chicken stuffed with truffles," Ellen said from the washstand. "But probably it takes a long time."

"What if it does," Ray said. "We'll be eating other things first."

He threw open the shutters and discovered that their room looked out on a painting by Dufy—the large, bare, open square surrounded by stone buildings, with the tricolor for accent, and the sky a rich, stained-glass blue. From another window, at the turning of the stairs on their way down to dinner, they saw the delicious garden, but it was dark, and no one was eating there now. At the foot of the stairs, they paused.

"You wanted the restaurant?" the concierge asked, and when they nodded, she came out from behind her mahogany railing and led them importantly down a corridor. The maître d'hôtel, in a grey business suit, stood waiting at the door of the dining room, and put them at a table for two. Then he handed them the menu with a flourish. They saw at a glance how expensive the dinner was going to be. A waitress brought plates, glasses, napkins, knives, and forks.

While Ellen was reading the menu, Ray looked slowly around the room. The *"élégante salle à manger"* looked like a hotel coffee shop. There weren't even any tablecloths. The walls were painted a dismal shade of off-mustard. His eyes came to rest finally on the stippled brown dado[3] a foot from his face. "It's a perfect room to commit suicide in," he said, and reached for the menu. A moment later he exclaimed, "I don't see the basket of ice cream!"

10   "It must be there," Ellen said. Don't get so excited."

"Well, where? Just show me?"

Together they looked through the two columns of desserts, without finding the marvel in question. "Jerry and Anne were here several days," Ellen said. "They may have had it in some other restaurant."

This explanation Ray would not accept. "It was the same dinner, I remember distinctly." The full horror of their driving all the way to Périgueux in order to eat a very expensive meal at the wrong restaurant broke over him. In a cold sweat he got up from the table.

"Where are you going?" Ellen asked.

"I'll be right back," he said, and left the dining room. Upstairs in their *15* room, he dug the "Guide Michelin" out of a duffel-bag. He had lost all faith in the "Guide Gastronomique," because of its description of the dining room; the person who wrote that had never set eyes on the Hôtel du Domino or, probably, on Périgueux. In the "Michelin," the restaurant of the Hôtel du Domino rated one star and so did the restaurant Le Montaigne, but Le Montaigne also had three crossed forks and spoons, and suddenly it came to him, with the awful clarity of a long-submerged memory at last brought to the surface through layer after layer of consciousness, that it was at Le Montaigne and not at the Hôtel du Domino that the Richardsons had meant them to eat. He picked up Ellen's coat and, still carrying the "Michelin," went back downstairs to the dining room.

"I've brought your coat," he said to Ellen as he sat down opposite her. "We're in the wrong restaurant."

"We aren't either," Ellen said. "And even if we were, I've *got* to have something to eat. I'm starving, and it's much too late now to go looking for—"

"It won't be far," Ray said. "Come on." He looked up into the face of the maître d'hôtel, waiting with his pencil and pad to take their order.

"You speak English?" Ray asked.

The maître d'hôtel nodded, and Ray described the basket of spun sugar *20* filled with different kinds of ice cream.

"And a spun-sugar bow," Ellen said.

The maître d'hôtel looked blank, and so Ray tried again, speaking slowly and distinctly.

"*Omelette?*" the maître d'hôtel said.

"No—ice cream!"

"*Glace,*" Ellen said. *25*

"*Et du sucre,*"[4] Ray said. "*Une—*" He and Ellen looked at each other. Neither of them could think of the word for "basket."

The maître d'hôtel went over to a sideboard and returned with another menu. "*Le menu des glaces,*" he said coldly. "*Vanille,*" they read, "*chocolat, pistache, framboise,*[5] *fraise,*[6] *tutti-frutti, praliné . . .*"

Even if the spun-sugar basket had been on the *menu des glaces* (which it wasn't), they were in too excited a state to have found it—Ray because of his fear that they were making an irremediable mistake in having dinner at this restaurant and Ellen because of the dreadful way he was acting.

"We came here on a pilgrimage," he said to the maître d'hôtel, in a tense, excited voice that carried all over the dining room. "We have these friends in America who ate in Périgueux, and it is absolutely necessary that we eat in the place they told us about."

30   "This is a very good restaurant," the maître d'hôtel said. "We have many *spécialités. Foie gras truffé,[7] poulet du Périgord noir,[8] truffes sous la cendre[9]—*"

"I know," Ray said, "but apparently it isn't the right one." He got up from his chair, and Ellen, shaking her head—because there was no use arguing with him when he was like this—got up, too. The other diners had all turned around to watch.

"Come," the maître d'hôtel said, taking hold of Ray's elbow. "In the lobby is a lady who speaks English very well. She will understand what it is you want."

In the lobby, Ray told his story again—how they had come to Périgueux because their friends in America had told them about a certain restaurant here, and how it was this restaurant and no other that they must find. They had thought it was the restaurant in the Hôtel du Domino, but since the restaurant of the Hôtel du Domino did not have the dessert that their friends in America had particularly recommended, little balls of ice cream in—

The concierge, her eyes large with sudden comprehension, interrupted him. "You want truffles?"

35   Out on the sidewalk, trying to read the "Michelin" map of Périgueux by the feeble light of a tall street lamp, Ray said, "La Montaigne has a star just like the Hôtel du Domino, but it also has three crossed forks and spoons, so it must be better than the hotel."

"All those crossed forks and spoons mean is that it is a very comfortable place to eat in," Ellen said. "It has nothing to do with the quality of the food. I don't care where we eat, so long as I don't have to go back there."

There were circles of fatigue under her eyes. She was both exasperated with him and proud of him for insisting on getting what they had come here for, when most people would have given in and taken what there was. They walked on a couple of blocks and came to a second open square. Ray stopped a man and woman.

"*Pardon, m'sieur,*" he said, removing his hat. "*Le restaurant La Montagne, c'est par là*"—he pointed—"*ou par là?*"[10]

"*La Montagne? Le restaurant La Montagne?*" the man said dubiously. "*Je regrette, mais je ne le connais pas.*"[11]

40   Ray opened the "Michelin" and, by the light of the nearest neon sign, the man and woman read down the page.

"*Ooh, LE MONTAIGNE!*" the woman exclaimed suddenly.

"*LE MONTAIGNE!*" the man echoed.

"*Oui, Le Montaigne,*" Ray said, nodding.

The man pointed across the square.

Standing in front of LeMontaigne, Ray again had doubts. It was much   *45*
larger than the restaurant of the Hôtel du Domino, but it looked much more
like a bar than a first-class restaurant. And again there were no tablecloths. A
waiter approached them as they stood undecided on the sidewalk. Ray asked to
see the menu, and the waiter disappeared into the building. A moment later, a
second waiter appeared. "*Le menu,*" he said, pointing to a standard a few feet
away. Le Montaigne offered many specialties, most of them *truffés*, but not the
Richardson's dessert.

"Couldn't we just go someplace and have an ordinary meal?" Ellen said. "I
don't think I feel like eating anything elaborate any longer."

But Ray had made a discovery. "The restaurant is upstairs," he said. "What
we've been looking at is the café, so naturally there aren't any tablecloths."

Taking Ellen by the hand, he started up what turned out to be a circular
staircase. The second floor of the building was dark. Ellen, convinced that the
restaurant had stopped serving dinner, objected to going any farther, but Ray
went on and, protesting, she followed him. The third floor was brightly lighted—
was, in fact, a restaurant, with white tablecloths, gleaming crystal, and the traditional dark-red plush upholstery, and two or three clients who were lingering
over the end of dinner. The maître d'hôtel, in a black dinner jacket, led them
to a table and handed them the same menu they had read downstairs.

"I don't see any roast chicken stuffed with truffles." Ellen said.

"Oh, I forgot that's what you wanted!" Ray said, conscience-stricken. "Did   *50*
they have it at the Domino?"

"No, but they had it *poulet noir*—and here they don't even have that."

"I'm so sorry," he said. "Are you sure they don't have it here?" He ran his
eyes down the list of dishes with truffles and said suddenly, "There it is!"

"Where?" Ellen demanded. He pointed to "*Tournedos aux truffes du Périgord.*"
"That's not chicken," Ellen said.

"Well, it's no good, then," Ray said.

"No good?" the maître d'hôtel said indignantly. "It's *very* good! *Le tour-*   *55*
nedos aux truffes du Périgord[12] is a *spécialité* of the restaurant!"

They were only partly successful in conveying to him that that was not
what Ray had meant.

No, there was no roast chicken stuffed with truffles.

No chicken of any kind.

"I'm very sorry," Ray said, and got up from his chair.

He was not at all sure that Ellen would go back to the restaurant in the   *60*
Hôtel du Domino with him, but she did. Their table was just as they had left it.
A waiter and a busboy, seeing them come in, exchanged startled whispers. The

maître d'hôtel did not come near them for several minutes after they had sat down, and Ray carefully didn't look around for him.

"Do you think he is angry because we walked out?" Ellen asked.

Ray shook his head. "I think we hurt his feelings, though. I think he prides himself on speaking English, and now he will never again be sure that he does speak it, because of us."

Eventually, the maître d'hôtel appeared at their table. Sickly smiles were exchanged all around, and the menu was offered for the second time, without the flourish.

"What is *les truffes sous la cendre?*" Ellen asked.

65 "It takes forty-five minutes," the maître d'hôtel said.

"*Le foie gras truffé,*" Ray said. "For two."

"*Le foie gras,* O.K.," the maître d'hôtel said. "*Et ensuite?*"[13]

"*Oeufs en gelée,*"[14] Ellen said.

"*Oeufs en gelée,* O.K."

70 "*Le poulet noir,*" Ray said.

"*Le poulet noir,* O.K."

"*Et deux Cinzano,*" Ray said, on solid ground at last, "*avec un morceau de glace et un zeste de citro. S'il vous plaît.*"[15]

The apéritif arrived, with ice and lemon peel, but the wine list was not presented, and Ray asked the waitress for it. She spoke to the maître d'hôtel, and that was the last the Ormsbys ever saw of her. The maître d'hôtel brought the wine list, they ordered the dry white *vin du pays*[16] that he recommended, and their dinner was served to them by a waiter so young that Ray looked to see whether he was in knee pants.

The pâté was everything the Richardsons had said it would be, and Ray, to make up for all he had put his wife through in the course of the evening, gave her a small quantity of his, which, protesting, she accepted. The maître d'hôtel stopped at their table and said, "Is it good?"

75 "Very good," they said simultaneously.

The *oeufs en gelée* arrived and were also very good, but were they any better than or even as good as the *oeufs en gelée* the Ormsbys had had in the restaurant of a hotel on the outskirts of Aix-en-Provence was the question.

"Is it good?" the maître d'hôtel asked.

"Very good," they said. "So is the wine."

The boy waiter brought in the *poulet noir*—a chicken casserole with a dark-brown Madeira sauce full of chopped truffles.

80 "Is it good?" Ray asked when the waiter had finished serving them and Ellen had tasted the *pièce de résistance.*[17]

"It's very good," she said. "But I'm not sure I can taste the truffles."

"I think I can," he said, a moment later.

"With the roast chicken, it probably would have been quite easy," Ellen said.

"Are you sure the Richardsons had roast chicken stuffed with truffles?" Ray asked.

"I think so," Ellen said. "Anyway, I know I've read about it."   *85*

"Is it good?" the maître d'hôtel, their waiter, and the waiter from a neighboring table asked, in succession.

"Very good," the Ormsbys said.

Since they couldn't have the little balls of various kinds of ice cream in a basket of spun sugar with a spun-sugar bow for dessert, they decided not to have any dessert at all. The meal came to an abrupt end with *café filtre*.

Intending to take a short walk before going to bed, they heard dance music in the square in front of Le Montaigne, and found a large crowd there, celebrating the annual fair of Périgueux. There was a seven-piece orchestra on a raised platform under a canvas, and a few couples were dancing in the street. Soon there were more.

"Do you feel like dancing?" Ray asked.   *90*

The pavement was not as bad for dancing as he would have supposed, and something happened to them that never happened to them anywhere in France before—something remarkable. In spite of their clothes and their faces and the "Michelin" he held in one hand, eyes constantly swept over them or past them without pausing. Dancing in the street, they aroused no curiosity and, in fact, no interest whatever.

At midnight, standing on the balcony outside their room, they could still hear the music, a quarter of a mile away.

"Hasn't it been a lovely evening!" Ellen said. I'll always remember dancing in the street in Périgueux."

Two people emerged from the cinema, a few doors from the Hôtel du Domino. And then a few more—a pair of lovers, a woman, a boy, a woman and a man carrying a sleeping child.

"The pâté was the best I ever ate," Ellen said.   *95*

"The Richardsons probably ate in the garden," Ray said. "I don't know that the dinner as a whole was all *that* good," he added thoughtfully. And then, "I don't know that we need to tell them."

"The poor people who run the cinema," Ellen said.

"Why?"

"No one came to see the movie."

"I suppose Périgueux really isn't the kind of town that would support a   *100* movie theatre," Ray said.

"That's it," Ellen said. "Here when people want to relax and enjoy themselves, they have an apéritif, they walk up and down in the evening air, they dance in the street, the way people used to do before there were any movies. It's another civilization entirely from anything we're accustomed to. Another world."

They went back into the bedroom and closed the shutters. A few minutes later, some more people emerged from the movie theatre, and some more, and some more, and then a great crowd came streaming out and, walking gravely, like people taking part in a religious procession, fanned out across the open square.

Notes

1. A beautiful and comfortable, justifiably famous establishment that Madame Lasgrezas efficiently runs. Given such a proprietor, you will find meals of great quality, served in an elegant dining room or in a delightful summer garden.
2. featured offering, specialty of the house
3. lower broad part of an interior wall covered in wallpaper, paint, or fabric
4. and of sugar
5. raspberry
6. strawberry
7. goose liver with truffles (rare edible mushrooms)
8. chicken casserole with a dark brown Madeira sauce with chopped truffles
9. grilled truffles
10. Is La Montagne restaurant over . . . or over there?
11. I'm sorry, but I never heard of it.
12. beef tenderloin with truffles from the region of Perigord
13. and after that?
14. eggs in aspic
15. Two Cinzanos (Italian red wine) with a little bit of ice and a lemon twist, if you please.
16. local wine
17. the principal dish of a meal

Engaging the Text

1. In what ways can Ray and Ellen's quest to locate the restaurant and have the meal their friends described be characterized as a "pilgrimage"? What is the effect of Maxwell's use of a term with religious overtones to describe their search? How does the contrast between the kind of pilgrimage people embarked on in past times and the one Maxwell describes illustrate a direction contemporary culture has taken?

2. As far as you can tell, what is Maxwell's opinion of his characters, Ray and Ellen? At what different points in the story do they misconstrue what is going on around them or draw inaccurate conclusions? How does Maxwell's use of the term *religious* in the final sentence suggest an ironic contrast between Ray and Ellen's quest and what the townspeople consider to be important?

3. Do Ray and Ellen need to be believe that their quest has been successful because they put so much effort into it? Is this a fair portrayal of the way

people deceive themselves when traveling abroad? To whom is this quest more important and why? Where in this story do Ray and Ellen switch roles? How does this quest affect the relationship between them?

Exploring Your Cultural Perspective

1. What values and qualities has French food come to signify for North Americans? If you have ever been in an expensive French restaurant (or any other expensive restaurant), describe in detail the part rituals play in the way wine and food is described and served. How do these features create an aura of privilege that, in some ways, is quasi-religious?

2. Maxwell's story is about the significance that a formal French meal has acquired for a North American couple. Yet many aspects of the formal meal cross cultural boundaries. Beyond their utilitarian function, what role do any of the following play in establishing the tone of a formal meal: tablecloths, cloth napkins, candles, serving spoons, wine glasses, proposing toasts? In what way does the formal meal remain the paradigm from which other food events (picnics, airline dinners, cocktail parties, fast-food meals) borrow their symbols, sequences, and categories?

3. Why do fancy canopies and ornate entryways to restaurants represent elevated status? To what extent have popular franchises, such as TGI Friday's or Bennigan's, appropriated architectural features intended to evoke upperclass associations? What other visual symbols of status do restaurants use, and what meanings do those symbols project?

CONNECTING THE TEXTS

1. How does Octavio Paz's analysis in "Hygiene and Repression" of the Puritan influence on North American culinary habits illustrate why the breakfast food innovations of John Harvey Kellogg and C. W. Post became so popular? Draw on material from Bill Bryson's "What's Cooking? Eating in America" and Paz's "Hygiene and Repression" to develop an argument as to whether elements of Puritanism persist in contemporary North American food preferences.

2. McDonald's embodies the logical outcome of trends that Bill Bryson describes in "What's Cooking? Eating in America." Drawing on Conrad P. Kottak's "Rituals at McDonald's" and Bryson's article, discuss the significance of McDonald's unique fusion of what appears to be an old-fashioned cottage with ultramodern glass walls and a color scheme that evokes an earlier time in a clean, efficient, modern setting. What insight does Bryson provide into the technology involved in creating fast-food chains

like McDonald's that offer predictable, convenient, standardized products? Is control over the environment one of the things we are buying? If so, why?

3. According to Octavio Paz in "Hygiene and Repression," North American cuisine is based on exclusions and a preoccupation with purity. Are these the same values that prevailed in early Christian communities, as Diane Ackerman describes them in "The Social Sense"? In a short essay, discuss the common fears underlying the food preferences of both cultures despite the millennia separating them.

4. In what way do the analyses by Dinitia Smith in "Did a Barnyard Schism Lead to a Religious One?" and Octavio Paz in "Hygiene and Repression" rest on the assumption that religious taboos concerning food reflect cultural prejudices? What role does the fear of contamination by the "other" play in these beliefs and world views? Drawing on both articles, write an essay in which you express your position on the issue of food taboos and religious intolerance.

5. The anthropologist Marvin Harris offers pragmatic explanations for religious food taboos that strip them of their theological underpinnings. In light of Harris's theories as cited by both Dinitia Smith in "Did a Barnyard Schism Lead to a Religious One?" and Diane Ackerman in "The Social Sense," compare and contrast the reasons Hindus don't eat beef and Jews and Muslims don't eat pork.

6. Fast food, as described by Conrad P. Kottak in "Rituals at McDonald's," serves as a modern variation of eating with one's hands, although plastic utensils are available. Drawing on articles by Kottak and Margaret Visser ("Fingers"), analyze how fast food has modified table manners. What would constitute a breach of etiquette at a fast-food franchise?

7. Have Ellen and Ray in William Maxwell's story "The Pilgrimage" shaken off the constraints of "hygiene and repression" that Octavio Paz identifies as the defining feature of North American culture? Or is their "pilgrimage" and the way they go about it really a form of labor rather than a pleasure-seeking quest?

8. Compare Margaret Visser's insights (in "Fingers") about prohibitions against using the left hand for eating in cultures in which it is reserved for profane functions with Dinitia Smith's discussion (in "Did a Barnyard Schism Lead to a Religious One?") of the division between pure and impure foods. In what ways do taboos operate in both etiquette and religion?

9. In what ways can Garrett Hongo's poem ("Who among You Knows the Essence of Garlic?") be understood as a reply to the values embodied in McDonald's as discussed by Conrad P. Kottak in "Rituals at McDonald's"?

10. Garrett Hongo (in "Who among You Knows the Essence of Garlic?") and Octavio Paz (in "Hygiene and Repression") agree that mainstream North America's antipathy

toward anything foreign leads to the exclusion of ethnic foods from the standard North American diet. How does Hongo's approach as a poet differ from that of Paz in getting this point across? How do each of them support their argument?

11. What role does the expression of individuality play in Eastern Europe under communism in Slavenka Drakulić's "Pizza in Warsaw, Torte in Prague" and in present-day communist China as portrayed in Guanlong Cao in "Chopsticks"?

12. Conrad P. Kottak in "Rituals at McDonald's" argues that McDonald's golden arches offer a secular equivalent of a communal religious experience. William Maxwell in "The Pilgrimage" suggests that Ray and Ellen's quest embodies the desire to obtain signs of status, taste, and social acceptance so fervent that it is tantamount to a religious "pilgrimage." In an essay, discuss the way both authors use religious values to add an ironic note.

WRITING ABOUT FOOD

1. What kinds of foods are customarily prepared for certain holidays, such as Easter, Christmas, Thanksgiving, Hanukkah, Kwanza, the end of Ramadan, or any other religious, ethnic, or cultural celebration? Research the evolution of any one of these holidays, paying attention to the social meanings that are embedded in the foods particular to it and the rituals governing how those foods are served.

2. Describe a visit to your favorite restaurant, including details drawn from all five senses (sight, sound, taste, touch, smell) in your account. Analyze the decor, architecture, employees' uniforms and greetings, specialties on the menu, displays, and other stylized features that create its distinctive image. To what social class does the restaurant cater? Do you go there just on special occasions or more frequently? Describe the most memorable meal you have had there, who you were with, your conversation, the cost, and who paid. To what extent does this restaurant reflect the values of the neighborhood in which it is located?

3. If money were no object, what would you serve at a party for your friends or on a special occasion, such as a wedding or college graduation? Create a detailed menu organized around a theme. For some ideas, you might visit the *Gourmet* magazine Web site at <http://www.epicurious.com>.

4. What do the first-class (Figure 2.11, page 138) and second-class (Figure 2.12, page 139) menus from the *Titanic* suggest about the era and about the social classes of its passengers? How do these menus compare with a typical meal today? What changes in patterns of taste have occurred, and to what do you attribute these changes?

R.M.S. "T I T A N I C."

APRIL 14, 1912

HORS D'ŒUVRE VARIÉS
OYSTERS

CONSOMME OLGA   CREAM OF BARLEY

SALMON. MOUSSELINE SAUCE. CUCUMBER

FILET MIGNONS LILI
SAUTE OF CHICKEN, LYONNAISE
VEGETABLE MARROW FARCIE

LAMB MINT SAUCE
ROAST DUCKLING. APPLE SAUCE
SIRLOIN OF BEEF CHATEAU POTATOES

GREEN PEAS   CREAMED CARROTS
BOILED RICE
PARMENTIER & BOILED NEW POTATOES

PUNCH ROMAINE

ROAST SQUAB & CRESS
COLD ASPARAGUS VINAIGRETTE
PÂTE DE FOIE GRAS
CELERY

WALDORF PUDDING
PEACHES IN CHARTREUSE JELLY
CHOCOLATE & VANILLA ECLAIRS
FRENCH ICE CREAM

FIGURE 2.11

5. Have you ever gone without food or water for religious or spiritual reasons? In a short essay, tell about your experiences. Describe the circumstances and any peer pressure surrounding your decision to fast. What psychological conflicts did you have to overcome? Did you complete the fast? What benefits did you gain? Would you do it again? Why or why not?

6. With several classmates, rent a videotape of *Babette's Feast,* a Danish film made in 1987; *The Big Night* (1996), about Italian-American restauranteurs; *Like Water for Chocolate* (1998), made in Mexico; *The Chef in Love* (1996), filmed in Soviet Georgia; or any other film in which the food from a particular country is important to the story. After viewing one or several of these films, discuss and compare your analyses of the way food exemplifies the unique values of the culture in the context of the story.

7. In what way have food-related terms drawn from other cultures become a kind of shorthand to express a unique way of looking at things? Discuss the cultural connota-

FIGURE 2.12

tions of one such term in a few paragraphs. For example, what associations has the term *masala* (a mixture of spices used in Indian cooking) acquired in nonfood-related contexts? Or how has the meaning of the term *salsa* broadened to refer to far more than a spicy tomato dip?

8. Investigate the origins, naming, evolution, and social history of any popular food. For example, the hot dog was originally called "a New York tube steak" around 1900, and German immigrants humorously called smoked frankfurter sausages *hundewurst,* "dog sausage," or *hundchen,* "little dogs" (reported by Irving Allen Lewis in *The City in Slang,* 1993). Use information from various sources, and address the significant social trends reflected in the item's popularity.

9. Explore the significance and history of a local or regional specialty, such as Key lime pie for Key West or saltwater taffy for Atlantic City (see Figure 2.14, page 140). Consult relevant Web sites to discover how the food item is integrated into the local folklore and its current role as a sign of the region in marketing to tourists. How have

FIGURE 2.13

regional festivals (such as the annual three-day event celebrating garlic in Gilroy, California) elevated certain foods into icons for towns or cities?

10. Since genetically engineered crops were first introduced in 1996, many foods containing genetically engineered ingredients—from infant formula to corn muffin mix to McDonald's McVeggie Burgers—have reached the consumer. Should food containing genetically engineered ingredients be labeled? Research the controversy surrounding the potential environmental risks posed by genetically engineered crops and the harm, if any, that these foods might cause to human health. Express your opinion in an essay, drawing on at least two sources.

CHAPTER 3

Cross (Cultural) Dressing

If you look good and dress well, you don't need a purpose in life.
—ROBERT PANTE (fashion consultant), *Dressing to Win*

In all cultures, clothing serves as a basic mode of communication. We signal who we are and how we wish to be perceived in very precise and defined ways. A motorcyclist's black leather jacket or the head-to-toe chadors worn by women in Islamic countries announce the values of a particular group, subculture, or social class. Consider the very different messages communicated by a three-piece suit (with a button-down shirt and conservative tie) and jeans, a flannel shirt, cowboy boots, and a Stetson hat.

CLOTHING AS SOCIAL CODE

Blue jeans, for example, are a uniquely American article of clothing, and their many transformations from the late 1800s to the present tell the story of how denim came to represent different (and often opposing) cultural meanings. Originally jeans were worn by gold miners, laborers, sailors, cowboys, and dock workers. In the 1960s, they were adopted by bikers, artists, hippies, and political activists as the uniform of the counterculture. In the 1970s and 1980s, they became designer-embossed symbols of affluence and leisure. More recently, oversized baggy jeans worn low on the hip (the hip-hop style of rappers) have communicated an antiauthority message. The humorist Dave Barry quipped (in his August 30, 1998, column "The ABC's of Shopping for School"), "If the pants do not contain enough material to make all the sails needed to

141

equip a full-size 19th-century whaling vessel then those pants are too small for your modern American boy." Farid Chenoune (in "Jeans and Black Leather: Gangs Don a Second Skin") observes that the antiauthority message of jeans, T-shirts, and leather jackets first appeared in the 1950s in association with motorcycle gangs.

Throughout the world, blue jeans serve as symbols of Westernization and have even been used as a form of currency on the black market. The prominent French designer Yves Saint Laurent paid tribute to the enduring power of jeans: "I wish I had invented blue jeans. They have expression, modesty, sex appeal, simplicity—all I hope for in my clothes." When embossed with designer logos, jeans become a status symbol. The distinctive stitching and copper rivets used by Levi Strauss in the 1840s (to reinforce the seams for California gold miners, who carried heavy ore samples) is an early example of a logo that later became a status symbol. Logos announce, "I can afford to buy this" and distinguish those who are "in" from those who are "out."

Roland Barthes studied the ways in which clothing can send messages (in such books as *The Fashion System*, 1967). Barthes discovered that society relies on carefully coded fashion taboos governing the interpretation of particular ensembles. For example, fashionably ripped jeans are clearly different from jeans in the same condition worn by someone who cannot afford new ones. Advertisers are quite adept at evoking such hidden fashion messages.

In the exclusive world of high fashion, the Chanel suit, the Armani jacket, Manolo's mules, and the Kelly bag have come to define the ultimate sine qua non ("without which, nothing") for the affluent. Dodie Kazanjian, a former writer for *Vogue* magazine, in "The Kelly Bag as Icon," explores the process by which these ultraexpensive handbags acquire their meaning. Kazanjian begins as an observer ("Like many women, I tended to dismiss the whole notion of couture as irrelevant, trivial, overpriced, and somewhat silly"), but the allure of high fashion gets the better of her. She confesses that her desire to obtain a Kelly bag (a Hermès handbag originally designed for Grace Kelly) has become an obsession, and we accompany her on her journey to procure one. Along the way, we gain insight into the mystique of designers' originals and the intangible aura (obtainable at a hefty price) of these sought-after icons.

We interpret the clothing others wear as a sign of how they wish to be perceived. Fashion magazines have great influence, as do dress-for-success books, when they treat clothing as the ultimate symbol of professional credibility. For women in the workplace, this unfortunately creates the double-bind of having to appear to be both feminine and businesslike. Deborah Tannen (in "There Is No Unmarked Woman") analyzes the unwanted attention directed toward women's clothing, makeup, and hairstyles in the business setting. In contrast, what men wear is largely taken for granted.

Clothing offers an immediate clue to the wearer's personal, political, and social values. Past societies even strictly regulated styles of clothing. In ancient Greece and Rome, the social rank of the wearer determined the type, color, and number of garments worn and the sorts of embroidery with which they could be trimmed. To dress above one's social class in these societies was considered a crime. The ever-changing kaleidoscope of fashion displayed in American culture reflects the enormous diversity of our society. How we dress announces our solidarity with groups that share our values and reveals subtleties of personal taste that define us as individuals within these groups.

BODY MODIFICATION

Germaine Greer, in "One Man's Mutilation Is Another Man's Beautification," extends the concept of dress to include forms of body decoration, and even scarification and mutilation, practiced in traditional cultures around the world. These body alterations are the "outward signs of the fulfillment of the rites of passage" that unite the initiate with the community in these cultures. Paradoxically, within our culture, these same practices indicate alienation and rejection of society.

Body modifications designed to match a prevailing concept of beauty within a particular culture can take a number of different forms, some of which appear "natural" within the culture but bizarre to outsiders. For example, the practice of foot binding lasted in ancient China for nearly a thousand years. In Chinese culture, small feet were regarded as a sign of elegance, breeding, and grace, and the willowy gait produced by foot binding was thought to resemble the movement of the lotus plant swaying in the wind. In "The Unfashionable Human Body," Bernard Rudofsky describes how bound feet were thought to enhance a woman's erotic appeal and suitability for marriage: the bride's shoe was "exhibited before the bridegroom's parents and figures as one of the deciding arguments in determining the price of purchase."

Valerie Steele and John S. Major, in "China Chic," explore the social and political meanings of the practice of foot binding. Their research discloses that the practice allowed the Chinese to maintain their distinct identity in the face of onslaughts from the invading Manchus from the North (whose women's feet were unbound). Steele and Major compare foot binding to the wearing of corsets as examples of practices that seem strange to us today but were considered quite "natural" and even desirable when in vogue. The deformities tolerated by Chinese women of old in the name of fashion provides a clue to why high heels caught on in the seventeenth century and remain popular today. Stiletto and spike heels deform the foot in ways comparable to foot binding, conveying sexiness, added height, and power while at the same time (paradoxi-cally) incapacitating the wearer.

CLOTHING AND CULTURAL IDENTITY

Alison Lurie has studied the cultural conventions that determine what a soci-ety considers to be fashionable at a particular time and suggests that clothing is a kind of language. In "The Language of Clothes," she explains how clothing acts as a complex system of signs that reflects the values of the surrounding culture. For example, in the 1950s the stereotypical outfit for the male bread-winner was a dark business suit (today, corporate types are called "suits"), while the housewife/homemaker was usually dressed in colorful, frilly, feminine attire. The relationship between fashion and social values again became appar-ent in the 1970s, when unisex clothes reflected the emerging equality of women and men.

We can understand how a particular article of clothing acquires meaning by adopting a cross-cultural perspective. We assume that men wear pants and women wear skirts. However, in Indonesia and throughout Southeast Asia, a wrapped skirt, or sarong, is standard male attire. Trousers, which in our cul-ture are symbols of masculinity, were originally worn by Middle Eastern women (and were called Turkish trousers). And although it is now customary for women to wear trousers, Western men cannot normally wear skirts—with the exception of the Scottish kilt, a national costume.

The significance of particular colors also illustrates different underlying cultural assumptions. For example, we tend to think of the physician's white coat as an emblem of the medical profession and the bride's white gown as a symbol of innocence. But in many Asian cultures, among them China and India, white symbolizes death. The underlying social values implicit in blue-collar (including its later variant, pink-collar) versus white-collar jobs also illus-trate how color-coding is used to validate class differences. Even something as seemingly inconsequential as the color of clothing can transmit powerful meanings in different social contexts.

Although we think of Western styles of dress as universal, many Middle Eastern cultures still require women to be veiled in public. Elizabeth W. and Robert A. Fernea, in "A Look behind the Veil," investigate the practice of pur-dah and its role in preserving Islamic values in a patriarchal culture. The rise of Islamic fundamentalism has strengthened adherence to this custom. Jan Goodwin (in "Tradition or Outrage," *Marie Claire*, March 1997) reports how in Iran, the chador—a black garment that envelopes a woman from head to toe—is the required form of clothing for females from the age of seven. In 1991, Iran's prosecutor-general stated that "any woman who rejects Islamic dress is an apostate" (apostasy is punishable by death). Yet, as Goodwin points out, for many Islamic women, the chador represents a return to respect for womanhood following the Iranian revolution of 1979. The power of this garment to represent both oppression and sanctity illustrates how the same article of clothing can resonate with different social and political meanings even within the same culture.

The kimono, in Japan, is as eloquent an expression of Japanese values as is the chador in the Middle East. The kimono has changed very little since it was first worn 1,200 years ago by the court ladies of the Nara period. The restrictions it imposes on a woman's posture and movements produce the distinctive gait that marks its wearer. Liza Dalby, the first non-Japanese to live as a geisha, tells us, in "Kimono," that the garment constitutes "a social code" replete with meanings about the wearer's social class and marital status. The exotic allure of geishas owes much to their wearing of the kimono. The continuing status of this garment can be inferred from its popularity among middle-class women in Japan who attend kimono schools and wear the kimono as a hobby.

In India, the sari (a five- or six-yard-long rectangle of silk or cotton cloth) is the traditional garment worn by women. The manner in which it is worn, as well as its color and texture, can express the wearer's social and marital status, age, occupation, religion, and region. Chitra Banerjee Divakaruni, in "Clothes," draws on the symbolism of the style and color of the sari to express the changing fortunes of her main character, or **protagonist.** Divakaruni counterpoints the meanings of the various saris worn by Mita with her Western attire as she attempts to assimilate into American culture. This story, as do all the selections in this chapter, helps us appreciate the fundamental role that clothing plays in communicating how we see ourselves within the context of our culture.

FARID CHENOUNE
Jeans and Black Leather: Gangs Don a Second Skin

Farid Chenoune holds a degree in modern literature from the University of Paris at the Sorbonne. His articles on fashion, literature, and social history appear on a regular basis in *Liberation, L'Express,* and *Vogue Hommes.* In "Jeans and Black Leather: Gangs Don a Second Skin," drawn from *A History of Men's Fashion* (1993), Chenoune correlates the appearance of leather jackets, T-shirts, and blue jeans with the breakdown in class distinctions that occurred in the mid-1950s. His latest work (with Farid Chenoline) is *Beneath It All: A Century of French Lingerie* (2000).

Thinking Critically

In what sense can fashion be considered a social testing ground in which people literally "try on" new self-images? What current styles reveal a conflict between mainstream and counterculture values? Can you identify another counterculture style that has moved into the fashion mainstream, as did leather jackets and blue jeans?

It's all leg movements. I don't do nothin' with my body.
> —ELVIS PRESLEY, quoted in Richard Horn,
> *Fifties Style, Then and Now,* 1985

It was hardly surprising, therefore, to find Teddy boys on the scene during outbreaks of vandalism as rock-and-roll swept over Great Britain. In May 1955, the American film *Blackboard Jungle,* with its tale of school rebels, hit London screens. The soundtrack of the film included Bill Haley and the Comets singing "Rock Around the Clock," a song that remained on the charts for nineteen weeks, selling some sixteen million copies the world over and becoming the musical manifesto of an entire generation. The riots that followed the screening of *Blackboard Jungle* in London's Elephant and Castle neighborhood were the first shocks of a quake that rattled Western countries right up until the mid-1960s. Gangs alarmed and excited the press from Hamburg to Tokyo in a remarkable wave of mimicry that produced Austro-German *halbstarken,* Japanese *taiyozoku,* Australian *bodgies,* French *gadjos* or *blousons noirs,* Swedish *skinknuttar* (i.e., "black leathers") and even Russian *stilyagi* (the appropriately named "groomed boys").

For the first time, these gangs lifted jeans and black leather jackets from the drab context of America's plains and suburbs. Such garb was no longer relegated to the work or leisure sphere, but was yanked into the harsh spotlight of high fashion. Of course, such clothes had already appealed to certain postwar European youths, in imitation of American GIs. Similarly, in the United States itself, motorcycle gangs had established their own hierarchy of black leather, with occasional allusions to the dark pomp of Nazi Germany. Here and there, a few highly snobbish circles had formulated an etiquette concerning a certain type of blue jeans and a certain way of wearing them. But such phenomena remained limited, almost unavowed.

It was through another channel—namely, the silver screen that so efficiently reflected twentieth-century behavior patterns—that attention was suddenly, almost brutally, drawn to two nonconformist figures: Marlon Brando in *The Wild One* (1953) and James Dean in *East of Eden* (1954) and *Rebel Without a Cause* (1955). Almost overnight, they forged a new fashion trinity—jeans, T-shirt, black leather jacket. Dark and heretical, this trinity emerged from fashion's waste lands, a world devoid of suit, shirt, tie and other trappings of white-collar society.

Like all pivotal events, this turning point has remained somewhat obscure even though extensively analyzed. Its symbolic aspect has been discussed at length—the emblematic value of such dress, its appeal to a generation in revolt against the social conformism of the 1950s, its significance to young people in search of their identity within the smothering, materialistic consumer society described in Vance Packard's influential 1960 book, *The Status Seekers.* Yet the material aspect of this pivotal shift, although immediately visible, has remained largely in the shadows.

In fact, the advent of jeans, T-shirt and leather jacket constituted an abrupt new crystallization of the slow and powerful subversion of dress codes by work clothes. It represented another stage in a struggle characterized by constant exchanges between upper and lower classes, between center and fringe, between establishment and nonconformists. But the special aura attached to it is also due to what might be called the *material moment* of this crystallization. It occurred just when the garment industry was congratulating itself for having vanquished, thanks to synthetic fibers, the last obstacles to the democratization of elegance and correct dress. These sturdy, wrinkle-free fabrics henceforth embodied the abstract ideal of the classic suit: clean surface, permanent shape, and rigid lines, as keenly demonstrated by the "permanent crease" in pants so vaunted in the 1950s. Yet this ideal remained supremely tangential to the body itself.

The soft and dirty carapace donned by Harley-Davidson "greasers" and other rebels without a cause was the malleable counterpart to the perfect mannequin look. Shrink-to-fit jeans, in particular, had to slowly *mold* themselves to fit the wearer. Wrinkles and creases in denim, like those in leather, were an expression of a real body's movements, postures, habits. This had always been a feature of work garments, and was therefore hardly new in itself. Far newer, however, was the fact that adolescents allergic to traditional rites of manhood (such as wearing a suit) were translating these *unfinished* garments, totally devoid of fashion vocabulary or grammar, into the direct expression of their identity crisis.

Perhaps this phenomenon should be seen as a precocious attempt—outrageous, desperate, fetishistic—to develop the *second skin* later invented by the fashion industry, that is to say a utopian garment free of all constraint and history, permitting the body to become the herald of a new subjectivity. Whatever the case, it is worth noting that the actors who brought these clothes to the screen and who became models for their generation—Marlon Brando, James Dean, Montgomery Clift, Paul Newman—were direct or indirect products of the Actor's Studio, where they learned that a character's moods and inner turmoil should first of all be expressed through the *body*.

Americans, particularly on the East coast, were all the more likely to reject conformist dress if they came from a working-class background (Presley had been a truckdriver). In the late fifties, the American Institute of Men's and Boys' Wear launched a campaign encouraging high school boys to "dress right," underscoring establishment disapproval of jeans and hostility toward black leather jackets. In France, *Le Monde* of 6 October 1960 congratulated the principal of a secondary school for banning black leather jackets. "Wearing a leather or denim jacket meant you were hood," recalls Roger Kaisermann, a.k.a. "Rodgers," a leather-toting member of the "Chez Riton" gang on rue Saint-Martin in Paris. The gang would zoom through flea-markets and amusement parks aboard their fashionable motor scooters (Spécial 50, Flandira, Gulietta or Flash Paloma), provoking rumbles in vacant lots on the outskirts of Paris to "show that you deserved the leather on your back." These toughs "all dressed alike" in American leather jackets (or sheepskin coats in winter) worn over a black, checked or polka-dot shirt, "low boots with pointed toes and metal taps" and, as the sixties dawned, the first bell-bottom pants.

Very quickly, however, black leather and denim went their separate ways. Leather was associated with the scourge of the chain-wielding, theater-smashing crowd, and was therefore shunned for a long time, even by young people. "Your jacket's a joke!" shouted the young florist to her hood of a boyfriend in the 1957 film *Ascenseur pour l'échafaud* ("Fast Lane to the Scaffold"). The black leather look remained so scandalous in France that in 1962, barely a year after the Palais des Sports was torn apart on 18 November 1961 by 5,000 fans of

leather-clad rocker Vince Taylor, the International Situationists could proclaim their goal of "translating the aggressiveness of the black leather crowd
onto the level of ideas" without sounding like drawing-room revolutionaries.

Unlike black leather jackets, blue jeans were adopted by middle-class   *10*
teenagers, the children of white-collar businessmen in gray flannel suits, and
therefore became more acceptable. In France, their non-conformist connotation also attracted adolescents described by *Le Monde* in 1957 as awkward, free,
unhappy and wild. The article in question concerned James Dean and novelist
Françoise Sagan, both symbols of "this century's affliction," what Pier Paolo
Pasolini characterized four years later as "the last trace of a sweetish, self-
indulgent romanticism." Wide, turned-up jeans could be seen in *L'Homme aux
clefs d'or* ("The Man with the Golden Keys"), a film depicting the small-time
underworld of privileged brats in a prep school in Lille, as well as in Marcel
Carne's 1959 film, *Les Tricheurs* ("The Cheaters"). The following year jeans, up
till then subject to import tariffs, were allowed to enter France duty-free, to
the great distress of the country's ten thousand tailors, who had remained deaf
to Maximilien Vox's 1943 prophecy: "I predict great success for the first major
tailor to declare the trouser crease dead."

Engaging the Text

1. In Chenoune's opinion, how did the advent of jeans, T-shirts, and leather
   jackets represent the subversion of the dress codes of the 1950s? What values did these articles of clothing embody?

2. What point does Chenoune make about the significance of this new kind of
   clothing that adapts itself to the wearer's body? What is the psychological
   significance of the "second skin," and how does clothing of this type differ
   from the way clothes usually function?

3. Is Chenoune's argument that new clothing styles function as a rite of passage plausible? Why or why not?

Exploring Your Cultural Perspective

1. Chenoune mentions several films (for example, *Rebel Without a Cause* with
   James Dean [1955]) that highlight clothing as a sign of nonconformist
   behavior. Watch one of these films, and analyze the relationship of the
   clothing the stars wear to the characters they portray and to the storyline.

2. At first glance, the outfit Chenoune describes might seem superficially to
   resemble the hip-hop style that first appeared in U.S. inner cities in the
   mid-1990s. What are the important differences between the two styles, in
   terms of the values they communicate and their origins?

DODIE KAZANJIAN
The Kelly Bag as Icon

In most societies social rank is expressed through exclusive access to finer materials, better craftsmanship, and distinctive styling. Unlike societies in which certain designs, fabrics, and colors are restricted to the elite, in the United States anyone who has $3,000 to spend on a handbag can display the symbol of wealth and class known as the Kelly bag. Dodie Kazanjian, a former senior writer for *Vogue* magazine who is currently on the staff of the *New Yorker,* describes her obsession with procuring this fashion icon while simultaneously mocking herself for it. She has also written (with Calvin Tomkins) *Alex: The Life of Alexander Lieberman* (1993) and (with Chesley McLaren) *Dodie Goes Shopping: And Other Adventures* (1999). The chapter reprinted here is from her book *Icons: The Absolutes of Style* (1995).

Thinking Critically

What does the term glamour *mean to you? How have advertising and the media influenced your views? Look through your wardrobe, and determine which clothes or accessories represent exclusivity and social prestige.*

For years and years, I've wanted the Kelly bag. To me, it's not just the supreme symbol of the world's most exclusive status boutique, Hermès, it's the ideal bag to carry. Roomy, stylish, exquisitely made, pickpocket proof with its twin closing straps and padlock—it's the bag for all seasons.

Over the years, though, whenever I got up the nerve to ask about one, the response was the same: As a salesman at Hermès announced to me a year ago, "Good heavens. There's a four-year waiting list." From his expression, it was obvious he thought I couldn't afford one.

But I kept seeing the Kelly bag around town, on the arms of New York's Chosen Ones—Brooke Hayward, Adele Chatfield-Taylor, Betty Bacall. How did they do it? I dreaded another humiliation. I had a vision of the dear old lady who once questioned the price of a brownie at Eli Zabar's E.A.T.; the proprietor snatched the morsel from her trembling fingers and ordered her to

"Leave my store!" Hope springs eternal, though; it seemed to me that with a recession on, the Kelly market might have loosened up a bit, and so, last fall, I decided to risk it once again.

The Kelly bag has been called the Kelly bag ever since the mid-1950s, when Grace Kelly was often photographed carrying one. Derived from a much larger piece of luggage, which was used to carry the saddles, bridles, and other riding tack of grand dukes and royals, it began its life as a ladies' handbag in 1930. In recent years, it has proliferated in various sizes, colors, and leathers, at prices ranging from $2,500 for a mini in calf up to $10,000 for the large-sized "croc." For about $30,000, you can get a version with a solid gold, diamond-studded padlock.

Not quite nervy enough to show my face in the Fifty-seventh Street Hermès boutique, I decide on a *coup de téléphone*. "I don't have anything in stock," says a saleslady named Marjorie. "And we're not taking special orders." To my surprise, she sounds genuinely sorry. "What color did you want, though?"   5

"Black," I say.

"Oh, that's the most difficult to come by. Everybody wants black."

Why, oh why, is this particular handbag so permanently out of reach? Perhaps because it's top-of-the-line Hermès, so well known it doesn't need the big "H" clasp that is on some other Hermès bags. Status, but quiet status. And Hermès itself is *unique au monde*, the three words that J. P. Morgan said were the most expensive he knew.

Five generations of the Hermès family have kept it that way. The business was started in 1837 by Thierry Hermès, just around the corner from its present world headquarters at 24 rue du Faubourg St.-Honoré in Paris. Its wholesale riding harnesses quickly became known as the best available. In 1879, Thierry's son, Émile-Charles, shifted to retail and added saddles and other riding gear. The Hermès saddlery catered to the greatest stables of France, the Imperial Russian Court, and wealthy South Americans. When the automobile unhorsed this market in the 1920s, Hermès shifted gears with great style, branching out into handbags and luggage. Clothing, clocks, watches, jewelry, silverware, gloves, and diaries followed. The famous Hermès hand-printed silk scarf first appeared in 1937.

The firm's worldwide growth in the fifties and sixties assured that the sun   10
would never set on the Hermès empire. It now has more than 250 sales outlets, and its 1990 sales totaled an estimated $460 million. And yet, the Kelly bag is still being made by hand, slowly and lovingly, on the fourth floor of 24 rue du Faubourg St.-Honoré; 9,000 are completed—and signed—each year by twelve skilled workers, who have apprenticed for ten years with a master, in the tradition that goes back to Thierry Hermès.

"Do you think it could take years before I get one?" I ask Marjorie.

"Yes and no."

Rumor has it that you can find a black Kelly bag in the Hong Kong Hermès, but I haven't been to Hong Kong lately. It seems hopeless.

But good heavens! Here I am going to the movies with Brooke Hayward and her beautiful medium-sized black Kelly bag—just what I long for. A little sullenly, I ask her how she got it.

15   "It's a copy," says Brooke. "I'd never dream of paying that much for a handbag."

A copy? *Bien entendu!* In this age of appropriation, the Kelly bag has been knocked off from Helsinki to Katmandu. Trust Brooke to find the right knockoff.

"I've been getting them for ten years," she says, "at a little store on Fifty-fourth Street."

I go there the next day. Kelly lookalikes on the walls, on the counters, on the floor; also fake Pradas, Célines, Guccis, and a couple of Mark Crosses and Bottega Venetas—all of them looking enough like the originals to fool a master shopper.

I ask for a medium-sized "Kelly" in black calf, and three models are promptly produced. How much? Three hundred and seventy-nine dollars and no waiting. The woman next to me is looking at a black lizard "Kelly" for $900. The store owner, a plump, talkative man in his shirtsleeves, is merrily playing to the clientele; holding a black "Kelly" against his hip, he says, "I brought this bag to America in 1952, before Grace Kelly ever saw it."

20   "Do you always have 'Kellys' in stock?" I ask.

"Always—except that this year, for the first time, I've been running out, so sometimes you'll have to wait a month."

These "Kellys" are made in Italy by the same people who make leather goods for Céline, Prada, and other well-known names. The owner of this boutique helped to channel his father's export-import business into handbags in 1950; his children now make this a three-generation concern. Within fifteen minutes, I have bought the last medium black calf "Kelly" he has in house. Three generations of knockoffs will never really match five generations of Hermès, but who's to know? As Julia Child would say, "Remember, you're alone in the kitchen—nobody's watching."

Ah, but I'm watching. I'm the original princess on the pea. So, when Marjorie from Hermès calls me two months later, out of the blue, and asks, "Are you still interested in a black Kelly?" my heart somersaults. I'm there when the store opens the next morning, wearing my pale pink "Napoleon" Hermès scarf. The bag has a softness and a glow to it, a quality beyond quality. It costs $2,800, but, with the right care, it will last thirty years or more. (Brooke admits that she gets a new copy every few years.)

"We just received a shipment of fifteen," Marjorie tells me. "None of the black calves will go out on the floor—some of our clients have been waiting four years." Then how is it that I can buy one? "Some people may have found them at one of our other boutiques. You're just lucky."

I weigh it in my hands, hold it against my hip. The line is unmistakably ele-   *25*
gant, inimitable, *unique au monde*. It's large enough to hold my hairbrush, my
tape recorder, my Filofax, and my dreams of glory. The seduction is complete.

I won't buy anything else this year. I promise. With my Kelly bag, I won't
have to.

Engaging the Text

1. How did the Kelly bag acquire such prestige that people are willing to pay
   an exorbitant price for it?

2. In what ways does Kazanjian mock her own compulsion to possess such an
   item? Does this tactic forestall the reader's potential disdain for someone so
   shallow?

3. According to Kazanjian, what are the pros and cons of knockoffs? Why
   didn't she simply buy a copy and leave it at that, as does her famous friend
   Brooke Hayward?

Exploring Your Cultural Perspective

1. How might the contents of handbags be thought of as archeological sites
   awaiting exploration? Describe the functional and cultural meanings of a
   few significant items commonly found in handbags.

2. For a brief period in North America, it was fashionable for men to carry
   small handbags. This is still the custom in Europe. Why do you think this
   fad did not last very long in North America? Do you think it was a good
   idea? Why or why not?

DEBORAH TANNEN

There Is No Unmarked Woman

Imagine how you would feel if every gesture you made and the clothing you wore were the subject of constant scrutiny and comment—that is, if these aspects of your life **marked** you. According to Deborah Tannen, this situation prevails for women in the workplace. Although Tannen was trained as a linguist, her research into the complex codes that govern communication between men and women is quite accessible in *You Just Don't Understand: Women and Men in Conversation* (1990) and *The Argument Culture: Stopping America's War of Words* (1999). The essay reprinted here originally appeared in the *New York Times Magazine* (1993).

Thinking Critically

As you read this piece, consider whether women's appearance in the workplace receives more scrutiny than does their male coworkers'.

Some years ago I was at a small working conference of four women and eight men. Instead of concentrating on the discussion I found myself looking at the three other women at the table, thinking how each had a different style and how each style was coherent.

One woman had dark brown hair in a classic style, a cross between Cleopatra and Plain Jane. The severity of her straight hair was softened by wavy bangs and ends that turned under. Because she was beautiful, the effect was more Cleopatra than plain.

The second woman was older, full of dignity and composure. Her hair was cut in a fashionable style that left her with only one eye, thanks to a side part that let a curtain of hair fall across half her face. As she looked down to read her prepared paper, the hair robbed her of bifocal vision and created a barrier between her and the listeners.

The third woman's hair was wild, a frosted blond avalanche falling over and beyond her shoulders. When she spoke she frequently tossed her head, calling attention to her hair and away from her lecture.

Then there was makeup. The first woman wore facial cover that made her   5
skin smooth and pale, a black line under each eye and mascara that darkened
already dark lashes. The second wore only a light gloss on her lips and a hint
of shadow on her eyes. The third had blue bands under her eyes, dark blue
shadow, mascara, bright red lipstick and rouge; her fingernails flashed red.

I considered the clothes each woman had worn during the three days of
the conference: In the first case, man-tailored suits in primary colors with
solid-color blouses. In the second, casual but stylish black T-shirts, a floppy
collarless jacket and baggy slacks or a skirt in neutral colors. The third wore a
sexy jump suit; tight sleeveless jersey and tight yellow slacks; a dress with gap-
ing armholes and an indulged tendency to fall off one shoulder.

Shoes? No. 1 wore string sandals with medium heels; No. 2, sensible, comfortable walking shoes; No. 3, pumps with spike heels. You can fill in the jewelry, scarves, shawls, sweaters—or lack of them.

As I amused myself finding coherence in these styles, I suddenly wondered
why I was scrutinizing only the women. I scanned the eight men at the table.
And then I knew why I wasn't studying them. The men's styles were unmarked.

The term "marked" is a staple of linguistic theory. It refers to the way language alters the base meaning of a word by adding a linguistic particle that has
no meaning on its own. The unmarked form of a word carries the meaning
that goes without saying—what you think of when you're not thinking anything special.

The unmarked tense of verbs in English is the present—for example, *visit.*   10
To indicate past, you mark the verb by adding *ed* to yield *visited.* For future,
you add a word: *will visit.* Nouns are presumed to be singular until marked for
plural, typically by adding *s* or *es,* so *visit* becomes *visits* and *dish* becomes *dishes.*

The unmarked forms of most English words also convey "male." Being
male is the unmarked case. Endings like *ess* and *ette* mark words as "female."
Unfortunately, they also tend to mark them for frivolousness. Would you feel
safe entrusting your life to a doctorette? Alfre Woodard, who was an Oscar
nominee for best supporting actress, says she identifies herself as an actor
because "actresses worry about eyelashes and cellulite, and women who are
actors worry about the characters we are playing." Gender markers pick up
extra meanings that reflect common associations with the female gender: not
quite serious, often sexual.

Each of the women at the conference had to make decisions about hair,
clothing, makeup and accessories, and each decision carried meaning. Every
style available to us was marked. The men in our group had made decisions,
too, but the range from which they chose was incomparably narrower. Men
can choose styles that are marked, but they don't have to, and in this group
none did. Unlike the women, they had the option of being unmarked.

Take the men's hair styles. There was no marine crew cut or oily longish hair falling into eyes, no asymmetrical, two-tiered construction to swirl over a bald top. One man was unabashedly bald; the others had hair of standard length, parted on one side, in natural shades of brown or gray or graying. Their hair obstructed no views, left little to toss or push back or run fingers through and, consequently, needed and attracted no attention. A few men had beards. In a business setting, beards might be marked. In this academic gathering, they weren't.

There could have been a cowboy shirt with string tie or a three-piece suit or a necklaced hippie in jeans. But there wasn't. All eight men wore brown or blue slacks and nondescript shirts of light colors. No man wore sandals or boots; their shoes were dark, closed, comfortable, and flat. In short, unmarked.

15   Although no man wore makeup, you couldn't say the men didn't wear makeup in the sense that you could say a woman didn't wear makeup. For men, no makeup is unmarked.

I asked myself what style we women could have adopted that would have been unmarked, like the men's. The answer was none. There is no unmarked woman.

There is no woman's hair style that can be called standard, that says nothing about her. The range of women's hair styles is staggering, but a woman whose hair has no particular style is perceived as not caring about how she looks, which can disqualify her from many positions, and will subtly diminish her as a person in the eyes of some.

Women must choose between attractive shoes and comfortable shoes. When our group made an unexpected trek, the woman who wore flat, laced shoes arrived first. Last to arrive was the woman in spike heels, shoes in hand and a handful of men around her.

If a woman's clothing is tight or revealing (in other words, sexy), it sends a message—an intended one of wanting to be attractive, but also a possibly unintended one of availability. If her clothes are not sexy, that too sends a message, lent meaning by the knowledge that they could have been. There are thousands of cosmetic products from which women can choose and myriad ways of applying them. Yet no makeup at all is anything but unmarked. Some men see it as a hostile refusal to please them.

20   Women can't even fill out a form without telling stories about themselves. Most forms give four titles to choose from. "Mr." carries no meaning other than that the respondent is male. But a woman who checks "Mrs." or "Miss" communicates not only whether she has been married but also whether she has conservative tastes in forms of address—and probably other conservative values as well. Checking "Ms." declines to let on about marriage (checking "Mr." declines nothing since nothing was asked), but it also marks her as either liberated or rebellious, depending on the observer's attitudes and assumptions.

I sometimes try to duck these variously marked choices by giving my title as "Dr."—and in so doing risk marking myself as either uppity (hence sarcastic responses like "Excuse *me*!") or an overachiever (hence reactions of congratulatory surprise like "Good for you!").

All married women's surnames are marked. If a woman takes her husband's name, she announces to the world that she is married and has traditional values. To some it will indicate that she is less herself, more identified by her husband's identity. If she does not take her husband's name, this too is marked, seen as worthy of comment: She has *done* something; she has "kept her own name." A man is never said to have "kept his own name" because it never occurs to anyone that he might have given it up. For him using his own name is unmarked.

A married woman who wants to have her cake and eat it too may use her surname plus his, with or without a hyphen. But this too announces her marital status and often results in a tongue-tying string. In a list (Harvey O'Donovan, Jonathan Feldman, Stephanie Woodbury McGillicutty), the woman's multiple name stands out. It is marked.

I have never been inclined toward biological explanations of gender differences in language, but I was intrigued to see Ralph Fasold bring biological phenomena to bear on the question of linguistic marking in his book *The Sociolinguistics of Language*. Fasold stresses that language and culture are particularly unfair in treating women as the marked case because biologically it is the male that is marked. While two X chromosomes make a female, two Y chromosomes make nothing. Like the linguistic markers *s*, *es*, or *ess*, the Y chromosome doesn't "mean" anything unless it is attached to a root form—an X chromosome.

Developing this idea elsewhere Fasold points out that girls are born with 25 fully female bodies, while boys are born with modified female bodies. He invites men who doubt this to lift up their shirts and contemplate why they have nipples.

In his book, Fasold notes "a wide range of facts which demonstrates that female is the unmarked sex." For example, he observes that there are a few species that produce only females, like the whiptail lizard. Thanks to parthenogenesis, they have no trouble having as many daughters as they like. There are no species, however, that produce only males. This is no surprise, since any such species would become extinct in its first generation.

Fasold is also intrigued by species that produce individuals not involved in reproduction, like honeybees and leaf-cutter ants. Reproduction is handled by the queen and a relatively few males; the workers are sterile females. "Since they do not reproduce," Fasold said, "there is no reason for them to be one sex or the other, so they default, so to speak, to female."

Fasold ends his discussion of these matters by pointing out that if language reflected biology, grammar books would direct us to use "she" to include males and females and "he" only for specifically male referents. But they don't. They tell us that "he" means "he or she," and that "she" is used only if the referent is specifically female. This use of "he" as the sex-indefinite pronoun is an innovation introduced into English by grammarians in the eighteenth and nineteenth centuries, according to Peter Mühlhäusler and Rom Harré in *Pronouns and People.* From at least about 1500, the correct sex-indefinite pronoun was "they," as it still is in casual spoken English. In other words, the female was declared by grammarians to be the marked case.

Writing this article may mark me not as a writer, not as a linguist, not as an analyst of human behavior, but as a feminist—which will have positive or negative, but in any case powerful, connotations for readers. Yet I doubt that anyone reading Ralph Fasold's book would put that label on him.

30   I discovered the markedness inherent in the very topic of gender after writing a book on differences in conversational style based on geographical region, ethnicity, class, age, and gender. When I was interviewed, the vast majority of journalists wanted to talk about the differences between women and men. While I thought I was simply describing what I observed—something I had learned to do as a researcher—merely mentioning women and men marked me as a feminist for some.

When I wrote a book devoted to gender differences in ways of speaking, I sent the manuscript to five male colleagues, asking them to alert me to any interpretation, phrasing, or wording that might seem unfairly negative toward men. Even so, when the book came out, I encountered responses like that of the television talk show host who, after interviewing me, turned to the audience and asked if they thought I was male-bashing.

Leaping upon a poor fellow who affably nodded in agreement, she made him stand and asked, "Did what she say accurately describe you?" "Oh, yes," he answered. "That's me exactly." "And what she said about women—does that sound like your wife?" "Oh yes," he responded. "That's her exactly." "Then why do you think she's male-bashing?" He answered, with disarming honesty, "Because she's a woman and she's saying things about men."

To say anything about women and men without marking oneself as either feminist or anti-feminist, male-basher or apologist for men seems as impossible for a woman as trying to get dressed in the morning without inviting interpretations of her character.

Sitting at the conference table musing on these matters, I felt sad to think that we women didn't have the freedom to be unmarked that the men sitting next to us had. Some days you just want to get dressed and go about your business. But if you're a woman, you can't, because there is no unmarked woman.

Engaging the Text

1. How does Tannen take concepts drawn from linguistic research and apply them to the social settings in which men's and women's appearance is evaluated?

2. What factors, in Tannen's view, explain why women's dress, hairstyles, and makeup are the subjects of such active scrutiny, whereas what men wear and how they appear are taken for granted as the norm? In what sense are women "marked" and men "unmarked"?

3. Does Tannen's use of Ralph Fasold's biologically based explanations of gender differences strengthen her argument? Why or why not? Write a few paragraphs supporting or challenging her assertions.

Exploring Your Cultural Perspective

1. Although Tannen downplays the possibility that men can also be "marked," are there specific ways in which they can be? What are these signals, and how do they differ from those that mark women? What cultural values are implicit in these differences? Do the appearances of males and females in your classes or place of work support Tannen's assertions about the extent to which women are marked in our culture? Write a short essay discussing your conclusions; support your findings with data based on personal observations.

2. If you are female, might you consider keeping your maiden name after you marry? Why or why not? What different signals does retaining your maiden name, relinquishing it, or adopting a hyphenated name send? If you are male, would you consider changing your name to your wife's or adding your wife's name to yours? Would you marry someone who refused to give up her maiden name? Why or why not?

GERMAINE GREER

One Man's Mutilation Is Another Man's Beautification

Just as clothing can communicate feelings, moods, social status, and even political alliances, more permanent body modifications are powerful indicators of how we define ourselves within our society. In this essay drawn from *The Madwoman's Underclothes* (1986), Germaine Greer explores the cultural significance of these ways of embellishing—and even mutilating—the human body. Greer is an Australian-born writer whose feminist perspective is embodied in such works as *The Female Eunuch* (1971), *Slip-shod Sibyls* (1995), and most recently, *The Whole Woman* (1999).

Thinking Critically

As you read, identify Greer's attitude toward the subject of body modification. Is she approving, sarcastic?

Humans are the only animals which can consciously and deliberately change their appearance according to their own whims. Most animals groom themselves, but humans are tempted to manipulate their appearance in ways much more radical than those open to other animals, not simply because they are able to use tools upon themselves, but also because of some peculiarities in the way in which humans are made. The human body is a curiously ambiguous structure, partaking of almost contradictory attributes. For example, humans are neither furry nor hairless, but variously naked, slightly hairy, and very hirsute. All these variations may be found on the body of a single individual at the same time. Humans are then confronted with a series of managerial problems: among the ways in which they express their cultural identities are the contrasting ways in which they handle these problems.

The Australian Aborigines used to conserve hair; not only did they not eliminate whatever hair was growing on their bodies, they collected extra human hair to work into a thick girdle for men to wear about their hips. We would look askance at anyone who could not bear to discard fallen hair, now that hair shirts are out of fashion, but sophisticated Western people often wear the hair of others as a postiche or toupee. Where the scalp-hunter once sought to augment his physical or psychic power by acquiring the hair of others, the literate people of the twentieth century feel that they will acquire youth and beauty through bought hair. They will even pay to have hair stitched into their scalps in a very costly and laborious development of the ancient practice of needle-working living flesh.

Some people identify themselves partly by their refusal to cut hair, as do the Sikhs, who twist the long silky hair of their beards together with what grows on their heads, tie the whole lot up in a chignon, and cover it with a turban. Others insist on the removal of any hair, wherever it is, and they too may choose a turban, this time to hide a bald head. Western conventions of hair management often appeal to younger or recalcitrant members of societies with strict rules for hair management because they find them more convenient; in fact, they are very subtle and difficult, requiring minute calculations of the degree of shagginess which is appropriate to age, and economic and social status. The rejection of traditional modes of hair management has less to do with convenience and common sense than with the desire to break out of the confinement of the group. A shaven Sikh might object that he is as much Sikh as ever; he may claim that his elimination of his identifying marks was simply to pour out the bath water while retaining the baby, but in fact he has summarily loosened his ties with his religious group in order to be accepted into another group. If he keeps his steel bracelet, which will be recognized by other Sikhs, it is because he does not wish to lose all the advantages connected with belonging to that group. When a Sikh takes his employer to court for refusing to allow him to wear his turban at work, it is not a mere formality. He is making a serious bid to limit his employer's power over his life.

ˑ The impact of technological culture can be measured by the degree of acceptance of Western conventions of body management throughout the world. Fashion, because it is beyond logic, is deeply revealing. Women all over the world have adopted, often in addition to their traditional accoutrements, four Western conventions: high-heeled shoes, lipstick, nail varnish, and the brassiere. The success of all of these fashions, which are not even remotely connected with comfort or common sense, is an indication of the worldwide acceptance of the Western notion that the principal duties of women are sexual attraction and vicarious leisure. The women who have accepted these fashions will justify their decision by saying that all four are more attractive than the alternatives. All that they are really saying is that they themselves were more attracted to alien styles than they were to the styles adopted by their mothers and grandmothers. To give the full answer would be to expose the tensions which are destroying traditional lifestyles all over the world. There is a slight traffic in the opposite direction. Distinguished lady professors of economics may reject high heels, lipstick, nail varnish, and brassiere, and adopt the dress of a Punjabi peasant laborer; Iranian girls may resume the chador. In each case the motive for the change is clearly political; what is not so often realized is that it is equally political when it happens the other way around.

5   Because what we do with our bodies is so revealing we try to insist that it has no meaning at all. A man whose hair is cut regularly and at great expense, who shaves his face in a careful pattern, will say that he is not concerned with his appearance, while a man with a beard will maintain that he simply cannot be bothered shaving, but the truth is that both have selected an image which they feel best expresses their characters and chosen social roles. The man with a beard probably shaves some part of his face and neck quite regularly, and definitely trims the beard itself. He may frequently be seen grooming it with his hands, patting and stroking it into his preferred shape. Between the shaggy bearded man and the smooth clean-shaven man there lies a vast range of tonsorial modes, all of which have meanings relative to each other. The man who grows his sideburns long is expressing something about his class and his age group. The man who lets his cheek whiskers grow in tufts or shaves his sideburns off is also projecting some part of a chosen self-image. All kinds of curious facial topiary are accepted provided that they have some pedigree within our cultural tradition. The association of such variations as curled and waxed mustaches, Mexican revolutionary mustaches, pencil mustaches, and toothbrush mustaches are endlessly subtle and constantly being remade.

In the recent past we came to accept long flowing hair as a possible masculine alternative; with the passing of time our initial reactions of outrage have softened into acceptance. Men's long curls are now a sign of nostalgia for the sixties, the last quiver of hippie energy, which was never anything to be feared. By contrast, the man who completely shaves his head still shocks us. It is as if he is flaunting a violence that he has done to himself. Other men, hairless through no choice of their own, may have wigs on the National Health to hide their embarrassing nakedness. Western youths whose heads are shaven in accordance with the practice of oriental monastics will wear wigs when they go to badger people in airports because shaven heads are so alienating to our sensibilities. The man who shaves his head and does not cover it is indulging in a form of indecent exposure, the purpose of which, as usual, is intimidation.

The shaving of women's heads is considered so disfiguring that it seemed adequate punishment for women who collaborated with the Nazis in the Second World War, and yet there are many cultures whose women shave all or part of their heads and would feel dirty or unkempt if they did not. Girls who shave off all the hair except what grows on the crown of their heads are doing no more than the Turkana women of Kenya have always done, but by doing it in a society where such styles have never been seen, they defy the accepted norms and court rejection. The coxcomb and its variants, sometimes called the

Mohawk or Mohican hairstyle, imitate the intimidating shapes of the advanced crests of fighting birds. A less daring version, for it can be tamed into smoothness when the wearer is in the haunts of the smooth, is the teased mop. The ferocity mimicked by the hairstyle is further expressed in the studded belts and armlets and earrings in the shape of a skull, but it is clearly a mere affectation. The camp aggressiveness of the display stands in inverse ratio to the social power wielded by the group. Their cultural uniformity is actually competitiveness and does not lead to solidarity.

In most societies which modify the body, the visible changes are outward signs of the fulfillment of the rites of passage. The acceptance of the newborn into the community at a naming ceremony or its equivalent may be marked by a ritual haircut, the shape of which may indicate his or her clan or totem. The approach of puberty may be signaled by circumcision or scarification or the adoption of a new hairstyle. The prelude to marriage may require further scarification or tattooing or fattening or a period of special body painting, while marriage itself may be signified by drastic changes in appearance, especially for women. The birth of children, achievement of elder status, or the death of a spouse bring the last changes. In classless societies where property is either held in common or kept to a minimum, all changes in status must involve changes in physical appearance. Where no one carries an identity card which will, say, permit him to drink in the company of adults, everyone who may must be distinguished by a sign. The achievement of these signs is one of the most important satisfactions of such societies. Before imperialists brought mirrors, such people could not confer the signs upon themselves: The recognition of a transition was given dramatic form by the ceremony of the conferring of signs in which the interested parties all acted as a group.

In Western society the outward signs of social status have withered into mere vestiges. Pubescent boys may live through intense dramas of hair cultivation, struggling for a mustache or bushy sideburns or simply longing to shave every day. Little girls may covet high heels and brassieres and long for the day that they can wear make-up, but the menarche will not be marked in any way: Marriageability will be signified only by the absence of an inconspicuous ring on the fourth finger of the left hand. In Jewish society, circumcision is still a rite of passage, but once the bar mitzvah is over, the initiate cannot be recognized by any other outward sign. Married women used to be expected to dress differently from girls: a pale echo of the sixteenth-century custom which required married women to wear closed bodices and hide their hair under a cap. This persisted into the twentieth century when married women were expected to wear hats on social occasions, but has now died out.

The disappearance of distinguishing marks of social status in industrial *10* societies is not meaningless, nor can it be construed to mean that human beings have outgrown such childish things. It is an accurate reflection of the fact that social relationships, particularly kinship relations, have been and are under intense pressure from economic relationships. The one insignia that is worn, in the United States more than in Europe but the strengthening of the trend is apparent, is the insignia of the employer. The family is no longer the dominant group and human beings are no longer differentiated on the grounds of their status within it. Instead they are differentiated by their consumer behavior, employment status, income, and possessions: The contrasts are so striking that it is considered indiscreet and tasteless to flaunt them by display of wealth. Instead the degrees of difference are signaled, more or less subtly, by grooming and by some carefully chosen attributes; hints to those who know how to take them are conveyed by the watch, the pen, the attaché case, the note case, the cuff links. Along with the indications of success are clues to other allegiances, the college ring, the lodge pin, the old school tie. Democracy and uniformity in outward appearance are necessitated by the extreme differentiation in economic circumstances, which might otherwise become a source of tension.

In tribal societies, where economic activity is static, limited as it is to the repetitive daily functions of survival, there is time to elaborate the paraphernalia of status considered in all but economic terms and immense satisfaction connected with doing so. The individual who proceeds through the stages all duly solemnized has conferred an elegance and order upon the struggle, and within that wider function there is scope for individual expression and aesthetic concerns.

The motives for Western beautification are very different. . . . People who are excluded from economic activity . . . cannot compensate by celebrating other forms of status for these have been eliminated. Unhappily, as the social roles which evolve out of family relationships ceased to command respect, the number of older people condemned to live for many years outside the sphere of economic activity in conditions of mere survival increased and will go on increasing. Among the displacement activities which this group must now concentrate on in order to beguile the time between retirement and the grave, there are a number connected with futile imitation of the group from which they have been excluded. As there is no prestige or power connected with being old, it is important to deny the aging process itself. Where once humans celebrated the achievement of seniority and longevity, they now invest as much energy or more in trying to resist the inevitable. Where hair coloring used to be done for fun, it is now done for camouflage.

A full head of strawberry blonde curls is only acquired by a sixty-year-old after regular orgies of dying, setting, and backcombing, all of which actually speed the degeneration of the scalp and the hair shaft. There is a good deal of pain involved as the dyes bite into sensitive old skin and the hot dryers tighten the hair, driving the pins still further into the old scalp. The ordeal is worth it if the sufferer sees herself rejuvenated by it; the suffering is an essential part of the prophylaxis, but it must be accompanied by words of tenderness and filial care from the torturers. We are not surprised to see the hairdresser as a shaman, hung about with amulets, his face suffused with long-suffering compassion. The payment of money for his services guarantees that the job has been well done; an old lady with a fifty-dollar hairstyle is still a person to be reckoned with. . . .

> *agree!*

. . . We are in the midst of a cultural upheaval in which the body, which for aeons was a holy thing, its excretions and its orifices feared and revered, is becoming reified. It is becoming a toy, an asset, a commodity, an instrumentality for human will, and the pace of the change is much too fast. The intolerability of pictures of stainless steel meticulously carving out faces and breasts, isolating the unwanted and throwing it in the trash, tells us that we are still superstitious. We still suspect that the fantasy which is being imposed upon the body is less potent and less various than the body itself. Yet we cannot ease our anxiety by sneering, for we know the callousness which characterizes our treatment of the old and obese. We can understand why people who have the money will endure pain and risk death rather than go on living inside the bodies which bear the marks of their own history. Cosmetic surgery is the secular version of confession and absolution. It has taken the place of all our lost ceremonies of death and rebirth. It is reincarnation.

Most societies reject the grossly deformed. All societies have notions of beauty and fitness to which they aspire: relatively non-neurotic societies tend to admire characteristics which are well-distributed among their people, because distance from the culturally recognized norm causes suffering. We are affected by our bodies just as our behavior marks them. Peculiar looking people tend to behave peculiarly. Criminologists have known for many years that cosmetic surgery may do more for a social delinquent than years of custody and psychiatric care, when it comes to rehabilitation.

Once we begin to sculpt the body to our own aesthetic requirements we enter a realm of shifting values to which there is no guide. In essence, beautification and mutilation are the same activity. The African women who practice genital mutilation do so primarily because they think the result is more attractive; the unreconstructed genitalia are disgusting to them. Very few Westerners really find the female genitalia beautiful, but most of them would be horrified, even nauseated, by the sight of an infibulated vagina. None of them, by contrast, would cry out in disgust at the sight of a mutilated penis, stripped of its foreskin; all of them would be unpleasantly affected by the sight of a sub-incised penis.

Some mutilations have an ulterior purpose; the biting off of little finger joints of the newborn by Aboriginal mothers may be a way of deflecting the attention of evil spirits who would covet a perfect child. The custom of branding sickly infants in India may incidentally eliminate the feebler ones before too much energy has been invested in their care, and even, perhaps, activate sluggish resistance to the pathogens in the environment. In any event, the brands are carefully placed. The endurance of pain, especially in poor communities where pain and discomfort are daily realities, is another important aspect of beautification/mutilation. Scarification is valued not only because it is symmetrically placed about the body and not only because it implies the achievement of new status, but because it hurts. Where survival is only achieved by constant effort, stoicism and willpower are immensely important. The young woman who lies unflinching while the circumciser grinds her clitoris off between two stones is proving that she will make a good wife, equal to all the anguish of child-bearing and daily toil, not only to the witnesses of her bravery, but more importantly, to herself.

Industrialized society is the first in which endurance of physical pain is not a condition of survival. We have identified pain as our enemy and have done our best to eradicate even its most manageable manifestations. Scars have no value for us and their aesthetic appeal has perished alongside their moral value. A few women might confess that they feel strangely drawn to men with scarred faces (or eye-patches or limps) but it is generally considered to be an aberrant taste. Yet, augmentation mammoplasty is no more after all than a raised scar. NO! The great difference between ancient and modern beautification/mutilation procedures is that nowadays we must conceal the fact of the procedure itself. The association of sculpted breasts with pain is anaphrodisiac, so much so, that a man who guesses that what he is admiring was produced by a knife, may lose all interest. Some women may boast of their cosmetic operations, but this is a safety valve against the possibility that they will be found out.

Most mutilations which have been accepted as beautiful are so by consensus; historically the most astonishing distortions have been admired, necks so elongated that they could not hold up the head unless supported by brass rings, teeth filed and knocked out, lips stretched to accommodate large discs, earlobes stretched until they hung down in large loops. However *outré* the punks may appear they are the merest beginners in the arts of mutilation. The admiration of certain disfigurements is an important part of the process of self-definition: Contempt for the same practices is one of the ways in which other groups insist upon their separateness. We are not surprised to find the greatest contrasts in groups living side by side. When genetic equipment and economic status are both very similar, contrasting cultural practices become immensely important; they become the expression of the group's introverted altruism. In most tribal societies the attitude is more or less pluralistic; a group of labret wearers, for example, will simply define themselves as labret wearers, without making any attempt to impose labrets on others or to deride them for being without them. Western industrial society, deluded perhaps by its own vastness and uniformity, is not pluralistic, but utterly convinced that its own practices are the product of enlightenment and ought to be followed by all progressive peoples. Thus Western women, fully accoutred with nail polish (which is incompatible with manual work), high-heeled shoes (disastrous for the posture and hence the back, and quite unsuitable for walking long distances over bad roads), and brassieres (which imitate the shape of a pubescent non-lactating breast rather than the useful organs to be found in most of the world) denounce female circumcision, without the shadow of a suspicion that their behavior is absurd.

Yet within this bland but crushing orthodoxy there are spores of something   20
different. Our unemployed young have reverted to tribal practices. They indulge in flamboyant mutilation/beautification which is not understood, let alone appreciated in our common judgment. Teenage daughters come to their parents' dinner parties covered with blue spots, with blue hair standing on end. Deviant groups cemented by shared ritual intoxication or guilt or ordeal or all of these are budding in our rotting inner cities, terrorizing us with raucous music and insulting doggerel. If they had the power to grow like a malignant organism and invade the whole of the body politic we might have reason to be afraid. Like millions of generations of body decorators before them, they have no economic activity beyond survival; they could be toughened by the necessity of existing on the little that society will mete out to them so that they accumulate the collective power to strike at its unprotected underbelly. Or they could fritter away their spare energy in intercommunal war, as gangs have always done. The body art of the urban deviant is unlike any which has appeared on earth before in that it has no socially constructed significance. There is . . . [no] . . . mutual decoration; no young warriors apply magical designs to each other's backs. No priests and witches or mothers and aunts confer new powers upon an initiate. The only human interactions we see are commercial. The manicurists, the cosmetologists, the surgeons, the hairdressers, the tattooists are all professionals. Between the dancer and the dance has been interposed the mirror; the clients have come to the professionals after long and lonely contemplation of the self which dissatisfies them. Individuals do not modify their bodies to please others or to clarify their relationship to others. Rather they inflict changes upon themselves in order to approximate to narcissistic needs which may have been projected on to putative others.

Inside the bodies they have reconstructed, the body builders live incommunicado. The illustrated men disappear behind designs imported from a highly structured alien culture into which they themselves could never be accepted. The body building, the tattooing, the cultivation of cockscombs, the driving of rings, bolts, barbs, and studs through labia, lobes, cartilage, nipples, foreskin are all displacement activities. A caged bird suffering from loneliness and sensory deprivation will turn upon itself and pluck out all its feathers or peck off its own leg. Middle-aged women rejected by their children will turn to surgery, restlessly beautifying/mutilating to no purpose, and a good deal of their activity will be directed against their sexuality. The body builders will proceed until they have become epicene monsters, all body hair shaved off so that the light can catch the slick greased muscles. . . . One of the most potent symbols among all natural symbols is the breast, not only the female breast but by extension the male simulacrum. Only groups doomed to extinction have ever attacked the nipples; cutting, piercing, and distorting them . . . is something hideously strange. . . . Attacks upon the genitalia and the secondary sexual characteristics are attacks upon the continuity of the species; they are only conceivable in lives which are confined to their own duration, on bodies which must be their own gratification, among human contacts which are fleeting and self-centered. . . .

The right to economic activity is no longer a right which our society can guarantee to everyone. We are on the brink of an era in which most people will be condemned to a life of enforced leisure and mere subsistence. It may very well be that these displacement activities will have to evolve into legitimate art forms involving a strong and healthy body decorated with skill, sophistication, and meaning. Perhaps human worker bees will some day be delighted by the displays of squads of human butterflies bred and trained to dance the drab streets as living works of art. It would be a great pity if the dazzling tradition of human body art were to perish in a waste of dreary conformity on the one hand and neurotic self-distortion on the other.

Engaging the Text

1. In what ways do the motives for body modification in tribal cultures differ from those in Western societies? Which examples in Greer's essay best illustrate the cultural forces that underlie the desire to decorate, modify, and even mutilate oneself?

2. Greer devotes a considerable portion of her essay to the body modification practices of women. Which features of her essay reveal an awareness of the unique pressures to which females are subjected in contemporary society?

3. How would you characterize Greer's attitude toward the customs she describes? How persuasive do you find her analysis? Do you disagree with her on some points—for example, her explanations for body piercing in Western cultures? Explain your reactions.

Exploring Your Cultural Perspective

1. What body modifications have you undergone or considered making? In what way would these changes either bring you into conformity with accepted norms or define you in opposition to those norms? Were any of the modifications associated with a rite of passage, that is, with the beginning of a new phase of your life? Describe your experiences and analyze their cultural meanings. In your opinion, why does Western society generally approve of ear piercing while disapproving to various degrees of other forms of body piercing (nose piercing, naval piercing, nipple piercing, genital piercing, or tongue piercing)?

2. Greer's tone in this piece is sharp and questioning. How does her style differ from that of a typical fashion magazine, such as *Vogue, Mademoiselle,* or *Esquire,* when she analyzes a feature of Western fashion? Greer treats the familiar and commonplace as if it were unfamiliar. Does this make her essay more or less effective? Why?

BERNARD RUDOFSKY

The Unfashionable Human Body

Bernard Rudofsky's views on the human body and the clothing worn in different cultures were the subject of his controversial exhibitions at New York's Museum of Modern Art from 1945 to 1965. The recipient of Ford, Fulbright, and Guggenheim fellowships, Rudofsky held professorships at Yale and at Tokyo's Waseda University. His books include *The Kimono Mind* (1965) and *The Unfashionable Human Body* (1971), from which this selection is drawn. His writings express astonishment at the extraordinary measures humans take to deform, mutilate, and otherwise constrict their bodies in the pursuit of fashion.

Thinking Critically

What current fashion practices require constricting the body in the interest of style in ways that would appear bizarre if they were not accepted as "normal"? As you read, consider how Rudofsky's examples illustrate his thesis that we make our bodies conform to fashion rather than making our clothes fit our bodies.

Every generation has its own demented ideas on supporting some part of the human anatomy. Older people still remember a time when everybody went through life ankle-supported. Young and old wore laced boots. A shoe that did not reach well above the ankle was considered disastrous to health. What, one asks, has become of ankle support, once so warmly recommended by doctors and shoe salesmen? What keeps our ankles from breaking down in these days of low-cut shoes?

Ankle support has given way to arch support; millions of shoe-buying people are determined to "preserve their metatarsal arch" without as much as suspecting that it does not exist. Nevertheless, the fiction of the arch is being perpetuated to help sell "supports" and "preservers" on an impressive scale.

The dread of falling arches is, however, a picayune affair compared to that other calamity, the feet's asymmetry. I am not talking about the difference within a single pair of feet, that is, the difference between the right and left foot of a person; I mean the asymmetry of the foot itself.

Few of us are truly aware that an undeformed foot's outline is *not* symmetrical. It is distinctly lopsided. Let us have a close look at it: The big toe extends from one to two inches beyond the fifth toe. More importantly, the five toes spread out fanlike. They do not converge to a point in front as one would expect from the shape of the shoe. Quite the contrary, they converge to a point in back of the heel. It should be obvious, even to the least observant person, that to conform to the outline of a shoe, the big toe ought to be in the place of the third one, i.e. in the center.

Shoe manufacturers have shown admirable patience with nature. Despite   5 or because of the absence of feet that live up to their commercial ideals of anatomy, they doggedly go on producing symmetrical shoes. And although their customers' feet have not changed in the course of time, they spare no effort and expense to come up every season with a new (symmetrical) shoe for the same old foot. (The pathological hate of the natural form of the foot is nowhere more forcibly expressed than in the commandments of the Shakers which say that "it is contrary to order to have right and left shoes.")

By some atavistic quirk of nature, every normal baby is born with undeformed feet. The forepart of the foot—measured across the toes—is about twice as wide as the heel. The toes barely touch each other and are as nimble as fingers. Were the child able to keep up his toe-twiddling, he might easily retain as much control over his feet as over his hands. Not that we see anything admirable in nimble toes; they strike us as freakish perhaps because we associate prehensile feet with primitive civilizations. To our twisted mind, the foot in its undamaged state is anachronistic, if not altogether barbaric. Ever since the shoe became the badge of admission to Western civilization—in rural countries such as Portugal and Brazil the government exhorts peasants to wear shoes in the name of progress—we look down on barefooted or sandaled nations.

Since wearing shoes is synonymous with wearing *bad* shoes, the modern shoe inevitably becomes an instrument of deformation. The very concept of the modern shoe does not admit of an intelligent solution; it is not made to fit a human foot but to fit a wooden last whose shape is determined by the whims of the "designer." Whereas a tailor allows for a customer's unequal shoulders and arms; an optometrist prescribes different lenses for the right and left eye, we buy shoes of identical size and dimensions for our right and left foot, conveniently forgetting—or ignoring—that, as a rule, they are not of the same width and length. Even in countries where it is still possible to find an artisan willing to make a pair of shoes to order, chances are that he works on mass-produced lasts and comes up with a product that, shapewise, is not much different from the industrial one.

In both the manufacturer's and the customer's opinion the shoe comes before the foot. It is less intended to protect the foot from cold and dirt than to mold it into a fashionable shape. Infants' very first shoes are liable to dislocate the bones, and bend the foot into the shoe shape. The child does not mind the interference; "never expect the child to complain that the shoe is hurting him," says podiatrist Dr. Simon Wikler, "for the crippling process is painless." According to a ten-year study of the Podiatry Society of the State of New York, 99 percent of all feet are perfect at birth, 8 percent have developed troubles at one year, 41 percent at the age of five, and 80 percent at twenty; "we limp into adulthood," the report concludes. "Medical schools," says Dr. DePalma, "fail almost completely in giving the student a sound grounding and a sane therapeutic concept of foot conditions." And in *Military Medicine* one reads that "there has been no objective test that could be readily incorporated in physical examinations, or taught to medical students, pediatricians, or physicians in military and industrial medicine, that would enable them to recognize deformities of the foot . . ." In sum, physicians leave it to the shoe designer to decide the fate of our feet.

To top it all, modern man, perhaps unknown to himself, is afflicted with a diffuse shoe-fetishism. Inherited prejudices derived from the Cinderella complex; practices whose origins and reasons escape him, and traditional obtuseness combine to make him tolerate the deformities inflicted by his shoes. In this respect his callousness matches that of the Chinese of old. In fact, if he ever felt a need to justify the shoes' encroachments on his anatomy, he could cite Lily feet (provided he had ever heard of them), the Chinese variety of the "correctly shaped" foot.

10   This exotic custom which lasted nearly one thousand years did not extend over the whole country; the Manchu, including the imperial family, never practiced foot-binding. Small feet are a racial characteristic of Chinese women, and the desire to still further reduce their size in the name of beauty and for reasons indicated earlier, seems to have been strong enough to make women tolerate irrevocable mutilation. As so often happens, people derive infinitely greater satisfaction from an artifact, however crude, than from nature's product. Besides, not only were a woman's stunted feet highly charged with erotic symbolism, they made her eligible for marriage. Without them she was reduced to spinsterhood. Her desirability as a love object was in direct proportion to her inability to walk. It ought to be easy for our women to understand the Chinese men's mentality; "every woman knows that to wear 'walking shoes'—as derogatory a term as 'sensible shoes'—puts a damper on a man's ardor. The effect of absurdly impractical shoes, on the other hand, is as intoxicating as a love potion. The girl child who puts on a pair of high-heeled shoes is magically propelled into womanhood."

Modern woman is not averse to maltreating her feet for reasons similar to those of her Chinese sisters, and therefore makes allowance for bunions, calluses, corns, ingrown toenails and hammer toes. But she draws the line at a major interference with her foot skeleton. Unwilling to bother with growing her own, organic high heels, she has to get along with artificial ones.

As costume props go, the high heel's history is relatively short. In the middle of the seventeenth century this new device for corrupting the human walk was added to the footwear of the elegant, putting them, as it were, on tiptoe. The ground, indoors and outdoors, came to a tilt, so to speak, and, for fashion's sake, people began to walk on a portable incline. As the ordinary folk continued to wear flat-bottomed shoes, heeled footwear, combined with a strutting walk, became a mark of distinction. Withal, the times were anything but favorable to the new invention. On the street the well-heeled had to avail themselves of a sedan chair to avoid the cobblestones underfoot, while indoors they found it difficult to negotiate the polished parquets and marble floors that were the pride of the epoch. And yet, men took to high heels as enthusiastically as women did. To judge from paintings of the time, fashionable men could not have cared less for "walking shoes."

Did men's high-heeled shoes and fine stockings turn a woman's head? Were women smitten with the sight of a man's well-turned ankle and slender leg? For whereas their own legs remained hidden by crinolines, men proudly displayed their calves and gave as much attention to them as to their wigs. Silicon injections still being centuries away, a skinny fellow made up by padding for any natural deficiency. Eventually, the French Revolution brought men and women down to earth. Dandies and *élégantes* wore paper-thin flat soles without, it seems, depriving themselves of their mutual attraction. Years later, when high heels reappeared on the fashionable scene, they were relegated to woman's domain; men never left the ground again.

In lucid moments we look with amazement at the fraud we perpetrate on ourselves—the bruises, mutilations, and dislocated bones—but if we feel at all uncomfortable, it is not for long. An automatic self-defense mechanism blurs our judgment, and makes right and wrong exchange places. Moreover, some violations of the body are sanctioned by religion, while others are simply the price of a man's admittance to his tribe, regardless of whether he lives in the bush or in a modern metropolis. The sense of superiority he derives from, say, circumcision is no less real than that of the owner of a pair of Lily feet. Physicians have always been of two minds about it; "to cut off the top of the uppermost skin of the secret parts," maintained the intrepid Dr. Bulwer, "is directly against the honesty of nature, and an injurious unsufferable trick put upon her." And a contemporary pediatrician, E. Noel Preston, writing in the *Journal of the American Medical Association*, considers circumcision "little better than mutilation." The very real dangers of the operation such as infection and hemorrhage outweigh the fancied advantages of cancer prevention. "If a child can be taught to tie his shoes or brush his teeth or wash behind the ears," said Dr. Preston, "he can also be taught to wash beneath his foreskin."

15   A change of allegiance may lead to double mutilation, as in the paradoxical phenomenon of uncircumcision: After the subjugation of Palestine by Alexander the Great, those Jews who found it desirable to turn into Gentiles, underwent a painful operation that restored to them the missing prepuce. (1 Cor. 7:18 ff; 1 Macc. 1:15)

Sometimes such mutilation reaches a high degree of ferocity. Among some Arabian tribes circumcision is performed as an endurance test for youths who have come of age; "it consists," writes the Hebrew scholar Raphael Patai, "in cutting off the skin across the stomach below the navel and thence down the thighs, after which it is peeled off, leaving the stomach, the pelvis, the scrotum, and the inner legs uncovered and flayed. Many young men are said to have succumbed to the ordeal which in recent times has been prohibited by the Saudi Arabian government." However, the custom has not disappeared, doubtless as a result of its sex appeal. The ceremony takes place in female company, that is, in the presence of the young men's brides-to-be, who may refuse to marry their intended if they betray their agony by as much as an air of discomfort.

Man's obsession with violating his body is not just of anthropological interest, it helps us to understand the irrationality of dress. The devices for interfering with human anatomy are paralleled by a host of contraptions that simulate deformation or are simply meant to cheat the eye: bustles, pads, heels, wedges, braguettes, brassières, and so forth. Once, thirty years marked the end of a woman's desirability. In time, this age limit was gradually extended and pushed to a point where it got lost altogether. In order not only to look eternally young but also fashionable, woman had to obey ever-changing body ideals. Thus a woman born at the turn of the century was a buxom maiden in accordance with the dictates of the day. Photographs testify to the generosity of her charms although her tender age ought to raise doubts about their authenticity. In the nineteen-twenties, when maturity and motherhood had come to her, pictures record an angular, lean, flat-chested creature. Since she did not want to renounce her attractiveness, she had to submit to an extremely unfeminine beauty ideal. Twenty years later, she was rotund again and commanded the undiminished attention of the other sex. Today, she is still in the running, ever ready to overhaul her body to prolong her youth beyond biological limits. She has inflamed three generations of men each loyal to a different image of perfection.

Alas, an aged body, however arresting and deceptive be the results of its updating and remodeling, imparts to its owner only a limited sense of youth.

It serves mainly as a stylish peg for clothes. In other words, it is the clothed body that triumphs, not the naked one. As Herbert Spencer said: "The consciousness of being perfectly dressed may bestow a peace such as religion cannot give."

Engaging the Text

1. How does the example of the wearing of high-laced boots for ankle support illustrate the generational nature of fashion trends? How does Rudofsky use the human foot's asymmetry to support his argument?

2. By alluding to the fairy tale of *Cinderella*, Rudofsky invokes the myth equating virtue with small foot size. How did this myth operate in China? How is modern woman's wearing of high heels similar to the deforming foot practices of the Chinese?

3. Do the connections Rudofsky perceives among fashions in feet (and footwear), circumcision, and devices for "interfering with human anatomy" support his thesis about the irrationality of fashion? Do you agree or disagree with his thesis? Why or why not?

Exploring Your Cultural Perspective

1. Investigate the history of some shoe-related custom (for example, tying shoes to the newlyweds' car; removing one's shoes upon entering a mosque, a Buddhist temple, or a Japanese home; or the symbolism of covered feet versus sandals). Write an essay describing your findings.

2. Examine the photographs in Figures 3.1 and 3.2 (page 176), and discuss the paradox of high heels that hobble but are perceived as sexy. What do these images suggest about the cultural values attached to being in the "height" of fashion?

FIGURE 3.1

FIGURE 3.2

VALERIE STEELE AND JOHN S. MAJOR

China Chic

Valerie Steele is chief curator of the Museum at the Fashion Institute of Technology (FIT). Steele organized a major exhibition at FIT to coincide with the 1999 publication of *China Chic: East Meets West.* She is the editor of *Fashion Theory: The Journal of Dress, Body, and Culture* and has also written *Paris Fashion: A Cultural History* (1998) and *Fashion and Eroticism* (2000). John S. Major is director of the China Council of the Asia Society. He is the author of *Heaven and Earth in Early Han Thought* (1993) and *The Silk Route: 7,000 Miles of History* (1996). The following essay, from *China Chic,* examines foot binding in the context of China's political, economic, and cultural history and its correspondence to fashions in the West.

Thinking Critically

Consider how foot binding in China (accomplished through dwarfing the foot by dislocating its bones) was a symbol of fashion just as high-heeled shoes are in the West. As you read, evaluate the causal relationships the authors identify between social pressures and the practice of foot binding.

Foot binding lasted for a thousand years. It apparently began in the declining years of the Tang dynasty and it persisted in remote areas of China until the middle of the twentieth century. Yet despite its manifest significance within Chinese history, foot binding has been the subject of surprisingly little scholarly research. Recently, however, scholars such as Dorothy Ko have begun to explore the subject—with surprising results. As Ko points out, "It is natural for modern-day reformers to consider footbinding a men's conspiracy to keep women crippled and submissive, but this is an anachronistic view that finds no support in the historical records."[1]

Many of the sources on which our understanding of foot binding are based are themselves highly problematic. Western missionaries attacked the "barbaric" practice of foot binding, but they did so within the context of a prejudiced and ignorant denunciation of many other aspects of Chinese civilization. Most of the

Chinese literature on the subject was written by men, who often emphasized the erotic appeal of foot binding. For a better understanding of foot binding, it is necessary to search for evidence of what Chinese women themselves thought about the practice. It is also necessary to place foot binding within its (changing) historical context. As Ko puts it, "Foot binding is not one monolithic, unchanging experience that all unfortunate women in each succeeding dynasty went through, but is rather an amorphous practice that meant different things to different people . . . It is, in other words, a situated practice."[2]

What did foot binding signify to the Chinese, and why did they maintain the practice for so long? Although historians do not know exactly how or why foot binding began, it was apparently initially associated with dancers at the imperial court and professional female entertainers in the capital. During the Song dynasty (960–1279) the practice spread from the palace and entertainment quarters into the homes of the elite. "By the thirteenth century, archeological evidence shows clearly that foot-binding was practiced among the daughters and wives of officials," reports Patricia Buckley Ebrey, whose study of Song women reproduces photographs of shoes from that period. The Fujian tomb of Miss Huang Sheng (1227–43), for example, contained shoes measuring between 13.3 and 14 cm. (5¼ to 5½ inches), while the Jiangxi tomb of Miss Zhou (1240–74) contained shoes that were 18 to 22 cm. (7 to 8⅝ inches) long.[3] Over the course of the next few centuries foot binding became increasingly common among gentry families, and the practice eventually penetrated the mass of the Chinese people.

Foot binding generally began between the ages of five and seven, although many poorer families delayed beginning for several years, sometimes even until the girl was an adolescent, so they could continue to benefit from her labor and mobility. First-person accounts of foot binding testify that the procedure was extremely painful. The girl's feet were tightly bound with bandages, which forced the small toes inward and under the sole of the foot, leaving only the big toe to protrude. Then the heel and toe were drawn forcefully together, breaking the arch of the foot.

5   This was the most extreme type of foot binding. However, many girls apparently had their feet "bound in less painful styles that 'merely' kept the toes compressed or limited the growth of the foot, but did not break any bones."[4] Nevertheless, there is no doubt that foot binding was a radical form of body modification. As early as the Song dynasty, Che Ruoshui made perhaps the first protest against foot binding. He wrote: "Little children not yet four or five *sui* [i.e. five to seven years old], who have done nothing wrong, nevertheless are made to suffer unlimited pain to bind [their feet] small. I do not know what use this is."[5]

In fact, foot binding served a number of uses. To begin with, as Ebrey suggests, by making the feet of Chinese women so much smaller than those of

Chinese men, it emphasized that men and women were different. Then, too, since only Chinese women bound their feet, the practice also served to distinguish between Chinese and non-Chinese. An investigation of the political situation suggests why this might have been thought desirable. At the time when foot binding began (in the late Tang) and spread (in the Song), China was in bad shape. Various foreign peoples who lived along the frontiers repeatedly raided and invaded China, sometimes conquering sizeable portions of Chinese territory and establishing their own dynasties on land that the Chinese regarded as properly theirs—as the Khitans did in the northeast when they defeated the Tang and established the Liao dynasty (907–1125), as the Tanguts did in the west when they established the XiXia Kingdom, and again as the Jürchens did in the north when they established the Jin dynasty (1115–1260) to succeed the Khitan Liao.

Although the Chinese managed to establish the Song dynasty in 960, after the turmoil that accompanied the fall of the Tang, it occupied only a portion of what had been Chinese territory, and even that portion decreased dramatically. Chinese men must often have been reminded of their military inferiority in the face of the aggressive "barbarians" encroaching from the north. Did they, perhaps, feel reassured about their strength and masculinity when they compared themselves to their crippled female counterparts? It may be possible to infer something of the sort when we analyze Song erotic poetry, devoted to the charms of tiny feet and a hesitant gait.

The suggestion that the spread of foot binding in the Song may have been related to the perceived need on the part of the Chinese gentry to emphasize the distinctions between men and women, Chinese and non-Chinese is strongly supported by Ebrey's analysis. "Because the ideal upper-class man was by Sung times a relatively subdued and refined figure, he might seem effeminate unless women could be made even more delicate, reticent, and stationary," she writes. In other words, anxieties about masculinity and national identity, rather than the desire to oppress women, *per se*, contributed to the spread of foot binding. "But," Ebrey adds, "we must also come to grips with women's apparently eager participation." A crucial element here, she argues, was the competition between wives and concubines. Chinese mothers may have become enthusiastic proponents of foot binding because small feet were regarded as sexually attractive, yet unlike the other tricks used by courtesans and concubines, there was nothing "forward" or "immodest" about having bound feet.[6]

The spread of foot binding during the Song dynasty also coincided with a philosophical movement known as Neo-Confucianism, which placed a pronounced ideological emphasis on female inferiority. (In Neo-Confucian metaphysics, the *yang* male principle was seen as superior to the *yin* female principle in both a cosmological and a moral sense.) Moreover, as already seen, political developments in the Song contributed to the demise of the great aristocratic families and the corresponding proliferation of gentry families, whose social and economic position was much more insecure, and whose predominant social function was to serve as bureaucrats. Members of this new class may have been especially receptive to foot binding, because the practice simultaneously provided reassurance about their social status, proper gender relations, and Chinese identity.

10   Foot binding may have been reassuring to the Chinese, but it did not prevent the Mongols from becoming the first foreigners to conquer all of China. Genghiz Khan unified the Mongols, and Kublai Khan established the Yuan dynasty (1279–1368). Similar anxieties about sexual and racial boundaries appeared again several centuries later toward the end of the Ming dynasty, when the Chinese began to be threatened by the Manchus. Moreover, when the Manchus succeeded in conquering China and establishing the Qing dynasty in the mid-seventeenth century, they passed edicts ordering Chinese men to shave their foreheads and Chinese women to cease foot binding.

The resulting "hysterical atmosphere" was "full of sexual overtones," since both cutting men's hair and unbinding women's feet were perceived by Chinese males almost as a symbolic mutilation or castration, which might even be worse than death. As Ko points out, "Although no one openly advocated footbinding, the very establishment of the Manchu dynasty created a need to re-emphasize the differences between 'we' and 'they' and between 'he' and 'she.' The ban on footbinding, thus doomed from the start, was rescinded in 1668, four years after its promulgation."[7]

Contrary to popular belief, it was not only the wealthy who bound their daughters' feet. By the Qing dynasty, the majority of Chinese women had bound feet—peasants included—although there did exist variations in the degree and type of foot binding. According to one Qing observer, "The practice of footbinding is more widespread in Yangzhou than in other places. Even coolies, servants, seamstresses, the poor, the old, and the weak have tiny feet and cramped toes."[8] Manchu women, however, did not bind their feet, nor did members of other ethnic minority groups. Indeed, under the Qing, Manchu women were specifically forbidden to bind their feet, which is intriguing, since it implies a desire to do so.

Because foot binding is usually interpreted today as a gruesome example of women's oppression, it is important to stress that women who experienced the practice rarely perceived it in those terms. Indeed, Ko has unearthed considerable evidence that many Chinese women felt proud of their bound feet, which they regarded as beautiful and prestigious. Foot binding was a central part of the women's world. The rituals surrounding foot binding were female-exclusive rituals, presided over by the women of the family, especially the girl's mother, who prayed to deities such as the Tiny Foot Maiden and the goddess Guanyin. According to Ko, these rituals "and the beliefs behind them help explain the longevity and spread of the custom."

> For all its erotic appeal to men, without the cooperation of the women
> concerned, footbinding could not have been perpetuated for a millen-
> nium. In defining the mother–daughter tie in a private space barred to
> men, in venerating the fruits of women's handiwork, and in the centrality
> of female-exclusive religious rituals, footbinding embodied the essential
> features of a woman's culture documented by the writings of the women
> themselves.[9]

Women wrote poems about lotus shoes and they exchanged them with friends.
Proverbs emphasized women's control over foot binding: "A plain face is given
by heaven, but poorly bound feet are a sign of laziness."[10]

Good mothers were supposed to bind their daughters' feet tightly so they
could make advantageous marriages, just as they made their sons study hard so
they could pass their examinations. The Victorian traveler Isabella Bird visited
China and reported that "The butler's little daughter, aged seven, is having her
feet 'bandaged' for the first time, and is in torture, but bears it bravely in the
hope of 'getting a rich husband' . . . The mother of this suffering infant says,
with a quiet air of truth and triumph, that Chinese women suffer less in the
process of being crippled than foreign women do from wearing corsets!"[11]

Indeed, Chinese and westerners alike not infrequently compared foot binding with corsetry, debating their relative injuriousness and irrationality. Yet   *15*
measurements of existing corsets and lotus shoes indicate that both the
sixteen-inch waist and the three-inch golden lotus were only achieved by a
minority of women. Writing at the turn of the century, the sociologist
Thorstein Veblen used foot binding (as well as such western fashions as corsets
and long skirts) as examples of what he called "conspicuous leisure," because
they supposedly indicated that the wearer could not perform productive labor.
Yet, contrary to popular belief, neither bound feet nor corsets prevented
women from working and walking; most Chinese women worked very hard,
albeit usually at home. Moreover, although foot binding was believed to ensure
female chastity by, literally, preventing women from straying, in fact women
were far more restricted by social and legal constraints.

Although for many centuries most Chinese men and women approved of
foot binding, the practice eventually ceased to be valorized as a way of emphasizing the beauty and virtue of Chinese women and/or the virility and civility
of Chinese men. Writing in the early nineteenth century, the novelist Li
Ruzhun attacked foot binding on the grounds that it oppressed women. His
novel *Flowers in the Mirror* included a satirical sequence about a country where
women ruled and men had their feet bound.

Missionary efforts undoubtedly played a role in the demise of foot binding, as the Chinese were made aware that Westerners thought the practice was

"barbaric," unhealthy, and oppressive to women. The Chinese girls who attended mission schools were taught that foot binding was bad. More significantly, however, growing numbers of young Chinese men (and a few educated Chinese women) began to reinterpret foot binding as a "backward" practice that hindered national efforts to resist western imperialism.

Chinese reformers began to discuss whether China could be strengthened *vis-à-vis* the West, if only Chinese women became stronger physically. This, in turn, seemed to depend on the elimination of what was increasingly regarded by progressive Chinese as the "feudal" practice of foot binding. Organizations such as the Natural Foot Society were founded, and struggled to change the idea that unbound female feet were "big" and ugly. Indeed, it was apparently difficult to convince the Chinese that foot binding was any more "unnatural" than other kinds of bodily adornment, such as clothing, jewelry, hairstyles, or cosmetics.[12]

There is even some evidence that the introduction of western high-heeled shoes, which give the visual illusion of smaller feet and produce a swaying walk, may have eased the transition away from the bound foot ideal. Manchu shoes were another alternative to lotus shoes in the early years of the anti-foot-binding movement, although with the rise of anti-Manchu nationalism at the time of the 1911 Revolution, this style disappeared.

20   Foot binding had never been mandated by any Chinese government. Indeed, various Qing rulers had sporadically attempted to abolish foot binding, without success. After the Qing dynasty was overthrown and a republic was declared, foot binding was outlawed. Laws alone would not have sufficed to end the practice, however, had it not already ceased to claim the allegiance of significant segments of the Chinese population, but once foot binding began to be regarded as "backward," modern-thinking Chinese increasingly attacked the practice.

Older brothers argued that their sisters should not have their feet bound, or should try to let their feet out—a process that was itself painful and only partly feasible. Sometimes husbands even abandoned wives who had bound feet, and looked for new, suitably modern brides. Obviously, these developments took place within the context of broader social change. The new generation of educated, urban Chinese increasingly argued that many aspects of traditional Chinese culture should be analyzed and improved. Women, as well as men, should be educated and should participate in athletic activities. Arranged marriages should be replaced by love matches. The Chinese nation should modernize and strengthen itself.

Notes

1. Dorothy Ko, *Teachers of the Inner Chambers: Women and Culture in Seventeenth-Century China* (Stanford: Stanford University Press, 1994), p. 148.
2. Dorothy Ko, "The Body as Attire: The Shifting Meanings of Footbinding in Seventeenth Century China," *Journal of Women's History* 8.4 (1997), p. 15.
3. Patricia Buckley Ebrey, *The Inner Quarters: Marriage and the Lives of Chinese Women in the Sung Period* (Berkeley: University of California Press, 1993), pp. 38–39.
4. Feng Jicai, *The Three-Inch Golden Lotus*, trans. David Wakefield (Honolulu: University of Hawaii Press, 1994), p. 236.
5. Cited in Ebrey, *The Inner Quarters*, p. 40.
6. Ebrey, *The Inner Quarters*, pp. 42–43.
7. Ko, *Teachers of the Inner Chambers*, p. 149.
8. Ibid., p. 263.
9. Ibid., p. 150.
10. Ibid., p. 171.
11. Isabella Bird, *The Golden Chersonese and the Way Thither* (first published London, 1883; reprinted, Singapore: Oxford University Press, 1990), p. 66.
12. Ko, "The Body as Attire," pp. 17–19.

Engaging the Text

1. What is the practice of foot binding? What political and social meanings did it communicate within the context of Chinese culture at the time it was practiced?

2. Why do Steele and Major draw a distinction between Western condemnation of foot binding and what the practice meant to Chinese women at the time?

Exploring Your Cultural Perspective

1. What do the kind of shoes you wear say about you? What are your favorite styles, heel heights, and colors? Given the choice between a pair of fashionable or comfortable shoes, which would you buy? Alternatively, compare the meanings communicated by various traditional shoe types—including moccasins, sandals, mules, boots, and clogs—and their modern variants.

2. The so-called "lotus foot" (named because the walk of the woman whose foot was bound was thought to resemble the swaying of the lotus plant in the wind) captivated the Chinese imagination such that the foot took on the role of a sexual object. In what way do "shoes that have no relationship to the natural foot shape" (high heels) communicate the same psychological meaning in the West?

ALISON LURIE
The Language of Clothes

Most of us are really quite adept at deciphering the range of meanings that clothing communicates. Alison Lurie, a professor of American literature at Cornell University, explains how we can understand fashion as a complex system of signs meant to communicate personal choices as well as a visible indicator of the social class of the wearer. Lurie is the author of several books, including the Pulitzer Prize–winning novel *Foreign Affairs* (1984; 1999). In this essay from *Human Ecology* (1991), Lurie explores the social codes and values that clothing conveys and the cultural conventions that determine what is considered fashionable at any particular time. Her latest works include *The Language of Clothes* (2000). Her other recent works include *The Last Resort: A Novel* (1999); a children's book, *Fabulous Beasts* (1999); and *Familiar Spirits: A Memoir of James Merriel and David Jackson* (2001).

Thinking Critically

To help you follow Lurie's line of thought, underline her key points and supporting examples as you read the piece.

For thousands of years human beings have communicated with one another first in the language of dress. Long before I am near enough to talk to you on the street, in a meeting, or at a party, you announce your sex, age and class to me through what you are wearing—and very possibly give me important information (or misinformation) as to your occupation, origin, personality, opinions, tastes, sexual desires and current mood. I may not be able to put what I observe into words, but I register the information unconsciously; and you simultaneously do the same for me. By the time we meet and converse we have already spoken to each other in an older and more universal language.

The statement that clothing is a language, though made occasionally with the air of a man finding a flying saucer in his backyard, is not new. Balzac, in *Daughter of Eve* (1830), observed that dress is a "continual manifestation of intimate thoughts, a language, a symbol." Today, as semiotics becomes fash-

184

ionable, sociologists tell us that fashion too is a language of signs, a nonverbal system of communication.

None of these theorists, however, has gone on to remark what seems obvious: that if clothing is a language, it must have a vocabulary and a grammar like other languages. Of course, as with human speech, there is not a single language of dress, but many: some (like Dutch and German) closely related and others (like Basque) almost unique. And within every language of clothes there are many different dialects and accents, some almost unintelligible to members of the mainstream culture. Moreover, as with speech, each individual has his own stock of words and employs personal variations of tone and meaning.

The vocabulary of dress includes not only items of clothing, but also hair styles, accessories, jewelry, make-up and body decoration. Theoretically at least this vocabulary is as large as or larger than that of any spoken tongue, since it includes every garment, hair style, and type of body decoration ever invented. In practice, of course, the sartorial resources of an individual may be very restricted. Those of a sharecropper, for instance, may be limited to five or ten "words" from which it is possible to create only a few "sentences" almost bare of decoration and expressing only the most basic concepts. A so-called fashion leader, on the other hand, may have several hundred "words" at his or her disposal, and thus be able to form thousands of different "sentences" that will express a wide range of meanings. Just as the average English-speaking person knows many more words than he or she will ever use in conversation, so all of us are able to understand the meaning of styles we will never wear.

MAGICAL CLOTHING

Archaeologists digging up past civilizations and anthropologists studying primitive tribes have come to the conclusion that, as Rachel Kemper [*Costume*] puts it, "Paint, ornament, and rudimentary clothing were first employed to attract good animistic powers and to ward off evil." When Charles Darwin visited Tierra del Fuego, a cold, wet, disagreeable land plagued by constant winds, he found the natives naked except for feathers in their hair and symbolic designs painted on their bodies. Modern Australian bushmen, who may spend hours decorating themselves and their relatives with patterns in colored clay, often wear nothing else but an amulet or two.

However skimpy it may be, primitive dress almost everywhere, like primitive speech, is full of magic. A necklace of shark's teeth or a girdle of cowrie shells or feathers serves the same purpose as a prayer or spell, and may magically replace—or more often supplement—a spoken charm. In the first instance a form of *contagious* magic is at work: the shark's teeth are believed to endow their wearer with the qualities of a fierce and successful fisherman. The cowrie shells, on the other hand, work through *sympathetic* magic: since they resemble the female sexual parts, they are thought to increase or preserve fertility.

In civilized society today belief in the supernatural powers of clothing—like belief in prayers, spells and charms—remains widespread, though we denigrate it with the name "superstition." Advertisements announce that improbable and romantic events will follow the application of a particular sort of grease to our faces, hair or bodies; they claim that members of the opposite (or our own) sex will be drawn to us by the smell of a particular soap. Nobody believes those ads, you may say. Maybe not, but we behave as though we did: look in your bathroom cabinet.

The supernatural garments of European folk tales—the seven-league boots, the cloaks of invisibility and the magic rings—are not forgotten, merely transformed, so that today we have the track star who can only win a race in a particular hat or shoes, the plainclothes cop who feels no one can see him in his raincoat and the wife who takes off her wedding ring before going to a motel with her lover.

Sympathetic or symbolic magic is also often employed, as when we hang crosses, stars or one of the current symbols of female power and solidarity around our necks, thus silently involving the protection of Jesus, Jehovah or Astarte. Such amulets, of course, may be worn to announce our allegiance to some faith or cause rather than as a charm. Or they may serve both purposes simultaneously—or sequentially. The crucifix concealed below the parochial-school uniform speaks only to God until some devilish force persuades its wearer to remove his or her clothes; then it acts—or fails to act—as a warning against sin as well as a protective talisman.

10   Articles of clothing, too, may be treated as if they had mana, the impersonal supernatural force that tends to concentrate itself in objects. When I was in college it was common to wear a particular "lucky" sweater, shirt or hat to final examinations, and this practice continues today. Here it is usually contagious magic that is at work: the chosen garment has become lucky by being worn on the occasion of some earlier success, or has been given to its owner by some favored person. The wearing of such magical garments is especially common in sports, where they are often publicly credited with bringing their owners luck. Their loss or abandonment is thought to cause injury as well as defeat. Actors also believe ardently in the magic of clothes, possibly because they are so familiar with the near-magical transforming power of theatrical costume.

FASHION AND STATUS

Clothing designed to show the social position of its wearer has a long history. Just as the oldest languages are full of elaborate titles and forms of address, so for thousands of years certain modes have indicated high or royal rank. Many societies passed decrees known as *sumptuary laws* to prescribe or forbid the wearing of specific styles by specific classes of persons. In ancient Egypt only those in high position could wear sandals; the Greeks and Romans controlled the type, color and number of garments worn and the sorts of embroidery with which they could be trimmed. During the Middle Ages almost every aspect of dress was regulated at some place or time—though not always with much success. The common features of all sumptuary laws—like that of edicts against the use of certain words—seem to be that they are difficult to enforce for very long.

Laws about what could be worn by whom continued to be passed in Europe until about 1700. But as class barriers weakened and wealth could be more easily and rapidly converted into gentility, the system by which color and shape indicated social status began to break down. What came to designate high rank instead was the evident cost of a costume: rich materials, superfluous trimmings and difficult-to-care-for styles, or as Thorstein Veblen later put it [in *The Theory of the Leisure Class*], Conspicuous Waste and Conspicuous Leisure. As a result, it was assumed that the people you met would be dressed as lavishly as their income permitted. In Fielding's *Tom Jones*, for instance, everyone judges strangers by their clothing and treats them accordingly; this is presented as natural. It is a world in which rank is very exactly indicated by costume, from the rags of Molly the gamekeeper's daughter to Sophia Western's riding habit "which was so very richly laced" that "Partridge and the post-boy instantly started from their chairs, and my landlady fell to her curtsies, and her ladyships, with great eagerness." The elaborate wigs characteristic of this period conferred status partly because they were both expensive to buy and expensive to maintain.

By the early eighteenth century the social advantages of conspicuous dress were such that even those who could not afford it often spent their money on finery. This development was naturally deplored by supporters of the status quo. In Colonial America the Massachusetts General Court declared its "utter detestation and dislike, that men or women of mean condition, should take upon them the garb of Gentlemen, by wearing Gold or Silver lace, or Buttons, or Points at their knees, or to walk in great Boots; or Women of the same rank to wear Silk or Tiffiny hoods, or Scarfes. . . ." What "men or women of mean condition"—farmers or artisans—were supposed to wear were coarse linen or wool, leather aprons, deerskin jackets, flannel petticoats and the like.

To dress above one's station was considered not only foolishly extravagant, but deliberately deceptive. In 1878 an American etiquette book complained,

> It is . . . unfortunately the fact that, in the United States, but too much attention is paid to dress by those who have neither the excuse of ample

means nor of social claims. . . . We Americans are lavish, generous, and ostentatious. The wives of our wealthy men are glorious in garb as are princesses and queens. They have a right so to be. But when those who can ill afford to wear alpaca persist in arraying themselves in silk . . . the matter is a sad one.

COLOR AND PATTERN

15 Certain sorts of information about other people can be communicated in spite of a language barrier. We may not be able to understand Welsh or the thick Southern dialect of the Mississippi delta, but when we hear a conversation in these tongues we can tell at once whether the speakers are excited or bored, cheerful or miserable, confident or frightened. In the same way, some aspects of the language of clothes can be read by almost anyone.

The first and most important of these signs, and the one that makes the greatest and most immediate impact, is color. Merely looking at different colors, psychologists have discovered, alters our blood pressure, heartbeat and rate of respiration, just as hearing a harsh noise or a harmonious musical chord does. When somebody approaches from a distance the first thing we see is the hue of his clothes; the closer he comes, the more space this hue occupies in our visual field and the greater its effect on our nervous system. Loud, clashing colors, like loud noises or loud voices, may actually hurt our eyes or give us a headache; soft, harmonious hues, like music and soft voices, thrill or soothe us. Color in dress is also like tone of voice in speech in that it can completely alter the meaning of what is "said" by other aspects of the costume: style, fabric and trimmings. Just as the words "Do you want to dance with me?" can be whispered shyly or flung as a challenge, so the effect of a white evening dress is very different from that of a scarlet one of identical fabric and pattern. In certain circumstances some hues, like some tones of voice, are beyond the bounds of polite discourse. A bride in a black wedding dress, or a stockbroker greeting his clients in a shocking-pink three-piece suit, would be like people screaming aloud.

Although color often indicates mood, it is not by any means an infallible guide. For one thing, convention may prescribe certain hues. The urban businessman must wear a navy blue, dark gray or (in certain regions) brown or tan suit, and can express his feelings only through his choice of shirt and tie, or tie alone; and even here the respectable possibilities may be very limited. Convention also alters the meaning of colors according to the place and time at which they are worn. Vermilion in the office is not the same as vermilion at a disco; and hot weather permits the wearing of pale hues that would make one look far more formal and fragile in midwinter.

There are other problems. Some people may avoid colors they like because of the belief or illusion that they are unbecoming, while others may wear colors they normally dislike for symbolic reason: because they are members or fans of a certain football team, for instance. In addition, some fashionable types may select certain hues merely because they are "in" that year.

Finally, it should be noted that the effect of any color in dress is modified by the colors that accompany it. In general, therefore, the following remarks should be taken as applying mainly to costumes composed entirely or almost entirely of a single hue.

The mood of a crowd, as well as that of an individual, can often be read in   *20* the colors of clothing. In the office of a large corporation, or at a professional convention, there is usually a predominance of conventional gray, navy, beige, tan and white—suggesting a general attitude of seriousness, hard work, neutrality, propriety and status. The same group of people at a picnic are a mass of lively, relaxed blue, red and brown, with touches of yellow and green. In the evening, at a disco, they shimmer under the rotating lights in dramatic combinations of purple, crimson, orange, turquoise, gold, silver and black.

Apart from the chameleon, man is the only animal who can change his skin to suit his background. Indeed, if he is to function successfully he must do so. The individual whose clothes do not fall within the recognized range of colors for a given situation attracts attention, usually (though not always) unfavorable attention. When a child puts its pet chameleon down on the earth and it does not turn brown, we know the creature is seriously ill. In the same way, men or women who begin to come to work in a conservative office wearing disco hues and a disco mood are regarded with anxiety and suspicion. If they do not blush a respectable beige, navy or gray within a reasonable length of time, their colleagues know that they will not be around for long.

Engaging the Text

1. According to Lurie, which cultural conventions determined the kinds of clothing that could be worn in societies in which questions of social class were important?

2. Which conventions govern the colors thought to be appropriate in different social settings?

3. In drawing **analogies** between clothes and speech, Lurie suggests equivalences between significant linguistic features (for example, vocabulary and syntax) and clothing styles and colors. Which of the examples Lurie cites to support her clothing-language analogy seem most persuasive? Does Lurie's analogy between clothing and language seem reasonable? Why or why not? Write a few paragraphs supporting or challenging her claim.

Exploring Your Cultural Perspective

1. Go through your wardrobe and classify the items of clothing you wear by the "statement" you want to make in different contexts. What is your favorite outfit? What do you think it says about you? Do you have an article of clothing that you feel brings you good luck? Describe the item, and explain how it came to have that meaning for you.

2. Analyze an advertisement for an item of clothing or an outfit, explaining how the ad was constructed to make the item or outfit appear desirable to the target audience. Also touch on the relationship between fashion and social status. (The controversial Benetton ads might be a good subject because they function more as vehicles for social commentary than as ads to sell clothes.)

ELIZABETH W. FERNEA AND ROBERT A. FERNEA

A Look behind the Veil

One of the most interesting examples of how clothes reflect cultural beliefs can be seen in the Middle Eastern custom of veiling women. Elizabeth W. Fernea and Robert A. Fernea have done extensive research in Iraq, Morocco, Egypt, and Afghanistan and are the authors of a number of books, including the award-winning *The Arab World: Personal Encounters* (1987) and its sequel, *The Arab World: Forty Years of Change* (1997). Elizabeth W. Fernea has also written *In Search of Islamic Feminism: One Woman's Global Journey* (1998) and is currently professor of Middle Eastern studies at the University of Texas at Austin.

Thinking Critically
As you read, consider the ways in which purdah defines how a woman must present herself in Middle Eastern cultures.

What objects do we notice in societies other than our own? Ishi, the last of a "lost" tribe of North American Indians who stumbled into 20th Century California in 1911, is reported to have said that the truly interesting objects in the white man's culture were pockets and matches. Rifa'ah Tahtawi, one of the first young Egyptians to be sent to Europe to study in 1826, wrote an account of French society in which he noted that Parisians used many unusual articles of dress, among them something called a belt. Women wore belts, he said, apparently to keep their bosoms erect, and to show off the slimness of their waists and the fullness of their hips. Europeans are still fascinated by the Stetson hats worn by American cowboys; an elderly Dutch lady of our acquaintance recently carried six enormous Stetsons back to The Hague as presents for the male members of her family.

Many objects signify values in society and become charged with meaning, a meaning that may be different for members of the society and for observers of that society. The veil is one object used in Middle Eastern societies that stirs strong emotions in the West. "The feminine veil has become a symbol: that of the slavery of one portion of humanity," wrote French ethnologist Germaine Tillion in 1966. A hundred years earlier, Sir Richard Burton, British traveler, explorer, and translator of the *Arabian Nights*, recorded a different view. "Europeans inveigh against this article [the face veil] . . . for its hideousness and jealous concealment of charms made to be admired," he wrote in 1855. "It is, on the contrary, the most coquettish article of woman's attire . . . it conceals coarse skins, fleshy noses, wide mouths and vanishing chins, whilst it sets off to best advantage what in these lands is most lustrous and liquid—the eye. Who has not remarked this at a masquerade ball?"

In the present generation, the veil and purdah, or seclusion, have become a focus of attention for Western writers, both popular and academic, who take a measure of Burton's irony and Tillion's anger to equate modernization of the Middle East with the discarding of the veil. "Iranian women return to veil in a resurgence of spirituality," headlines one newspaper; another writes, "Iran's 16 million women have come a long way since their floor-length cotton veil officially was abolished in 1935." The thousands of words written about the appearance and disappearance of the veil and of purdah do little to help us understand the Middle East or the cultures that grew out of the same Judeo-Christian roots as our own. The veil and the all-enveloping garments that inevitably accompany it (the *milayah* in Egypt, the *abbayah* in Iraq, the *chadoor* in Iran, the *yashmak* in Turkey, the *burqa* in Afghanistan, and the *djellabah* and the *haik* in North Africa) are only the outward manifestations of a cultural pattern and idea that is rooted deep in Mediterranean society.

"Purdah" is a Persian word meaning curtain or barrier. The Arabic word for veiling and secluding comes from the root *hajaba*. A *hijab* is an amulet worn to keep away the evil eye; it also means a diaphragm used to prevent conception. The gatekeeper or doorkeeper who guards the entrance to a government minister's office is a *hajib*, and in casual conversation a person might say, "I want to be more informal with my friend so-and-so, but she always puts a *hijab* (barrier) between us."

5   In Islam, the Koranic verse that sanctions the barrier between men and women is called the Sura of the *hijab* (curtain): "Prophet, enjoin your wives, your daughters and the wives of true believers to draw their veils close round them. That is more proper, so that they may be recognized and not molested. Allah is forgiving and merciful."

Certainly seclusion and some forms of veiling had been practiced before the time of Muhammad, at least among the upper classes, but it was his followers who apparently felt that his women should be placed in a special category. According to history, the *hijab* was established after a number of occasions on which Muhammad's wives were insulted by people who were coming to the mosque in search of the prophet. When chided for their behavior, they said they had mistaken Muhammad's wives for slaves. The *hijab* was established, and in the words of the historian Nabia Abbott, "Muhammad's women found themselves, on the one hand, deprived of personal liberty, and on the other hand, raised to a position of honor and dignity."

The veil bears many messages and tells us many things about men and women in Middle East society; but as an object in and of itself it is far less important to members of the society than the values it represents. Nouha al Hejailan, wife of the Saudi Arabian ambassador to London, told Sally Quinn of *The Washington Post*, "If I wanted to take it all off (her *abbayah* and veil), I would have long ago. It wouldn't mean as much to me as it does to you." Early Middle Eastern feminists felt differently. Huda Sh'arawi, an early Egyptian activist who formed the first Women's Union, made a dramatic gesture of removing her veil in public to demonstrate her dislike of society's attitudes toward women and her defiance of the system. But Basima Bezirgan, a contemporary Iraqi feminist, says, "Compared to the real issues that are involved between men and women in the Middle East today, the veil is unimportant." A Moroccan linguist who buys her clothes in Paris laughs when asked about the veil. "My mother wears a *djellabah* and a veil. I have never worn them. But so what? I still cannot get divorced as easily as a man, and I am still a member of my family group and responsible to them for everything I do. What is the veil? A piece of cloth."

"The seclusion of women has many purposes," states Egyptian anthropologist Nadia Abu Zahra. "It expresses men's status, power, wealth, and manliness. It also helps preserve men's image of virility and masculinity, but men do not admit this; on the contrary they claim that one of the purposes of the veil is to guard women's honor." The veil and purdah are symbols of restriction, to men as well as to women. A respectable woman wearing a veil on a public street is signaling, "Hands off. Don't touch me or you'll be sorry." Cowboy Jim Sayre of Deadwood, South Dakota, says, "If you deform a cowboy's hat, he'll likely deform you." In the same way, a man who approaches a veiled woman is asking for trouble; not only the woman but also her family is shamed, and serious problems may result. "It is clear," says Egyptian anthropologist Ahmed Abou Zeid, "that honor and shame which are usually attributed to a certain individual or a certain kinship group have in fact a bearing on the total social structure, since most acts involving honor or shame are likely to affect the existing social equilibrium."

Veiling and seclusion almost always can be related to the maintenance of social status. Historically, only the very rich could afford to seclude their women, and the extreme example of this practice was found among the sultans of prerevolutionary Turkey. Stories of these secluded women, kept in harems and guarded by eunuchs, formed the basis for much of the Western folklore concerning the nature of male-female relationships in Middle East society. The stereotype is of course contradictory; Western writers have never found it necessary to reconcile the erotic fantasies of the seraglio with the sexual puritanism attributed to the same society.

10   Poor men could not always afford to seclude or veil their women, because the women were needed as productive members of the family economic unit, to work in the fields and in cottage industries. Delta village women in Egypt have never been veiled, nor have the Berber women of North Africa. But this lack of veiling placed poor women in ambiguous situations in relation to strange men.

"In the village, no one veils, because everyone is considered a member of the same large family," explained Aisha bint Mohammed, a working-class wife of Marrakech. "But in the city, veiling is *sunnah*, required by our religion." Veiling is generally found in towns and cities, among all classes, where families feel that it is necessary to distinguish themselves from other strangers in the city.

Veiling and purdah not only indicate status and wealth, they also have some religious sanction and protect women from the world outside the home. Purdah delineates private space, distinguishes between the public and private sectors of society, as does the traditional architecture of the area. Older Middle Eastern houses do not have picture windows facing the street, nor walks leading invitingly to front doors. Family life is hidden from strangers; behind blank walls may lie courtyards and gardens, refuges from the heat, the cold, the bustle of the outside world, the world of non-kin that is not to be trusted. Outsiders are pointedly excluded.

Even within the household, among her close relatives, a traditional Muslim woman veils before those kinsmen whom she could legally marry. If her maternal or paternal male cousins, her brothers-in-law, or sons-in-law come to call, she covers her head, or perhaps her whole face. To do otherwise would be shameless.

The veil does more than protect its wearers from known and unknown intruders; it can also be used to conceal identity. Behind the anonymity of the veil, women can go about a city unrecognized and uncriticized. Nadia Abu Zahra reports anecdotes of men donning women's veils in order to visit their lovers undetected; women may do the same. The veil is such an effective disguise that Nouri Al-Said, the late prime minister of Iraq, attempted to escape death by wearing the *abbayah* and veil of a woman; only his shoes gave him away.

15   Political dissidents in many countries have used the veil for their own ends. The women who marched, veiled, through Cairo during the Nationalist demonstrations against the British after World War I were counting on the strength of Western respect for the veil to protect them against British gunfire. At first they were right. Algerian women also used the protection of the

veil to carry bombs through French army checkpoints during the Algerian revolution. But when the French discovered the ruse, Algerian women discarded the veil and dressed like Europeans to move about freely.

The multiple meanings and uses of purdah and the veil do not explain how the pattern came to be so deeply embedded in Mediterranean society. Its origins lie somewhere in the basic Muslim attitudes about men's roles and women's roles. Women, according to Fatima Mernissi, a Moroccan sociologist, are seen by men in Islamic societies as in need of protection because they are unable to control their sexuality, are tempting to men, and hence are a danger to the social order. In other words, they need to be restrained and controlled so that society may function in an orderly way.

The notion that women present a danger to the social order is scarcely limited to Muslim society. Anthropologist Julian Pitt-Rivers has pointed out that the supervision and seclusion of women is also to be found in Christian Europe, even though veiling was not usually practiced there. "The idea that women not subjected to male authority are a danger is a fundamental one in the writings of the moralists from the Archpriest of Talavera to Padre Haro, and it is echoed in the modern Andalusian *pueblo*. It is bound up with the fear of ungoverned female sexuality which had been an integral element of European folklore ever since prudent Odysseus lashed himself to the mast to escape the sirens."

Pitt-Rivers is writing about Mediterranean society, which, like all Middle Eastern societies, is greatly concerned with honor and shame rather than with individual guilt. The honor of the Middle Eastern extended family, its ancestors and its descendants, is the highest social value. The misdeeds of the grandparents are indeed visited on the children. Men and women always remain members of their natal families. Marriage is a legal contract but a fragile one that is often broken; the ties between brother and sister, mother and child, father and child are lifelong and enduring. The larger family is the group to which the individual belongs and to which the individual owes responsibility in exchange for the social and economic security that the family group provides. It is the group, not the individual, that is socially shamed or socially honored.

Male honor and female honor are both involved in the honor of the family, but each is expressed differently. The honor of a man, *sharaf*, is a public matter, involving bravery, hospitality, piety. It may be lost, but it may also be regained. The honor of a woman, *'ard*, is a private matter involving only one thing, her sexual chastity. Once lost, it cannot be regained. If the loss of female honor remains only privately known, a rebuke—and perhaps a reveiling—may be all that takes place. But if the loss of female honor becomes public knowledge, the other members of the family may feel bound to cleanse the family name. In extreme cases, the cleansing may require the death of the offending female member. Although such killings are now criminal offenses in the Middle East, suspended sentences are often given, and the newspapers in Cairo and Baghdad frequently carry sad stories of runaway sisters "gone bad" in the city and revenge taken upon them in the name of family honor by their brothers or cousins.

20   This emphasis on female chastity, many say, originated in the patrilineal society's concern with the paternity of the child and the inheritance that follows the male line. How does a man know that the child in his wife's womb is his own, and not that of another man? Obviously he cannot know unless his wife is a virgin at marriage. From this consideration may have developed the protective institutions called variously purdah, seclusion, or veiling.

Middle Eastern women also look upon seclusion as practical protection. In the Iraqi village where we lived from 1956 to 1958, one of us (Elizabeth) wore the *abbayah* and found that it provided a great sense of protection from prying eyes, dust, heat, flies. Parisian ladies visiting Istanbul in the 16th Century were so impressed by the ability of the all-enveloping garment to keep dresses clean of mud and manure and to keep women from being attacked by importuning men that they tried to introduce it into French fashion.

Perhaps of greater importance for many women reared in traditional cultures is the degree to which their sense of personal identity is tied to the use of the veil. Many women have told us that they felt self-conscious, vulnerable, and even naked when they first walked on a public street without the veil and *abbayah*—as if they were making a display of themselves.

The resurgence of the veil in countries like Morocco, Libya, and Algeria, which have recently established their independence from colonial dominance, is seen by some Middle Eastern and Western scholars as an attempt by men to reassert their Muslim identity and to reestablish their roles as heads of families. The presence of the veil is a sign that the males of the household are once more able to assume the responsibilities that were disturbed or usurped by foreign colonial powers.

But a veiled woman is seldom seen in Egypt or in many parts of Lebanon, Syria, Iran, Tunisia, Turkey, or the Sudan. And as respectable housewives have abandoned the veil, in some of these Middle Eastern countries prostitutes have put it on. They indicate their availability by manipulating the veil in flirtatious ways, but as Burton pointed out more than a century ago, prostitutes are not the first to discover the veil's seductiveness. Like women's garments in the West, the veil can be sturdy, utilitarian, and forbidding—or it can be filmy and decorative, hinting at the charms beneath it.

25   The veil is the outward sign of a complex reality. Observers are often deceived by the absence of that sign, and fail to see that in most Middle East-

ern societies (and in many parts of Europe) basic attitudes are unchanged. Women who have taken off the veil continue to play the old roles within the family, and their chastity remains crucial. A woman's behavior is still the key to the honor and the reputation of her family.

In Middle Eastern societies, feminine and masculine continue to be strong polarities of identification. This is marked contrast to Western society, where for more than a generation social critics have been striving to blur distinctions in dress, in status, and in type of labor. Almost all Middle Eastern reformers (most of whom are middle and upper class) are still arguing from the assumption of a fundamental difference between men and women. They do not demand an end to the veil (which is passing out of use anyway) but an end to the old principles, which the veil symbolizes, that govern patrilineal society. Middle Eastern reformers are calling for equal access to divorce, child custody, and inheritance; equal opportunities for education and employment; abolition of female circumcision and "crimes of honor"; and a law regulating the age of marriage.

An English woman film director, after several months in Morocco, said in an interview, "This business about the veil is nonsense. We all have our veils, between ourselves and other people. That's not what the Middle East is about. The question is what veils are used for, and by whom." The veil triggers Western reactions simply because it is the dramatic, visible sign of vexing questions, questions that are still being debated, problems that have still not been solved, in the Middle East or in Western societies.

Given the biological differences between men and women, how are the sexes to be treated equitably? Men and women are supposed to share the labor of society and yet provide for the reproduction and nurture of the next generation. If male fear and awe of woman's sexuality provokes them to control and seclude women, can they be assuaged? Rebecca West said long ago that "the difference between men and women is the rock on which civilization will split before it can reach any goal that could justify its expenditure of effort." Until human beings come to terms with this basic issue, purdah and the veil, in some form, will continue to exist in both the East and the West.

References

Abou-Zeid, Ahmed, "Honor and Shame among the Bedouins of Egypt," *Honor and Shame: The Values of Mediterranean Society*, ed. by J. G. Peristiany, University of Chicago Press, 1966.

Fernea, Elizabeth Warnock, *Guests of the Sheik: An Ethnology of an Iraqi Village*, Doubleday/Anchor, 1969.

Fernea, Elizabeth Warnock, and Basima Qattan Bezirgan, eds., *Middle Eastern Muslim Women Speak*, University of Texas Press, 1977.

Levy, Reuben, *The Social Structure of Islam*, Cambridge University Press, 1965.

Mernissi, Fatima, *Beyond the Veil: Male-Female Dynamics in a Modern Muslim Society*, Schenkman Publishing Company, 1975.

Pitt-Rivers, Julian, *The Fate of Schechem: or The Politics of Sex*, Cambridge University Press, 1977.

Engaging the Text

1. Why, according to the authors, is the practice of veiling women in Middle Eastern countries most frequently encountered in affluent, male-dominated extended families? What attitudes toward female sexuality help explain the veiling of women and the practice of purdah?

2. The authors use interviews and the testimony of experts to support their analysis as to why veiling and purdah continue to exist in Middle Eastern societies. Do you detect a bias on the authors' part either for or against this practice? Explain your answer.

3. How is the practice of veiling tied in with other important cultural values and institutions in Middle Eastern societies?

Exploring Your Cultural Perspective

1. Select one of the following, and write an essay in response. Create a dialogue between someone who is in favor of the practice of veiling and someone who is very much against it. If you were a woman living in a society where wearing the chador was a matter of personal choice, would you choose to do so or not? Explain your answer. If you were a man in that society, would you prefer to see women completely veiled? Why or why not?

2. What current views on the question of *hijab* can you discover by consulting either of the following Web sites: The Muslim Women's Home Page <http://www.albany.edu/~ha4934/sisters.html> or Understanding Islam <http://darkwing.uoregon.edu/~kbatarfi/islam.html>? To what extent have traditional cultural values changed since the Ferneas did their groundbreaking study in 1979? You might consider recent laws in Afghanistan that make it a crime for women to appear in public without veils.

3. Does the photograph in Figure 3.3 communicate what Fernea and Fernea say about purdah? Why or why not?

FIGURE 3.3

LIZA DALBY

Kimono

Liza Dalby received a doctorate in anthropology from Stanford University. Dalby, who is fluent in Japanese, became the only non-Japanese ever accepted by geisha during a yearlong residence in Kyoto. The profession of geisha originated in the eighteenth century. As their popularity grew, geisha became society's fashion arbiters, and their sophisticated style had a great impact on the art, music, and literature of nineteenth-century Japan. The world of the geisha offers a unique glimpse into a disciplined and glamorous way of life that is quintessentially Japanese. Dalby is the author of *Kimono: Fashion in Culture* (1993). Her latest work is *The Tale of Murasaki* (2000). This piece, a chapter drawn from her book *Geisha* (1998), provides insight into the social codes embodied in the kimono, the traditional costume worn by geisha.

Thinking Critically
As you read this selection, consider what the kimono communicates about Japanese cultural values.

A month after I returned to the United States, I was invited to appear on the "To Tell the Truth" television show because of my odd distinction of being the only non-Japanese ever to have become a geisha. The object for the panelists would be to guess the identiy of the real "geisha anthropologist," so I had dressed myself and the two women pretending to be me in cotton kimono. As we walked through the program's format during rehearsal, each of us was to announce, "My name is Liza Crihfield," then step ten paces to our seats facing the panel at stage left. The director shook her head in dismay before we even took our places. "Stop," she called. "You've just given it away."

After my year-long training as a geisha, the technique of walking gracefully in a kimono had become second nature. The two poseurs, though they had diligently studied my research proposal in order to anticipate questions from the panel, could not, in an afternoon, master the art of walking. It was quite obvious who was who before we even opened our mouths.

Repeatedly I showed them the technique of sliding one foot, pigeon-toed, in front of the other with knees slightly bent. I tried to convey how the shoulders should have a barely perceptible slope, how the arms should be carried gracefully, close to the body. We tried to minimize the contrast. They made great efforts to mimic an authentic movement, while I attempted to recreate the clumsiness of my own first experience in wearing kimono. Even so, on the show the next day, none of the panelists except Bill Cullen was fooled a bit. I am convinced that our body language had "told the truth."

Learning to wear kimono properly was one of the most difficult aspects of my geisha training. But it was essential so that I could fit without awkwardness into a group of geisha. No one gives geisha formal lessons in how to wear kimono. Most of them have learned how to move gracefully in kimono by virtue of their practice of Japanese dance. Awkward gestures are noticed immediately by the watchful mothers, who seldom fail to utter a reproof to a fidgety maiko.

When I lived in Pontochō, the sardonic old auntie who worked at the Mitsuba invariably had some critical remark when I checked in for okāsan's approval of my outfit before going off to a teahouse engagement. I usually managed to put together a feasible color combination of kimono, obi, and *obi-age* (the sheer, scarf-like sash that is tied so as to be barely visible above the obi), but it was many months before I could proceed on my way to a party without something having to be untied and retied properly. Only when I reached the point where I could put on the entire outfit in less than twenty minutes by myself did I finally win the grudging respect of the old auntie who tended the inn.

THE LANGUAGE OF KIMONO

Wearing kimono is one of the things that distinguishes geisha from other women in Japan. Geisha wear their kimono with a flair just not seen in middle-class ladies who, once or twice a year, pull out their traditional dress to attend a wedding, a graduation, or perhaps a retirement ceremony. They are uncomfortable in the unaccustomed garment, and it shows.

To the untutored eye, the kimono a geisha chooses are much the same as those any other Japanese woman might wear. The resplendent trailing black robe with deep reverse décolletage is the geisha's official outfit, but she actually wears it infrequently. Her usual garment is an ankle-length, medium-sleeve silk kimono in slightly more subdued colors than those other women wear. The subtle differences in sleeve openings, in color, or in the manner of tying the obi that set a geisha apart are not immediately obvious, even to many Japanese. But together with her natural way of wearing the outfit, such cues are visible to an observer who is sensitive to the language of kimono. A connoisseur will know the wide vocabulary of elements that varies according to the region, class, age, and profession of the wearer. He or she will be able to recognize a geisha easily.

The elements of the kimono costume in fact constitute a social code. This was revealed to me when I inadvertently mixed up some of them early in my geisha career, before I had acquired an appropriate wardrobe from the taller geisha in the neighborhood. In the beginning, the only kimono I owned was one that Yuriko, my well-to-do middle-aged friend in Tokyo, had given me. It was a lovely burnt orange color with a pattern of weeping willow branches in brown shot with gold. She had worn it a few times many years ago, before she had married. Now the colors were inappropriate to her age, and besides, she told me, she never wore kimono any more. She doubted she could even tie the obi by herself.

When okāsan first asked me to help her out at a party at the Mitsuba so I could see the geisha's side of the affair, I gladly agreed and planned to wear my only kimono. As she helped me put it on, she remarked that, lovely as it was, it would be entirely unsuitable in the future. It was the sort of thing a stylish bourgeois young lady might wear, not a geisha. It would have to do for that evening, though. She loaned me a tea-green obi with a pale cream orchid dyed into the back and gave me an old obi-age sash that she had worn as an apprentice many years ago.

10   The obi-age was of sheer white silk with a pattern of scattered fans done in a dapple-effect tie-dying technique called *kanoko*. Okāsan slipped it over the pad that held the back loop of the obi secure, and as she tied it in the front she said, "Here is a trick for keeping the front knot in place. All the geisha tie their obi-age this way." She made a little loose slipknot in one end, making sure the red fan pattern showed at the front of the knot, then drew the other end through. The effect was of a simply knotted sash, but without the bulk of both ends tied together. She smoothed and tucked this light sash down behind the top of the obi, so that only a glimpse of the red and white was visible. At the time, I was reminded of letting a bit of lace show at the neckline of a blouse. Since the obi-age is technically considered part of the "kimono underwear," my thought was more apt than I first realized.

Still wearing this outfit, I went out after the party. Later than evening I met a pair of college teachers at a nearby bar. We struck up a conversation, and I told them a bit about the circumstances of my being in Japan. The bartender, half listening in, finally exclaimed, "Aha, now I realize what was bothering me about you. You said you were a student, and I could tell that you're an unmarried young lady from a proper family. Your kimono is perfectly appropriate. But I think it's your sash, something about the way it's tied, that struck me as odd for a young lady—something too much like a geisha about it." As I had not yet said anything about the precise subject of my study, I was astounded at the acuity of the man's eye.

Incongruent as it was, my outfit that evening expressed my odd position rather well. Not exactly an *ojōsan*, a demure young lady, not yet a geisha, I was attired in disparate elements of each style, so I presented an odd aspect to someone with a perspicacious eye for dress. The bartender had received all the messages my outfit conveyed but was puzzled at the totality, as well he might have been.

KIMONO WEARERS

Mono means "thing," and with *ki-* from *kiru*, "to wear," kimono originally meant simply "a garment." Not all things to wear are kimono, however. Today, the relevant distinction is between *yōfuku*, "Western apparel," and *wafuku*, "native apparel": kimono. Western clothes, following all the latest fashion trends, are what most Japanese women wear most of the time. Some women don't even own a kimono, and many, like my friend Yuriko in Tokyo, have forgotten how to wear those they have tucked away in the Japanese equivalent of cedar chests. Few if any social occasions in Japan now would exclude a woman because she was not dressed in kimono.

Most women own a black kimono dyed with the family crest that they will pull out of a drawer for a few highly formal occasions. This garment was probably the main item in their wedding trousseaux. Families are encouraged to buy their young daughters the gaudy, long-sleeved *furisode*-style kimono for New Year, so a woman often has one of these packed away from her girlhood as well. Such occasional use means that most Japanese women are nearly as unaccustomed to the proper manner of wearing kimono as a foreigner would be. They sigh with relief when they can finally unwind the stiff obi from around their waists and slip back into comfortable Western clothes.

As my eye became educated to the niceties of kimono, I was more and more struck by how many women who put one on fail to achieve a graceful demeanor. A good time to view masses of kimono is the New Year holiday. Young girls, who trudge to school in loafers all year, suddenly mince about in traditional *zōri* that match their long-sleeved kimono. Arms swinging, knees pumping up and down as they do in skirts, the girls flock on the streets like pinioned flamingos. Colorful and clumsy, they brighten the bleak January streets briefly before donning their familiar blue and white school uniforms again at the end of holidays. Women over fifty generally feel more at home than this in kimono. They probably wore the traditional dress as children and feel a pang of nostalgia when they put it on. *15*

Middle-class women of means are now rediscovering the conspicuous display afforded by kimono. The wearing of wafuku, as opposed to the Cacharel skirts and Dior blouses of their friends, has become a fashionable hobby.

A woman who would blanch at spending two hundred dollars on a dress could easily justify spending five times as much on a kimono. After all, a kimono is an investment. It won't go out of style, it can accommodate thickening midriffs without alteration, and it can be passed on to one's daughters. In the status game, it is difficult to spend more than a thousand dollars on even the most skillfully tailored Western dress. But with kimono, one can easily wear thousands of dollars on one's back without looking too obvious. The expensive yet understated possibilities of kimono are ideally suited to this aspect of fashion one-upmanship.

Yet the wearing of kimono is not without problems in modern Japan. Aside from the matter of expense, kimono inherently belong to a different style and pace of life. That life still thrives here and there, but usually under special circumstances—as are found, for example, in the geisha world. Few would call the beautiful kimono a practical garment for modern living.

Floors versus Chairs

The kimono was once part of a cultural totality that embraced every aspect of daily life. The garment was influenced by, and in turn it influenced, canons of feminine beauty that enhanced some parts of the body (nape, ankle, and hip) and concealed others (waist, legs, and bosom). Not surprisingly, the kimono flatters a figure found most often in Japanese women: a long waist and long thigh but small bust and short calf. Cultural notions of ideal beauty seem to influence actual physical characteristics, however; as Western notions of long-legged, big-bosomed glamour have affected postwar Japan, amazingly, such physical types seem to have blossomed. The cultivation of this new type of figure does not bode well for the kimono.

The wearing of kimono was also perfectly integrated into the arrangement of living space in the traditional Japanese home. Much of the activity of daily life was conducted close to the floor, on low tables where people knelt, not sat, to accomplish tasks. To Japanese, a shod foot treading the floor inside the house would be as gauche as shoes on a Westerner's dining room table. Floors were clean enough to permit trailing garments, and the wives of wealthy men let their robes swirl about their feet as they glided down polished halls from one tatami mat room to another. The trailing hem contributed to the overall balance of the outfit, creating an effect of elegance. Again, nowadays one must look to the geisha's formal kimono to see what that style was like. Ordinary modern kimono are adjusted, by a fold at the waist, to reach only the ankle. The line, rather than flowing, is somewhat stiff and tubular.

20   The integration of cultural elements that formed the whole of which kimono was a part has now fragmented. The single most nefarious artifact

in this respect is the chair. Chairs are antithetical to kimono, physically and aesthetically.

Women who wear kimono of course sit on chairs, but the garment is poorly adapted to this posture; it is designed for sitting on the floor. When Americans sit on the floor, this implies a greater degree of relaxation than does sitting on a chair. Not so in Japan. A chair is comfortable and relaxed compared to the straight-spine posture required to sit properly on the tatami floor. There are two different verbs meaning "to sit" in Japanese, depending on whether it is on the floor or in a chair. If in a chair, then one literally "drapes one's hips" there.

When, out of determination to show the Japanese that we understand etiquette, we Westerners endure a tea ceremony or traditional banquet sitting on the floor, after thirty minutes our knees are jelly and our legs so benumbed they refuse to obey our brain's directive to stand. We are consoled that young Japanese have much the same problem. Part of the exhaustion we feel is due to the gradual slumping of our unsupported backs. Skirts ride up, pants become constricting, narrow belts bite into our waists. But the kimono that became disheveled and kept us perched uncomfortably at the edge of a chair now offers back support with the obi, and it turns out to be almost comfortable in the posture for which it was designed.

The back view of a kneeling kimono-clad woman shows off the garment to its best advantage. The obi often has a large single design woven or painted on the back part, which forms a large, flat loop in the common style of tying known as *taiko*, (drum). This flat drum, not quite a square foot in area, is framed by the contrasting color of the kimono. I have often been struck by the artfulness of a seated figure, Japanese style. In a chair, the drum of the obi is not only hidden from view, it is a positive nuisance, as it prevents one from sitting back.

The fact that the back view of a kimono-clad figure is such an aesthetic focus has to do, I think, with the way a traditional Japanese room is arranged and how a woman in public (such as a geisha) moves and is viewed on a social occasion. At a banquet, low, narrow tables are laid end to end, forming a continuous row that parallels three sides of the room. People sit on individual flat square cushions along the outer edge of this U-shaped arrangement. In effect, everyone sits next to someone, but nobody sits across from anyone else.

The seating positions are hierarchical: the places of highest status are in front of the alcove, and the lowest are those closest to the entrance. People usually have a keen sense of where they stand vis-à-vis one another's status in Japan, so the problem of where they sit is solved with a minimum of polite protestation. When everyone has taken a seat, the banquet can begin. After it has started, however, people leave their original places to wander across the center of the room, squatting temporarily in front of different personages to make a toast or have a short conversation. This center space is a no-man's- 25 land, ringed as it is by the prescribed statuses of the proper seats on the other side of the tables. Here more relaxed conviviality can occur.

When geisha attend upon a banquet, they often move into the center free space, kneeling for a few minutes across from one guest after another. As they do so, their backs are turned toward an entire row of tables on the other side of the room. The first time I was a guest at a traditional banquet, I noticed the beauty of the backs of the geisha as they talked with other guests. Upon reflection, it hardly seems accidental that the view from that particular vantage point was so striking.

Engaging the Text

1. In what way does the kimono serve as a complex signaling system that embodies and communicates traditional Japanese values?

2. Dalby says that "chairs are antithetical to kimono, physically and aesthetically." What does she mean by this, and how does this insight provide a glimpse into a traditional world that modern Japanese remember somewhat nostalgically?

Exploring Your Cultural Perspective

1. Describe some costumes of contemporary Western culture that share some of the features of the kimono. These might include a ball gown or white tie and tails, which symbolize elegance and refinement and are expensive and uncomfortable. To what extent do these outfits perform the same function in Western culture that the kimono does in Japan?

2. How does clothing in the United States govern how one sits? Does it make a difference whether you are wearing formal or informal clothing? What are some differences between the ways that men and women are supposed to sit?

3. In your opinion, was becoming a geisha for Dalby simply an exercise in fieldwork? Might she have chosen to remain in Japan in this profession? What does your answer tell you about your cultural assumptions?

CHITRA BANERJEE DIVAKARUNI
Clothes

Chitra Banerjee Divakaruni grew up in India, earned a PhD in English at the University of California, Berkeley, and is currently a professor at Foothill College in California. This short story is drawn from her collection *Arranged Marriage* (1995), which won the American Book Award. She has also written *The Mistress of Spices* (1997), *Sister of My Heart* (1999), and *Black Candle: Poems about Women from India, Pakistan, and Bangladesh* (2000). Divakaruni is especially adept at dramatizing the struggles of women from India who attempt to adjust to life in the United States.

Thinking Critically

As you read, underline and annotate the passages where the story dramatizes how the outfits worn by the main character reflect important changes in her life. In what way do different outfits in your wardrobe symbolize different sides of your personality?

The water of the women's lake laps against my breasts, cool, calming. I can feel it beginning to wash the hot nervousness away from my body. The little waves tickle my armpits, make my sari float up around me, wet and yellow, like a sunflower after rain. I close my eyes and smell the sweet brown odor of the *ritha* pulp my friends Deepali and Radha are working into my hair so it will glisten with little lights this evening. They scrub with more vigor than usual and wash it out more carefully, because today is a special day. It is the day of my bride-viewing.

"Ei, Sumita! Mita! Are you deaf?" Radha says. "This is the third time I've asked you the same question."

"Look at her, already dreaming about her husband, and she hasn't even seen him yet!" Deepali jokes. Then she adds, the envy in her voice only half hidden, "Who cares about friends from a little Indian village when you're about to go live in America?"

I want to deny it, to say that I will always love them and all the things we did together through my growing-up years—visiting the *charak* fair where we always ate too many sweets, raiding the neighbor's guava tree summer after-noons while the grown-ups slept, telling fairy tales while we braided each other's hair in elaborate patterns we'd invented. *And she married the handsome prince who took her to his kingdom beyond the seven seas.* But already the activities of our girlhood seem to be far in my past, the colors leached out of them, like old sepia photographs.

5   His name is Somesh Sen, the man who is coming to our house with his parents today and who will be my husband "if I'm lucky enough to be chosen," as my aunt says. He is coming all the way from California. Father showed it to me yesterday, on the metal globe that sits on his desk, a chunky pink wedge on the side of a multicolored slab marked *Untd. Sts. of America.* I touched it and felt the excitement leap all the way up my arm like an electric shock. Then it died away, leaving only a beaten-metal coldness against my fingertips.

For the first time it occurred to me that if things worked out the way every-one was hoping, I'd be going halfway around the world to live with a man I hadn't even met. Would I ever see my parents again? *Don't send me so far away,* I wanted to cry, but of course I didn't. It would be ungrateful. Father had worked so hard to find this match for me. Besides, wasn't it every woman's des-tiny, as Mother was always telling me, to leave the known for the unknown? She had done it, and her mother before her. *A married woman belongs to her hus-band, her in-laws.* Hot seeds of tears pricked my eyelids at the unfairness of it.

"Mita Moni, little jewel," Father said, calling me by my childhood name. He put out his hand as though he wanted to touch my face, then let it fall to his side. "He's a good man. Comes from a fine family. He will be kind to you." He was silent for a while. Finally he said, "Come, let me show you the special sari I bought in Calcutta for you to wear at the bride-viewing."

"Are you nervous?" Radha asks as she wraps my hair in a soft cotton towel. Her parents are also trying to arrange a marriage for her. So far three families have come to see her, but no one has chosen her because her skin-color is con-sidered too dark. "Isn't it terrible, not knowing what's going to happen?"

I nod because I don't want to disagree, don't want to make her feel bad by saying that sometimes it's worse when you know what's coming, like I do. I knew it as soon as Father unlocked his mahogany *almirah* and took out the sari.

10   It was the most expensive sari I had ever seen, and surely the most beauti-ful. Its body was a pale pink, like the dawn sky over the women's lake. The color of transition. Embroidered all over it were tiny stars made out of real gold *zari* thread.

"Here, hold it," said Father.

The sari was unexpectedly heavy in my hands, silk-slippery, a sari to walk carefully in. A sari that could change one's life. I stood there holding it, want-ing to weep. I knew that when I wore it, it would hang in perfect pleats to my feet and shimmer in the light of the evening lamps. It would dazzle Somesh and his parents and they would choose me to be his bride.

When the plane takes off, I try to stay calm, to take deep, slow breaths like Father does when he practices yoga. But my hands clench themselves on to the folds of my sari and when I force them open, after the *fasten seat belt* and *no smoking* signs have blinked off, I see they have left damp blotches on the delicate crushed fabric.

We had some arguments about this sari. I wanted a blue one for the journey, because blue is the color of possibility, the color of the sky through which I would be traveling. But Mother said there must be red in it because red is the color of luck for married women. Finally, Father found one to satisfy us both: midnight-blue with a thin red border the same color as the marriage mark I'm wearing on my forehead.

It is hard for me to think of myself as a married woman. I whisper my new   *15* name to myself, Mrs. Sumita Sen, but the syllables rustle uneasily in my mouth like a stiff satin that's never been worn.

Somesh had to leave for America just a week after the wedding. He had to get back to the store, he explained to me. He had promised his partner. The store. It seems more real to me than Somesh—perhaps because I know more about it. It was what we had mostly talked about the night after the wedding, the first night we were together alone. It stayed open twenty-four hours, yes, all night, every night, not like the Indian stores which closed at dinnertime and sometimes in the hottest part of the afternoon. That's why his partner needed him back.

The store was called *7-Eleven*. I thought it a strange name, exotic, risky. All the stores I knew were piously named after gods and goddesses—*Ganesh Sweet House, Lakshmi Vastralaya for Fine Saris*—to bring the owners luck.

The store sold all kinds of amazing things—apple juice in cardboard cartons that never leaked; American bread that came in cellophane packages, already cut up; canisters of potato chips, each large grainy flake curved exactly like the next. The large refrigerator with see-through doors held beer and wine, which Somesh said were the most popular items.

"That's where the money comes from, especially in the neighborhood where our store is," said Somesh, smiling at the shocked look on my face. (The only places I knew of that sold alcohol were the village toddy shops, "dark, stinking dens of vice," Father called them.) "A lot of Americans drink, you know. It's a part of their culture, not considered immoral, like it is here. And really, there's nothing wrong with it." He touched my lips lightly with his finger. "When you come to California, I'll get you some sweet white wine and you'll see how good it makes you feel. . . ." Now his fingers were stroking my cheeks, my throat, moving downward. I closed my eyes and tried not to jerk away because after all it was my wifely duty.

20   "It helps if you can think about something else," my friend Madhavi had said when she warned me about what most husbands demanded on the very first night. Two years married, she already had one child and was pregnant with a second one.

I tried to think of the women's lake, the dark cloudy green of the *shapla* leaves that float on the water, but his lips were hot against my skin, his fingers fumbling with buttons, pulling at the cotton night-sari I wore. I couldn't breathe.

"Bite hard on your tongue," Madhavi had advised. "The pain will keep your mind off what's going on down there."

But when I bit down, it hurt so much that I cried out. I couldn't help it although I was ashamed. Somesh lifted his head. I don't know what he saw on my face, but he stopped right away. "Shhh," he said, although I had made myself silent already. "It's OK, we'll wait until you feel like it." I tried to apologize but he smiled it away and started telling me some more about the store.

And that's how it was the rest of the week until he left. We would lie side by side on the big white bridal pillow I had embroidered with a pair of doves for married harmony, and Somesh would describe how the store's front windows were decorated with a flashing neon Dewar's sign and a lighted Budweiser waterfall *this big*. I would watch his hands moving excitedly through the dim air of the bedroom and think that Father had been right, he was a good man, my husband, a kind, patient man. And so handsome, too, I would add, stealing a quick look at the strong curve of his jaw, feeling luckier than I had any right to be.

25   The night before he left, Somesh confessed that the store wasn't making much money yet. "I'm not worried, I'm sure it soon will," he added, his fingers pleating the edge of my sari. "But I just don't want to give you the wrong impression, don't want you to be disappointed."

In the half dark I could see he had turned toward me. His face, with two vertical lines between the brows, looked young, apprehensive, in need of protection. I'd never seen that on a man's face before. Something rose in me like a wave.

"It's all right," I said, as though to a child, and pulled his head down to my breast. His hair smelled faintly of the American cigarettes he smoked. "I won't be disappointed. I'll help you." And a sudden happiness filled me.

That night I dreamed I was at the store. Soft American music floated in the background as I moved between shelves stocked high with brightly colored cans and elegant-necked bottles, turning their labels carefully to the front, polishing them until they shone.

Now, sitting inside this metal shell that is hurtling through emptiness, I try to remember other things about my husband: how gentle his hands had been, and his lips, surprisingly soft, like a woman's. How I've longed for them through those drawn-out nights while I waited for my visa to arrive. He will be standing at the customs gate, and when I reach him, he will lower his face to mine. We will kiss in front of everyone, not caring, like Americans, then pull back, look each other in the eye, and smile.

But suddenly, as I am thinking this, I realize I cannot recall Somesh's face.   *30*
I try and try until my head hurts, but I can only visualize the black air swirling outside the plane, too thin for breathing. My own breath grows ragged with panic as I think of it and my mouth fills with sour fluid the way it does just before I throw up.

I grope for something to hold on to, something beautiful and talismanic from my old life. And then I remember. Somewhere down under me, low in the belly of the plane, inside my new brown case which is stacked in the dark with a hundred others, are my saris. Thick Kanjeepuram silks in solid purples and golden yellows, the thin hand-woven cottons of the Bengal countryside, green as a young banana plant, gray as the women's lake on a monsoon morning. Already I can feel my shoulders loosening up, my breath steadying. My wedding Benarasi, flame-orange, with a wide *palloo* of gold-embroidered dancing peacocks. Fold upon fold of Dhakais so fine they can be pulled through a ring. Into each fold my mother has tucked a small sachet of sandalwood powder to protect the saris from the unknown insects of America. Little silk sachets, made from *her* old saris—I can smell their calm fragrance as I watch the American air hostess wheeling the dinner cart toward my seat. It is the smell of my mother's hands.

I know then that everything will be all right. And when the air hostess bends her curly golden head to ask me what I would like to eat, I understand every word in spite of her strange accent and answer her without stumbling even once over the unfamiliar English phrases.

Late at night I stand in front of our bedroom mirror trying on the clothes Somesh has bought for me and smuggled in past his parents. I model each one for him, walking back and forth, clasping my hands behind my head, lips pouted, left hip thrust out just like the models on TV, while he whispers applause. I'm breathless with suppressed laughter (Father and Mother Sen must not hear us) and my cheeks are hot with the delicious excitement of conspiracy. We've stuffed a towel at the bottom of the door so no light will shine through.

I'm wearing a pair of jeans now, marveling at the curves of my hips and thighs, which have always been hidden under the flowing lines of my saris.

I love the color, the same pale blue as the *nayantara* flowers that grow in my parents' garden. The solid comforting weight. The jeans come with a close-fitting T-shirt which outlines my breasts.

35   I scold Somesh to hide my embarrassed pleasure. He shouldn't have been so extravagant. We can't afford it. He just smiles.

The T-shirt is sunrise-orange—the color, I decide, of joy, of my new American life. Across its middle, in large black letters, is written *Great America*. I was sure the letters referred to the country, but Somesh told me it is the name of an amusement park, a place where people go to have fun. I think it a wonderful concept, novel. Above the letters is the picture of a train. Only it's not a train, Somesh tells me, it's a roller coaster. He tries to explain how it moves, the insane speed, the dizzy ground falling away, then gives up. "I'll take you there, Mita sweetheart," he says, "as soon as we move into our own place."

That's our dream (mine more than his, I suspect)—moving out of this two-room apartment where it seems to me if we all breathed in at once, there would be no air left. Where I must cover my head with the edge of my Japan nylon sari (my expensive Indian ones are to be saved for special occasions—trips to the temple, Bengali New Year) and serve tea to the old women that come to visit Mother Sen, where like a good Indian wife I must never address my husband by his name. Where even in our bed we kiss guiltily, uneasily, listening for the giveaway creak of springs. Sometimes I laugh to myself, thinking how ironic it is that after all my fears about America, my life has turned out to be no different from Deepali's or Radha's. But at other times I feel caught in a world where everything is frozen in place, like a scene inside a glass paperweight. It is a world so small that if I were to stretch out my arms, I would touch its cold unyielding edges. I stand inside this glass world, watching helplessly as America rushes by, wanting to scream. Then I'm ashamed. Mita, I tell myself, you're growing westernized. Back home you'd never have felt this way.

We must be patient. I know that. Tactful, loving children. That is the Indian way. "I'm their life," Somesh tells me as we lie beside each other, lazy from lovemaking. He's not boasting, merely stating a fact. "They've always been there when I needed them. I could never abandon them at some old people's home." For a moment I feel rage. You're constantly thinking of them, I want to scream. But what about me? Then I remember my own parents, Mother's hands cool on my sweat-drenched body through nights of fever, Father teaching me to read, his finger moving along the crisp black angles of the alphabet, transforming them magically into things I knew, water, dog, mango tree. I beat back my unreasonable desire and nod agreement.

Somesh has bought me a cream blouse with a long brown skirt. They match beautifully, like the inside and outside of an almond. "For when you begin working," he says. But first he wants me to start college. Get a degree, perhaps in teaching. I picture myself in front of a classroom of girls with blond pigtails and blue uniforms, like a scene out of an English movie I saw long ago in Calcutta. They raise their hands respectfully when I ask a question. "Do you really think I can?" I ask. "Of course," he replies.

I am gratified he has such confidence in me. But I have another plan, a   *40* secret that I will divulge to him once we move. What I really want is to work in the store. I want to stand behind the counter in the cream-and-brown skirt set (color of earth, color of seeds) and ring up purchases. The register drawer will glide open. Confident, I will count out green dollars and silver quarters. Gleaming copper pennies. I will dust the jars of gilt-wrapped chocolates on the counter. Will straighten, on the far wall, posters of smiling young men raising their beer mugs to toast scantily clad redheads with huge spiky eyelashes. (I have never visited the store—my in-laws don't consider it proper for a wife— but of course I know exactly what it looks like.) I will charm the customers with my smile, so that they will return again and again just to hear me telling them to have a nice day.

Meanwhile, I will the store to make money for us. Quickly. Because when we move, we'll be paying for two households. But so far it hasn't worked. They're running at a loss, Somesh tells me. They had to let the hired help go. This means most nights Somesh has to take the graveyard shift (that horrible word, like a cold hand up my spine) because his partner refuses to.

"The bastard!" Somesh spat out once. "Just because he put in more money he thinks he can order me around. I'll show him!" I was frightened by the vicious twist of his mouth. Somehow I'd never imagined that he could be angry.

Often Somesh leaves as soon as he has dinner and doesn't get back till after I've made morning tea for Father and Mother Sen. I lie mostly awake those nights, picturing masked intruders crouching in the shadowed back of the store, like I've seen on the police shows that Father Sen sometimes watches. But Somesh insists there's nothing to worry about, they have bars on the windows and a burglar alarm. "And remember," he says, "the extra cash will help us move out that much quicker."

I'm wearing a nightie now, my very first one. It's black and lacy, with a bit of a shine to it, and it glides over my hips to stop outrageously at mid-thigh. My mouth is an O of surprise in the mirror, my legs long and pale and sleek from the hair remover I asked Somesh to buy me last week. The legs of a movie star. Somesh laughs at the look on my face, then says, "You're beautiful." His voice starts a flutter low in my belly.

"Do you really think so," I ask, mostly because I want to hear him say it   *45* again. No one has called me beautiful before. My father would have thought it inappropriate, my mother that it would make me vain.

Somesh draws me close. "Very beautiful," he whispers. "The most beautiful woman in the whole world." His eyes are not joking as they usually are. I want to turn off the light, but "Please," he says, "I want to keep seeing your face." His fingers are taking the pins from my hair, undoing my braids. The escaped strands fall on his face like dark rain. We have already decided where we will hide my new American clothes—the jeans and T-shirt camouflaged on a hanger among Somesh's pants, the skirt set and nightie at the bottom of my suitcase, a sandalwood sachet tucked between them, waiting.

I stand in the middle of our empty bedroom, my hair still wet from the purification bath, my back to the stripped bed I can't bear to look at. I hold in my hands the plain white sari I'm supposed to wear. I must hurry. Any minute now there'll be a knock at the door. They are afraid to leave me alone too long, afraid I might do something to myself.

The sari, a thick voile that will bunch around the waist when worn, is borrowed. White. Widow's color, color of endings. I try to tuck it into the top of the petticoat, but my fingers are numb, disobedient. It spills through them and there are waves and waves of white around my feet. I kick out in sudden rage, but the sari is too soft, it gives too easily. I grab up an edge, clamp down with my teeth and pull, feeling a fierce, bitter satisfaction when I hear it rip.

There's a cut, still stinging, on the side of my right arm, halfway to the elbow. It is from the bangle-breaking ceremony. Old Mrs. Ghosh performed the ritual, since she's a widow, too. She took my hands in hers and brought them down hard on the bedpost, so that the glass bangles I was wearing shattered and multicolored shards flew out in every direction. Some landed on the body that was on the bed, covered with a sheet. I can't call it Somesh. He was gone already. She took an edge of the sheet and rubbed the red marriage mark off my forehead. She was crying. All the women in the room were crying except me. I watched them as though from the far end of a tunnel. Their flared nostrils, their red-veined eyes, the runnels of tears, salt-corrosive, down their cheeks.

50 It happened last night. He was at the store. "It isn't too bad," he would tell me on the days when he was in a good mood. "Not too many customers. I can put up my feet and watch MTV all night. I can sing along with Michael Jackson as loud as I want." He had a good voice, Somesh. Sometimes he would sing softly at night, lying in bed, holding me. Hindi songs of love, *Mere Sapnon Ki Rani*, queen of my dreams. (He would not sing American songs at home out of respect for his parents, who thought they were decadent.) I would feel his warm breath on my hair as I fell asleep.

Someone came into the store last night. He took all the money, even the little rolls of pennies I had helped Somesh make up. Before he left he emptied the bullets from his gun into my husband's chest.

"Only thing is," Somesh would say about the night shifts, "I really miss you. I sit there and think of you asleep in bed. Do you know that when you sleep you make your hands into fists, like a baby? When we move out, will you come along some nights to keep me company?"

My in-laws are good people, kind. They made sure the body was covered before they let me into the room. When someone asked if my hair should be cut off, as they sometimes do with widows back home, they said no. They said I could stay at the apartment with Mrs. Ghosh if I didn't want to go to the crematorium. They asked Dr. Das to give me something to calm me down when I couldn't stop shivering. They didn't say, even once, as people would surely have in the village, that it was my bad luck that brought death to their son so soon after his marriage.

They will probably go back to India now. There's nothing here for them anymore. They will want me to go with them. You're like our daughter, they will say. Your home is with us, for as long as you want. For the rest of your life. *The rest of my life.* I can't think about that yet. It makes me dizzy. Fragments are flying about my head, multicolored and piercing sharp like bits of bangle glass.

I want you to go to college. Choose a career. I stand in front of a classroom of 55 smiling children who love me in my cream-and-brown American dress. A faceless parade straggles across my eyelids: all those customers at the store that I will never meet. The lace nightie, fragrant with sandalwood, waiting in its blackness inside my suitcase. The savings book where we have $3605.33. *Four thousand and we can move out, maybe next month.* The name of the panty hose I'd asked him to buy me for my birthday: sheer golden-beige. His lips, unexpectedly soft, woman-smooth. Elegant-necked wine bottles swept off shelves, shattering on the floor.

I know Somesh would not have tried to stop the gunman. I can picture his silhouette against the lighted Dewar's sign, hands raised. He is trying to find the right expression to put on his face, calm, reassuring, reasonable. *OK, take the money. No, I won't call the police.* His hands tremble just a little. His eyes darken with disbelief as his fingers touch his chest and come away wet.

I yanked away the cover. I had to see. *Great America, a place where people go to have fun.* My breath roller-coasting through my body, my unlived life gathering itself into a scream. I'd expected blood, a lot of blood, the deep red-black of it crusting his chest. But they must have cleaned him up at the hospital. He was dressed in his silk wedding *kurta.* Against its warm ivory his face appeared remote, stern. The musky aroma of his aftershave lotion that someone must have sprinkled on the body. It didn't quite hide that other smell, thin, sour, metallic. The smell of death. The floor shifted under me, tilting like a wave.

I'm lying on the floor now, on the spilled white sari. I feel sleepy. Or perhaps it is some other feeling I don't have a word for. The sari is seductive-soft, drawing me into its folds.

Sometimes, bathing at the lake, I would move away from my friends, their endless chatter. I'd swim toward the middle of the water with a lazy backstroke, gazing at the sky, its enormous blueness drawing me up until I felt weightless and dizzy. Once in a while there would be a plane, a small silver needle drawn through the clouds, in and out, until it disappeared. Sometimes the thought came to me, as I floated in the middle of the lake with the sun beating down on my closed eyelids, that it would be so easy to let go, to drop into the dim brown world of mud, of water weeds fine as hair.

60 Once I almost did it. I curled my body inward, tight as a fist, and felt it start to sink. The sun grew pale and shapeless; the water, suddenly cold, licked at the insides of my ears in welcome. But in the end I couldn't.

They are knocking on the door now, calling my name. I push myself off the floor, my body almost too heavy to lift up, as when one climbs out after a long swim. I'm surprised at how vividly it comes to me, this memory I haven't called up in years: the desperate flailing of arms and legs as I fought my way upward; the press of the water on me, heavy as terror; the wild animal trapped inside my chest, clawing at my lungs. The day returning to me as searing air, the way I drew it in, in, in, as though I would never have enough of it.

That's when I know I cannot go back. I don't know yet how I'll manage, here in this new, dangerous land. I only know I must. Because all over India, at this very moment, widows in white saris are bowing their veiled heads, serving tea to in-laws. Doves with cut-off wings.

I am standing in front of the mirror now, gathering up the sari. I tuck in the ripped end so it lies next to my skin, my secret. I make myself think of the store, although it hurts. Inside the refrigerated unit, blue milk cartons neatly lined up by Somesh's hands. The exotic smell of Hills Brothers coffee brewed black and strong, the glisten of sugar-glazed donuts nestled in tissue. The neon Budweiser emblem winking on and off like a risky invitation.

I straighten my shoulders and stand taller, take a deep breath. Air fills me— the same air that traveled through Somesh's lungs a little while ago. The thought is like an unexpected, intimate gift. I tilt my chin, readying myself for the arguments of the coming weeks, the remonstrations. In the mirror a woman holds my gaze, her eyes apprehensive yet steady. She wears a blouse and skirt the color of almonds.

Engaging the Text

1. At different points in the story, Mita acquires saris of different colors and fabrics and also wears Western clothing, such as jeans and T-shirts. How does Divakaruni use these outfits as an index to chart the crucial changes in Mita's life?

2. In what sense can this story be understood, not only as a personal tragedy but also as a tragedy of the immigrant experience? What insight does the story offer into the unique challenges that immigrants face? What is at stake for someone who comes to the United States to start a new life?

3. Embedded in Divakaruni's story are many details that dramatize the ways in which Indian culture differs from U.S. culture. What are some of these differences, and what do they imply about the differences in value systems between India and the United States?

Exploring Your Cultural Perspective

1. As Divakaruni describes them, what do saris (see Figure 3.4) suggest about women's identity in Indian culture? What other aspects of Divakaruni's story support this perception? Information on saris can be found at <http://www. shakti.clara.net/sari/expo> and at <http://www.incore.com/india/commun. dress.html>.

2. How would you explain the fascination of North Americans with "pashmina" shawls? What does this fashion trend suggest about North American culture?

FIGURE 3.4

CONNECTING THE TEXTS

1. Would Deborah Tannen's analysis in "There Is No Unmarked Woman" hold up when applied to the counterculture styles described by Farid Chenoune in "Jeans and Black Leather: Gangs Don a Second Skin"? Why or why not?

2. In what sense can body piercing, tattooing, and scarification, as discussed by Germaine Greer in "One Man's Mutilation Is Another Man's Beautification," communicate meaning in the same way that clothing can, as discussed by Alison Lurie in "The Language of Clothes"? What do these modifications "say" about the wearer and about the prevailing social values in the culture in which they are practiced?

3. In what significant way does the perspective on foot binding voiced by Valerie Steele and John S. Major in "China Chic" differ from that of Bernard Rudofsky in "The Unfashionable Human Body" in terms of whether Chinese women themselves were in favor of this practice?

4. In its own way, the wearing of kimono, as described by Liza Dalby in "Kimono," imposes as many constraints on the human form and its natural movement as do the deformations Bernard Rudofsky identifies in "The Unfashionable Human Body." Discuss the cultural codes that these restrictions communicate in both the East and the West.

5. The protagonist in Chitra Banerjee Divakaruni's story "Clothes" wears different kinds of clothing at crucial points in her life. How do these different outfits signal important changes in her status based on the meaning these clothes have in Indian culture? How do they function as a kind of language, as Alison Lurie describes the concept in "The Language of Clothes"?

6. After reading Germaine Greer's article "One Man's Mutilation Is Another Man's Beautification," consider why the ensemble Farid Chenoune describes in "Jeans and Black Leather" is part of the same fashion system as body piercing and tattooing. What do these have in common, and what do they collectively communicate? What important differences exist between rock and punk styles, and how do each of these "tribes" define themselves through what they wear?

7. In what ways does the Kelly bag (as described by Dodie Kazanjian) represent many of the same values to North Americans and Europeans that the kimono does for the Japanese (as described by Liza Dalby)?

8. In what ways do both the Kelly bag (as described by Dodie Kazanjian) and the elaborate shoes made to fit the "lotus foot," (see Valerie Steele and John S. Major's "China Chic") symbolize femininity and status?

9. Drawing on Deborah Tannen's analysis in "There Is No Unmarked Woman," discuss what signals are communicated by the practice of *hijab* (that is, covering one's

face, head, and body) for Muslim women, as Elizabeth Fernea and Robert Fernea explain it in "A Look behind the Veil." What assumptions about the autonomy of women emerge in both essays?

10. Compare and contrast the meanings that veiling expresses in Middle Eastern societies, as described by Elizabeth Fernea and Robert Fernea in "A Look behind the Veil," with that of the kimono of Japanese culture, as described by Liza Dalby in "Kimono."

11. Kimono wearers are clearly "marked" (as Deborah Tannen uses the term in "There Is No Unmarked Woman"), even more than are Japanese women who wear Western clothes. What tendencies does the wearing of the kimono accentuate, and how does a kimono define, or "mark," its wearers? Discuss this concept as it relates to Liza Dalby's essay "Kimono."

12. In what ways do clothes represent various aspects of life to their wearers, as shown by the saris in Chitra Divakaruni's story "Clothes," and the wearing of the veil, as described by Elizabeth Fernea and Robert Fernea in "A Look behind the Veil"?

WRITING ABOUT CLOTHING

1. In what ways do saris in India, veils and chadors in Middle Eastern cultures, and kimonos in Japan express very precise but different meanings about the ways in which women in each of these cultures should present themselves?

2. The history of the T-shirt parallels that of jeans in that both were working-class apparel that made the transition to carriers of emblems and slogans. What sign system governs the wearing of T-shirts displaying the names of places? Would you be more or less likely to wear a shirt emblazoned with the name of a place you had visited or wanted to go to (as Mita in the short story "Clothes" wears a T-shirt that says "Great America")? Explain your answer.

3. What assumptions about future fashions can you make from the clothing worn by characters in science-fiction films such as *Star Trek*? To what extent are these functional unisex outfits an index to their designers' views of what society might be like in the future?

4. Do you believe that students attending public schools should be required to wear uniforms? Why or why not?

5. Is it a good idea to dress twins in identical clothing? Why or why not? Support your argument by citing research on the subject.

6. What features of military uniforms communicate authority? How does the rank of the wearer affect the appearance of the uniform so that it communicates a hierarchy

of power? Do some research to find out how many different kinds of uniforms exist for different occasions. You might consult the Uniform Support Center Web site at <http://www.navy-nex.com>. How do prison uniforms express the opposite of military uniforms?

7. Have you ever misjudged someone because of the way he or she was dressed, or were you ever misjudged because of your dress? Describe the circumstances and the clothing that led to the misperception, and explain the cultural context in which the judgment was made.

8. Why did dark business suits and white shirts, which in previous times were associated with uncool corporate types, make a comeback in such popular films as *Men in Black* (1997) and *The Blues Brothers* (1980 and 1998)? What function do sunglasses and hats play in modifying the conventional meaning of this outfit?

9. What assumptions govern the outfits worn by clowns or mimes? How do these outfits distort normal clothing, and to what effect?

10. How do today's hairstyles reflect societal and generational attitudes? What changes in hairstyles have you witnessed, and what is their significance?

11. Popular opinion holds that there is a correlation between the length of women's skirts and the economic state of the country. Shorter skirts are supposed to signify prosperity, and longer ones a recession. Is this simply a myth? Examine pictures in fashion magazines during bull and bear markets, and write about your findings.

12. The articles of clothing worn by religious practitioners have a symbolism all their own. Select a few religious sects, and investigate the meanings of their traditional outfits (for example, the clothing worn by Buddhists, Dervishes, Hindus, Orthodox Jews, Shinto priests, Sufis, Sikhs, Christians, Moslems, or Zoroastrians). You might start your investigation with the *Encyclopaedia Britannica*'s discussion of religious dress at <http://www.search.eb.com>.

CHAPTER 4

Gender (Mis) Representation

Because of our social circumstances, male and female are really two cultures and their life experiences are utterly different.
—KATE MILLETT (b. 1934, U.S. feminist writer), *Sexual Politics*

Biology might determine our sex, but culture shapes our **gender:** each of us assimilates our society's ideas of what it means to be male or female. The social meanings that our culture attaches to the specific behaviors of men and women influence how we see ourselves and the roles we assume. These gender roles differ strikingly from culture to culture and have varied widely throughout history. The writers whose readings are included in this chapter help us understand how we acquire our concepts of sexual identity and how cultural expectations, pressures, and values shape the choices we make.

SIGNS OF GENDER

Let's examine, for example, the widespread belief in the West that the color pink is for girls and blue is for boys. We may think these associations are perfectly "natural," but they are actually a rather recent innovation, dating to the turn of the twentieth century. Before that, blue (which was thought to be more "delicate" and "dainty") was the color most frequently linked with girls, whereas pink (considered a stronger color) was thought more suitable for boys. Paris designers sparked the shift to blue for boys and pink for girls in the 1920s.

This change in color coding of gender identity is just one example of the ways in which society reformulates gender roles. Brian Pronger uses the phrase "sexual mythologies" to characterize the ever-changing representations of masculinity and femininity that society prescribes. We may accept these roles as "natural," but in Pronger's view, they are created to legitimize the ongoing power relationships between men and women in a society.

The popular film *Boys Don't Cry* (1999) illustrates the difficulty people have in accepting the gender roles of their society. The movie dramatizes the predicament of a young Midwestern woman who feels compelled to dress and act as if she were a man. She attracts a young woman who loves her and enemies who are threatened by her ambiguous sexuality. Her search for identity brings her face to face with the limitations of traditional gender roles as society conventionally defines them.

Like this film (which is based on a true story), recent controversies over sex reassignment of infants illustrate the power society aggregates to itself to determine gender roles. After their son's circumcision had been botched, David Reimer's parents allowed doctors to surgically alter him and subsequently raised him as a girl alongside his twin brother. This landmark case, reported by John Colapinto in his book *As Nature Made Him: The Boy Who Was Raised as a Girl* (2000), had initially been cited as an example of the success of sex reassignment for newborns with injured or irregular genitals.

When he was growing up, David was not told he had been born a male. Despite hormone treatments, however, he never really felt like a girl and, when informed of the reality at age fourteen, made the decision to live as a man and to undergo a series of operations designed to reconstruct the male organ. His observations are poignant:

> It just seems that they implied that you're nothing if your penis is gone. The second you lose that, you're nothing, and they've got to do surgery and hormones to turn you into something. Like you're a zero. [. . .] If a woman lost her breasts, do you turn her into a guy? To make her feel "whole and complete"?

David's experience illustrate society's rejection of people who do not fit into defined gender roles. Now in his thirties, David is married with two adopted children.

The widespread assumption in the West that gender roles must fit traditional patterns is also challenged by the recognition accorded to alternative gender roles in many other cultures, including India. For example, the *hijras* (as described by Serena Nanda in *Neither Man nor Woman: The Hijras of India* [1990]) are a religious community of men who have undergone an operation to remove their genitals and who dress and act like women. They occupy a special niche in Indian society, are believed to possess powers to bless and curse, and are treated with respect.

By contrast, in the West, a departure from stereotypical gender roles often meets with intolerance and violence. Recent attempts to toughen laws against hate crimes (such as the 1998 murder of Matthew Shepard, a University of Wyoming college student who was killed because he was gay) reflect the deep-seated nature of these prejudices.

MEN, RACE, AND SOCIAL CLASS

Stereotyped gender roles, especially in the United States, are further complicated by race. For example, surviving as a black male in a white society, according to Richard Majors and Janet Mancini Billson, means adopting a "cool pose." For many young black males, staying "cool" is critical to the core of masculine identity—and is very similar to the concept of appearing tough, in control, and thoroughly "macho" in Hispanic culture. It may well be that those who are different (gays, blacks) are forced to adopt exaggerated **personas** (public facades or images) to protect themselves from mainstream society's rejection.

The response of blue-collar white males to the same type of cultural expectations that underlie the black "cool pose" and Hispanic "machismo" illustrates the influence of social class on gender roles. A well-known white performer who embodies and projects this **myth** (social construct or belief) of masculinity is Bruce Springsteen. His public persona and his songs, as Gareth Palmer points out in "Bruce Springsteen and Authentic Masculinity," express what it means to be a "real" man in a working-class culture. Interestingly, the women in his songs are depicted as "decorative angels," a **stereotype** (standardized, oversimplified picture) that is as much as a myth of femininity as being macho or cool are myths of masculinity.

WOMEN, MOTHERHOOD, AND BODY IMAGE

Myths of femininity have long revolved around the definition of motherhood. However, in the past few decades, new birth technologies (in vitro fertilization, surrogate parenting, artificial insemination) have redefined what it means to be a mother. Anne Taylor Fleming, in "Sperm in a Jar," tells us that she deferred having a child during the 1970s and 1980s (when women were freeing themselves from traditional gender roles) and now has turned to technology to become a mother.

It is surely a paradox that at the same time Western women are enjoying a newfound freedom, they are also responding to cultural pressures to reshape their appearance. In "Never Just Pictures," Susan Bordo examines the way in which the supermodel image has been promulgated (through media and advertising) as the ideal female body. She analyzes how women are coerced into feeling about themselves if they cannot reach this almost unattainable goal of being as thin as a supermodel. The idealized woman who has it all, a career and a family, must now also compete with media images.

The extent to which these unrealistic and unattainable myths have permeated advertising can be judged by the increasing numbers of young women who suffer from eating disorders. The tragic consequences for girls who buy into the prevailing culture script are the subject of Marge Piercy's satiric poem "Barbie Doll." The Barbie doll, of course, is the cultural icon that symbolizes the feminine ideal of a perfect body and promotes the values and interests of a consumer culture.

Although these myths help determine the ways in which American and other Western women see themselves, in many Middle Eastern countries women are subject to far more drastic forms of coercion. In Saudi Arabia, Egypt, Yemen, Somalia, and other Middle Eastern and East African countries, female children are routinely circumcised. These cultures view the procedure as the means for guaranteeing chastity and thereby preserving the patriarchal order. Waris Dirie, in "The Tragedy of Female Circumcision," describes how traumatic this experience was for her and argues movingly for its elimination. Female circumcision may well go the way of foot binding in China and *suttee* (or widow burning) in India.

Viewed together, the accounts of Susan Bordo and Waris Dirie as well as Marge Piercy's poem all illustrate the various measures different societies use to keep women in their prescribed gender roles. These works show us how women are viewed as property or objects by the males who dominate and control these cultures.

MEN AND WOMEN

The socioeconomic dependence of women on men, especially in non-Western cultures, also requires us to reconsider our assumptions about social equality, political power, and economic opportunities. Fatima Mernissi, in "The French Harem," describes her life in a harem in Morocco (which at the time was under French colonial occupation). Life in the harem was communal, involving eating together at set hours and a total lack of privacy. Although the movies depict harem life as exotic, in reality, it was not only physically restrictive but psychologically demeaning.

The kind of polygamous society Mernissi describes is but one of the many permutations marriage takes around the world. In many cases, what appears to be "natural" is in fact determined by the history and customs of the culture. In

Japan and India, for example, marriages still are arranged as they have been for generations. In both societies, a complex series of negotiations—involving the caste and social class of the prospective bride and groom; a dowry; and in some cases, advance viewing of the intended mate—culminate in elaborate weddings and, surprisingly, few divorces.

Although the idea of an arranged marriage may challenge our concept of free choice, consider what the personal ads in the classified sections say about our culture. They suggest that looking for a suitable mate can be a lonely and potentially embarrassing experience. The search for mates in the United States has moved away from the traditional realms of family and church into new areas such as personal ads, dating services, and the workplace. This shift reflects a dramatic change in American culture.

Monique Proulx, in "Feint of Heart," has written a story about people who should be quite familiar to us. They are suspicious of conventional ideas about marriage and value their freedom. These characters believe they have divested themselves of the gender roles that have so bedeviled men and women in the past. Whether they are any happier because of their "modern" values is the theme of Proulx's story.

All the selections in "Gender (Mis) Representation" illustrate the profound insight of Kate Millet's observation about the "life experiences" of men and women. Most important, they show that power is the ultimate factor in determining how gender roles are played out in various societies.

BRIAN PRONGER
Sexual Mythologies

The relative advantages enjoyed by men simply by virtue of their sex make it quite clear that gender is akin to a class system. These issues and the process by which attributes such as individualism and aggression come to define masculinity in any given culture can be understood as a kind of myth. Brian Pronger develops this line of reasoning in this selection from *The Arena of Masculinity: Sports, Homosexuality, and the Meaning of Sex* (1990). Pronger disputes what is commonly thought to be the universally accepted myth of masculinity and in "Sexual Mythologies" shows how these values are socially constructed.

Thinking Critically

Notice how Pronger establishes his dominant theme in the opening paragraph by drawing attention to the distinction between sex and gender. Take a moment to reflect on why children in most cultures are usually given the paternal surname.

There is an important distinction between sex and gender. Sex is a physiological distinction that is drawn between male and female, whereas gender is a cultural distinction that divides power between men and women. There are four categories of sexual physiological distinction. Genetic sex, male or female, and phenotypic sex (that is, the manifested, observable structure), male or female. The genetic sex of an individual is determined by the presence or absence of the "Y" chromosome. If an individual has an "X" and a "Y" chromosome, he is genetically male. If she has two "X" chromosomes she is genetically female.[1] Judging genetic sex is possible only by the examination of DNA under an electron microscope—a procedure that is usually followed only when there are other chromosomal medical problems.

The phenotypic sex is physically determined by the action of certain hormones that are responsible for the development of internal and external genitalia and the secondary sex characteristics that appear at puberty (such as the development of facial hair in males and breast development in females). The action of androgen, the male sex hormone, brings about the development of male genitals; the absence of this hormone allows for the development of female genitalia. It is only in the eighth week of embryonic development that genitalia become distinguished as male or female—until that point, the phenotypic sex of the embryo is undifferentiated. Interestingly, the difference between male and female genitalia and physiologies in general is only one of emphasis. A penis is an elongated version of the clitoris, the scrotum is labia that have fused. The action of hormones affects the extent of genital development. Sometimes, at birth, it is difficult to tell whether a baby is phenotypically male or female. Doctors then decide whether the child will be regarded as a male or a female. It is a very important decision in a patriarchal culture, the application of a major distinction, one that determines the status and therefore possibilities an individual may have in his or her life. This absolute distinction drawn between men and women is made on the basis of a physical attribute as minor as the degree of genital development. A development that is the result of the level of activity of hormones—a level that can and frequently is adjusted by the administration of drugs.

Before continuing, some mention should be made of the role of reproduction in the construction of gender. Much has been written on this subject, so there is little point in going into details here. Although it is a fact that, generally speaking, women must carry a child to term for the reproduction of the species, there is no reason to believe that they must be tied to that role. The slogan of the women's liberation movement, "biology is not destiny," should no longer be debatable. The nobler history of humanity is the history of the ability of the human mind and of culture to overcome the dictates of biology and "nature" in the service of a better life, one that is not the mere slave of biological impulses and the "forces of nature." The quest for an egalitarian organization of society in which people choose how to organize child-rearing is just one example of our ability to organize life as we see fit. In actual practice, reproduction has only a small role in sexual relations between people. This is amply proved by the fact that for growing numbers of people in heterosexual relations, contraception is becoming the norm and pregnancy is often the unwanted outcome of heterosexual relations in which contraception either failed or was ignored. There can be no doubt that the use of sexuality goes well beyond a desire to reproduce.

In a culture that is dominated by gender, in which gender is like a class system, giving power to men and withholding it from women, all aspects of a person's life will be influenced by his or her gender. By peering at a baby's little genitals, an enormous decision is reached regarding its sex and future.[2] From that point, every effort is made by the child's family and society to develop a distinct application of masculine or feminine gender. Whereas sex is a physiological distinction, gender is a cultural distinction.[3] Sex is socially neutral, gender is not. Without gender, physical sex is a mere biological fact; outside of gender, sexual characteristics are no more significant than any other physical characteristic. Therefore, it is gender that makes physical sex meaningful in social, cultural, and sexual contexts.

5   The idea that there is a "natural" difference between men and women presupposes a dichotomy between these genders that would have to be universal, that is, present in all cultures, throughout history, with variations being nothing more than anomalies. The sociologist R. W. Connell points out that the notion of dichotomous sexes is not universal. He refers to the work of fellow sociologists Suzanne Kessler and Wendy McKenna. They argue that most research, both of a scientific and popular nature, works within a "cultural framework in which the 'natural attitude' is to take gender as strictly dichotomous and unchanging. What they call 'gender attribution,' the social process 'by which we construct our world of two genders,' is sustained despite the failure of human reality on almost any count to be simply dimorphic."[4] For instance, anthropological literature on *berdache*, North American Indian transvestites who were socially accepted as women, indicates that gender is not always assigned on the basis of the biological differences of male and female.[5] This indicates, moreover, that one can choose gender.

disagree

    Connell, essentially arguing against biological determinism, offers another important criticism of the notion that there is a "natural difference" between men and women. "The idea of natural difference is that of a passively suffered condition, like being subject to gravity. If human life were in its major internal structures—gender being one—so conditioned, human history would be inconceivable. For history depends on the transcendence of the natural through social practice."[6]

    Gender, understood as a cultural phenomenon, is a mythic world that polarizes the sexes, giving them social and psychic significance and status. Myths have great power. According to Roland Barthes, myth is a type of speech.[7] It is a form of communication, a way of transmitting meaning that fuels the understanding people have of themselves and their culture. When a subject is treated mythically, it has an aura; there is a sense that the way it is presented in myth is the way it has always been—the subjects of myths are timeless, eternal, and necessarily true.

    Myths describe "nature." But anthropology has taught us that what is considered "natural" varies extensively from one culture to another.[8] When we say something is "natural," we are pretending that somehow it is the product of "Nature," which is a force greater than ourselves. But, in fact, to say something is natural is to make a judgment; what we are really saying when we say that a phenomenon is natural is that it fits our view of the world—a view that is the product of tradition.[9] Myths operate as received wisdom; they enjoy the power of being traditional ways of seeing things. Tradition has its own authority.[10] People bow to tradition. To question tradition is to have the wrong attitude toward it. The myth of gender, being traditional, brings with it the sense that the content of the myth is authoritative. Gender myth communicates the traditional division of power in our culture between males and females, making that division seem natural, ahistorical, universal, and necessarily the way things must be.

Gender myth exaggerates the minor physiological differences between male and female, transforming them into opposites. There is a metamorphosis in which relatively slight physical variation becomes an absolute distinction; these physical variations become the basis for the mythic hierarchical division of the world into men and women, commonly known as the "opposite sexes." People live their lives and understand each other in the context of the myth of gender. A multitude of gestures, physical attributes, and attitudes are interpreted in the light of masculine and feminine gender myth. Gender is a way of seeing things; it is a worldview, a *weltanschauung*. The physical characteristics of sex become mythic signs of gender.

Masculinity and femininity are interpretive context that assign value to   *10* gestures and attitudes that are in themselves valueless. These values are along a spectrum of power, with masculine being powerful and feminine powerless. When a man behaves in a way that is interpreted as masculine, he is placed in this spectrum of power. This power need not be actualized; in fact, it usually is not.[11] The power is mythic. For example, while in the gym working out with weights, a man may without good reason drop the weights to the floor so they make more noise than is necessary; simultaneously he will grunt. Because aggressive noise-making is a masculine gesture, such behavior in the weight room is meant to indicate a man's sense of his place in the myth. The interpretation of gesture as masculine is an invocation of the mythic world of gender power; it endows that gesture with such power. Acknowledging or accepting the power that's been invoked by the interpretation of a gesture as masculine is a matter of faith in the gender myth. It's similar to a Catholic priest at the Eucharist claiming to invoke the power of God so that bread and wine become body and blood. Whether or not they actually become body and blood is beside the point; to those who care, the bread and wine have been changed: they are endowed with a new meaning.

The myth of gender creates and supports differences between males and females that consolidate men's power over women. Keeping in mind that the myth of masculinity and femininity is cultural and therefore the product of historical developments and subject to social change, it can be argued that this myth plays a role in the division of labor and the structure of power in our society.

The central fact about this structure in the contemporary capitalist world is the subordination of women. This fact is massively documented, and has enormous ramifications—physical, mental, interpersonal, cultural—whose effects on the lives of women have been the major concerns of feminism. *One of the central facts about masculinity, then, is that men in general are advantaged by the subordination of women.*[12]

The gender categories of masculine and feminine are fundamental to the structure of patriarchal power and how it works. Men are in a position of power over women. This difference in mythic power is blatantly realized in the social sphere. Women are discouraged, in some cases prohibited, from competing with men in economic or professional life. In our culture and many others, they frequently act as unpaid servants and bear children who will perpetuate the *man's* lineage—children are usually given the paternal surname. The high incidence of men's violence against women in their homes and on the streets is now a well-documented fact. This violence is the most obvious social manifestation of mythic gender power.

Gender is a myth that justifies, expresses, and supports the power of men over women. As such, it is an important tool for giving men that hegemony. Remembering that Barthes said that myth is a form of speech that endows its subject with a sense of ahistorical universality and necessity,[13] we can see how the myth justifies hegemonic gender relations. The notion that the dominant and subordinate positions of men and women respectively are dependent upon social and historical influences is alien to the mythical understanding of masculinity and femininity. Until the blossoming of modern feminism, almost everyone in Western culture assumed that gender was somehow a fundamental feature of one's sex, that the power men have over women is natural and universal. Because it is the effect of myth to enshrine social relations in the false prestige of the "natural order of things," challenging the social order is seen as going against nature.[14] Certainly, this is a traditional accusation leveled against feminists demanding equality for women. Through the myth, gender is justified by being a "natural" aspect of the way things are.

As examination of the nature of power reveals the way that gender myth expresses and supports masculine and feminine power relations. Michel Foucault offers a comprehensive definition of power.

> Power must be understood in the first instance as the multiplicity of *force relations*, immanent in the sphere in which they operate and which constitute their own organization; as the *process* which, through ceaseless struggles and confrontations transforms, strengthens, or reverses them; as the *support* which these force relations find in one another, thus forming a chain or a system, or on the contrary, the disfunctions and contradictions

which isolate them from one another; and lastly as the *strategies* in which they take effect, whose general design or institutional crystallization is embodied in the state apparatus, in the formulation of the law, in the various social hegemonies.[15]

Gender myth, while attempting to polarize the relations between men and women, allows for extensive interplay within those relations, which indicates that the respective dominant and subordinate positions of men and women constitute a "multiplicity of *force relations.*" The "battle of the sexes," that is, the fact that masculinity and femininity are expressed and played off one another, thereby realizing their power relations, is the *process* that "transforms, strengthens, or reverses" those relations. The complementarity of masculinity and femininity, strength and weakness, dominance and submission, function as the "*support* which these force relations find in one another." And finally, the institutionalizations of patriarchal hegemony and privilege in law, medicine, religion, commerce, sport, and so on, clearly function as the "*strategies*" through which the force relations of masculinity and femininity "take effect."

The gender myth involves three related axes: physical sex (male/female), sociocultural status (man/woman), and signs of gender (masculine/feminine).

As discussed earlier, *physical sex* is a matter of being male or female, that is, having the "X" or "Y" chromosome and the phenotypic results of it: male or female genitalia and secondary sex characteristics.

Sociocultural status is what it means to be a man or a woman in our culture. The gender order is hierarchical and divided into two. Men are superior to women. This is the birthright of men and exists independently of any individual merit. Being a man automatically places one on the positive side of power. This status is changing. Men's birthright is being challenged by women and the superior status of men is slowly being eroded. Although it is changing in practice, remnants of this classlike system remain in people's thinking. Certainly at a conscious level, many are attempting to dismantle the superior position of men; there are now laws prohibiting discrimination against women. Subconsciously, though, even in enlightened circles, women are still often understood as inferior to men by both men and women. The reasons for this are deeply psychic, emanating out of the fundamental sense that one has of one's own position in a patriarchal world.

The *signs of gender* are various gestures—by which I mean assorted body deportments, clothing customs, hair styles, and complex behaviors such as "being a football player"—that indicate the forcefulness or significance that one's gender is supposed to take. The mythic division of power is expressed and secured through the complex relationship between the spectrum of masculinity and femininity and the use of it by men and women. At one end of the spectrum, a man behaving in a way that is interpreted as masculine is powerful; at the other end, a women interpreted as feminine is not powerful.[16] In a rigidly gendered society, men would be completely masculine and women completely feminine. The world is not so simple. Some women do not embrace the enervated life of femininity entirely and some men do not take up a purely masculine one. Men, however, can exert considerable power over women by using masculinity. Women complement that power by being subordinate in femininity.

20   From infancy, one's family and society work very hard to convince one of one's place in the fundamental sexist division of power in our society; this is the process of learning one's gender. The ways in which gender are learned are well known and therefore need only a passing reference here.[17] Boys and girls are usually given respectively masculine and feminine names; as they learn those names they simultaneously learn whether they are boys or girls. Mother says to her child, "Bobby's a big boy," or "Cynthia is a sweet little girl." The physical treatment of little boys is rough and aggressive compared to that of little girls. Boys wear clothes designed for activity; girls' little dresses are delicate and inhibit active behavior. And so on. Most people grow up with a strong sense of where they belong in the gender order. One day I was playing with the three-year-old son of a friend of mine. He wanted to know why I wear an earring. "It makes you look like a girl," he said. He was surprised that I would do something that would make me look like a girl. Although he was too young to read, he was fully aware of a sign of gender (an earring). Moreover, he saw it as a contradiction for a man to wear feminine paraphernalia. That episode illustrates that at a very young age, a child knows not only the signs of gender, but also the importance of adhering to the gender that one has been assigned. It also indicates a basic intuition that gender is fluid, that is, that it is possible for a male to dress or behave as a woman.

Gender is deeply personal. One's relation to gender is a matter of one's relation to power. The fundamental meaning of being a man or being a woman in our culture lies in their relative mythic powers. Gender is a kind of prison. It is difficult to think about another person without thinking of his or her gender. For example, if you meet a person briefly you may well forget most everything about them; it is very unlikely, however, that you will forget whether they were a man or a woman. We are usually aware of the gender of the person with whom we are having sex; it's difficult to conceive of sexual relations in which gender would have no place in the experience. Because gender is fundamentally a matter of power, knowing a person's gender is essentially a matter of knowing their status within the myth of gender power. This is a way of knowing that emanates out of one's earliest infantile adjustments to the mythic patriarchal discourse of power. This discourse has been thousands of years in the making and operates like a language that imbues our thinking or being in a way that is quite similar to the profound influence of ancient Greek meta-physics.[18] Our earliest cultural experience of ourselves and others has been mediated by the language, the discourse of patriarchy. As long as we continue to see the world through the gender myth, as divided into men and women, we will continue to see a relative patriarchal status for each.

It is essential to point out that this interpretation can be conscious or sub-conscious. For the most part, it is *subconscious*. Almost all men and women dress, cut their hair, and carry themselves in such a way that their gender is obvious. Those who present themselves in a convincingly androgynous way make most others uneasy. The fact that in English and many other languages, it is difficult to refer to someone without using a masculine or feminine pronoun, illustrates the way in which gender imbues our language and therefore culture. The ten-dency to interpret people and their behavior in light of the myth of gender remains, for the most part, in the subconscious mind because it is a fundamen-tal, accepted, and largely unquestioned way of seeing things. Although in the 1970s, feminism did draw elements of this thinking from the depths of the sub-conscious, making them explicit and open to criticism, such "consciousness-raising" is no longer fashionable.

The mythical interpretation of gender emerges from the individual's per-sonal experience as it confronts culture. *Culture* is the world of meaning or sig-nificance in which one finds oneself.[19] For the most part we don't choose it; we are, as Heidegger would say, "thrown" into it. In any culture there are many "languages." Of course, tongues such as English, French, and Swahili are lan-guages. Born and educated in Pakistani culture, one will probably understand and speak Urdu. One's experience will be filtered through the grammar, vocab-ulary, and literature of Urdu. Although the language is common to all who speak it, depending on one's experience and creativity, one is able to fashion unique statements with it. Myths are languages also. Just as the Urdu tongue subconsciously guides one's thinking and therefore experience, so too gender myth filters experience without our being aware of it for the most part. The culture that imparts the myth of gender offers its standard language of gender, its signs of gender. Depending on one's experience and creativity, one is able to use that culture, to employ those myths and their signs in one's own way.

Just as the myth affects the thinking of people, so too people affect the nature of the myth. Different people have encountered our culture and its gen-der myth in different ways. This means there is great variability in the notions people have of gender. Gender may be a major concern or a minor one. Some may see the myth as an authentic view of the social difference between male and female; others may see the myth as the tool of the patriarchal oppression of women. Some dismiss the myth; others cherish it.

Anthropology has shown us that the gestures that constitute masculine and feminine gender vary significantly from culture to culture.[20] This illustrates

25

that nothing is inherently masculine or feminine; rather, masculinity and femininity are dependent on cultural conventions. The masculine and feminine constitution of gender varies not only from culture to culture, but also from group to group within a culture and from person to person within a group. The signs of gender are profoundly influenced by other cultural factors such as class and ethnicity. What may be seen as masculine by one class may be considered effeminate by another. Interpretations of gender are idiosyncratic in the extreme. Nevertheless, there is some basic agreement on the nature of masculinity and femininity in North American and British culture.

It's illuminating to see how the dictionaries define "masculine," "feminine," and related words. A number of important themes emerge. Power is the distinguishing feature of masculinity, whereas lack of power is the distinguishing feature of femininity. The *Oxford English Dictionary* (OED) defines "masculine" as "having the appropriate excellences of the male sex; manly, virile, vigorous, powerful." The OED defines "feminine" as "the characteristics of, peculiar or proper to a woman." "Woman" is defined not only as "an adult female human being," but also "with allusion to qualities generally attributed to the female sex, . . . their position of inferiority or subjection." Interestingly, whereas "masculine" is defined in terms of "excellences," the OED offers a depreciative use of "feminine," which is "womanish, effeminate." It is in this depreciative use that the powerlessness that is associated with femininity is borne out. *Webster's Third New International Dictionary of the English Language* (1976) defines "effeminate" as "lacking manly strength of purpose; exhibiting weakness." *The Dictionary of Contemporary American Usage* (Random House, 1957) says that "effeminate" "is a term of contempt, applied to actions or qualities in a man that would be fitting in a woman." The OED defines "effeminate" as "to make womanish or unmanly; to enervate; to grow weak, languish." Four of the OED definitions of "enervate" make explicit the dearth of power that our concept of feminism indicates. "1. Wanting in strength of character; spiritless, unmanly, effeminate. 2. Wanting in bodily strength or physical power. 3. To weaken mentally or morally; to destroy the capacity for vigorous effort of intellect or will. 4. To render ineffectual."

It is important to note that the dictionaries suggest that although masculinity and femininity are seen as attributes of males and females respectively, they are not *necessarily* attributable to those respective sexes. These definitions leave open the possibility for masculine women and feminine men. *The Dictionary of Contemporary American Usage* says that "Masculine applies to the qualities that properly characterize men as compared to women. If applied to a woman, it suggests something incongruous with her femininity (Large shoulders gave her a masculine appearance) or conveys a compliment (She had a logical, masculine mind)."

Masculinity is seen as superior to femininity.* It is more socially acceptable for a woman to be masculine than for a man to be feminine because it is more acceptable to take power than it is to relinquish it.[21] Because in patriarchal culture it is generally accepted that it is better to be powerful than weak, masculine things are usually seen to be superior to feminine things.

By reference to the myth of gender, one can interpret the behavior of others in the context of the spectrum of power between men and women. One can invite interpretations of one's own actions within these mythic contexts by behaving in ways that play on the myth of gender. One's clothes, carriage, and body all become signs of gender. The characteristics of male and female physical sex become signs of gender. It is in the context of gender myth that muscles have masculine significance and breasts feminine. The importance of the phallus lies in its mythic significance as the organ of masculinity, the sign of men's power.

Notes

1. There are "chromosomal abnormalities" in which there are variations in the number of X and Y chromosomes. Although such variations raise some interesting questions about the attribution of gender, their incidence is too rare to warrant discussion here.
2. See John Money, *Sexual Signatures* (Boston: Little Brown, 1975).
3. That gender is a cultural category without biological basis is now well established. Cross-cultural studies indicate that gender is constituted differently in different cultures. Some societies have more than two genders and others have as many as six. See William H. Dubay, *Gay Identity* (Jefferson, N.C.: McFarland, 1987) p. 44.

   Margaret Mead's famous iconoclastic study of seven remote societies of the South Seas illustrated that our conceptions of masculinity and feminity for men and women respectively are not reproduced in all cultures, thereby illustrating the cultural foundations of gender. See Margaret Mead, *Male and Female* (New York: William Morrow, 1949).

---

*There are feminist arguments that try to claim respectability for femininity by affirming the positive traits that are attributed to it and downplaying the negative. It is only by adoption of a masculine standard, they say, that physical strength, aggressiveness, and so on are seen as superior and that "feminine" attributes are seen as inferior. These arguments usually amount to a dangerous form of "essentialism" positing women as biologically predisposed to care and nurture. This is not only unfounded biologically, psychologically, anthropologically, and sociologically, it is also oppressive to women, keeping them in their traditional labor. The superiority of masculinity consists not in ethical superiority, by any means. The superiority of masculinity lies in its (unethical) ability to subjugate others. Males and females are inherently neither inferior nor superior, only the myth of gender makes it so.

4. Robert W. Connell, *Gender and Power* (Cambridge, England: Polity Press, 1987) p. 76. He is referring to Suzanne Kessler and Wendy McKenna, *Gender* (Chicago: University of Chicago Press, 1985).

5. There is also evidence that females in North American Indian culture crossed gender. See Evelyn Blackwood, "Sexuality and Gender in Certain Native American Tribes," *Signs* 10, no. 4 (Autumn 1984): 27–42. For a review of the literature on *berdache*, see Charles Callender and Lee M. Kochems, "The North American Berdache," *Current Anthropology* 24, no. 4 (Aug.–Oct., 1983): 443–70.

6. Connell, *op. cit.*, p. 77.

7. See Roland Barthes, *Mythologies*, 2nd ed., trans. Annette Lavers (London: Paladin, 1973) pp. 109ff.

8. See Mead, *Male and Female*.

9. Paul Carter, *The Road to Botany Bay* (London: Faber, 1987).

10. See Hannah Arendt's introduction to Walter Benjamin, *Illuminations* (New York: Harcourt, Brace and World, 1968).

11. The myths of gender are not the same as the actual subjugation of women by men. The *exercise* of men's power over women is the actual forcing of women in sexual acts, the using of them as cheap domestic labor, the marginalization of them in the workforce. While the myths are instrumental in the power men have over women in that they justify and create a context for that power, they are one step removed from the actual seizing of power. Whereas it's true that men sometimes actualize their power and behave aggressively and violently, some more frequently than others, allusion to the gender myth is more or less constant.

12. T. Carrington, B. Connell and J. Lee, "Toward a New Sociology of Masculinity," *Theory and Society* 14, no. 5 (1985): p. 590. Emphasis mine.

13. Barthes, *Mythologies*, p. 151.

14. In *Mythologies*, Barthes says that the principle of myth is that it transforms history into nature, p. 129.

15. Michel Foucault, *The History of Sexuality*, vol. 1, trans. Robert Hurley (New York: Vintage, 1978) pp. 92–93. Emphasis mine.

16. It is essential to note that masculinity is not the only expression or instrument of power. Capital, class, and the control of information are just three examples of other instruments of power.

17. See Money, *Sexual Signatures*.

18. Here I am drawing a parallel with Heidegger's argument about the insidiousness of Hellenic thought.

19. The anthropologist Clifford Geertz, paraphrasing Max Weber, said that "man [sic] is an animal suspended in webs of significance he himself has spun." In *The Interpretation of Cultures* (New York: Basic Books, 1973) p. 5.

20. See Salvatore Cucchiari, "The Gender Revolution and the Transition from Biosexual Horde to Patrilocal Band," *Sexual Meanings*, ed. by Sherry B. Ortner and Harriet Whitehead (Cambridge, England: Cambridge University Press, 1981) pp. 31–79. See also Mead, *Male and Female*.

21. G. Blachford, "Male Dominance in the Gay World," *The Making of the Modern Homosexual*, ed. Kenneth Plummer (London: Hutchinson, 1981) p. 187.

Engaging the Text

1. What are some of the customary signs of gender associated with masculinity and femininity, and what unspoken cultural **agendas** (plans) do they implement? How does accepting Pronger's thesis that gender roles are culturally produced and not biologically determined alter our perceptions about what is natural and normal?

2. What do the insights of Roland Barthes and Michel Foucault add to Pronger's argument? Do their theories make Pronger's argument more effective? Why or why not?

3. According to Pronger, how does the language used to characterize masculinity and femininity reinforce gender stereotypes?

Exploring Your Cultural Perspective

1. Based on your own observations of children, what gender messages and expectations do they receive from infancy on? Is Pronger correct when he asserts, "Because gender is fundamentally a matter of power, knowing a person's gender is essentially a matter of knowing their status within the myth of gender power"? Explain your answer.

2. Are there some jobs for which men are better suited than women? If so, why? Do you agree or disagree with Pronger's statement that "gender myth exaggerates the minor physiological differences between male and female, transforming them into opposites"? Write a few paragraphs explaining your answer.

RICHARD MAJORS AND
JANET MANCINI BILLSON

Cool Pose

Richard Majors is an associate professor of psychology at the University
of Wisconsin, Eau Claire. Cofounder of the National Council of African
American Men and the *Journal of African American Males Studies,* he has
written (with Jo Joliffe) *The Black Education Revolution* (1999). Janet
Mancini Billson is professor of sociology and women's studies at Rhode
Island College. She is the author of *Keepers of the Culture: The Power of
Tradition in Women's Lives* (1995) and *Pathways to Manhood: Young Black
Males Struggle for Identity* (1996). In the following selection from *Cool
Pose: The Dilemmas of Black Manhood in America* (1992), Majors and Billson
explain that acting detached, fearless, and aloof is a strategy for emo-
tional survival for black men in white society.

Thinking Critically

*As you read, notice the organizational structure of the piece: a problem-
solution format. As an aid to following the authors' train of thought, underline and annotate passages in which they define what they see as the problem of black male identity and explain how the "cool pose" is a solution.*

*The cat seeks through a harmonious combination of charm . . . the proper
dedication to his "kick" and unrestrained generosity to make of his day to
day life itself a gracious work of art.*[1]

For many African-American males, the character that best exemplifies the
expressive life-style is the cool cat. Like other forms of cool pose, being a cool
cat provides a way to accentuate the self. The cool cat is an exceptional artist of
expressiveness and flamboyant style. He creates his unique identity by artfully
dipping into a colorful palette of clothes and hairstyles that set him apart from

the ordinary. His nonverbal gestures—his walk and handshakes, for example— are mixed with high verbal agility. He can be found "rapping it down to a woman" with a flair and virtuosity that others envy. He does not simply drive a car—he "leans" (drives with one arm) and sets his neighbors talking about his self-assured risk-taking. The cool cat is the consummate actor. His performance may also be characterized by deftly manipulative and deceptive strategies.

Black males put great emphasis on style and acting cool. Appearing suave, urbane, and charming is at the heart of being a cool cat. The black male is supremely skilled at utilizing cultural symbols in a way that stamps his personal mark on all encounters. This allows him to elevate his sense of pride and control. He can broadcast strength and masculinity or shore up flagging status and dignity.

PORTRAIT OF THE COOL CAT

The portrait of a typical cool cat is usually that of a young black male found on the streets of American cities. He is probably unemployed, may be involved in drugs or alcohol, and has limited education. He is involved in some kind of hustling activity and is probably from a low-income, beleaguered family. Some embrace values of education and work and are marked by self-assurance. For example, in *Strategic Styles*, Mancini describes Hank as a "together guy" who exudes confidence and autonomy, as well as flamboyance; he states simply, "I got my own way in everything. I don't copy nothing from nobody."[2]

McCord and his colleagues in *Life Styles in the Black Ghetto* characterize the cool cat as a young man who spends his time on street corners, in pool halls, or in "running some type of racket." He has a distinctive style. Firestone defines the cool cat as a man who combines charm, dedication to his "kick," and unusual generosity to make everyday life a balanced and "gracious work of art" that contributes in some way to a pleasant, aesthetic life-style. The cool cat is unruffled, self-assured, and eminently cool in the face of emergencies.

CLOTHES AND THE COOL CAT

Few African-American males now wear the *dashikis* of the Black Revolution, 5 but clothes are still used to make fashion and status statements. Clothes help the black male attract attention and enhance his self-image. After all, in a society that has kept blacks invisible, it is not surprising that seemingly flamboyant clothes might be worn to heighten visibility.

Clothes can also contribute to violence and fighting, even death, among young black males. For example, some gangs use baseball caps or colors to symbolize gang membership. Gangs have been known to kill youths for wearing the wrong colors or clothes. They have also fought, occasionally to death, over brand name clothes (such as Georgio and Gucci items), basketball sneakers, or gold chains. Black fraternities often use jackets to indicate membership and solidarity.

To style is the ultimate way hustlers attempt to act cool. Clothes are a portable and creative expression of styling. The interest in colorful male plumage begins in the early teens when attention-getting costumes earn the young cat his place on center stage. He begins to establish his own personal signature in dress, hairstyle, and language. To "style," "front off," "friend," "high sign," or "funk" all mean to show off or upstage others in a highly competitive war of masculine self-presentation. A young black woman describes how she compliments the cool cats in her life: "You all dressed up and you have your apple hat on, your flairs, and your boots and you walkin' down the street lookin' at all d' people, so you goin' style wid the lookin' good. Be more less flamboyant. . . . He's decked to kill! Da's what we [young women] tell 'em."[3]

Getting "clean" and dressing with style is an important way to get over in the world. Some teens see the world as a constant stage—a series of personal performances. They earn street applause for being clean and having style. Folb notes that because how you dress says so much about who you are, black males often resent wearing work-related uniforms. The uniform de-styles them. Folb quotes a youth who is contemplating quitting his job as groundskeeper aide for the County of Los Angeles: "I like to get clean and stay sharp."[4]

Hudson calls the attire of the hustler flashy and flamboyant and stresses that clothing is a central part of a hustler's front. In order to make money, he must look like he already has money (somewhat akin to the Madison Avenue grey flannel suit or recent evocations for yuppies to "dress for success"). He cannot expect to "take off some fat suckers" if he looks like a "greaseball."

10   When a hustler starts making money, he immediately puts his wardrobe together in order to establish prestige with his audience. A monologue by well-known black recording artist Lou Rawls describes a popular young hustler on the South Side of Chicago who epitomizes the cool cat style:

> Every Friday evening about 4:30 he would be standing there because his girlfriend works at Walgreen's . . . and on Friday, the eagle flies. He was wearing the very popular silk mohair wool worsted—continental to the bone—$250 hustler's suit . . . a pair of highly shined hustler's alligator shoes . . . white on white tab collar shirt, a very thin hustler's necktie . . . a very large artificial diamond stick pin in place . . . a hustler's hairdo . . . a process . . . hustler's shades on, cigarette in hand, a very broad smile on his face . . . staring hard and elated at what he saw . . . his automobile parked

at the curb . . . white on white on white. The hustlers call them hogs, the trade name is Cadillac . . . (As the hustler is standing on the corner, he sees his wife approaching with a razor in hand, screaming at him): You no good jiving farmer . . . the rent's not paid and the baby is hungry and needs shoes and you're out here hustling and carrying on . . . (He says): Baby, you can have this car and anything you want. Just don't cut my new suit. I just got it out of the pawn shop and I've got to have my front so I can keep on making my game.[5]

COOL WHEELS

Cars also underscore the significance of style and feature heavily in "making the game." Hustlers and others in the ghetto value and treasure their automobiles. The more expensive the automobile, the more valid is the hustler's claims to have made it. As the expression goes, "he is doing good in this town."

From an early age, black teens see cars as a status symbol. Many learn to pop the ignition so they can take joyrides—preparation perhaps for organized car theft later in life. Cars allow visible, conspicuous display of status—a perfect way for the cool cat to stage his performance literally throughout the community.

One stylized type of physical posturing noted by Folb is "leaning" or "low-riding," in which the driver (and sometimes the passenger) sits so low in his seat that only the top of his head is visible and his eyes peer out over the steering wheel. Low-riding is designed to draw attention to both driver and car—a performance that may be specifically directed toward females. Folb quotes a young woman's perception of these performances:

> Leanin' that's when a dude be leanin' so hard like he's layin' down in d' car. Da's what they do in their cars. Lean like, "I'm jus' the man." But guys in low-ridin' cars lean and low ride 'cause they know they gotta be funky and they say, "Well, the car be lookin' good, I gotta look good."[6]

For the cool cat, driving a Cadillac (or other luxury car) is important for more than just transportation. Cadillac-type cars epitomize class because of their reputation and because they take up a great deal of physical space. They symbolize being seen—a critical experience for those who have been invisible in this country for so long. The cool cat feels, "If I can drive a stylish car like this, it proves to myself and others that I am as important as anyone else. I haven't given up. I am going to make it." The cool cat often sacrifices other economic goods in his life or his family's life to have a big luxury car as a way to make such a statement.

LAME TO THE BONE

15   If style is the ultimate way to act cool, cool cats must have definite beliefs as to what represents nonstylistic behavior. Being called "lame to the bone" or "uncool" is the ultimate insult in black teenage vernacular. Being lame means to be socially incompetent, disabled, or crippled—a sissy. The "lame brand" does not even know how to talk to females; he may appear frightened of them. Folb reports:

> Dudes be talkin' to d' young lady, he run aroun', shootin' marbles. Not too situated . . . Dumb sucker have no girls, don't know where everything is . . . stone SUCKER! Sissy boy, hangin' 'round his momma all the time. Dedicated to d' home front. He don't know what's happ'nin'. He like a school book chump . . . stupid, ignorant, hide in d' books all d' time—like a bookworm. He square to d' wood! . . . Don't get high, don't smoke no weed. Show 'im a reefer, he wouldn't even know what it is! . . . Uncoordinated. He cain't fight or nothin'. Like he followin' you everplace you go . . . wanna be wid everybody but don't do nothin' . . . They can't catch on to what's happ'nin'."[7]

For those who are lame, there is probably no hope of rehabilitation.

Half-stepping means to do something halfway and is a form of being lame or uncool. A person who is not appropriately dressed for an occasion is not mounting the correct performance. If he is giving a party, he should not dress the way he would for school or work, in off-brand tennis shoes or Levis, or wrinkled clothing: "Don't come half-steppin', come fiendish, righteously dap to a tee, silk to the bone. Or like a date. Like you dress yo'self up—some bad-boy bell bottom, nice shirt. Don't half step. Get yo'self together brother."[8]

WHY IS STYLE SO IMPORTANT?

We might ask why style is so important to cool cats. Styling helps cool cats draw attention to the self and communicates creativity. The African-American man in this country has been "nobody" for generations. The purpose of styling, then, is to paint a self-portrait in colorful, vivid strokes that makes the black male "somebody."

The extravagant, flashy clothes often worn by cool cats, the blaring ghetto-blasters playing earsplitting music as they walk or drive down the street, signify their need to be seen and heard. Styling is an antidote to invisibility and silence, a hope in a hopeless world, a defense against multiple attacks on cultural and personal integrity. It is proactive rather than defensive. Styling lets the black male show others that he is alive, and reminds himself as well.

The cool cat styles for the cosmetic effect (how he looks) and to symbolize the messages he wants to portray: "No matter how poor I am or what has happened to me in the past, this shows that I can still make it . . . and with class."

Irrespective of race or class, it is not enough to survive or just live from day to day in a social vacuum. Rather, individuals have a genuine need to know that they can make a contribution to their own welfare and personal growth and that they have control over their own destiny. That they can be noticed and can better their lives.   20

Perkins writes that black children internalize the roles that will allow them to perform on the only stage they know: the black ghetto colony. The cool cat and similar roles are adopted because they have great survival value, not just because they elicit applause from the immediate audience. Black children learn how to be cool under the most extenuating circumstances because being cool is a clear advantage. Perkins adds that when a situation is fraught with danger or anxiety (becomes "uptight"), the most sophisticated response is being cool, "hip," or "together." Cool stabilizes the situation and either minimizes or ignores threats that cannot be easily dealt with in other ways.

Firestone sees the "idea cat" as a person who is adequate to any situation. He adopts a cool image in order to deal with status and identity problems in a society that denies equal access. Foster hypothesizes that as the black man's drive for middle-class status in the North was thwarted by racism, a cool street-corner life-style evolved. White racism in urban areas both stimulates and perpetuates street-corner behavior. Whereas other ethnic groups have been allowed to assimilate after a period of initial bigotry, doors have remained impermeable to African-Americans. (Foster notes that where the doors have been opened for black males, a highly organized street life-style is not as likely to develop.) In most places in America, those doors remain at least partially closed.

The cool cat life-style has long functioned as a means to enhance the black male's ability to survive the harsh effects of racism and social oppression. Because of a lack of resources, services, goods, information, and jobs, lower-income blacks often have hours of free time on their hands. The cool cat life-style provides a kind of stimulation and entertainment. Something is always going on or being contemplated. Those who live in the ghetto often view cool cats as fashionable, hip, cool, and chic. This glamorized life-style helps the black male to achieve balance—entertainment and stimulation counter frustration and boredom.

Being a cool cat is one route toward creative masculinity, toward recognition. It helps black males to survive, to style and act cool, to show disdain for the white man and the Protestant work ethic, and to show pride and dignity. It enhances manhood, commands respect, vents bitterness and anger, establishes a sense of control, expresses artistry, accentuates the self, and provides a form of amusement.

LIFE ON THE STREETS

25   For cool cats who like to style, the streets are the best place to hustle and earn
a living. The streets are exhilarating, perilous, electric with possibilities, and
lush with social meaning. As with some other groups, such as Hispanics, the
streets are the main stage of daily life for black males. For whites and for middle-
class blacks, the streets are just concrete pathways of neutrality and practicality,
perhaps even of danger. For young blacks, especially those who live in impoverished inner-city neighborhoods, the streets become the community living
room, the sports arena, the recreation hall, the marketplace, and the political
forum. Drug deals, hanging out, love affairs, gang rivalries, and training in
conventional wisdom all take place in the streets.

The streets are a school of life that easily competes with the dry, often irrelevant pap squeezed between pages of books in nearby school buildings. H. Rap
Brown remembers his own early years in the ghetto. He says the streets are
where "young bloods" seek and gain control and where they receive their most
relevant education: "I learned how to talk in the streets, not from reading about
Dick and Jane going to the zoo and all that simple shit. Sometimes I wonder
why I ever bothered to go to school. Practically everything I know I learned on
the corner."[9]

Phil talks about how the streets are his home and the place he learned to
keep his true feelings to himself: "I am a street person. A street person will not
tell The Man everything. Like you can't be too honest, man. Go ahead and be
honest, you goin' wish you had not. You don't tell the truth all the time. You're
screwing yourself up! I learned that shit from the white man."

Streets are where it happens—it being whatever holds emotional valence for
the young black male. Streets are beyond parental control. Streets respond to
the authority of youth and gangs, rather than of age, parents, teachers, or police.
The streets train for criminality, not conventionality. For many, the streets
become home for most of the day and night. Home (meaning house) becomes a
place to catch a few hours of sleep and to dress for the next main stage (street)
performance. For others, the streets become home, literally—or their coffin.

A young black boy raised by a prostitute mother and an alcoholic father
remembers when he began to develop the street-smart ways of a cool cat, liking the taste of cheap liquor, and meeting all the neighborhood's cats—the
gamblers, pimps, bootleggers, and hustlers:

> I knew the ministers, teachers, and deacons of the church who came to the
> district to do no preaching or teaching. I knew the city and county offi-
> cials who, in secret, slipped me quarters whenever they came for their
> share of the "dirty money" or just seeking the favor of the ladies . . . I
> remember the sharp gamblers who spent their spare time hanging around

with my beautiful mother. They played with me and taught me the tricks of the trade. At nine, I knew how to ink and crimp the other guy's cards between my fingers. I remember the flashy clothes of the gamblers and pimps and sharp automobiles.[10]

The young boy's early training in such illegal activities as pimping, gambling, bootlegging, and prostitution prepared him for the fast life. He wanted to grow up to be just like these role models, reflecting the urgency of black males in the ghetto who are exposed to alternative life-styles and roles during their tenderest years. If they learn their lessons well, they can survive later as cool hustlers. *30*

HUSTLING TO FILL THE VOID

The cool cat life-style is a survival strategy par excellence because this role develops as a reaction to racism and social oppression. The art of hustling, expressed in various forms of deceptive and manipulative activities, is the cool cat's greatest weapon against poverty and social inequality. Hustling becomes the African-American male's original and indigenous means of waging a private war on poverty. Some believe that hustling is a more successful antipoverty weapon than the government has invented to date.

Foster writes that hustling, as a profession, is a way of life for many black men. It requires only a "degree from the streets." Horton asked some black males, "When a dude needs bread (money), how does he get it?" The universal response was "the hustle." Hustling, as the primary street activity, becomes the economic foundation for everyday life and sets the tone of social activities as well.

Hustling for the cool cat represents not only an alternative economic form, but an alternative form of masculinity. Black males have accepted the basic masculine goals, norms, and standards of our society (such as wanting to work and provide for a family), but unlike white males, they lack the means to achieve these masculine goals. Resolute attempts to work hard in legitimate jobs are, for many black males, met with being the last hired and first fired, low pay, insult, or lack of promotion. Playing the American game according to the standard rules does not necessarily lead to upward social or occupational mobility.

The constant pressure to prove his manhood without mainstream tools has left many black males feeling angry and bitter. They feel that they have been locked out of the American mainstream. The cool cat life-style is a way to mock whites and the Protestant work ethic by exploiting, rapping, conning, the "pimping game," and other hustling roles.

35   Hustling roles say to the white man: "Hustling makes me feel like a man and allows me to survive. But more important, I hustle, white man, because it is something you hate, and it therefore defies the principles you are most proud of . . . the Protestant work ethic. And even though I realize this life-style can potentially destroy me, at least I make a strong statement to you, white man, that no matter what happens by this hustling, I was in control, not you, and this is all that matters."

Hustling compensates for lack of income, goods and services, and status. It gives the cool cat a kit bag of identity tools for creating a sense of power, prestige, pride, and manhood. The road to mainstream American success is opened, at least for the moment or for the day. The oppressed man can use cool and hustling as his best chance to advance financially and socially and to feel important.

Foster believes that considerable talent is expended in pulling off the street-corner hustle. If racism and exploitation by whites had not pulled the plug on legitimate means for establishing masculinity, illegal outlets would not have thrived. He argues that countless young black males—cool cats and hustlers supreme—who have shown talent in their pursuit of the illegitimate game, would have shown extreme giftedness in the pursuit of mainstream avenues to success.

The street corner hustlers might have become more aggressive salesmen, businessmen, or politicians under more favorable conditions. But in the face of restricted opportunities, lack of middle-class black role models, and confronted with the successful models of the hustler and pimp, the young black male is tempted to take the street route to success. Ironically, the street man and the mainstream man both want the same thing. Both want to make it and to be seen by their families and friends as secure and successful—as somebody. But each sees a different road as the logical one to take.

Hudson offers an intriguing idea: although hustling might appear to be diametrically opposed to the Protestant ethic, it is actually an extension of it. He hypothesizes that the hustler's society may be deviant, but it is an adaptive, systematic form of deviance that struggles toward mainstream rewards and goals.

40   Survival dictates the cool cat's course. He accepts the expressive, cool path of the street because he quickly or eventually comes to believe that conventional routes are congested or closed off to him. For the cool cat who travels the road of hustling, conning, and gaming, pitfalls, as well as fame, may be around the corner.

Notes

1. H. Firestone, "Cats, Kicks and Color," *Social Problems* 1957, Vol. 5, p. 5.
2. J .K. Mancini, *Strategic Styles: Coping in the Inner City* (Hanover, N.H.: University Press of New England, 1981), p. 164.

3. E. Folb, *Runnin' down some lines: The Language and Culture of Black Teenagers* (Cambridge, Ma.: Harvard University Press, 1980), pp. 109–10; see also M. L. Knapp, "The Field of Nonverbal Communication: An Overview," in *On Speech Communication*, ed. C. J. Stewart and B. Kendall (New York: Holt, Rinehart and Winston, 1978).
4. *Ibid.*
5. B. Dworkin and S. Dworkin, *Cool: Young Adults in the Negro Ghetto*, unpublished manuscript, Washington University, St. Louis, Mo.
6. Folb 1980, 112, 115.
7. Folb 1980, 38.
8. Folb 1980, 42.
9. H. R. Brown, *Die Nigger Die!* (New York: Dial Press, 1969).
10. W. J. McCord, et al., *Life Styles in the Black Ghetto* (New York: W. W. Norton, 1969), p. 129.

Engaging the Text

1. How can the "cool pose" be understood as a carefully crafted persona based on power and control? Why would such a pose be especially important for black males who have limited control and limited access to conventional power and resources?

2. In what different areas does maintaining a cool exterior reveal itself as a way to enhance manhood? How do the distinctive cool styles in clothing, cars, and conversation reinforce this image?

Exploring Your Cultural Perspective

1. How persuasive do you find Majors and Billson's argument that the "cool pose" is not so much a manipulation as a survival strategy? What limitations does this persona entail?

2. To what extent do the articles and advertisements in popular magazines geared to an African American audience, such as *Essence* and *Ebony*, make use of the "cool pose" **archetype** (perfect example) to appeal to their audience? For example, what features of the "cool pose" are exemplified in the photograph of the popular singer Maxwell (Figure 4.1, page 248)?

FIGURE 4.1

GARETH PALMER

Bruce Springsteen and Authentic Masculinity

Gareth Palmer is a senior lecturer in media production at the University of Salford, England. His publications include "The Cosby Show" in *Critical Survey* and "Noel's House Party" in *Interface*. The essay reprinted here appeared in *Sexing the Groove: Popular Music and Gender*, edited by Sheila Whiteley (1997). Palmer argues that Bruce Springsteen's image of blue-collar masculinity embodies male dissatisfaction with this traditional gender role.

Thinking Critically

As you read this article, underline what you consider to be the key points in Palmer's analysis. In the margins, note your responses to what Palmer says, including examples that illustrate or contradict his position. Consider the various reasons that Palmer offers for Springsteen's popularity.

Since the mid-1970s the combined disciplines of philosophy, anthropology and cultural theory have set about deconstructing the "crisis of masculinity." Masculinity was revealed as a complex ideological construction whose intellectual power resulted from its historically validated claims to reason and whose physical power is destined by anatomy. Masculinity is a performance covering an emptiness, a cultural bribe, and a prime victim of the "disturbing fragmentation of the social and cultural era."[1] But men do not constitute one homogeneous group experiencing the same type of masculinity. They are all negotiating their own masculinities via systems of identification. For example, professional men are subject to entrepreneurial definitions of manhood which are quite different from those promoted in blue-collar culture. In view of this, it might perhaps be more accurate to say that masculinities are going through crises.

The exploration of masculinities has been the subject of extensive debate over the last decade. Groups ranging from punk Straight-Edge to the so-called Men's Movement in cultural politics have sought to define themselves in the negative: i.e. we are not nurturers or home-makers. In these models, masculinity is about exclusion and a rigid self-policing of identity. Given the changes in the post-industrial world it may be that such constructions are no longer tenable. However, these definitions of manliness are still prevalent in the world of signs. Films such as *Terminator, Die Hard,* and *Judge Dredd* and the hyper-macho posturing of rock stars such as Bon Jovi and Aerosmith are evidence of a desperate attempt to assert the continuing validity of the externally rampant male in a world which has little need of him. The humour that accompanies these performances helps diffuse the criticism but fails to disguise the desire to reassert the dominant male of patriarchy.

What is always true is that masculinity is not a gendered inevitability but something constructed by a variety of agencies through signs. The aim of this chapter is to examine the work of Bruce Springsteen as a dominant force in promoting and signifying masculinity. In the first section, Springsteen is examined as a writer mapping the signifiers of the Western onto contemporary blue-collar culture. His figures patrol borders, real and metaphorical. They capture and keep their womenfolk, and they struggle with their fathers who are represented as embodiments of the patriarchal law. The tragedy of these figures lies in their inability to abandon the carefully drawn markers of masculinity which prevents escape into the world of feeling.

In the second section I shall discuss how Springsteen's performance, in a variety of formats, is another valuable indication of what his masculinity "means." The rock aesthetic "depends crucially on an argument about authenticity."[2] Thus, it is argued that Springsteen's performance can be interpreted as that of a man striving for authentic masculinity, and this will be discussed through an analysis of his relationship with his fans, his videos and his "look."

SPRINGSTEENS' WORLD

Fathers and Sons

5 Since the industrial revolution the father has represented the breadwinner in the home, but changes in the industrial and economic base have threatened this position. In XY magazine, a review of Stephen Biddulph's *Manhood* inadvertently reveals the bias towards the father that is the root of many definitions of masculinity and the need to reassert this power:

> Many men have missed out on good close relationships with their fathers and few of us have had close intimate relationships with other men.[3]

Springsteen responds to these changes by exploring the three stages that are said to be typical in the relationship between father and son—adoration, rebellion and *rapprochement*. What informs each stage is the power the father has as a mythical figure. The tragedy is that the son becomes disenchanted with the failure of his father to match the ideal. And although the ideal is eventually questioned it never loses its hold.

In the first stage masculinity is understood through a child's eyes as a pose or posture such as a way of walking. The Springsteen narrator remembers the image as an authentic sign of masculinity which he hopes will get him through his wedding day:

> All I can remember is being five years old
> following your footsteps in the sand
> tryin' hard to walk like a man[4]

In the second stage comes the rebellion crucial to masculine development and which has become the mainstay of much rock and roll. The force of the narrative here is directed against the father's fatigue and lethargy. Springsteen's sons want their fathers to be role models and yet whether as parents, husbands, friends or workers each boy sees only failure and despair. The father remains a powerful but negative presence expressing the sullen resentment of men who have not been taught to articulate beyond resentful grunts. It often boils down to the elementary "this town ain't big enough for the both of us" of the western.

> Daddy worked his whole life, for nothing but the pain.
> Now he walks these empty rooms looking for something to blame,
> You inherit the sins, you inherit the flames,
> Adam raised a Cain.[5]

The father is continually defeated by the work process and can offer his family only an embittered husk at the end of the day. In songs like "Factory," father is "walking through them gates in the rain" like one of the automatons in *Metropolis*. He can't escape his dull torment nor can he comprehend it. The only way this father can express his anger is to fight "and just you better believe boy, somebody's gonna get hurt tonight." But even this rage is a futile gesture directed at others emasculated by a lack of power in the workplace.

In reflective moments father takes son out in his used car to look at the Mansion on the Hill—signifier of an enduring class divide in Springsteen's world. No words are spoken in this mute communion as father and son gaze at this remote prize. The heroism of this still quiet figure is underscored by the son's growing understanding that his father's failure may be down to some problems in the economy. But by then it is too late—the process of alienation has completely removed his father from the world of feeling and communication is difficult. Not surprisingly the boy swears never to be in the same situation: "They ain't gonna do to me/What I watched them do to you."[6] He wants to take charge, gain control: "It's a town full of losers and I'm pullin' out of here to win,"[7] but escape is difficult as the hero always stops behind state lines, where the highway ends. All around him are cages and prisons—real and metaphorical.

At the end of the long day's journey into night Springsteen's fathers are alone staring into an emptiness they can neither articulate or efface. Their prime function in the home is to provide a dull mute force against which the son—like all sons—must struggle to break free. This struggle itself is given mythic proportions by Springsteen's use of biblical imagery to frame the conflicts in this urban landscape, perhaps suggesting that conflicts between fathers and sons inhere in the nature of their relationship. The empty prize of masculinity is won by following a primitive code of loyalty which functions to limit its adherents. Men are condemned to be active, independent and dominating. Any hint of passivity or feeling risks fracturing the ideal.

10   The tragedy for those figures lies in the lack of alternatives offered to industrial man. Blue-collar culture is presented as relegating feeling to the feminine but its own sign-ideals of masculinity have disappearing referents. Springsteen presents the poses and gestures as a temporary haven from having to confront the failure of an unattainable masculine ideal. In the grim real world fathers and sons are left with few places to pitch the flimsy tent of masculinity. Where else can the anger go but into the domestic sphere, where men try to assert the masculine fantasy of control they have been taught is at the root of their identity as men?

Springsteen's characters experience a despair that has no object to focus upon. They know that what they have isn't working but they don't know what to do to change things: "But it's a sad man who lives in his own skin and can't stand the company."[8]

Girls/Family

Springsteen's female characters faithfully recreate the divide between good-time girl and wife that is rooted in the western. Occasionally a woman is a buddy but more usually women are decorative angels whose beauty is worn down as they become disenchanted with the husks of men their husbands have become.

Women first have to be captured then placed in the home where they come to represent the ambiguous prize of domesticity. The comforts women offer necessarily entail the end of those essential wanderings that define masculinity. "Racing in the Streets" is typical in that the "little girl" is the prize which the hero wins in a race. However, she ends up alone and "crying on the porch of her daddy's house, all her pretty dreams are torn." Beyond expressing despair the heroine has little to do or say. Women are mysterious, impenetrable and other. No optimistic end is possible, for both men and women are locked into blinkered positions on what is and is not their role.

Springsteen's women do not exist as characters in their own right but as signifiers of domesticity and commitment against which men define their masculinity. Men's right to "fool around" becomes a part of their self-definition. The good times are celebrated in numbers like "Sherry Darlin" and "Born to Run" which show women offering sensual delights. Here Springsteen expresses a true blue-collar authentic sexuality—"Lovin' you is a man's job." In these moments the hero is at one with a million rock stars demonstrating their commitment to a primitive model of sexual politics. At the risk of overstating the case, when Springsteen is rockin', his lyrics display increasing levels of crudity. It's almost as if the crowd-pleasers are designed with simple pictures in mind. Simply wrapping this up in a humorous package smuggles in the mythology propelling it. The difference between Springsteen and the rest is that the pessimism informing his more sombre numbers reveals the narrator/hero as a sensitive type "after all."

If we look at the language Springsteen uses we may gain an insight into his conception of women. For example in *The River*, an album considered one of his most profound and reflective, Springsteen offers one of the most restricted readings of women to emerge from an adult-rocker in some time. In nine of the twenty tracks women are referred to as "little girls." Further to this they are seen as hopeless figures in need of men to protect them via marriage, thus perpetuating the male/female divide of patriarchy. But the crudity of this picture is overlooked because Springsteen is seen as an authentic figure who lived in this world and can write authoritatively of it.

Perhaps Springsteen's pessimism helps underscore his authenticity. The good times don't last long and marriage is never far away. When the hero gets Mary pregnant in *The River*, "man that was all she wrote." A union card and wedding soon follow. As the hero figure moves from boyhood to adulthood he encounters further frustrations. Masculinity becomes a paradox of power and discipline. Man is encouraged to be a breadwinner which gives him certain power but it also represents a prison which denies him opportunities for independence and freedom which are the core of mythic masculinity. Springsteen's figures repeat a cycle of behaviour, the futility of which they realise too late. They are tempted by the cultural bribe of a masculinity which promises to give them identity but which remains unattainable and leaves them unfulfilled.

Some of the most touching moments come when Springsteen's heroes are close to their womenfolk, for example, in "Drive All Night" when they "lie in the heat of the night like prisoners all our lives." But perhaps it is revealing that these moments occur when the women in question are asleep—only then and in abstract can they be celebrated, only in silence can the true man whisper such devotions. Here then in another western myth—that of the strong silent type whose heart may be tender, but whose loyalty to a primitive code of masculinity with self-control at its core disqualifies him from expressing himself. The cautious Bill Horton can't believe his luck when he finds and marries a beautiful woman but he is haunted by the mystery of her and can't relax:

> Billy felt a coldness rise up inside him that he couldn't name
> Just as the words tattooed 'cross his knuckles
> he knew would always remain.[9]

Women's essential otherness is not something a man can understand so he stands apart, at best a witness to his remoteness.

Since *Darkness on the Edge of Town* Springsteen's figures have more moments of uncertainty and indecision when they become aware of their limitations as men. Sometimes the hero feels jealous or full of self-doubt: "Is that you baby or just a brilliant disguise?"[10] This is the most modern aspect of Springsteen—that which allows a crack in the edifice of masculinity and reveals the new insecurity of male identity.

Moss has suggested a progression in Springsteen's representation of women which sees them go from flesh-pots to love objects.[11] For example in "Spare Parts" the heroine brings up a child alone after being abandoned by an irresponsible man. As Springsteen himself defined it, this is a song about a woman "struggling to understand the value of her own independent existence."[12] But it is difficult to see a clear development as simplistic representations in songs dot all of Springsteen's albums. Thus on *Lucky Town* we hear: "All I need is your sweet kiss/To get me feeling like a real man."[13]

20   In tracing Springsteen's career we can note odd disjunctions between a rhetoric that expresses support for women as individuals with rights, and very narrow, stereotypical representations. In early songs like "Mary, Queen of Arkansas" the gender identity is confused: "You're not man enough for me to hate or woman enough for kissing." In the 1970s and 1980s women are honoured with romantic lines such as "You ain't a beauty but hey you're alright"[14] or celebrated as sexual figures in "Candy's Room." In the 1990s the only "advance" offered is the "honest" one that the hero has "feet of clay."[15]

If we take an overview of Springsteen's entire lyrical output it is perhaps instructive to note that if women are given an occupation it is most often that of hooker. In this way women are preserved as sad and mysterious—innocent of true love and corrupted by the world. The hooker's body is literally in service to a masculinity founded on ownership and control. She has no character and is there simply to fulfil fantasies—the ultimate of which is "all she wants is me."[16] It is precisely this fantasy that men need in order to sustain the belief that a hooker is a forlorn individual simply looking for the right man to "take charge" of her situation. Each visit is an opportunity to celebrate true masculinity and to take refuge in the fantasy that she can make fleetingly real. The man's body remains his own possession and crucial to his sense of identity. He cannot be corrupted by his visits to the hooker for he preserves the mind/body distinction. He is in control while the woman within, the threatening other of the unconscious, is symbolically controlled by his dominance of the hooker. Man is pure mind, women are flesh, the territory to be colonised and controlled. As long as he works within this framework man will maintain the distance he feels necessary to his self-definition.

Work

David Morgan has written of how "Work, in both the general and specific sense, is assumed to be a major basis of identity and what it means to be a man."[17] Work is one of the key sites where masculine identity is formed and yet men have a complex relationship to their work: Men need to work in order to survive and yet it can destroy them. The loss of the industrial base and the computerisation of many processes coupled with the erosion of union power and the loss of apprenticeship schemes has meant that men are left with fewer opportunities to define their masculinity. Springsteen's songs articulate the problems facing workers coming to terms with this transformed industrial landscape.

If we were to catalogue the occupations of Springsteen's characters, we would note that the predominant ones are factory hand and mechanic. Also significant are carnival workers, dockers, construction workers, police and hookers. It will be noted that these jobs are principally concerned with physical displays of masculinity—a disappearing world.

In Springsteen's world the men who work in factories see them as "mansions of pain" offering little reward in terms of self-respect. The simple truths that emerge from such situations are that after such work men need to reassert their masculine power in some way. This often involves them in a great deal of "face work," the exaggerated claims to potency that Adler saw as crucial to the construct of masculinity.

The work of the mechanic links to the mythic America where cars, like 25 horses, explore unknown territories. Cars are where men perform some of the last rituals of masculinity for a culture that has little need of them. After work, or in place of work, men work on their cars. The car represents an escape from the parental home and an opportunity to break free—although no one ever really escapes. The careful reconstruction of a classic car represents homage to an unfulfilled dream of freedom.

Another significant site for Springsteen's figures is the carnival. The middle-class flâneur visit the carnival to experience forbidden pleasures as it represents a licensed arena for experiment. But in Springsteen's world it has only a little tawdry glamour. The workers demythologise what they do while the hero sees only metaphors in the creaking motions of the Big Dipper and the Tunnel of

Love. The carnival is a dark and dangerous place not because it is threatening or mysterious but because it foreshadows the grim world of marriage and disappointment to follow.

> It ought to be easy ought to be simple enough
> Man meets woman and they fall in love
> But the house is haunted and the ride gets rough
> And you've got to learn to love with what you can't rise above
> If you want to ride down into this tunnel of love[18]

The police/state troopers are the physical embodiments of the law and the state. But these men are not overworked for the limits are imprinted in the minds of these young workers. Borders are significant in that they represent the limits of the possible. If masculinity is about policing boundaries then these visits to imprecise borders are significant, for here men go through the tests they feel they must endure. It is at borders that men discover the limits of themselves and encounter culturally defined standards for masculine behaviour. On *Darkness on the Edge of Town* the possibilities of transgressing class boundaries are tested only to re-establish those relations of dominance which represent masculine identity. The narrator sings of an old flame who married into money:

> Well if she wants to see me
> you can tell her that I'm easily found
> Tell her there's a spot out near . . . the bridge
> and tell her—there's a darkness on the edge of town . . .[19]

On *Nebraska* lawmen express codes both ancient and inappropriate for the modern world: "man leaves his wife and family—that man ain't no good."[20] Growing up in blue-collar culture means developing an awareness of the Law. This is either the law of the father embodied in the police and resented in a sullen way, or the unwritten laws of loyalty to the community. Adherence to laws gives men an identity. But the limitations of these laws are written on the body and deny men access to the world of feeling. Eventually the borders are internalised and passed down as the natural limitations of "what a man's gotta do."

In many Springsteen narratives the dead weight of tradition presses its characters into blind obedience to laws they don't understand but pass on to their sons. The powerlessness is eloquent in its simplicity but rather self-defeating. A man joins the union in the same way that he would join any organisation his friends did. But it doesn't seem terribly effective in this industrial land—perhaps an all too relevant comment on life within Springsteen's blue-collar milieu.

Masculinity is culturally and historically variable but not in Springsteen's world. The fact that men are now addressed as consumers, care-givers, objects of desire, etc. is never allowed to intrude on the landscape. Springsteen is holding on to the traditional icons of masculinity in the monument valley of rock. Given the rather bleak universe that Springsteen has built, how are we to explain its enduring popularity? It may be that those listening to his songs hear and take comfort in his clear definitions of men and women. The cracks of doubt in this masculine persona and the powerful pessimism give it authority and a point of identification. It may be a despairing picture but it's also a conservative one which many living in the new industrial revolutions might relate to.

Notes

1. Frosh S. (1994) *Sexual Difference: Masculinity and Psychoanalysis*, London: Routledge, p. 91.
2. Pfeil, F. (1995) *White Guys*, London: Verso, p. 78.
3. Review of Biddulph, S. *Manhood*, in *XY Magazine*, Summer 1995.
4. "Walk Like a Man" on *Tunnel of Love* (1987) Zomba Music Pub. Ltd. (Bruce Springsteen).
5. "Adam Raised a Cain" on *Darkness on the Edge of Town* (1978) © Bruce Springsteen, CBS Records.
6. "Independence Day," from *The River*, CBS Records, Intersong Ltd., 1980.
7. "Thunder Road," from *Born to Run*, CBS Records, 1976.
8. "Living Proof," from *Human Touch*, Columbia Records, 1992.
9. "Cautious Man," from *Tunnel of Love*, CBS Records, 1987.
10. "Brilliant Disguise," from *Tunnel of Love*, CBS Records, 1987.
11. Moss, P. (1992) "Where Is the Promised Land? Class and Gender in Bruce Springsteen's Rock Lyrics," *Geografiska* 74 B: 3.
12. Quote from Springsteen, introducing "Spare Parts" on his video anthology.
13. "Real Man," from *Lucky Town*, Columbia Records, 1992.
14. "Thunder Road," from *Born to Run*, CBS Records, 1976.
15. "Man's Job," from *Human Touch*, Columbia, 1992.
16. "Candy's Room," from *Darkness on the Edge of Town*, CBS Records, 1978.
17. Morgan, D. (1992) *Discovering Men*, London: Routledge, p. 76.
18. "Tunnel of Love," from album of the same name, CBS Records, 1987.
19. "Darkness on the Edge of Town," from album of the same name, CBS Records, 1978.
20. "State Trooper," from *Nebraska*, CBS Records, 1982.

Engaging the Text

1. In what way is the concept of the worker and work itself an essential component of the Springsteen image? What features of his performance and lyrics strengthen this association?

2. How do the ways in which women are depicted in Springsteen's songs support the masculine identity he creates?

FIGURE 4.2

3. In your opinion, what is Palmer's underlying attitude toward Springsteen? Does he admire him, or does he think Springsteen has perpetuated a hoax? Explain your answer.

Exploring Your Cultural Perspective

1. Analyze how one of your current favorite male performers projects masculinity through his songs and his style.

2. How accurate do you feel Springsteen's portrayal of masculinity is? Focus on one of Palmer's topics: fathers and sons, girls/family, or work.

3. What essential features of Bruce Springsteen's stage persona does Figure 4.2 communicate?

ANNE TAYLOR FLEMING

Sperm in a Jar

A variety of procedures for treating infertility have become common-place in our culture, yet we don't necessarily consider the emotional impact of these technologies on the recipients. Anne Taylor Fleming takes us on a personal journey that reflects the attitudes of many in a generation who are ambivalent toward this technology. Fleming has written many articles for *Glamour, Vogue, Woman's Day,* and the *New York Times,* in which this essay first appeared (1994). She expanded these ideas in her 1995 book *Motherhood Deferred: A Woman's Journey.* Fleming's recent works include *Sophie is Gone* (1996) and *This Means Mischief* (1997).

Thinking Critically

Fleming draws on her personal experiences to illustrate how technologic interventions have changed our ideas about motherhood. If you were unable to have a child, which, if any, of the many approaches to becoming a parent would you consider? Alternatively, would you simply adopt a child? Why or why not?

On a beautiful spring day in 1988 I am driving down the Santa Monica free-way with a jar of my sixty-year-old husband's sperm in my purse, en route to the Institute for Reproductive Research at the Hospital of the Good Samaritan in downtown Los Angeles. He is at home sleeping after having yielded up this specimen, and I am gingerly maneuvering through the heavy morning traffic with my stash, careful not to swerve or speed lest I upset my cargo or get stopped by a cop.

This is what we have come to, after sixteen years of marriage: this clinical breeding. Oh, my, how did I get here? I ask myself as I park the car, surrender the sperm to the lab technician, and take my place in the waiting room. What quirk of fate, of timing, of biology, has brought me to this clinic, presided over by Dr. Richard Marrs, one of the new crop of infertility experts who do the procreative bidding of those of us who cannot do it on our own? A soft-spoken forty-year-old Texan with a specialty in reproductive endocrinology, Dr. Marrs spouts abbreviations for all the out-of-body pregnancy procedures—I.V.F. (in-vitro fertilization), GIFT (gamete intra-Fallopian transfer), ZIFT (zygote intra-Fallopian transfer), IUI (intra-uterine insemination), ITI (intertubal insemination)—with optimism and assurance. His waiting room is full of anxious women from all over the country, from all over the world.

I am one of them, this sisterhood of the infertile. At thirty-eight, I have entered the high-tech world of postsexual procreation. As I look around at the other women—some in blue jeans, like me, some in suits en route to work, just stopping by to get a shot of sperm before heading out to do battle in corporate America—I smile a small, repressed smile at them and for them. We have sailed together into a strange, surreal country, the Country of the Disembodied Pro-creators, mutually dedicated to practicing biological warfare against our very own bodies in the hope of reversing time, cheating fate, and getting our hands on an embryo, a baby, a life.

We're hard-core, those of us here. Last-ditchers. And there's a kind of stubborn, exhilarating pride radiating from us. No wimps, we. Toting our small white paper bags of hypodermic needles and hundreds of dollars' worth of fertility drugs, we shoot up once or twice daily with the expertise of junkies, our hips tight and swollen like cheeks with wads of tobacco in them. We are fearless, Amazonian in our baby hunger, bereft. The small waiting room vibrates with our hope.

5   "Anne."

I go into an examining room, strip from the waist down and take my place in the stirrups. The doctor appears. Boyish and solicitous, his hair beginning to gray like that of many of his patients, he is perfectly cast for his role as pro-creative assistant to a bunch of desperate women. Gently he inserts the dildo-like scanner and, voilà, my ovaries appear as if by magic on the grainy screen next to me. The doctor and I count together: One, two, three, on the left side; one, two, on the right.

"You have the ovaries of a twenty-five-year-old," he says, reaching for the syringe of my husband's sperm, now washed and sorted and counted. And with one deft whoosh through a thin catheter inserted up through my vagina and cervix, the sperm are sent spinning into my uterus.

I feel nothing, no pain; but strangely enough, tears hover. There is something in the matter-of-fact gentleness with which the doctor folds my legs back up off the stirrups that affects me, a reminder of touch and flesh, normal pro-creation instead of this cold, solo breeding. I hold the tears until the doctor leaves. In my supine position, which I must maintain for at least fifteen minutes, I imagine the sperm settling in, looking around after their frantic, accelerated journey. I implore my eggs to make their move, to come down my Fallopian tubes into the sperm's frenzied midst, there to be pursued and penetrated.

I drifted into a reverie, remembering being pursued and won and indeed penetrated myself as a young college girl in Northern California in the late 1960s. I remember the wonderfully sticky smells that hung over those years, an erotic brew of sweat and incense and marijuana. I remember the aromatic afternoons in bed in my small dorm room, the sun filtering in through the redwoods, the light filigreed across our skin and the spines of my books—Rousseau and Thoreau and Marx and Marcuse. From a record player down the hall Janis Joplin wailed about freedom. A cocoon of passion and politics, of pine trees and patchouli oil. Armed with my contraceptives and my fledgling feminism, I was on the cusp of a fabulous journey. My sisters and I were. We were the golden girls of the brave new world, ready, willing and able to lay our contraceptively endowed bodies across the chasm between the feminist mystique and the world the feminists envisioned. Strong, smart, educated, we were the beneficiaries of unique historical timing, when the doors were opening, the old male-female roles were falling and the world was ours to conquer: the world of men, of lawyers and doctors, astronauts and poets. I wanted in that world. I wanted to matter. I wanted to be somebody. I wanted to send dazzling words out into that world.

Babies didn't cross my mind back then. And not for a long, long time after. 10 I took contraception for granted: birth-control pills briefly in my late teens, then a diaphragm. It became not only a fixed part of my body but also a fixed part of my mind—entrenched, reflexive, the ticket to my female freedom. Not for me an unexpected pregnancy, the fate of women throughout the millennia.

In the early 1970s, when my husband, Karl, whispered above me about wanting to have a baby, I shrank from his ardor. I couldn't imagine it, didn't even feel the connection between lovemaking and baby making, so methodically had I put contraception—and ambition—between my womb and pregnancy. I had been adamant, powerful in my rebuff of the sperm ejaculated into my body, the sperm I am now importuning to do its fertilizing dance.

After all those years of sex without procreation, here I lie, engaged in this procreation without sex. It is a stunning reversal, a cosmic joke. It contains my history, that arc—from all that sex to no sex—a lifetime of trying to be somebody, my whole own woman in the latter half of twentieth-century America, a lifetime of holding motherhood at bay. The nurse gently knocks and I am released. On the freeway heading home, I am already beginning the fourteen-day countdown to the pregnancy test—am I, am I not; am I, am I not—a moment-by-moment monitoring, an imaginary ear to the womb intent on picking up any uterine sign of life.

In my hope and in my angst, I am tempted to roll down the window and shout: "Hey, hey, Gloria! Germaine! Kate! Tell us: How does it feel to have ended up without babies, children, flesh of your flesh? Did you mean to thumb your noses at motherhood, or is that what we heard or intuited for our own needs? Simone, Simone de Beauvoir and Virginia Woolf, can you wade in here too, please, share any regrets, my barren heroines from the great beyond? Tell me: Was your art worth the empty womb—predicated on it, in fact—no children to divert attention, to splinter the focus? Can you tell me, any of you: Am I going to get over this?"

The clouds do not part; no feminist goddess peers down with a benediction on my emptiness. I am on my own here, an agnostic midlife feminist sending up silent prayers to the fertility gods on high. (I also send up apologies to the mothers of yore, the station-wagon moms with their postpartum pounds who felt denigrated in the liberationist heyday by the young, lean, ambitious women like me so intent on making our way.) In my most aggrieved moments I think of infertility as comeuppance for having so fervently and so long delayed motherhood. The data are irrefutable: Fertility declines with age.

15   How could something as primal as this longing to procreate have been so long repressed, so long buried? Not only am I infertile but, worse, a cliché, a humbled renegade haunting the natural imagination, held up as some sort of dupe of feminism, rather a double dupe of the sexual revolution and the women's revolution.

I will persevere in this pregnancy quest. I know that about myself. And as I turn into the driveway I breathe a pride-filled sigh. I can manage this. If it doesn't work this time, I will try again next month and the next. I will be optimistic, as dogged in my pursuit of motherhood as in everything else: Our Lady of the Stirrups, shooting up and running up and down the smoggy L.A. freeways with jars of sperm if need be.

Dr. Marrs and I are having our procreative postmortem. It has been only a matter of months, but it seems a thousand years ago that I was here. After countless inseminations and surgical procedures, I still do not have a baby. He says the only thing left to offer women like me is—and I almost want to cover my ears because I know full well what's coming—those damn donor eggs. That's the panacea now for us older women who aren't getting pregnant even with high-tech intervention. Am I willing to buy eggs from another woman to make embryos with my husband's sperm and carry them as my own—if I can carry them? This is a daunting new edge to dance on somehow.

He says the odds for donor eggs on an I.V.F. or GIFT procedure go as high as a 25 to 33 percent success rate per cycle, no matter the recipient's age. Big, fat, juicy odds from where I'm sitting. So, are eggs and sperm totally analogous finally, equally purchasable? Is this the logical reduction of liberation, this absolute biological equality?

It strikes me as conceptual hanky-panky—my husband's sperm and another woman's egg. I imagine a stranger floating in my amniotic fluid. What do I tell this child, and when? Ninety percent of the couples who buy eggs do so anonymously, I am told—most clinics won't do otherwise—the same way couples have been buying sperm for so many years. They simply pretend to all concerned that the baby is 100 percent genetically theirs.

Can I do that, be matched with a woman whose physical characteristics   *20* approximate mine and just carry the conceit on to the grave? No. I would have to know that down the road my child could see and meet his or her biological mother. I get dizzy with the moral and emotional ramifications of this. But I am not ready to shut the door, especially since doctors can work their magic even on postmenopausal women. Still, do I really want to be a fifty-year-old first-time mother?

Isn't that finally beyond the limit, procreating in the final trimester of life? Do I want it so bad—to have someone, anyone, doing somersaults in my gut? I can't answer. In fact, there is one other alternative that will allow me my own embryo—not a pregnancy but an embryo. Gestational surrogacy. Rent-a-womb.

A friend of proven fertility has offered to try to carry my embryos for me. It is one of those offers that transcends love. Why not? I can make them, that we know; and she can certainly carry them, or at least has carried her own. But in an offhand moment she says ebulliently, "I'll breast feed them too for a few days, just to get them started," and something in me tenses despite the overweening generosity of her offer.

My babies? You will breast feed my babies? And in that instant I have a sharp inkling of how fine the lines are in all this talk of scrambled eggs and borrowed wombs.

In the meantime, I mourn. Karl doesn't really. We have survived. As the father of four grown sons, he feels no stubborn need for our baby, as I do, as the younger husbands of my friends do. His detachment is faintly annoying but mostly restful.

For me now, it's over, and I set about, as is my writer's wont, trying to   *25* reckon with all the mixed messages and complicated choices faced by women over the last decades, looking for clues always to my delayed and unconsummated motherhood. True, those bedeviling baby-making possibilities remain, and I toss them around in the days and weeks and months after I have officially declared my independence from Dr. Marrs and his seductive magic. But I don't begrudge anyone else's choices. Going through this, with all the disapproval from various quarters—friend and foe, feminist and counterfeminist—I am aware of how lonely some decisions can be.

Engaging the Text

1. After considering the range of options that might make it possible for her to have a child, Fleming rejects all the choices. What are her reasons for doing so?

2. What sense do you get of Fleming's personality and her feelings about the procedure she undergoes? How does Fleming's use of irony make her narrative more effective? Why didn't Fleming get pregnant earlier in her life when she had the chance? Does the disparity in ages between Fleming (she is 38) and her husband (he is 60) affect your response to her essay? Why or why not?

3. The freedom to postpone having children that characterized the 1970s has now exacted an unforeseen price in the lives of many women (and men). How would you characterize the shift in values that took place in the United States between then and now?

Exploring Your Cultural Perspective

1. How have new technologies transformed traditional concepts of what it means to be a mother? Can parents have the same relationship with a child produced through a sperm bank, frozen embryo, donor egg, in vitro fertilization, or surrogate parent as with a child conceived the old-fashioned way? Why or why not?

2. Reports from Japan suggest a dramatic shift away from the traditional Asian preference for male heirs. Surveys show that up to seventy-five percent of young Japanese parents now prefer baby girls because they are seen as easier to raise, more likely to bond emotionally with their parents, and more likely to look after their elderly parents. By 1999, Japanese clinics offered sex-selection techniques comparable to the infertility treatments discussed by Anne Taylor Fleming. By contrast, China's one-child policy, which you can find out more about on the Internet, has resulted in a disproportionate number of male children. How do you feel about selecting the sex of your children?

SUSAN BORDO
Never Just Pictures

Susan Bordo is professor of English and women's studies at the University of Kentucky and was awarded the Singletary Chair of Humanities. Bordo's book *Unbearable Weight: Feminism, Western Culture and the Body* (1993) examines the myths, ideologies, and pathologies of the modern female body. She is also the author of *The Male Body: A New Look at Men in Public and Private* (1999). "Never Just Pictures" first appeared in *Twilight Zones: The Hidden Life of Cultural Images from Plato to O. J.* (1997).

Thinking Critically
Before you read Bordo's essay, which raises questions about the images of women presented in advertising, think about some current ads for women's products. Do the ads encourage women to be dissatisfied with the way they look? Whether you are male or female, what part, if any, do the media play in your concept of how you should look?

BODIES AND FANTASIES

When Alicia Silverstone, the svelte nineteen-year-old star of *Clueless*, appeared at the Academy Awards just a smidge more substantial than she had been in the movie, the tabloids ribbed her cruelly, calling her "fatgirl" and "buttgirl" (her next movie role is Batgirl) and "more *Babe* than babe."[1] Our idolatry of the trim, tight body shows no signs of relinquishing its grip on our conceptions of beauty and normality. Since I began exploring this obsession it seems to have gathered momentum, like a spreading mass hysteria. Fat is the devil, and we are continually beating him—"eliminating" our stomachs, "busting" our thighs, "taming" our tummies—pummeling and purging our bodies, attempting to make them into something other than flesh. On television, infomercials hawking miracle diet pills and videos promising to turn our body parts into steel have become as commonplace as aspirin ads. There hasn't been a tabloid cover in the past few years that didn't boast of an inside scoop on some star's diet regime, a "fabulous" success story of weight loss, or a tragic relapse. (When they can't come up with a current one, they scrounge up an old one; a few weeks ago the *National Inquirer* ran a story on Joan Lunden's fifty-pound weight loss fifteen years ago!) Children in this culture grow up knowing that you can never be thin enough and that being fat is one of the worst things one can be. One study asked ten- and eleven-year-old boys and girls to rank drawings of children with various physical handicaps; drawings of fat children elicited the greatest disapproval and discomfort, over pictures of kids with facial disfigurements and missing hands.

Psychologists commonly believe that girls with eating disorders suffer from "body image disturbance syndrome": they are unable to see themselves as anything but fat, no matter how thin they become. If this is a disorder, it is one that has become a norm of cultural perception. Our ideas about what constitutes a body in need of a diet have become more and more pathologically trained on the slightest hint of excess. This ideal of the body beautiful has largely come from fashion designers and models. (Movie stars, who often used to embody a more voluptuous ideal, are now modeling themselves after the models.) They have taught us "to love a woman's pelvis, her hipbones jutting out through a bias-cut gown . . . the clavicle in its role as a coat hanger from which clothes are suspended."[2] (An old fashion industry justification for skinniness in models was that clothes just don't "hang right" on heftier types.) The fashion industry has taught us to regard a perfect healthy, nonobese body [. . .] as an unsightly "before" ("Before CitraLean, no wonder they wore swimsuits like that"). In fact, those in the business have admitted that models have been getting thinner since 1993, when Kate Moss first repopularized the waif look. British models Trish Goff and Annie Morton make Moss look well fed by comparison,[3] and recent ad campaigns for Jil Sander go way beyond the thin-body-as-coat-hanger paradigm to a blatant glamorization of the cadaverous, starved look itself.[. . .] More and more ads featuring anorexic-looking young men are appearing too.

The main challenge to such images is a muscular aesthetic that *looks* more life-affirming but is no less punishing and compulsion-inducing in its demands on ordinary bodies. During the 1996 Summer Olympics—which were reported with unprecedented focus and hype on the fat-free beauty of muscular bodies—commentators celebrated the "health" of this aesthetic over anorexic glamour. But there is growing evidence of rampant eating disorders among female athletes, and it's hard to imagine that those taut and tiny Olympic gymnasts—the idols of preadolescents across the country—are having regular menstrual cycles. Their skimpy level of body fat just won't support it. During the Olympics I heard a commentator gushing about how great it was that the 1996 team was composed of eighteen- and nineteen-year-old women rather than little girls.

To me it is far more disturbing that these nineteen-year-olds still *look* (and talk) like little girls! As I watched them vault and leap, my admiration for their tremendous skill and spirit was shadowed by thoughts of what was going on *inside* their body—the hormones unreleased because of insufficient body fat, the organ development delayed, perhaps halted.

Is it any wonder that despite media attention to the dangers of starvation dieting and habitual vomiting, eating disorders have spread throughout the culture?[4] In 1993 in *Unbearable Weight* I argued that the old clinical generalizations positing distinctive class, race, family, and "personality" profiles for the women most likely to develop an eating disorder were being blasted apart by the normalizing power of mass imagery. Some feminists complained that I had not sufficiently attended to racial and ethnic "difference" and was assuming the white, middle-class experience as the norm. Since then it has been widely acknowledged among medical professionals that the incidence of eating and body-image problems among African American, Hispanic, and Native American women has been grossly underestimated and is on the increase.[5] Even the gender gap is being narrowed, as more and more men are developing eating disorders and exercise compulsions too. (In the mid-eighties the men in my classes used to yawn and pass notes when we discussed the pressure to diet; in 1996 they are more apt to protest if the women in the class talk as though it's their problem alone.)

The spread of eating disorders, of course, is not just about images. The   5 emergence of eating disorders is a complex, multilayered cultural "symptom," reflecting problems that are historical as well as contemporary, arising in our time because of the confluence of a number of factors.[6] Eating disorders are overdetermined in this culture. They have to do not only with new social expectations of women and ambivalence toward their bodies but also with more general anxieties about the body as the source of hungers, needs, and physical vulnerabilities not within our control. These anxieties are deep and long-standing in Western philosophy and religion, and they are especially acute in our own time. Eating disorders are also linked to the contradictions of consumer culture, which is continually encouraging us to binge on our desires at the same time as it glamorizes self-discipline and scorns fat as a symbol of laziness and lack of willpower. And these disorders reflect, too, our increasing fascination with the possibilities of reshaping our bodies and selves in radical ways, creating new bodies according to our mind's design.

The relationship between problems such as these and cultural images is complex. On the one hand, the idealization of certain kinds of bodies foments and perpetuates our anxieties and insecurities, that's clear. Glamorous images of hyperthin models certainly don't encourage a more relaxed or accepting attitude toward the body, particularly among those whose own bodies are far from that ideal. But, on the other hand, such images carry fantasized solutions *to* our anxieties and insecurities, and that's part of the reason why they are powerful. They speak to us not just about how to be beautiful or desirable but about how to get control of our lives, get safe, be cool, avoid hurt. When I look at the picture of a skeletal and seemingly barely breathing young woman [. . .], for example, I do not see a vacuous fashion ideal. I see a visual embodiment of what novelist and ex-anorexic Stephanie Grant means when she says in her autobiographical novel, *The Passion of Alice*, "If I had to say my anorexia was about any single thing, I would have said it was about living without desire. Without longing of any kind."[7]

Now, this may not seem like a particularly attractive philosophy of life (or a particularly attractive body, for that matter). Why would anyone want to look like death, you might be asking. Why would anyone want to live without desire? But recent articles in both the *New Yorker* and the *New York Times* have noted a new aesthetic in contemporary ads, in which the models appear dislocated and withdrawn, with chipped black nail polish and greasy hair, staring out at the viewer in a deathlike trance, seeming to be "barely a person." Some have called this wasted look "heroin chic": ex-model Zoe Fleischauer recalls that "they wanted models that looked like junkies. The more skinny and fucked-up you look, the more everybody thinks you're fabulous."[8]

Hilton Als, in the *New Yorker*, interprets this trend as making the statement that fashion is dead and beauty is "trivial in relation to depression."[9] I read these ads very differently. Although the photographers may see themselves as ironically "deconstructing" fashion, the reality is that no fashion advertisement can declare fashion to be dead—it's virtually a grammatical impossibility. Put that frame around the image, whatever the content, and we are instructed to find it glamorous. These ads are not telling us that beauty is trivial in relation to depression, they are telling us that depression is beautiful, that being wasted is *cool* [. . .]. The question then becomes not "Is fashion dead?" but "Why has death become glamorous?"

Freud tells us that in the psyche death represents not the destruction of the self but its return to a state prior to need, thus freedom from unfulfilled longing, from anxiety over not having one's needs met. Following Freud, I would argue that ghostly pallor and bodily disrepair, in "heroin chic" images, are about the allure, the safety, of being beyond needing, beyond caring, beyond desire. Should we be surprised at the appeal of being without desire in a culture that has invested our needs with anxiety, stress, and danger, that has made us craving and hungering machines, creatures of desire, and then repaid us with addictions, AIDS, shallow and unstable relationships, and cutthroat competition for jobs and mates? To have given up the quest for fulfillment, to be unconcerned with the body or its needs—or its vulnerability—is much wiser than to care.

So, yes, the causes of eating disorders are "deeper" than just obedience to   *10* images. But cultural images themselves *are* deep. And the way they become imbued and animated with such power is hardly mysterious. Far from being the purely aesthetic inventions that designers and photographers would like to have us believe they are—"It's just fashion, darling, nothing to get all politically steamed up about"—they reflect the designers' cultural savvy, their ability to sense and give form to flutters and quakes in the cultural psyche. These folks have a strong and simple motivation to hone their skills as cultural Geiger counters. It's called the profit motive. They want their images and the products associated with them to sell.

The profit motive can sometimes produce seemingly "transgressive" wrinkles in current norms. Recently designers such as Calvin Klein and Jil Sander have begun to use rather plain, ordinary-looking, unmadeup faces in their ad campaigns. Unlike the models in "heroin chic" ads, these men and women do not appear wasted so much as unadorned, unpolished, stripped of the glamorous veneer we have come to expect of fashion spreads. While many of them have interesting faces, few of them qualify as beautiful by any prevailing standards. They have rampant freckles, moles in unbeautiful places, oddly proportioned heads. Noticing these ads, I am first wondered whether we really were shifting into a new gear, more genuinely accepting of diversity and "flaws" in appearance. Then it suddenly hit me that these imperfect faces were showing up in clothing and perfume ads only and the *bodies* in these ads were as relentlessly normalizing as ever—not one plump body to complement the facial "diversity."

I now believe that what we are witnessing here is a commercial war. Clothing manufacturers, realizing that many people—particularly young people, at whom most of these ads are aimed—have limited resources and that encouraging them to spend all their money fixing up their faces rather than buying clothes is not in their best interests, are reasserting the importance of body over face as the "site" of our fantasies. In the new codes of these ads a too madeup look signifies a lack of cool, too much investment in how one looks. "Just Be," Calvin Klein tells us in a recent CK One ad. But looks—a lean body—still matter enormously in these ads, and we are still being told *how* to be—in the mode which best serves Calvin Klein. And all the while, of course, makeup and hair products continue to promote their own self-serving aesthetics of facial perfection.

Notes

1. I give great credit to Alicia Silverstone for her response to these taunts. In *Vanity Fair* she says, "I do my best. But it's much more important to me that my brain be working in the morning than getting up early and doing exercise. . . . The most

important thing for me is that I eat and that I sleep and that I get the work done, but unfortunately . . . it's the perception that women in film should look a certain way" ("Hollywood Princess," September 1996, pp. 292–294). One wonders how long she will manage to retain such a sane attitude!

2. Holly Brubach, "The Athletic Aesthetic," *The New York Times Magazine*, June 23, 1996, p. 51.

3. In early 1996 the Swiss watch manufacturer Omega threatened to stop advertising in British *Vogue* because of *Vogue's* use of such hyperthin models, but it later reversed this decision. The furor was reminiscent of boycotts that were threatened in 1994 when Calvin Klein and Coca-Cola first began to use photos of Kate Moss in their ads. In neither case has the fashion industry acknowledged any validity to the charge that their imagery encourages eating disorders. Instead, they have responded with defensive "rebuttals."

4. Despite media attention to eating disorders, an air of scornful impatience with "victim feminism" has infected attitudes toward women's body issues. Christina Hoff-Sommers charges Naomi Wolf (*The Beauty Myth*) with grossly inflating statistics on eating disorders and she poo-poos the notion that women are dying from dieting. Even if some particular set of statistics is inaccurate, why would Sommers want to deny the reality of the problem, which as a teacher she can surely see right before her eyes?

5. For the spread of eating disorders in minority groups, see, for example, "The Art of Integrating Diversity: Addressing Treatment Issues of Minority Women in the 90's," in *The Renfrew Perspective*, Winter 1994; see also Becky Thompson, *A Hunger So Wide and So Deep* (Minneapolis: University of Minnesota Press, 1994).

6. See my *Unbearable Weight* (Berkeley: University of California Press, 1993).

7. Stephanie Grant, *The Passion of Alice* (New York: Houghton Mifflin, 1995), 58.

8. Zoe Fleischauer quoted in "Rockers, Models, and the New Allure of Heroin," *Newsweek*, August 26, 1996.

9. Hilton Als, "Buying the Fantasy," *The New Yorker*, October 10, 1996, p. 70.

Engaging the Text

1. How do the pervasive eating disorders so common in U.S. culture suggest an underlying confusion in values associated with being fat?

2. Bordo draws on an unusually broad range of sources in framing her argument. Are these scholarly and academic works necessary to offset the pop-culture nature of her subject? Without them, would her argument seem less substantial? Why or why not?

3. What relationships between classes, men and women, and ethnic minorities and mainstream society underlie Bordo's thesis? What role do the media and advertising play as part of a system that urges women to shape, monitor, and re-form their bodies to fit cultural stereotypes?

" I WANT TO BE THIN LIKE ALLY McBEAL, STACKED LIKE BARBIE and ETERNALLY YOUNG LIKE A SUPERMODEL....
NOW IF YOU'LL EXCUSE ME, I HAVE TO GO VOMIT MY HAPPY MEAL. "

FIGURE 4.1

Exploring Your Cultural Perspective

1. Bordo views the implications of "heroin chic" images in advertisements as particularly ominous. In your opinion, what are these ads really saying? Do you agree with Bordo's analysis of them? Explain your answer.

2. Our attitudes toward food are invariably connected with cultural messages about losing weight and being thin. Analyze the promotional claims for any weight loss program, pill, diet, or exercise video, and in a short essay, discuss how cultural values are interwoven with the message. To what extent has your own self-image been determined by prevailing cultural expectations?

3. In your opinion, does the cartoon in Figure 4.3 ring true?

MARGE PIERCY
Barbie Doll

Since the introduction of the Barbie doll as a children's toy in the 1950s, its unattainable image of perfection has made it a cultural icon. Marge Piercy explores the negative consequences of such an unreachable role model in the following poem, which originally appeared in her collection *Circles in the Water* (1982). Her latest works include *City of Darkness: City of Light* (1997) and *The Art of Blessing the Day: Poems with a Jewish Theme* (1999).

Thinking Critically
Before you read this poem, think about the qualities that in your opinion constitute ideal feminine beauty. What part have advertising and the mass media played in shaping your ideal?

This girlchild was born as usual
and presented dolls that did pee-pee
and miniature GE stoves and irons
5 and wee lipsticks the color of cherry candy.
Then in the magic of puberty, a classmate said:
You have a great big nose and fat legs.

She was healthy, tested intelligent,
possessed strong arms and back,
10 abundant sexual drive and manual dexterity.
She went to and fro apologizing.
Everyone saw a fat nose on thick legs.

She was advised to play coy,
exhorted to come on hearty,
15 exercise, diet, smile and wheedle.
Her good nature wore out
like a fan belt.

So she cut off her nose and her legs
and offered them up.

In the casket displayed on satin she lay
with the undertaker's cosmetics painted on,   *20*
a turned-up putty nose,
dressed in a pink and white nightie.
Doesn't she look pretty? everyone said.
Consummation at last.
To every woman a happy ending.   *25*

Engaging the Text

1. How do the dolls and toys given to the "girlchild" convey society's expectations? How does she change herself in response to them?

2. How does the contrast between the girl's natural attributes and the changes she is encouraged to make convey Piercy's opinion about what society considers worthy?

3. Why does Piercy introduce such an extreme image in the final stanza of the poem? Is it ironic? Why or why not? How does it underscore her point? Discuss whether Piercy makes the Barbie doll a scapegoat for prevailing cultural attitudes.

Exploring Your Cultural Perspective

1. What do women's magazines reveal about the cultural pressures on women to reshape themselves in physical ways (through diet, exercise, and surgery) and psychological ways that corresponds to Piercy's critique? Two resources for examining how women are encouraged to suppress their natural selves in the interests of attracting a husband include Ellen Fein and Sherrie Schneider's books *The Rules: Time-tested Secrets for Capturing the Heart of Mr. Right* (1995) and *The Rules II* (1997). What does the popularity of these books (a total of 41 weeks on the *New York Times* bestseller list) suggest about American culture?

2. Pretend you are a Barbie or a Ken doll. Write a defense of yourself emphasizing the needs you meet and the way in which you function as a valid role model. For example, how might "Holiday Girl Barbie," a $200 porcelain production of a Barbie doll, justify her cost?

WARIS DIRIE

The Tragedy of Female Circumcision

The supermodel Waris Dirie was born in Somalia and as a child underwent the genital mutilation that is customary in that and in other Islamic countries, including the Sudan, Saudi Arabia, Egypt, Libya, and Yemen. Her experience, as told to Laura Ziv, first appeared in the March 1996 issue of *Marie Claire* magazine. Dirie's autobiography, *Desert Flower: The Extraordinary Journey of a Desert Nomad,* written with Cathleen Miller, was published in 1998.

Thinking Critically

Dirie draws on personal experience to protest the practice of female circumcision. As you read, note how she explains the significance of her personal struggle to bring this issue to public awareness.

In my profession as a model, people sometimes tell me I'm beautiful, but they don't know what lies beneath the surface. Let me tell you who I am and where I come from.

I was born in Somalia, East Africa, one of 12 children. I don't really know how old I am. I'm around 28. In Africa, there is no time, no watch, no calendar. My family is nomadic. When I was a child, we moved around every day, looking for food and water. We slept on the ground in the open air. I spent my time running around barefoot, with the whole desert before me. There was nothing to plan, no tomorrow. We lived every day as it came.

I had never heard anything about the western world, but somehow I knew there was something else outside Africa. I had never even seen a white person. But I always wanted to be different, so I asked my cousin, "Where do you go to become white?" They said, "If you leave Africa, you become white because there is no sun."

When I was about 5 years old, my father decided it was time for me to be circumcised. I remember it so clearly that if I think about it, I'll throw up. The woman who did it called herself a "professional cutter," but she was just an old gypsy who traveled around with her bag. My mother sat me down and said,

"Be a good girl; don't move. I don't have the energy to hold you down." The old woman held a dirty razor blade, and I could see the dried blood on it from the person she had cut before me. I opened my legs, closed my eyes, and blocked my mind. I did it for my mother. The woman didn't just cut the clitoris—she cut everything, including the labia. She then sewed me up tightly with a needle. All I could feel was pain. After I had been cut, I lay on the floor in agony. They tied my legs together to stop me from walking, so that I wouldn't rip open. I was on my back for a month. I couldn't eat, I couldn't think, I could not do anything. I turned black, blue, and yellow. I couldn't urinate—the pee just dripped out of me. After three weeks my mother found someone else to open me up a tiny bit to give me a space to pee because I was getting so sick. I bled for the next two, three months. I nearly died. I wanted to die at the time—I had given up on life.

One of my younger sisters and two of my cousins died from the procedure. 5 My mother has had it done, like her mother, grandmothers, and great-grandmothers before her. You can't escape it. They catch you, tie you down, and then do it. It's done for men. They think if you haven't been circumcised, you're going to sleep around. They cut you so that you won't be horny. It has nothing to do with religion. Neither the Bible nor the Koran talks about female circumcision anywhere. Men invented the custom so that sexual pleasure is nonexistent for women—sex is just for men. When you marry, the man forces himself in or cuts you with a knife. When you give birth, they unsew you. Once the baby has come out, they sew you back up again. It continues like this. A woman who has ten children is sewn up and opened like a piece of material.

One day, when I was about 13, my father came to me on the sand. "I have found a man for you," he said. "You are getting married. Aren't you happy?" He had sold me for five camels to a 60-year-old man. I met this man the next day. He looked so old. I thought, "There has got to be more to life." That was the second I decided to leave Africa. I told my mother. I was her favorite. "Do what you want," she said. "Be safe, be happy, and don't forget me." She gave me the biggest hug and cried.

I left that night for Mogadishu, the Somali capital, where I knew I had an aunt. I ran through the desert for about ten days, pushing myself to keep going until I was ready to drop. I had nothing on me, just a piece of cloth on my waist. When it was dark and tribesmen were asleep, I would drink milk from their camels. When I reached Mogadishu, I just stood there like a zombie, I was so scared. I told people I was looking for my aunt, and eventually I found her. One day, one of my uncles came to see her. He was the Somali ambassador in England and was looking for a girl to work at his residence in London. When I heard this, I begged my aunt to convince him to take me. I had no idea where I would be going, but I knew it would be out of Africa. My uncle agreed.

I had never seen an airplane before. Looking back, it was hilarious, because I remember that in the plane, I was desperate to go to the toilet. I only knew how to pee outside in the bush. Eventually, I couldn't hold it any longer. I had watched people go to the little cabin at the back of the plane, so I did the same, but I was frightened that if I touched something, the plane would blow up. I didn't know how to flush, so I filled the toilet with cups of water so it wouldn't look like I had just peed!

I arrived in London in December. I was about 14. I worked as a servant in my uncle's residence for four years. Every day, I would get up at 6 A.M., then cook and clean without stopping until midnight. I never had a day off.

10   The culture shock for me in England was huge. I didn't speak English. I couldn't read or write. But I knew right from the start that I was different from white women. I was aware that what had been done to me when I was 5 doesn't happen in western culture. I was angry and completely frustrated. I wanted to be the same as the girls around me. I kept saying to myself, "Why me? Why?" It was something I had to learn to live with.

Men would often bother me. I used to accompany my little cousin to school every day and men would stare at me, or blow me kisses. I'd ignore them, not knowing what was going on. One man in particular approached me all the time. I thought he was disgusting and dirty like the others. One day, he followed me home and introduced himself to my aunt. He said he was a photographer and wanted to take pictures of me. My aunt refused. I was disappointed.

I had heard about Iman, the Somalian supermodel. I had covered my wall with photographs of her that I'd cut from magazines. To me, she looked like a typical Somali woman, but when I came to the western world, I found out that she was rich and famous.

Shortly afterward, my ambassador uncle's term of office ended and he wanted to take me back to Somalia. But I didn't want to go back. The day before we were due to leave London, I buried my passport in the garden and told him I had lost it. He was furious because there was no time to issue another one, and the family was forced to leave without me.

I was free at last. That day, I went to Oxford Street, London's main shopping street, and spotted a Somali woman—I know what my people look like. I told her that I had nowhere to stay. She was living at the YMCA and helped me get a room there. The next day, I got a day job scrubbing floors at McDonald's and started night school.

15   Meanwhile, I kept in touch with the photographer and he took some pictures of me. One day, a modeling agency called. They wanted to sign me on. At my first job casting, for a calendar, the photographer asked me to take off my top. I stormed out. That night, the modeling agency tracked me down and yelled, "What on earth are you doing? Do you know how much you could earn

on this job?" I had no idea. In England, the Pirelli calendar with its topless supermodels has a cult status. But I thought I'd have to have sex with the photographer and preferred to go back to my McDonald's, scrubbing the floor. When I realized all I had to do was smile at the camera for 2500 pounds ($4000), I went back the next day and took my shirt off. I got the job and my photograph was chosen for the cover of the calendar. That day changed my life.

I've been modeling ever since. I find it ridiculous that people pay me just for how I look. When I landed a job at Revlon, the cosmetics company, the ad I was in had a headline that said: "The most beautiful women in the world wear Revlon." I thought, "Wait a minute, I'm not that pretty. I'm OK." It took a long time for me to say "Thank you" when someone said, "You're so pretty." My mother, on the other hand, is beautiful. She is beautiful inside.

I hadn't been back to Somalia for 15 years when BBC television approached me last year and said they wanted to do a documentary on my life. I said to them, "Let's make a deal. I'll do the program only if you take me back to Africa so I can see my family again." It's too dangerous for me to go back there alone because of the civil war. They agreed.

Being back there after so long was incredible—I had missed my family so much. In the West, you hear only about the bad in Africa, the starvation and war, but to me, Africa is still a magical place. But I wish Africans had clean water to drink, could grow trees and send their children to school.

None of my family understands how I make a living, except my mother. She's proud of me. I begged her to come back with me to London, but she doesn't want to leave Somalia. When it was time for me to go, I was overwhelmed with emotion. It had felt so good to be back in Africa—I am at home there.

As for the future, I'm very romantic about getting married and having kids. *20* But it took me a long time to start dating. First of all, sex is not important to me. Second, I need to know a man well before I get close. When I see a man, or when he touches me, I want him to keep a distance. Men are loving and say, "It's OK. I'm not going to eat you. What's the matter? Don't you like sex?" They don't understand because I don't tell them what happened to me.

I now have a beautiful boyfriend and, yes, I fall in love and can have a physical relationship like everyone else. Being circumcised doesn't mean I've lost every feeling in my body. But female circumcision changes your whole life, not just sex. And I still have health problems associated with it. Every month, my periods are very heavy and last a long time. I have to lock myself up for three days because it hurts so badly. I went to doctors everywhere and they all said, "There's nothing we can do." I've been opened up, but it still doesn't help. It used to make me really, really depressed, but I have to live with it. I try to enjoy my life and I consider myself very lucky. There's nothing I can do about what happened to me. I can't turn back the clock.

Whoever came up with female circumcision should be tortured, because it is torture. It has got nothing at all to do with male circumcision, where they just cut off an extra piece of skin. Female circumcision is mutilation. It is brutal, cruel, and unnecessary.

It's very painful for me to talk about this subject because it is so deeply personal. And I don't want anybody's sympathy. But it's time for me to tell the world and swallow my pride in order to save my sisters in Africa. I want to be an ambassador on their behalf because they can't stick up for themselves. I've seen them suffer from it and die from it. I was strong enough to survive and I want to make a difference. I can talk because I've experienced the pain. I want female circumcision to stop. Now! Today! If only I could make that happen, I would drop everything. Even if I just save one woman from this torture, it would be worth it.

Engaging the Text

1. What role does female circumcision play in Somalian culture? Why is something that Westerners perceive as so horrendous considered natural and normal in other cultures?

2. Dirie says that "neither the Bible nor the Koran talks about female circumcision anywhere." Why does she mention this, and how does it undercut arguments for female circumcision?

3. How does Dirie's experience reflect Somalian cultural attitudes toward women?

Exploring Your Cultural Perspective

1. How does the value placed on female virginity differ in Somalian culture and in contemporary U.S. society? What explains the differences?

2. Drawing on Dirie's essay, explore the relationship between freedom of choice and law and custom. In terms of who controls what a woman can do with her body, are there analogies between the ongoing abortion debate in the United States and Dirie's account? You might research current U.S. efforts to outlaw female circumcision among immigrants who wish to continue the practice. One source of information is the Female Genital Mutilation Education and Networking Project's Web site at <http://www.fgmnetwork.org/>.

FATIMA MERNISSI
The French Harem

Fatima Mernissi was raised in Fez, Morocco. She is a distinguished scholar whose approach is that of a feminist sociologist. Mernissi currently teaches at the University of Mohammed V in Rabat, Morocco. Among her published works are *Islam and Democracy: Fear of the Modern World* (1992) and *Dreams of Trespass: Tales of a Harem Girlhood* (1994), from which the following selection is taken. In it, Mernissi recalls her childhood as an inhabitant of a harem (from an Arabic word meaning "forbidden"), which she characterizes as a domain in which women are almost completely isolated from the world. Mernissi has also written *Scheherazade Goes West: Different Cultures, Different Harems* (2001).

Thinking Critically

As you read, pay particular attention to Mernissi's word choices and how they express her personal feelings toward the institution of the harem. How do you think you would react to the lack of freedom that defines harem life?

Our house gate was a definite *hudud*, or frontier, because you needed permission to step in or out. Every move had to be justified and even getting to the gate was a procedure. If you were coming from the courtyard, you had to first walk down an endless corridor, and then you came face to face with Ahmed, the doorkeeper, who was usually sitting on his throne-like sofa, always with his tea tray by his side, ready to entertain. Since the right of passage always involved a rather elaborate negotiating process, you were invited either to sit beside him on his impressive sofa, or to face him, duly relaxed on the out-of-place "fauteuil d'França," his hard, shabby, upholstered easy chair that he had picked out for himself on a rare visit to the *joutya*, or local flea market. Ahmed often had the youngest of his five children on his lap, because he took care of them whenever his wife Luza went to work. She was a first-rate cook and accepted occasional assignments outside our home when the money was good.

Our house gate was a gigantic stone arch with impressive carved wooden doors. It separated the women's harem from the male strangers walking in the streets. (Uncle's and Father's honor and prestige depended on that separation, we were told.) Children could step out of the gate, if their parents permitted it, but not grownup women. "I would wake up at dawn," Mother would say now and then. "If I only could go for a walk in the early morning when the streets are deserted. The light must be blue then, or maybe pink, like at sunset. What is the color of the morning in the deserted, silent streets?" No one answered her questions. In a harem, you don't necessarily ask questions to get answers. You ask questions just to understand what is happening to you. Roaming freely in the streets was every woman's dream. Aunt Habiba's most popular tale, which she narrated on special occasions only, was about "The Woman with Wings," who could fly away from the courtyard whenever she wanted to. Every time Aunt Habiba told that story, the women in the courtyard would tuck their caftans into their belts, and dance away with their arms spread wide as if they were about to fly. Cousin Chama, who was seventeen, had me confused for years, because she managed to convince me that all women had invisible wings, and that mine would develop too, when I was older.

Our house gate also protected us from the foreigners standing a few meters away, at another equally busy and dangerous frontier—the one that separated our old city, the Medina, from the new French city, the Ville Nouvelle. My cousins and I would sometimes slip out of the gate when Ahmed was busy talking or napping, to take a look at the French soldiers. They dressed in blue uniforms, wore rifles on their shoulders, and had small gray eyes that were always alert. They often tried to talk to us children, because the adults never spoke with them, but we were instructed never to answer back. We knew that the French were greedy and had come a long way to conquer our land, even though Allah had already given them a beautiful one, with bustling cities, thick forests, luscious green fields, and cows much bigger than ours that gave four times as much milk. But somehow the French needed to get more.

Because we lived on the frontier between the old city and the new, we could see how different the French Ville Nouvelle was from our Medina. Their streets were large and straight, and lit by bright lights in the night. (Father said that they squandered Allah's energy because people did not need that much bright light in a safe community.) They also had fast cars. Our Medina streets were narrow, dark, and serpentine—filled with so many twists and turns that cars could not enter, and foreigners could not find their way out if they ever dared to come in. This was the real reason the French had to build a new city for themselves: they were afraid to live in ours.

5   Most people walked on foot in the Medina. Father and Uncle had their mules, but poor people like Ahmed had only donkeys, and children and women had to walk. The French were afraid to walk. They were always in their cars.

Even the soldiers would stay in their cars when things got bad. Their fear was quite an amazing thing to us children, because we saw that grownups could be as afraid as we could. And these grownups who were afraid were on the outside, supposedly free. The powerful ones who had created the frontier were also the fearful ones. The Ville Nouvelle was like their harem; just like women, they could not walk freely in the Medina. So you could be powerful, and still be the prisoner of a frontier.

Nonetheless, the French soldiers, who often looked so very young, afraid, and lonely at their posts, terrorized the entire Medina. They had power and could hurt us.

One day in January 1944, Mother said, King Mohammed V, backed by nationalists all over Morocco, went to the top-ranking French colonial administrator, the Résident Général, to make a formal demand for independence. The Résident Général got very upset. How dare you Moroccans ask for independence! he must have screamed, and to punish us, he launched his soldiers into the Medina. Armored cars forced their way as far as they could into the serpentine streets. People turned to Mecca to pray. Thousands of men recited the anxiety prayer, consisting of one single word repeated over and over for hours when one is faced with disaster: "*Ya Latif, Ya Latif, Ya Latif!*" (O Sensitive One!) *Ya Latif* is one of the hundred names of Allah, and Aunt Habiba often said it was the most beautiful one of all because it describes Allah as a source of tender sympathy, who feels your sorrow and can help you. But the armed French soldiers, trapped in the narrow streets, surrounded by chants of "*Ya Latif*" repeated thousands of times, became nervous and lost control. They started shooting at the praying crowds and within minutes, corpses were falling on top of each other on the mosque's doorstep, while the chants were still going on inside. Mother said that Samir and I were barely four at the time and no one noticed us watching from our gate as the blood-soaked corpses, all dressed in the ceremonial white prayer *djellaba*, were carried back home. "For months afterward, you and Samir had nightmares," she said, "and you could not even see the color red without running to hide. We had to take you to the Moulay Driss sanctuary many Fridays in a row to have the *sharifs* (holy men) perform protection rituals over you, and I had to put a Koranic amulet under your pillow for a whole year before you slept normally again." After that tragic day, the French walked around carrying guns with them in plain view all the time, while Father had to ask permission from many different sources just to keep his hunting rifle, and even then, had to keep it concealed unless he was in the forest.

All these events puzzled me and I talked about them often with Yasmina, my maternal grandmother, who lived on a beautiful farm with cows and sheep and endless fields of flowers, one hundred kilometers to the west of us, between Fez and the Ocean. We visited her once a year, and I would talk to her about frontiers and fears and differences, and the why of it all. Yasmina knew a lot about fear, all kinds of fears. "I am an expert on fear, Fatima," she would tell me, caressing my forehead as I played with her pearls and pink beads, "And I will tell you things when you are older. I will teach you how to get over fears."

Often, I could not sleep the first few nights on Yasmina's farm—the frontiers were not clear enough. There were no closed gates to be seen anywhere, only wide, flat, open fields where flowers grew and animals wandered peaceably about. But Yasmina explained to me that the farm was part of Allah's original earth, which had no frontiers, just vast, open fields without borders or boundaries, and that I should not be afraid. But how could I walk in an open field without being attacked? I kept asking. And then Yasmina created a game that I loved, to help put me to sleep, called *mshia-f-lekhla* (the walk in the open fields). She would hold me tight as I lay down, and I would clasp her beads with my two hands, close my eyes, and imagine myself walking through an endless field of flowers. "Step lightly," Yasmina would say, "so you can hear the flowers' song. They are whispering, '*salam, salam*' (peace, peace.)" I would repeat the flowers' refrain as fast as I could, all danger would disappear, and I would fall asleep. "*Salam, salam*," murmured the flowers, Yasmina, and I. And the next thing I knew, it was morning and I was lying in Yasmina's big brass bed, with my hands full of pearls and pink beads. From outside came the mixed music of breezes touching the leaves and birds talking to one another, and no one was in sight but King Farouk, the peacock, and Thor, the fat white duck.

10   Actually, Thor was also the name of Yasmina's most hated co-wife, but I could only call the woman Thor when thinking about her silently to myself. When I said her name out loud, I had to call her Lalla Thor. *Lalla* is our title of respect for all important women, just as *Sidi* is our title of respect for all important men. As a child, I had to call all important grownups Lalla and Sidi, and kiss their hands at sunset, when the lights were turned on and we said *msakum* (good evening). Every evening, Samir and I would kiss everyone's hands as quickly as we could so we could return to our games without hearing the nasty remark, "Tradition is being lost." We got so good at it that we managed to rush through the ritual at an incredible speed, but sometimes, we were in such a hurry that we would trip over each other and collapse onto the laps of important people, or even fall down on the carpet. Then everyone would start laughing. Mother would laugh until there were tears in her eyes. "Poor dears," she would say, "they already are tired of kissing hands, and it is only the beginning."

But Lalla Thor on the farm, just like Lalla Mani in Fez, never laughed. She was always very serious, proper, and correct. As the first wife of Grandfather Tazi, she had a very important position in the family. She also had no housekeeping duties, and was very rich, two privileges that Yasmina could not abide. "I could not care how rich this woman is," she would say, "she ought to be working like the rest of us. Are we Muslims or not? If we are, everyone is equal. Allah said so. His prophet preached the same." Yasmina said that I should never accept inequality, for it was not logical. That was why she named her fat white duck Lalla Thor.

Engaging the Text

1. What features of communal life in the harem made the chance to get out so exciting?

2. Given the political situation of being governed by a foreign power (the French), how might life in the harem be seen as a way to uphold Moroccan identity?

3. How did Yasmina's farm provide a refuge for Mernissi? What values did her grandmother communicate that so greatly influenced Mernissi?

Exploring Your Cultural Perspective

1. To what extent has privacy become an increasingly rare luxury in modern culture? How important is it to you? Can you imagine living in a communal setting of the kind Mernissi describes? Why or why not?

2. How are harems depicted in films, on television, and in fairy tales? In what ways do these portrayals differ from Mernissi's description? What assumptions are part of the Hollywood image of harem life that are missing from Mernissi's real-life account? In a short essay, discuss the significance of the Western myth of the harem as exotic, the "other," and speculate on what that myth says about Western culture. You might consult Edward Said's classic critical work *Orientalism* (1978), a lively analysis of how the West has created cultural stereotypes about the East, and *Harem: The World behind the Veil* by Alev Lytle Croutier (1997).

MONIQUE PROULX

Feint of Heart

Monique Proulx was born in Quebec City, Canada, in 1952. She is best known for her short stories, including "Feint of Heart," the title story of her 1983 collection, *Sans coeur et sans reproche*. This bittersweet story follows the relationship of two young people in Quebec City whose pose of world-weary sophistication interferes with their finding happiness. Proulx has also written *Invisible Man at the Window*, translated into English by Matt Cohen (1995).

Thinking Critically

As you read Proulx's story, pay particular attention to how the narrator becomes another character whose ironic, yet sympathetic, reactions to the events are as important as those of Françoise and Benoît.

Might as well come right out with it: love stories don't do much for me. They rarely loosen my tear ducts. Other people's love stories, that is, the ones Guy des Cars will be cranking out until Cupid himself, with heaving stomach, sticks him full of arrows to shut him up. Or the ones that limp across our movie and TV screens and fill our nights with sweet, gritty fantasies. Love stories are personal, if you want my opinion: either you have one or you don't, and if you don't have one life's disgusting enough without some honey-tongued sadist purring his into your ear. But a love story of your own: well, that's another matter altogether. Once you've known love in all its force and fragility, words just can't describe the dizzying eddies that sweep us to the heights—and who cares about other people's love stories when you're drifting into the regions of interstellar bliss, which is perhaps the only reality that matters after all. But enough of that. Whether you like it or not I'm going to tell you the story of Françoise and Benoît in love: because you're a bunch of hopeless romantics—yes, I can see it in your eyes that drip with emotion whenever you see a beautiful, banal young couple exchange a peck on the cheek, not to mention a cavernous kiss—because fresh-sliced heart served up with no matter what revolting sauce is your favourite gourmet treat, you sentimental anthropophagist creeps, and for a lot of other reasons that are none of your business.

But let's get one thing straight right away: this is a perfectly ordinary story, not at all rife with dramatic incident. The "heroes" are heroic in name only: there isn't a single case of creeping, insidious leukemia, and neither protagonist suffers from even the tiniest fatal cerebral lesion. They're normal, ordinary folks, as healthy as can be expected, given their propensity for alcohol, nicotine, animal fats and the various controlled substances they turn to for life's little pleasures. So you've been warned, and don't come whining to me if the conclusion isn't bloody enough for your liking.

Among today's young intelligentsia there's an impressive clique of misguided perfectionists who, in the name of Independence, complicate their lives beyond belief. I'll get back to that. For the moment, let's just say that Françoise and Benoît were members in good standing when they first met in a little bar on rue Saint-Jean, which will remain anonymous unless the owner offers me drinks on the house for at least ten days running.

It was a Monday night in winter—quiet, nothing out of the ordinary. As soon as Françoise walked into the bar with a suicidal-looking friend at her side, her sleepwalker's shuffle—was it chance or fate—took her to the very back, right next to the seat where Benoît was peacefully reading. On the chair beside him sat an ill-defined individual, considerably the worse for drink, the sort of quiet old bum you often see in bars, who occasionally turns out to be PhD in mathematics or a former Nobel Peace Prize laureate. Françoise took a seat without looking at anyone, the friend flopped down beside her with a melodramatic whoosh, Benoît's eyes stayed glued to his book and the bum muttered something unintelligible. Time passed.

The friend—let's call her Marie, she's just a bit player here—had been   5
delivering an endless, monotonous litany of complaints about life, love, death and other profound matters for some time, to judge by Françoise's weary silence, when suddenly the bum made a sound like a death rattle—guttural and rather frightening. All heads turned his way, including those of a small group of individuals—the only other customers in the bar—sitting a few tables away. The septuagenarian dipsomaniac hadn't succumbed to a run-of-the-mill heart attack. On the contrary, his cheeks had suddenly gone purple and he was pointing, stupefied, at the walls of the bar, emitting lugubrious noises all the while. Finally he yelped something intelligible: "Horrible! Hideous! Horrible!"

Curious heads turned away from the bum and converged upon the apparent cause of this vast spill of emotion: the walls of the bar. There was nothing special about the aforesaid walls, aside from the fact that they were covered with paintings by a local artist. It's true that the artist in question was inordinately prone to formless, provocative dribbles and smears, but who, in these troubled, permissive and culturally undistinguished times, can boast of his or her ability to distinguish the beautiful from the ugly? So. The bum did *not* approve of the work of the artist in question; in fact, he clearly disapproved. The small group a few tables away from Françoise, Benoît and company resumed their discussion somewhat resentfully. Benoît gave the bum an approving snicker, Françoise gave the sorry-looking pictures an amused glance, friend Marie tried to resume her dreary soliloquy—in short, everything was just about back to normal. The old man wasn't impressed; he stood up and started shrieking insults at the pictures, threatening to slice them to shreds if they weren't removed from his sight.

"Garbage!" he yelled. "Trash! Makes me puke!"

And so forth. Now, among the small group of individuals seated, as I mentioned, a few tables away, were some friends of the maligned artist, and they were beginning to think the joke had gone a bit far. A tall, bearded man got up, almost knocking over his chair in the process, and waved his fist at the bum.

"If that old wreck doesn't shut up, I'll bust his jaw!"

10   The old wreck, delighted and encouraged by the attention, only stepped up the abuse, producing new, ever more eloquent epithets. The tall, bearded man stomped over to him.

Then Benoît stood and calmly laid his book on the table.

"I think they're ugly too," he said blandly. "In fact, I think they're hideous, repugnant and stercoraceous."

Which cleared the deck for action. The artist's fan club sent their table flying, Benoît and the bearded man prepared for battle, the panic-stricken waiter burst into the fray—and the little old man, with a snort, began to take the pictures off the wall.

Suddenly a firm, strident voice rose from the budding scuffle and, surprisingly, paralyzed the crowd.

15   "Monsieur Riopelle! That's enough! Sit down, Monsieur Riopelle."

Françoise was tugging gently at the old bum's arm, forcing him to leave the pictures be. She pushed him onto a chair, holding him in a firm yet respectful grip.

"Calm down, Monsieur Riopelle. Young artists deserve a break too—don't they, Monsieur Riopelle?"

After a long, stunned silence, the artist's fan club slowly took their seats again, and it's here that my story, or rather the story of Françoise and Benoît, really gets underway.

Now you weren't born yesterday and you're well aware that that bum was no more Jean-Paul Riopelle than I'm Simone de Beauvoir. Françoise and Benoît found themselves at the same table, doubled over—discreetly—in the same uncontrollable laughter. Friend Marie had finally gone, the group at the other table was gradually breaking up, the old bum—who was nothing more or less than a full-time rubby—sank into a comatose slumber. For our hero and heroine, though, their chattering, their mutual glee, and their delight in each other's wit were endless, and now Françoise's hand finds its way, as if by chance, onto Benoît's thigh, and in their eyes there dances an odd sort of shared glimmer that now and then reduces them to silence, and here they are, a little later, fused and confused in Françoise's big double bed, laughing harder and harder through all the blazing pores of their skin.

Now let's be frank. This nocturnal liaison was not, in itself, exceptional—   20
not for Françoise, and not for Benoît. Both were happily bound for thirty and they were accustomed to light-hearted, effervescent flings, tossed off as voraciously as champagne, just for a few spins of the clock. They were familiar with sudden yearnings for passion that would draw them inexorably into the bed of a stranger with an ever-so-sensual voice encountered in some smoky bar.

At times the fling would have happy consequences: a one-night stand would turn into a regular lover, for a while at least, and the relationship would develop into one of affectionate complicity, free of hassles.

Other times, the fling would turn out to be a full-fledged disaster: after awakening to a vague anxiety bordering on disgust, one would be astonished to find oneself beside some pale, nondescript stranger with whom no communication was possible, but who, behind the veil of the previous night's alcoholic vapours, had seemed brilliant.

To get back to the case in question, everything had been proceeding as smooth as silk from the moment Françoise and Benoît first made contact until the next day when they parted. In fact, they hadn't slept very well. It was as if, in the course of their mutual explorations, their bodies had set off a series of flash fires they couldn't extinguish, and their consuming hilarity kept them awake all night. Hunger finally tugged them from bed the next morning, their eyes rimmed in black, aching all over, but in a splendid mood regardless, and they carried right on with their giggles and winks and confessions. The omelette was good. Benoît—surprise!—knew how to make filtered coffee, and Françoise—oh, joy!—wasn't a grow-your-own-granola type. In a word, they were enraptured as they parted at Françoise's door, repeating how enjoyable it had been and so on and so forth. Then came the last peck on the cheek, the final wink and giggle, and a nonchalant, "Be seeing you. Take care." And so it began.

Françoise devoted the rest of the week to her usual activities with a surplus of energy and zeal that she didn't, at the time, find suspect. Her "usual activities," it should be said, would normally have been enough to consume the vitality of half a dozen less dynamic souls. Françoise was a born activist, and the financial problems of one Philémon Tremblay, Third Avenue, unemployed—one-armed, asbestositic, tubercular—and the tribulations of one Roberte Roberge, rue Couillard, tenant—grappling with rent increases directly proportional to the size of her giant cockroaches—gave her serious difficulty in sleeping. Françoise could be found in any association that proposed direct action to improve the fate of the world in general, and the quality of her neighbours' lives in particular.

25   Benoît didn't sit still either, in the days that followed, but was active in his own inward and reflective way, which often resembled mere daydreaming. He was a teaching assistant at Laval University, in the literature department actually, but what he did there was closer to revolutionary sociology than literary studies. There was a kind of serene, spontaneous authority in his most innocuous presentations ("Why are the poor not interested in reading?" "Is feminist literature authentically progressive?" "Who really stands to profit from the book-publishing industry?") that had the knack of stimulating passionate discussions among his students and even, at time—to his great astonishment—provoking outside the university stormy demonstrations and the distribution of frankly subversive tracts that claimed to be inspired by him.

Whatever, the week passed normally, or almost: it wasn't until Friday night that Philémon Tremblay's money problems and Roberte Roberge's bugs aroused in Françoise only a sort of irritable indifference, and she suddenly started thinking about Benoît and the night they'd spent together. In fact, she realized she'd been thinking about it nonstop, insidiously, despite the variety of tasks she had compelled herself to carry on with, and that wasn't normal for a why-not-round-off-the-evening sort of fling. She even caught herself glaring at her phone, which was silent—or might as well have been, if you know what I mean—and getting vaguely depressed and wondering if he'd call and telling herself he wouldn't and remembering his hands so soft and velvet and that adorable dimple in his chin and thinking maybe she ought to go back to the little bar 'cause you never know and then saying no, he probably has a wife and five kids—the interesting ones always do.

As there'd been a tacit agreement not to broach the subject of another meeting or any formal commitment, and as he himself hadn't dared to contravene it—out of pride or God knows what ridiculous principle—Benoît, for his part, was concocting, along with his lecture notes, some complex manoeuvres that would allow him to see Françoise again, without making it too obvious. There was the telephone, of course—because he'd made a note of her number without being too obvious—but wouldn't such a primitive mode of communication risk the displeasure of a woman who transcended, without effort, it seemed, such petty, practical details of everyday life? (I know . . .) There remained—of the measures that wouldn't seem too obvious—the chance encounter. Benoît had peeked several times inside the little bar on rue Saint-Jean—which will remain anonymous unless the owner, etc.—and he hadn't seen Françoise (she wasn't there, she was waiting, at home, by the telephone), and that was all it took to convince him that she didn't care if she ever saw him again, she was so beautiful, so free, so far above the petty, practical details of everyday life, and undoubtedly had her hands full coping with the earnest attentions of a dozen men more interesting than he was.

Right. A pair of idiots, I grant you. But be patient, there's worse to come.

As there's a limit to everything, even to the blackest streak of lousy luck and the crassest stupidity, they finally ran into one another at the newsstand near Françoise's apartment, where Benoît—oddly enough—had been buying his papers for two weeks. They recognized each other at once, obviously, but didn't even exchange a peck on the cheek, overwhelmed as they were by an all-consuming stupefaction that had them stammering nonsense about the snow that would or wouldn't fall and the weather past and future. But they did manage, with an unconvincing air of nonchalance, to make a date for that evening. "If you aren't tied up, that is. . . . " That night found them at his place or hers, it really doesn't matter, and this time Cupid's aim was right on target. He took their breath away, turned their legs to jelly, flung them together like molten lava. They saw each other the next day and the day after that and every night afterwards for weeks and weeks and always there was the same electrifying ardour, the same unalloyed delirium.

This might be the place to bring up independence again, with a capital 30 "I"—no, my lambs, you haven't been forgotten—in the name of which we make so many sacrifices, especially once it's hardened into a virtue.

It pleased both Françoise and Benoît to consider themselves—eyes modestly lowered, though, as befitted their leftish convictions—part of a mature and highly developed elite, utterly dedicated to the examination and liberation of the self, which had learned how to function on its own (that's what Independence means after all, or something pretty close, with all due respect to my two-volume dictionary). On the subject of love, it follows that they both had airy theories (rather unlike those of John Paul II), which condemned both systematic lumping into couples and unhealthy possessiveness. I'm not telling you anything new when I point out that, when you profess to hold certain theories with a modicum of sincerity, the trouble starts when you have to make them conform with reality.

In the beginning, euphoria came easily. It was its own begetter. They were swept along by an incredibly powerful current they hardly dared believe in, that left them exhausted and fulfilled.

Every day as dusk began to fall, Françoise would pick Benoît up at the university or wait for him with a pretended nonchalance at the back of a café or throw herself into the preparation of a gargantuan dinner for two that she knew she'd only pick at, for the emotions of love paralyzed her stomach and her appetite as surely as a bout of nausea. Every day, Benoît would twitch with impatience until late afternoon when he'd see Françoise's indefinable smile, and he never wearied of swooping her up in a violent embrace, of feeling her reel with desire against him, of cooing spectacular trivia into her ear that would melt both their hearts and cause them, with sudden gravity, to exchange a look that left them all a-flutter.

Until . . . Right. Until they take fright as they realize to what extent the well-oiled gears of their lives have unquestionably been disturbed. They start to daydream, to find more and more suspect the peace of mind and security in which they've lately been submerged up to the neck. Françoise, who's always been a lyrical advocate of the need for creative independence and sanctifying solitude, glumly discovers that she NEEDS Benoît: she turns to him at night with undeniable eagerness and rapture that leave her awash with guilt; he turns up at any hour of the day, nesting at the very core of her thoughts, even though she was sure she was safe among her tenants and her jobless. . . . She seems to be in the process of succumbing to feminine atavism, getting caught in the time-worn role of the near-wife devoured by the Other.

35   As for Benoît, he finds himself overreacting to a friendly jibe by one of his students who saw him with Françoise. He suddenly has the disagreeable impression that his image has betrayed him, that he's gradually lost control of his own emotions, that he's playing the bashful lover in a caricature of a melodrama that has nothing to do with him, that's totally at odds with his libertarian principles. . . . He begins to doubt the authenticity of his inexplicable, all-consuming feeling for Françoise. He thinks it's unhealthy, mawkish, restricting—in a word, conformist. The evidence is clear: he's well on the way to giving in to petit bourgeois happiness.

In short, it's Benoît who strikes the first blow. Boldly and manfully. He unplugs his phone and plays dead for several days. Françoise, concerned and saddened by his abrupt silence, finally runs into him one night as she's strolling, woebegone, through the Latin Quarter. Having spotted him through a café window, she unthinkingly heads inside and makes her way toward him. He greets her with torrents of affection, as if nothing has changed, enquires about her health and the well-being of the unemployed Philémon Tremblay. He gets lost in a woolly discourse on the latest Altman film which he's just seen at the Cartier with Manon or Sandra or Marie who, as it happens, is even now at his side and whose thigh he is almost absent-mindedly patting. Françoise plays along as if nothing was wrong, smiles pleasantly at Manon or Sandra or Marie, dazzlingly outdoes him on the subject of Altman's style—so peculiarly engaging and so unexpectedly American—then finally gets up, gives Benoît an excessively polite kiss, flashes a charming smile at Manon or Sandra or Marie, and leaves the café—distraught, knees quaking, and with an uncontrollable desire to throw up and scream. She drags herself home, upbraiding herself aloud and giving herself inward kicks to ward off the real pain. Oh, it was nothing to get worked up about, just a passing fancy she'd inflated like some prepubescent crush, that's all. . . . Françoise is almost relieved, despite the frightful ache that's spreading through her belly: now, at least, she can go on believing that there's no such thing as love. She stretches out on her bed, flicks on the TV, forbids herself to cry and eventually falls into a dreamless sleep, as though nothing had happened: stoicism is a precondition for Independence.

First thing the next morning, though, who should phone but Benoît—all sweetness and light, and secretly ravaged by a nagging anxiety that kept him awake all night. What if Françoise was so hurt by his inexplicable behaviour that she refused to see him again. . . . But no—Françoise speaks in her usual voice, pleasant and warm, tells him she's fine, and they make a date for that night. Miraculously, they get together as if nothing had happened: with their usual passion and fire, laughing and embracing like old accomplices. Françoise asks no questions, Benoît offers no confession. They maintain a tacit silence about what *may* have happened the night before—and the days before that.

And so the tone is set. Benoît is convinced he was right to introduce those breathing spaces into their relationship—not only does Françoise not hold it against him, she seems to be welcoming the change with her unshakeable good humour; perhaps deep down she was even hoping for it. And so Benoît multiplies his meetings with Manon or Sandra or Marie, sets up others with Sylvie, Laura and Julie, and banishes guilt from both his vocabulary and his daily life. By behaving as if nothing has happened, Françoise finally convinces herself she's living through a healthy, normal situation, one that's even somehow privileged (traditional couples are so quick to give in to possessiveness and neurotic jealousy . . .) and that her relationship with Benoît is turning out to be, basically, completely satisfying, giving her exactly what she needs. After all, don't they see each other at least twice a week, and isn't it absolutely sensational, fantastically passionate, every time? What more could she ask? It's only the remnants of romantic culture, decadent vestiges she hasn't had time to shed, that still make her start painfully and feel an acute, inexplicable anguish whenever she sees Benoît exchange familiar, tender gestures with someone else. . . . And then she decides that a meaningful quickie or two would do her a world of good, so she goes back to cruising, a tried-and-true activity at which, I might add, she excelled before Benoît came into her life. So now it's Benoît's turn to feel something like an icy swell rising in him as he sees Françoise's indefinable smile reflected in someone else's eyes, as he sneaks a peek at her sensual hand brushing against a leg other than his. But there are new ground rules now, and there's nothing to do but carry on in the same offhand, swaggering manner, to nervously gulp down the rest of his beer and look around for a woman to go home with tonight, so he won't be outdone.

And then one night Françoise is sitting with a friend—sure, let's call her Marie. Why not?—in the little bar from the beginning of the story, and as a matter of fact she's just launched into a loud, clear discourse on the merits and advantages of her relationship with Benoît when who should walk in but . . . He spots Françoise and gives her a knowing wink. He sits at a table with a gorgeous blonde—yet another one—whom he clearly already knows, as he starts up passionate conversation punctuated with furtive fondling and inconsequential little kisses—inconsequential, Françoise tells herself, recognizing at once the vague cramp that even now is clenching her guts, though it doesn't stop her from pursuing with increased fervour her discourse on the fidelity, yes, the sort of inner, visceral fidelity, that marks her relationship with Benoît, even though, from all appearances, even though . . . And then, suddenly, she stops talking. Breaks off in mid-sentence with no warning, just like that. She doesn't even pretend to be following the conversation, but slumps into an odd sort of torpor from which her friend Marie can't shake her. When the gorgeous blonde gets up to go to the can or straight to hell—who cares—Françoise glides over to Benoît and tells him in a hoarse little voice, without giving him time for a smile or a kiss, that she has just discovered that she doesn't have the knack for being super cool, so she's pulling out, giving up, she's tired of stomach aches, she's exhausted from making up stories for herself. Benoît is silent, she utters a definitive goodnight that sounds like a farewell, and now she's outside, encased in an Olympian calm, friend Marie hard on her heels.

40   We find them both much later, in another bar, needless to say, unwinding into strong drink the never-ending skein of female rancour—he was never capable of love, I should have known, when I think of what I invested in that relationship, God, women are crazy to love the way we do, so much for nothing, waiter, five more beers, five beers to help me forget that times are tough and men are wimps. . . . Françoise is awash in a sort of lyric intoxication. She's found herself even though she's lost Benoît; at least this pain is unequivocal, with no little tricks, it'll be easier to assuage, to cauterize it, starting tonight with that dish with the bedroom eyes who's been hovering around, whom she brutally decides to pick up—for her libido, only her libido, and also to warm up the left side of her big double bed—the nights are so chilly now.

When she eventually goes home on the arm of the stranger who may with a little luck turn out to be a good lover, Françoise finds Benoît—who else!—haggard and shivering on her landing, his eyes distorted by something wet that looks like tears. He tells her he loves her—what else!—that he doesn't want to lose her, all in a tone that cannot be mistaken, on the landing of an aging apartment, in the slanting pre-dawn light, with a stranger planted there like a coat-rack, who finally takes off because nobody's paying any attention to him.

So there it is. I've reached the epilogue, dear hearts. But where's the ending, the real ending, how does it *really* end (a bang? a whimper? fireworks or cold shower?), you ask with the look of a lustful pterodactyl. All right. I can see right through your new-wave hairdo. I know what's on your mind. Maybe Françoise and Benoît get married—sure, why not—it's still done. It's been all the rage for the past few years, in fact, amazingly popular with the under-twenty-fives. Don't get your hopes up, my little badgers. After all, I did make it clear that Françoise and Benoît were intelligent youngsters, well aware of life or, at least, a few of the primary truths, starting with this one: the marital arts are inevitably, every single time, transformed into martial arts. Okay, fine, so you resign yourselves, sighing like a duck-billed platypus being stroked the wrong way. Whether they marry or not, whether they have children or not, Françoise and Benoît might well enjoy a long and flawless happiness, for all eternity. Sure. Don't get me wrong—I'd like that, too. But things don't turn out that way in real life, where love isn't organized by those chaps from Hollywood or Harlequin. So let me tell you what happens to Françoise and Benoît: after all the twists and turns and torturous manoeuvres through which we've followed them, they finally reach a workable compromise between independence and commitment—which is rare, ultra-rare. In fact, their relationship is very special, a passionate, gripping love affair that lasts three years. Or five. Or eight. And then one day they decide to split up because it's time, because they'd only hurt each other if they tried to revive what's already dead between then, because nothing lasts forever, alas, and they have high standards and abhor pretense. I'm not saying they burned all their bridges. No. When you've achieved an intense, almost total communion with someone—which is rare—when you've lived a real-life love story, in a word, you never really leave each other altogether: there's a neatly laid-out compartment in your heart that no one else can fill.

Listen: only last year, on the anniversary of the day they met, Françoise received from Benoît—special delivery—a big rectangular package. She was home with some friends and a passing lover—Max, let's call him, or Pierre or Victor-Hippolyte—when she opened the parcel. It was a print, a reproduction of a weird-looking hairy owl, pasted like a party favour onto a hazy landscape. When she recognized the picture that had got Monsieur Riopelle so worked up, Françoise laughed. Then, if you must know, she started to blubber, blubbered like a calf, like a Magdalene, blubbered hard enough to bust a gut, tirelessly, inconsolably, till we had to call Benoît to help us calm her down.

And that's why alcohol and Colombian gold and lovely lavender stories exist. That's why I've told you about Françoise and Benoît, and that's why I'm on my way to down a few little carafes of plonk. There are truths that are difficult to digest, there are truths to be swallowed a spoonful at a time, slowly, slowly, so as not to upset the stomach. This one, for example.

If you're strong, you know that life's a road on which you're always alone, *45* even with love, even if people have halted along the way to engage our emotions. We must carry on, carry on to the end, till we can touch the little light that's shining just for us, till we can embrace its light, a special little light for each of us, at the end, at the very end of the road.

Engaging the Text

1. What traits initially define Françoise and Benoît? How does the narrator's commentary frame the action of the story? In your opinion, would the story

have been more effective if it had been told from Françoise's—rather than the omniscient narrator's—point of view? Why or why not?

2. The world Proulx reveals to us might be considered a subculture. What are its identifying characteristics and values, and how do they permeate the personal relationships within it? If Françoise and Benoît had met in another environment, do you think the outcome would have been different? Why or why not?

3. What elements in the story make the reader aware of the extent to which the characters' conceptions of themselves differ from how they really are? Discuss whether this story can be considered a tragedy.

Exploring Your Cultural Perspective

1. Have you ever known a couple who were like the characters in "Feint of Heart"? How did their story end? To what extent were their reactions influenced by the surrounding culture?

2. Rewrite a scene from either Françoise's or Benoît's perspective, and compare it with the original omniscient (all-knowing) third-person narrative.

CONNECTING THE TEXTS

1. Which facets of masculinity described by Richard Majors and Janet Mancini Billson in "Cool Pose" would appear to be social constructed from Brian Pronger's perspective in "Sexual Mythologies"?

2. Playing it cool is the theme in Richard Majors and Janet Mancini Billson's essay "Cool Pose" and in Monique Proulx's short story "Feint of Heart," although her characters are French Canadians. In what sense might the "cool pose" be considered a way to offset emotional vulnerability as well as a tactic for survival in both works? Identify and evaluate what symbolic gestures indicate coolness for the black males in "Cool Pose" and for the characters in "Feint of Heart."

3. What common elements unite Springsteen's enactment of blue-collar masculinity, as analyzed by Gareth Palmer in "Bruce Springsteen and Authentic Masculinity," with the "cool pose" described by Richard Majors and Janet Mancini Billson? What important differences separate them?

4. As an icon of masculinity (described by Gareth Palmer in "Bruce Springsteen and Authentic Masculinity"), Springsteen's public persona is complex. What insights does

Brian Pronger in "Sexual Mythologies" provide into this kind of persona? Give examples to support your argument.

5. In what ways do both Anne Taylor Fleming's memoir "Sperm in a Jar" and Susan Bordo's discussion in "Never Just Pictures" reveal a radical reassessment of the options that are open to women today?

6. Despite her recent makeover, Barbie (as described in Marge Piercy's poem "Barbie Doll") would seem to demonstrate many of Susan Bordo's points in "Never Just Pictures." What fundamental critique of society's intolerance toward the overweight do Bordo and Piercy present?

7. Are the stereotyped roles that men are forced to play according to Brian Pronger in "Sexual Mythologies" as harmful as those forced upon women as Susan Bordo describes in "Never Just Pictures"?

8. Compare the pressures and coercive techniques both Eastern and Western cultures use to reshape women into images that serve the interests of society. Write a short essay drawing on Marge Piercy's poem "Barbie Doll" and Waris Dirie's account in "The Tragedy of Female Circumcision."

9. What sexual mythology discussed by Brian Pronger in "Sexual Mythologies" does Marge Piercy condemn in "Barbie Doll"?

10. Compare Brian Pronger's analysis in "Sexual Mythologies" with Waris Dirie's account of female circumcision in terms of the way in which females are deprived of power. In the societies where it is practiced, female circumcision is thought to be natural and normal. Evaluate Dirie's conclusion that female circumcision exists to support the sexual power structure.

11. Discuss the extent to which women in Morocco, as described by Fatima Mernissi in "The French Harem," are more or less confined than those Susan Bordo describes in "Never Just Pictures."

12. How do role playing and the presumed importance of being independent figure prominently in Monique Proulx's "Feint of Heart" and in Brian Pronger's analysis in "Sexual Mythologies"?

WRITING ABOUT GENDER

1. How do current practices relating to dating, courtship, marriage, and child rearing differ from the customs your parents or grandparents followed? Interview a member of your family, and write an essay reporting your findings.

2. Is it possible to raise a child free from the gender stereotyping so prevalent in our society? For example, what books would you read to the child; what toys, games, and clothing would you buy? As part of your research project, you might visit a toy store and the infant/toddlers clothing department to see whether they carry gender-neutral items.

3. Does society have a double standard regarding sexual behavior for men and women? Do attitudes vary from culture to culture? If so, how? Assuming the persona of a reporter or journalist, analyze one instance of a double standard that you have experienced or witnessed. Be sure to address the five W's (when, what, who, where, and why); describe objectively the people, places, actions, and dialogue involved; and analyze the double standard.

4. To what extent do children's television shows, such as Saturday morning cartoons, promote expectations of how boys and girls should act, dress, and talk and what they should value? Select a typical show, and analyze the societal expectations it promotes.

5. If you have a sibling of the other sex, compare the way he or she was raised with your own experiences. How did the messages your parents, relatives, and society conveyed to your brother or sister differ from those they communicated to you? What cultural factors explain the differences?

6. Fairy tales (for example, Cinderella, Sleeping Beauty, Little Red Riding Hood) play an important role in shaping gender expectations. How do women's magazines, advertisements, romance novels, and soap operas reinforce these values? What messages do traditional fairy tales send boys compared with girls? For the full text of many fairy tales, see the Online Book Initiative site under "Fairy Tales" at <gopher://ftp.std.com/11/obi/book/Fairy.Tales>.

7. What network or cable television shows, movies, or Web sites offer broad insights into contemporary cultural values regarding gender roles? (Examples might include the films *In and Out* [1997] and *American Beauty* [1999] or the TV sitcoms *Will and Grace* and *Friends*.) Do these presentations reveal a shift in societal attitudes toward previously marginalized or ostracized groups?

8. How do magazines marketed to men (*Esquire, Gentleman's Quarterly, Men's Journal*) or women (*Glamour, Vogue*) instruct their readers on appropriate gender roles? Locate an example in one of these magazines, and describe the message being conveyed. By contrast, how do cutting-edge magazines (such as online "zines") redefine conventional gender roles?

9. What common labels for men and women rely on metaphors associated with food (for example, calling a man a "hunk" or a "stud muffin" and a woman a "dish" or a "honey bun")? What attitudes do these labels evoke? How do the foods selected allude to underlying cultural codes regarding gender roles? Write a few paragraphs on the origins, uses, and meanings of these or similar terms.

10. How has the theme of cross-dressing been treated in such films as *The Birdcage* (1998), *The Crying Game* (1992), and *Boys Don't Cry* (1999)? Why, in most cases, does society react negatively to men who dress like women and women who dress like men?

11. In a short paper, analyze the iconography and mythology of blondeness in our society, focusing on the different set of cultural signals that being blonde sends according to gender. For women, for example, some connotations attached to being blonde include sexuality, fertility, vitality, health, perfection, innocence, and at the other extreme, flightiness, and the "dumb blonde" stereotype. The story is quite different for men. Do people take blonde men seriously?

CHAPTER 5

Language Matters

*"One does not inhabit a country; one inhabits a language.
That is our country, our fatherland—and no other."*
—E. M. CIORAN (1911–1995, Rumanian-born French philosopher),
Anathemas and Admirations

Language is the quintessential means by which we grasp the world around us. It allows us to employ symbolic means to think and talk about objects that are not physically present and events that are not now occurring. The impulse to communicate is one of the most fundamental human needs and is the basis of all cultures and civilizations.

Consider the sheer complexity of what human beings must learn to communicate with one another. Research has shown that all children come into the world equipped with a prodigious variety of linguistic capabilities that unfold in clearly defined stages. A child's emerging ability to produce an unbelievable number of sentences is one of the most distinctive properties of being human. Noam Chomsky, the renowned American linguist, has argued for the existence of a "language instinct" that allows children to master their particular culture's language and to create and understand novel combinations of words and sentence constructions they have never encountered. Although the capacity to acquire language (and to perceive grammar, syntax, and structure) is most likely innate, social and cultural contexts determine the ways in which we grasp the connotations (which are far more important than the literal meanings) of words and phrases. By some estimates, children at the age of eighteen months can add a new word to their vocabulary every two hours.

LANGUAGE AND REALITY

The writers whose works are included in this chapter discuss the complex, subtle, and often unseen ways in which language not only shapes perception but (as rhetoric) can also be used to manipulate behavior. The fundamental insight elaborated by the Swiss philosopher Ferdinand de Saussure (1857–1913) is that everything we think, know, and experience is constructed by language, not simply reflected by it. Saussure rejected the prevailing view that language was *referential* (that is, that words label a preexisting reality), proposing instead that language is *conceptual* and plays an active role in constructing reality for us.

The validity of Saussure's insight is demonstrated by the experiences of autistic children, who are unable to understand abstract words or ideas without processing them as concrete images. Temple Grandin's account of her battle with autism, in "Thinking in Pictures," shows us how vital language is to our comprehension of the world. Without it, people, events, and experiences would remain an undifferentiated flux of stimuli, isolating us as are autistic children.

The mediating role that language plays in constructing reality also helps explain the enormous difficulties many people have acquiring fluency in a second language. As Luc Sante describes it in "Lingua Franca," growing up in Belgium (where French is one of the three official languages) linked all of his early experiences to the French language. When he moved to the United States, he found that English was less real to him than French: "As a boy, I lived in French; now, I live in English. The words don't fit, because languages are not equivalent to one another." Sante was unable to transfer the profound and unbreakable emotional associations he had formed as a child between certain French words and the corresponding experiences simply by learning the English words for the same events.

We can see the same process at work in Barbara Mellix's account "From Outside, In." Mellix grew up in a community in which she spoke black English. She undertook the task of mastering standard English, enrolled in a college composition class, and discovered that by learning a different version of English, she also became a different person. Mellix's essay raises the interesting question of who decides what standard English should be. What cultural forces determine which idioms and dialects are perceived as legitimate and which as inferior? When we realize that what we consider "standard" English (now spoken worldwide by nearly 400 million people) began as a dialect of an obscure Germanic tribe that invaded England in AD 600, we can appreciate how accident and circumstance over time can produce what is later perceived as being the norm. Defenders of black English (or Ebonics) have included the distinguished American novelist James Baldwin. He believed that black English evolved as a means by which blacks who came from different tribes in Africa and did not speak the same language could communicate with each other, and thus survive. Since the 1960s, many African Americans have adopted African names as a way of resisting the influence of the dominant white culture and affirming their heritage.

LANGUAGE AND POWER

Throughout history, groups have often asserted their dominance over others by imposing their language or dialect. The Kenyan writer Ngũgĩ wa Thiong'o has written eloquently on the damaging psychological effect of the British prohibition against the speaking of native languages after their colonization of Kenya in the early part of the twentieth century: "The language of my education was no longer the language of my culture." Thiong'o makes it clear that communication and culture are interdependent; when you damage one, you destroy the other. These issues are dramatized in John Agard's satirical look (in his poem "Listen mr oxford don") at the linguistic effects of British colonialism in Guyana. Agard brings considerable wit and humor to his analysis of how dialect functions as a marker of social class in determining what forms of English are judged to be correct.

   The deep-seated relationship between language and social acceptability illustrates how political forces determine what is considered proper English. One of the most striking creative works to dramatize this connection is Anthony Burgess's book *A Clockwork Orange*. Burgess creates a dialect of English (based on slang, substandard grammar, and invented words drawn from Slavic languages) to underscore the gap in social class between his working-class narrator and the upper-class doctors and hospital administrators charged with reforming his behavior.

LANGUAGE AND IDENTITY

The lack of understanding between social classes and cultures is also expressed in stereotypes. Stereotypes can be dangerous because they portray people in terms of a single trait, often misrepresenting them in the process. Luis Alberto Urrea experienced the misrepresentation of stereotyping firsthand as someone born in Tijuana to an American mother and a Mexican father. In "Nobody's Son," Urrea reminds us of the large number of English words that were originally borrowed from Spanish and condemns the disparaging terms used to characterized Mexican Americans. Urrea's experience is typical of the bilingual confusion of children of immigrant parents, who must learn to communicate using a new language in a new culture.

Amy Tan is less concerned that her parents spoke to her in Chinese while she answered them in English than with the presumption that Chinese people are "discreet and modest" because the Chinese language has no words for "yes" and "no." Tan, in "The Language of Discretion," refutes this misperception and offers valuable insight into the way language differences can isolate immigrants from mainstream culture.

LANGUAGE AND BEHAVIOR

As social creatures, we spend a great deal of time talking to one another, sharing how we feel and communicating information. The experiences Kyoko Mori describes in "Polite Lies" suggest that the intricate social ritual we call conversation relies on culturally enforced rules. Raised in Japan, Mori emigrated to the United States when she was twenty. When she returned to her homeland, she found herself frustrated by the elaborate rituals of politeness that governed conversations. Mori's account reveals that the language of a culture contains the key to understanding the unspoken rules of behavior and customs that hold a society together. Bernard Rudofsky relates an example of the relationship between language and culture in *The Kimono Mind: An Informal Guide to Japan and the Japanese* (1965):

> One day Isamu let himself be persuaded to dine at my Tokyo apartment and, after he had slowly eaten a lobster bisque, a chateaubriand, and a chocolate mousse, I asked him whether he had liked the food.
>
> It is not his way to blurt out an opinion; a thoughtful man, he takes his time.
>
> "No rice," he finally decided. "A meal without rice is no meal."
>
> He was far from being rude. In fact, he could not have expressed himself more felicitously. The Japanese language itself bears out his point: the word *gohan* stands for both, a meal and boiled rice. The two are synonymous.

In the conversations we have been referring to, the participants are face to face and can rely on a range of verbal and nonverbal signals to determine whose turn it is to speak and how the dialogue should proceed. The Internet has produced an entirely new kind of interaction, however, with relaxed codes of propriety and behavior. Gary Chapman points out in "Flamers: Cranks, Fetishists, and Monomaniacs" that the anonymity of cyberspace encourages people to behave in ways that would be unacceptable in face-to-face conversations.

The selections in this chapter show us in a variety of ways that the most pervasive impact of language is often the most invisible. The social dimension of language is closely connected to our cultural identity and influences both how we see ourselves and how others perceive us. The psychological aspect of language is equally important: those who have an interest in convincing us to believe something or buy something are often quite skillful at using language to persuade us. An awareness of how language can be used to manipulate our behavior reduces the likelihood that we will be deceived into acting against our own best interests.

TEMPLE GRANDIN

Thinking in Pictures

Dr. Temple Grandin is a gifted animal scientist who has designed one third of all the livestock handling facilities in the United States. Her account of the difficulties she faced as an autistic child offers a rare glimpse into the unusual cognitive processes at the heart of how we learn language. The following selection is drawn from her 1996 autobiography, *Thinking in Pictures: And Other Reports from My Life with Autism*. She has also written (with Margaret M. Scariano) *Emergence: Labeled Autistic* (1996) and *Animal Welfare and Meat Science* (1999).

Grandin tells us that autistic children cannot understand abstract meanings; they must be able to visualize ideas as concrete images. For example, the phrase "to bridge a gap" can be grasped only as an image of a bridge over a chasm. The difficulties autistic children encounter in processing information this way helps explain their isolation.

Thinking Critically

One of the tasks Grandin sets for herself is to explain why those who are autistic find it so difficult to communicate with others. To better understand Grandin's challenge, try to conceive of an abstract idea (for example, charity or love) by relying only on concrete images. How does Gary Larson's cartoon (Figure 5.1, page 304) use humor to convey this idea?

PROCESSING NONVISUAL INFORMATION

Autistics have problems learning things that cannot be thought about in pictures. The easiest words for an autistic child to learn are nouns, because they directly relate to pictures. Highly verbal autistic children like I was can sometimes learn how to read with phonics. Written words were too abstract for me to remember, but I could laboriously remember the approximately fifty phonetic sounds and a few rules. Lower-functioning children often learn better by association, with the aid of word labels attached to objects in their

FIGURE 5.1

environment. Some very impaired autistic children learn more easily if words are spelled out with plastic letters they can feel.

Spatial words such as "over" and "under" had no meaning for me until I had a visual image to fix them in my memory. Even now, when I hear the word "under" by itself, I automatically picture myself getting under the cafeteria tables at school during an air-raid drill, a common occurrence on the East Coast during the early fifties. The first memory that any single word triggers is almost always a childhood memory. I can remember the teacher telling us to be quiet and walking single-file into the cafeteria, where six or eight children huddled under each table. If I continue on the same train of thought, more and more associative memories of elementary school emerge. I can remember the teacher scolding me after I hit Alfred for putting dirt on my shoe. All of these memories play like video-tapes in the VCR in my imagination. If I allow my mind to keep associating, it will wander a million miles away from the word "under," to submarines under the Antarctic and the Beatles song "Yellow Sub-marine." If I let my mind pause on the picture of the yellow submarine, I then hear the song. As I start humming the song and get to the part about people coming on board, my association switches to the gangway of a ship I saw in Australia.

I also visualize verbs. The word "jumping" triggers a memory of jumping hurdles at the mock Olympics held at my elementary school. Adverbs often trigger inappropriate images—"quickly" reminds me of Nestle's Quik—unless they are paired with a verb, which modifies my visual image. For example, "he ran quickly" triggers an animated image of Dick from the first-grade reading book running fast, and "he walked slowly" slows the image down. As a child, I left out words such as "is," "the," and "it," because they had no meaning by themselves. Similarly, words like "of" and "an" made no sense. Eventually I learned how to use them properly, because my parents always spoke correct English and I mimicked their speech patterns. To this day certain verb conjugations, such as "to be," are absolutely meaningless to me.

When I read, I translate written words into color movies or I simply store a photo of the written page to be read later. When I retrieve the material, I see a photocopy of the page in my imagination. I can then read it like a TelePrompTer. It is likely that Raymond, the autistic savant depicted in the movie *Rain Man*, used a similar strategy to memorize telephone books, maps, and other information. He simply photocopied each page of the phone book into his memory. When he wanted to find a certain number, he just scanned pages of the phone book that were in his mind. To pull information out of my memory, I have to replay the video. Pulling facts up quickly is sometimes difficult, because I have to play bits of different videos until I find the right tape. This takes time.

When I am unable to convert text to pictures, it is usually because the text 5 has no concrete meaning. Some philosophy books and articles about the cattle futures market are simply incomprehensible. It is much easier for me to understand written text that describes something that can be easily translated into pictures. The following sentence from a story in the February 21, 1994, issue of *Time* magazine, describing the Winter Olympics figure-skating championships, is a good example: "All the elements are in place—the spotlights, the swelling waltzes and jazz tunes, the sequined sprites taking to the air." In my imagination I see the skating rink and skaters. However, if I ponder too long on the word "elements," I will make the inappropriate association of a periodic table on the wall of my high school chemistry classroom. Pausing on the word "sprite" triggers an image of a Sprite can in my refrigerator instead of a pretty young skater.

Teachers who work with autistic children need to understand associative thought patterns. An autistic child will often use a word in an inappropriate manner. Sometimes these uses have a logical associative meaning and other times they don't. For example, an autistic child might say the word "dog" when he wants to go outside. The word "dog" is associated with going outside.

In my own case, I can remember both logical and illogical use of inappropriate words. When I was six, I learned to say "prosecution." I had absolutely no idea what it meant, but it sounded nice when I said it, so I used it as an exclamation every time my kite hit the ground. I must have baffled more than a few people who heard me exclaim "Prosecution!" to my downward-spiraling kite.

Discussions with other autistic people reveal similar visual styles of thinking about tasks that most people do sequentially. An autistic man who composes music told me that he makes "sound pictures" using small pieces of other music to create new compositions. A computer programmer with autism told me that he sees the general pattern of the program tree. After he visualizes the skeleton for the program, he simply writes the code for each branch. I use similar methods when I review scientific literature and troubleshoot at meat plants. I take specific findings or observations and combine them to find new basic principles and general concepts.

My thinking pattern always starts with specifics and works toward generalization in an associational and nonsequential way. As if I were attempting to figure out what the picture on a jigsaw puzzle is when only one third of the puzzle is completed, I am able to fill in the missing pieces by scanning my video library. Chinese mathematicians who can make large calculations in their heads work the same way. At first they need an abacus. the Chinese calculator, which consists of rows of beads on wires in a frame. They make calculations by moving the rows of beads. When a mathematician becomes really skilled, he simply visualizes the abacus in his imagination and no longer needs a real one. The beads move on a visualized video abacus in his brain.

ABSTRACT THOUGHT

Growing up, I learned to convert abstract ideas into pictures as a way to understand them. I visualized concepts such as peace or honesty with symbolic images. I thought of peace as a dove, an Indian peace pipe, or TV or newsreel footage of the signing of a peace agreement. Honesty was represented by an image of placing one's hand on the Bible in court. A news report describing a person returning a wallet with all the money in it provided a picture of honest behavior.

10   The Lord's Prayer was incomprehensible until I broke it down into specific visual images. The power and the glory were represented by a semicircular rainbow and an electrical tower. These childhood visual images are still triggered every time I hear the Lord's Prayer. The words "thy will be done" had no meaning when I was a child, and today the meaning is still vague. Will is a hard concept to visualize. When I think about it, I imagine God throwing a lightning bolt. Another adult with autism wrote that he visualized "Thou art

in heaven" as God with an easel above the clouds. "Trespassing" was pictured as black and orange no trespassing signs. The word "Amen" at the end of the prayer was a mystery: a man at the end made no sense.

As a teenager and young adult I had to use concrete symbols to understand abstract concepts such as getting along with people and moving on to the next steps of my life, both of which were always difficult. I knew I did not fit in with my high school peers, and I was unable to figure out what I was doing wrong. No matter how hard I tried, they made fun of me. They called me "work-horse," "tape recorder," and "bones" because I was skinny. At the time I was able to figure out why they called me "workhorse" and "bones," but "tape recorder" puzzled me. Now I realize that I must have sounded like a tape recorder when I repeated things verbatim over and over. But back then I just could not figure out why I was such a social dud. I sought refuge in doing things I was good at, such as working on reroofing the barn or practicing my riding prior to a horse show. Personal relationships made absolutely no sense to me until I developed visual symbols of doors and windows. It was then that I started to understand concepts such as learning the give-and-take of a relationship. I still wonder what would have happened to me if I had not been able to visualize my way in the world.

Engaging the Text

1. How did Grandin's high school experiences illustrate the limitations she and others who are autistic experience when trying to communicate with other people?

2. What is unusual about the way in which Grandin understands the meanings of words? What function do associative thought processes and retrieval of images from memory play in how she makes sense of what she reads?

3. Grandin uses analogies to make the complex subject of autism easier to understand. How does this rhetorical strategy clarify the unique manner that those with autism use to grasp ideas?

Exploring Your Cultural Perspective

1. The cognitive processes of those who are autistic are similar to the stages through which we all pass when we learn language. To what extent are your associative thought processes and methods of understanding new words and ideas similar to or different from those described by Grandin? Give some examples.

2. Without being able to call upon abstractions with which to generalize, we would find ourselves in a situation similar to the one described by Jonathan

Swift in Book III of *Gulliver's Travels* (1727). There, Gulliver, on a visit to a "school of languages," learns of a "Scheme for Entirely Abolishing All Words Whatsoever." The rationale behind this unlikely enterprise is that "since words are only names for things, it would be more convenient for all men to carry about them, such things as were necessary to express the particular business they are to discourse on." Thus, instead of speaking, citizens would carry sacks filled with the physical objects about which they wished to converse, and a "conversation" would appear as follows:

> If a man's business be very great and of various kinds, he must be obliged in proportion to carry a greater bundle of Things upon his back unless he can afford one or two strong servants to attend him. I have often beheld two of those sages almost sinking under the weight of their packs like peddlers among us who when they meet in the streets would lay down their loads, open their sacks and hold conversation for an hour together, then put up their implements, help each other to resume their burdens and take their leave.

How does this amusing caricature of a conversation without speech dramatize the disadvantages of being unable to use abstractions to symbolize qualities or express ideas?

LUC SANTE

Lingua Franca

Luc Sante (pronounced "Luke Sahnt") was born in Belgium in 1954 and emigrated to the United States in 1959. He was educated at Columbia University and is the author of *Low Life: Lures and Snares of Old New York* (1991), *Evidence* (1992), and "Lingua Franca," which first appeared in *The Anchor Essay Annual: Best of 1998*. This essay is from a work in progress titled *The Factory of Facts*, a memoir in which Sante reflects on what it was like to be brought up in two cultures with two different languages (French and English).

Thinking Critically

As you read, notice how Sante uses his personal experiences to raise the broader theme of the way one's identity is connected to the language one speaks. Have you ever tried to make yourself understood in another language that you did not speak well? What got lost in the translation?

In order to write of my childhood I have to translate. It is as if I were writing about someone else. As a boy, I lived in French; now, I live in English. The words don't fit, because languages are not equivalent to one another. If I say, 'I am a boy; I am lying in my bed; I am sitting in my room; I am lonely and afraid,' attributing these thoughts to my eight-year-old self, I am being literally correct but emotionally untrue. Even if I submit the thoughts to indirect citation and the past tense I am engaging in a sort of falsehood. I am playing ventriloquist, and that eight-year-old, now made of wood and with a hinged jaw, is sitting on my knee, mouthing the phrases I am fashioning for him. It's not that the boy couldn't understand those phrases. It is that in order to do so, he would have to translate, and that would mean engaging an electrical circuit in his brain, bypassing his heart.

If the boy thought the phrase, 'I am a boy', he would picture Dick or Zeke from the school books, or maybe his friends Mike or Joe. The word 'boy' could not refer to him; he is *un garçon*. You may think this is trivial, that *garçon* simply means 'boy', but that is missing the point. Similarly, *maman* and *papa* are people; 'mother' and 'father' are notions. *La nuit* is dark and filled with fear, while 'the night' is a pretty picture of a starry field. The boy lives in *une maison* with a house on either side. His *coeur* is where his feelings dwell, and his heart is a blood-pumping muscle. For that matter, his name is Luc, pronounced *lük*; everybody around, though, calls him 'Luke', which is an alias, a mask.

He regards the English language with a curiosity bordering on the entomological. Watching the *Amerloques* moving around in their tongue is like seeing lines of ants parading through tunnels, bearing sections of leaves. He finds it funny, often enough. In school, for instance, when nutrition is discussed, the elements of a meal are called 'servings', a word that always conjures up images of footmen in claw-hammer coats bearing covered dishes. Since he knows that his classmates, however prosperous their parents might be, aren't likely to have servants, he substitutes the familiar advertising icon of Mother entering the room with a trussed turkey on a platter, which is no less alien or ridiculous. He gathers that this scene has some material basis in the lives of Americans, although it appears to him contrived beyond belief. American life, like the English language, is fascinating and hopelessly phoney.

His vantage point is convenient, like a hunter's blind. He has some struggles with the new language—it will be years, for example, before his tongue and teeth can approximate the 'th' sound, and in the meantime he will have to tolerate laughter every time he pronounces 'third' as 'turd'—but at the same time he is protected. No one will ever break his heart with English words, he thinks. It is at home that he is naked. If the world outside the door is a vast and apparently arbitrary game, inside lies the familiar, which can easily bruise or cut him. No, his parents aren't monsters, nothing like that, although they may not appreciate their own power. Anyway, he has raised and nurtured enough monsters by himself to inflict pain without need of assistance. The French language is a part of his body and his soul, and it has a latent capacity for violence. No wonder he has trouble navigating between the languages at first: they are absurdly different, doors to separate and unequal universes. Books might allege they are the same kind of item, like a pig and a goat, but that is absurd on the face of it. One is tissue and the other is plastic. One is a wound and the other is a prosthesis.

5   Of course, the French language would not be so intimate, wrenching, and potentially dangerous to him if he had remained in a French-speaking world. There he would be bombarded by French of all temperatures, flavours, connotations. His friends, his enemies, his teachers, his neighbours, the newspaper, the radio, the billboards, people on the street, pop songs, movies, assembly instructions, lists of ingredients, shouting drunks, mumbling lunatics, indifferent officials, all would transmit in French. Pretty girls would speak French. He would pick up slang, poesy, academese, boiler-plate, specialized jargon, cant, nonsense. He would not only hear French everywhere but absorb it uncon-

sciously all the time. He would learn the kind of things no dictionary will tell you: for example that apparent synonyms are in reality miles apart, each with its own calluses of association. By and by, *je* would become more than his private self, would find itself shoulder to shoulder with the *je* of a million others. There would be traffic and commerce between inner life and outer world. A great many things would go without saying, be taken for granted. It would seem as though language had arisen from the ground, had always been and would always be.

Instead French festers. It is kept in darkness and fed meagrely by the spoonful. It isn't purposely neglected, of course; there is nothing intentionally punitive about the way it is sequestered and undernourished. On the contrary: it is cherished, cosseted, rewarded for just being, like an animal in a zoo. But like that animal it can only enjoy a semblance of its natural existence. Its memory of the native habitat grows sparser all the time, and its attempts at normality become play-acting, become parody, become rote. Its growth has been stunted, and it correspondingly retains many infantile characteristics. Even as the boy grows gradually tougher and more worldly in English, he carries around a French internal life whose clock has stopped. He is unnaturally fragile, exaggeratedly sensitive in his French core. Not surprisingly, he resents this, wants to expunge it, destroy it, pour salt on its traces to prevent regeneration.

What does this say about the boy's view of his family circumstances? That is a complicated matter. French is his soul, and it is also a prison, and the same terms could be applied to his family. At home he is alone with his parents; no one else exists. It is stifling and comforting in equal measure. Out in the world he is entirely alone. He is terrified but he is free. Or potentially free, anyway; he's too young to know. But one of the things that sustains him in the world is the knowledge of his French innards. He can feel superior about it (his peers don't possess anything equivalent, and they'll never have any idea what it feels like) but it is simultaneously a source of shame. At home he may be alone with his parents, but while they have an awesome power over his infant core, his growing English self is something they don't know and can't touch. You can take all these propositions as mathematical equations. Work them out, forwards or backwards, and you will always arrive at the same reduction, the same answer: he is alone.

My attempt to put any sort of words in the boy's mouth is doomed. He doesn't yet have a language. He has two tongues: one is all quivering, unmediated, primal sensation, and the other is detached, deliberate, artificial. To give a full accounting he would have to split himself in two. But I don't know whether I might not have to do the same myself, here and now. To speak of my family, for example, I can hardly employ English without omitting an emotional essence that remains locked in French, although I can't use French, either, unless I am willing to sacrifice my critical intelligence. Could I, employing English, truly penetrate my parents' decision to emigrate? I was born in Verviers, in south-eastern Belgium, birthplace of everyone bearing my last name for at least 800 years. The city was dominated by its textile industry for nearly a millennium, but that industry began to die in the 1950s, and my father was out of a job, and no others were to be had. The notice of bankruptcy of my father's employer was posted in French; the agonized conversations between my parents were conducted in French; the war bride and her brother, my father's childhood friends, invited my parents to consider joining them in New Jersey, phrasing their inducements in French. I now understand such grave adult matters, but I understand them in English. A chasm yawns between languages, between my childhood and my present age. But there is an advantage hidden in this predicament: French is an archaeological site of emotions, a pipeline to my infant self. It preserves the very rawest, deepest, least guarded feelings.

If I stub my toe, I may profanely exclaim, in English, 'Jesus!' But in agony, such as when I am passing a kidney stone, I might cry, *'Petit Jésus!'* with all the reverence of nursery religion. Others have told me that when I babble in feverish delirium or talk in my sleep, I do so in French. Preserved, too, in French, is a world of lost pleasures and familial comforts. If someone says, in English, 'Let's go visit Mr and Mrs X,' the concept is neutral, my reaction is determined by what I think of Mr and Mrs X. On the other hand, if the suggestion is broached in French, *'Allons dire bonjour'*, the phrasing affects me more powerfully than the specifics. *'Dire bonjour'* calls up a train of associations: for some reason I see my great-uncle Jules Stelmes, dead more than thirty years, with his fedora and his enormous white moustache and his soft dark eyes. I smell coffee and the raisin bread called *cramique*, hear the muffled bong of a parlour clock and the repetitive commonplaces of chit-chat in the drawling accent of the Ardennes, people rolling their Rs and leaning hard on their initial Hs. I feel a rush-caned chair under me, see white curtains and a starched tablecloth, can almost tap my feet on the cold ceramic tiles, maybe the *trompe l'oeil* pattern that covered the entire floor surface of my great-uncle Albert Remacle's farmhouse in Viville. I am sated, sleepy, bored out of my mind.

10   The triggers that operate this mechanism are the simplest, humblest expressions. They are things that might be said to a child or said often within a child's hearing. There are common comestibles: *une tasse de café, une tartine, du chocolat*. There are interjections and verbal place-markers: *sais-tu, figure-toi, je t'assure, mon Dieu*. And, naturally, there are terms of endearment. In my family, the use of someone's first name was nearly always an indication of anger or a prelude to bad news. My parents addressed me as *fifi, chou* (cabbage), *lapin* (rabbit), *vî tchèt* (meaning 'old cat' in Walloon, the native patois of southern Belgium) *petit coeur*. If I'd done something mischievous, my father would laugh and call me *cûrêye* (Walloon for 'carcass' or 'spavined horse'—like saying, 'you're rotten'); if I'd made myself especially comfortable, such as by taking up

most of the couch, he'd shake his head and grin and call me *macrale* (Walloon for 'witch'). I regularly got called *tièsse èl aîr* (head in the clouds; Walloon). If my mother was teasing me in mock anger, she'd call me a *petit chenapan* (little scamp); if it was my father, he'd be likely to say *'t'es ô tièssetou'* ('you're a stubborn one', in Walloon). My father's real anger was rare and grave; my mother's boiled over quickly even if it faded just as fast. She might call me a *vaurien* (good-for-nothing) or a *sale gosse* (dirty kid), an *èstèné* (an idiot, literally 'bewildered'; Walloon) or a *singlé* (a simpleton) or a *nolu* (a nullity; Walloon). If I'd really stung her, though, she'd yell *chameau!* (camel), and I liked that, because she was acknowledging I had some kind of power. There are worse words, which still have the capacity to make me cringe: *cochon* (pig), *crapuleux* (vile, vicious), *crotté* (filthy), *mâssî* (ditto; Walloon). Those words are woven through the fabric of my early adolescence.

A few years ago, early in the morning, I was waiting to cross a street in Liège. I wasn't quite awake yet, and was lost in thought, so that when I heard someone shout *'Fais attention! Regarde!'* I immediately stiffened. All of a sudden I was back at the age of eight or nine, being reproved by my parents. As it happened, there was a small boy standing next to me, holding a tray of empty coffee cups which he was returning to the café opposite; his father, manning a flea-market booth behind us, had observed the kid putting a toe into the street unmindful of oncoming traffic. It can easily happen to me, when faced with some officious fracophone creep, shopkeeper or librarian or customs agent, that I lose thirty years and two feet off my height. If I haven't briefed myself beforehand, I crumple. This can happen even though I've kept my French alive internally through reading, as well as occasional conversations with friends. But even in such circumstances I can find myself tripped up, suddenly sprawled. I can be reading something truly scabrous, something by Georges Bataille, say, turning the pages as an imperturbable adult, and then a turn of phrase will shock me, not some description of outlandish vice but rather a perfectly innocent locution lying in the midst of the smut. It will throw everything else into a new relief. Suddenly it is as if one of my aunts had looked up from her coffee and started spewing obscenities.

Since I live almost entirely in English now, I can regard French with some of the same detachment and sense of the ridiculous with which I once regarded my adopted tongue. If I walk into an American discount store and the loudspeaker starts braying 'Attention shoppers!' I will consign the noise to the realm of static, switch off its ability to reach me except as an irritant. On the other hand, if I am in a Belgian supermarket and the loudspeaker begins its recital, nearly always in a polished female murmur rather than the American male bark: *'Monsieur, madame, nous vous conseillons . . .'* I am bemused, imagining the rapport between the voice and its sleek, well-dressed target, someone so exquisitely put together that he or she can purchase low-fat frozen entrées with a withering superiority, as if picking out a *grand cru classé*. I am never the 'you' of American advertising because I consciously slam the door, but in French I am never given the opportunity to spurn the come-on. I am excluded at the gate. Naturally there is a class factor involved—in French I revert to proletarian status as easily as to childhood—but the exclusion is also due to my status as a counterfeit Belgian, an American pretender.

I can cross the border between English and French, although I can't straddle it. Years ago, when I worked behind the cash register in a store, I resented the demands of the customers and sometimes went out of my way to be rude to them, to put them in their place. After work, though, I might go to some other shop, and there, trying to find out whether the shirt came in a larger size or a darker colour, would find myself resenting the arrogance and apathy of the clerks. I had jumped from one side of the fence to the other. I could no more simultaneously occupy the mentality of clerk and client than I could bat a ball to myself in the outfield. Each claim effaced the other. It was useless to try and apportion blame; customers and clerks were both rude and both justified, were in fact interchangeable. This insight is perhaps the closest I've ever got to understanding the psychology that lies behind nationalism. The situation is a bit like one of the famous optical illusions, in which the silhouettes of two facing profiles form the outline of a vase. You can see the vase, and then you can see the profiles, but you can't see both images at once.

Engaging the Text

1. In what ways are Sante's memories of his childhood filtered through the French language he spoke when he was growing up? Why is French a more visceral experience for him than is English?

2. As he learns to speak English and his French languishes, Sante experiences a sense of loss. In what way is the language he is no longer encouraged to speak like an earlier self from which he feels increasingly disconnected?

3. Which of the many examples Sante presents communicate the unbreakable bond between his early life experiences and the French words connected with them?

Exploring Your Cultural Perspective

1. Why are the expressions we learned in childhood and hear again as adults capable of transporting us back to a former time? Has this happened to you? Describe such an experience.

2. If you are fluent in two languages, in which one do you think, dream, or talk? Does the language depend on the circumstances?

BARBARA MELLIX

From Outside, In

Barbara Mellix teaches composition and fiction writing at the University of Pittsburgh, where she earned her MFA in creative writing in 1986. Her first published short story appeared in the Summer 1987 issue of the *Pennsylvania Review*, and "From Outside, In" first appeared in the Summer 1987 issue of the *Georgia Review*. For Mellix, who grew up speaking black English, the experience of learning standard English transformed her life.

Thinking Critically

Recent controversies about Ebonics have made people more conscious of the bond between language and **community** *(a social group whose members share common characteristics). Do you speak a dialect that connects you to your community but separates you from mainstream culture? As you read this piece, think about the role language plays in freeing or limiting you in your social interactions, particularly those outside your peer group.*

Two years ago, when I started writing this paper, trying to bring order out of chaos, my ten-year-old daughter was suffering from an acute attack of boredom. She drifted in and out of the room complaining that she had nothing to do, no one to "be with" because none of her friends were at home. Patiently I explained that I was working on something special and needed peace and quiet, and I suggested that she paint, read, or work with her computer. None of these interested her. Finally, she pulled up a chair to my desk and watched me, now and then heaving long, loud sighs. After two or three minutes (nine or ten sighs), I lost my patience. "Looka here, Allie," I said, "you too old for this kinda carryin' on. I done told you this is important. You wronger than dirt to be in here haggin' me like this and you know it. Now git on outta here and leave me off before I put my foot all the way down."

I was at home, alone with my family, and my daughter understood that this way of speaking was appropriate in that context. She knew, as a matter of fact, that it was almost inevitable; when I get angry at home, I speak some of my finest, most cherished black English. Had I been speaking to my daughter in this manner in certain other environments, she would have been shocked and probably worried that I had taken leave of my sense of propriety.

Like my children, I grew up speaking what I considered two distinctly different languages—black English and standard English (or as I thought of them then, the ordinary everyday speech of "country" coloreds and "proper" English)—and in the process of acquiring these languages, I developed an understanding of when, where, and how to use them. But unlike my children, I grew up in a world that was primarily black. My friends, neighbors, minister, teachers—almost everybody I associated with every day—were black. And we spoke to one another in our own special language: *That sho is a pretty dress you got on. If she don' soon leave me off I'm gon tell her head a mess. I was so mad I could'a pissed a blue nail. He all the time trying to low-rate somebody. Ain't that just about the nastiest thing you ever set ears on?*

Then there were the "others," the "proper" blacks, transplanted relatives and one-time friends who came home from the city for weddings, funerals, and vacations. And the whites. To these we spoke standard English. "Ain't?" my mother would yell at me when I used the term in the presence of "others." "You *know* better than that." And I would hang my head in shame and say the "proper" word.

5   I remember one summer sitting in my grandmother's house in Greeleyville, South Carolina, when it was full of the chatter of city relatives who were home on vacation. My parents sat quietly, only now and then volunteering a comment or answering a question. My mother's face took on a strained expression when she spoke. I could see that she was being careful to say just the right words in just the right way. Her voice sounded thick, muffled. And when she finished speaking, she would lapse into silence, her proper smile on her face. My father was more articulate, more aggressive. He spoke quickly, his words sharp and clear. But he held his proud head higher, a signal that he, too, was uncomfortable. My sisters and brothers and I stared at our aunts, uncles, and cousins, speaking only when prompted. Even then, we hesitated, formed our sentences in our minds, then spoke softly, shyly.

My parents looked small and anxious during those occasions, and I waited impatiently for our leave-taking when we would mock our relatives the moment we were out of their hearing. "Reeely," we would say to one another, flexing our wrists and rolling our eyes, "how dooo you stan' this heat? Chile, it just too hy*ooo*-mid for words." Our relatives had made us feel "country," and this was our way of regaining pride in ourselves while getting a little revenge in the bargain. The words bubbled in our throats and rolled across our tongues, a balming.

As a child I felt this same doubleness in uptown Greeleyville where the whites lived. "Ain't that a pretty dress you're wearing!" Toby, the town policeman, said to me one day when I was fifteen. "Thank you very much," I replied, my voice barely audible in my own ears. The words felt wrong in my mouth, rigid, foreign. It was not that I had never spoken that phrase before—it was common in black English, too—but I was extremely conscious that this was an occasion for proper English. I had taken out my English and put it on as I did my church clothes, and I felt as if I were wearing my Sunday best in the middle of the week. It did not matter that Toby had not spoken grammatically correct English. He was white and could speak as he wished. I had something to prove. Toby did not.

Speaking standard English to whites was our way of demonstrating that we knew their language and could use it. Speaking it to standard-English-speaking blacks was our way of showing them that we, as well as they, could "put on airs." But when we spoke standard English, we acknowledged (to ourselves and to others—but primarily to ourselves) that our customary way of speaking was inferior. We felt foolish, embarrassed, somehow diminished because we were ashamed to be our real selves. We were reserved, shy in the presence of those who owned and/or spoke *the* language.

My parents never set aside time to drill us in standard English. Their forms of instruction were less formal. When my father was feeling particularly expansive, he would regale us with tales of his exploits in the outside world. In almost flawless English, complete with dialogue and flavored with gestures and embellishment, he told us about his attempt to get a haircut at a white barbershop; his refusal to acknowledge one of the town merchants until the man addressed him as "Mister"; the time he refused to step off the sidewalk uptown to let some whites pass; his airplane trip to New York City (to visit a sick relative) during which the stewardesses and porters—recognizing that he was a "gentleman"—addressed him as "Sir." I did not realize then—nor, I think, did my father—that he was teaching us, among other things, standard English and the relationship between language and power.

My mother's approach was different. Often, when one of us said, "I'm gon wash off my feet," she would say, "And what will you walk on if you wash them off?" Everyone would laugh at the victim of my mother's "proper" mood. But it was different when one of us children was in a proper mood. "You think you are so superior," I said to my oldest sister one day when we were arguing and she was winning. "Superior!" my sister mocked. "You mean I'm acting 'biggidy'?" My sisters and brothers sniggered, then joined in teasing me. Finally, my mother said, "Leave your sister alone. There's nothing wrong with using proper English." There was a half-smile on her face. I had gotten "uppity," had "put on airs" for no good reason. I was at home, alone with the family, and

10

I hadn't been prompted by one of my mother's proper moods. But there was also a proud light in my mother's eyes; her children were learning English very well.

Not until years later, as a college student, did I begin to understand our ambivalence toward English, our scorn of it, our need to master it, to own and be owned by it—an ambivalence that extended to the public-school classroom. In our school, where there were no whites, my teachers taught standard English but used black English to do it. When my grammar-school teachers wanted us to write, for example, they usually said something like, "I want y'all to write five sentences that make a statement. Anybody git done before the rest can color." It was probably almost those exact words that led me to write these sentences in 1953 when I was in the second grade:

> The white clouds are pretty.
> There are only 15 people in our room.
> We will go to gym.
> We have a new poster.
> We may go out doors.

Second grade came after "Little First" and "Big First," so by then I knew the implied rules that accompanied all writing assignments. Writing was an occasion for proper English. I was not to write in the way we spoke to one another: The white clouds pretty; There ain't but 15 people in our room; We going to gym; We got a new poster; We can go out in the yard. Rather I was to use the language of "other": clouds *are*, there *are*, we *will*, we *have*, we *may*.

My sentences were short, rigid, perfunctory, like the letters my mother wrote to relatives:

> Dear Papa,
>
> How are you? How is Mattie? Fine I hope. We are fine. We will come to see you Sunday. Cousin Ned will give us a ride.
>
> Love,
Daughter

The language was not ours. It was something from outside us, something we used for special occasions.

But my coloring on the other side of that second-grade paper is different. I drew three hearts and a sun. The sun has a smiling face that radiates and envelops everything it touches. And although the sun and its world are enclosed in a circle, the colors I used—red, blue, green, purple, orange, yellow, black—indicate that I was less restricted with drawing and coloring than I was with writing standard English. My valentines were not just red. My sun was not just a yellow ball in the sky.

By the time I reached the twelfth grade, speaking and writing standard English had taken on new importance. Each year, about half of the newly graduated seniors of our school moved to large cities—particularly in the North—to live with relatives and find work. Our English teacher constantly corrected our grammar: "Not 'ain't,' but 'isn't.'" We seldom wrote papers, and even those few were usually plot summaries of short stories. When our teacher returned the papers, she usually lectured on the importance of using standard English: "I *am;* you *are;* he, she, or it *is,*" she would *say,* writing on the chalkboard as she spoke. "How you gon git a job talking about 'I is,' or 'I isn't' or 'I ain't'?"

In Pittsburgh, where I moved after graduation, I watched my aunt and   *15* uncle—who had always spoken standard English when in Greeleyville—switch from black English to standard English to a mixture of the two, according to where they were or who they were with. At home and with certain close relatives, friends, and neighbors, they spoke black English. With those less close, they spoke a mixture. In public and with strangers, they generally spoke standard English.

In time, I learned to speak standard English with ease and to switch smoothly from black to standard or a mixture, and back again. But no matter where I was, no matter what the situation or occasion, I continued to write as I had in school:

> Dear Mommie,
>
> How are you? How is everybody else? Fine I hope. I am fine. So are Aunt and Uncle. Tell everyone I said hello. I will write again soon.
>
> > Love,
> > Barbara

At work, at a health insurance company, I learned to write letters to customers. I studied form letters and letters written by co-workers, memorizing the phrases and the ways in which they were used. I dictated:

> Thank you for your letter of January 5. We have made the changes in your coverage you requested. Your new premium will be $150 every three months. We are pleased to have been of service to you.

In a sense, I was proud of the letters I wrote for the company: they were proof of my ability to survive in the city, the outside world—an indication of my growing mastery of English. But they also indicate that writing was still mechanical for me, something that didn't require much thought.

Reading also became a more significant part of my life during those early years in Pittsburgh. I had always liked reading, but now I devoted more and more of my spare time to it. I read romances, mysteries, popular novels. Looking back, I realize that the books I liked best were simple, unambiguous: good versus bad and right versus wrong with right rewarded and wrong punished, mysteries unraveled and all set right in the end. It was how I remembered life in Greeleyville.

Of course I was romanticizing. Life in Greeleyville had not been so very uncomplicated. Back there I had been—first as a child, then as a young woman with limited experience in the outside world—living in a relatively closed-in society. But there were implicit and explicit principles that guided our way of life and shaped our relationships with one another and the people outside—principles that a newcomer would find elusive and baffling. In Pittsburgh, I had matured, become more experienced: I had worked at three different jobs, associated with a wider range of people, married, had children. This new environment with different prescripts for living required that I speak standard English much of the time, and slowly, imperceptibly, I had ceased seeing a sharp distinction between myself and "others." Reading romances and mysteries, characterized by dichotomy, was a way of shying away from change, from the person I was becoming.

But that other part of me—that part which took great pride in my ability to hold a job writing business letters—was increasingly drawn to the new developments in my life and the attending possibilities, opportunities for even greater change. If I could write letters for a nationally known business, could I not also do something better, more challenging, more important? Could I not, perhaps, go to college and become a school teacher? For years, afraid and a little embarrassed, I did no more than imagine this different me, this possible me. But sixteen years after coming north, when my youngest daughter entered kindergarten, I found myself unable—or unwilling—to resist the lure of possibility. I enrolled in my first college course: Basic Writing, at the University of Pittsburgh.

20   For the first time in my life, I was required to write extensively about myself. Using the most formal English at my command, I wrote these sentences near the beginning of the term:

> One of my duties as a homemaker is simply picking up after others. A day seldom passes that I don't search for a mislaid toy, book, or gym shoe, etc. I change the Ty-D-Bol, fight "ring around the collar," and keep our laundry smelling "April fresh." Occasionally, I settle arguments between my children and suggest things to do when they're bored. Taking telephone messages for my oldest daughter is my newest (and sometimes most aggravating) chore. Hanging the toilet paper roll is my most insignificant.

My concern was to use "appropriate" language, to sound as if I belonged in a college classroom. But I felt separate from the language—as if it did not and could not belong to me. I couldn't think and feel genuinely in that language, couldn't make it express what I thought and felt about being a housewife.

A part of me resented, among other things, being judged by such things as the appearance of my family's laundry and toilet bowl, but in that language I could only imagine and write about a conventional housewife.

For the most part, the remainder of the term was a period of adjustment, a time of trying to find my bearings as a student in a college composition class, to learn to shut out my black English whenever I composed, and to prevent it from creeping into my formulations; a time for trying to grasp the language of the classroom and reproduce it in my prose; for trying to talk about myself in that language, reach others through it. Each experience of writing was like standing naked and revealing my imperfection, my "otherness." And each new assignment was another chance to make myself over in language, reshape myself, make myself "better" in my rapidly changing image of a student in a college composition class.

But writing became increasingly unmanageable as the term progressed, and by the end of the semester, my sentences sounded like this:

> My excitement was soon dampened, however, by what seemed like a small voice in the back of my head saying that I should be careful with my long awaited opportunity. I felt frustrated and this seemed to make it difficult to concentrate.

There is a poverty of language in these sentences. By this point, I knew that the clichéd language of my Housewife essay was unacceptable, and I generally recognized trite expressions. At the same time, I hadn't yet mastered the language of the classroom, hadn't yet come to see it as belonging to me. Most notable is the lifelessness of the prose, the apparent absence of a person behind the words. I wanted those sentences—and the rest of the essay—to convey the anguish of yearning to, at once, become something more and yet remain the same. I had the sensation of being split in two, part of me going into a future the other part didn't believe possible. As that person, the student writer at that moment, I was essentially mute. I could not—in the process of composing— use the language of the old me, yet I couldn't imagine myself in the language of "others."

I found this particularly discouraging because at midsemester I had been writing in a much different way. Note the language of this introduction to an essay I had written then, near the middle of the term:

> Pain is a constant companion to the people in "Footwork." Their jobs are physically damaging. Employers are insensitive to their feelings and in many cases add to their problems. The general public wounds them further by treating them with disgrace because of what they do for a living. Although the workers are as diverse as they are similar, there is a definite link between them. They suffer a great deal of abuse.

The voice here is stronger, more confident, appropriating terms like "physically damaging," "wounds them further," "insensitive," "diverse"—terms I couldn't have imagined using when writing about my own experience—and shaping them into sentences like, "Although the workers are as diverse as they are similar, there is a definite link between them." And there is the sense of a personality behind the prose, someone who sympathizes with the workers: "The general public wounds them further by treating them with disgrace because of what they do for a living."

What caused these differences? I was, I believed, explaining other people's thoughts and feelings, and I was free to move about in the language of "others" so long as I was speaking of others. I was unaware that I was transforming into my best classroom language my own thoughts and feelings about people whose experiences and ways of speaking were in many ways similar to mine.

25   The following year, unable to turn back or to let go of what had become something of an obsession with language (and hoping to catch and hold the sense of control that had eluded me in Basic Writing), I enrolled in a research writing course. I spent most of the term learning how to prepare for and write a research paper. I chose sex education as my subject and spent hours in libraries, searching for information, reading, taking notes. Then (not without messiness and often-demoralizing frustration) I organized my information into categories, wrote a thesis statement, and composed my paper—a series of paraphrases and quotations spaced between carefully constructed transitions. The process and results felt artificial, but as I would later come to realize I was passing through a necessary stage. My sentences sounded like this:

> This reserve becomes understandable with examination of who the abusers are. In an overwhelming number of cases, they are people the victims know and trust. Family members, relatives, neighbors and close family friends commit seventy-five percent of all reported sex crimes against children, and parents, parent substitutes and relatives are the offenders in thirty to eighty percent of all reported cases. While assault by strangers does occur, it is less common, and is usually a single episode. But abuse by family members, relatives and acquaintances may continue for an extended period of time. In cases of incest, for example, children are abused repeatedly for an average of eight years. In such cases, "the use of physical force is rarely necessary because of the child's trusting, dependent relationship with the offender. The child's cooperation is often facilitated by the adult's position of dominance, an offer of material goods, a threat of physical violence, or a misrepresentation of moral standards."

The completed paper gave me a sense of profound satisfaction, and I read it often after my professor returned it. I know now that what I was pleased with was the language I used and the professional voice it helped me maintain. "Use better words," my teacher had snapped at me one day after reading the notes I'd begun accumulating from my research, and slowly I began taking on the language of my sources. In my next set of notes, I used the word "vacillating"; my professor applauded. And by the time I composed the final draft, I felt at ease with terms like "overwhelming number of cases," "single episode," and "reserve," and I shaped them into sentences similar to those of my "expert" sources.

If I were writing the paper today, I would of course do some things differently. Rather than open with an anecdote—as my teacher suggested—I would begin simply with a quotation that caught my interest as I was researching my paper (and which I scribbled, without its source, in the margin of my notebook): "Truth does not do so much good in the world as the semblance of truth does evil." The quotation felt right because it captured what was for me the central idea of my essay—an idea that emerged gradually during the making of my paper—and expressed it in a way I would like to have said it. The anecdote, a hypothetical situation I invented to conform to the information in the paper, felt forced and insincere because it represented—to a great degree—my teacher's understanding of the essay, *her* idea of what in it was most significant. Improving upon my previous experiences with writing, I was beginning to think and feel in the language I used, to find my own voices in it, to sense that how one speaks influences how one means. But I was not yet secure enough, comfortable enough with the language to trust my intuition.

Now that I know that to seek knowledge, freedom, and autonomy means always to be in the concentrated process of becoming—always to be venturing into new territory, feeling one's way at first, then getting one's balance, negotiating, accommodating, discovering one's self in ways that previously defined "others"—I sometimes get tired. And I ask myself why I keep on participating in this highbrow form of violence, this slamming against perplexity. But there is no real futility in the question, no hint of that part of the old me who stood outside standard English, hugging to herself a disabling mistrust of a language she thought could not represent a person with her history and experience. Rather, the question represents a person who feels the consequence of her education, the weight of her possibilities as a teacher and writer and human being, a voice in society. And I would not change that person, would not give back the good burden that accompanies my growing expertise, my increasing power to shape myself in language and share that self with "others."

"To speak," says Frantz Fanon, "means to be in a position to use a certain syntax, to grasp the morphology of this or that language, but it means above all to assume a culture, to support the weight of a civilization."* To write

---

Black Skin, White Masks (1952; rpt. New York: Grove Press, 1967), pp. 17–18.

means to do the same, but in a more profound sense. However, Fanon also says that to achieve mastery means to "get" in a position of power, to "grasp," to "assume." This, I have learned—both as a student and subsequently as a teacher—can involve tremendous emotional and psychological conflict for those attempting to master academic discourse. Although as a beginning student writer I had a fairly good grasp of ordinary spoken English and was proficient at what Labov calls "code-switching" (and what John Baugh in *Black Street Speech* terms "style shifting"), when I came face to face with the demands of my status as a black and a speaker of one of the many black English vernaculars—a traditional outsider. For the first time, I experienced my sense of doubleness as something menacing, a built-in enemy. Whenever I turned inward for salvation, the balm so available during my childhood, I found instead this new fragmentation which spoke to me in many voices. It was the voice of my desire to prosper, but at the same time it spoke of what I had relinquished and could not regain: a safe way of being, a state of powerlessness which exempted me from responsibility for who I was and might be. And it accused me of betrayal, of turning away from blackness. To recover balance, I had to take on the language of the academy, the language of "others." And to do that, I had to learn to imagine myself a part of the culture of that language, and therefore someone free to manage that language, to take liberties with it. Writing and rewriting, practicing, experimenting, I came to comprehend more fully the generative power of language. I discovered—with the help of some especially sensitive teachers—that through writing one can continually bring new selves into being, each with new responsibilities and difficulties, but also with new possibilities. Remarkable power, indeed. I write and continually give birth to myself.

Engaging the Text

1. What does Mellix feel she gained in making the transition from black English to standard English? What did she lose? What part did writing play in helping her discover her new self?

2. What prompted Mellix to begin her journey? How do the extracts from notes and letters she wrote along the way illustrate her progress?

3. What factors explain the prestige of "standard English" for Mellix? Does this correspond to your view of it? Why or why not?

Exploring Your Cultural Perspective

1. In what way do Mellix's experiences separate her from African Americans who defend the use of Ebonics and/or adopt African names to affirm their

identity? Write a synthesis essay defending your position on this issue. External sources could include James Baldwin's "If Black English Isn't a Language, Then Tell Me, What Is?" (*New York Times*, 29 July 1979, op-ed), interviews with African American educators, and works by such writers as Toni Morrison. For a Web site that presents both sides of the debate, see the Center for Applied Linguistics site at <http://www.cal.org/ebonics/ebcal.htm>.

2. Do you express yourself differently in different contexts? For example, are there words you use with your friends that you wouldn't use at home or in the classroom? What is your purpose in "switching codes," as described by Mellix?

JOHN AGARD

Listen mr oxford don

John Agard (born in Guyana in 1930) is a poet, short story writer, and journalist. He is a frequent contributor to Guyana's newspaper *Sunday Chronicle*, and his poetry has been collected in *Shoot Me with Flowers* (1985). In the following poem, Agard uses West Indian dialect to satirize cultural intolerance for forms of English deemed to be inferior.

Thinking Critically

Consider the extent to which dialect functions as a marker of social class. As you read this poem, evaluate whether the speaker is educated.

Me not no Oxford don
me a simple immigrant
from Clapham Common
I didn't graduate
5 I immigrate

But listen Mr Oxford don
I'm a man on de run
and a man on de run
is a dangerous one

10 I ent have no gun
I ent have no knife
but mugging de Queen's English
is the story of my life

I dont need no axe
15 to split/up yu syntax
I dont need no hammer
to mash up yu grammar

I warning you Mr Oxford don
I'm a wanted man
and a wanted man   *20*
is a dangerous one

Dem accuse me of assault
on de Oxford dictionary
imagin a concise peaceful man like me
dem want me serve time   *25*
for inciting rhyme to riot

but I tekking it quiet
down here in Clapham Common

I'm not a violent man Mr Oxford don
I only armed wit muh human breath   *30*
but human breath
is a dangerous weapon

So mek dem send one big word after me
I ent serving no jail sentence
I slashing suffix in self-defence   *35*
I bashing future wit present tense
and if necessary

I making de Queen's English accessory/to my offence

Engaging the Text

1. The speaker's witty assault on the linguistic authorities focuses on a "Mr
   Oxford don." What is an "Oxford don," and why does Agard choose this
   person to represent mainstream British culture?

2. What norms of standard English, grammar, and usage does the speaker violate? In what way does his mastery of nonstandard English disprove the
   "crimes" of which he stands accused?

3. Implicit in the poem is a conflict between different social classes and forms
   of language deemed to be the most correct. What "story" does the poem
   tell about the speaker's life and his status as an outsider?

Exploring Your Cultural Perspective

1. In what ways is this poem similar to the lyrics of a rap song? Can you identify a rap song that has an especially compelling message? In your opinion,

why have rap and rap artists been so controversial—for example, Eminem (winner of MTV's 2000 award for best male performer and for best video)?

2. How do you imagine the speaker in this poem might make his living? Do you think there is a correlation between social status and language? Use your personal observations to explain your answer.

ANTHONY BURGESS

A Clockwork Orange

Anthony Burgess (1917–1993), a prolific and entertaining writer of biographies, essays, and novels, is best known for *A Clockwork Orange* (1962), from which the following selection is taken. This darkly surreal comic novel about a violent fifteen-year-old juvenile delinquent who is behaviorally conditioned by the state to be "normal" is a masterpiece of linguistic invention. For this novel, set sometime in the future, Burgess created a futuristic slang (called Nadsat) that is a hybrid of English and Russian. (See the glossary insert on page 333.) His last published work was *A Mouthful of Air: Language, Languages . . . Especially English* (1992).

Thinking Critically

As you read, consider the linguistic means that Burgess uses to create a portrait of a violent antisocial teenager. How does his invented language communicate the subculture to which his protagonist belongs? Have you and your friends ever used jargon or invented your own slang to keep others from knowing what you were talking about?

I could not believe, brothers, what I was told. It seemed that I had been in that vonny mesto for near ever and would be there for near ever more. But it had always been a fortnight and now they said the fortnight was near up. They said: "Tomorrow, little friend, out out out." And they made with the old thumb like pointing to freedom. And then the white-coated veck who had tolchocked me and who had still brought me my trays of pishcha and like escorted me to my everyday torture said: "But you still have one real big day in front of you. It's to be your passing-out day." And he had a leery smeck at that.

I expected this morning that I would be ittying as usual to the sinny mesto in my pyjamas and toofles and over-gown. But no. This morning I was given my shirt and underveshches and my platties of the night and my horrorshow kickboots, all lovely and washed or ironed or polished. And I was even given my cut-throat britva that I had used in those old happy days for fillying and dratsing. So I gave with the puzzled frown at this as I got dressed, but the white-coated under-veck just like grinned and would govoreet nothing, O my brothers.

I was led quite kindly to the same old mesto, but there were changes there. Curtains had been drawn in front of the sinny screen and the frosted glass under the projection holes was no longer there, it having perhaps been pushed up or folded to the sides like blind or shutters. And where there had been just the noise of coughing kashl kashl kashl and like shadows of lewdies was now a real audience, and in this audience there were litsos I knew. There was the Staja Governor and the holy man, the charlie or charles as he was called, and the Chief Chasso and this very important and well-dressed chelloveck who was the Minister of the Interior or Inferior. All the rest I did not know. Dr. Brodsky and Dr. Branom were there, though not now white-coated, instead they were dressed as doctors would dress who were big enough to want to dress in the heighth of fashion. Dr. Branom just stood, but Dr. Brodsky stood and govoreeted in a like learned manner to all the lewdies assembled. When he viddied me coming in he said: "Aha. At this stage, gentlemen, we introduce the subject himself. He is, as you will perceive, fit and well nourished. He comes straight from a night's sleep and a good breakfast, undrugged, unhypnotized. Tomorrow we send him with confidence out into the world again, as decent a lad as you would meet on a May morning, unvicious, unviolent, if anything—as you will observe—inclined to the kindly word and the helpful act. What a change is here, gentlemen, from the wretched hoodlum the State committed to unprofitable punishment some two years ago, unchanged after two years. Unchanged, do I say? Not quite. Prison taught him the false smile, the rubbed hands of hypocrisy, the fawning greased obsequious leer. Other vices it taught him, as well as confirming him in those he had long practiced before. But, gentlemen, enough of words. Actions speak louder than. Action now. Observe, all."

I was a bit dazed by all this govoreeting and I was trying to grasp in my mind that like all this was about me. Then all the lights went out and then there came on two like spotlights shining from the projection-squares, and one of them was full on Your Humble and Suffering Narrator. And into the other spotlight there walked a bolshy big chelloveck I had never viddied before. He had a lardy like litso and a moustache and like strips of hair pasted over his near-bald gulliver. He was about thirty or forty or fifty, some old age like that, starry. He ittied up to me and the spotlight ittied with him, and soon the two spotlights had made like one big pool. He said to me; very sneery: "Hello heap of dirt. Pooh, you don't wash much, judging from the horrible smell." Then, as if he was like dancing, he stamped on my nogas, left, right, then he gave me a finger-nail flick on the nose that hurt like bezoomny and brought the old tears to my glazzies, then he twisted at my left ooko like it was a radio dial. I could slooshy titters and a couple of real horrorshow hawhawhaws coming from like the audience. My nose and nogas and ear-hole stung and pained like bezoomny, so I said:

"What do you do that to me for? I've never done wrong to you, brother." 5

"Oh," this veck said, "I do this"—flickflicked nose again—"and that"—twisted smarting ear-hole—"and the other"—stamped nasty on right noga—"because I don't care for your horrible type. And if you want to do anything about it, start, start, please do." Now I knew that I'd have to be real skorry and get my cut-throat britva out before this horrible killing sickness whooshed up and turned the like joy of battle into feeling I was going to snuff it. But, O brothers, as my rooker reached for the britva in my inside carman I got this like picture in my mind's glazzy of this insulting chelloveck howling for mercy with the red red krovvy all streaming out of his rot, and hot after this picture the sickness and dryness and pains were rushing to overtake, and I viddied that I'd have to change the way I felt about this rotten veck very very skorry indeed, so I felt in my carmans for cigarettes or for pretty polly, and, O my brothers, there was not either of these veshches. I said, like all howly and blubbery:

"I'd like to give you a cigarette, brother, but I don't seem to have any." This veck went:

"Wah wah. Boohoohoo. Cry, baby." Then he flickflick-flicked with his bolshy horny nail at my nose again, and I could slooshy very loud smecks of like mirth coming from the dark audience. I said, real desperate, trying to be nice to this insulting and hurtful veck to stop the pains and sickness coming up:

"Please let me do something for you, please." And I felt in my carmans but could find only my cut-throat britva, so I took this out and handed it to him and said: "Please take this, please. A little present. Please have it." But he said:

"Keep your stinking bribes to yourself. You can't get round me that way." 10 And he banged at my rooker and my cut-throat britva fell on the floor. So I said:

"Please, I must do something. Shall I clean your boots? Look, I'll get down and lick them." And, my brothers, believe it or kiss my sharries, I got down on my knees and pushed my red yahzick out a mile and a half to lick his grahzny vonny boots. But all this veck did was to kick me not too hard on the rot. So then it seemed to me that it would not bring on the sickness and pain if I just gripped his ankles with my rookers tight round them and brought this grahzny bratchny down to the floor. So I did this and he got a real bolshy surprise, coming down crack amid loud laughter from the vonny audience. But viddying him on the floor I could feel the whole horrible feeling coming over me, so I gave him my rooker to lift him up skorry and up he came. Then just as he was going to give me a real nasty and earnest tolchock on the litso Dr. Brodsky said:

"All right, that will do very well." Then this horrible veck sort of bowed and danced off like an actor while the lights came up on me blinking and with my rot square for howling. Dr. Brodsky said to the audience: "Our subject is, you see, impelled towards the good by, paradoxically, being impelled towards evil. The intention to act violently is accompanied by strong feelings of physical distress. To counter these the subject has to switch to a diametrically opposed attitude. Any questions?"

"Choice," rumbled a rich deep goloss. I viddied it belonged to the prison charlie. "He has no real choice, has he? Self-interest, fear of physical pain, drove him to that grotesque act of self-abasement. Its insincerity was clearly to be seen. He ceases to be a wrongdoer. He ceases also to be a creature capable of moral choice."

"These are subtleties," like smiled Dr. Brodsky. "We are not concerned with motive, with the higher ethics. We are concerned only with cutting down crime—"

15   "And," chipped in this bolshy well-dressed Minister, "with relieving the ghastly congestion in our prisons."

"Hear hear," said somebody.

There was a lot of govoreeting and arguing then and I just stood there, brothers, like completely ignored by all these ignorant bratchnies, so I creeched out:

"Me, me, me. How about me? Where do I come into all this? Am I like just some animal or dog?" And that started them off govoreeting real loud and throwing slovos at me. So I creeched louder still, creeching: "Am I just to be like a clockwork orange?" I didn't know what made me use those slovos, brothers, which just came like without asking into my gulliver. And that shut all those vecks up for some reason for a minoota or two. Then one very thin starry professor type chelloveck stood up, his neck like all cables carrying like power from his gulliver to his plott, and he said:

"You have no cause to grumble, boy. You made your choice and all this is a consequence of your choice. Whatever now ensues is what you yourself have chosen." And the prison charlie creeched out:

20   "Oh, if only I could believe that." And you could viddy the Governor give him a look like meaning that he would not climb so high in like Prison Religion as he thought he would. Then loud arguing started again, and then I could slooshy the slovo Love being thrown around, the prison charles himself creeching as loud as any about Perfect Love Casteth Out Fear and all that cal. And now Dr. Brodsky said, smiling all over his litso:

"I am glad, gentlemen, this question of Love has been raised. Now we shall see in action a manner of Love that was thought to be dead with the Middle Ages." And then the lights went down and the spotlights came on again, one on your poor and suffering Friend and Narrator, and into the other there like rolled or sidled the most lovely young devotchka you could ever hope in all your jeezny, O my brothers, to viddy. That is to say, she had real horror-show groodies all of which you could like viddy, she having on platties which

🌐 SELECTIONS FROM GLOSSARY OF NADSAT LANGUAGE

Words that don't seem to be of Russian origin are distinguished by asterisks.

bezoomny: mad	mesto: place
Bog: God	minoota: minute
bolshy: big, great	noga: foot, leg
bratchny: bastard	ooko: ear
britva: razor	pishcha: food
cal: feces	platties: clothes
carman: pocket	pletcho: shoulder
* charles, charlie: chaplain	plott: body
chasso: guard	* pretty polly: money
chelloveck: person, man, fellow	rock, rooker: hand, arm
creech: to shout or scream	rot: mouth
devotchka: girl	sharries: buttocks
dratsing: fighting	shoot: fool
* filly: to play or fool with	* sinny: cinema
glazz: eye	skorry: quick, quickly
goloss: voice	sloosh, slooshy: to hear, to listen
govoreet: to speak or talk	slovo: word
grahzny: dirty	smeck: laugh
gromky: loud	* snuff it: to die
groody: breast	* Staja: State Jail
gulliver: head	starry: ancient
horrorshow: good, well	tolchock: to hit or push; blow, beating
* in-out in-out: copulation	toofles: slippers
itty: to go	veck: (see chelloveck)
jeezny: life	veshch: thing
keeshkas: guts	viddy: to see or look
krovvy: blood	von: smell
lewdies: people	yahzick: tongue
litso: face	

came down down down off her pletchoes. And her nogas were like Bog in His Heaven, and she walked like to make you groan in your keeshkas, and yet her litso was a sweet smiling young like innocent litso. She came up towards me with the light like it was the like light of heavenly grace and all that cal coming with her, and the first thing that flashed into my gulliver was that I would like to have her right down there on the floor with the old in-out real savage, but skorry as a shot came the sickness, like a like detective that had been watching round a corner and now followed to make his grahzny arrest. And now the von of lovely perfume that came off her made me want to think of starting to like heave in my keeshkas, so I knew I had to think of some new like way of thinking about her before all the pain and thirstiness and horrible sickness come over me real horrorshow and proper. So I creeched out:

"O most beautiful and beauteous of devotchkas, I throw like my heart at your feet for you to like trample all over. If I had a rose I would give it to you. If it was all rainy and cally now on the ground you could have my platties to walk on so as not to cover your dainty nogas with filth and cal." And as I was saying all this, O my brothers, I could feel the sickness like slinking back. "Let me," I creeched out, "worship you and be like your helper and protector from the wicked like world." Then I thought of the right slovo and felt better for it, saying: "Let me be like your true knight," and down I went again on the old knees, bowing and like scraping.

And then I felt real shooty and dim, it having been like an act again, for this devotchka smiled and bowed to the audience and like danced off, the lights coming up to a bit of applause. And the glazzies of some of these starry vecks in the audience were like popping out at this young devotchka with dirty and like unholy desire, O my brothers.

"He will be your true Christian," Dr. Brodsky was creeching out, "ready to turn the other cheek, ready to be crucified rather than crucify, sick to the very heart at the thought even of killing a fly." And that was right, brothers, because when he said that I thought of killing a fly and felt just that tiny bit sick, but I pushed the sickness and pain back by thinking of the fly being fed with bits of sugar and looked after like a bleeding pet and all that cal. "Reclamation," he creeched. "Joy before the Angels of God."

25   "The point is," this Minister of the Inferior was saying real gromky, "that it works."

"Oh," the prison charlie said, like sighing, "it works all right, God help the lot of us."

Engaging the Text

1. In what sense does the phrase "a clockwork orange" (a Cockney phrase that Burgess said he meant to stand for "the application of a mechanistic morality to a living organism") characterize the bizarre condition into which the narrator has been transformed? What was he like before?

2. How does the unusual language the narrator uses define him in terms of his social class? How does he use language differently from the way his examiners use it? What does his language imply about his psychological state?

3. How does the attitude of the experimenters and scientists toward their human subject differ from that of the prison chaplain? What is the significance of the chaplain's final remark?

Exploring Your Cultural Perspective

1. Investigate how "Spanglish" (a hybrid of English and Spanish) permits the expression of aspects of Latino culture within contemporary American society. Identify some typical Spanglish words or expressions. As part of your research, you might visit the pocho.com Web site at <http://pocho.com> and consult the glossary at <http://www.generationmex.com>. Compare Spanglish to the Russian/English slang in Burgess's "A Clockwork Orange." How do these two hybrid languages foster group identity?

2. Rent the film *A Clockwork Orange* (1971), directed by Stanley Kubrick, and after viewing it, discuss the role that Burgess's invented language plays in dramatizing the differences in social class between Alec and his doctors.

LUIS ALBERTO URREA
Nobody's Son

Luis Alberto Urrea's bicultural experiences have given him a unique perspective. Born in Tijuana, Mexico, to an American mother and a Mexican father, he was raised in San Diego and is a 1977 graduate of the University of California. After working as a film extra, Urrea spent four years (1978–1982) as a volunteer with Spectrum Ministries, a Protestant organization providing food, clothing, and medicine to the poor on the Mexican side of the border. In 1982, he taught expository writing at Harvard. Urrea currently lives in Boulder, Colorado. His latest works include *Across the Wire: Life and Hard Times on the Mexican Border* (1993); a novel, *In Search of Snow* (1994); *Nobody's Son: Notes from an American Life* (1998), in which the following essay appeared, and *Vatos* (with Alberto Urrea, 2000).

Thinking Critically
Notice how Urrea sets up the dominant theme in the opening paragraph when he raises the issue of his identity as a Mexican American. As you read, observe how he uses the subject of language to develop this theme. Can you identify some common words that have come into English from other languages? What are their origins?

My mom said, "I'm so sick of your God-damned Mexican bullshit!" I was in bed with my wife at the time. It was 7:30 in the morning. My wife was white. So was my mother.

Apparently, the issue of my identity was troubling Mom. She was a good Republican. She tended to work up a good cuss when she was beyond her limit of endurance. I must have come to represent a one-man wave of illegal aliens to her as she sipped her coffee and looked out at a tender New England dawn.

I had finally gotten away from the border. I was teaching writing, at Harvard no less. She saw this development as being due to the force of her own will. That's the GOP for you, I'd say in our frequent and spirited political squabbles—taking credit for someone else's achievements while demonizing their ethnicity. (Did you know that *squabble* is a Scandinavian word? So what, you ask? Just keep it in mind, that's all.)

I was still being called Mexican, Chicano, Hispanic, Latino, Mexican American, Other. These Ivy-League types were taking my name seriously. It drove my mother to distraction.

She barged through the door shouting anti-Mexican rhetoric. Whither   5
goest Mom goest the nation.

We had a miniature Proposition 187 anti-immigration rally right there in my bedroom.

"You are *not* a Mexican!" she cried. "Why can't you be called *Louis* instead of *Luis*?"

Go, Mom.

"Louis *Woodward* or Louis *Dashiell.* One of *my* names. I'm warning you—someday, they're going to come for you, and you'll be sorry."

They.   10

I've been on the lookout for those scoundrels all my life. So has much of my family. (When I mention my family, I mean Mexicans. The Americans were held at bay by my mother for reasons I only later understood. It turns out she was ashamed of the Mexicans. "They spit on the floor," she insisted, though I never saw my *abuelita* hawk up a big one and splash it in the corner. If your mama's saying it, it must be true.) Many of my relatives were afraid of the border patrol. Others were afraid of the Mexican government. Still others were afraid of Republican white people and Democratic black people. Cops. And perhaps my white relatives back East were afraid of all these things, too. But mostly, I got to thinking, they must have been scared of me. I was one of them, but I was also one of *them.*

They.

"They," Wendell Berry writes, "will want you to kneel and weep / and say you should have been like them."

It's a poem called "Do Not Be Ashamed." I read it whenever I'm called upon to give a commencement speech at college graduations. It's not a political poem. It's not a liberal or conservative poem. It's a human poem.

Most students seem to understand what Berry's talking about.   15

He goes on to say:

And once you say you are ashamed,
reading the page they hold out to you,
then such light as you have made
in your history will leave you.
They will no longer need to pursue you.
You will pursue them, begging forgiveness.

They.

You can almost see thought bubbles above the students' heads as they listen. *Honkies,* some are thinking. *Liberals,* and *minorities,* and *commies.* And certainly

666 and *the Antichrist* bubble about up in the air: *Hispanics, Yankees, blacks, queers. Democrats. Women. Men.*

My mother thought: *Mexicans.*

20   My father, a Mexican, thought: *gringos.*

I, for one, think *They* are the ones with the words. You know, the Words. The ones they called my dad and me—like *wetback. Spic. Beaner. Greaser. Pepper-belly. Yellow-belly. Taco-bender. Enchilada-breath.*

That was my wife's phrase. She thought it was cute. She's gone now.

So is my mom.

"Dad?" I said. "What's a greaser?"

25   He used to tell me I was no *God-damned gringo.* I was, however, white. *Speak Spanish, pendejo!* was a common cry when I spoke some unacceptable English phrase. Utterly forbidden English in our house included many taboos, among them: *my old man* (he was sure this was disrespectful and implied he wasn't a virile young thing); *big daddy* (he was certain this meant big penis); *you're kidding* (another disrespect, suggesting he didn't tell the truth at all times—he didn't); *easy rider* (he thought this meant a man married to a whore); *chicano* (from chicanery).

His only word for *them* was *gringo.* He didn't see it as all that bad. He said it came from the Mexican-American War. The pop hit the American soldiers sang in those days was "Green Grow the Lilacs." Green grows/*gringos.* It seemed altogether benign compared to yellow bellies.

I had been called "greaser" by the son of a retired Navy petty officer in my new, all-white neighborhood. We had fled from the ethnic cleansing taking place in Shelltown, California, to which we had hurried from Tijuana. I couldn't quite fathom the name. Surely I wasn't greasy? But I *felt* greasy. And the vivid image of grease, of some noxious *Mexican* grease, collided in my mind with the word "wetback." And suddenly I was certain that my back was wet with grease. A grease I couldn't see. I had an image in my mind of the back of my shirt soaked through with cooking oil and sticking to me, glistening sickeningly in the sun. Everybody could see the grease drooling down my spine. Except me.

My father was whiter than my mother. If he had become an American citizen, he would have voted for Nixon. Twice. Most Mexican immigrants—both "legal" and "illegal"—would vote Republican if given a chance, except the Republicans scare them, so they're forced to support the Clintons and Carters of this nation. It has been estimated that by 2050, Latinos will be the majority population of the world. Not only will America be "brown," but it will also be the home of the new Democrats. The Institutional Revolutionary Catholic Democratic Party ticket of John Kennedy Jr. and Edward James Olmos will sweep the elections. The paradigm will shift, as they say: the bogeyman will become the *chupacabras*. Bullfights at the county fair. Baja California will be the fifty-first state. The Buchanan Brigade Aryan Militia will mount an offensive in the Malibu Hills, holding nineteen gardeners and twelve nannies hostage. NASA will land the first lowrider on the moon. Just watch.

"Greaser," my father replied.

I believe he had prepared himself for this. On our first day in the neigh-   *30* borhood, he'd been chased out of our driveway by an irate white man. You don't spend two decades living as a Mexican guest of Southern California without becoming fully aware of the genocidal urge that percolates in the human heart.

Dad transformed before my eyes into a college lecturer.

"During the Americans' westward expansion," he intoned, "the settlers traveled in covered wagons. When they reached the West—Arizona, Texas, California—they often needed repair work done on their wagons after such a long hard trip. A large part of this work consisted of *greasing* the axles, which had dried out. The only ones who had the skill to fix the wagons were Mexicans. Mexicans greased the axles. You see? *Greasers.* So when they call you that, hold your head up. It's a badge of honor. We helped build America."

He's gone now, too.

The last time I was interviewed by the Mexican press, I was in Mexico City, the self-appointed home of all true Mexicans. I was startled to find out that I was not a true Mexican. I was any number of things: I was an American, I was "just" a Chicano, I was a *norteño* (which, in Mexico City, is like saying you're one of the Mongol horde). I was lauded for speaking Spanish "just like" a Mexican, or chided for having what amounted to a cowboy accent. That I was born in Tijuana didn't matter a bit: Tijuana, I was informed, is no-man's-land. Mexicans don't come from Tijuana. Tijuanans come from Tijuana.

That I was an American citizen was apparently a *faux pas*. That I wrote in   *35* English was an insult. That I was blue-eyed, however, allowed me to pass for Mexican high society.

I will say this for Mexico City, though: people in La Capital have perfect manners. For all its travails and crises, Mexico City is the most civil city I've ever visited. Imagine a city where a cabbie returns your tip to you because you've paid him too much for his services. Imagine this same city reporting a stunning 700 assaults every day.

In the great museum, you can see a famous Aztec mask. One half of it is a smiling face. The other half is a skull.

I was told by the editor of the newspaper to be out of town by the time the interview appeared. Someone somewhere decided that what I had to say was somehow dangerous. I thought this was a joke. Then an editor took me to the foyer where several of the paper's reporters had been executed. *All I'm saying*, I protested, *is that poor people should be treated with respect.* She lit a cigarette and said, *Be out of town.*

Things that seemed perfectly clear to me turned confusing and opaque.

40   In the interview, I offered the often-quoted comment from *By the Lake of Sleeping Children* that I, as a son of the border, had a barbed-wire fence neatly bisecting my heart. The border, in other words, ran through me. The journalist said, "Aha!" and scribbled with real vigor.

When the article came out, however, the comment had been transformed. I'm still not sure what it means. It said: "If you were to cut Urrea's heart open, you would find a border patrol truck idling between his ribs."

I was going to write, "Meanwhile, back home . . ." But where is home? Home isn't just a place, I have learned. It is also a language. My words not only shape and define my home. Words—not only for writers—*are* home. Still, where exactly is that?

Jimmy Santiago Baca reminds us that "Hispanics" are immigrants in our own land. By the time Salem was founded on Massachusetts Bay, any number of Urreas had been prowling up and down the Pacific coast of our continent for several decades. Of course, the Indian mothers of these families had been here from the start. But manifest destiny took care of us all—while we greased the wheels.

Them wagons is still rollin'.

45   I saw a hand-lettered sign on television. It was held up by a woman in stretch pants and curlers, and it said: America For Americans. A nearby man held up a sign exhorting the universe to speak English or go home.

The official language of the United States.

Well, sure. We speak English and, apparently, Ebonics. I want to call Chicano slang Aztonics while we're at it. *Orale*, Homes—we down, *¿qué no? Simón, vato*—let's trip out the *rucas* of the school board, *ese! Ese torcido rifa, locos!*

It's all English. Except for the alligator, which is a Spanish word. Lariat, too, is a Spanish word.

In fact, here's a brief list, in no particular order: It might help you score points in a trivia parlor game someday. All words borrowed from Spanish:

Chaps
Savvy
Palaver
Hoosegow
Palomino

Coyote
Pinto
Marijuana
Vamoose
Stampede
Buckaroo
Adobe
Saguaro
Rodeo
Ranch
Rancher
Patio
Key (as in Florida Keys)
Florida
Sarsaparilla
Navajo
Nevada
Machete
Texas
Alfalfa
Bonanza
Bronco
Calaboose
Canyon
Colorado
Fandango
Foofaraw
Guacamole
Hackamore
Beef jerky
Lasso
Abalone
Vanilla
Chocolate
Cigar

For example. Perfectly acceptable English. Nary an Aztonic word in sight.   *50*

You don't believe me about beef jerky, do you? I find it a little hard to believe, my own self. What's more American than a hunk of jerky? Cowboys, rednecks, crackers, wrestlers, mountain men gnaw away on planks of jerked beef!

Winfred Blevins, in the marvelous *Dictionary of the American West*, notes: "The word is an Americanized version of the Spanish term for jerked meat, *charqui*."

I don't know what we're going to do. Forget about purifying the American landscape, sending all those ethnic types packing back to their homelands. Those illegal humans. (A straw-hat fool in a pickup truck once told my Sioux brother Duane to go back where he came from. "Where to?" Duane called. "South Dakota?")

The humanoids are pretty bad, but how will we get rid of all those pesky foreign *words* debilitating the United States?

55   Those Turkish words (like *coffee*). Those French words (like *maroon*). Those Greek words (like *cedar*). Those Italian words (like *marinate*). Those African words (like *marimba*).

English! It's made up of all these untidy *words*, man. Have you noticed?

Native American (*skunk*), German (*waltz*), Danish (*twerp*), Latin (*adolescent*), Scottish (*feckless*), Dutch (*waft*), Caribbean (*zombie*), Nahuatl (*ocelot*), Norse (*walrus*), Eskimo (*kayak*), Tatar (*horde*) words! It's a glorious *wreck* (a good old Viking word, that).

Glorious, I say, in all of its shambling mutable beauty. People daily speak a quilt work of words, and continents and nations and tribes and even enemies dance all over your mouth when you speak. The tongue seems to know no race, no affiliation, no breed, no caste, no order, no genus, no lineage. The most dedicated Klansman spews the language of his adversaries while reviling them.

It's all part of the American palaver and squawk.

60   *Seersucker:* Persian.

Sandalwood: Sanskrit.

Grab a dictionary. It's easy. You at home—play along.

The $64,000 question for tonight: What the hell are we speaking? What language (culture, color, race, ethnicity) is this anyway? Who are we?

Abbott: Aramaic.

65   *Yo-yo:* Philippino.

Muslin: Iraqi.

Yogurt: Turkish.

I love words so much. Thank God so many people lent us theirs or we'd be forced to point and grunt. When I start to feel the pressure of the border on me, when I meet someone who won't shake my hand because she has suddenly discovered I'm half Mexican (as happened with a landlady in Boulder), I comfort myself with these words. I know how much color and beauty we Others really add to the American mix.

My advice to anyone who wants to close the border and get them Messkins out is this: *don't dare start counting how many of your words are Latin, Baby.*

70   America—there's a Mexican in the woodpile.

Engaging the Text

1. How does the anecdote with which Urrea begins his essay affirm his view of himself as Mexican? In what way does this episode open the door to his exploration of how language is used to ostracize others?

2. Urrea tackles the issue of his Mexican identity from many different perspectives. Why is it ironic that although Urrea identified himself as being Mexican, he was not seen that way in Mexico?

3. What role does Urrea's examination of the origin of English words borrowed from Spanish play in his essay? How is this section connected to the broader question of the way ethnic identity is constructed through language?

Exploring Your Cultural Perspective

1. The United States is increasingly becoming a contact zone where people from many different cultures interact. Many people of diverse ethnic and racial backgrounds must choose how to identify themselves, as Urrea did. Consult the Internet to discover the public's reaction to the new categories used in the 2000 long-form U.S. Census questionnaire, a copy of which is available at <http://www.census.gov/dmd/www/infoquest.html>. Discuss the significance of public resistance to the Census in general and to the particular categories used.

2. Urrea closely analyzes the concealed inferences of some of the terms used to demean Mexicans—thereby diminishing their impact. Do the same for other objectionable ethnic epithets.

AMY TAN

The Language of Discretion

Amy Tan was born in Oakland, California, in 1952 into a family of immigrants from China. After studying linguistics, she worked with disabled children. She began writing fiction in the mid-1980s. Tan's first novel, *The Joy Luck Club* (1989), was widely praised for its depiction of the relationship between Chinese mothers and their U.S.-born daughters. Tan has also written *The Kitchen God's Wife* (1991), *The Hundred Secret Senses* (1995), and *The Bonesetter's Daughter* (2001). "The Language of Discretion" first appeared in *The State of Language* (1990). Growing up in a family in which only Chinese was spoken gave Tan an unusual perspective on the way English speakers stereotype the Chinese, and vice versa.

Thinking Critically

Tan's analysis is a complicated one, and taking notes will help you follow it. Underline and annotate those parts of the selection in which Tan explores language-related stereotypes. If you speak two languages, in which one do you think, dream, or express anger?

At a recent family dinner in San Francisco, my mother whispered to me: "Sau-sau [Brother's Wife] pretends too hard to be polite! Why bother? In the end, she always takes everything."

My mother thinks like a *waixiao*, an expatriate, temporarily away from China since 1949, no longer patient with ritual courtesies. As if to prove her point, she reached across the table to offer my elderly aunt from Beijing the last scallop from the Happy Family seafood dish.

Sau-sau scowled, "*B'yao, zhen b'yao!*" (I don't want it, really I don't!) she cried, patting her plump stomach.

5   "Take it! Take it!" scolded my mother in Chinese.

"Full, I'm already full," Sau-sau protested weakly, eyeing the beloved scallop.

"Ai!" exclaimed my mother, completely exasperated. "Nobody else wants it. If you don't take it, it will only rot!"

At this point, Sau-sau sighed, acting as if she were doing my mother a big favor by taking the wretched scrap off her hands.

My mother turned to her brother, a high-ranking communist official who was visiting her in California for the first time: "In America a Chinese person could starve to death. If you say you don't want it, they won't ask you again forever."

My uncle nodded and said he understood fully: Americans take things quickly because they have no time to be polite.

I thought about this misunderstanding again—of social contexts failing in   *10*
translation—when a friend sent me an article from the *New York Times Magazine* (24 April 1988). The article, on changes in New York's Chinatown, made passing reference to the inherent ambivalence of the Chinese language.

Chinese people are so "discreet and modest," the article stated, there aren't even words for "yes" and "no."

That's not true, I thought, although I can see why an outsider might think that. I continued reading.

If one is Chinese, the article went on to say, "One compromises, one doesn't hazard a loss of face by an overemphatic response."

My throat seized. Why do people keep saying these things? As if we truly were those little dolls sold in Chinatown tourist shops, heads bobbing up and down in complacent agreement to anything said!

I worry about the effect of one-dimensional statements on the unwary and   *15*
guileless. When they read about this so-called vocabulary deficit, do they also conclude that Chinese people evolved into a mild-mannered lot because the language only allowed them to hobble forth with minced words?

Something enormous is always lost in translation. Something insidious seeps into the gaps, especially when amateur linguists continue to compare, one-for-one, language differences and then put forth notions wide open to misinterpretation: that Chinese people have no direct linguistic means to make decisions, assert or deny, affirm or negate, just say no to drug dealers, or behave properly on the witness stand when told, "Please answer yes or no."

Yet one can argue, with the help of renowned linguists, that the Chinese are indeed up a creek without "yes" and "no." Take any number of variations on the old language-and-reality theory stated years ago by Edward Sapir: "Human beings . . . are very much at the mercy of the particular language which has become the medium for their society. . . . The fact of the matter is that the 'real world' is to a large extent built up on the language habits of the group."*

———

*Edward Sapir, *Selected Writings*, ed. D. G. Mandelbaum (Berkeley and Los Angeles, 1949).

This notion was further bolstered by the famous Sapir-Whorf hypothesis, which roughly states that one's perception of the world and how one functions in it depends a great deal on the language used. As Sapir, Whorf, and new carriers of the banner would have us believe, language shapes our thinking, channels us along certain patterns embedded in words, syntactic structures, and intonation patterns. Language has become the peg and the shelf that enables us to sort out and categorize the world. In English, we see "cats" and "dogs"; what if the language had also specified *glatz*, meaning "animals that leave fur on the sofa," and *glotz*, meaning "animals that leave fur and drool on the sofa"? How would language, the enabler, have changed our perceptions with slight vocabulary variations?

And if this were the case—of language being the master of destined thought—think of the opportunities lost from failure to evolve two little words, *yes* and *no*, the simplest of opposites! Ghenghis Khan could have been sent back to Mongolia. Opium wars might have been averted. The Cultural Revolution could have been sidestepped.

20   There are still many, from serious linguists to pop psychology cultists, who view language and reality as inextricably tied, one being the consequence of the other. We have traversed the range from the Sapir-Whorf hypothesis to est and neurolinguistic programming, which tell us "you are what you say."

I too have been intrigued by the theories. I can summarize, albeit badly, ages-old empirical evidence: of Eskimos and their infinite ways to say "snow," their ability to *see* the differences in snowflake configurations, thanks to the richness of their vocabulary, while non-Eskimo speakers like myself founder in "snow," "more snow," and "lots more where that came from."

I too have experienced dramatic cognitive awakenings via the word. Once I added "mauve" to my vocabulary I began to see it everywhere. When I learned how to pronounce *prix fixe*, I ate French food at prices better than the easier-to-say *à la carte* choices.

But just how seriously are we supposed to take this?

Sapir said something else about language and reality. It is the part that often gets left behind in the dot-dot-dots of quotes: ". . . No two languages are ever sufficiently similar to be considered as representing the same social reality. The worlds in which different societies live are distinct worlds, not merely the same world with different labels attached."

25   When I first read this, I thought, Here at last is validity for the dilemmas I felt growing up in a bicultural, bilingual family! As any child of immigrant parents knows, there's a special kind of double bind attached to knowing two languages. My parents, for example, spoke to me in both Chinese and English; I spoke back to them in English.

"Amy-ah!" they'd call to me.

"What?" I'd mumble back.

"Do not question us when we call," they scolded me in Chinese. "It is not respectful."

"What do you mean?"

"Ai! Didn't we just tell you not to question?"   *30*

To this day, I wonder which parts of my behavior were shaped by Chinese, which by English. I am tempted to think, for example, that if I am of two minds on some matter it is due to the richness of my linguistic experiences, not to any personal tendencies toward wishy-washiness. But which mind says what?

Was it perhaps patience—developed through years of deciphering my mother's fractured English—that had me listening politely while a woman announced over the phone that I had won one of five valuable prizes? Was it respect—pounded in by the Chinese imperative to accept convoluted explanations—that had me agreeing that I might find it worthwhile to drive seventy-five miles to view a time-share resort? Could I have been at a loss for words when asked, "Wouldn't you like to win a Hawaiian cruise or perhaps a fabulous Star of India designed exclusively by Cartier and Van Arpels?"

And when this same woman called back a week later, this time complaining that I had missed my appointment, obviously it was my type A language that kicked into gear and interrupted her. Certainly, my blunt denial—"Frankly I'm not interested"—was as American as apple pie. And when she said, "But it's in Morgan Hill," and I shouted, "Read my lips. I don't care if it's Timbuktu," you can be sure I said it with the precise intonation expressing both cynicism and disgust.

It's dangerous business, this sorting out of language and behavior. Which one is English? Which is Chinese? The categories manifest themselves: passive and aggressive, tentative and assertive, indirect and direct. And I realize they are just variations of the same theme: that Chinese people are discreet and modest.

Reject them all!   *35*

If my reaction is overly strident, it is because I cannot come across as too emphatic. I grew up listening to the same lines over and over again, like so many rote expressions repeated in an English phrasebook. And I too almost came to believe them.

Yet if I consider my upbringing more carefully, I find there was nothing discreet about the Chinese language I grew up with. My parents made everything abundantly clear. Nothing wishy-washy in their demands, no compromises accepted: "Of course you will become a famous neurosurgeon," they told me. "And yes, a concert pianist on the side."

In fact, now that I remember, it seems that the more emphatic outbursts always spilled over into Chinese: "Not that way! You must wash rice so not a single grain spills out."

I do not believe that my parents—both immigrants from mainland China—are an exception to the modest-and-discreet rule. I have only to look at the number of Chinese engineering students skewing minority ratios at Berkeley, MIT, and Yale. Certainly they were not raised by passive mothers and fathers who said, "It is up to you, my daughter. Writer, welfare recipient, masseuse, or molecular engineer—you decide."

40   And my American mind says, See, those engineering students weren't able to say no to their parents' demands. But then my Chinese mind remembers: Ah, but those parents all wanted their sons and daughters to be *pre-med.*

Having listened to both Chinese and English, I also tend to be suspicious of any comparisons between the two languages. Typically, one language—that of the person doing the comparing—is often used as the standard, the benchmark for a logical form of expression. And so the language being compared is always in danger of being judged deficient or superfluous, simplistic or unnecessarily complex, melodious or cacophonous. English speakers point out that Chinese is extremely difficult because it relies on variations in tone barely discernible to the human ear. By the same token, Chinese speakers tell me English is extremely difficult because it is inconsistent, a language of too many broken rules, of Mickey Mice and Donald Ducks.

Even more dangerous to my mind is the temptation to compare both language and behavior *in translation.* To listen to my mother speak English, one might think she has no concept of past or future tense, that she doesn't see the difference between singular and plural, that she is gender blind because she calls my husband "she." If one were not careful, one might also generalize that, based on the way my mother talks, all Chinese people take a circumlocutory route to get to the point. It is, in fact, my mother's idiosyncratic behavior to ramble a bit.

Sapir was right about differences between two languages and their realities. I can illustrate why word-for-word translation is not enough to translate meaning and intent. I once received a letter from China which I read to non-Chinese speaking friends. The letter, originally written in Chinese, had been translated by my brother-in-law in Beijing. One portion described the time when my uncle at age ten discovered his widowed mother (my grandmother) had remarried—as a number three concubine, the ultimate disgrace for an honorable family. The translated version of my uncle's letter read in part:

> In 1925, I met my mother in Shanghai. When she came to me, I didn't have greeting to her as if seeing nothing. She pull me to a corner secretly and asked me why didn't have greeting to her. I couldn't control myself and cried, "Ma! Why did you leave us? People told me: one day you ate a beancake yourself. Your sister in-law found it and sweared at you, called your names. So . . . is it true?" She clasped my hand and answered imme-

diately, "It's not true, don't say what like this." After this time, there was a few chance to meet her.

"What!" cried my friends. "Was eating a beancake so terrible?"

Of course not. The beancake was simply a euphemism; a ten-year-old boy   *45* did not dare question his mother on something as shocking as concubinage. Eating a beancake was his equivalent for committing this selfish act, something inconsiderate of all family members, hence, my grandmother's despairing response to what seemed like a ludicrous charge of gluttony. And sure enough, she was banished from the family, and my uncle saw her only a few times before her death.

While the above may fuel people's argument that Chinese is indeed a language of extreme discretion, it does not mean that Chinese people speak in secrets and riddles. The contexts are fully understood. It is only to those on the *outside* that the language seems cryptic, the behavior inscrutable.

I am, evidently, one of the outsiders. My nephew in Shanghai, who recently started taking English lessons, has been writing me letters in English. I had told him I was a fiction writer, and so in one letter he wrote, "Congratulate to you on your writing. Perhaps one day I should like to read it." I took it in the same vein as "Perhaps one day we can get together for lunch." I sent back a cheery note. A month went by and another letter arrived from Shanghai. "Last one perhaps I hadn't writing distinctly," he said. "In the future, you'll send a copy of your works for me."

I try to explain to my English-speaking friends that Chinese language use is more *strategic* in manner, whereas English tends to be more direct; an American business executive may say, "Let's make a deal," and the Chinese manager may reply, "Is your son interested in learning about your widget business?" Each to his or her own purpose, each with his or her own linguistic path. But I hesitate to add more to the pile of generalizations, because no matter how many examples I provide and explain, I feel that it appears defensive and only reinforces the image: that Chinese people are "discreet and modest"—and it takes an American to explain what they really mean.

Why am I complaining? The description seems harmless enough (after all, the *New York Times Magazine* writer did not say "slippery and evasive"). It is precisely the bland, easy acceptability of the phrase that worries me.

I worry that the dominant society may see Chinese people from a limited—   *50* and limiting—perspective. I worry that seemingly benign stereotypes may be part of the reason there are few Chinese in top management positions, in mainstream political roles. I worry about the power of language: that if one says anything enough times—in *any* language—it might become true.

Could this be why Chinese friends of my parents' generation are willing to accept the generalization?

"Why are you complaining?" one of them said to me. "If people think we are modest and polite, let them think that. Wouldn't Americans be pleased to admit they are thought of as polite?"

And I do believe anyone would take the description as a compliment—at first. But after a while, it annoys, as if the only things that people heard one say were phatic remarks: "I'm so pleased to meet you. I've heard many wonderful things about you. For me? You shouldn't have!"

These remarks are not representative of new ideas, honest emotions, or considered thought. They are what is said from the polite distance of social contexts: of greetings, farewells, wedding thank-you notes, convenient excuses, and the like.

55 It makes me wonder though. How many anthropologists, how many sociologists, how many travel journalists have documented so-called "natural interactions" in foreign lands, all observed with spiral notebook in hand? How many other cases are there of the long-lost primitive tribe, people who turned out to be sophisticated enough to put on the stone-age show that ethnologists had come to see?

And how many tourists fresh off the bus have wandered into Chinatown expecting the self-effacing shopkeeper to admit under duress that the goods are not worth the price asked? I have witnessed it.

"I don't know," the tourist said to the shopkeeper, a Cantonese woman in her fifties. "It doesn't look genuine to me. I'll give you three dollars."

"You don't like my price, go somewhere else," said the shopkeeper.

You are not a nice person," cried the shocked tourist, "not a nice person at all!"

60 "Who say I have to be nice," snapped the shopkeeper.

"So how does one say 'yes' and 'no' in Chinese?" ask my friends a bit warily.

And here I do agree in part with the *New York Times Magazine* article. There is no one word for "yes" or "no"—but not out of necessity to be discreet. If anything, I would say the Chinese equivalent of answering "yes" or "no" is dis*crete*, that is, specific to what is asked.

Ask a Chinese person if he or she has eaten, and he or she might say *chrle* (eaten already) or perhaps *meiyou* (have not).

Ask, "So you had insurance at the time of the accident?" and the response would be *dwei* (correct) or *meiyou* (did not have).

65 Ask, "Have you stopped beating your wife?" and the answer refers directly to the proposition being asserted or denied: stopped already, still have not, never beat, have no wife.

What could be clearer?

As for those who are still wondering how to translate the language of discretion, I offer this personal example.

My aunt and uncle were about to return to Beijing after a three-month visit to the United States. On their last night I announced I wanted to take them out to dinner.

"Are you hungry?" I asked in Chinese.

"Not hungry," said my uncle promptly, the same response he once gave   70
me ten minutes before he suffered a low-blood-sugar attack.

"Not too hungry," said my aunt. "Perhaps you're hungry?"

"A little," I admitted.

"We can eat, we can eat," they both consented.

"What kind of food?" I asked.

"Oh, doesn't matter. Anything will do. Nothing fancy, just some simple   75
food is fine."

"Do you like Japanese food? We haven't had that yet," I suggested.

They looked at each other.

"We can eat it," said my uncle bravely, this survivor of the Long March.

"We have eaten it before," added my aunt. "Raw fish."

"Oh, you don't like it?" I said. "Don't be polite. We can go somewhere else."   80

"We are not being polite. We can eat it," my aunt insisted.

So I drove them to Japantown and we walked past several restaurants featuring colorful plastic displays of sushi.

"Not this one, not this one either," I continued to say, as if searching for a Japanese restaurant similar to the last. "Here it is," I finally said, turning into a restaurant famous for its Chinese fish dishes from Shandong.

"Oh, Chinese food!" cried my aunt, obviously relieved.

My uncle patted my arm. "You think Chinese."   85

"It's your last night here in America," I said. "So don't be polite. Act like an American."

And that night we ate a banquet.

Engaging the Text

1. What language-based stereotypes does Tan analyze to discover the concealed inferences they mask?

2. Tan's relationship with her mother reflects the different cultural perspectives of and the tensions between an immigrant parent and a child born in the United States. What are these differences, and how are they involved in Tan's efforts to understand the connection between culture and language?

3. What part does the Sapir-Whorf hypothesis play in Tan's analysis? Do her experiences tend to support this theory? How plausible does this concept appear to you? Write a short essay defending your position. Be sure to acknowledge and refute opposing viewpoints.

Exploring Your Cultural Perspective

1. What different "Englishes" do you use with friends, family, teachers, and in different social settings? "Translate" a conversation about the same subject into several of these Englishes.

2. If you lived in a family in which you were the only English-speaking member, what unique challenges might you face as the translator?

KYOKO MORI

Polite Lies

Kyoko Mori was born in Japan in 1957 and emigrated to the United States when she was twenty. She currently teaches creative writing at St. Norbert's College in De Pere, Wisconsin. She has written two volumes of fiction for young adults, *Shizuko's Daughter* (1993) and *One Bird* (1995). Her acclaimed memoir, *The Dream of Water* (1995), delves into her traumatic experiences as a child in Japan: her mother committed suicide, and her father was emotionally abusive. In the following selection from her 1997 book, *Polite Lies: On Being a Woman Caught between Cultures*, Mori expands on what she sees as a defining feature of Japanese culture: courtesy intertwined with pretense. Mori has recently written *Stone Field, True Arrow* (2000).

Thinking Critically

Mori draws on her own experiences to raise the larger issue of how the Japanese use language to avoid unwanted interactions. Under what circumstances can courtesy be used as a form of evasion?

I don't like to go to Japan because I find it exhausting to speak Japanese all day, every day. What I am afraid of is the language, not the place. Even in Green Bay, when someone insists on speaking to me in Japanese, I clam up after a few words of general greetings, unable to go on.

I can only fall silent because thirty seconds into the conversation, I have already failed at an important task: while I was bowing and saying hello, I was supposed to have been calculating the other person's age, rank, and position in order to determine how polite I should be for the rest of the conversation. In Japanese conversations, the two speakers are almost never on an equal footing: one is senior to the other in age, experience, or rank. Various levels of politeness and formality are required according to these differences: it is rude to be too familiar, but people are equally offended if you are too formal, sounding snobbish and untrusting. Gender is as important as rank. Men and women practically speak different languages; women's language is much more indirect

353

and formal than men's. There are words and phrases that women are never supposed to say, even though they are not crude or obscene. Only a man can say *damare* (shut up). No matter how angry she is, a woman must say, *shizukani* (quiet).

Until you can find the correct level of politeness, you can't go on with the conversation: you won't even be able to address the other person properly. There are so many Japanese words for the pronoun *you*. *Anata* is a polite but intimate *you* a woman would use to address her husband, lover, or a very close woman friend, while a man would say *kimi*, which is informal, or *omae*, which is so informal that a man would say this word only to a family member; *otaku* is informal but impersonal, so it should be used with friends rather than family. Though there are these various forms of *you*, most people address each other in the third person—it is offensive to call someone *you* directly. To a woman named Hanako Maeda, you don't say, "Would you like to go out for lunch?" You say, "Would Maeda-san (Miss Maeda) like to go out for lunch?" But if you had known Hanako for a while, maybe you should call her Hanako-san instead of Maeda-san, especially if you are also a woman and not too much younger than she. Otherwise, she might think that you are too formal and unfriendly. The word for *lunch* also varies: *hirumeshi* is another casual word only a man is allowed to say, *hirugohan* is informal but polite enough for friends, *ohirugohan* is a little more polite, *chushoku* is formal and businesslike, and *gochushoku* is the most formal and businesslike.

All these rules mean that before you can get on with any conversation beyond the initial greetings, you have to agree on your relationship—which one of you is superior, how close you expect to be, who makes the decisions and who defers. So why even talk, I always wonder. The conversation that follows the mutual sizing-up can only be an empty ritual, a careful enactment of our differences rather than a chance to get to know each other or to exchange ideas.

5   Talking seems especially futile when I have to address a man in Japanese. Every word I say forces me to be elaborately polite, indirect, submissive, and unassertive. There is no way I can sound intelligent, clearheaded, or decisive. But if I did not speak a "proper" feminine language, I would sound stupid in another way—like someone who is uneducated, insensitive, and rude, and therefore cannot be taken seriously. I never speak Japanese with the Japanese man who teaches physics at the college where I teach English. We are colleagues, meant to be equals. The language I use should not automatically define me as second best.

Meeting Japanese-speaking people in the States makes me nervous for another reason. I have nothing in common with these people except that we speak Japanese. Our meeting seems random and artificial, and I can't get over the oddness of addressing a total stranger in Japanese. In the twenty years I lived in Japan, I rarely had a conversation with someone I didn't already know. The only exception was the first day of school in seventh grade, when none of us knew one another, or when I was introduced to my friends' parents. Talking to clerks at stores scarcely counts. I never chatted with people I was doing business with. This is not to say that I led a particularly sheltered life. My experience was typical of anyone—male or female—growing up in Japan.

In Japan, whether you are a child or an adult, ninety-five percent of the people you talk to are your family, relatives, old friends, neighbors, and people you work or go to school with every day. The only new people you meet are connected to these people you already know—friends of friends, new spouses of your relatives—and you are introduced to them formally. You don't all of a sudden meet someone new. My friends and I were taught that no "nice" girl would talk to strangers on trains or at public places. It was bad manners to gab with shopkeepers or with repair people, being too familiar and keeping them from work. While American children are cautioned not to speak with strangers for reasons of safety, we were taught not to do so because it wasn't "nice." Even the most rebellious of us obeyed. We had no language in which we could address a stranger even if we had wanted to.

Traveling in Japan or simply taking the commuter train in Kobe now, I notice the silence around me. It seems oppressive that you cannot talk to someone who is looking at your favorite painting at a museum or sitting next to you on the train, reading a book that you finished only last week. In Japan, you can't even stop strangers and ask for simple directions when you are lost. If you get lost, you look for a policeman, who will help you because that is part of his job.

A Japanese friend and I got lost in Yokohama one night after we came out of a restaurant. We were looking for the train station and had no idea where it was, but my friend said, "Well, we must be heading in the right direction, since most people seem to be walking that way. It's late now. They must be going back to the station, too." After about ten minutes—with no train station in sight yet—my friend said that if she had been lost in New York or Paris, she would have asked one of the people we were following. But in her own country, in her own language, it was unthinkable to approach a stranger.

For her, asking was not an option. That's different from when people in *10* the Midwest choose not to stop at a gas station for directions or flag down a store clerk to locate some item on the shelves. Midwestern people don't like to ask because they don't want to call attention to themselves by appearing stupid and helpless. Refusing to ask is a matter of pride and self-reliance—a matter of choice. Even the people who pride themselves on never asking know that help is readily available. In Japan, approaching a stranger means breaking an unspoken rule of public conduct.

The Japanese code of silence in public places does offer a certain kind of protection. In Japan, everyone is shielded from unwanted intrusion or attention, and that isn't entirely bad. In public places in the States, we all wish, from time to time, that people would go about their business in silence and leave us alone. Just the other day in the weight room of the YMCA, a young man I had never met before told me that he had been working out for the last two months and gained fifteen pounds. "I've always been too thin," he explained. "I want to gain twenty more pounds, and I'm going to put it all up here." We were sitting side by side on different machines. He indicated his shoulders and chest by patting them with his hand. "That's nice," I said, noncommittal but polite. "Of course," he continued, "I couldn't help putting some of the new weight around my waist, too." To my embarrassment, he lifted his shirt and pointed at his stomach. "Listen," I told him. "You don't have to show it to me or anything." I got up from my machine even though I wasn't finished. Still, I felt obligated to say, "Have a nice workout," as I walked away.

I don't appreciate discussing a complete stranger's weight gain and being shown his stomach, and it's true that bizarre conversations like that would never happen in a Japanese gym. Maybe there is comfort in knowing that you will never have to talk to strangers—that you can live your whole life surrounded by friends and family who will understand what you mean without your saying it. Silence can be a sign of harmony among close friends or family, but silent harmony doesn't help people who disagree or don't fit in. On crowded trains in Kobe or Tokyo, where people won't even make eye contact with strangers, much less talk to them, I feel as though each one of us were sealed inside an invisible capsule, unable to breathe or speak out. It is just like my old dream of being stuck inside a spaceship orbiting the earth. I am alarmed by how lonely I feel—and by how quietly content everyone else seems to be.

Engaging the Text

1. Why is having to speak Japanese on her return to Japan a stressful experience for Mori? What sorts of things does a Japanese speaker evaluate at the start of a conversation?

2. Provide some examples of how conversations in Japan differ from those in the United States. What aspects of American conversations does Mori find embarrassing?

3. Why is having a sense of private space important to the Japanese? How does the code of silence in public contribute to this? In what ways does Mori's recurrent dream serve as a metaphor for her return trips to Japan?

Exploring Your Cultural Perspective

1. The next time you are in an elevator, observe the protocols that govern conversations and interactions between strangers and compare them with those that prevail in Japan. For information about the latter, see the report by

Terry Caesar in "In and Out of Elevators in Japan" (February 2000) in the online *Journal of Mundane Behavior* at <http://www.mundanebehavior.org/issues/v1n1/caesar.htm>. (This journal provides analyses of ordinary events in the lives of people in different societies.) Discuss your conclusions in a short essay.

2. Do you prefer people who say exactly what they think or those who are polite but leave you wondering what they really think? To what extent are these different styles culturally based? Make a case for one style over the other.

GARY CHAPMAN

Flamers: Cranks, Fetishists, and Monomaniacs

According to Gary Chapman, the anonymity of cyberspace has produced some bizarre forms of interaction in which people insult, or
"flame," each other, adopt fantasy personas, and generally behave in
ways they never would in face-to-face interactions. Chapman is the
coordinator of the Twenty-first Century Project at the LBJ School of
Public Affairs at the University of Texas at Austin. He writes the syndicated column "Innovations" for the *Los Angeles Times* and covers cyberspace for the *New Republic* magazine. The following essay first appeared
in the April 10, 1995, issue of the *New Republic*.

Thinking Critically

*As you read this essay, observe Chapman's tone. Where does he use irony
and humor to make his analysis simultaneously understated and incisive?
Do you behave differently in cyberspace than you do in everyday life? If so,
how does your behavior differ? What might account for the differences?*

A joke floating around the Internet: Q: How many Internet contributors does
it take to change a light bulb? A: What are you trying to say, you worthless,
scumbag jerk? Computer networks are increasingly hyped as a new medium of
virtuous democratic and social discourse, the cyber version of the Acropolis. A
Time magazine reviewer recently called the Internet "the ultimate salon" of
conversation, and *The Utne Reader* is promoting "electronic salons" to soothe
the anomie and coarseness of contemporary life. Author Howard Rheingold
has celebrated the "virtual community" as a source of solace and fraternity, and
columnist David Broder has written paeans to the new spirit of civic participation allegedly found on computer networks.

Electronic conversations—if that's what they are to be called—on the
Internet and various other computer networks such as America Online, Prodigy and CompuServe, are certainly a new and interesting feature of American
social life and manners. The terabytes of gab on these systems, engaging millions of people, are perhaps the first display of the direct voice of the American

people in an ongoing, semi-organized, public forum. People are talking about everything under the sun—politics, pet care, even deliberate gibberish. Consequently, politicians, pollsters, reporters, marketers and social analysts are keenly interested in what our fellow citizens are thinking and saying on-line. Electronic conversations, to our benefit, allow people to circumvent the managed public dialogue that politicians and P.R.-types try to shape to serve their own ends.

But the evidence of public virtue in cyberspace is so far more discouraging and alarming than noble and salutary. Electronic salons already contain broken furniture and have mud on their walls. The notorious phenomenon of "flaming"—issuing a nasty and often profane diatribe—is now a familiar sociological curiosity. UseNet news groups—open, topical conversations accessible over the Internet and other systems—have become vast libraries of pyrotechnic insults. Mark Dery, editor of a new book, *Flame Wars*, offers a few choice examples: "You syphilitic bovine harpy." "You heaving purulent mammoth." "You twitching gelatinous yolk of rancid smegma." You get the idea. Many retorts are merely terse, obscene snarls, but Internet users have also developed a competition in rococo, smart-alecky taunts, such as this one: "Your reply was most impressive. You seem to have the ability to respond to e-mail with either profanity, inanity or pointless threats of physical violence. Why don't you try those pills the doctor gave you, and take a nice long rest. It may do you no good, but I am sure the remainder of the viewers would be pleased by the absence of your moronic and asinine diatribes." It's hard to imagine such exchanges at a PTA meeting or a cocktail party. Electronic communication is providing a disturbing glimpse of what may be smoldering, heretofore unsaid, in the minds of many Americans.

More generally, electronic conversations appear to be prone to misinterpretation, sudden and rapidly escalating hostility between participants, and a weird kind of implosion when the conversants express their anger with sulking silence. This may be because, unlike in face-to-face conversation, there are no visual cues, what linguist Peter Farb calls "paralanguage." It may also be because people who are completely removed from one another physically can assault each other verbally without fear of bodily harm, a suggestion that our evolutionary heritage is still at work in restraining our behavior in everyday encounters.

Electronic anonymity also encourages fantasy life, often tilting toward the dark side. Dedicated network denizens frequently inhabit alter egos attached to their computer names. Some computer users have identities in cyberspace that correspond to exotic names, such as Phreak or Acid, two well-known hacker monikers, rather than to their prosaically named real-world personae. While a middle-class, suburban white man may tend not to adopt a nom d'ordinateur, millions of electronic Walter Mittys nationwide do take on a more aggressive personality behind a computer and a modem—ferociously pouring out their otherwise sublimated middle-class angst.

A cyberspace alter ego often goes beyond a new name and a release of inhibition. Network users lie, sometimes spectacularly. Pavel Curtis, a Xerox researcher who runs a fascinating Multi-User Dimension (or mud)—a kind of a "virtual world" within the Internet with its own simulated geography, characters and interactions—reports that a significant portion of people logging into his system switch genders for the identities they assume. Most common are young men who portray themselves as women; indeed, it's become a rule of thumb that any sexually aggressive female on this mud is really a man. Peter Lewis, *The New York Times*'s cyberspace reporter, tells a story about a man who conducted a protracted and intimate electronic romance over the Internet with a pen pal, who said she was a 26-year-old graduate student. When he met her in person, he learned that she was in fact a 13-year-old girl.

As the French discovered in their national Minitel system, sex often dominates electronic encounters. The majority of messages on Minitel have been advertisements for sex or sex talk, and, national character notwithstanding, Americans are no slackers in this regard. Computer communication seems to bring out the id screaming for attention. In February, a University of Michigan student, Jake Baker, was arrested for posting to the university's computer network a graphic fantasy of the rape, torture and murder of a fellow student; though such stories are common on a few news groups, Baker actually named his victim, which police interpreted as a threat. A reporter for *Computer Life* magazine posed on the Internet as a 15-year-old cheerleader and got more than thirty e-mail messages of a sexual nature, including requests for her panties and her telephone number. Harassment of women is so common that women often pretend to be men to avoid sexually suggestive e-mail.

Bigotry and misogyny are prevalent as well. As Amy Harmon noted recently in *The Los Angeles Times*, bigots are showing up on computer networks with increasing frequency because they can't get a hearing anywhere else. Networks are a cheap means for white supremacists and neo-Nazis to get their hate messages to thousands of people at once. The Simon Wiesenthal Center has protested to Prodigy about frequent anti-Semitic rants on that system. Prodigy officials are caught, to their embarrassment, in a tug-of-war between freedom of speech and the basic civilities that many users expect.

Finally, the general quality of the rhetoric on the Internet is discouraging in itself. Even without all the cranks, poseurs, charlatans, fetishists, single-issue monomaniacs, sex-starved lonely hearts, mischievous teenagers, sexists, racists and right-wing haranguers many participants in unstructured Internet conversations have little of interest to say but a lot of room in which to say it. Goofy opinions and comical disregard for facts are rampant. Spelling is haphazard and even simple typos sometimes produce absurd flaming firefights. Nearly every reasonable discussion is sooner or later discovered by someone with a hobby horse or an abrasive personality or both, and there are few reliable ways to shunt such people elsewhere. It's pretty clear, too, that quite a few messages come from people who must be drunk; there are as yet no sobriety checkpoints on the "information superhighway." The new electronic Acropolis seems to foster rhetoric stylistically closer to Beavis and Butthead than to Pericles.

Fifteen years ago, the forerunner of the Internet, the Arpanet, was used almost exclusively by top computer scientists and other elite engineers and sci- *10* entists, who tend to be a refined bunch, partial to classical music and good books. Many are now appalled by what networking has become. Some have dropped off the net altogether.

This suggests that the Internet may be on a path similar to that followed by television and other communications media: the introduction of the masses so alienates well-educated, cosmopolitan people that they abandon the medium or resort to a specialized class of cultural material that advertises its disdain for mass tastes. There are already signs that this is happening on the Internet: while veterans of the net have tended to narrow their presence to a select group of exclusive and low-profile mailing lists, more recent users are complaining loudly about the influx of hundreds of thousands of newcomers via America Online, "newbies" who are stumbling around the net asking greenhorn questions and committing faux pas of "netiquette." Many people with pressing schedules are starting to regard the cacophonous noise as a waste of time. Their exits raise the proportion of nuts, creeps and boors. Thus an inevitable backlash against the lofty hype surrounding the Internet is building, such as in Cliff Stoll's new book, *Silicon Snake Oil: Second Thoughts on the Information Highway.*

This all sounds like an anti-democratic trend, in contrast to the democratization that computer networks are supposed to both exemplify and support. Is cyberspace already sorting itself into two camps, a jaded, invisible elite and a teeming mass of wrassling rubes? This image wouldn't be unusual in the history of American popular culture. It seems clear that cultural polarization and low behavior in cyberspace reflect trends in American society as a whole, but the peculiar features of computer communication are amplifying the decline of our national mores and manners, and, at the same time, giving us an unprecedented bird's-eye view of what we've become.

Of course, we can always hope that computer networks are undergoing a metamorphosis from childhood to adolescence these days, with an anticipated maturation into adulthood sometime in the future. We'll have to develop manners in cyberspace just as we have in our everyday, real-world encounters, and that could entail a long process of evolution and refinement. If we don't develop virtual manners, cyberspace will continue to resemble a mud wrestling event. But if we can treat each other with respect over e-mail, we may go a long way toward solving some of the basic dilemmas of democracy.

Engaging the Text

1. Why does cyberspace encourage people to create personas different from their real selves? Is Chapman's premise valid?

2. In what sense, according to Chapman, is the Internet in a phase akin to adolescence? What consequences, if any, does this have? In a few paragraphs, challenge or support Chapman's claim.

Exploring Your Cultural Perspective

1. The Internet as a social institution has been the subject, either directly or indirectly, of a number of films, including *The Net* (1995) and *Matrix* (1999). As a form, science fiction often dramatizes the hopes and fears aroused by new social phenomena. In a short essay, address the way in which the Internet is becoming an integral feature of modern culture.

2. What does the preponderance of sex-related Web sites suggest about U.S. culture? Does this situation, as Chapman believes, amplify "the decline of our national mores and manners?" In your view, has the Internet instigated or simply accelerated ongoing sexual trends?

3. What are the merits of belonging to a "virtual" community? In an essay, explore one or several of the following issues, drawing on your own experiences:

   - How are the problems one has to contend with in a virtual community similar to or different from those in real-world communities?

   - To what extent do virtual communities meet the needs of their "members" in a way that real communities do not?

   - Have you ever posted a message or responded to one on a community bulletin board? How did that experience differ from a face-to-face conversation?

   - Would you consider online dating as a way of getting to know someone before meeting in person?

   - Who polices virtual communities?

   - What useful information (medical, legal, personal, business, finance) have you found online?

   - To what extent do virtual communities serve as a local bar, bistro, coffee shop, or other traditional meeting place?

CONNECTING THE TEXTS

1. In what ways do Luc Sante's difficulties in learning English (as described in "Lingua Franca") correspond to Temple Grandin's disorder (in "Thinking in Pictures")? Write an essay exploring the insights these articles offer into how people acquire language.

2. What insights into the connection between language and cultural identity do the essays by Barbara Mellix ("From Outside, In") and Luis Alberto Urrea ("Nobody's Son") provide?

3. How does John Agard's poem "Listen mr oxford don" illustrate the same themes of language and prejudice that Luis Alberto Urrea discusses in "Nobody's Son"? What insights do both authors provide about the way language functions as a marker of social class?

4. Part of the speaker's crime in John Agard's poem is his "impolite" use of language. Compare this with how Kyoko Mori addresses the same issue in her essay "Polite Lies."

5. Luc Sante focuses on the split consciousness produced by two languages in "Lingua Franca." How does Luis Alberto Urrea's perspective in "Nobody's Son" differ from Sante's?

6. In what way are the Japanese imprisoned in cocoons of politeness (described by Kyoko Mori in "Polite Lies") in much the same way as are autistic children, as described by Temple Grandin in "Thinking in Pictures"?

7. Kyoko Mori (in "Polite Lies") and Amy Tan (in "The Language of Discretion") bring different perspectives to the function of polite language in Japanese and Chinese cultures. Write a synthesis essay in which you add your own observations to the insights of Mori and Tan on the way polite language functions in these two Asian countries and in the United States.

8. The question of how to define himself as a result of knowing two languages is the main focus of Luc Sante's life. In what ways do Sante's conclusion in "Lingua Franca" and Amy Tan's conclusions in "The Language of Discretion" differ?

9. The concrete nature of the images that a child absorbs register with unusual force on both Luc Sante in "Lingua Franca" and Temple Grandin in "Thinking in Pictures." What insights do both accounts offer into the connection between perception and language?

10. How do both Gary Chapman's "Flamers: Cranks, Fetishists, and Monomaniacs" and Anthony Burgess's "A Clockwork Orange" raise the issue of what the government's role should be in controlling deviant behavior?

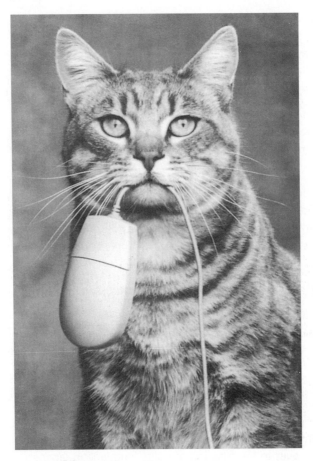

FIGURE 5.2

11. In what ways does language function as a marker of social class in "A Clockwork Orange" and in Barbara Mellix's article "From Outside, In"? What might be the significance of Nadsat's being a hybrid of English and Russian? (Keep in mind that this novel was written during the Cold War between the United States and the Soviet Union and that it is set in some unspecified future.)

WRITING ABOUT LANGUAGE

1. What would a typical day be like if you could not read or write? Record all your activities, and explain how each would be different if you were illiterate.

2. Do you swear when you are angry? What metaphors and social attitudes underlie the expressions you use?

FIGURE 5.3

3. How does a "page" on a computer screen differ from a conventional page of text in terms of the user's/reader's interaction with it? What are the social implications of the difference?

4. What cybertalk expressions are part of your vocabulary? What ideas do they allow you to express that you would not otherwise be able to convey?

5. Trace the evolution of any cyber term (you might consult the *Oxford English Dictionary*), illustrating how it was used when it originally appeared and what it means now.

6. In what ways are Figure 5.2 and Figure 5.3 a kind of text that can be interpreted much as you would a written text? For each, specify the message it communicates and discuss how the picture serves as a sign of commonly understood cultural values.

CHAPTER 6

Otherness

I am an invisible man. . . . I am a man of substance, of flesh and bone,
fiber and liquids—and I might even be said to possess a mind. I am
invisible, understand, simply because people refuse to see me.
—RALPH ELLISON (1914–1994, African American author), *The Invisible Man*

The popular NBC sitcom *3rd Rock from the Sun* featured John Lithgow as Dick
Solomon, the High Commander of an investigative team from another planet
sent to Earth to learn about the so-called advanced civilization of humans. Part
of the appeal of these alien "others" was their ability to see things as they really
were—or to misunderstand them as they tried to fit into society on Earth. This
good-natured series raised some interesting points about our creation and our
perceptions of the **other.** All societies create myths about those whom they
consider deviant, abnormal, or simply different. What societies tag as the other
varies from culture to culture, but the need to divide "us" from "them" is displayed throughout history.

   In this chapter, we examine **myths**—cultural views—about various groups
that have been stigmatized, ostracized, and made into scapegoats. Designation
of a group as the other is often a response by members of the society who perceive themselves to be threatened by qualities they project onto the group. It is
in this sense that value judgments based on perceived important differences
between groups are a matter of cultural perspective. A culture's values often
determine who is the group in power, or in-group, and who is considered the
other, or out-group.

   The most rudimentary form of otherness is connected to the idea of the
double, or the *doppelganger,* a supposed ghostly double of a living person. In

literature and films, the idea of this subversive shadow self underlies the concept of the evil alter ego. The most famous example is Jekyll and Hyde. Recently, genetic engineering has led us to reconsider the distinction between the self and the other. In "A Clone Is Born," Gina Kolata reports that technology that would allow the cloning of humans now exists. The clone is a radical form of the other that leads us to examine our own presumed individuality. The human clone as other raises some important ethical and moral issues: would a clone be entitled to the same rights (such as social security benefits) as the original person? Would it be defined as a lesser human being, for example, whose organs could be removed for transplantation to the original person? Would it be regarded as a soulless replicant, as in science fiction films? It is quite likely that human clones would be dehumanized and seen as the other— as minorities and social outcasts have been. Would our society even permit the creation of human clones, should this become possible?

When we critically analyze what makes a group an other, we can identify significant forms of behavior and then assess how underlying cultural **codes** and **value systems** have been projected onto these behaviors. By discovering how otherness is constructed, we can determine whose interests these **mythologies** serve and also suggest how these stereotypes can be debunked.

THE PHYSICALLY FLAWED AS OTHER

Each of the writers in this chapter assails a particular myth. Lennard J. Davis in "Visualizing the Disabled Body" shows how "disability" is a cultural phenomenon and how "normalcy" is a constructed ideology that has existed in European thought only since the mid-nineteenth century. Davis believes that the myth of the disabled "other" is the direct consequence of the formulation of the "average"; those who did not fit this "norm" were perceived as less than human, and taken to the extreme, even monstrous.

In "Autobiography of a Face," Lucy Grealy describes how, as a result of cancer, part of her jaw was removed and she underwent a series of reconstructive surgeries that were not only painful in themselves but were made more so because of the way people rejected her. Her narrative takes us inside the mind and heart of one who is viewed as the other. Both Davis's analysis and Grealy's narrative suggest that people who are perceived as deformed others arouse anxiety. "Normal" people find it easier to ostracize them than to cope with their own anxiety and fears. Only through self-determination and personal courage can someone designated as "deformed" overcome this stigma.

Paul Monette's experiences, related in "Borrowed Time: An AIDS Memoir," demonstrate how a culture can use an illness to legitimize treating its victims as outcasts. Although societies arrive at the construction of the other by different routes, they invariably establish precautions to protect the social order from what are perceived as sources of contamination. The consequences of this attitude are the subject of Bruce Springsteen's song "Streets of Philadelphia." The lyrics, written for the 1994 film *Philadelphia*, tell the story of society's rejection of those who suffer from AIDS.

The predicament of those who are ostracized because of differences in appearance or because they are ill, poor, or of a lower social class can tell us a great deal about a society's threshold of tolerance toward those who are different. For example, in America those who are homeless and in India those who are known as the untouchables are shunned as the other. Being an untouchable, like being homeless, means that one has very little control over one's life. In America, being categorized as the other (based on one's social class) is often associated with racial discrimination because minorities often receive limited education, have the least political clout, earn the lowest incomes, and work in menial occupations with little hope of advancement.

SOCIAL CONSTRUCTION OF THE OTHER

Around the world, a wide range of qualities are used as a basis on which to construct otherness. Constance Classen in "The Odour of the Other" points out that odors can serve as markers for cultural identity in societies that use them to establish distinctions based on class and race. For example, among the Dassenetch of southeastern Ethiopia, the smell of everything associated with cattle is considered good, whereas odors associated with fish are considered to be noxious. Those whose odor places them in the category of the other, according to this distinction, are excluded and even subject to persecution. Classen's analysis reveals that, because odors cross distances and nullify social barriers, the concept of the other has its basis in a fear of contamination.

In past eras, primordial fears were projected in the mythology and folklore of the "undead," whose best-known form is the vampire. The vampire myth underwent an amazing transformation from Transylvanian folklore to Hollywood. Originally, the idea of the vampire arose in Eastern Europe in the eighteenth century. Unlike the glamorous Hollywood versions of Dracula, these vampires didn't wear cloaks or belong to the upper classes but were cantankerous peasants who, it was believed, returned after death to torment their neighbors. Paul Barber, who has written definitively on the subject (in "The Real Vampire"), has analyzed the psychological mechanisms at work in the construction of the vampire legend. In essence, societies project their fears onto those already in disfavor ("the godless, people of different faiths, sorcerers, and prostitutes") and re-create them as the dreaded other. Barber also draws attention to the similarities between the social construction of the vampire as the other in Europe in the 1750s and contemporary attitudes toward those with AIDS.

CONTAINMENT OF THE OTHER

Once a society determines that a group is to be cast into the role of other, it employs a variety of control mechanisms and social rituals to make sure that these others not only are contained but also play their preassigned role in the culture. Gino Del Guercio in "The Secrets of Haiti's Living Dead" reveals how secret voodoo societies in Haiti act as judge, jury, and executioner to punish criminals whom the law is powerless to touch. The threat of being made into a zombie is an effective social control mechanism designed to ensure order in Haitian society. Zombies are considered the "living dead," who have been resurrected from their graves, deprived of free will, and enslaved. More likely than not, they are already outcasts who have committed crimes and have gone unpunished by the conventional system of justice.

In an international context, the other can be a nation that is stigmatized. In his story "The Wedgwood Tea Set," Milorad Pavić blends surrealism and fantasy within a realistic framework to demonstrate how otherness can have a geopolitical dimension.

The readings that follow illuminate a variety of ways different cultures determine who is to be designated as the other. In each case they help us to identify the specific myths responsible and to evalute the ways in which those designations reflect dominant values in particular cultures.

GINA KOLATA

A Clone Is Born

With the cloning of a lamb named Dolly on July 5, 1996, it became possible to duplicate a mammal from a single cell. From the onset of this technological advance, the need to distinguish clones from originals has transformed the other into a fantastic new realm. Would human clones be seen as less equal than their originals? Would they be viewed as organ donors, and might they even go the mythological route of zombies and vampires? As science journalist for the *New York Times*, Kolata discusses the profound ethical implications of human cloning in this chapter from her book *Clone: The Road to Dolly and the Path Ahead* (1998).

Thinking Critically

Notice how Kolata has integrated a broad range of sources into her article. As an aid to seeing how she develops her analysis, underline and annotate the passages that contain these expert opinions. Evaluate how Kolata uses them to develop her thesis that "cloning is a metaphor and a mirror." Under what circumstances, if any, would you consider being cloned?

Many people wonder if this is a miracle for which we can thank God, or an ominous new way to play God ourselves.
— NANCY DUFF, Princeton Theological Seminary

On a soft summer night, July 5, 1996, at 5:00 P.M., the most famous lamb in history entered the world, head and forelegs first. She was born in a shed, just down the road from the Roslin Institute in Roslin, Scotland, where she was created. And yet her creator, Ian Wilmut, a quiet, balding, fifty-two-year-old embryologist, does not remember where he was when he heard that the lamb, named Dolly, was born. He does not even recall getting a telephone call from John Bracken, a scientist who had monitored the pregnancy of the sheep that gave birth to Dolly, saying that Dolly was alive and healthy and weighed 6.6 kilograms, or 14.5 pounds.

It was a moment of remarkable insouciance. No one broke open champagne. No one took pictures. Only a few staff members from the institute and a local veterinarian who attended the birth were present. Yet Dolly, a fluffy creature with grayish-white fleece and a snow-white face, who looked for all the world like hundred of other lambs that dot the rolling hills of Scotland, was soon to change the world.

When the time comes to write the history of our age, this quiet birth, the creation of this little lamb, will stand out. The events that change history are few and unpredictable. In the twentieth century, there was the discovery of quantum theory, the revolutionary finding by physicists that the normal rules of the visible world do not apply in the realm of the atom. There was Einstein's theory of general relativity, saying that space and time can be warped. There was the splitting of the atom, with its promise of good and evil. There was the often-overlooked theorem of mathematician Kurt Gödel, which said that there are truths that are unknowable, theorems that can be neither proved nor disproved. There was the development of computers that transformed Western society.

In biology and medicine, there was the discovery of penicillin in the 1940s, and there was James Watson and Francis Crick's announcement, in 1953, that they had found the structure of DNA, the genetic blueprint. There was the conquest of smallpox that wiped the ancient scourge from the face of the earth, and the discovery of a vaccine that could prevent the tragedy of polio. In the 1980s, there was the onslaught of AIDS, which taught us that plagues can afflict us still.

In politics, there were the world wars, the rise and fall of communism, and   5
the Great Depression. There is the economic rise of Asia in the latter part of the century, and the ever-shifting balance of the world's powers.

But events that alter our very notion of what it means to be human are few and scattered over the centuries. The birth of Dolly is one of them. "Analogies to Copernicus, to Darwin, to Freud, are appropriate," said Alan Weisbard, a professor of law and medical ethics at the University of Wisconsin. The world is a different place now that she is born.

Dolly is a clone. She was created not out of the union of a sperm and an egg but out of the genetic material from an udder cell of a six-year-old sheep. Wilmut fused the udder cell with an egg from another sheep, after first removing all genetic material from the egg. The udder cell's genes took up residence in the egg and directed it to grow and develop. The result was Dolly, the identical twin of the original sheep that provided the udder cells, but an identical twin born six years later. In a moment of frivolity, as a wry joke, Wilmut named her Dolly after Dolly Parton, who also was known, he said, for her mammaries.

Until Dolly entered the world, cloning was the stuff of science fiction. It had been raised as a possibility decades ago, then dismissed, relegated to the realm of the kooky, the fringy, something that serious scientists thought was simply not going to happen anytime soon.

Yet when it happened, even though it involved but one sheep, it was truly fantastic, and at the same time horrifying in a way that is hard to define. In 1972, when Willard Gaylin, a psychiatrist and the founder of the Hastings Center, an ethics think tank, mistakenly thought that science was on the verge of cloning, he described its awesome power: "One could imagine taking a single sloughed cell from the skin of a person's hand, or even from the hand of a mummy (since cells are neither 'alive' or 'dead,' but merely intact or not intact), and seeing it perpetuate itself into a sheet of skin tissue. But could one really visualize the cell forming a finger, let alone a hand, let alone an embryo, let alone another Amenhotep?"

10   And what if more than one clone is made? Is it even within the realm of the imaginable to think that someday, perhaps decades from now, but someday, you could clone yourself and make tens, dozens, hundreds of genetically identical twins? Is it really science fiction to think that your cells could be improved beforehand, genetically engineered to add some genes and snip out others? These ideas, that so destroy the notion of the self, that touch on the idea of the soul, of human identity, seemed so implausible to most scientists that they had declared cloning off-limits for discussion.

Even ethicists, those professional worriers whose business it is to raise alarms about medicine and technology, were steered away from talk of cloning, though they tried to make it a serious topic. In fact, it was one of the first subjects mentioned when the bioethics field came into its own in the late 1960s and early 1970s. But scientists quashed the ethicists' ruminations, telling them to stop inventing such scary scenarios. The ethicists were informed that they were giving science a bad name to raise such specters as if they were real possibilities. The public would be frightened, research grants might dry up, scientists would be seen as Frankensteins, and legitimate studies that could benefit humankind could be threatened as part of an anti-science backlash.

Daniel Callahan, one of the founders of the bioethics movement and the founder, with Gaylin, of the Hastings Center, recalled that when he and others wanted to talk about cloning, scientists pooh-poohed them. They were told, he said, that "there was no real incentive for science to do this and it was just one of those scary things that ethicists and others were talking about that would do real harm to science."

Now, with the birth of Dolly, the ethicists were vindicated. Yes, it was a sheep that was cloned, not a human being. But there was nothing exceptional about sheep. Even Wilmut, who made it clear that he abhorred the very idea of cloning people, said that there was no longer any theoretical reason why humans could not clone themselves, using the same methods he had used to clone Dolly. "There is no reason in principle why you couldn't do it." But, he added, "all of us would find that offensive."

The utterly pragmatic approach of Wilmut and many other scientists, however, ignores the awesome nature of what was accomplished. Our era is said to be devoted to the self, with psychologists and philosophers battling over who can best probe the nature of our identities. But cloning pares the questions down to their essence, forcing us to think about what we mean by the self, whether we are our genes or, if not, what makes us *us*. "To thine own self be true" goes the popular line from Shakespeare—but what is the self?

We live in an age of the ethicist, a time when we argue about pragmatism   *15* and compromises in our quest to be morally right. But cloning forces us back to the most basic questions that have plagued humanity since the dawn of recorded time: What is good and what is evil? And how much potential for evil can we tolerate to obtain something that might be good? We live in a time when sin is becoming one of those quaint words that we might hear in church but that has little to do with our daily world. Cloning, however, with its possibilities for creating our own identical twins, brings us back to the ancient sins of vanity and pride: the sins of Narcissus, who so loved himself, and of Prometheus, who, in stealing fire, sought the powers of God. In a time when we hear rallying cries of reproductive freedom, of libertarianism and the rights of people to do what they want, so long as they hurt no one else, cloning, by raising the possibility that people could be made to order like commodities, place such ideas against the larger backdrop of human dignity.

So before we can ask why we are so fascinated by cloning, we have to examine our souls and ask, What exactly so bothers many of us about trying to replicate our genetic selves? Or, if we are not bothered, why aren't we?

We want children who resemble us. Even couples who use donor eggs because the woman's ovaries have failed or because her eggs are not easily fertilized, or who use donor sperm because the man's sperm is not viable, peruse catalogs of donors to find people who resemble themselves. We want to replicate ourselves. Several years ago, a poem by Linda Pastan, called "To a Daughter," was displayed on the walls of New York subways. It read:

Knit two, purl two,
I make of small boredoms
a fabric
to keep you warm.
Is it my own image
I love so
in your face?

I lean over your sleep,
Narcissus over
his clear pool,
ready to fall in—
to drown for you
if necessary.

Yet if we so love ourselves, reflected in our children, why is it so terrifying to so many of us to think of seeing our exact genetic replicas born again, identical twins years younger than we? Is there a hidden fear that we would be forcing God to give us another soul, thereby bending God to our will, or, worse yet, that we would be creating soul-less beings that were merely genetic shells of humans? After all, in many religions, the soul is supposed to be present from the moment of conception, before a person is born and shaped by nurture as well as nature. If a clone is created, how could its soul be different from the soul of the person who is cloned? Is it possible, as molecular biologist Gunther Stendt once suggested, that "a human clone would not consist of real persons but merely of Cartesian automata in human shape"?

Or is it one thing for nature to form us through the vagaries of the genetic lottery, and another for us to take complete control, abandoning all thoughts of somehow, through the mixing of genes, having a child who is like us, but better? Normally, when a man and a woman have a child together, the child is an unpredictable mixture of the two. We recognize that, of course, in the hoary old joke in which a beautiful but dumb woman suggests to an ugly but brilliant man that the two have a child. Just think of how wonderful the baby would be, the woman says, with my looks and your brains. Aha, says the man. But what if the child inherited *my* looks and *your* brains?

Theologians speak of the special status of a child, born of an act of love between a man and a woman. Of course, we already routinely employ infertility treatments, like donor eggs, semen banks, and frozen embryos, that have weakened these ties between the parents and the child. But, said Gilbert Meilaender, a Lutheran theologian, cloning would be "a new and decisive turn on this road." Cloning entails the *production*, rather than the creation, of a child. It is "far less a surrender to the mystery of the genetic lottery," he said, and "far more an understanding of the child as a product of human will."

20 Elliott Dorff, a rabbi at the University of Judaism in Los Angeles, said much the same thing. "Each person involved has to get out of himself or herself in order to make and have a child." But if a person can be reproduced through cloning, that self-surrender is lost, and there is danger of self-idolization.

Cloning also poses a danger to our notion of mortality, Dorff said. The biblical psalm says, "Teach us to number our days so that we can obtain a heart of wisdom," he recalled. "The sense that there is a deadline, that there is an end to all of this, forces us to make good use of our lives."

In this age of entertainment, when philosophical and theological questions are pushed aside as too difficult or too deep, cloning brings us face-to-face with our notion of what it means to be human and makes us confront both the privileges and limitations of life itself. It also forces us to question the powers of science. Is there, in fact, knowledge that we do not want? Are there paths we would rather not pursue?

The time is long past when we can speak of the purity of science, divorced from its consequences. If any needed reminding that the innocence of scientists was lost long ago, they need only recall the comments of J. Robert Oppenheimer, the genius who was a father of the atomic bomb and who was transformed in the process from a supremely confident man, ready to follow his scientific curiosity, to a humbled and stricken soul, wondering what science had wrought.

Before the bomb was made, Oppenheimer said, "When you see something that is technically sweet you go ahead and do it." After the bomb was dropped on Hiroshima and Nagasaki, in a chilling speech at the Massachusetts Institute of Technology in 1947, he said: "In some sort of crude sense which no vulgarity, no humor, no overstatement can quite extinguish, the physicists have known sin; and this is a knowledge which they cannot lose."

As with the atom bomb, cloning is complex, multilayered in its threats and its promises. It offers the possibility of real scientific advances that can improve our lives and save them. In medicine, scientists dream of using cloning to reprogram cells so we can make our own body parts for transplantation. Suppose, for example, you needed a bone-marrow transplant. Some deadly forms of leukemia can be cured completely if doctors destroy your own marrow and replace it with healthy marrow from someone else. But the marrow must be a close genetic match to your own. If not, it will lash out at you and kill you. Bone marrow is the source of the white blood cells of the immune system. If you have someone else's marrow, you'll make their white blood cells. And if those cells think you are different from them, they will attack.

Today, if you need marrow, you have to hope that a sister, brother, parent, or child happens to have bone-marrow cells that are genetically compatible with your own. If you have no relative whose marrow matches yours, you can search in computer databases of people who have volunteered to donate their marrow, but your chances of finding someone who matches you are less than one in twenty thousand—or one in a million if your genetic type is especially rare.

But suppose, instead, that scientists could take one of your cells—any cell—and merge it with a human egg. The egg would start to divide, to develop, but it would not be permitted to divide more than a few times. Instead, technicians would bathe it in proteins that direct primitive cells, embryo cells, to become marrow cells. What started out to be a clone of you could grow into a batch of your marrow—the perfect match.

25

More difficult, but not inconceivable, would be to grow solid organs, like kidneys or livers, in the same way.

Another possibility is to create animals whose organs are perfect genetic matches for humans. If you needed a liver, a kidney, or even a heart, you might be able to get one from a pig clone that was designed so it had human proteins on the surface of its organs. The reason transplant surgeons steer away from using animal organs in humans, even though there is a dire shortage of human organs, is that animals are so genetically different from people. A pig kidney transplanted into a human is just so foreign that the person's immune system will attack it and destroy it. But cloning offers a different approach. Scientists could take pig cells, for example, and add human genes to them in the laboratory, creating pig cells that were coated with human proteins. Then they could make cloned pigs from those cells. Each pig would have organs that looked, to a human immune system, for all the world like a human organ. These organs could be used for transplantation.

30 Cloning could also be used to make animals that are living drug factories—exactly the experiment that Ian Wilmut's sponsor, a Scottish company called PPL Therapeutics, Ltd., wants to conduct. Scientists could insert genes into laboratory cells that would force the cells to make valuable drugs, like clotting factors for hemophiliacs. Then they could clone animals from those cells and create animals that made the drugs in their milk. The only step remaining would be to milk the clones and extract the drugs.

Another possibility would be to clone prize dairy cows. The average cow produces about fifteen thousand pounds of milk annually, but world champion milk producers make as much as forty thousand pounds of milk a year. The problem for breeders is that there are, apparently, so many genes involved in creating one of these phenomenal cows that no one has learned how to breed them the old-fashioned way. But if you had a cow that produced forty thousand pounds of milk a year, you could clone her and make a herd.

Zoologists might clone animals that are on the verge of extinction, keeping them alive and propagating when they might otherwise have vanished from the earth.

The possibilities are limitless, scientists say, and so, some argue, we should stop focusing on our hypothetical fears and think about the benefits that cloning could bring.

Others say that cloning is far from business as usual, far from a technical advance, and that we should be wary of heading down such a brambly path.

35 But was the cloning of Dolly really such a ground-shifting event? After all, the feat came as a climax to years of ever more frightening, yet dazzling, technological feats, particularly in the field of assisted reproduction. Each step, dreaded by some, cursed by others, welcomed by many more, soon grew to be

part of the medical landscape, hardly worthy of comment. And so, with this history as background, some asked why, and how, anyone thought cloning could be controlled—or why anyone would want to. Besides, some asked, why was cloning any different in principle from some of the more spectacular infertility treatments that are accepted with hardly a raised eyebrow?

The infertility revolution began in 1978, when Louise Brown was born in England, the world's first test-tube baby. After more than a decade of futile efforts, scientists finally had learned to fertilize women's eggs outside their bodies, allowing the first stages of human life to begin in a petri dish in a laboratory. The feat raised alarms at the time. It was, said Moshe Tendler, a professor of medical ethics and chair of the biology department at Yeshiva University, "matchmaking at its most extreme, two reluctant gametes trying to be pushed together whether they liked it or not."

But in vitro fertilization flourished despite its rocky start, nourished by the plaintive cries of infertile couples so unjustly condemned to be barren, and justified by the miracle babies—children who were wanted so badly that their parents were willing to spend years in doctors' offices, take out loans for tens of thousands of dollars, and take their chances of finally, ultimately, failing and losing all hope of having a child who bore their genes. The doctors who ran the clinics soothed the public's fears. In vitro fertilization was not horrifying, they said. It was just a way to help infertile couples have babies.

The federal government quickly got out of the business of paying for any research that even peripherally contributed to the manipulation of human embryos, but in vitro fertilization clinics simply did research on their own, with money from the fees they charged women for infertility treatments, and so the field advanced, beyond the purview of university science, with its federal grants and accompanying strict rules and regulations.

"There are no hard-and-fast rules; there is no legislation," said Arthur Wisot, the executive director of the Center for Advanced Reproductive Care in Redondo Beach, California. "This whole area of medicine is totally unregulated. We don't answer to anyone but our peers."

Nearly every year, the fertility clinics would take another step. Recently, they began advertising something they called intercytoplasmic sperm injection, or I.C.S.I., in which they could get usable sperm even from men who seemed to make none, or whose sperm cells were misshapen or immotile and simply unable to fertilize an egg. The scientists would insert a needle into a man's testicle and remove immature sperm, which were little more than raw genes. They would inject these nascent sperm into an egg to create an embryo. Medical scientists later discovered that many of these men had such feeble sperm because the genes that controlled their sperm production were mutated. When the sperm, carrying the mutated gene, were used to make a baby boy, the boy would grow up with the same mutated genes and he, too, would need

40

I.C.S.I. to have a baby. Some scientists worried that there might be other consequences of such a mutation.

But the infertility doctors and many infertile couples were unconcerned by the possibility that this technique might be less of an unqualified boon than it at first appeared. And the I.C.S.I. advertisements continued unabated.

Infertility doctors also learned to snip a cell from a microscopic embryo and analyze it for genetic defects, selecting only healthy embryos to implant in a woman's womb. They learned that there is no age barrier to pregnancy: Women who had passed the age of menopause could still carry a baby if they used eggs from a younger woman, fertilized in a laboratory. Even women in their early sixties have gotten pregnant, and while some doctors have said they do not want to participate in creating such pregnancies, others say that it is really up to the women whether they want to become mothers at such an advanced age.

Infertility clinics are even learning to do the ultimate prenatal testing: fishing fetal cells out of a pregnant woman's blood and analyzing them for genetic defects. It is, said Tendler, "the perfect child syndrome. We can now take 5 cc of a woman's blood when she is seven to nine weeks pregnant, do 191 genetic probes on that cell, and decide whether that baby is going to make it or not."

The latest development involves methods to sort sperm, separating those sperm with Y chromosomes, which would create boys, from those with X chromosomes, which would create girls. Soon parents can have the ultimate control over the sex of their babies.

45   At the same time, molecular biologists learned to snip genes out of cells and to sew others in, engineering cells to order. Infertility clinics expect, before long, to be able to add genes to human embryos—or delete genes that could cause disease or disability—creating a perfect child before even implanting an embryo into a woman's womb.

At first, the feats of reproductive scientists were the objects of controversy and shock. But we have become accustomed to their achievements. And it is hard to argue against the cries that couples have a right to reproductive freedom. Many have suffered for years, yearning for a child of their own. If they want to create babies, and are paying with their own money, who has the right to tell them no?

These days, when infertility doctors introduce a new method to the public, or when their techniques disrupt what we have thought of as the natural order, there is, at first, a ripple of surprise, or sometimes dismay, but then that reaction fades and all we remember is that there seemed to be reports of one more incredible technological trick.

Even newspapers are becoming blasé. One Sunday in April, about six weeks after the cloning of Dolly was announced, I was attending a meeting of a federal commission that was assessing cloning. I crept out of the meeting to call a national news editor at *The New York Times* and inform him of the meeting's progress. He said there was something else he wanted to ask me about. There was a story out of Florida, he said, about a woman who just gave birth to her own grandchild. Was that news, he asked me?

I assured him that it was not news. Several years ago, another woman had done the same thing, and we'd reported it on page 1. The woman's daughter had been born with ovaries but not a uterus, so the mother carried the baby for the daughter. That story had come and gone, no longer even worth a raised eyebrow.

So when Dolly was born, in this age of ever-more-disarming scientific   *50* advances, some worried that her birth might be greeted with a brief shiver, then forgotten, like the woman who gave birth to her own grandchild. Leon Kass, a biochemist turned philosopher, at the University of Chicago, warned that to react as though cloning were just another infertility treatment would be to miss the point of Dolly. He worried that we may be too jaded by previous triumphs of technological wizardry to take cloning as seriously as we should. He quoted Raskolnikov, the protagonist of Fyodor Dostoyevsky's *Crime and Punishment:* "Man gets used to everything—the beast."

It is true, of course, that the revolution in infertility treatments set the stage for people to think about cloning a human. Were it not for the proficiency of doctors in manipulating human eggs and sperm, it would not be feasible to even think of transferring the chromosomes of an adult cell into a human egg. But there is an intellectual chasm between methods that result in a baby with half its genes from the mother and half from the father and cloning, which would result in a baby whose genes are identical to those of an adult who was cloned.

Human cloning, Kass said, would be "something radically new, both in itself and in its easily foreseeable consequences. The stakes here are very high indeed." Until now "we have benefited mightily from the attitude, Let technology go where it will and we can fix any problems that might arise later." But, he said, "that paradigm is open to question." Now we are "threatened with really major changes in human life, even human nature." And even if an absolute prohibition on cloning cannot be made effective, "it would at least place the burden on the other side to show the necessity" of taking this awesome step.

What is at issue, Kass said, "is nothing less than whether human procreation is going to remain human, whether children are going to be made rather than begotten, and whether it is a good thing, humanly speaking, to say yes to the road which leads, at best, to the dehumanized rationality of *Brave New World.*" And so "What we have here is not business as usual, to be fretted about for a while and then given our seal of approval, not least because it appears to be unusual." Instead, he said, "the future of humanity may hang in the balance."

The cloning debate, Kass said, is so much more than just an argument about one more step in assisted reproduction. "This is really one of those critical moments where one gets a chance to think about terribly important things. Not just genetics and what is the meaning of mother and father and kinship, but also the whole relationship between science and society and attitudes toward technology." Cloning, he said, "provides the occasion as well as the urgent necessity of deciding whether we shall be slaves of unregulated progress and ultimately its artifacts or whether we shall remain free human beings to guide our technique towards the enhancement of human dignity."

55   He quoted the theologian Paul Ramsey: "Raise the ethical questions with a serious and not a frivolous conscience. A man of frivolous conscience announces that there are ethical quandaries ahead that we must urgently consider before the future catches up with us. By this he often means that we need to devise a new ethics that will provide the rationalization for doing in the future what men are bound to do because of the new actions and interventions science will have made possible. In contrast, a man of serious conscience means to say in raising urgent ethical questions that there may be some things that men should never do. The good things that men do can be made complete only by the things they refuse to do."

Yet if there is one lesson of cloning it is that there is no uniformly accepted way to think about the ethical questions that it elicits, and no agreement, even among the most thoughtful and well-informed commentators, about what is right and what is wrong. Many—but by no means all—theologians tended to condemn the notion of human cloning. Many ethicists were similarly repelled, but others asked instead, who would be harmed, and why are we so sure that harm would ensue? While theologians cited religious traditions and biblical proscriptions, lawyers cited reproductive rights and said that it would be very hard to argue that it was illegal to clone oneself. In the meantime, some ethicists said they'd heard from in vitro fertilization clinics, which—operating already outside the usual rules that bind scientists, and looking for paying customers—were extremely interested in investigating cloning.

The diversity of opinions extended even to interpretations of identical passages from the Bible. One priest and Catholic theologian argued from Genesis that cloning would be against God's will. An orthodox rabbi and theologian argued from the same passage that cloning should not be proscribed.

The priest, Albert Moraczewski, of the National Conference of Catholic Bishops, was invited to explain the Catholic point of view by a presidential commission that was asked to make recommendations on whether cloning should be permitted. He began by saying that the cloning of humans would be an affront to human dignity. Then he spoke of the familiar story of Adam and Eve, told in the Book of Genesis, in which God gave humans dominion "over

the creatures that swim in the sea, that fly in the air, or that walk the earth."
And he spoke of God's order. "The Lord God gave man this order: 'You are
free to eat from any of the trees of the garden except the tree of knowledge of
good and bad.'"

Moraczewski explained that according to the Catholic interpretation,
"Adam and Eve were given freedom in the garden but with one limitation,
which if transgressed would lead to death. Accordingly, human beings have
been granted intelligence and free will so that human beings can search for,
and recognize, the truth and freely pursue the good."

Cloning, he said, would exceed "the limits of the delegated dominion given   *60*
to the human race. There is no evidence that humans were given the power to
alter their nature or the manner in which they come into existence."

He added that couples who clone a child would be dehumanizing the act
of procreating and treating their child as an object, attempting to "design and
control the very identity of the child."

Moraczewski concluded by quoting John Paul II: "The biological nature
of every person is untouchable."

The next day, Moshe Tendler, an Orthodox Jewish rabbi, spoke to the commission. He, too, started with Genesis, and with the same quotation. But his
interpretation of it, from the Jewish tradition, was very different.

"This knowledge of good and evil has always confused theologians and
certainly the layman," Tendler said. "If Adam and Eve did not know of good
and evil, how could they have sinned? They knew good and evil. The tree of
good and evil is the tree that allows you to think that you can reevaluate, you
can set another yardstick for what is good and what is evil."

The Jewish tradition says that humans are obliged to help master our   *65*
world, according to Tendler, as long as they do not transgress into areas where
they would attempt to contravene God. It would not be in character with the
Jewish tradition to have a technology that could have outcomes that are good—
like preserving the family line of a Holocaust survivor who had no other living
relatives—and decide, ahead of time, not to use it for fear of its evil consequences. "We are bound by good and evil as given to us by divine imperative.
And we knew pretty well in most areas what is good and what is evil until
cloning came along and now we are not so sure what is good and what is evil.

"So, cloning, it is not intrinsically good or evil," Tendler said. The question, really, is whether particular applications of cloning might be a transgression by humans into the domain of God.

"I will give you a simile or metaphor of a guest invited to your house,"
Tendler said. "You ask them to be comfortable, help themselves, there is cake
in the cake box and fruits in the refrigerator, and coffee in the coffeemaker."
When you wake up, he continued, you're pleased to see that your guest did
as you suggested. "But if he should move your sofa to the other side of the

wall because he thought that that is where it really belongs, you will not invite him again."

God, Tendler added, says, "Make yourselves comfortable in my world, but you are guests in my house, do not act as if you own the place. Don't you rearrange my furniture."

He spoke also of a metaphor from the Talmud. "The question was posed, 'Is there not a time when you say to the bee, neither your honey nor your sting'?" And so, he asked, are we really prepared to ban cloning, to give up the honey, because we are so afraid of the sting?

70   On the other hand, some wonder whether we might not want to squash the bee. Nancy Duff, a theologian at the Princeton Theological Seminary, argued from Protestant tradition that, at the very least, all thoughts of human cloning should be put on hold. "Many people wonder if this is a miracle for which we can thank God, or an ominous new way to play God ourselves," she said. "At the very least, it represents the ongoing tension between faith and science."

But there is also a secular point of view, one that asks how persuasive, after all, are the hypothetical harms of cloning, and whether they are great enough to override the right that people have to reproductive freedom. John Robertson, a law professor at the University of Texas in Austin, who specializes in ethics and reproductive law, said he is unconvinced by those who argue that cloning is somehow too unnatural, too repugnant, too contrary to the laws of God, to proceed with. "In assessing harm, deviation from traditional methods of reproduction, including genetic selection of offspring characteristics, is not in itself a compelling reason for restriction when tangible harm to others is not present." He argued that cloning is not significantly different from other methods our society now accepts as ethical, and which are now being actively studied in research laboratories throughout the world. He referred to methods for adding genes or correcting faulty ones, in an attempt to cure diseases like muscular dystrophy or cystic fibrosis, which, although not yet possible, is expected to occur before too long.

"Cloning enables a child with the genome of another embryo or person to be born," Robertson said. "The genome is taken as it is. Genetic alteration, on the other hand, will change the genome of a person who could have been born with their genome intact." So what is the greater intervention? Given a choice of a child who is a clone or no child at all—a choice that could befall infertile couples—how bad is it to allow them to have a clone? Robertson asked. "If a loving family will rear the child, it is difficult to see why cloning for genetic selection is per se unacceptable."

A compelling argument, said Daniel Brock, a philosopher and ethicist at Brown University. Is the right to clone part of our right to reproductive freedom? he asked. He said that although he is not certain that cloning could be protected in this way because it is not, strictly speaking, reproduction, it might nonetheless fall into that broad category. And, he added, if the right to have yourself cloned is treated as a reproductive right, "that creates the presumption that it should be available to people who want to use it without government control."

Brock, for one, thinks that the public reaction to cloning is overblown. "The various harms are usually speculative," he said. "It is difficult to make the claim that these harms are serious enough and well-enough established to justify overriding the claim that cloning should be available." The public, he said, "has a tendency to want to leap ahead to possibilities that we're not even sure are possible."

Ruth Macklin, an ethicist at Albert Einstein College of Medicine, raised 75 similar questions about whether fears of cloning are reasonable. "One incontestable ethical requirement is that no adult person should be cloned without his or her consent," Macklin said. "But if adult persons sought to have themselves cloned, would the resulting individual be harmed by being brought into existence in this way? One harm that some envisage is psychological or emotional distress to a person who is an exact replica of another. Some commentators have elevated this imagined harm to the level of a right: the right to control our own individual genetic identity. But it is not at all clear why the deliberate creation of an individual who is genetically identical to another living being (but separated in time) would violate anyone's rights."

After all, Macklin said, if the cloned person was not created from the cell of another, he or she would not have been born. Is it really better never to have existed than to exist as a clone? "Evidence, not mere surmise, is required to conclude that the psychological burdens of knowing that one was cloned would be of such magnitude that they would outweigh the benefits of life itself."

Macklin even took on those who argued that cloning violates human dignity. Those who hold that view, she said, "owe us a more precise account of just what constitutes a violation of human dignity if no individuals are harmed and no one's rights are violated. Dignity is a fuzzy concept and appeals to dignity are often used to substitute for empirical evidence that is lacking or sound arguments that cannot be mustered."

Kass argued, however, that such utterly pragmatic language obscures the moral significance of what is being contemplated. He quoted Bertrand Russell: "Pragmatism is like that warm bath that heats up so imperceptibly that you don't know when to scream."

The clashing viewpoints, said Ezekiel J. Emanuel, a doctor and ethicist at the Dana-Farber Cancer Institute in Boston, who was a member of the president's commission that was studying cloning, seem to indicate "a moral values gap." And so, he added, how people react to cloning "depends a lot on one's world outlook, as it were. How much you might weigh these other values depends a lot on how you understand yourself and your place in the world."

80 And that, in the end, is what cloning brings to the fore. Cloning is a metaphor and a mirror. It allows us to look at ourselves and our values and to decide what is important to us, and why.

It also reflects the place of science in our world. Do we see science as a threat or a promise? Are scientists sages or villains? Have scientists changed over the years from natural philosophers to technologists focused on the next trick that can be played on nature?

Freud once said that, sometimes, a cigar is just a cigar. But so far, we have not reached a point where a clone is just a clone. As the social and cultural history of cloning continues, the questions and the insights into who we are, who we are becoming, and who we want to be grow ever deeper. Dolly, it now seems, is more a beginning than an end.

Engaging the Text

1. How are the issues raised by cloning qualitatively different from those produced by treatments for infertility? How would the relationship between a parent and a cloned offspring be different from that between a parent and an offspring produced through, for example, artificial insemination?

2. Kolata includes numerous quotations from scientists, theologians, and ethicists in her piece. On what points do these experts agree or disagree? Is there a consensus as to the advisability of cloning humans? In your opinion, is cloning an example of a procedure that is technologically feasible but ethically objectionable? Why or why not?

3. Does Kolata seem to be a neutral observer reporting as a science journalist? Does she have a detectable personal opinion about the subject? As far as you can tell, what is her attitude toward cloning?

Exploring Your Cultural Perspective

1. Recently, a couple had a child so the child could serve as a bone marrow donor for another of their children, who had leukemia. Does this differ from creating a clone for the sole purpose of harvesting tissues and organs? Why or why not?

2. Currently, genetic screening can predict whether someone will develop Huntington's disease or have genetic defects that will lead to other diseases. In addition, some scientists suggest that some personality traits—such as depression, aggression, and shyness—may be influenced by heredity. Will

FIRST ROW (L-R): CINDY, CINDY, RALPH, RALPH, CINDY, RALPH.
SECOND ROW (L-R): RALPH, CINDY, RALPH, RALPH, CINDY, RALPH, CINDY, CINDY.

FIGURE 6.1

our future look like that in the 1997 science fiction film *Gattaca*, about a society in which one's DNA determines every aspect of one's life? This scenario may be becoming more likely given the successful mapping (in 2000) of the human chromosome in an effort known as the Human Genome Project. In a short essay, examine the implications of such a future.

3. Do you think the scenario depicted in the cartoon in Figure 6.1 could ever come true? Why or why not?

LENNARD J. DAVIS
Visualizing the Disabled Body

The modern concept of "disability" originated in the nineteenth century as a result of the Industrial Revolution and the need to define the ideal worker. Lennard J. Davis, who was born to parents who were deaf and who "uttered" his first words in sign language, shows us how the idea of what is "normal" (and "abnormal") is rooted in socially constructed myths. These concepts have had great influence in shaping depictions of deformity in literature and films. This essay is drawn from *Enforcing Normalcy: Disability, Deafness and the Body* (1995). Davis is currently a professor and graduate director of English at SUNY-Binghamton. His most recent work is *My Sense of Silence: Memoirs of a Childhood with Deafness* (2000).

Thinking Critically

To what extent have the mass media shaped your concept of beauty and ugliness? What does the shift of descriptive terms from "handicapped" to "disabled" to "differently abled" suggest about changes in social attitudes?

A human being who is first of all an invalid is all *body, therein lies his inhumanity and his debasement. In most cases he is little better than a carcass—.*
> —THOMAS MANN, *The Magic Mountain*

. . . the female is as it were a deformed male.
> —ARISTOTLE, *Generation of Animals*

When I begin to wish I were crippled—even though I am perfectly healthy—or rather that I would have been better off crippled, that is the first step towards butoh.
> —TATSUMI HIJIKATA, co-founder of the Japanese
> performance art/dance form *butoh*

She has no arms or hands, although the stump of her upper right arm extends just to her breast. Her left foot has been severed, and her face is badly scarred, with her nose torn at the tip, and her lower lip gouged out. Fortunately, her facial mutilations have been treated and are barely visible, except for minor scarring visible only up close. The big toe of her right foot has been cut off, and her torso is covered with scars, including a particularly large one between her shoulder blades, one that covers her shoulder, and one covering the tip of her breast where her left nipple was torn out.

Yet she is considered one of the most beautiful female figures in the world. When the romantic poet Heinrich Heine saw her he called her 'Notre-Dame de la Beauté.'

He was referring to the Venus de Milo.

Consider too Pam Herbert, a quadriplegic with muscular dystrophy, writing her memoir by pressing her tongue on a computer keyboard, who describes herself at twenty-eight years old:

> I weigh about 130 pounds; I'm about four feet tall. It's pretty hard to get an accurate measurement on me because both of my knees are permanently bent and my spine is curved, so 4' is an estimate. I wear size two tennis shoes and strong glasses; my hair is dishwater blonde and shoulder length. (Browne et al., eds, 1985, 147)

In this memoir, she describes her wedding night:

5

> We got to the room and Mark laid me down on the bed because I was so tired from sitting all day. Anyway, I hadn't gone to the bathroom all day so Mark had to catheterize me. I had been having trouble going to the bathroom for many years, so it was nothing new to Mark, he had done it lots of times before.
>
> It was time for the biggest moment of my life, making love. Of course, I was a little nervous and scared. Mark was very gentle with me. He started undressing me and kissing me. We tried making love in the normal fashion with Mark on top and me on the bottom. Well, that position didn't work at all, so then we tried laying on our sides coming in from behind. That was a little better. Anyway, we went to sleep that night a little discouraged because we didn't have a very good lovemaking session. You would have thought that it would be great, but sometimes things don't always go the way we want them to. We didn't get the hang of making love for about two months. It hurt for a long time. (ibid., 155)

I take the liberty of bringing these two women's bodies together. Both have disabilities. The statue is considered the ideal of Western beauty and eroticism, although it is armless and disfigured. The living woman might be considered by many 'normal' people to be physically repulsive, and certainly without erotic allure. The questions I wish to ask is why does the impairment of the Venus de Milo in no way prevent 'normal' people from considering her beauty, while Pam Herbert's disability becomes the focal point for horror and pity?

In asking this question, I am really raising a complex issue. On a social level, the question has to do with how people with disabilities are seen and why, by and large, they are de-eroticized. If, as I mentioned earlier, disability is a cultural phenomenon rooted in the senses, one needs to inquire how a disability occupies a field of vision, of touch, of hearing; and how that disruption or distress in the sensory field translates into psycho-dynamic representations. This is more a question about the nature of the subject than about the qualities of the object, more about the observer than the observed. The 'problem' of the disabled has been put at the feet of people with disabilities for too long.

Normalcy, rather than being a degree zero of existence, is more accurately a location of bio-power, as Foucault would use the term. The 'normal' person (clinging to that title) has a network of traditional ableist assumptions and social supports that empowers the gaze and interaction. The person with disabilities, until fairly recently, had only his or her own individual force or will. Classically, the encounter has been, and remains, an uneven one. Anne Finger describes it in strikingly visual terms by relating an imagined meeting between Rosa Luxemburg and Antonio Gramsci, each of whom was a person with disabilities, although Rosa is given the temporary power of the abled gaze:

> We can measure Rosa's startled reaction as she glimpses him the misshapen dwarf limping towards her in a second-hand black suit so worn that the cuffs are frayed and the fabric is turning green with age, her eye immediately drawn to this disruption in the visual field; the unconscious flinch; the realization that she is staring at him, and the too-rapid turning away of the head. And then, the moment after, the consciousness that the quick aversion of the gaze was as much of an insult as the stare, so she turns her head back but tries to make her focus general, not a sharp gape. Comrade Rosa, would you have felt a slight flicker of embarrassment? shame? revulsion? dread? of a feeling that can have no name?

In this encounter what is suppressed, at least in this moment, is the fact that Rosa Luxemburg herself is physically impaired (she walked with a limp for her whole life). The emphasis then shifts from the cultural norm to the deviation; Luxemburg, now the gazing subject, places herself in the empowered position of the norm, even if that position is not warranted.

Disability, in this and other encounters, is a disruption in the visual, auditory, or perceptual field as it relates to the power of the gaze. As such, the disruption, the rebellion of the visual, must be regulated, rationalized, contained. Why the modern binary—normal/abnormal—must be maintained is a complex question. But we can begin by accounting for the desire to split bodies into two immutable categories: whole and incomplete, abled and disabled, normal and abnormal, functional and dysfunctional.

In the most general sense, cultures perform an act of splitting (*Spaltung*, to   10
use Freud's term). These violent cleavages of consciousness are as primitive as our thought processes can be. The young infant splits the good parent from the bad parent—although the parent is the same entity. When the child is satisfied with the parent, the parent is the good parent; when the child is not satisfied, the parent is bad. As a child grows out of the earliest phases of infancy, she learns to combine those split images into a single parent who is sometimes good and sometimes not. The residue of *Spaltung* remains in our inner life, personal and collective, to produce monsters and evil stepmothers as well as noble princes and fairy godmothers.

In this same primitive vein, culture tends to split bodies into good and bad parts. Some cultural norms are considered good and others bad. Everyone is familiar with the 'bad' body: too short or tall, too fat or thin, not masculine or feminine enough, not enough or too much hair on the head or other parts of the body, penis or breasts too small or (excepting the penis) too big. Furthermore, each individual assigns good and bad labels to body parts—good: hair, face, lips, eyes, hands; bad: sexual organs, excretory organs, underarms.

The psychological explanation may provide a reason why it is imperative for society at large to engage in *Spaltung*. The divisions whole/incomplete, able/disabled neatly cover up the frightening writing on the wall that reminds the hallucinated whole being that its wholeness is in fact a hallucination, a developmental fiction. *Spaltung* creates the absolute categories of abled and disabled, with concomitant defenses against the repressed fragmented body.

But a psychological explanation alone is finally insufficient. Historical specificity makes us understand that disability is a social process with an origin. So, why certain disabilities are labeled negatively while others have a less negative connotation is a question tied to complex social forces (some of which I have tried to lay out in earlier chapters). It is fair to say, in general, that disabilities would be most dysfunctional in postindustrial countries, where the ability to perambulate or manipulate is so concretely tied to productivity, which in itself is tied to production. The body of the average worker, as we have seen, becomes the new measure of man and woman. Michael Oliver, citing Ryan and Thomas (1980), notes:

> With the rise of the factory . . . [during industrialization] many more disabled people were excluded from the production process for 'The speed of factory work, the enforced discipline, the time-keeping and production norms—all these were a highly unfavourable change from the slower, more self-determined and flexible methods of work into which many handicapped people had been integrated.' (1990, 27)

Both industrial production and the concomitant standardization of the human body have had a profound impact on how we split up bodies.

We tend to group impairments into categories either of 'disabling' (bad) or just 'limiting' (good). For example, wearing a hearing aid is seen as much more disabling than wearing glasses, although both serve to amplify a deficient sense. But loss of hearing is associated with aging in a way that nearsightedness is not. Breast removal is seen as an impairment of femininity and sexuality, whereas the removal of a foreskin is not seen as a diminution of masculinity. The coding of body parts and the importance attached to their selective function or dysfunction is part of a much larger system of signs and meanings in society, and is constructed as such.

15   'Splitting' may help us to understand one way in which disability is seen as part of a system in which value is attributed to body parts. The disabling of the body part or function is then part of a removal of value. The gradations of value are socially determined, but what is striking is the way that rather than being incremental or graduated, the assignment of the term 'disabled,' and the consequent devaluation, are total. That is, the concept of disabled seems to be an absolute rather than a gradient one. One is either disabled or not. Value is tied to the ability to earn money. If one's body is productive, it is not disabled. People with disabilities continue to earn less than 'normal' people and, even after the passage of the Americans with Disabilities Act, 69 percent of Americans with disabilities were unemployed (*New York Times*, 27 October 1994, A:22). Women and men with disabilities are seen as less attractive, less able to marry and be involved in domestic production.

The ideology of the assigning of value to the body goes back to preindustrial times. Myths of beauty and ugliness have laid the foundation for normalcy. In particular, the Venus myth is one that is dialectically linked to another. This embodiment of beauty and desire is tied to the story of the embodiment of ugliness and repulsion. So the appropriate mythological character to compare the armless Venus with is Medusa. Medusa was once a beautiful sea goddess who, because she had sexual intercourse with Poseidon at one of Athene's temples, was turned by Athene into a winged monster with glaring eyes, huge teeth, protruding tongue, brazen claws, and writhing snakes for hair. Her hideous appearance has the power to turn people into stone, and Athene eventually completes her revenge by having Perseus kill Medusa. He finds Medusa by stealing the one eye and one tooth shared by the Graiae until they agree to help him. Perseus then kills Medusa by decapitating her while looking into his brightly polished shield, which neutralizes the power of her appearance; he then puts her head into a magic wallet that shields onlookers from its effects. When Athene receives the booty, she uses Medusa's head and skin to fashion her own shield.

In the Venus tradition, Medusa is a poignant double. She is the necessary counter in the dialectic of beauty and ugliness, desire and repulsion, wholeness and fragmentation. Medusa is the disabled woman to Venus's perfect body. The story is a kind of allegory of a 'normal' person's intersection with the disabled body. This intersection is marked by the power of the visual. The 'normal' person sees the disabled person and is turned to stone, in some sense, by the visual interaction. In this moment, the normal person suddenly feels self-conscious, rigid, unable to look but equally drawn to look. The visual field becomes problematic, dangerous, treacherous. The disability becomes a power derived from its otherness, its monstrosity, in the eyes of the 'normal' person. The disability must be decapitated and then contained in a variety of magic wallets. Rationality, for which Athene stands, is one of the devices for containing, controlling, and reforming the disabled body so that it no longer has the power to terrorize. And the issue of mutilation comes up as well because the disabled body is always the reminder of the whole body about to come apart at the seams. It provides a vision of, a caution about, the body as a construct held together willfully, always threatening to become its individual parts—cells, organs, limbs, perceptions—like the fragmented, shared eye and tooth that Perseus ransoms back to the Graiae.

I have been concentrating on the physical body, but it is worth considering for a moment the issue of madness. While mental illness is by definition not related to the intactness of the body, nevertheless, it shows up as a disruption in the visual field. We 'see' that someone is insane by her physical behavior, communication, and so on. Yet the fear is that the mind is fragmenting, breaking up, falling apart, losing itself—all terms we associate with becoming mad. With the considerable information we have about the biological roots of mental illness, we begin to see the disease again as a breaking up of 'normal' body chemistry: amino acid production gone awry, depleted levels of certain polypeptide chains or hormones. Language production can become fragmentary, broken, in schizophrenic speech production. David Rothman points out that in eighteenth- and nineteenth-century America, insanity was seen as being caused by the fragmented nature of 'modern' life—particularly the pressures brought to bear on people by a society in which economic boundaries were disappearing. This fragmenting of society produced a fragmentation of the individual person. So the asylums that sprung up during this period recommended a cure that involved a removal from the urban, alienated, fragmented environment to rural hospitals in which order and precision could be restored. 'A precise schedule and regular work became the two characteristics of the best private and public institutions. . . . The structure of the mental hospital would counteract the debilitating influences of the community' (Rothman 1971, 144).

As Rothman notes, 'Precision, certainty, regularity, order' were the words that were seen as embodying the essence of cure (ibid., 145). The mind would be restored to 'wholeness' by restoring the body through manual labor. However, needless to add, one had to have a whole body to have a whole mind. The general metaphor here continues to be a notion of wholeness, order, clean boundaries, as opposed to fragmentations, disordered bodies, messy boundaries.

If people with disabilities are considered anything, they are or have been considered creatures of disorder—monsters, monstrous. Leslie Fiedler has taken some pains to show this in his book *Freaks*. If we look at Mary Shelley's *Frankenstein*, we find some of the themes we have been discussing emerge in novelistic form. First, we might want to note that we have no name for the creation of Dr Frankenstein other than 'monster.' (This linguistic lapsus is usually made up for in popular culture by referring to the creature itself as 'Frankenstein,' a terminology that confuses the creator with the created.) In reading the novel, or speaking about it, we can only call the creature 'the monster.' This linguistic limitation is worth noting because it encourages the reader to consider the creature a monster rather than a person with disabilities.

20 We do not often think of the monster in Mary Shelley's work as disabled, but what else is he? The characteristic of his disability is a difference in appearance. He is more than anything a disruption in the visual field. There is nothing else different about him—he can see, hear, talk, think, ambulate, and so on. It is worth noting that in popular culture, largely through the early film versions of the novel, the monster is inarticulate, somewhat mentally slow, and walks with a kind of physical impairment. In addition, the film versions add Ygor, the hunchbacked criminal who echoes the monster's disability in his own. Even in the recent film version by Kenneth Branagh, the creature walks with a limp and speaks with an impediment. One cannot dismiss this filtering of the creature through the lens of multiple disability. In order for the audience to fear and loathe the creature, he must be made to transcend the pathos of a single disability. Of course, it would be unseemly for a village to chase and torment a paraplegic or a person with acromegaly. Disabled people are to be pitied and ostracized; monsters are to be destroyed; audiences must not confuse the two.

In the novel, it is clear that Dr Frankenstein cannot abide his creation for only one reason—its hideous appearance. Indeed, the creature's only positive human contact is with the blind old man De Lacey, who cannot see the unsightly features. When De Lacey's family catches a glimpse of the creature, the women faint or run, and the men beat and pursue him. His body is a zone of repulsion; the reaction he evokes is fear and loathing. The question one wants to ask is why does a physical difference produce such a profound response?

The answer, I believe, is twofold. First, what is really hideous about the creature is not so much his physiognomy as what that appearance suggests.

The *corps morcelé* makes its appearance immediately in the construction of the monster. Ironically, Dr Frankenstein adapts Zeuxis's notion of taking ideal parts from individuals to create the ideal whole body. As he says, 'I collected bones from charnel houses. . . . The dissecting room and the slaughter-house furnished many of my materials' (Shelley 1990, 54–5). From these fragments, seen as loathsome and disgusting, Frankenstein assembles what he wishes to create—a perfect human. It is instructive in this regard to distinguish the Boris Karloff incarnation of the creature—with the bolt through his neck—or Branagh's grotesquely sewn creature, from the image that Mary Shelley would have us imagine. Dr Frankenstein tells us:

> His limbs were in proportion, and I had selected his features as beautiful. Beautiful!—Great God! His yellow skin scarcely covered the work of muscles and arteries beneath; his hair was of a lustrous black and flowing; his teeth of a pearly whiteness; but these luxuriances only formed a more horrid contrast with his watery eyes, that seemed almost of the same colour as the dun white sockets in which they were set, his shrivelled complexion and straight black lips. (ibid., 57)

What then constitutes the horror? If we add up the details, what we see is a well-proportioned man with long black hair, pearly white teeth, whose skin is somewhat deformed—resulting in jaundice and perhaps a tightness or thinness of the skin, a lack of circulation perhaps causing shriveling, watery eyes and darkened lips. This hardly seems to constitute horror rather than, say, pathos.

What is found to be truly horrifying about Frankenstein's creature is its composite quality, which is too evocative of the fragmented body. Frankenstein's reaction to this living *corps morcelé* is repulsion: 'the beauty of the dream vanished, and breathless horror and disgust filled my heart' (ibid., 57). Frankenstein attempted to create a unified nude, an object of beauty and harmony—a Venus, in effect. He ended up with a Medusa whose existence reveals the inhering and enduring nature of the archaic endlessly fragmented body, endlessly repressed but endlessly reappearing.

Works Cited

Browne, S. E., D. Connors, and N. Stern, eds. *With the Power of Each Breath: A Disabled Women's Anthology.* Pittsburg: PA: Cleis Press, 1985.

Oliver, Michael. *The Politics of Disablement: A Sociological Approach.* New York: St. Martin's Press, 1990.

Rothman, David. *The Discovery of the Asylum: Social Order and Disorder in the New Republic.* Boston: Little, Brown, 1971.

Shelley, Mary. *Frankenstein, or the Modern Prometheus.* Oxford: Oxford University Press, 1990.

Engaging the Text

1. How does the contrast Davis draws between the Venus de Milo and Pam Herbert dramatize the different standards people apply to classic works of art and to real people with disabilities?

2. In what ways did the Industrial Revolution's need for strong, healthy workers who could withstand long hours in a factory shape modern-day concepts of who is "normal" and who is disabled?

3. How does the phenomenon known as splitting help explain why we stereotype those with disabilities? Do you agree with Davis's view that "disability is a cultural phenomenon rooted in the senses"? Why or why not?

Exploring Your Cultural Perspective

1. How have films such as *Mask* (1985), *Shine* (1992), *Forrest Gump* (1994), *Mr. Holland's Opus* (1995), and *Sling Blade* (1996) depicted those with disabilities? Rent one or more of these films and analyze how the mythology of disability is portrayed. What insight do these films offer about our society that would explain why this **genre** (type of film) is so popular?

2. If you have ever been physically incapacitated or have a disability, write about your experiences in a way that helps others understand your situation. What overt and subtle psychological aspects of discrimination must those with disabilities endure every day?

LUCY GREALY

Autobiography of a Face

When Lucy Grealy was nine, half of her jaw was removed because of cancer. She subsequently underwent years of reconstructive surgery. This experience, traumatic in itself, was made worse by other people's reactions to her disfigurement. The intolerance and rejection she experienced empowered her to become self-reliant. Grealy's compelling account of her journey toward self-acceptance is drawn from her 1994 memoir, *Autobiography of a Face*. She has also written a collection of essays, *As Seen on TV: Provocations* (2000).

Thinking Critically

As you read Grealy's memoir, consider whether beauty is an absolute or a relative concept, one that is culturally determined.

It was only when I got home from the hospital that I permitted myself to look more closely at my new face. It was still extremely swollen (it would be months before it went down), and a long thin scar ran the length of it. In the middle of the scar was the island of pale skin from my hip. Placing my hand over the swollen and discolored parts, I tried to imagine how my face might look once it was "better." If I positioned the angle of my face, the angle of my hand, and the angle of the mirror all just right, it looked okay.

Actually, in my mind, my face looked even better than okay, it looked beautiful. But it was a beauty that existed in the future, a possible future. As it was, I hated my face. I turned my thoughts inward again, and this strange fantasy of beauty became something very private, a wish I would have been ashamed to let anyone in on. Primarily it was a fantasy of relief. When I tried to imagine being beautiful, I could only imagine living without the perpetual fear of being alone, without the great burden of isolation, which is what feeling ugly felt like.

The beginning of high school was a couple of months away. Each day I checked my face in private, wondering what I would look like by my first day at a new school. I expected to have a second "revising" operation before school started, but as it turned out I would have to wait at least another three months, a span of time that seemed useless and insurmountable. What was the point, if I still had to walk into school that first day looking like this?

There was only one solution, and that was to stop caring. I became pretentious. I picked out thick books by Russian authors and carted them around with me. Sometimes I even read them. *Anna Karenina, The Brothers Karamazov, Dead Souls.* I read *Jude the Obscure* simply because I liked the title, and anything else that sounded difficult and deep. Often I missed the subtle nuances of these books, but they presented a version of the world in which honor and virtue and dedication to the truth counted. The stories comforted me, though it didn't escape my attention that these qualities were ascribed primarily to men. The women might be virtuous as well, but their physical beauty was crucial to the story.

5   On the first day of school I rode the bus, entered my strange homeroom, and went through my day of classes as invisibly as possible. By now my hair was long, past my shoulders, and I walked around with my head bent, my dark blond hair covering half my face. Having decided against seeking anything as inconsequential as social status, I spent the days observing my peers with a perfectly calibrated air of disinterest. I remained the outsider, like so many of the characters I had read about, and in this role I found great comfort. Doubtless I was more keenly aware of the subtleties of the various dramas and social dances of my classmates than they were themselves.

For the most part I was left alone. People were a bit more mature, and it was rare that anyone openly made fun of me. But I was still braced for the teasing. Every time I saw someone looking at me, I expected the worst. Usually they just looked the other way and didn't register much interest one way or the other. Then, just as I would start to relax, to let my guard down, some loud-mouthed boy would feel a need to point out to his friends how ugly I was.

One day when I went to my English class, I found a copy of Hesse's *Siddhartha*, his version of the story of Buddha, lying on my chair. My notions of Buddhism were sketchy at best, but the opening pages immediately reminded me of the messages of grace, dignity, and light that I'd first encountered in those Christian publications, which had long since ceased arriving in the mail. I'd almost forgotten about my quest for enlightenment, imagining my momentous meeting with the great guru. Now, after so much time and so much loss, I took it as a sign that someone had left this book on my chair. Desire and all its painful complications, I decided, was something I should and would be free of.

Two months after school started, the long-awaited revision operation was scheduled. I started focusing on the upcoming date, believing that my life would finally get started once I had the face I was "supposed" to have. Logically I knew that this was only one of many operations, but surely it would show promise, offer a hint of how it was all going to turn out.

When I woke up in recovery the day after the operation, I looked up to see a nurse wearing glasses leaning over me. Cautiously I looked for my reflection in her glasses. There I was, my hair messed and my face pale and, as far as I could tell, looking exactly the same as before. I reached up and felt the suture line. A few hours later, when I was recovered enough to walk unaided to the bathroom, I took each careful step toward the door and geared myself up to look in the mirror. Apart from looking like I'd just gotten over a bad case of flu, I looked just the same. The patch of paler skin was gone, but the overall appearance of my face was no different from before.

I blamed myself for the despair I felt creeping in; again it was a result of having expectations. I must guard against having any more. After all, I still had it pretty good by global standards. "I have food," I told myself. "I have a place to sleep." So what if my face was ugly, so what if other people judged me for this. That was their problem, not mine. This line of reasoning offered less consolation than it had in the past, but it distanced me from what was hurting most, and I took this as a sign that I was getting better at detaching myself from my desires.

When I returned to school I had resolved that my face was actually an asset. It was true I hated it and saw it as the cause of my isolation, but I interpreted it as some kind of lesson. I had taught myself about reincarnation, how the soul picks its various lives with the intent of learning more and more about itself so that it may eventually break free of the cycle of karma. Why had my soul chosen this particular life, I asked myself; what was there to learn from a face as ugly as mine? At the age of sixteen I decided it was all about desire and love.

Over the years my perspective on "what it was all about" has shifted, but the most important point then was that there *was* a reason for this happening to me. No longer feeling that I was being punished, as I had during the chemo, I undertook to see my face as an opportunity to find something that had not yet been revealed. Perhaps my face was a gift to be used toward understanding and enlightenment. This was all noble enough, but by equating my face with ugliness, in believing that without it I would never experience the deep, bottomless grief I called ugliness, I separated myself even further from other people, who I thought never experienced grief of this depth. Not that I did not allow others their own suffering. I tried my best to be empathic because I believed it was a "good" emotion. But in actuality I was judge and hangman, disgusted by peers who avoided their fears by putting their energy into things as insubstantial as fashion and boyfriends and gossip.

I tried my best, but for the most part I was as abysmal at seeking enlightenment as I had once been at playing dodge ball. No matter how desperately I wanted to catch that ball, I dropped it anyway. And as much as I wanted to love everybody in school and to waft esoterically into the ether when someone called me ugly, I was plagued with petty desires and secret, evil hates.

I hated Danny in my orchestra class because I had a crush on him and knew that he would never have a crush on me. Anger scared me most of all, and I repressed every stirring. Every time I felt hatred, or any other "bad" thought, I shooed it away with a broom of spiritual truisms. But the more I tried to negate my feelings, the more they crowded in. I not only harbored hatred for Danny even while I had a crush on him, I also hated Katherine, the girl in orchestra *he* had a crush on. Trying to repress that feeling, I found myself hating Katherine's cello, of all things, which she played exquisitely well. The cycle eventually ended with me: I hated myself for having even entertained the absurd notion that someone like Danny could like me.

15   I didn't begrudge Danny his crush on Katherine. She was pretty and talented, so why shouldn't he want her? I was never going to have anyone want me in that way, so I mustn't desire such a thing; in this way I could be grateful to my face for "helping" me to see the error of earthly desire. This complicated gratitude usually lasted for about five minutes before giving way to depression, plain and simple.

When my father's insurance money came, and before we learned of the accumulated tax debt we owed, my mother generously kept her promise and bought me another horse. Her registered name was even more silly than Sure Swinger, so I simply called her Mare. I kept her at Snowcap, a more professional and better-kept stable than Diamond D. There I undertook learning to ride seriously. I fell in love with Mare just as I had with Swinger, and again I had bad luck. Not long after I got her, she broke her leg while turned out in a field. As she limped pathetically onto the trailor to be taken away, they told me they could sell her as a brood mare, but I knew she was too old for this and would be put down shortly. Again my heart was broken, but this time I saw it in much more self-pitying terms. I told myself that anything I loved was doomed, and even as I was aware of my own overblown melodrama, just as I had been that night I nearly collapsed on the hospital floor, I took a strange comfort in this romantic, tragic role.

Luckily, the owners of Snowcap permitted me to continue on at the barn as their exercise rider. This was ideal. Not only did I get to ride horses for free, sometimes as many as six a day, and gain a great deal of experience in the process, but it also gave my life a center. I withstood school all day, knowing I would go straight to the barn afterward and stay there until eight or nine o'clock at night. The barn became the one place where I felt like myself, and I relished the physicality of riding, performing acts I was good at, feeling a sense of accomplishment. I spent as little time at home as possible.

During the tenth grade I had one more operation to work on shaping the free flap, and the results seemed as trivial and ineffectual to me as the last time. The following summer I spent every day with the horses. One day when it was too hot to get very much accomplished, I went along for the ride on an errand with some people from the stable. We got caught in traffic on the main road, and as we crept along at a snail's pace, I looked out the window and got lost in my own world. A bakery storefront, its door set at a very odd angle, caught my attention, reminding me of something I couldn't quite put my finger on. Then I remembered that I had been to this town some ten or twelve years earlier with my father. He loved to go out for a drive on a Sunday and explore the area, and Sarah and I loved to accompany him. We'd stand up in the back seat and sing songs with him, songs from his own distant childhood, so familiar and lovely to him that we could both hear that strange, sad love in his voice as we sang. Unexpectedly, and consciously for the first time since his death, I missed my father.

The one time I had visited him in the hospital, I had to wait outside in the hallways briefly. The smells and sounds were so familiar—the sweet disinfectant and wax, always an aroma of overcooked food in the background, the metallic clinks of IV poles as they were pushed along the floor on their stands. Yet I was only visiting, passing through. I had felt alone and without purpose, unidentified, not sure how to act. How, more than a year after his death, I again didn't know how to act. I didn't want to ignore the grief or even get over it, because that would mean I hadn't loved my father. When my horse died, I had cried almost continuously for days. The loss was pure and uncomplicated. Loving my father had been a different matter. I finally and suddenly found myself consumed with a longing for his presence.

I started imagining my father standing next to me in the hospital, visiting   20 me. With all my might I strained to hear the background noises of the hospital, feel the starch of the sheets, and hear my father's footsteps approaching, hear the rustle of his clothes as he stood near me, his cough to see if I was awake. I'd imagine opening my eyes very slowly, very carefully, and try to see him, standing beside my hospital bed. All I could conjure was the vaguest of outlines, a passing detail that only seemed to obscure the rest of him: how his watch fitted on his wrist, how he would trace the edge of his ear with one finger.

Spending as much time as I did looking in the mirror, I thought I knew what I looked like. So it came as a shock one afternoon toward the end of that summer when I went shopping with my mother for a new shirt and saw my face in the harsh fluorescent light of the fitting room. Pulling the new shirt on over my head, I caught a glimpse of my reflection that was itself being reflected in a mirror opposite, reversing my face as I usually saw it. I stood there motionless, the shirt only halfway on, my skin extra pale from the lighting, and saw how asymmetrical my face was. How had that happened? Walking up to the mirror, reaching up to touch the right side, where the graft had been put in only a year before, I saw clearly that most of it had disappeared, melted away into nothing. I felt distraught at the sight and even more distraught that it had taken so long to notice. My eyes had been secretly working against me, making up for the asymmetry as it gradually reappeared. This reversed image of myself was the true image, the way other people saw me.

I felt like such a fool. I'd been walking around with a secret notion of promised beauty, and here was the reality. When I saw Dr. Baker a few weeks later, I wanted desperately to ask him what had gone wrong, but I found myself speechless. Besides, I knew that the graft had been reabsorbed by my body—the doctor had warned me it might happen. He spoke of waiting a few years before trying any more big operations, of letting me grow some more. We spoke about a series of minor operations that would make readjustments to what was already there, but there was only vague talk of any new grafts, of putting more soft tissue or bone in place. Sitting in his expensively decorated office, I felt utterly powerless. Realizing I was going to have to change my ideals and expectations was one thing, but knowing what to replace them with was another.

That unexpected revelation in the store's fitting room mirror marked a turning point in my life. I began having overwhelming attacks of shame at unpredictable intervals. The first one came as I was speaking to Hans, my boss at the stable. He was describing how he wanted me to ride a certain horse. I was looking him in the eye as he spoke, and he was looking me in the eye. Out of nowhere came an intense feeling that he shouldn't be looking at me, that I was too horrible to look at, that I wasn't worthy of being looked at, that my ugliness was equal to a great personal failure. Inside I was churning and shrinking, desperate for a way to get out of this. I took the only course of action I knew I was any good at: I acted as if nothing were wrong. Steadying myself, breathing deeply, I kept looking him in the eye, determined that he should know nothing of what I was thinking.

That summer I started riding horses for Hans in local schooling shows. In practice I always wore a helmet with my hair hanging loose beneath it, but etiquette required that during shows my hair be tucked neatly up beneath the helmet, out of sight. I put this off until the very last minute, trying to act casual as I reached for the rubber band and hair net. This simple act of lifting my hair and exposing my face was among the hardest things I ever had to do, as hard as facing Dr. Woolf, harder than facing operations. I gladly would have undergone any amount of physical pain to keep my hair down. No one at the show grounds ever commented to me about it, and certainly no one there was going to make fun of me, but I was beyond that point. By then I was perfectly capable of doing it all to myself.

The habits of self-consciousness, of always looking down and hiding my   25
face behind my hair or my hand, were so automatic by now that I was blind to
them. When my mother pointed out these habits to me in the hope of making
me stop, telling me they directed even more attention to my face, she might as
well have been telling me to change the color of my eyes.

I fantasized about breakthroughs in reconstructive surgery, about winning
the lottery and buying my own private island, about being abducted by space
aliens who'd fix me up and plop me back in the midst of a surprised public.
And there were still acts of heroism waiting to be thrust upon me, whole bus-
loads of babies to be saved and at least one, there had to be at least one out
there, wise older man who would read about my heroism in the papers, fall in
love with my inner beauty, and whisk me away from the annoyance of existence as defined by Spring Valley High School.

During the eleventh and twelfth grades I had several small operations. The
hospital was the only place on earth where I didn't feel self-conscious. My face
was my battle scar, my badge of honor. The people in the plastic surgery ward
hated their gorgeously hooked noses, their wise lines, their exquisitely thin
lips. Beauty, as defined by society at large, seemed to be only about who was
best at looking like everyone else. If *I* had my original face, an undamaged face,
I would know how to appreciate it, know how to see the beauty of it. Yet each
time I was wheeled down to the surgical wing, high on the drugs, I'd think to
myself, *Now, now I can start my life, just as soon as I wake up from this operation.*
And no matter how disappointed I felt when I woke up and looked in the mirror, I'd simply postpone happiness until the next operation. I knew there would
always be another operation, another chance for my life to finally begin.

In the wake of my recurring disappointment I'd often chide myself for
thinking I'd ever be beautiful enough, good enough, or worthy enough of
someone else's love, let alone my own. Who cared if I loved my own face if no
one else was going to? What was beauty for, after all, if not to attract the attention of men, of lovers? When I walked down a street or hallway, sometimes
men would whistle at me from a distance, call me *Baby*, yell out and ask me my
name. I was thin, I had a good figure, and my long blond hair, when I bothered
to brush it, was pretty. I would walk as fast as possible, my head bent down, but
sometimes they'd catch up with me, or I'd be forced to pass by them. Their
comments would stop instantly when they saw my face, their sudden silence
potent and damning.

Life in general was cruel and offered only different types of voids and
chaos. The only way to tolerate it, to have any hope of escaping it, I reasoned,
was to know my own strength, to defy life by surviving it. Sitting in math class,
I'd look around and try to gauge who among my classmates could have lived
through this trauma, certain that none of them could. I had already read a great
deal about the Holocaust, but now we were reading first-person accounts by

Elie Wiesel and Primo Levi in social studies. I was completely transported by their work, and the more I absorbed of their message, the more my everyday life took on a surreal quality. Now everything, *everything*, seemed important. The taste of salt and peanut butter and tomatoes, the smell of car fumes, the small ridge of snow on the inside sill of a barely open window. I thought that this was how to live in the present moment, to resee the world: continuously imagine a far worse reality. At these moments, the life I was leading seemed unimportant, uncomplicated. Sometimes I could truly find refuge in the world of my private senses, but just as often I disingenuously affected a posture of repose, using it as a weapon against people I envied and feared, as a way of feeling superior to and thus safe from them.

30   After the section on the Holocaust, my social studies class moved on to art history. One day I walked into class late and found the lights off. My teacher was just about to show slides. Giacometti's sculptures flashed on the wall, their elongated arms simultaneously pointing toward and away from the world, while their long legs held them tall and gracefully but tenuously. Next were de Chirico's paintings, with the shadows from unseen others falling directly across the paths of the visible. I had seen Munch's "The Scream" and had identified it with my own occasional desire to let out a howl, but it was only at that moment, sitting in that darkened classroom, that I understood the figure might not be screaming himself but shielding his ears from and dropping his mouth open in shock at the sound of someone, or something, else's loud, loud lament. Matisse's paintings seemed to be about how simple it was to see the world in a beautiful way. Picasso's were about how complex, how difficult, beauty was.

The poems we read in English class had similar effects on me. My taste was not always sophisticated, but I did read poetry by Keats, Emily Dickinson, and Wallace Stevens, which moved me in ways I couldn't understand. It was, in part, the very lack of understanding that was so moving. I would read Keats's "Ode to a Nightingale" and feel that something important and necessary was being said here, but the moment I tried to examine the words, dissect the sentences, the meaning receded.

Senior year I applied to and was accepted at Sarah Lawrence College with a generous scholarship. Not sure what to do with my life, I decided to work toward medical school. The day senior class yearbook photos were taken, I purposefully cut school, and I threw away all the subsequent notices warning that unless I attended the makeup shoot, my photo would not appear in the yearbook.

Engaging the Text

1. How does Grealy's disfigurement sensitize her to the depiction of the other in paintings and works of literature?

2. In what way do the horses Grealy cares for, the books she reads, and the writing to which she is committed provide a refuge for her? How would you characterize the style and tone of Grealy's account?

3. What occasionally allowed Grealy to get beyond feelings of shame about her appearance? How did she struggle with the cultural conditioning that many people internalize?

Exploring Your Cultural Perspective

1. Compare the current popularity of cosmetic surgery to reconstruct people's faces and bodies to match an idealized "norm" with Grealy's account of reconstruction to achieve an approximation of normalcy. In what sense do these procedures illustrate society's intolerance toward those who look different? If money were not an issue, would you "fix" your face through cosmetic surgery? Why or why not?

2. Is there something in your life that serves the same function that horses, books, and writing did for Grealy? Describe what that refuge is and the satisfactions it provides.

3. The premise of the classic *Twilight Zone* episode "The Eye of the Beholder" was based on a startling reversal of expectations. A woman considered beautiful by "normal" standards undergoes an operation to transform her so that she will look like everyone else in a society whose people appear—by our standards—grotesque. What does this suggest about how beauty is culturally determined? (See Figures 6.2 and 6.3 on page 404. To see more images from this episode, go to the Web site Pete's Twilight Zone at <http://members.fortunecity.com/tzarchive/picture_pages/tzpictures042.html>.

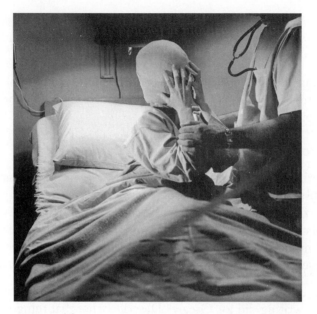

FIGURE 6.2

FIGURE 6.3

PAUL MONETTE

Borrowed Time: An AIDS Memoir

Before the emergence of AIDS in the early 1980s, homosexuality had begun to gain a level of acceptance previously denied it in American society. Paul Monette (who died of AIDS in 1995) is an eloquent witness to the horrifying physical and psychological effects of this disease. Monette was a distinguished writer of poetry, novels, and autobiographical volumes. His nonfiction works include *Borrowed Time: An AIDS Memoir* (1988), which was nominated for a National Book Critics Circle Award, and *Becoming a Man: Half a Life Story* (1992), which won the National Book Award for nonfiction. He is also the author of *Last Watch of the Night: Essays Too Personal and Otherwise* (1994) and (posthumously) *Sanctuary: A Tale of Life in the Woods* (1997).

Thinking Critically

As you read this essay, think about Monette's analysis of the profound effects of AIDS on society. In what ways are people with AIDS thought of as being the other?

I don't know if I will live to finish this. Doubtless there's a streak of self-importance in such an assertion, but who's counting? Maybe it's just that I've watched too many sicken in a month and die by Christmas, so that a fatal sort of realism comforts me more than magic. All I know is this: The virus ticks in me. And it doesn't care a whit about our categories—when is full-blown, what's AIDS-related, what is just sick and tired? No one has solved the puzzle of its timing. I take my drug from Tijuana twice a day. The very friends who tell me how vigorous I look, how well I seem, are the first to assure me of the imminent medical breakthrough. What they don't seem to understand is, I used up all my optimism keeping my friend alive. Now that he's gone, the cup of my own health is neither half full nor half empty. Just half.

Equally difficult, of course, is knowing where to start. The world around me is defined now by its endings and its closures—the date on the grave that follows the hyphen. Roger Horwitz, my beloved friend, died of complications of AIDS on October 22, 1986, nineteen months and ten days after his diagnosis. That is the only real date anymore, casting its ice shadow over all the secular holidays lovers mark their calendars by. Until that long night in October, it didn't seem possible that any day could supplant the brute equinox of March 12—the day of Roger's diagnosis in 1985, the day we began to live on the moon.

The fact is, no one knows where to start with AIDS. Now, in the seventh year of the calamity, my friends in L.A. can hardly recall what it felt like any longer, the time before the sickness. Yet we all watched the toll mount in New York, then in San Francisco, for years before it ever touched us here. It comes like a slowly dawning horror. At first you are equipped with a hundred different amulets to keep it far away. Then someone you know goes into the hospital, and suddenly you are at high noon in full battle gear. They have neglected to tell you that you will be issued no weapons of any sort. So you cobble together a weapon out of anything that lies at hand, like a prisoner honing a spoon handle into a stiletto. You fight tough, you fight dirty, but you cannot fight dirtier than it.

I remember a Saturday in February 1982, driving Route 10 to Palm Springs with Roger to visit his parents for the weekend. While Roger drove, I read aloud an article from *The Advocate:* "Is Sex Making Us Sick?" There was the slightest edge of irony in the query, an urban cool that seems almost bucolic now in its innocence. But the article didn't mince words. It was the first in-depth reporting I'd read that laid out the shadowy nonfacts of what till then had been the most fragmented of rumors. The first cases were reported to the Centers for Disease Control (CDC) only six months before, but they weren't in the newspapers, not in L.A. I noted in my diary in December '81 ambiguous reports of a "gay cancer," but I know I didn't have the slightest picture of the thing. Cancer of the *what*? I would have asked, if anyone had known anything.

5   I remember exactly what was going through my mind while I was reading, though I can't now recall the details of the piece. I was thinking: How is this not me? Trying to find a pattern I was exempt from. It was a brand of denial I would watch grow exponentially during the next few years, but at the time I was simply relieved. Because the article appeared to be saying that there was a grim progression toward this undefined catastrophe, a set of preconditions—chronic hepatitis, repeated bouts of syphilis, exotic parasites. No wonder my first baseline response was to feel safe. It was *them*—by which I meant the fast-lane Fire Island crowd, the Sutro Baths, the world of High Eros.

Not us.

I grabbed for that relief because we'd been through a rough patch the previous autumn. Till then Roger had always enjoyed a sort of no-nonsense good health: not an abuser of anything, with a constitutional aversion to hypochondria, and not wed to his mirror save for a minor alarm as to the growing dimensions of his bald spot. In the seven years we'd been together I scarcely remember him having a cold or taking an aspirin. Yet in October '81 he had struggled with a peculiar bout of intestinal flu. Nothing special showed up in any of the blood tests, but over a period of weeks he experienced persistent symptoms that didn't neatly connect: pains in his legs, diarrhea, general malaise. I hadn't been feeling notably bad myself, but on the other hand I was a textbook hypochondriac, and I figured if Rog was harboring some kind of bug, so was I.

The two of us finally went to a gay doctor in the Valley for a further set of blood tests. It's a curious phenomenon among gay middle-class men that anything faintly venereal had better be taken to a doctor who's "on the bus." Is it a sense of fellow feeling perhaps, or a way of avoiding embarrassment? Do we really believe that only a doctor who's *our* kind can heal us of the afflictions that attach somehow to our secret hearts? There is so much magic to medicine. Of course we didn't know then that those few physicians with a large gay clientele were about to be swamped beyond all capacity to cope.

The tests came back positive for amoebiasis. Roger and I began the highly toxic treatment to kill the amoeba, involving two separate drugs and what seems in memory thirty pills a day for six weeks, till the middle of January. It was the first time I'd ever experienced the phenomenon of the cure making you sicker. By the end of treatment we were both weak and had lost weight, and for a couple of months afterward were susceptible to colds and minor infections.

It was only after the treatment was over that a friend of ours, diagnosed *10* with amoebas by the same doctor, took his slide to the lab at UCLA for a second opinion. And that was my first encounter with lab error. The doctor at UCLA explained that the slide had been misread; the squiggles that looked like amoebas were in fact benign. The doctor shook his head and grumbled about "these guys who do their own lab work." Roger then retrieved his slide, took it over to UCLA and was told the same: no amoebas. We had just spent six weeks methodically ingesting poison for no reason at all.

So it wasn't the *Advocate* story that sent up the red flag for us. We'd been shaken by the amoeba business, and from that point on we operated at a new level of sexual caution. What is now called safe sex did not use to be so clearly defined. The concept didn't exist. But it was quickly becoming apparent, even then, that we couldn't wait for somebody else to define the parameters. Thus every gay man I know has had to come to a point of personal definition by way of avoiding the chaos of sexually transmitted diseases, or STD as we call them in the trade. There was obviously no one moment of conscious decision, a bolt of clarity on the shimmering freeway west of San Bernardino, but I think of that day when I think of the sea change. The party was going to have to stop. The evidence was too ominous: *We were making ourselves sick.*

Not that Roger and I were the life of the party. Roger especially didn't march to the different drum of *so many men, so little time*, the motto and anthem of the sunstruck summers of the mid-to-late seventies. He'd managed not to carry away from his adolescence the mark of too much repression, or indeed the yearning to make up for lost time. In ten years he had perhaps half a dozen contacts outside the main frame of our relationship, mostly when he was out of town on business. He was comfortable with relative monogamy, even at a time when certain quarters of the gay world found the whole idea trivial and bourgeois. I realize that in the world of the heterosexual there is a generalized lip service paid to exclusive monogamy, a notion most vividly honored in the breach. I leave the matter of morality to those with the gift of tongues; it was difficult enough for us to fashion a sexual ethics just for us. In any case, I was the one in the relationship who suffered from lost time. I was the one who would go after a sexual encounter as if it were an ice cream cone—casual, quick, good-bye.

But as I say, who's counting? I only want to make it plain to start with that we got very alert and very careful as far back as the winter of '82. That gut need for safety took hold and lingered, even as we got better again and strong. Thus I'm not entirely sure what I thought on another afternoon a year and a half later, when a friend of ours back from New York reported a conversation he'd had with a research man from Sloan-Kettering.

"He think all it takes is one exposure," Charlie said, this after months of articles about the significance of repeated exposure. More tenaciously than ever, we all wanted to believe the whole deepening tragedy was centered on those at the sexual frontiers who were fucking their brains out. The rest of us were fashioning our own little Puritan forts, as we struggled to convince ourselves that a clean slate would hold the nightmare at bay.

15   Yet with caution as our watchword starting in February of '82, Roger was diagnosed with AIDS three years later. So the turning over of new leaves was not to be on everybody's side. A lot of us were already ticking and didn't even know. The magic circle my generation is trying to stay within the borders of is only as real as the random past. Perhaps the young can live in the magic circle, but only if those of us who are ticking will tell our story. Otherwise it goes on being *us* and *them* forever, built like a wall higher and higher, till you no longer think to wonder if you are walling it out or in.

Engaging the Text

1. How is Monette's account of coming to terms with AIDS personally also a reflection of mainstream culture's recognition of the problem?

2. Discuss how Monette came to understand the way in which AIDS placed still another barrier between heterosexuals and homosexuals.

3. What stylistic effect does Monette achieve by interweaving memories with commentary? Does this device prevent his account from becoming self-pitying? Why or why not?

Exploring Your Cultural Perspective

1. On the Internet, research the Supreme Court ruling of June 25, 1998, that those diagnosed as HIV positive are entitled to full disability benefits, even if they are asymptomatic, and discuss how this decision has altered public perception. Write an argumentative essay in which you identify the controversy surrounding the issue, state your position in a clear thesis, and present evidence to support your view. Acknowledging opposing viewpoints will make your essay more persuasive.

2. Rent a copy of the film *And the Band Played On* (1993), *Philadelphia* (1994), or *Indian Summer* (1996) and analyze it to discover how it portrays those with AIDS. What insights does the film offer as to why society stigmatizes some diseases but not others?

BRUCE SPRINGSTEEN

Streets of Philadelphia

The impact of AIDS has seldom been dramatized with greater poignancy than in the lyrics for the song "Streets of Philadelphia" by Bruce Springsteen. From the film *Philadelphia*, which stars Tom Hanks and Denzel Washington, this song won the 1994 Academy Award for best original song. In the film Hanks plays a lawyer who is dismissed from a prestigious Philadelphia law firm when it is learned that he has AIDS. Washington plays the lawyer who agrees to take on his suit against the firm. In the course of the movie, Hanks's condition worsens, and the initially homophobic Washington comes to recognize that Hanks is just like anyone else who is dying painfully and too soon. Springsteen has given innumerable U.S. and international concert tours, and he received the Grammy Award for best male rock vocalist in 1984, 1987, and 1994. His albums include *Born to Run* (1975), *Born in the U.S.A.* (1984), *Tunnel of Love* (1987), and *Bruce Springsteen's Greatest Hits* (1995), and *Live in New York City* (2001).

Thinking Critically

As you read, consider how this song (written and performed by a celebrity of Springsteen's magnitude) could change the public perception of AIDS victims.

I was bruised and battered: I couldn't tell what I felt.
I was unrecognizable to myself.
Saw my reflection in a window and didn't know my own face.
Oh, brother are you gonna leave me wastin' away on the streets of
    Philadelphia.
5 Ain't no angel gonna greet me: it's just you and I, my friend.
And my clothes don't fit me no more: I walked a thousand miles just to slip
    this skin.

I walked the avenue till my legs felt like stone.
I heard the voices of friends vanished and gone.
At night I could hear the blood in my veins
Just as black and whispering as the rain   *10*
On the streets of Philadelphia.
Ain't no angel gonna greet me: it's just you and I, my friend.
And my clothes don't fit me no more: I walked a thousand miles just to slip
   this skin.

The night has fallen, I'm lying awake.
I can feel myself fading away.   *15*
So, receive me, brother, with your faithless kiss.
Or will we leave each other alone like this
On the streets of Philadelphia?

Ain't no angel gonna greet me: it's just you and I, my friend.
And my clothes don't fit me no more: I walked a thousand miles just to slip   *20*
   this skin.

Engaging the Text

1. How would you characterize the voice you hear in these lyrics? What images convey the speaker's sense of "losing himself" as a result of having AIDS?

2. How does being acknowledged as a person become a central theme in the song? At what point in the lyrics does the speaker appeal for this recognition?

3. Rent a copy of the 1994 film *Philadelphia* and evaluate how the song "Streets of Philadelphia" was used to evoke certain moods at different points in the movie. How does reading the lyrics differ from hearing Springsteen sing the song (on his *Greatest Hits* CD, 1995).

Exploring Your Cultural Perspective

1. To communicate the speaker's feelings effectively, Springsteen had to avoid depicting those with AIDS in a sentimental or stereotyped fashion. In your opinion, did he succeed? What impact do these lyrics have on you?

2. Analyze another song about a social issue. How do the words and the music influence the emotional response of listeners?

CONSTANCE CLASSEN

The Odour of the Other

Odor is both a personal and a social phenomenon, but what is considered to be fragrant or foul-smelling is not as absolute as we might imagine. The perception of odor varies from culture to culture and is often a means by which the in-group validates the exclusion of others. Constance Classen's analysis of how odors serve as signifiers of cultural identity reveals that odor is truly in the nose of the beholder. Classen teaches at Harvard, where she specialized in the cross-cultural study of sensory symbolism. "The Odour of the Other" is drawn from *Worlds of Sense: Exploring the Senses in History and Across Cultures* (1993). Her most recent works include *Aroma: The Cultural History of Smell* (1995) and *The Color of Angels: Cosmology, Gender and the Aesthetic Imagination* (1998).

Thinking Critically

In what way does the perception of smell provide a subtle means for including or excluding groups of people? How might odor become another way to divide "us" from "them"?

By exploring the ways in which olfactory symbolism is used to express themes of identity and difference in diverse cultures, including that of the West, I hope to show here the extent to which olfactory codes pervade classificatory thought, not only in "exotic" highly olfactory-conscious societies, but even in our own, rather "deodorized" society. To this end I will bring together examples of such symbolism from a wide variety of cultures. At the same time, the examination of how odours are used to categorize "others" in different societies, provides an important insight, or better, "inscent," into the construction of concepts of "oneness" and "otherness," and their basic similarities and differences across cultures.

ODOURS AND CLASS

The ascription of different characteristic odours to different races and different social groups is a universal trait and one which has a certain empirical basis:

body odours can differ among ethnic groups, due partly to the different foods consumed and partly to genetic factors. While all peoples give off odours, however, most people are so accustomed to their own personal and group scents as to not be aware of them and only notice the odours of others. Edmund Carpenter, for instance, reports the following interchange from his anthropological fieldwork among the Inuit:

> One day when Kowanerk [an Inuit woman] and I were alone, she looked up from the boot she was mending to ask, without preamble, "Do we smell?"
> "Yes."
> "Does the odor offend you?"
> "Yes."
> She sewed in silence for a while, then said, "You smell and it's offensive to us. We wondered if we smelled and if it offended you."

The widespread role of odour as a marker of social identity and difference led one early twentieth-century scientist to hypothesize that olfactory affinities and antipathies are an important means of group preservation. Whether this is true or not, the odour of the other does in fact often serve as a scapegoat for certain antipathies towards the other. This principle can be found to operate when members of one culture attribute an exaggeratedly offensive odour to members of another culture for whom they feel animosity for unrelated reasons. In the anti-Semitic Europe of the Middle Ages, for example, it was believed by many that Jews emitted a reek so horrible that they could only rid themselves of it by Christian baptism or by drinking the blood of a Christian child!

Blacks have also traditionally been assigned a foul odour by mainstream Western culture, evidenced both in descriptions by early European anthropologists of the "stench" of Africans, and in white stereotypes of "repulsive-smelling" blacks in the American South. John Dollard writes in *Caste and Class in a Southern Town*:

> Among beliefs which profess to show that Negro and white people cannot intimately participate in the same civilization is the perennial one that Negroes have a smell extremely disagreeable to white people . . . White people generally regard this argument as a crushing final proof of the impossibility of close association between the races.

White Westerners, in turn, are often, to their surprise, perceived as foul-smelling by members of other cultures and races.

It is evident in most such cases that the stench ascribed to the other is far less a response to an actual perception of the odour of the other than a potent metaphor for the social decay it is feared the other, often simply by virtue of its being "other," will cause in the established order. On a small scale we say that something or someone "stinks" when it or they disagree with our notion of propriety, on a large scale we apply this metaphor to whole groups of people. Therefore, while we may feel an antipathy towards something or someone because its or their odour offends us, we may equally ascribe an offensive odour to something because we feel an antipathy for it (or indeed the two elements may operate simultaneously so as to reinforce each other).

5   The use of olfactory symbolism as a means of expressing and regulating cultural identity and difference is found in a great many societies. A particularly well-elaborated example of the olfactory classification of different social groups is provided by the Tukano-speaking tribes of the Colombian Amazon. According to this Amazonian culture, all members of a tribe share the same general body odour which is said to mark the territory of the tribe in the same way that animals mark their territories through odour. This territorial odour is called *mahsá sëríri*, and has the metaphorical meaning of "sympathy" or "tribal feeling."

The specific odour of each tribal group is considered to be caused by the different foods it customarily eats. Thus, it is said of the intermarrying Desana, Pira-Tapuya and Tukano tribes that the Desana, who are hunters, smell of meat, the Pira-Tapuya, associated with fishing, smell of fish, and the Tukano, associated with agriculture, of roots. It is held to be possible to recognize the distinct "odour trails" laid down by these different exogamic groups within the general communal territory. Indeed, when travelling from one region to another, members of these tribes continually sniff the air and remark on the different territorial and tribal odours. These distinct group odours all have different symbolic associations which serve to order the interaction between one tribe and another. Odour thus functions in this Amazonian society as a marker of tribal identity and territory, and as a regulator of intertribal relations.

The establishment of social boundaries through recourse to olfactory markers can take place within communities as well as between them. It is common, for instance, for the dominant class in a society to characterize itself as pleasant-smelling, or inodorate, and the subordinate class as foul-smelling. In ancient Greece, for example, Socrates opposed the use of perfume by men on the principle that it masked the natural olfactory distinctions between freemen and slaves: "If you perfume a slave and a freeman, the difference of their birth produces none in the smell; and the scent is perceived as soon in the one as in the other."

In nineteenth- and early twentieth-century Europe, the principal olfactory distinction was between the upper class, who lived in clean, inodorate or fragrant environment and used light delicate scents, and the working class, who lived in a dirty, foul-smelling environment, and used heavy coarse scents. Somerset Maugham wrote in 1927:

In the West we are divided from our fellows by our sense of smell . . . I do not blame the working man because he stinks, but stink he does. It makes social intercourse difficult to persons of a sensitive nostril.

George Orwell likewise argued that the "real secret of class distinctions in the West" could be "summed up in four frightful words . . . *The lower classes smell*." It is odour, according to Orwell, which serves to make the class barrier impassable:

Race-hatred, religious hatred, differences of education, of temperament, of intellect, even differences of moral code, can be got over; but physical repulsion cannot.

The social hierarchy of smell described by Maugham and Orwell is also evidenced in the imaginative literature of the period. In *My Lady Ludlow* by Elizabeth Gaskell, for example, the superfine sensibility of an aristocrat is described in terms of her olfactory preferences:

The choice of odours was what my lady piqued herself upon, saying nothing showed birth like a keen susceptibility of smell. We never named musk in her presence . . . her opinion on the subject was believed to be, that no scent derived from an animal could ever be of a sufficiently pure nature to give pleasure to any person of good family.

Indeed, even musky-scented flowers were suspect. If a suitor of one of Lady Ludlow's maids appeared wearing an offending sprig in his buttonhole, "she was afraid that he liked coarse pleasures, and I am not sure if she did not think that his preference for this coarse sweetness did not imply a probability that he would take to drinking."

If the olfactory delicacy of the upper class was due to the fineness of its sense of smell, the olfactory promiscuity indulged in by the working class was reputed to be the result of a dull sense of smell. As a Victorian perfumer explains:

Among the lower orders, bad smells are little heeded; in fact "noses have they, but they smell not"; and the result is, a continuance to live in an atmosphere laden with poisonous odours, whereas anyone with the least power of smelling retained shuns such odours, as they would anything else that is vile or pernicious.

As these citations make plain, the working classes' apparent proclivity for "disreputable" odours was considered an index of their propensity for all else that was disreputable. As is also evident, these olfactory class distinctions were not thought to be based on mere social circumstance, but rather on fundamental differences in the quality of the sense of smell itself between the classes.

The odour of the proletarian other in nineteenth-century Europe was *10* often real enough: many workers did reek of the filthy conditions in which they lived and worked. The disapprobation accorded this reek by the middle and upper classes, however, was as much a product of certain social sensibilities as of natural olfactory sensibilities. Orwell, for example, admits as much by saying that "even 'lower class' people whom you knew to be quite clean—servants, for instance—were faintly unappetising. The smell of their sweat, the very texture of their skins were mysteriously different from yours."

Indeed, in previous centuries members of the European aristocracy had reeked just as much as anyone. The typical stench of the elaborate wigs affected by the eighteenth-century nobility, for instance, led one English writer of the time to comment that he had had "the honour of smelling in the most unsavoury manner very many heads of the first rank," "rank" wittily conveying here both class and reek. So closely associated were certain "foul" odours with the nobility of the day, that, according to the contemporary playwright Sebastien Chamfort, one provincial gentleman, on returning home from Versailles, ordered his servants to urinate around his manor so that his home would acquire the same aristocratic aroma as that famed court. Thus while certain odours, such as that of urine, tend to be universally disliked, cultural norms can make these odours a matter of indifference or even of appeal. Just as "beauty is in the eye of the beholder," so "fragrance is in the nose of the smeller."

With this in mind, let us turn to the rigorous olfactory class division effected by the Dassanetch of Southwestern Ethiopia. The Dassanetch divide themselves into cattle-raising pastoralists and fishermen. As cattle are of pre-eminent practical and symbolic importance for the Dassanetch, pastoralists are regarded as greatly superior to fishermen. Each of these two social groups is identified with the odour of the species of animal it depends on for its livelihood. The Dassanetch, in fact, believe that humans are naturally inodorate and that their odours are acquired through contact with their particular environments.

The value accorded cattle by the Dassanetch is such that the smell of everything associated with cattle is considered good, and the pastoralists do all they can to augment their identification with this prestigious odour:

> They often wash their hands in cattle urine; men smear manure on their bodies to advertise the fertility of their herds; and nubile girls and fertile women smear *ghee* [liquid butter] on their shoulders, heads, hair and bosoms to ensure fertility . . . The Dassanetch explicitly say that the smell of *ghee* serves to attract men and is the "perfume," so to speak, of women.

While other odours, such as those of flowers, are also considered good by the Dassanetch, the odour of cattle has the added characteristic of serving as a marker of group identity for the pastoralists.

As pastoralists are identified with the odour of cattle in Dassanetch society, so fishermen and their families are identified with the odour of fish. Unlike cattle, however, fish are symbolically suspect: they are considered to exist outside the natural cycles of weather and sexuality, so fundamental to the well-being and procreation of cattle. Fish, and the fishermen who are associated with them, are therefore said by the pastoralists to be foul-smelling. The supposed acyclical nature of fish makes their odour particularly noxious for, "unlike other bad smells, which come and go, stimulate awareness, and evaporate, the bad smell of fish is a kind of stagnation and is permanently connected with [fishermen]." This belief is the foul odour of fishermen is so strongly held by the "upper-class" pastoralists that they will hold their noses when walking by fishermen's huts. Although a certain amount of interchange takes place between the two groups, usually to the advantage of the pastoralists, the social and olfactory barriers between them are so rigidly established as to prevent any merging of identities.

It is noteworthy that for most outsiders the smell of the Dassanetch pastoralists, perfumed with butter, manure and cattle urine, would probably be more repellent than that of the fishermen, who apparently do not make any special effort to give themselves a piscine odour. Nonetheless, the social and olfactory codes of Dassanetch society state definitively that pastoralists are good-smelling and fishermen bad-smelling. Evidently, here again the standards of olfactory classification are being strongly influenced by cultural considerations. The odour of cattle is held to be superior to that of fish by the Dassanetch because cattle are considered superior to fish. The odour of pastoralists, who are identified with cattle and form the elite within Dassanetch society, is therefore considered good, while that of fishermen, who are identified with the inferior fish, is considered bad.

The odour of the fisherman other is classified as foul by the dominant pastoralists, however, not only because fish and fishermen constitute an "inferior" and "alien" group, but also—as seems to be the rule in such cases—because the pastoralists perceive them as threatening decay within their own community. For the pastoralists, the world of fish and fishermen, independent as it apparently is from periodic cycles, represents a world without order which can disrupt the orderly cycles on which their own bovine world depends. The pastoralists' repugnance to the odour of fish and fishermen is thus above all a repugnance to the disorder which it represents. This repugnance is heightened by the fear that disorder, like odour, has the ability to transgress boundaries. The pastoralists, for example, believe that "the bad smell of fishermen can infect the cattle."

The fact that the two groups are not entirely separate but constitute one interdependent community probably only increases the pastoralists' concern to safeguard their own identity and social structure from external forces of corruption. Even within the general order of a society, therefore, certain peoples can represent disorder from the perspective of the dominant class and as a result be attributed the foul smell of decay.

WHEN ONE BECOMES OTHER

In *Gulliver's Travels*, when Gulliver returns home from his voyages, he finds that he cannot abide the odour of his family. Even after having been home for five years, Gulliver can still barely tolerate the smell of other humans. He states:

> I began last week to permit my wife to sit at dinner with me, at the far-thest end of a long table . . . Yet the smell of a [human] continuing very offensive, I always keep my nose well stopped with rue, lavender, or tobacco leaves.

This olfactory antipathy was instilled in Gulliver during his stay in a land in which human-like creatures, called Yahoos, manifested all the coarsest vices, and horse-like creatures, called Houyhnhmns, the highest virtues. On return-ing home after this experience Gulliver found that his cultural and olfactory antipodes had become inverted: he felt at odds with his own kind, and at one with horses:

> The first money I laid out [on returning] was to buy two young stone-horses, which I keep in a good stable, and next to them the groom is my greatest favourite; for I feel my spirits revived by the smell he contracts in the stable. My horses understand me tolerably well; I converse with them at least four hours every day. They are strangers to bridle or saddle; they live in great amity with me, and friendship to each other.

For Gulliver humans had become the threatening other, dangerous "brutes" who leave the earth "reeking with the blood of its inhabitants," while nature had come to represent harmony and order. The olfactory consequence of this was that the odour of humans become repulsive to Gulliver, and the odour of horses attractive.

The olfactory reversal described so strikingly in *Gulliver's Travels* can be found in actual tales of journeys in which travelers are assimilated into other cultures and odours. One such case deals with a young white man, Manuel Cordova, who was captured by an Amazonian tribe in the early twentieth cen-tury. Cordova's first olfactory impression of his captors was that they had a strange, musky odour. In turn, the Amazonians apparently did not consider Cordova to have quite the right "odour of culture," for, as part of their rite of tribal initiation, they brushed Cordova's body with fragrant leaves and bathed him with a fragrant liquid.

20   After a period of living with the tribe, Cordova became "attuned" to its olfactory traits. Eventually, however, he began to long to return to his own people. "It was at this time," he states, "that I began to notice again the smell

of these people, a strange, persistent musky odor that I began to dislike." As his dissatisfaction with tribal life grew, Cordova found that the "overpowering musky smell" of the tribe "nauseated" him. The Indians had once more become "other" for Cordova and he returned to the world of whites. One can imagine that, without the cultural and olfactory re-reversal that Cordova experienced before returning to his own people, he would have found himself in a similar predicament to Gulliver on his return home.

A similar "olfactory reversal" is sometimes described as occurring after a journey to the world of the supernatural. An example of this is found in the legend of the twelfth-century Dutch mystic, Christina Mirabilis. Christina, on resurrecting shortly after her death, found that her experience of the divine fragrance had rendered her unable to abide the odour of humans. It was only after she immersed herself in a baptismal fount and was symbolically born again that she was once again able to tolerate the odour of humans and live among them.

One's own odour is also often altered through association with the supernatural in the traditions of different cultures. In the West holy persons were believed to manifest an "odour of sanctity," signalling the presence of the Holy Spirit, while the wicked manifested the stench of the Devil. Similarly, among the Warao of Venezuela, the bad breath of the sorcerer indicates that he has recently returned from a journey to the foul underworld.

Those persons who come into the presence of supernatural beings without undergoing the correct olfactory transformation are experienced as "other" by such beings. In a legend of the Andes the daughter of a mountain deity falls in love with a human and tries to hide him in her home. Her parents discover the man by his foul odour, however, and he is forced to leave the supernatural abode. In ancient Egypt the dead king had to be perfumed with incense in order to be accepted by the gods:

> The use of [incense] in assuring the divinity of the dead king is important, for when he goes to the Horizon or the West he is most easily accepted by the gods when he is like them, and being like them means among other things that "your scent is as their scent . . ."

For the ancient Egyptians, incense was the scent of the gods. By acquiring this scent, the king affirmed his basic identity with the gods: "My sweat is the sweat of Horus, my odour is the odour of Horus."

One can become other not only through contact with others, but also through a change in one's social status, which often produces a corresponding change in one's olfactory status (and vice versa). In Bororo society, for instance, new parents, who constitute a particularly anomalous class, are surrounded by olfactory taboos: they are not supposed to engage in strenuous labour because the odours of sexual fluids would be harmful to their child. New mothers are not allowed to prepare food for others for their "stench" would be communicated through the food and harm those who ate it. In parts of Southern Europe, the anomalous nature of couples who contracted what was considered a social inappropriate marriage was traditionally signaled by incensing the couple's house with foul smoke. In such cases, olfactory symbolism is used to mark a person's separation, temporary or permanent, from cultural norms.

25   Significantly, individuals who feel themselves to be cut off from society can sometimes attribute a foul odour to themselves. Such persons imagine that their bodies give off putrid emanations, often as a result of an inherent fault or evil within themselves, which cause them to be socially isolated. Interestingly, this disorder is particularly found in Japan. The sufferers tend to be timid young men, who believe that the odours they emit are so repugnant that they avoid contact with others, and constantly wash and deodorize themselves. This disorder would seem to be a literal actualization of the expression "to be in ill odour," meaning to be in a state of social disfavour. One feels that, in some intrinsic way, one is "other" within one's society, and one imagines that this "otherness" is communicated to one's fellows through a distinguishing evil odour.

. . .

Odours are symbolically employed by many cultures to serve as identifying marks of different classes of beings. The attractive/repulsive nature of olfactory experience makes odour a particularly useful symbolic vehicle for categorizing different groups according to cultural values, as it invests classificatory systems with a strong emotive power. The inhalation of a foul odour, for instance, produces the immediate physical repugnance a society might demand its members feel in response to a particular class of people. To characterize a certain group as foul-smelling, therefore, is to render it repellent at a very basic physical and emotional level, and not simply at a cognitive level. Likewise, to characterize a group as fragrant is to render it attractive, although this attractiveness may be tempered by connotations of underlying danger.

Such categorizations are not always absolute, for the same group may sometimes be characterized as fragrant, and sometimes as foul. In the West, for example, a woman may be a fragrant maiden in one context, and a foul witch in another. Similarly, among the Tukano, deer are sometimes seen as "clean, sleek forest maidens, sweet scented and seductive," and sometimes as "repulsive bitches in heat." This ambivalence of odour indicates the ambivalent attitudes of the dominant group towards those others it finds attractive on one level and repellent on another.

As a rule, the dominant group in a society ascribes to itself a pleasant or neutral smell within this system of olfactory classification. What constitutes a "pleasant" (or "unpleasant") odour is by no means universally agreed upon, however. For the Dassanetch of Ethiopia, the odour of cow manure is "pleasant" and serves as the identifying olfactory mark of the dominant group. In the West, where the odour of manure is considered "unpleasant," to identify a group as smelling of manure would be to place it in a position of exclusion and inferiority. Fragrance and foulness must therefore always be understood within a specific cultural context.

It is not only the strong emotional appeal of smell which makes odours useful for classifying others, but also the fact that it can be perceived at a distance and does not require intimate contact to be experienced. Thus, to label a group "foul," one does not need to have had any close association with it. At the same time, the ability of odours to travel through space renders them capable of crossing barriers.

This transitive character of odour symbolically expresses the ability of different classes of beings to transcend class boundaries. The foul other can invade one; the fragrant other, absorb one. Odour therefore comes to symbolize not only the qualities of the other, but also the ability of the other to disrupt one's own order. The disintegrative power of the odour of the other can be controlled through practices of strict separation of groups with different olfactory and cultural values, or through the use of powerful opposing odours—a classic example of the latter practice being the widespread use of fragrance to ward off evil spirits.

The very ability of odour to break down barriers, which renders it so dangerous in one regard, also makes it, however, a powerful force for integration. The incense employed in a religious ritual, for instance, serves not only to unite humans and gods, but also to unite the participants in the rite. With regard to this characteristic of odour, a shared smell can give the partakers a strong "we" feeling, while an interchange of personal or other odours between individuals and groups, such as takes place in many forms of greetings, can serve as a basis for the recognition and mediation of mutual differences.

Engaging the Text

1. How does Classen's analysis shed light on the ways in which different societies use odors as markers of social identity and difference? Why do odors elicit such a strong impulse to segregate people into groups?

2. What comparisons and contrasts does Classen use to emphasize important differences between in-groups and out-groups in various societies? Why is this organizational strategy particularly well suited to her discussion?

3. Classen includes a number of surprising quotes from such well-known authors as Socrates, Somerset Maugham, George Orwell, and Jonathan

Swift. In what sense do these quotes from literary sources strengthen Classen's argument?

Exploring Your Cultural Perspective

1. Discuss marketing techniques used to give value to specific aromas in contemporary U.S. culture (for example, car sprays that simulate a "new car smell").

2. What products do you use to mask or eliminate "offensive" odors? Which odors do you particularly like and particularly dislike? Explain why.

PAUL BARBER

The Real Vampire

The stories and legends about the "undead" reflected in the myth of the vampire tell us a great deal about the terror felt by Europeans several hundred years ago. The widespread paranoia produced by inexplicable deaths and the fear that evildoers had returned from the dead fostered the idea of the vampire. In "The Real Vampire" (which first appeared in the October 1990 issue of *Natural History*), Paul Barber discloses that the vampires of old were quite different from Hollywood's fictional portrayals. A research associate with the Fowler Museum of Cultural History, University of California, Los Angeles, Barber is the author of *Vampires, Burial and Death: Folklore and Reality* (1988). Studying how the vampire legend came into being can help us better understand how contemporary societies create new others, such as those with AIDS, in response to modern fears.

Thinking Critically

As you read Barber's essay, notice the range of evidence that he uses to develop his analysis. Consider the extent to which your concept of the vampire has been influenced by films, literature, Halloween costumes, and other artifacts of popular culture. What class-related values are implicit in Hollywood's depiction of the vampire?

I saw the Count lying within the box upon the earth, some of which the rude[1] falling from the cart had scattered over him. He was deathly pale, just like a waxen image, and the red eyes glared with the horrible vindictive look which I knew too well . . .

The eyes saw the sinking sun, and the look of hate in them turned to triumph.

But, on the instant, came the sweep and flash of Jonathan's great knife. I shrieked as I saw it shear through the throat; whilst at the same moment Mr. Morris's bowie knife plunged into the heart.

---

[1]*rude:* ignorant peasant—*Ed.*

It was like a miracle; but before our very eyes, and almost in the drawing of a breath, the whole body crumbled into dust and passed from our sight.
—BRAM STOKER, *Dracula*

If a typical vampire of folklore were to come to your house this Halloween, you might open the door to encounter a plump Slavic fellow with long fingernails and a stubbly beard, his mouth and left eye open, his face ruddy and swollen. He would wear informal attire—a linen shroud—and he would look for all the world like a disheveled peasant.

If you did not recognize him, it would be because you expected to see—as would most people today—a tall, elegant gentleman in a black cloak. But that would be the vampire of fiction—the count, the villain of Bram Stoker's novel and countless modern movies, based more or less on Vlad Tepes, a figure in Romanian history who was a prince, not a count; ruled in Walachia, not Transylvania; and was never viewed by the local populace as a vampire. Nor would he be recognized as one, bearing so little resemblance to the original Slavic revenant (one who returns from the dead)—the one actually called *upir* or *vampir.* But in folklore, the undead are seemingly everywhere in the world, in a variety of disparate cultures. They are people who, having died before their time, are believed to return to life to bring death to their friends and neighbors.

We know the European version of the vampire best and have a number of eyewitness accounts telling of the "killing" of bodies believed to be vampires. When we read these reports carefully and compare their findings with what is now known about forensic pathology, we can see why people believed that corpses came to life and returned to wreak havoc on the local population.

Europeans of the early 1700s showed a great deal of interest in the subject of the vampire. According to the *Oxford English Dictionary,* the word itself entered the English language in 1734, at a time when many books were being written on the subject, especially in Germany.

5   One reason for all the excitement was the Treaty of Passarowitz (1718), by which parts of Serbia and Walachia were turned over to Austria. The occupying forces, which remained there until 1739, began to notice, and file reports on, a peculiar local practice: exhuming bodies and "killing" them. Literate outsiders began to attend such exhumations. The vampire craze was an early "media event," in which educated Europeans became aware of practices that were by no means of recent origin.

In the early 1730s, a group of Austrian medical officers were sent to the Serbian village of Medvegia to investigate some very strange accounts. A number of people in the village had died recently, and the villagers blamed the deaths on vampires. The first of these vampires, they said, had been a man named Arnold Paole, who had died some years before (by falling off a hay wagon) and had come back to haunt the living.

To the villagers, Paole's vampirism was clear: When they dug up his corpse, "they found that he was quite complete and undecayed, and that fresh blood had flowed from his eyes, nose, mouth, and ears; that the shirt, the covering, and the coffin were completely bloody; that the old nails on his hands and feet, along with the skin, had fallen off, and that new ones had grown; and since they saw from this that he was a true vampire, they drove a stake through his heart, according to their custom, whereby he gave an audible groan and bled copiously."

This new offensive by the vampires—the one that drew the medical officers to Medvegia—included an attack on a woman named Stanacka, who "lay down to sleep fifteen days ago, fresh and healthy, but at midnight she started up out of her sleep with a terrible cry, fearful and trembling, and complained that she had been throttled by the son of a Haiduk by the name of Milloe, who had died nine weeks earlier, whereupon she had experienced a great pain in the chest and became worse hour by hour, until finally she died on the third day."

In their report, *Visum et Repertum* (Seen and Discovered), the officers told not only what they had heard from the villagers but also, in admirable clinical detail, what they themselves had seen when they exhumed and dissected the bodies of the supposed victims of the vampire. Of one corpse, the authors observed, "After the opening of the body there was found in the *cavitate pectoris* a quantity of fresh extravascular blood. The *vasa* [vessels] of the *arteriae* and *venae*, like the *ventriculis cordis*, were not, as is usual, filled with coagulated blood, and the whole *viscera*, that is, the *pulmo* [lung], *hepar* [liver], *stomachus*, *lien* [spleen], *et intestina* were quite fresh as they would be in a healthy person." But while baffled by the events, the medical officers did not venture opinions as to their meaning.

Modern scholars generally disregard such accounts—and we have many of them—because they invariably contain "facts" that are not believable, such as the claim that the dead Arnold Paole, exhumed forty days after his burial, groaned when a stake was driven into him. If that is untrue—and it surely seems self-evident that it must be untrue—then the rest of the account seems suspect. 10

Yet these stories invariably contain details that could only be known by someone who had exhumed a decomposing body. The flaking away of the skin described in the account of Arnold Paole is a phenomenon that forensic pathologists refer to as "skin slippage." Also, pathologists say that it is no surprise that Paole's "nails had fallen away," for that too is a normal event. (The Egyptians knew this and dealt with it either by tying the nails onto the mummified corpse or by attaching them with little golden thimbles.) The reference to "new nails" is presumably the interpretation of the glossy nail bed underneath the old nails.

Such observations are inconvenient if the vampire lore is considered as something made up out of whole cloth. But since the exhumations actually took place, then the question must be, how did our sources come to the conclusion they came to? That issue is obscured by two centuries of fictional vampires, who are much better known than the folkloric variety. A few distinctions are in order.

The folklore of the vampire comes from peasant cultures across most of Europe. As it happens, the best evidence of actual exhumations is from Eastern Europe, where the Eastern Orthodox church showed a greater tolerance for pagan traditions than the Catholic church in Western Europe.

The fictional vampire, owing to the massive influence of Bram Stoker's *Dracula*, moved away from its humble origin. (Imagine Count Dracula—in formal evening wear—undergoing his first death by falling off a hay wagon.)

15   Most fiction shows only one means of achieving the state of vampirism: people become vampires by being bitten by one. Typically, the vampire looms over the victim dramatically, then bites into the neck to suck blood. When vampires and revenants in European folklore suck blood—and many do not—they bite their victims somewhere on the thorax. Among the Kashubes, a Slavic people of northern Europe, vampires chose the area of the left breast; among the Russians, they left a small wound in the area of the heart; and the Danzig (now Gdansk), they bit the victim's nipples.

People commonly believe that those who were different, unpopular, or great sinners returned from the dead. Accounts from Russia tell of people who were unearthed merely because while alive they were alcoholics. A more universal category is the suicide. Partly because of their potential for returning from the dead or for drawing their nearest and dearest into the grave after them, suicides were refused burial in churchyards.

One author lists the categories of revenants by disposition as "the godless [people of different faiths are included], evildoers, suicides, sorcerers, witches, and werewolves; among the Bulgarians the group is expanded by robbers, highwaymen, arsonists, prostitutes, deceitful and treacherous barmaids and other dishonorable people."

A very common belief, reported not only from Eastern Europe but also from China, holds that a person may become a revenant when an animal jumps over him. In Romania there is a belief that a bat can transform a corpse into a vampire by flying over it. This circumstance deserves remark if only because of its rarity, for as important as bats are in the fiction of vampires, they are generally unimportant in the folklore. Bats came into vampire fiction by a circuitous route: the vampire bat of Central and South America was named after the vampire of folklore, because it sucks (or rather laps up) blood after biting its victim. The bat was then assimilated into the fiction: the modern (fictional) vampire is apt to transform himself into a bat and fly off to seek his victims.

Potential revenants could often be identified at birth, usually by some defect, as when (among the Poles of Upper Silesia and the Kashubes) a child was born with teeth or a split lower lip or features viewed as somehow bestial—for example, hair or a taillike extension of the spine. A child born with a red caul, or amniotic membrane, covering its head was regarded as a potential vampire.

The color red is related to the undead. Decomposing corpses often acquire   20
a ruddy color, and this was generally taken for evidence of vampirism. Thus, the folkloric vampire is never pale, as one would expect of a corpse; his face is commonly described as florid or of a healthy color or dark, and this may be attributed to his habit of drinking blood. (The Serbians, referring to a red-faced, hard-drinking man, assert that he is "blood red as a vampire.")

In various parts of Europe, vampires, or revenants, were held responsible for any number of untoward events. They tipped over Gypsy caravans in Serbia, made loud noises on the frozen sod roofs of houses in Iceland (supposedly by beating their heels against them), caused epidemics, cast spells on crops, brought on rain and hail, and made cows go dry. All these activities attributed to vampires do occur: storms and scourges come and go, crops don't always thrive, cows do go dry. Indeed, the vampire's crimes are persistently "real-life" events. The issue often is not whether an event occurred but why it was attributed to the machinations of the vampire, an often invisible villain.

Bodies continue to be active long after death, but we moderns distinguish between two types of activity: that which we bring about by our will (in life) and that which is caused by other entities, such as microorganisms (in death). Because we regard only the former as "our" activity, the body's posthumous movements, changes in dimension, or the like are not real for us, since we do not will them. For the most part, however, our ancestors made no such distinction. To them, if after death the body changed in color, moved, bled, and so on (as it does), then it continued to experience a kind of life. Our view of death has made it difficult for us to understand earlier views, which are often quite pragmatic.

Much of what a corpse "does" results from misunderstood processes of decomposition. Only in detective novels does this process proceed at a predictable rate. So when a body that had seemingly failed to decompose came to the attention of the populace, theories explaining the apparent anomaly were likely to spring into being. (Note that when a saint's body failed to decompose it was a miracle, but when the body of an unpopular person failed to decompose it was because he was a vampire.) But while those who exhumed the bodies of suspected vampires invariably noted what they believed was the lack of decomposition, they almost always presented evidence that the body really was decomposing. In the literature, I have so far found only two instances of exhumations that failed to yield a "vampire." (With so many options, the body almost certainly will do something unexpected, hence scary, such as showing blood at the lips.) Our natural bias, then as now, is for the dramatic and the exotic, so that an exhumation that did not yield a vampire could be expected to be an early dropout from the folklore and hence the literature.

But however mythical the vampire was, the corpses that were taken for vampires were very real. And many of the mysteries of vampire lore clear up when we examine the legal and medical evidence surrounding these exhumations. "Not without astonishment," says an observer at the exhumation of a Serbian vampire in 1725, "I saw some fresh blood in his mouth, which, according to the common observation, he had sucked from the people killed by him." Similarly, in *Visum et Repertum*, we are told that the people exhuming one body were surprised by a "plumpness" they asserted had come to the corpse in the grave. Our sources deduced a cause-and-effect relationship from these two observations. The vampire was larger than he was because he was full to bursting with the fresh blood of his victims.

25   The observations are clinically accurate: as a corpse decomposes, it normally bloats (from the gases given off by decomposition), while the pressure from the bloating causes blood from the lungs to emerge at the mouth. The blood is real, it just didn't come from "victims" of the deceased.

But how was it that Arnold Paole, exhumed forty days after his death, groaned when his exhumers drove a stake into him? The peasants of Medvegia assumed that if the corpse groaned, it must still be alive. But a corpse does emit sounds, even when it is only moved, let alone if a stake were driven into it. This is because the compression of the chest cavity forces air past the glottis, causing a sound similar in quality and origin to the groan or cry of a living person. Pathologists shown such accounts point out that a corpse that did not emit such sounds when a stake was driven into it would be unusual.

To vampire killers who are digging up a corpse, anything unexpected is taken for evidence of vampirism. Calmet, an eighteenth-century French ecclesiastic, described people digging up corpses "to see if they can find any of the usual marks which leads them to conjecture that they are the parties who molest the living, as the mobility and suppleness of the limbs, the fluidity of the blood, and the flesh remaining uncorrupted." A vampire, in other words, is a corpse that lacks rigor mortis, has fluid blood, and has not decomposed. As it happens, these distinctions do not narrow the field very much: Rigor mortis is a temporary condition, liquid blood is not at all unusual in a corpse (hence the "copious bleeding" mentioned in the account of Arnold Paole), and burial slows down decomposition drastically (by a factor of eight, according to a standard textbook on forensic pathology). This being the case, exhumations often yielded a corpse that nicely fit the local model of what a vampire was.

None of this explains yet another phenomenon of the vampire lore—the attack itself. To get to his victim, the vampire is often said to emerge at night from a tiny hole in the grave, in a form that is invisible to most people (sorcerers have made a good living tracking down and killing such vampires). The modern reader may reject out of hand the hypothesis that a dead man, visible or not, crawled out of his grave and attacked the young woman Stanacka as related in *Visum et Repertum*. Yet in other respects, these accounts have been quite accurate.

Note the sequence of events: Stanacka is asleep, the attack takes place, and she wakes up. Since Stanacka was asleep during the attack, we can only conclude that we are looking at a culturally conditioned interpretation of a nightmare—a real event with a fanciful interpretation.

The vampire does have two forms: one of them the body in the grave; the other—and this is the mobile one—the image, or "double," which here appears as a dream. While we interpret this as an event that takes place within the mind of the dreamer, in nonliterate cultures the dream is more commonly viewed as either an invasion by the spirits of whatever is dreamed about (and these can include the dead) or evidence that the dreamer's soul is taking a nocturnal journey. *30*

In many cultures, the soul is only rather casually attached to its body, as is demonstrated by its habit of leaving the body entirely during sleep or unconsciousness or death. The changes that occur during such conditions—the lack of responsiveness, the cessation or slowing of breathing and pulse—are attributed to the soul's departure. When the soul is identified with the image of the body, it may make periodic forays into the minds of others when they dream. The image is the essence of the person, and its presence in the mind of another is evidence that body and soul are separated. Thus, one reason that the dead are believed to live on is that their image can appear in people's dreams and memories even after death. For this reason some cultures consider it unwise to awaken someone suddenly: he may be dreaming, and his soul may not have a chance to return before he awakens, in which case he will die. In European folklore, the dream was viewed as a visit from the person dreamed about. (The vampire is not the only personification of the dream: the Slavic *mora* is a living being whose soul goes out of the body at night, leaving it as if dead. The *mora* first puts men to sleep, and then frightens them with dreams, chokes them, and sucks their blood. Etymologically, *mora* is cognate with the *mare* or nightmare, with German *Mahr*, and with the second syllable of the French *cauchemar*.

When Stanacka claimed she was attacked by Milloe, she was neither lying nor even making an especially startling accusation. Her subsequent death (probably from some form of epidemic disease; others in the village were dying too) was sufficient proof to her friends and relatives that she had in fact been attacked by a dead man, just as she had said.

This is why our sources tell us seemingly contradictory facts about the vampire. His body does not have to leave the grave to attack the living, yet the evidence of the attack—the blood he has sucked from his victims—is to be seen on the body. At one and the same time he can be both in the grave in his physical form and out of it in his spirit form. Like the fictional vampire, the vampire of folklore must remain in his grave part of the time—during the day—but with few exceptions, folkloric vampires do not travel far from their home towns.

And while the fictional vampire disintegrates once staked, the folkloric vampire can prove much more troublesome. One account tells that "in order to free themselves from this plague, the people dug the body up, drove a consecrated nail into its head and stake through its heart. Nonetheless, that did not help: the murdered man came back each night." In many of these cases, vampires were cremated as well as staked.

35 In Eastern Europe the fear of being killed by a vampire was quite real, and the people devised ways to protect themselves from attacks. One of the sources of protection was the blood of the supposed vampire, which was baked in bread, painted on the potential victim, or even mixed with brandy and drunk. (According to *Visum et Repertum*, Arnold Paole had once smeared himself with the blood of a vampire—that is, a corpse—for protection.) The rationale behind this is a common one in folklore, expressed in the saying "similia similiis curantur" (similar things are cured by similar things). Even so, it is a bit of a shock to find that our best evidence suggests that it was the human beings who drank the blood of the "vampires," and not the other way around.

Perhaps foremost among the reasons for urgency with which vampires were sought—and found—was sheer terror. To understand its intensity we need only recall the realities that faced our informants. Around them people were dying in clusters, by agencies that they did not understand. As they were well aware, death could be extremely contagious: if a neighbor died, they might be next. They were afraid of nothing less than death itself. For among many cultures it was death that was thought to be passed around, not viruses and bacteria. Contagion was meaningful and deliberate, and its patterns were based on values and vendettas, not on genetic predisposition or the domestic accommodations of the plague-spreading rat fleas. Death came from the dead who, through jealousy, anger, or longing, sought to bring the living into their realm. And to prevent this, the living attempted to neutralize or propitiate the dead until the dead became powerless—not only when they stopped entering dreams but also when their bodies stopped changing and were reduced to inert bones. This whole phenomenon is hard for us to understand because although death is as inescapable today as it was then, we no longer personify its causes.

In recent history, the closest parallel to this situation may be seen in the AIDS epidemic, which has caused a great deal of fear, even panic, among people who, for the time being at least, know little about the nature of the disease. In California, for instance, there was an attempt to pass a law requiring the quarantine of AIDS victims. Doubtless the fear will die down if we gain control over the disease—but what would it be like to live in a civilization in which all diseases were just as mysterious? Presumably one would learn—as was done in Europe in past centuries—to shun the dead as potential bearers of death.

Engaging the Text

1. What fears and historical conditions existed in cultures in which the legend of the vampire evolved? What unusual features distinguished the corpses that were believed to be those of vampires?

2. What are the differences between the fictional vampires of Bram Stoker and Hollywood and the "real" vampires described by Barber?

Exploring Your Cultural Perspective

1. The concept of the vampire is based on a tradeoff between immortality, on one hand, and a permanent subhuman existence as a night-feeding creature who cannot live in sunlight, on the other. Would you find this tradeoff appealing? Why or why not?

2. Do any of the film or television portrayals of vampires (such as those in *The Addams Family* and *Buffy the Vampire Slayer*) come close to the "real" vampires Barber describes? What do these portrayals suggest about contemporary cultural attitudes toward vampires? For further research, consult Web sites on vampire lore, among them the Vampirism Research Institute site at <http://users.aol.com/lirielmc/private/vri.htm>.

GINO DEL GUERCIO
The Secrets of Haiti's Living Dead

According to voodoo belief, zombies are the "living dead," who have been reanimated by malevolent sorcerers. In reality, researchers have discovered that certain drugs can simulate a deathlike trance and that the threat of zombification serves as a form of social control in Haitian culture. This essay by Gino Del Guercio describes the findings of Wade Davis, a Harvard-trained ethnobotanist, which formed the basis for Davis's book *The Serpent and the Rainbow* (1985) and for a later film of the same name (1988). Del Guercio has written, produced, and directed documentaries for PBS, the Discovery Channel, and the Arts and Entertainment channel. His most recent works are *Transistorized!* (1999) and *Nerds 2.01* (2000), a three-hour PBS series focusing on the Internet. He also served as an advisor on the 1998 film *Stigmata*.

Thinking Critically
Zombies are not actually dead but are the products of pharmacology and mind control. As you read, consider the extent to which your concept of zombies is influenced by films and TV.

Five years ago, a man walked into l'Estére, a village in cental Haiti, approached a peasant woman named Angelina Narcisse, and identified himself as her brother Clairvius. If he had not introduced himself using a boyhood nickname and mentioned facts only intimate family members knew, she would not have believed him. Because, eighteen years earlier, Angelina had stood in a small cemetery north of her village and watched as her brother Clairvius was buried.

The man told Angelina he remembered that night well. He knew when he was lowered into his grave, because he was fully conscious, although he could not speak or move. As the earth was thrown over his coffin, he felt as if he were floating over the grave. The scar on his right cheek, he said, was caused by a nail driven through the casket.

The night he was buried, he told Angelina, a voodoo priest raised him from the grave. He was beaten with a sisal whip and carried off to a sugar plantation in northern Haiti where, with other zombies, he was forced to work as a slave. Only with the death of the zombie master were they able to escape, and Narcisse eventually returned home.

Legend has it that zombies are the living dead, raised from their graves and animated by malevolent voodoo sorcerers, usually for some evil purpose. Most Haitians believe in zombies, and Narcisse's claim is not unique. At about the time he reappeared, in 1980, two women turned up in other villages saying they were zombies. In the same year, in northern Haiti, the local peasants claimed to have found a group of zombies wandering aimlessly in the fields.

But Narcisse's case was different in one crucial respect; it was documented. 5 His death had been recorded by doctors at the American-directed Schweitzer Hospital in Deschapelles. On April 30, 1962, hospital records show, Narcisse walked into the hospital's emergency room spitting up blood. He was feverish and full of aches. His doctors could not diagnose his illness, and his symptoms grew steadily worse. Three days after he entered the hospital, according to the records, he died. The attending physicians, an American among them, signed his death certificate. His body was placed in cold storage for twenty hours, and then he was buried. He said he remembered hearing his doctors pronounce him dead while his sister wept at his bedside.

At the Centre de Psychiatrie et Neurologie in Port-au-Prince, Dr. Lamarque Douyon, a Haitian-born, Canadian-trained psychiatrist, has been systematically investigating all reports of zombies since 1961. Though convinced zombies were real, he had been unable to find a scientific explanation for the phenomenon. He did not believe zombies were people raised from the dead, but that did not make them any less interesting. He speculated that victims were only made to *look* dead, probably by means of a drug that dramatically slowed metabolism. The victim was buried, dug up within a few hours, and somehow reawakened.

The Narcisse case provided Douyon with evidence strong enough to warrant a request for assistance from colleagues in New York. Douyon wanted to find an ethnobotanist, a traditional-medicines expert, who could track down the zombie potion he was sure existed. Aware of the medical potential of a drug that could dramatically lower metabolism, a group organized by the late Dr. Nathan Kline—a New York psychiatrist and pioneer in the field of psychopharmacology—raised the funds necessary to send someone to investigate.

The search for that someone led to the Harvard Botanical Museum, one of the world's foremost institutes of ethnobiology. Its director, Richard Evans Schultes, Jeffrey professor of biology, had spent thirteen years in the tropics studying native medicines. Some of his best-known work is the investigation of curare, the substance used by the nomadic people of the Amazon to poison their darts. Refined into a powerful muscle relaxant called D-tubocurarine, it is now an essential component of the anesthesia used during almost all surgery.

Schultes would have been a natural for the Haitian investigation, but he was too busy. He recommended another Harvard ethnobotanist for the assignment, Wade Davis, a 28-year-old Canadian pursuing a doctorate in biology.

10   Davis grew up in the tall pine forests of British Columbia and entered Harvard in 1971, influenced by a *Life* magazine story on the student strike of 1969. Before Harvard, the only Americans he had known were draft dodgers, who seemed very exotic. "I used to fight forest fires with them," Davis says. "Like everybody else, I thought America was where it was at. And I wanted to go to Harvard because of that *Life* article. When I got there, I realized it wasn't quite what I had in mind."

Davis took a course from Schultes, and when he decided to go to South America to study plants, he approached his professor for guidance. "He was an extraordinary figure," Davis remembers. "He was a man who had done it all. He had lived alone for years in the Amazon." Schultes sent Davis to the rain forest with two letters of introduction and two pieces of advice: wear a pith helmet and try ayahuasca, a powerful hallucinogenic vine. During that expedition and others, Davis proved himself an "outstanding field man," says his mentor. Now, in early 1982, Schultes called him into his office and asked if he had plans for spring break.

"I always took to Schultes's assignments like a plant takes to water," says Davis, tall and blond, with inquisitive blue eyes. "Whatever Schultes told me to do, I did. His letters of introduction opened up a whole world." This time the world was Haiti.

Davis knew nothing about the Caribbean island—and nothing about African traditions, which serve as Haiti's cultural basis. He certainly did not believe in zombies. "I thought it was a lark," he says now.

Davis landed in Haiti a week after his conversation with Schultes, armed with a hypothesis about how the zombie drug—if it existed—might be made. Setting out to explore, he discovered a country materially impoverished, but rich in culture and mystery. He was impressed by the cohesion of Haitian society; he found none of the crime, social disorder, and rampant drug and alcohol abuse so common in many of the other Caribbean islands. The cultural wealth and cohesion, he believes, spring from the country's turbulent history.

15   During the French occupation of the late eighteenth century, 370,000 African-born slaves were imported to Haiti between 1780 and 1790. In 1791, the black population launched one of the few successful slave revolts in history, forming secret societies and overcoming first the French plantation owners and then a detachment of troops from Napoleon's army, sent to quell the revolt. For the next hundred years Haiti was the only independent black republic in the Caribbean, populated by people who did not forget their African heritage. "You can almost argue that Haiti is more African than Africa," Davis says. "When the west coast of Africa was being disrupted by colonialism and

the slave trade, Haiti was essentially left alone. The amalgam of beliefs in Haiti is unique, but it's very, very African."

Davis discovered that the vast majority of Haitian peasants practice voodoo, a sophisticated religion with African roots. Says Davis, "It was immediately obvious that the stereotypes of voodoo weren't true. Going around the countryside, I found clues to a whole complex social world." Vodounists believe they communicate directly with, indeed are often possessed by, the many spirits who populate the everyday world. Vodoun society is a system of education, law, and medicine; it embodies a code of ethics that regulates social behavior. In rural areas, secret vodoun societies, much like those found on the west coast of Africa, are as much or more in control of everyday life as the Haitian government.

Although most outsiders dismissed the zombie phenomenon as folklore, some early investigators, convinced of its reality, tried to find a scientific explanation. The few who sought a zombie drug failed. Nathan Kline, who helped finance Davis's expedition, had searched unsuccessfully, as had Lamarque Douyon, the Haitian psychiatrist. Zora Neale Hurston, an American black woman, may have come closest. An anthropological pioneer, she went to Haiti in the Thirties, studied vodoun society, and wrote a book on the subject, *Tell My Horse*, first published in 1938. She knew about the secret societies and was convinced zombies were real, but if a powder existed, she too failed to obtain it.

Davis obtained a sample in a few weeks.

He arrived in Haiti with the names of several contacts. A BBC reporter familiar with the Narcisse case had suggested he talk with Marcel Pierre. Pierre owned the Eagle Bar, a bordello in the city of Saint Marc. He was also a voodoo sorcerer and had supplied the BBC with a physiologically active powder of unknown ingredients. Davis found him willing to negotiate. He told Pierre he was a representative of "powerful but anonymous interests in New York," willing to pay generously for the priest's services, provided no questions were asked. Pierre agreed to be helpful for what Davis will only say was a "sizable sum." Davis spent a day watching Pierre gather the ingredients—including human bones—and grind them together with mortar and pestle. However, from his knowledge of poison, Davis knew immediately that nothing in the formula could produce the powerful effects of zombification.

Three weeks later, Davis went back to the Eagle Bar, where he found 20 Pierre sitting with three associates. Davis challenged him. He called him a charlatan. Enraged, the priest gave him a second vial, claiming that this was the real poison. Davis pretended to pour the powder into his palm and rub it into his skin. "You're a dead man," Pierre told him, and he might have been, because this powder proved to be genuine. But, as the substance had not actually touched him, Davis was able to maintain his bravado, and Pierre was impressed. He agreed to make the poison and show Davis how it was done.

The powder, which Davis keeps in a small vial, looks like dry black dirt. It contains parts of toads, sea worms, lizards, tarantulas, and human bones. (To obtain the last ingredient, he and Pierre unearthed a child's grave on a nocturnal trip to the cemetery.) The poison is rubbed into the victim's skin. Within hours he begins to feel nauseated and has difficulty breathing. A pins-and-needles sensation afflicts his arms and legs, then progresses to the whole body. The subject becomes paralyzed; his lips turn blue for lack of oxygen. Quickly—sometimes within six hours—his metabolism is lowered to a level almost indistinguishable from death.

As Davis discovered, making the poison is an inexact science. Ingredients varied in the five samples he eventually acquired, although the active agents were always the same. And the poison came with no guarantee. Davis speculates that sometimes instead of merely paralyzing the victim, the compound kills him. Sometimes the victim suffocates in the coffin before he can be resurrected. But clearly the potion works well enough often enough to make zombies more than a figment of Haitian imagination.

Analysis of the powder produced another surprise. "When I went down to Haiti originally," says Davis, "my hypothesis was that the formula would contain *concombre zombi*, the 'zombie's cucumber,' which is a *Datura* plant. I thought somehow *Datura* was used in putting people down." *Datura* is a powerful psychoactive plant, found in West Africa as well as other tropical areas and used there in ritual as well as criminal activities. Davis had found *Datura* growing in Haiti. Its popular name suggested the plant was used in creating zombies.

But, says Davis, "there were a lot of problems with the *Datura* hypothesis. Partly it was a question of how the drug was administered. *Datura* would create a stupor in huge doses, but it just wouldn't produce the kind of immobility that was key. These people had to appear dead, and there aren't many drugs that will do that."

25   One of the ingredients Pierre included in the second formula was a dried fish, a species of puffer or blowfish, common to most parts of the world. It gets its name from its ability to fill itself with water and swell to several times its normal size when threatened with predators. Many of these fish contain a powerful poison known as tetrodotoxin. One of the most powerful nonprotein poisons known to man, tetradotoxin turned up in every sample of zombie powder that Davis acquired.

Numerous well-documented accounts of puffer fish poisoning exist, but the most famous accounts come from the Orient, where *fugu* fish, a species of puffer, is considered a delicacy. In Japan, special chefs are licensed to prepare *fugu*. The chef removes enough poison to make the fish nonlethal, yet enough remains to create exhilarating physiological effects—tingles up and down the spine, mild prickling of the tongue and lips, euphoria. Several dozen Japanese die each year, having bitten off more than they should have.

"When I got hold of the formula and saw that it was the *fugu* fish, that suddenly threw open the whole Japanese literature," says Davis. Case histories of *fugu* poisoning read like accounts of zombification. Victims remain conscious but unable to speak or move. A man who had "died" after eating *fugu* recovered seven days later in the morgue. Several summers ago, another Japanese poisoned by *fugu* revived after he was nailed into his coffin. "Almost all of Narcisse's symptoms correlated. Even strange things such as the fact that he said he was conscious and could hear himself pronounced dead. Stuff that I thought had to be magic, that seemed crazy. But, in fact, that is what people who get *fugu*-fish poisoning experience."

Davis was certain he had solved the mystery. But far from being the end of his investigation, identifying the poison was, in fact, its starting point. "The drug alone didn't make zombies," he explains. "Japanese victims of puffer-fish poisoning don't become zombies, they become poison victims. All the drug could do was set someone up for a whole series of psychological pressures that would be rooted in the culture. I wanted to know why zombification was going on," he says.

He sought a cultural answer, an explanation rooted in the structure and beliefs of Haitian society. Was zombification simply a random criminal activity? He thought not. He had discovered that Clairvius Narcisse and "Ti Femme," a second victim he interviewed, were village pariahs. Ti Femme was regarded as a thief. Narcisse had abandoned his children and deprived his brother of land that was rightfully his. Equally suggestive, Narcisse claimed that his aggrieved brother had sold him to a *bokor*, a voodoo priest who dealt in black magic; he made cryptic reference to having been tried and found guilty by the "masters of the land."

Gathering poisons from various parts of the country, Davis had come into direct contact with the vodoun secret societies. Returning to the anthropological literature on Haiti and pursuing his contacts with informants, Davis came to understand the social matrix within which zombies were created.

Davis's investigations uncovered the importance of the secret societies. These groups trace their origins to the bands of escaped slaves that organized the revolt against the French in the late eighteenth century. Open to both men and women, the societies control specific territories of the country. Their meetings take place at night, and in many rural parts of Haiti the drums and wild celebrations that characterize the gatherings could be heard for miles.

Davis believes the secret societies are responsible for policing their communities, and the threat of zombification is one way they maintain order. Says Davis, "Zombification has a material basis, but it also has a societal logic." To the uninitiated, the practice may appear a random criminal activity, but in rural vodoun society, it is exactly the opposite—a sanction imposed by recognized authorities, a form of capital punishment. For rural Haitians, zombification is an even more severe punishment than death, because it deprives the subject of his most valued possessions: his free will and independence.

The vodounists believe that when a person dies, his spirit splits into several different parts. If a priest is powerful enough, the spiritual aspect that controls a person's character and individuality, known as *ti bon ange*, the "good little angel," can be captured and the corporeal aspect, deprived of its will, held as a slave.

From studying the medical literature on tetrodotoxin poisoning, Davis discovered that if a victim survives the first few hours of the poisoning, he is likely to recover fully from the ordeal. The subject simply revives spontaneously. But zombies remain without will, in a trance-like state, a condition vodounists attribute to the power of the priest. Davis thinks it possible that the psychological trauma of zombification may be augmented by *Datura* or some other drug; he thinks zombies may be fed a *Datura* paste that accentuates their disorientation. Still, he puts the material basis of zombification in perspective: "Tetrodotoxin and *Datura* are only templates on which cultural forces and beliefs may be amplified a thousand times."

35   Davis has not been able to discover how prevalent zombification is in Haiti. "How many zombies there are is not the question," he says. He compares it to capital punishment in the United States: "It doesn't really matter how many people are electrocuted, as long as it's a possibility." As a sanction in Haiti, the fear is not of zombies, it's of becoming one.

Davis attributes his success in solving the zombie mystery to his approach. He went to Haiti with an open mind and immersed himself in the culture. "My intuition unhindered by biases served me well," he says. "I didn't make any judgments." He combined this attitude with what he had learned earlier from his experiences in the Amazon. "Schultes's lesson is to go and live with the Indians as an Indian." Davis was able to participate in the vodoun society to a surprising degree, eventually even penetrating one of the Bizango societies and dancing in their nocturnal rituals. His appreciation of Haitian culture is apparent. "Everybody asks me how did a white person get this information? To ask the question means you don't understand Haitians—they don't judge you by the color of your skin."

As a result of the exotic nature of his discoveries, Davis has gained a certain notoriety. He plans to complete his dissertation soon, but he has already finished writing a popular account of his adventures. To be published in January by Simon and Schuster, it is called *The Serpent and the Rainbow*, after the serpent that vodounists believe created the earth and the rainbow spirit it married. Film rights have already been optioned; in October Davis went back to Haiti with a screenwriter. But Davis takes the notoriety in stride. "All this attention is funny," he says. "For years, not just me, but all Schultes's students have had extraordinary adventures in the line of work. The adventure is not the end point, it's just along the way of getting the data. At the Botanical Museum, Schultes created a world unto itself. We didn't think we were doing anything above the ordinary. I still don't think we do. And you know," he adds, "the Haiti episode does not begin to compare to what others have accomplished—particularly Schultes himself."

Engaging the Text

1. How is the threat of zombification intended to deter crimes against the community and to punish those untouched by the conventional justice system? How did it operate in the cases of Clairvius Narcisse and "Ti Femme"?

2. Why is it significant that, as Del Guercio reports, "Haiti was the only independent black republic in the Caribbean, populated by people who did not forget their African heritage"? How does this help explain the unique institution of zombification and its function in Haitian life?

3. In what way is zombification quite a different phenomenon from what has been presented in movies? How do Haitian beliefs about the nature of the soul explain why zombies (created by certain poisonous drugs) are found in Haitian culture, whereas Japanese victims who survive the same poisons do not become zombies?

Exploring Your Cultural Perspective

1. What similarities exist between the processes used by various religious cults (such as Heaven's Gate, the Exclusive Brethren Cult, Hare Krishnas, the People's Temple, Sun Myong Moon) to enlist and program their members and the methods of the vodoun priests? What comparable roles do positive and negative reinforcement and psychological conditioning play?

2. What do you think of zombification as a means of social control? How does it compare with imprisonment as a means of punishing criminals?

MILORAD PAVIĆ
The Wedgwood Tea Set

The condition of otherness can have a political dimension that has seldom been represented with such ingenuity as in this story by Milorad Pavić. One of the best known contemporary Serbian writers, Pavić is credited with the invention of "hyperfiction," a kind of storytelling that creates a sense of open-endedness by blending fantasy with realistic narratives. Pavić was born in 1929 in Belgrade (in the former Yugoslavia). His work has been translated into many languages, and he has been nominated for the Nobel Prize for literature. He received the Nin Award in 1984 for *Dictionary of the Khazars: A Lexicon Novel in 100,000 Words*. His other notable works include *Landscape Painted with Tea* (1988), *The Inner Side of the Wind* (1993), and *Last Love in Constantinople: A Tarot Novel for Divination* (1999). "The Wedgwood Tea Set," translated by Darka Topali, first appeared in English in *The Prince of Fire*, edited by R. J. Gorup and M. Obradovic (1998).

Thinking Critically

As you read, underline and annotate passages that establish conflict between the two characters. Be alert to clues that the situation may not be as it appears.

In the story you are about to read, the protagonists' names will be given at the end instead of the beginning.

At the capital's mathematics faculty, my younger brother, who was a student of philology and military science, introduced us to each other. Since she was searching for a companion with whom to prepare for Mathematics I, we began studying together, and as she did not come from another town as I did, we studied in her parents' big house. Quite early each morning, I passed by the shining Layland-Buffalo car, which belonged to her. In front of the door I would stoop down and look for a stone, put it in my pocket, ring the doorbell, and go upstairs. I carried no books, notebooks, or instruments; everything stayed at her place and was always ready for work. We studied from seven to nine, then we were served breakfast and would continue till ten; from ten to eleven we would usually go over the material already covered. All that time, I would be holding the stone in my hand. In case I should doze off, it would fall on the floor and wake me up before anyone noticed. After eleven she would continue to study, but not I. So we prepared for the mathematics exam every day except Sunday, when she studied alone. She very quickly realized that I could not keep up with her and that my knowledge lagged more and more behind hers. She thought that I went home to catch up on the lessons I had missed, but she never said a thing. "Let everyone like an earthworm eat his own way through," she thought, aware that by teaching another she wasn't teaching herself.

When the September term came, we agreed to meet on the day of the examination and take the exam together. Excited as she was, she didn't have time to be especially surprised that I didn't show up and that I did not take the exam, either. Only after she had passed the exam did she ask herself what had happened to me. But I didn't appear till winter. "Why should every bee gather honey, anyway?" she concluded, but still asked herself sometimes, "What's he up to? He is probably one of those smile-carriers, who buys his merchandise in the East, and sells it in the West, or vice versa . . ."

When Mathematics II was on the agenda, she suddenly met me one morning, noticing with interest the new patches on my elbows and the newly grown hair, which she had not seen before. It was again the same. Each morning I would come at a certain hour, and she would descend through the green and layered air, as if through water full of cool and warm currents, open the door for me, sleepy, but with that mirror-breaking look of hers. She would watch for one moment how I squeezed out my beard into the cap and how I took off my gloves. Bringing together the middle finger and the thumb, with a decisive gesture I would simultaneously turn them inside out, thus taken them both off with the same movement. When that was over, she would immediately go to work. She made up her mind to study with all her strength, which happened daily. With untiring will and regularity, she delved into all details of the subject, no matter if it was morning, when we started out fresh, after breakfast, or toward the end, when she worked a bit more slowly but not skipping a single thing. I would still quit at eleven, and she would soon notice again that I couldn't concentrate on what I was doing, that my looks grew old in an hour, and that I was behind her again. She would look at my feet, one of which was always ready to step out, while the other was completely still. Then they would change positions.

When the January term arrived, she had the feeling that I could not pass the exam, but she was silent, feeling a trifle guilty herself. "Anyway," she concluded, "should I kiss his elbow to make him learn? If he cuts bread on his head, that's his own affair . . ."

When I didn't show up then either, she was nevertheless surprised, and after finishing the exam looked for the list of candidates to check whether I was perhaps scheduled for the afternoon or some other day. To her great surprise, my name wasn't on the list for that day at all—or any other day, for that matter. It was quite obvious: I hadn't even signed up for that term.

When we saw each other again in May, she was preparing Concrete. When she asked me if I was studying for the exams I had not taken before, I told her that I, too, was preparing Concrete, and we continued to study together as in the old times, as if nothing had happened. We spent the whole spring studying, and when the June term came, she had already realized that I would not appear this time, either, and that she wouldn't be seeing me till fall. She watched me pensively with beautiful eyes so far apart that there was space between them for an entire mouth. And naturally, things were the same once again. She took and passed the Concrete exam, and I didn't even bother to come. Returning home satisfied with her success, but totally puzzled as far as my position was concerned, she noticed that, in the hurry of the previous day, I had forgotten my notebooks. Among them she caught sight of my student's booklet. She opened it and discovered with astonishment that I was not a student of mathematics at all, but of something else, and that I had been passing my exams regularly. She recalled the interminable hours of our joint study, which for me must have been a great strain without purpose, a big waste of time, and she asked the inevitable question: what for? Why did I spend all that time with her studying subjects that had nothing to do with my interests and the exams I had to pass? She started thinking and came to one conclusion: one should always be aware of what is passed over in silence. The reason for all that was not the exam but she herself. Who would have thought that I would be so shy and unable to express my feelings for her? She immediately went to the rented room where I lived with a couple of people my age from Asia and Africa, was surprised by the poverty she saw, and received the information that I had gone home. When they also gave her the address of a small town near Salonica, she took her Buffalo without hesitation and started off toward the Aegean coast in search of me, having made up her mind to act as if she had discovered nothing unusual. So it was.

She arrived at sunset and found the house she had been told about wide open, with a great white bull tied to a nail, upon which fresh bread was impaled. Inside she noticed a bed, on the wall an icon, below the icon a red tassel, a pierced stone tied to a string, a top, a mirror, and an apple. A young naked person with long hair was lying on the bed, tanned by the sun, back turned to the window and resting on one elbow. The long ridge of the spine, which went all the way down the back and ended between the hips, curving slightly, vanished beneath a rough army blanket. She had the impression that the girl would turn any moment and that she would also see her breasts, deep, strong, and glowing in the warm evening. When that really took place, she saw that it was not a woman at all lying on the bed. Leaning on one arm I was chewing my moustache full of honey, which substituted for dinner. When she was noticed and brought into the house, she could still not help thinking of that first impression of finding a female person in my bed. But that impression, as well as the fatigue from a long drive, were soon forgotten. From a mirror-bottomed plate she received a double-dinner: for herself and her soul in the mirror: some beans, a nut, and fish, and before the meal a small silver coin, which she held, as did I, under the tongue while eating. So one supper fed all four of us: the two of us and our two souls in the mirrors. After dinner she approached the icon and asked me what it represented.

"A television set," I told her. In other words, it is the window to another world which uses mathematics quite different from yours.

"How so?" she asked.

"Quite simple," I answered. "Machines, space crafts, and vehicles built on the basis of your quantitative mathematical evaluations are founded upon three elements, which are completely lacking in quantity. These are: singularity, the point, and the present moment. Only a sum of singularities constitutes a quantity; singularity itself is deprived of any quantitative measurement. As far as the point is concerned, since it doesn't have a single dimension, not width or height or length or depth, it can undergo neither measurement nor computation. The smallest components of time, however, always have one common denominator: that is the present moment, and it, too, is devoid of quantity and is immeasureable. Thus, the basic elements of your quantitative science represent something to whose very nature every quantitative approach is alien. How then should I believe in such a science? Why are machines made according to these quantitative misconceptions of such a short lifespan, three, four or more times shorter than the human ones? Look, I also have a white 'buffalo' like you. Only, he is made differently from yours, which was manufactured at Layland. Try him out and you will see that in a way he is better than the one you own."

"Is he tame?" she asked, smiling.

"Certainly," I answered. "Go ahead and try."

In front of the door she stroked the big white bull and slowly climbed onto his back. When I also mounted him, turning my back to the horns and facing her, I drove him by the sea, so that he had two feet in the water and the other two feet on the sand. She was surprised at first when I started to undress her. Piece by piece of her clothing fell into the water; then she started unbuttoning me. At one moment she stopped riding on the bull and started riding on me, feeling that I was growing heavier and heavier inside her. The bull beneath us did everything that we would otherwise have had to do ourselves, and she could tell no longer who was driving her pleasure, the bull or I. Sitting upon the double lover, she saw through the night how we passed by a forest of white

10

cypresses, by people who were gathering dew and pierced stones on the seashore, by people who were building fires inside their own shadows and burning them up, by two women bleeding light, by a garden two hours long, where birds sang in the first hour and evening came in the second, where fruit bloomed in the first and there was a blizzard behind the winds. Then she felt that all the weight from me had passed into her and that the spurred bull had suddenly turned and taken her into the sea, leaving us finally to the waves that would separate us . . .

15   However, she never told me a word about her discovery. In the fall, when she was getting ready to graduate and when I offered to study with her again, she was not the least bit surprised. As before, we studied every day from seven until breakfast and then until half past ten; only now she did not try to help me master the subject I was doing and also stayed after ten-thirty for half an hour, which separated us from the books. When she graduated in September, she wasn't surprised at all when I didn't take the examination with her.

She was really surprised when she did not see me any more after that. Not that day, nor the following days, weeks, or examination terms. Never again. Astonished, she came to the conclusion that her assessment of my feelings for her was obviously wrong. Confused at not being able to tell what it was all about, she sat one morning in the same room in which we had studied together for years; then she caught sight of the Wedgewood [sic] tea set, which had been on the table since breakfast. Then she realized. For months, day after day, with tremendous effort and an immeasurable loss of time and energy, I had worked with her only in order to get a warm breakfast every morning, the only meal I was able to eat during those years. Having realized that, she asked herself another thing. Was it possible that in fact I hated her?

At the end, there is one more obligation left: to name the protagonists of this story. If the reader has not thought of it already, here is the answer. My name is the Balkans. Hers, Europe.

Engaging the Text

1. What kind of relationship does the narrator have with the girl with whom he studies? What easily overlooked details suggest that the situation is not as it appears?

2. Once you discovered the protagonist's true circumstances, what insight did you gain into what appeared to be a purely personal relationship?

3. Why is the title of the piece significant? What did it suggest to you before you read the story, and how did you understand its meaning afterward? How does this story differ from traditional fiction? Based on these differences, how would you define the term *hyperfiction*?

Exploring Your Cultural Perspective

1. Drawing on Pavić's story as a model, create your own realistic short story whose characters function as representatives of some current relationship between countries. Infuse your story with fantastic elements and seemingly innocuous clues whose true meaning is disclosed only at the end. For more information on hyperfiction and on Milorad Pavić, consult the Web site <http://www.khazars.com>.

2. Pavić's depiction of student life is especially telling in his revelation of how little power and control the narrator has over his own destiny. To what extent have your experiences as a student made you aware of the inequities in social class and political clout that affect many students?

CONNECTING THE TEXTS

1. How do the personal experiences Lucy Grealy relates in "Autobiography of a Face" illustrate Lennard J. Davis's theories in "Visualizing the Disabled Body"?

2. Bruce Springsteen in "Streets of Philadelphia" describes how AIDS victims are ostracized. In what sense is the way people with AIDS are treated a contemporary manifestation of society's need to construct the concepts of "normal" and "abnormal," as discussed by Lennard J. Davis in "Visualizing the Disabled Body"?

3. Lucy Grealy believed that people viewed her as "monstrous" because of her disfigured face. What insights do Grealy (in "Autobiography of a Face") and Paul Barber (in "The Real Vampire") offer into the psychological processes underlying society's creation of the monster?

4. What cultural mythologies about illness are evident in the ways homosexuals with AIDS are stigmatized, according to Paul Monette in "Borrowed Time: An AIDS Memoir," and the ways in which those who look different are treated, as described by Lucy Grealy in "Autobiography of a Face"?

5. In what ways do the life experiences of the narrator in Bruce Springsteen's "Streets of Philadelphia" differ in content and tone from Paul Monette's memoir "Borrowed Time: An AIDS Memoir"?

6. Compare how Bruce Springsteen uses song lyrics (in "Streets of Philadelphia") for social commentary and how Milorad Pavić (in "The Wedgwood Tea Set") uses fiction to make political points. Are imaginative works such as these better suited to dramatize social criticism than is nonfiction? Why or why not?

7. What factors reinforce social boundaries and class prejudices in Milorad Pavić's story "The Wedgwood Tea Set" in ways that are similar to different societies' use of

odors as markers of social identity, as described by Constance Classen in "The Odour of the Other"?

8. In creating the other, compare the role played by the sense of sight (as described by Lennard J. Davis in "Visualizing the Disabled Body") with the role played by the sense of smell (according to Constance Classen in "The Odour of the Other").

9. In "The Real Vampire," Paul Barber suggests that contemporary attitudes toward those with AIDS parallel the fears that led to construction of the vampire as the other in Europe two hundred years ago. Do you agree? Why or why not? Does a comparable folklore of AIDS exist (see Paul Monette's "Borrowed Time: An AIDS Memoir")?

10. What cultural differences might explain why, in Haiti, the "undead" are seen as slaves controlled by voodoo masters (see Gino Del Guercio's "The Secrets of Haiti's Living Dead"), whereas in Eastern Europe, the "undead" are feared as rampant evildoers (as described by Paul Barber in "The Real Vampire")?

11. In what ways do political agendas and class interests determine who is perceived as the other in Milorad Pavić's story "The Wedgwood Tea Set" and in Paul Monette's account "Borrowed Time: An AIDS Memoir"?

WRITING ABOUT OTHERNESS

1. Movies and television series such as *The X-Files* and *Alien Nation* use the science fiction format to depict the other. Select an episode of one of these or another science fiction series and analyze the social and cultural issues it presents in disguised form. You might consult the official *X-Files* Web site at <http://www.foxhome.com/trustno1> or the *Alien Nation* site at <http://www.scifi.com/alienation/>.

2. Many films rely on the audience's assumption that a twisted body signifies a twisted psyche. Why do you think so many film villains are depicted as deformed, scarred, mutilated, or otherwise not physically whole (for example, in the James Bond films or their recent spoofs, the Austin Powers films)? Conversely, other films use the hero's or heroine's disability as a sign of his or her humanity, such as Christy Brown's *My Left Foot* (1989) and David Lynch's *Edward Scissorhands* (1990). In a short essay, explore the range of cultural meanings disability can convey.

3. In television shows set in hospitals, such as *ER*, doctors speak about patients and their conditions in jargon that sometimes dehumanizes the patients. The same can be said of lawyers and their clients on such shows as *Law and Order* and *The Practice*. Watch one of these shows, and analyze the specialized language professionals use to transform the nonprofessional patient or client into the other.

4. How does *Psycho* (1960), *Rosemary's Baby* (1968), *The Stepford Wives* (1975), or another more recent horror film, such as *Scream III* (2000), represent the other as your next-door neighbor, friend, or mate? Why is this so frightening?

5. What techniques do magazines such as *Essence, Ebony* (for African American readers), *Hispanic* (for Latino readers), or *Transpacific* (for Asian readers) use to lessen the dominant culture's perception that these groups are the other?

6. To what extent have immigrants been viewed as the other and subjected to restrictive immigration and naturalization laws? How do current immigration quotas compare with past quotas, and how do they reflect underlying cultural agendas?

7. Has the concept of the other become a marketable commodity for TV talk shows and tabloids? For example, consider how people are encouraged to project themselves as victims of abuse, dysfunction, and discrimination for the entertainment of audiences of such shows as these: Jerry Springer, Jenny Jones, Maury Povich, Sally Jesse Raphael. What does the commercial exploitation of victimhood signify about U.S. culture?

8. To what extent is AIDS portrayed as a disease that afflicts others (Haitians, drug users, blacks, gay men) who are already stigmatized by mainstream society? If those most likely to contract AIDS had not already been others, how might the perception and treatment of the disease have been different? How was the story of Ryan White (a young hemophiliac who contracted AIDS from a blood transfusion) used in an attempt to "reconstruct" the disease? Write an essay in which you explore the social construction of the meaning of AIDS.

9. Using the library and the Internet, research the use of robots or replicants as the other in literature and film (for example, the replicants in the 1982 film *Blade Runner* are described as "more human than humans"). You might visit *Blade Runner* Web sites (you'll find one at <http://www.voyagerco.com/CC/sfh/bladerunner.html>) or consult *The Official Bladerunner Online Magazine* at <http://madison.tdsnet. com/bladerunner>.

10. Blacks and Jews have historically been classified as the other (see Figure 6.4 on page 448). This shared predicament has in past eras produced a strong alliance between the two groups in their struggle for social justice. Yet in recent times this alliance has disintegrated. Research and report on the causes of this fracture and its implications. A valuable source is *Bridges and Boundaries: African Americans and American Jews,* edited by Jack Salzman (1992).

11. What important idea does African American artist Gary Simmons communicate using monogrammed towels in Figure 6.5 (page 449), which conventionally bear "His" and "Hers" inscriptions?

Saranac Inn

ON

Upper Saranac Lake

Adirondack Mountains

New York

Harrington Mills, President

John M. Kirby, Manager

Willard Boyce, Supt.

FIGURE 6.4

12. The film still in Figure 6.6, from the classic *Star Trek* episode "Let This Be Your Last Battlefield," makes an important point about how the other is socially constructed. The two characters depicted in the illustration are enemies. What point does the picture make, and why is it so effective?

13. Consider how the events of September 11, 2001, have transformed American popular culture in terms of the socially constructed mythologies of disease and the groups now seen as the other?

FIGURE 6.5

FIGURE 6.6

CHAPTER 7

That's Entertainment!

Every country gets the circus it deserves. Spain gets bullfights. Italy gets the Catholic church. America gets Hollywood.
> —Erica Jong (b. 1942, U.S. fiction and nonfiction writer),
> *How to Save Your Own Life*

A scene in Frank McCourt's best-selling autobiography *Angela's Ashes* (1996) suggests that for previous generations, entertainment was closely connected to folk traditions: "There's a gramophone in Mrs. O'Connor's playing an Irish jig or reel and boys and girls are dancing around kicking their legs out and keeping their hands to their sides." Although McCourt is referring to Ireland in the 1930s, the idea of making your own entertainment is something of a lost art that survives in square dances, bluegrass festivals, choral singing, barbershop quartets, and other forms connected to the popular culture of past eras. By contrast, most of today's Americans expect to be continually entertained without having to move from their couches.

CULTURAL ICONS

What a society regards as entertainment can tell us a great deal about that culture. For example, Elvis Presley, who made a profound impression on popular culture, offers us a way to understand how entertainment not only mirrors American life but can also transform it. In "Dead Elvis," Greil Marcus speculates that before his death (and even twenty-five years later) Elvis represented a symbol of possibility in American life. He blended white country music with black rhythm and blues at about the same time (1954) that the Supreme Court ruled racial segregation unconstitutional. Elvis was among those rare performers who permeate the popular psyche and become cultural icons that serve as points of reference in our own lives. These icons project patterns of public behavior that reflect and reinforce cultural values.

As an archetype of American morality in the 1950s and 1960s, Doris Day had this kind of influence. Sandra Tsing Loh speculates in "The Return of Doris Day" that the cycle of public morality as reflected in movie heroines has come full circle, beginning with Doris Day's "good girl" image. The evolution of female antiheroines (such as Madonna) in the 1970s and 1980s has led to the return of the "good girl" in the 1990s, according to Loh. She speculates that the public has grown weary of "yesterday's swampy girls/ . . . who reigned in the go-go eighties."

TELEVISION TRENDS

This return to traditional value is not apparent in nightly TV news broadcasts. Neil Postman and Steve Powers in "TV News as Entertainment" assert that the purpose of TV nightly news shows has changed—from providing real information to being just another form of amusement. Intelligent commentary that put events in perspective has been replaced by sensational images, stirring music, and glitzy graphics. Stories that are visually exciting take precedence over those that are simply informative, and images of violence and destruction actually become the news. The attempt to hold onto viewers may have spurred this transformation. As the number of network and cable TV stations has expanded and as access to the Internet has grown, Americans do not automatically tune to the major networks (NBC, CBS, or ABC) for news as they did until the 1970s. The shift in news coverage may also reflect a cultural change in that Americans have become accustomed to regarding information as a form of entertainment.

Because entertainment originally was associated with the visual-effects characteristic of movies, television viewers have come to expect the same kind of exciting visual images, special effects, and dramatic scenes on the small screen as well. With the concept of the home theater, as TV screens have become larger and sound reproduction more dramatic, this trend has grown even more pronounced. As a cultural phenomenon, television has come to occupy an important place in American life. As one wit observed, "The human is faced with a cruel choice: work or daytime television." Americans under age 50 have never known a world without television. Researchers at the Annenberg School of Communication estimate that children will have spent more hours watching TV (30,000 hours) before entering school than they will spend in classrooms during the course of their education. We might expect that a child's perceptions and expectations of the world would be fundamentally shaped during these impressionable years. Television at all levels offers vicarious rather than real experiences and may create a quick-fix mentality.

One of the most inventive satires on Americans' addiction to television is the novel *Being There* (1971), penned by the late Polish-born author Jerzy Kosinski. The main character, a retarded gardener named Chance who is illiterate, interprets everything that happens in real life according to what he has seen on television. Through a series of mishaps, Chance is interviewed on an evening talk show as an authority on economics. Kosinski's satire of the triumph of style over substance in America becomes sharper when Chance is later considered a candidate for the vice presidency. Kosinski's premise is not that exaggerated when we think of the extent to which politics is dominated by television and the campaign for president is staged as a series of made-for-TV events.

Modern TV talk shows, in the view of Charles Oliver in "Freak Parade," are the contemporary equivalents of carnival side shows. Millions of viewers tune in to see the bizarre spectacles that often border on violence. According to Tom Shachtman in *The Inarticulate Society* (1996), the language used on these shows by everyone, including the educated hosts, has been "dumbed down"—it's marked by poor grammar and misused terms that debase English. Producers find ingenious new ways to boost ratings by showing ever more abysmal and dysfunctional domestic relationships. To a certain degree, our society has come to define entertainment as passive vicarious sensationalism.

Long before TV talk shows exploited people's miseries for the sake of entertainment, an unusually prescient short story, "The Enormous Radio" by John Cheever, dramatized an analogous situation. A young urban couple discover that their new radio allows them to listen to their neighbors' private conversations. Gradually, the wife becomes addicted to these confessions and begins to pity (and feel superior to) her neighbors—in the same way that today's television audiences react to the guests on talk shows.

An early representative of this trend was *All in the Family* (1971), a series originally intended as a satire on bigotry. A radical departure from earlier family shows such as *The Adventures of Ozzie and Harriet*, this series liberated the sitcom and opened the door to caricatured depictions of moral and social issues. This loosening of social and moral constraints on what could be said and shown on television can be considered a precursor to today's Jerry Springer–type shows.

Television shows can tell us much about the surrounding culture at the time they are popular. For example, the popularity of *Survivor* and other reality-based shows in 2000 may suggest some unpleasant truths about contemporary American culture. The contrast between this series and, for example, *Friends* in the 1990s is dramatically expressed by the titles. On the other hand, *Will & Grace*, an over-the-top sitcom depicting an alternate lifestyle, won the Emmy in 2000.

HOLLYWOOD STEREOTYPES AND ARCHETYPES

Along with TV, movies also provide a context for interpreting the meaning of events in our own lives. Even the most ordinary film can reveal a great deal about the social concerns and cultural mood of the time. For example, in "Asian Women in Film: No Joy, No Luck," Jessica Hagedorn analyzes why films (ranging from *The World of Suzie Wong* [1960] to *The Joy Luck Club* [1993]) depict Asian women in stereotyped ways: as either treacherous seductresses or martyred victims. According to Hagedorn, these representations are so pervasive and enduring that they have gained legitimacy. Such stereotypes give a false picture of the culture they purport to represent.

The popular sci-fi, fantasy, and horror film genres are particularly well suited to the symbolic acting out of society's repressed racial anxieties. For example, the 1989 film *Alien Nation* (later made into a TV series) has attracted a cult following and can certainly be read as an allegory of race relationships in the United States. Ed Guerrero in *Framing Blackness: The African American Image in Film* (1993) speculates that

> The film's setting and historical moment [Los Angeles in the 1990s], combined with the rapid growth of its newcomer population, their containment in a ghetto, and their begrudging acceptance on the urban scene, form a specific and complex mediation of the social tensions and concerns over undocumented and uncontrolled Latino immigration into Los Angeles. (47)

Hollywood has long since ceased to be simply a place where American films are made and has become an icon representing fantasy throughout the world. In no small part this is due to the mythic dimension of movies. *Titanic* (1997) is an apt example of the film that taps into universal archetypes to reveals important cultural messages. Christopher Vogler in *The Writer's Journey* (1998) considers the film the modern-day equivalent of a Greek tragedy whose protagonists brought catastrophe upon themselves (because of their pride in constructing a technological marvel). The film's director, James Cameron, summed up why the film appealed to audiences on so many levels in a March 28, 1998, letter to the *Los Angeles Times: Titanic* "intentionally incorporates universals of human experience and emotion that are timeless—and familiar because they reflect our basic emotional fabric. By dealing in archetypes, the film touches people in all cultures and of all ages."

ASIAN FILMS, ASIAN CULTURES

Hollywood's worldwide influence underlies R. K. Narayan's account of the "Misguided 'Guide.'" Bombay (known as "Bollywood") film producers proposed making his succesful novel *The Guide* into a movie. Narayan humorously recounts how his authentic depiction of life in a fictional south Indian village became a grandiose Hollywood-type extravaganza. The attempt to make the film commercially successful (i.e., to make it attractive to audiences accustomed to Western films) caused it to lose the distinctive essence of the culture the novel's author had captured.

The films that come out of Hong Kong use martial arts to emphasize action and feature story lines that reflect the Confucian values of benevolence, honor, and morality. In "A Dirty Job," film star Jackie Chan describes how, as an underpaid apprentice, he volunteered (twice) to perform a life-endangering stunt that catapulted him to stardom. Implicit in Chan's account is that showing bravery and moral integrity, both quintessential Asian values, is essential to gaining recognition for one's abilities.

It is ironic that although people throughout the world enjoy films made in Hollywood, Vietnamese immigrants in the United States find little to relate to in American-made movies, according to Jesse W. Nash in "Confucius and the VCR." Instead they prefer to rent films made in Taiwan and Hong Kong. These films more accurately reflect their cultural values: loyalty to one's family, clan, or state; the Confucian tradition of showing respect; and being a good son or daughter.

The selections in this chapter encourage you to assess the role that entertainment (especially via the media) plays in Eastern and Western cultures. They offer a great deal of insight into how various forms of entertainment not only reflect but also transform societal values.

GREIL MARCUS

Dead Elvis

Greil Marcus is a highly regarded writer on rock and roll music and has written many articles for *Rolling Stone* magazine. The author of *Mystery Train* (1975), which was nominated for a National Book Critics Circle Award, Marcus currently writes a bimonthly column for Salon.com. Among his recent works are *Invisible Republic: Bob Dylan's Basement Tapes* (1997) and *Double Trouble: Bill Clinton and Elvis Presley in a Land of No Alternative* (2000). According to Marcus, Elvis's ride to fame during his lifetime and his posthumous celebrity status is a vivid case of public mythmaking. In this chapter from *Dead Elvis: A Chronicle of a Cultural Obsession* (1991), Marcus analyzes the meaning of America's continuing obsession with Elvis so many years after his death.

Thinking Critically

Marcus argues that Elvis redefined what it means to be an American. To help you follow Marcus's line of thought, underline and annotate those passages in which he develops his thesis.

In 1981 I was invited to speak at the third annual Salute to Memphis Music, held as it had been the previous years at the Memphis State University on August 16, the anniversary of Elvis Presley's death. Given the location, I misunderstood the forum; I expected an academic symposium, with an audience of teachers and students. Instead there were testimonials and reminiscences from those who had known the King— friends, relatives, his dentist's wife—and one speaker from elsewhere. The audience was mostly Southern, white, middle-aged, and working class.

I had two props. I ran a video of Elvis's performance of "Tryin' to Get to You" from his comeback television special; as the crowd on the video burst into wild applause, so did the crowd in Memphis. I brought out an Elvis whiskey bottle, twisted off the head, and poured bourbon—Missouri bourbon, of all things—out of the neck and into a glass.

That was Elvis in 1968, facing an audience for the first time in nine years; and that was Elvis today, four years after his death. Nobody, I think, knows what to make of this: the singing and the bottle. The contradiction is too big. Contrasts and contradictions have always been the language in which Elvis has been talked about: the polite rebel, the gospel rocker, the country boy in Hollywood. True folk artist and commodity fetish. Clean living model for the nation's youth with his own drugstore. Why, said the promoter, with this boy I could reach—everyone.

Even in that video of Elvis sitting on stage with Scotty Moore and D. J. Fontana, reinventing his music on the spot—the performance is about an hour long, we saw only a favorite moment—there's a contradiction. Elvis laughs while drawing the deepest passion out of himself: that's no contradiction. He merely removes a bit of the edge from a performance almost too powerful to grasp all at once—removes the edge for himself, and for us. It takes him a while to get warmed up, the first few numbers are formal run-throughs or self parodies, but once Elvis takes the electric guitar from Scotty Moore and begins to lead the music, we're in a new world. To take a line from Albert Werthheimer, a photographer who traveled with Elvis in 1956, responding to this music isn't a matter of taste, it's a matter of whether you're a living, breathing human being. But then Elvis sets down the guitar. Strings come up, and he puts on a solemn face. He walks to the edge of the little stage, raises a hand mike, and begins to sing a song called "Memories."

5   It's a rotten song: funeral music. Worse than that: music for a commercial advertising a mortuary. Elvis, naturally, sings with true reverence. What the performance says is this: What I just did (I didn't know I had it in me), what you just saw (you didn't think I had it in me), wasn't real. It might have been the greatest music of his life, it might be a central moment in American culture—but we'll chalk it up to nostalgia. Memories. Fifties stuff, the old songs. Remember where you were when you first heard Elvis sing "Tryin' to Get to You" like that? Forget that you can't remember where you were when you first heard Elvis sing "Tryin' to Get to You" like that—he never did before, and he never did again.

"They're going to let me do what I want," Elvis says at the beginning of the performance, talking like a prisoner out on parole. Later, he tells the crowd there's time for only one more song; another audience is coming in. The crowd doesn't boo, but they let him know they're disappointed. "Hey, I just work here," Elvis says. Then he hoists the guitar again and sings rhythm and blues—and offers a metaphor for the possibilities of life that makes almost every job, every love affair, every religious experience, every presidential candidate—save, perhaps, Franklin Roosevelt—seem like a shoddy compromise.

What I'm getting at is this: Elvis was too big, too complex—too much—for any of us to quite take in, to see all at once, to understand. He was too big, finally, for us to live with. To use a psychological term, he was too big for us to incorporate into ourselves. He confounds us. Like Medusa, you can't look at him head on. So we look sideways. From one angle, we see the young man who untangled and rewove the strands of American identity with "Good Rockin' Tonight"; from another angle, we hear that same young man declare Kay Starr his favorite female singer—insisting, in not so many words, that such an image of American identity, fixed and sterile, will do just fine. We may not be comfortable with such a contradiction, but what we're truly uncomfortable with, I think, is bigger still: the possibility that this is no contradiction at all. Millions of people found comfort precisely in this contradiction: without it, they wouldn't have been comfortable with the Elvis who got into fights, who did a bump and grind on stage, who sang "Hound Dog."

As long as Elvis was alive—as long as there was still some possibility of a resolution to his career—some last confession, perhaps, or some unheard, unknown, unimaginable musical synthesis—this was fascinating, but it wasn't exactly a problem. Sure, I may be making too much of Elvis singing a stupid, life-denying tune only seconds after singing a tune I think would do as a version of life itself: this was, we can say, just a touch the producer added. It had nothing to do with the *real* Elvis. "I just work here," he says—but what does *that* mean? This moment was planned, it was in the script, and we can say what counts is what happened during those moments that couldn't be planned, that couldn't be scripted, and we saw what happened then. That kind of talk was good enough, some years ago. But now we seize on smaller things, we try to find meaning in them, because Elvis's story, and his music, is at times so grand, so unsettling, and we're desperate to understand. Some part of us is wrapped up in some part of Elvis Presley. What part? What happens? What happens is what critic Paul Nelson said happened with Bob Dylan: "People would search through his trash, his dropped cigarette butts, looking for a sign. The scary thing is, they'd find it."

It's troubling; we can't ever understand. Elvis's story has been told again and again, the litany of his success and failure has been recited until it seems like an old blessing and an older curse, and the tale explains everything but what we want to know: how did he do that? Why did I respond? Freud lets us off the hook. Halfway through his psychobiography of Leonardo da Vinci—after pinning down da Vinci's vulture fantasy, after explaining why da Vinci painted what he painted, why he designed his flying machines—even after explaining the reasons behind the *way* da Vinci painted his paintings and designed his flying machines—after all that, Freud said, now we come to the question of genius. In other words, okay, paintings; all right, flying machines. But why so profound? Well, Freud said, we all know a genius is incomprehensible.

This is part of the problem with Elvis. Yes, he was a genius, but not the *10* kind we're accustomed to. Was he even an artist? He didn't even write his own songs. So we listen to writers and news analysts—the people who turned up on television when Elvis died—tell us that if Elvis hadn't brought together white country music and black blues, and thus changed the contours and the symbolism of American life, changed the symbols by which we interpret our culture to ourselves, interpret what it means to be American, then someone else would have done the same. It's in the momentum of history, we're told; in 1954, the very year the Supreme Court ruled racial segregation unconstitutional, it was in the cards. But you can listen to every proto-rockabilly singer—to some very good ones, like Roy Hall, who one day sat down with a black friend and wrote "Whole Lotta Shakin' Goin' On," and recorded one of the first versions of that song—and what you hear in Elvis simply isn't there. You can listen to Jimmie Rodgers and Hank Williams, both originals, neither of whom would have existed without the blues, and it isn't there. You can listen to Elvis at the very beginning and it is there; you just can't tell what it is. All the sociological and musicological explanations about Elvis's boyhood and his background and his taste and his favorite radio stations won't explain it. You can go right to the edge, and then it all vanishes.

America is a young country, as countries go. Because of that, and because it's a polyglot country, filled with people of all sorts, made out of a clash of languages and regions and religions, and because it's based in crime, in slavery and the extermination of the Indians, and because it's based in a war, the Civil War, a war that has yet to be fully settled, we're uncertain about what it is to be American—uncertain, and eager for a nice, neat definition. There have been a lot of them, some enforced by law and some set forth in poetry. This is our great subject, but of late it's been narrowed down, as if we've given up on the question, on our story. Now we ask, what does it mean to be a black American? A white Southern American? An Italian American? A Jewish American? We're relatively comfortable with these questions. But if we chance to encounter a figure like Herman Melville, or Abraham Lincoln, Emily Dickinson, William Faulkner, Howlin' Wolf, or Elvis Presley, they blow these neat questions apart.

For some years now, I've thought of Elvis in terms of blues singers like Robert Johnson and punk bands like the Sex Pistols or X—the Los Angeles group that's just put out a tune called "Back 2 the Base," the best song about Elvis since Bill Parsons' "The All American Boy"—and I've thought of Elvis in terms of Melville and Lincoln and Faulkner. Some people have been interested in the notion of looking at Elvis this way, and some people have been irritated, but what has actually upset people is the argument that Elvis belongs in this company because he was, in a way that we don't quite understand, conscious. He knew what he was doing. If he had redefined what it means to be American, it was because he meant to. He wanted change. He wanted to confuse, to disrupt, to tear it up. He was not, in any important manner, a folk artist, as RCA once called him and as timid folk have called him ever since—he was not an exemplar of "the people." Watch him as he first appeared on television in 1956, watch the way he moves, what he says, how he says it: the willfulness, the purpose, is unmistakable. And yet so many of us missed it: as we watched, we drew a veil over the man bent on saying what he meant.

It wasn't only the idea of the conscious actor that led me to place Elvis and Lincoln and Melville together, though—it was as much the sense of mystery in the speeches, the novels, the music. No one knows how to explain the grace in Lincoln's Second Inaugural Address. No one knows how to explain the unholy power of the chapter in *Moby-Dick* called "The Whiteness of the Whale," the chapter that makes you wish that you too were on the ship, on the hunt. And no one knows how to explain the music I showed on the video. "I don't get it," a musician friend said of Elvis's guitar playing, as we watched that video a few weeks ago. "Those are such easy chords."

With each of these examples there is a presentation, an acting out, a fantasy, a performance, not of what it means to be American—to be a creature of history, the inheritor of certain crimes, wars, ideas, landscapes—but rather a presentation, an acting out, a fantasy of what the deepest and most extreme possibilities and dangers of our national identity are. We read, or we listen, or with Lincoln we read and we imagine ourselves listening, then and there, on the spot, and we gasp. We get it. We feel ennobled and a little scared, or very scared, because we are being shown what could be, because we realize what we are, and what we are not. We pull back.

We can't explain, but we can explain away. Melville was not much talked 15 about until the 1920s, but after that he slowly became an academic industry, and his best books have stood up against the shallowest and the most pretentious analysis. The *TV Guide* listing for the film of *Moby-Dick* provides all the summation that's really necessary: "An American epic in which the mad captain of a whaling ship chases a white whale." That's enough for us to respond to. Lincoln has been an enigma, a saint, and a reproach ever since he was made a martyr. Faulkner took the curse of the Civil War upon himself and watched as his characters struggled to escape it, which he never permitted them to do. And yet each of them has been whittled down; a great attempt has been made to make these people, and their legacies, manageable. Melville? Central figure of the nineteenth-century American literary renaissance. Lincoln? Keeper of our national soul. Faulkner? Mississippi's truest voice.

The same thing is going to happen to Elvis. It's already happening; the process is well advanced. There is less mystery every day. To many people, Elvis was no sort of creator, just an uneducated country boy with a smart manager and a gullible, thrill-seeking public to exploit. There's no aura of genius, of mystery, surrounding him; the very idea is ludicrous. To many who revere Elvis, the absence of genius is just as vital: their Elvis is a kind of innocent, passive, a hero because of where he came from and where he went. His death adds a layer of guilt to the story—Elvis's guilt, and the guilt of those who loved him but could not save him—and so this image is very powerful, a closed, imploding circle. To other Americans, Elvis is just a name, a joke, a few scandals. Or he is a symbol of rebellion. Or he existed only in 1954 and 1955, when he recorded for Sun Records here in Memphis, before he was swallowed up and spit out by big business and mass culture. To say that this last idea of Elvis ignores most of his music, its complexity and its contradictions, the seeming gap I began with, is no strong criticism: all of these ideas of Elvis ignore most of his music, as each denies every other. In every case, a piece of Elvis for Everyone, and no effort to discover why an everyone even comes into play, no attempt to seek out the whole story, to take it on its own terms, to say what those terms might be.

People have always talked about the real Elvis. We have a reason for attempting to find the real Elvis on tape, on the video we watched, or we have a motive in the invisible but undeniable connection between the video and the bottle. But as the bottle says, the real Elvis now seems more than anything else a question of marketing. There is an audience out there, right here: find it, map it, service it, use it up. The idea of Elvis as a market is the idea that Elvis *can* be used up. What have we seen, then, since Elvis's death? What do we see as the market brings him down to size?

One result of Elvis's death was a lot more to hear and a lot more to watch. Videos like the one we saw, at first pirate tapes, now official products available anywhere. Scores of new records, most of them bootlegs of very early live shows, TV appearances, dozens of later concerts, even of the famous Million Dollar Quartet sessions from 1956. Almost secret albums containing the talk that went on in the Sun studio between Elvis, Sam Phillips, and Scotty Moore when the first songs were being cut. Endless repackagings of recordings already issued. But this is for a relatively small legion of fans, not for the country itself. The country itself is aware of something very different: of Elvis as an emptied, triumphantly vague symbol of displaced identity.

The country is aware of Elvis as a weird icon: as a T-shirt, a black velvet wall hanging, an emblem of working-class bad taste or upper-class camp, an ashtray, a $200 baby doll with a porcelain head marked down to $125, a commemorative limited-edition dinner plate. The country is aware of Elvis as he's been worshipfully caricatured by thousands of Elvis imitators, and sneering imitators of Elvis imitators, like the TV comedian Andy Kaufman—who, twice removed, a knowing parody of a parody that doesn't know it is a parody, in some aspect of his act wants to get it across that in fact he loves Elvis, would in some part of his soul give up a limb to feel as Elvis must have felt when he sang as, in his best moments, he sang, and who, as a comedian on TV, in this context of camp layered over bad taste, cannot begin to get such a thing across. The country is aware of Elvis as he is presented in TV movies: just one more confused star, an ordinary boy with a bit of talent and a bit of nerve who lost his way. Someone we can all easily identify with, and just as easily feel different from, safe from.

We've had scores of books in which the Elvis who first attracted our at-   *20*
tention is unrecognizable: books full of nice memories, books full of awful
tales. We're going to get more of the last: Albert Goldman's forthcoming
biography—it will be published next month, there will be ads everywhere, it
will be excerpted in your newspapers and reviewed in *Time* and *Newsweek*—
may have enough dirt in it to bury everything else. Goldman is a vulture with
no interest in his subject; he's already made hundreds of thousands of dollars
from his book and he'll make more. He's got, as they say, a lot of good stories.
So what if he doesn't know, or care, what he's talking about—doesn't know,
that is, why the world is at such a point that a book about Elvis Presley could
make so much money? What we want to know is why a certain person sang in
a certain way, and why that touched us, why that simple confluence of circumstances changed the country, and the world—but since those are difficult questions, mysteries that will never be solved but also the only questions worth asking, we can be led to settle for every last quirk, rumor, failing, perversion, and
we may be led to believe, finally, perhaps, that the real questions are not so
important, or even real at all. A certain person, singing in a certain way—
maybe it wasn't quite what it seemed. Anyway it was a long time ago.

As we form or accept the idea of Elvis that America will live with, or live
without, whether it is an idea of beauty or an idea of squalor, we are moving farther and farther away from the source of that idea: Elvis Presley's music. But
even the story, the life, is losing it's shape; it's being reshaped to fit into old boxes.
The scandal books and loving memoirs tell the same story in the end, an old
story that is not, in any particular sense, Elvis's story: he got what he wanted but
he lost what he had. He was cut off from his roots; he fell from grace. See what
happens to American heroes; see what we do to them. We've always loved this
story: the artist or the leader dies for our sins, after permitting us to enjoy them.

Such mythologizing predated Elvis's death, but it's gathered irresistible
force since. A dead person is vulnerable in ways a living person is not, and it's
not simply that you can't libel the dead. When the subject of a book is living,
he or she can always make that book into a lie by acting in a new way. A dead
person can be summed up and dismissed. And Elvis is especially vulnerable,
because for much of America he has always been a freak.

Let me quote James Wolcott, a columnist for the *Village Voice*. "Elvis," he
writes, "is a figure whose significance shrinks with each passing season. . . . As
a musical artist he doesn't exist—he doesn't begin to exist." Wolcott is a snob
but he's not a fool, and he's not an old hack with a grudge against rock 'n' roll.
Wolcott is twenty-eight, and he's written well about rock 'n' roll; he was one of
the first writers to spread the word about punk. But now he's most interested
in making a name for himself, in attracting attention, and this is one way of
doing it: such a complete dismissal of Elvis Presley has not really been heard,
in an interesting publication, since the fifties.

What exactly is Wolcott saying? "As a musical artist he doesn't exist—he doesn't begin to exist"—even as simple musicology such a statement has no meaning unless we're willing to wipe out most of the history of American popular music, most of blues, country, and rock 'n' roll, from ancient Child ballads like "Barbara Allen" to the Sex Pistols' "Anarchy in the U.K." It has no meaning unless we're willing to write off that music as a bad joke, a trick we played on ourselves. Wolcott's line tells us we can forget it—but we shouldn't forget that a great proportion of the American public has always believed precisely what Wolcott wrote. With Elvis dead, we're going to hear a lot more of this: as ridicule, and as silence.

25   There are other ways in which Elvis, dead, is vulnerable, other ways in which he is being dismissed. Alice Walker is a black writer from Georgia who once wrote a great, shattering novel called *The Third Life of George Copeland*. She recently published a short story called "Nineteen Fifty-five." It's about a white pop singer who records a song by a blues singer, a black woman. The record makes the pop singer famous, rich, powerful. He feels guilty, though—not because he used the woman's song, though he is grateful, but because, after singing the song hundreds of times, on record, on television, all over the country, he still doesn't understand it. So he plies the woman with gifts: a car, a house. He brings her on TV to sing the song with him; he has her over to his house, hoping she'll tell him the secret. Finally he dies—alone, fat, ruined, helpless, too young—dies because he couldn't understand the music that made him a star. He couldn't solve the mystery; he couldn't even find it.

Now, there is truth in this story: the truth that, in the music Elvis sang, there is a mystery. But that was hardly the point Alice Walker was making. Her point was blunt—blunt enough that even the reviewer for the *New York Times* recognized that "Nineteen Fifty-five" was a parable about Elvis, Willie Mae Thornton, and "Hound Dog"—a song Thornton was the first to record but which, as it happens, she did not write. The story isn't, in the end, a real piece of fiction—a story that generates its own reason for being—it's an argument about the nature of American culture: about how white America was sold, and happily bought, a bill of goods, and about how black America was bilked. The white boy robs the black woman—pays her, yes, dutifully, piously, even, but some things can never be paid for—and dies of guilt.

This story has no more meaning than the statement that as a musical artist Elvis doesn't exist, but a search for meaning is not at issue here. The story is an object that will insulate those predisposed to accept it, and that they will turn some readers away from music they might have otherwise heard, or that they have already heard. Never mind that part of what needs to be understood is not the mystery of Willie Mae Thornton's "Hound Dog"—a recording that is good, but ordinary, a piece of genre music—but the mystery of Elvis's "Hound Dog," which was a sound for which no one was prepared. Listen: the idea that

Elvis didn't understand this song is bewildering. But if we accept that we don't have to talk about Elvis—a person who did a particular thing at a particular time, for particular reasons—then the story fits neatly into various cultural prejudices, some of which are those of American blacks, and more of which are those white, middle-class Americans, and it makes perfect sense.

Writing about Elvis's death, rock critic Lester Bangs talked about how Elvis had given a generation a sense of itself as a generation, and how, well before Elvis died, those who had once felt that felt it no longer, "I can guarantee you one thing," he wrote: "we will never again agree on anything as we agreed on Elvis." Today it is clear that Elvis's fans, people who get some sense of life through some reflection of this person, don't speak the same language, which may tell us that they, we, never did. We have an Elvis who is dissolving into sentiment, an Elvis who has nothing to do with sex, drugs, misery, tragedy, anger, resentment, simply a perfect man. We have an Elvis dissolving in horror and crime. We have an Elvis dissolving in shared myths that existed long before he did and that will exist long after. We have an Elvis whose work is being dissolved by the facts of his life, as anyone's work can be dissolved by the facts of his or her life.

There is a way to respond to this. It's to place ourselves in confrontation with Elvis's music—all of it, pieces at a time, trying to understand what's there, what isn't, how the music was made, how it communicates, how it fails to communicate. We have to understand that not every little boy or girl can grow up to be Elvis Presley. We have to understand that if Elvis is an exemplar of the American dream, that tells something about the limits of the American dream—because Elvis was unique, talented in a way that no one else in this century was talented, as Howlin' Wolf was talented like no one else in our history in so far as we know it, neither of them missing parts of a formula, but pieces that made everything else fall into place around them.

British critic Simon Frith sheds some light on the morass that is now 30 Elvis—on our ability to encompass the Elvis of 1968, singing "Tryin' to Get to You," and the Elvis of the bourbon bottle. "Our joyous response to music," Frith writes, "is a response not to meanings but to the making of meanings. This response involves self abandonment, as the terms we usually use to construct and hold ourselves together suddenly seem to float free. Think of Elvis Presley. In the end this is the only way we can explain his appeal: not in terms of what he 'stood for,' socially or personally, but by reference to the *grain* of his voice. Elvis Presley's music was thrilling because he dissolved the symbols that had previously put adolescence together. He celebrated—more sensually, more voluptuously than any other rock and roll singer—the act of symbol creation itself."

I disagree with Frith at the end—Elvis didn't just, or even principally, dissolve the symbols that had put adolescence together, he dissolved the symbols that had put America together. As his career went on, those symbols regained their shape, and surrounded him, trapped him, made it hard for us to see him at all, made it nearly impossible to see him as anything more than a simple symbol of all the other symbols. But the grain of his voice remained—that element in his voice that rubbed against, that rubbed raw, so much that we had taken for granted, as finished and sealed. That element told its own story: it changed, it disappeared, it reappeared, it kept on making symbols, submitting to old symbols, then casting them off. And we still hear it happen. Today we did.

Simon Frith's words are just a beginning. The surface has only been scratched, and the surface has been covered up. It's so covered with debris we can't even see the scratches, can't feel them as we run our fingers over the old 45s.

Every once in a while, though someone gets it right. Someone pins it down—not the answer, but the reality of the question. Someone reminds you that, no, it wasn't an illusion; it wasn't a trick. The insistence we've heard in Elvis's music that nothing is settled, that nothing is final, that there are new things under the sun, comes home. And because of the grime crusted over the records, this now happens less often, less directly, when one listens to the music than when someone else catches what is there, and finds new words for it.

William Price Fox is a North Carolina novelist who once wrote a terrific trash novel called *Ruby Red*, about two country girls who sing their way to success and perdition in Nashville; when he wrote about the way their voices intertwined, you could hear it. Earlier this year he published a novel called *Dixiana Moon*, about a young New Yorker and an old Southern hustler who join forces to stage the ultimate revival show. One night, driving through the South, the New Yorker picks up an old Sun single on the radio. "Wonder what he was like," he says to his carny mentor. "He wasn't like anyone," says the would-have-been Colonel Parker. "You start trying to compare Elvis to something and you can forget it. . . . All you can do with a talent that big and that different is sort of point at it when you see it going by, and maybe listen for the ricochet." We are the ricochet.

Engaging the Text

1. Marcus claims that "Elvis was too big, too complex—too much—for any of us to quite take in, to see all at once, to understand," How does Marcus solve this problem for his readers? For example, what is the significance of the italic headnote in providing a framework for his analysis?

2. How does Marcus tap into the mythic dimension of Elvis by linking him with two renowned Americans, Abraham Lincoln and Herman Melville? Why does he do this?

3. What role does Marcus see himself playing in relationship to Elvis's memory? How does he characterize other chroniclers?

FIGURE 7.1

Exploring Your Cultural Perspective

1. Films, books, newspaper articles, magazine covers, kitsch artifacts, and song lyrics suggest that Elvis has permeated popular culture. Locate one of these items, and analyze the meaning it ascribes to Elvis. A good source of ideas is Elvis Presley's Graceland at <http://www.elvispresley.com>. See especially the section on "Elvisology."

2. Compare the very different cultural meanings of Graceland and of the Taj Mahal in Agra, India, as national shrines. What is the history behind each one? What common elements do they share? For information on the Taj Mahal, go to <http://rubens.anu.edu.au/student.projects/tajmahal/home.html>.

3. In what way does the picture in Figure 7.1 capture the nature of Elvis's posthumous appeal, as Marcus discusses?

SANDRA TSING LOH

The Return of Doris Day

In the mid-1990s, something strange started to happen in American film and popular culture: the "good girl" image returned from exile to oust her "bad girl" counterpart. The reasons for this, according to Sandra Tsing Loh in "The Return of Doris Day," reflect a fundamental cultural shift that testifies to the enduring power of the good girl archetype. This essay first appeared in the September 1995 issue of *Buzz*. Loh has also written *Depth Takes a Holiday: Essays from Lesser Angeles* (1996), *If You Lived Here, You'd Be Home by Now* (1997), and *A Year in Van Nuys* (2001).

Thinking Critically

Loh gives an account of her life as an erstwhile "good girl" before reflecting on its cultural significance. In your opinion, what explains the enduring appeal of the good girl or girl-next-door archetype in America?

The seventies and eighties were tough times for us Good Girls. As polite people, we like to do what's expected of us. Unfortunately, what was expected, in our sexual heyday, was for Girls to be . . . anything but Good.

In junior high, I dutifully grappled with whatever icky senior boy that Spin the Bottle sent me. By college, my sisters and I had graduated to smoking pot and swimming nude in the Sierras, sleeping with men on the first date (or before—you're welcome!), and developing evasive "mumble vaguely and give back rubs" routines if forced into a threesome.

We were lost, I tell you. Lost. But not anymore. Recently I was faced with a Nude Hot Tub Situation. It was a tame one by the eighties standards. The tub was vast, the night was dark, and my companions were three platonic male friends—thirtysomethings like me stooped with worry, hardly a threat.

"C'mon!" I heard that inner coach urging me. It was the voice born in 1975, when everyone in my junior high had Chemin de Fer jeans and Candie's sandals. *Don't be a drag*, it said. *Take off your clothes and jump in!*

5   But then, for the first time, I heard another voice. Clear as a bell, it was the soaring soprano of Mary Martin in *South Pacific*, or perhaps Shirley Jones in *Oklahoma!* It sang:

I've got a guy!
A really great guy!
He makes me as high
As an elephant's eye!

Or something to that effect. It was like a light bulb going on. Suddenly I felt right with my world—fresh, natural, confident, all the panty-shield adjectives. It was so simple, so clear. The wandering days of these breasts were over.

"If you'd known me in my twenties," I lecture my hot tub companions, as though sharing an amazing story from ancient lore, "you would have seen my boobs and seen them often!" I'm in the water now, but demurely covered in my white cotton T-shirt from Victoria's Secret. (A white cotton T-shirt is typical of what we women actually *buy* there.) "But no more." I lift a teacherly finger. "Today, I feel much more liberated keeping my shirt on. I don't have to prove anything anymore. I can turn the world on with a smile!" I hear myself excitedly half-singing, flashing on Mary Tyler Moore.

My treatise is cut short by the arrival of two 24-year-old modern dancers who rip off towels and flash their naked pink everything. The men's attention snaps away with the zing of taut bungee cords. But I don't feel bad. I know it's only I, Goody Two Shoes, who feels that wonderful glowing specialness inside.

I. GOOD GIRLS: A CLEANED AND BUFFED THUMBNAIL HISTORY

Were our moms actually right way back when? Maybe so. Because like it or not, these days Good Girls are back in. Demure behavior is suddenly clever, fashionable, even attractive.

Who *is* the nineties Good Girl? She is: (a) spunky; (b) virginal; (c) busy   10 with purposeful activity. But not obsessively so. Her hormones are in balance. Brave chin up, she works within society's rules, finds much to celebrate in her immediate surroundings, makes the best of her lot. Good Girls don't challenge the status quo.

Good Girls have been around a long time in Western culture. The star of the very first novel in English? A Good Girl! We find her in Samuel Richardson's 1740 opus, *Pamela*. In it, Pamela's resistance to sex charges five-hundred-plus pages of narrative tension; it's so effective a gambit that Good Girls (typically poor but beautiful governesses) become the very foundation of the eighteenth- and nineteenth-century novel.

It is in twentieth-century America, however, that we start to see the rowdy Good Girl. She does more than keep her knees crossed. In fact, if so moved, she may even spread her legs boldly akimbo! (If only to punctuate a funny singalong.)

The forties and fifties brought the U.S. Good Girl her two most sacred boons: World War II, and Rodgers & Hammerstein. The former yielded new busy-but-virginal archetypes like Rosie the Riveter, the Andrews Sisters, and the Chipper Navy Nurse. The latter fleshed out the canon via the Feisty Governess of the past (Anna in *The King and I*), the Chipper Navy Nurse of the semipresent (Nellie Forbush in *South Pacific*), even the boldly innovative Frisky Nun of the future (Julie Andrews in *The Sound of Music*). Indeed, Frisky Nun proved so popular she'd soon hop mediums and become TV's *The Flying Nun* (comical ex-Gidget Sally Field). Even *The Mary Tyler Moore Show*—a milestone in the modern Good Girl's progress—almost had Moore playing a version of Frisky Nun. Laugh no more at winged hats: in the past, Frisky Nun was a female star's emancipated alternative!

The quintessential Good Girl of midcentury America—indeed the mother of all modern Good Girls—was Doris Day. We mean, of course, Nubile Doris Day, in her guise as pert, urban, apartment-dwelling career girl (*Pillow Talk*), opposed to harangued suburban housewife (*Please Don't Eat the Daisies*). Never mind that Doris typically chucked her career at the end of the film for Rock Hudson; what mattered was that while Doris *was* a Good Girl, she was hardly a nun—in fact, she was quite sexy in her spunky purposefulness.

15   It was too bad that Doris stayed mainly in the movies, for the most perfect form for the American Good Girl remains the musical. Here emerges a unique symbiosis: on the one hand, the musical needs the Good Girl's soprano, her can-do optimism, the soaring love songs only she can inspire. On the other, not to put too fine a point on it, the Good Girl needs the musical. The musical could *create* Good Girls where there once were none. Example: where, outside the musical, do you find the rarest of beings—the ethnic Good Girl? Sure, ethnic girls can have hearts o' gold, but in the real world they—can we say it?—tend to be a bit sassy. Happily, the musical has the miraculous power to freshen, sanitize, uplift even ethnicities who might feel too irked with society to be Good. We see Jewish Good Girls: Tevye's daughters in *Fiddler on the Roof*. (Imagine "Matchmaker, Matchmaker" done in dialogue on a hot afternoon in Queens—another tale entirely.) It also gave us Yentl. Hm. *West Side Story* produces Latina Good Girl Maria (Natalie Wood, but we quibble). *Flower Drum Song* yields that mousy Asian Good Girl whose name no one can remember (not Nancy Kwan, the other one). *The Wiz* even gives us a black Good Girl: Diana Ross (who was never that Good again).

As we move into the late seventies, however, even white Good Girls are hard to come by. There's a general Fall of the Musical (we could discuss Andrew Lloyd Webber, but why?)—and Fall of Filmic Good Girls. We lose our bright, dependable, pony-tailed stars—our June Allysons, Shirley Joneses, Julie Andrewses. We collapse into the nude/seminude group therapy "line" musicals: *Oh! Calcutta!*, *Pippin*, the exhaustingly confessional *A Chorus Line*. By 1977, we have, God forbid, Liza Minnelli trying to play an ex-WAC in *New York, New York*. Liza Minnelli? The eyelashes alone would have scared Our Boys.

And you know why we saw this fall, this demise, this dismal sinking? Because national hope is failing. No one whistles a happy tune. We're moving into bad times for optimism. Bad times for patriotism. Bad times for Good Girls. Forrest Gump drifts out of touch with Jenny . . . and America itself becomes very *dark*.

II. THE ENDURING POWER OF GOOD GIRLS

If Good Girls are back in the nineties, what does that imply? That we've come full circle? Forgiven Mom and Dad? We're in love with a wonderful guy? More deeply, does the Good Girl's resurgence signal an uplift in national character, a kind of neo-fifties patriotism, a return to what we might call, without irony, American values?

We have no idea—Good Girls are notoriously poor at political analysis. All we know is, we look around and Good Girls seem to be all over the place, winning again.

Look how they flourish, in the very bosom of our society! Good girls are our great: morning-show hosts (Katie Couric now, Jane Pauley before); figure skaters (Nancy Kerrigan vanquishing Tonya Harding now, Dorothy Hamill vanquishing all those foreigners before); country singers (Reba, Tammy & Co. now; Dolly Parton before); middle-of-the-road pop stars (Whitney Houston, Paula Abdul now; Linda Ronstadt before); goyische straight gals to nervous Jewish comics (Sally to Harry, Helen Hunt to Paul Reiser now; Diane Keaton to Woody Allen before); Peter Pans (Sandy Duncan now-ish, Mary Martin way before); androgynous gals (Ellen DeGeneres now, Nancy Drew's pal boyish George before); astronauts (Sally Ride); Australians (Olivia Newton-John); MTV newspersons (Tabitha Soren); princesses (Di). 20

Can a video vixen be Good? Absolutely. Look at ex-Aerosmith girl and rising star Alicia Silverstone. You thought she was Drew Barrymore, but she's not. In Amy Heckerling's surprise summer hit *Clueless* (loosely based on Jane Austen's *Emma!*), Silverstone played Cher, a fashion-obsessed virgin ("You see how picky I am about my shoes, and *they* only go on my feet!"). Alicia the person is very spunky, clean, convincingly virginal, attends Shakespeare camp, takes tap-dancing lessons, and loves animals!

Good Girl accessories are in. Look what Hillary Clinton did for the headband—an astounding semiotic statement. Look how she reinvented cookie baking. Too-thin Nancy Reagan in her let-them-eat-cake Adolfo suit is over. Today, posing as a Good Girl—as clever Hillary does—seems powerfully subversive.

Look how even yesterday's swampy girls are cleaning up. Jane Seymour bounced back from whatever seamy B-stuff she was doing to triumph today as Dr. Quinn, Medicine Woman. Consider post-Donald Ivana, her pertness and brave industry recalling the Czech girl skier of yore. Even Sharon Stone seems downright nice. She makes an effort to dress "up" for press briefings and is so polite, modest, funny! (She showed us her home in *In Style*—the essence of nice! Is a *Redbook* cover in her future?)

And why not? Being a Good Girl pays off. Look how well Meg Ryan/Sandra Bullock films are doing. These girls don't titillate by getting naked. Why? They can turn the world on with a smile!

25   Even the musical is coming back! Via Disney, we have Belle and the Little Mermaid, even Princess Jasmine and Pocahontas. Look how ethnic! Maybe there *is* a place called Hope.

III. THE NASTIEST TRUTH OF ALL

But what is the bottom-line appeal of the Good Girl? Why do we urban nineties women want to *be* her? It's not as uncalculated as one might think. The Good Girl's draw is that she is the opposite of Bad. And Bad is something we no longer want to be.

You remember Bad Girl—she who reigned in the go-go eighties. Bad Girl is very Bad. Ow. She needs a spanking, she wants it, but beware of giving it to her because ironically it is you (or, more likely, Michael Douglas) who will suffer afterward.

Good Girl's opposite, Bad Girl, has out-of-control hormones. Bad Girl comes from a wildly dysfunctional family; her past makes her do strange, erratic things. Bad Girl tells us something is terribly wrong with society. Bad Girl challenges the status quo. Bad Girl uses sex for everything but love and babies: it's power, self-expression, psychosis, hate, revolt, revenge.

What we have in Bad Girl is Power Slut. Like Madonna in, well, ninety percent of her oeuvre. Joan Collins in *Dynasty*. Glenn Close in *Fatal Attraction*. Sharon Stone in *Basic Instinct*. Demi Moore in *Disclosure*. (Sure those last few are technically nineties, but anything written by Joe Eszterhas is really quite eighties, no?)

30   Good feminists we, we have saluted Bad Girl/Power Slut's right to exist, to demolish, to flourish in her own dark way. But the nagging question remains: Is this a good behavior model for us? Is Bad Girl's life healthy, happy, productive? Does she get enough love? Even more creepily we ask: Is she aging well?

Because the fact is, even we—once-nubile twentysomething gals who gamboled defiantly topless in the mountain streams of yore—feel ourselves gently softening with age each day. The drama in the bathroom no longer centers around the scale. Forget that—we've gained and lost the same fifteen pounds so often that the cycle has become like an old pal, natural as our monthly period.

But our skin! Each new wrinkle tells us there's no going back. No wonder our obsessions have become all Oil of Olay, Clinique moisturizer, antiwrinkle cream!

And while we hate to be unsupportive of our Badder sisters, we can't help noticing that, well, Bad Girlhood seems so bad *for* you. Look at Heidi Fleiss—drawn and witchy and actually too thin at 29. Partying, prostitution, cocaine, and, heck, the eighties don't wear well on a gal. And look at spooky seventy-something *Cosmo* girl Helen Gurley Brown, a.k.a. "the Crypt Keeper in capri pants," as she is known to AM-radio wag Peter Tilden.

Even the indestructible Madonna is looking a bit exhausted. Sure she's a zillionaire and superpowerful and has been on top forever. Her *Sex* book broke every boundary, sold tons. But it must be tough, we secretly think, for Madonna to greet her 5,012th weekend with only those girly dancing boys with the weird hair for company. Sean is off having babies with Robin Wright (a Good Girl, if oddly skinny). Geez: Madonna's going to be 40 soon. If she keeps hanging onto Bad Girl, soon she'll be Old Crone girl. Can we women age with dignity? By what strategy will we engineer fabulous forties, fifties, sixties, and beyond? (My God—a healthy woman of 65 today can expect to live to 83! Almost half our life will be spent being 50 or older!)

As we drift past our midthirties, we begin to question the idea of relentlessly pushing the boundaries of society, psychology, and biology. Will we end up like tart-talking Roseanne? We used to love her. We still do, but it's 1995 now and we are confused. She had a hit show, but still she felt the need for plastic surgery, butt tattoos, Tom Arnold tattoos, a Tom Arnold divorce, she hates her family, belched the anthem, lit her farts (or could if she'd wanted), married her bodyguard and has had a new baby, like, surgically implanted . . . where? Is this feminism? Help!

We will not go like that. (Anyway, we can't afford to.) We women are survivors, and we are battening down our hatches . . . for the future. 35

IV. THE GOOD GIRL MANIFESTO

Herewith, then, a declaration of our principles:

1. We're no longer promiscuous. Diseases suck. And so do noncommittal men our age (often spoiled for commitment by all that free sex we gave them in the sixties, seventies, and eighties). There's really no point. We can do it ourselves.

2. We're tailing down on booze and drugs. Eight glasses of water a day—better for the skin.

3. We're trying not to be anorexic. That seems very eighties. Then again, we don't want to be fat. As a result, we're just a wee bit bulimic. Sorry! We know this is not good.

40

4. We're *trying* to envision a future without plastic surgery. We try to keep happy, confident, glowing, nonlifted, fortysomething earth mothers Meryl/Cybill/Susan foremost in our minds. (See Nivea wrinkle cream ad: a blond mom in white feels good about her face, baby splashing in the background.)

5. We're trying to love our parents again. Their mortality weighs heavily upon us. When a parent dies, we peruse the photo album, weep while contemplating their jauntily hopeful forties hats, the huge families they came from. We feel suddenly lonely.

6. Were the forties and fifties really so bad? Gee, we feel nostalgic. We yearn for old love songs and old movies. At least our filmic Good Girl heroines do. (See Meg Ryan in *Sleepless in Seattle*, Marisa Tomei in *Only You*.) Although I must tell you: if I hear Harry Connick Jr. singing "It Had to Be You" again on the soundtrack of one more light romantic comedy, I will kill someone.

7. We're drawn to stuff that seems traditional, even if it isn't. Laura Ashley sheets. Coach bags. *Martha Stewart Living*.

8. We're back to white cotton underpants. (And as Victoria's Secret tells us, cotton is sexy again!)

45

9. We love our pets—our very own Disney familiars. (If we are starring in a movie, we can be expected to talk to our cat or dog in a very cute way. Starlets who need their tawdry images to be cleaned up can be expected to join PETA.)

10. We believe in true love, but we don't expect to find it in Rock Hudson. That's a dream of the past. Urban Lotharios *never* settle down—we've learned that, unlike Doris, we can't domesticate them through interior design.

That's why we're looking for love in all new places. Maybe we find it via a much younger man (a third of today's women already do). Maybe we find it by falling in love again with the family (like Sandra Bullock does in *While You Were Sleeping*). Maybe we find it in our children, postdivorce.

Consider that the template for the female sitcom today is not single newsgal Mary Tyler Moore, but single mom Murphy Brown, divorced mom Brett Butler, divorced mom Cybill. Exhusbands are reduced to comic characters sticking their heads in the door, like Howard the neighbor on the old *Bob Newhart Show*. In these days, when conception's becoming increasingly immaculate, maybe we have a baby without a guy.

Or maybe, hell, we find love for a few beautiful days with a fiftysomething shaman/photographer called Robert Kincaid with a washboard stomach. Maybe we never see him again after that. But today's Good Girl is tough and prudent—a little bit of love and she says, uncomplainingly, "I'm fine. I'm full. I have plenty."

Then goes outside and, into the air, high above her head, throws not her   *50*
bra . . . but her hat.

Engaging the Text

1. Provide some examples of ways in which Loh's anecdotes based on her own experiences make her analysis more effective.

2. What qualities have come to define the "good girl"? In Loh's view, what is the relationship between "good girl" and "bad girl" images? What factors explain why, in some decades, one is "in" and the other is "out"? In a short essay, challenge or support Loh's claims, drawing on your own observations.

3. Loh wrote her essay in 1995. Have pop stars (in films and music) changed the way they present themselves since then?

Exploring Your Cultural Perspective

1. How prominent is the "good girl" archetype in both the articles and the advertising in women's magazines, such as *Ladies' Home Journal* and *Vogue*? To what extent do the ads and articles in *Glamour* still present the "bad girl" archetype?

FIGURE 7.2

FIGURE 7.3

2. Write a few paragraphs comparing Doris Day's appeal with that of Madonna. (For a picture of Doris Day, see Figure 7.2 on page 473. Madonna's many incarnations include those shown in Figure 7.3.)

NEIL POSTMAN AND STEVE POWERS

TV News as Entertainment

In the past, the nightly TV news, delivered by authoritative figures like Walter Cronkite, reported factually and objectively on world matters. Today, according to the authors, news broadcasts have become money-making spectacles—forms of theater—with stories illustrated by compelling visual images. Neil Postman has criticized the emergence of this sensationalistic tabloid mentality in such books as *Amusing Ourselves to Death* (1985) and *Conscientious Objections* (1992). A professor of media ecology at New York University, Postman was instrumental in the movement to radically reform education that was sparked by his book (with Charles Weingartner) *Teaching as a Subversive Activity* (1969). His most recent book is *Building a Bridge to the Eighteenth Century: How the Past Can Improve Our Future* (1999). Steve Powers is a journalist and news reporter. The following essay is from their 1992 book *How to Watch TV News*.

Thinking Critically

What does the media coverage of such events as the O. J. Simpson trial, the Jon Benet Ramsey murder, the Elian Gonzalez custody case, and the post–September 11, 2001, events, to mention but a few examples, suggest about how North Americans' concept of news has changed?

When a television news show distorts the truth by altering or manufacturing facts (through re-creations), a television viewer is defenseless even if a re-creation is properly labeled. Viewers are still vulnerable to misinformation since they will not know (at least in the case of docudramas) what parts are fiction and what parts are not. But the problems of verisimilitude posed by re-creations pale to insignificance when compared to the problems viewers face when encountering a straight (no-monkey-business) show. All news shows, in a sense, are re-creations in that what we hear and see on them are attempts to represent actual events, and are not the events themselves. Perhaps, to avoid ambiguity, we might call all news shows "re-presentations" instead of

475

"re-creations." These re-presentations come to us in two forms: language and pictures. The question then arises: what do viewers have to know about language and pictures in order to be properly armed to defend themselves against the seductions of eloquence (to use Bertrand Russell's apt phrase)? . . .

[Let us look at] the problem of pictures. It is often said that a picture is worth a thousand words. Maybe so. But it is probably equally true that one word is worth a thousand pictures, at least sometimes—for example, when it comes to understanding the world we live in. Indeed, the whole problem with news on television comes down to this: all the words uttered in an hour of news coverage could be printed on one page of a newspaper. And the world cannot be understood in one page. Of course, there is a compensation: television offers pictures, and the pictures move. Moving pictures are a kind of language in themselves, but the language of pictures differs radically from oral and written language, and the differences are crucial for understanding television news.

To begin with, pictures, especially single pictures, speak only in particularities. Their vocabulary is limited to concrete representation. Unlike words and sentences, a picture does not present to us an idea or concept about the world, except as we use language itself to convert the image to idea. By itself, a picture cannot deal with the unseen, the remote, the internal, the abstract. It does not speak of "man," only of *a* man; not of "tree," only of *a* tree. You cannot produce an image of "nature," any more than an image of "the sea." You can only show a particular fragment of the here-and-now—a cliff of a certain terrain, in a certain condition of light; a wave at a moment in time, from a particular point of view. And just as "nature" and "the sea" cannot be photographed, such larger abstractions as truth, honor, love, and falsehood cannot be talked about in the lexicon of individual pictures. For "showing of" and "talking about" are two very different kinds of processes: individual pictures give us the world as object; language, the world as idea. There is no such thing in nature as "man" or "tree." The universe offers no such categories or simplifications; only flux and infinite variety. The picture documents and celebrates the particularities of the universe's infinite variety. Language makes them comprehensible.

Of course, moving pictures, video with sound, may bridge the gap by juxtaposing images, symbols, sound, and music. Such images can present emotions and rudimentary ideas. They can suggest the panorama of nature and the joys and miseries of humankind.

5   Picture—smoke pouring from the window, cut to people coughing, an ambulance racing to a hospital, a tombstone in a cemetery.

Picture—jet planes firing rockets, explosions, lines of foreign soldiers surrendering, the American flag waving in the wind.

Nonetheless, keep in mind that when terrorists want to prove to the world that their kidnap victims are still alive, they photograph them holding a copy of a recent newspaper. The dateline on the newspaper provides the proof that the photograph was taken on or after that date. Without the help of the written word, film and videotape cannot portray temporal dimensions with any precision. Consider a film clip showing an aircraft carrier at sea. One might be able to identify the ship as Soviet or American, but there would be no way of telling where in the world the carrier was, where it was headed, or when the pictures were taken. It is only through language—words spoken over the pictures or reproduced in them—that the image of the aircraft carrier takes on specific meaning.

Still, it is possible to enjoy the image of the carrier for its own sake. One might find the hugeness of the vessel interesting; it signifies military power on the move. There is a certain drama in watching the planes come in at high speeds and skid to a stop on the deck. Suppose the ship were burning: that would be even more interesting. This leads to an important point about the language of pictures. Moving pictures favor images that change. That is why violence and dynamic destruction find their way onto television so often. When something is destroyed violently it is altered in a highly visible way; hence the entrancing power of fire. Fire gives visual form to the ideas of consumption, disappearance, death—the thing that burned is actually taken away by fire. It is at this very basic level that fires make a good subject for television news. Something was here, now it's gone, and the change is recorded on film.

Earthquakes and typhoons have the same power. Before the viewer's eyes the world is taken apart. If a television viewer has relatives in Mexico City and an earthquake occurs there, then he or she may take a special interest in the images of destruction as a report from a specific place and time; that is, one may look at television pictures for information about an important event. But film of an earthquake can be interesting even if the viewer cares nothing about the event itself. Which is only to say, as we noted earlier, that there is another way of participating in the news—as a spectator who desires to be entertained. Actually to see buildings topple is exciting, no matter where the buildings are. The world turns to dust before our eyes.

Those who produce television news in America know that their medium   *10* favors images that move. That is why they are wary of "talking heads," people who simply appear in front of a camera and speak. When talking heads appear on television, there is nothing to record or document, no change in process. In the cinema the situation is somewhat different. On a movie screen, closeups of a good actor speaking dramatically can sometimes be interesting to watch. When Clint Eastwood narrows his eyes and challenges his rival to shoot first, the spectator sees the cool rage of the Eastwood character take visual form, and the narrowing of the eyes is dramatic. But much of the effect of this small movement depends on the size of the movie screen and the darkness of the theater, which make Eastwood and his every action "larger than life."

The television screen is smaller than life. It occupies about 15 percent of the viewer's visual field (compared to about 70 percent for the movie screen). It is not set in a darkened theater closed off from the world but in the viewer's ordinary living space. This means that visual changes must be more extreme and more dramatic to be interesting on television. A narrowing of the eyes will not do. A car crash, an earthquake, a burning factory are much better.

With these principles in mind, let us examine more closely the structure of a typical newscast, and here we will include in the discussion not only the pictures but all the nonlinguistic symbols that make up a television news show. For example, in America, almost all news shows begin with music, the tone of which suggests important events about to unfold. The music is very important, for it equates the news with various forms of drama and ritual—the opera, for example, or a wedding procession—in which musical themes underscore the meaning of the event. Music takes us immediately into the realm of the symbolic, a world that is not to be taken literally. After all, when events unfold in the real world, they do so without musical accompaniment. More symbolism follows. The sound of teletype machines can be heard in the studio, not because it is impossible to screen this noise out, but because the sound is a kind of music in itself. It tells us that data are pouring in from all corners of the globe, a sensation reinforced by the world map in the background (or clocks noting the time on different continents). The fact is that teletype machines are rarely used in TV news rooms, having been replaced by silent computer terminals. When seen, they have only a symbolic function.

Already, then, before a single news item is introduced, a great deal has been communicated. We know that we are in the presence of a symbolic event, a form of theater in which the day's events are to be dramatized. This theater takes the entire globe as its subject, although it may look at the world from the perspective of a single nation. A certain tension is present, like the atmosphere in a theater just before the curtain goes up. The tension is represented by the music, the staccato beat of the teletype machines, and often the sight of news workers scurrying around typing reports and answering phones. As a technical matter, it would be no problem to build a set in which the newsroom staff remained off camera, invisible to the viewer, but an important theatrical effect would be lost. By being busy on camera, the workers help communicate urgency about the events at hand, which suggests that situations are changing so rapidly that constant revision of the news is necessary.

The staff in the background also helps signal the importance of the person in the center, the anchor, "in command" of both the staff and the news. The anchor plays the role of host. He or she welcomes us to the newscast and welcomes us back from the different locations we visit during the filmed reports.

15   Many features of the newscast help the anchor to establish the impression of control. These are usually equated with production values in broadcasting.

They include such things as graphics that tell the viewer what is being shown, or maps and charts that suddenly appear on the screen and disappear on cue, or the orderly progression from story to story. They also include the absence of gaps, or "dead time," during the broadcast, even the simple fact that the news starts and ends at a certain hour. These common features are thought of as purely technical matters, which a professional crew handles as a matter of course. But they are also symbols of a dominant theme of television news: the imposition of an orderly world—called "the news"—upon the disorderly flow of events.

While the form of a news broadcast emphasizes tidiness and control, its content can best be described as fragmented. Because time is so precious on television, because the nature of the medium favors dynamic visual images, and because the pressures of a commercial structure require the news to hold its audience above all else, there is rarely any attempt to explain issues in depth or place events in their proper context. The news moves nervously from a warehouse fire to a court decision, from a guerrilla war to a World Cup match, the quality of the film most often determining the length of the story. Certain stories show up only because they offer dramatic pictures. Bleachers collapse in South America: hundreds of people are crushed—a perfect television news story, for the cameras can record the face of disaster in all its anguish. Back in Washington, a new budget is approved by Congress. Here there is nothing to photograph because a budget is not a physical event; it is a document full of language and numbers. So the producers of the news will show a photo of the document itself, focusing on the cover where it says "Budget of the United States of America." Or sometimes they will send a camera crew to the government printing plant where copies of the budget are produced. That evening, while the contents of the budget are summarized by a voice-over, the viewer sees stacks of documents being loaded into boxes at the government printing plant. Then a few of the budget's more important provisions will be flashed on the screen in written form, but this is such a time-consuming process—using television as a printed page—that the producers keep it to a minimum. In short, the budget is not televisable, and for that reason its time on the news must be brief. The bleacher collapse will get more time that evening.

While appearing somewhat chaotic, these disparate stories are not just dropped in the news program helter-skelter. The appearance of a scattershot story order is really orchestrated to draw the audience from one story to the next—from one section to the next—through the commercial breaks to the end of the show. The story order is constructed to hold and build the viewership rather than place events in context or explain issues in depth.

Of course, it is a tendency of journalism in general to concentrate on the surface of events rather than underlying conditions; this is as true for the newspaper as it is for the newscast. But several features of television undermine whatever efforts journalists may make to give sense to the world. One is that a television broadcast is a series of events that occur in sequence, and the sequence is the same for all viewers. This is not true for a newspaper page, which displays many items simultaneously, allowing readers to choose the order in which they read them. If newspaper readers want only a summary of the latest tax bill, they can read the headline and the first paragraph of an article, and if they want more, they can keep reading. In a sense, then, everyone reads a different newspaper, for no two readers will read (or ignore) the same items.

But all television viewers see the same broadcast. They have no choices. A report is either in the broadcast or out, which means that anything which is of narrow interest is unlikely to be included. As NBC News executive Reuven Frank once explained:

> A newspaper, for example, can easily afford to print an item of conceivable interest to only a fraction of its readers. A television news program must be put together with the assumption that each item will be of some interest to everyone that watches. Every time a newspaper includes a feature which will attract a specialized group it can assume it is adding at least a little bit to its circulation. To the degree a television news program includes an item of this sort . . . it must assume that its audience will diminish.

20   The need to "include everyone," an identifying feature of commercial television in all its forms, prevents journalists from offering lengthy or complex explanations, or from tracing the sequence of events leading up to today's headlines. One of the ironies of political life in modern democracies is that many problems which concern the "general welfare" are of interest only to specialized groups. Arms control, for example, is an issue that literally concerns everyone in the world, and yet the language of arms control and the complexity of the subject are so daunting that only a minority of people can actually follow the issue from week to week and month to month. If it wants to act responsibly, a newspaper can at least make available more information about arms control than most people want. Commercial television cannot afford to do so.

But even if commercial television could afford to do so, it wouldn't. The fact that television news is principally made up of moving pictures prevents it from offering lengthy, coherent explanations of events. A television news show reveals the world as a series of unrelated, fragmentary moments. It does not—and cannot be expected to—offer a sense of coherence or meaning. What does this suggest to a TV viewer? That the viewer must come with a prepared mind—information, opinions, a sense of proportion, an articulate value system. To the TV viewer lacking such mental equipment, a news program is only a kind of rousing light show. Here a falling building, there a five-alarm fire, everywhere the world as an object, much without meaning, connections, or continuity.

FIGURE 7.4

Engaging the Text

1. Why have TV news programs become a form of theater, according to Postman and Powers? How is this transformation related to TV as a medium?

2. What factors determine what is and is not reported and how news stories are constructed?

3. How do the examples that Postman and Powers offer (a new U.S. budget; arms control) illustrate the failure of TV to present information citizens might need to be better informed?

Exploring Your Cultural Perspective

1. What objectives govern the reporting of political news in terms of how conflicts are manufactured, managed, and then resolved? In what sense are these supposedly objective news accounts the contemporary media equivalent of the "bread and circuses" used to divert the public in ancient Rome?

2. Is there any truth to the cartoon in Figure 7.4? Why or why not?

FIGURE 7.5

3. Choose a story that has been reported on the news every day for weeks or month—one that has begun to appear more like a theatrical event than a news report. How has the story been transformed into an ongoing soap opera? For example, what do the pictures in Figures 7.5 and 7.6 convey about the part imagery played in the media's marketing of the Elian Gonzalez saga (1999–2000).

FIGURE 7.6

CHARLES OLIVER
Freak Parade

The public appetite for tacky, sleazy, and bizarre spectacles on daytime TV talk shows is apparently endless, judging by the ingenuity the producers display in presenting new oddities on a daily basis. Charles Oliver sees these shows as the modern-day equivalent of the carnival "freak shows." Oliver writes on national issues for *Investor's Business Daily*. This essay first appeared in the April 1995 issue of *Reason* magazine.

Thinking Critically
As you read, think of how you would expand on or counter Oliver's claims about the formats, themes, and typical guests on daytime TV talk shows. How offensive would a TV talk show have to be for you to turn it off?

Bearded ladies. Siamese twins. Men and women who weigh more than 300 pounds each. Tattooed men. These are just a few of the guests to grace the stages of daytime talk shows in recent months. If those examples remind you of a carnival sideshow, there's a reason.

In the nineteenth century and for the first few decades of this century, carnivals crisscrossed the United States, providing entertainment to people in small towns. Carnivals catered to the dark side of man's need for spectacle by allowing people to escape temporarily from their dull everyday lives into a world that was dark, sleazy, and seemingly dangerous. Of course, the danger wasn't real, and the ultimate lure of the carnival was that you could safely return from its world to your everyday life.

Television and regional amusement parks took their toll on the carnival. Today, the few carnivals in existence are generally sad collections of rickety rides and rigged games. But man's need for dark spectacle hasn't gone away, and a new generation of entrepreneurs has found a way to allow people to experience the vicarious thrill of the dark, the sleazy, and the tawdry—all without leaving the safety of their homes.

The gateways to this dark world are daytime talk shows Phil Donahue created the mold for this genre, and Oprah Winfrey carried it to perhaps its greatest success. Both their shows are essentially women's magazines on the air, alternating celebrity profiles, services-oriented features, discussion of political issues, and more exploitative episodes. Both mix the tawdry with the serious. Donohue was the man who gave us daytime debates between presidential candidates, and he was also the man who wore a skirt on a show devoted to cross dressing.

However, a new generation of hosts has emerged that trades almost exclu-   5
sively in the sleaze their audiences demand: Geraldo, Montel, Ricki, Jerry. Their names may not be familiar to you, but they have millions of viewers. "Oprah" alone is watched by seven million households each day. Each has managed to recreate the carnival in a contemporary setting.

One of the main attractions of the old carnivals were the "hoochie coochie" dancers. Men would eagerly wait in line, enticed by the talker's promise that these women would "take it off, roll it up, and throw it right at you." This was the origin of modern striptease. Today, the heirs of Little Egypt[1] are a staple on daytime television. In fact, they are so common that producers really have to try to come up with new angles. Male strippers, female strippers, old strippers, grossly overweight strippers, amateur strippers—these are just a few of the variations that I saw on the daytime talk shows in just one four-week period. Of course, these people didn't just talk about their profession; they inevitably demonstrated it. While the television viewer could see the naughty bits only in digitized distortions, the live audiences for these shows were treated to an eyeful.

However, most of the strippers on these shows are attractive young women. Given that the audience for daytime talk is also women, this seems like a strange choice of guests. I can only assume that at least some of the women who watch these shows are intrigued by the profession and wonder what it would be like to be a stripper. By presenting these women strippers—indeed, by actually taking their cameras into clubs for performances—talk shows give those women viewers the chance to live out their fantasies vicariously without risking any of the dangers involved. Based upon the comments offered, female audience members generally seem to sympathize with the strippers who appear on these shows, usually defending them against those brought on to attack the profession.

Of course, at times the subject of stripping is simply an excuse for these shows to engage in emotional voyeurism. A perfect example was an episode of "Jerry Springer" dealing with strippers and family members who disapproved of how they earned their money. Naturally, the strippers couldn't just talk to

---

[1]*Little Egypt:* A once popular carnival dancer.

their parents and siblings; they had to demonstrate their art to them. So while the assembled families and the studio audience watched, the girls stripped naked.

On one side of a split television screen, the home audience saw a lovely young girl strip down to her distorted birthday suit. On the other side, her family, some of them crying, averted their eyes and tried to ignore the hooting and catcalls of the audience.

10   It was tacky; it was sleazy. It was the perfect daytime moment. Whoever thought of it is a veritable P. T. Barnum[2] of the airwaves. At once, this sordid mess provides the viewer with the voyeuristic thrill of seeing a family conflict that one really shouldn't observe, the vicarious thrill of stripping before an audience, and, ultimately, the confirmation that a dull, "normal" lifestyle is superior to that of the women on the show.

An important part of carnivals was the freak show, an assortment of real and contrived physical oddities: pinheads, fat people, bearded ladies. While the carnival talkers would try to entice people into the sideshow tents with come-ons about the scientific oddities inside, the real lure of these attractions wasn't intellectual curiousity. It was terror and pity. The customer could observe these people and think to himself that no matter how bad his life seemed at times, it could be much, much worse.

Daytime talk shows have their own version of the freak show. Indeed, on her now-defunct show, Joan Rivers had actual sideshow freaks. These were politically correct "made" freaks (people who had purposefully altered their bodies), not natural ones. The guest who drew the biggest reaction from the audience was a man who lifted heavy weights attached to earrings that pierced various parts of his body. (I've actually seen this guy perform, and I can say that the audience didn't see his most impressive piece of lifting. But there was no way that it could have been shown on television, at least not without some serious digitizing of the screen.)

More often, talk shows will feature people with physical conditions similar to those who were attractions in sideshows. I've seen various shows do episodes on women with facial hair, and the lives of the very large are always a popular topic. One episode of "Jerry Springer" featured greeting card models who weigh more than 300 pounds. In typical fashion these women were not dressed as they presumably would be in everyday life, but in revealing lingerie. So much better for gawking, I guess.

---

[2]*P. T. Barnum:* Phineas Taylor Barnum (1810–1891), American circus operator and promoter.

Again, the host will set up one of these shows with some remarks about understanding these people, and to their credit, many of the guests on these programs do try to maintain their dignity. The greeting card models seemed a happy, boisterous lot of people. But more often guests are asked to tell tales of discrimination and broken hearts. It's easy to conclude that they were invited on the show so that the audience could feel sorry for them and feel superior to them.

And speaking of feeling superior, how could anyone help but laugh at and   *15* feel better than the endless parade of squabbling friends and relatives who pass through these shows? Judging from the looks of guests on some of these shows, you'd think the producers comb every trailer park and housing project in the nation looking for them. In fact, most are solicited through telephone numbers given during the show: "Are you a white transsexual stripper whose family disapproves of your Latino boyfriend? Call 1-800-IMA-FREK."

The guests then are invited on the show, where they battle it out for the amusement of the audience. A typical example was a show hosted by Ricki Lake on the topic of promiscuity. Ricki began by introducing Shannon, a girl who claimed her best friend Keisha sleeps around too much. Amid much whooping from the audience, Shannon detailed her friend's rather colorful sex life: "It ain't like she getting paid."

Then Keisha came out and accused Shannon of being the one who sleeps around too much. They spent an entire segment arguing. After the break Ricki introduces a mutual friend of the two and asked the question everyone in the audience now wanted to know:"Which one is the real slut?" A dramatic pause. The emphatic answer: "Both of them." The audience erupts.

Conflict is a key element on the new breed of talk shows. Physical fights seem to break out on Ricki Lake's show more frequently than at hockey games. These conflicts are not always mere arguments between friends or family members. Often, there are clear-cut good guys whom the audience is supposed to cheer and bad guys whom the audience boos. These episodes resemble the low-brow morality plays of professional wrestling.

Pro wrestling, in fact, had its origins in the carnival. Sometimes the resemblance to pro wrestling is quite pronounced. Daytime talk shows have a fascination with the Ku Klux Klan. It seems a week doesn't go by without one show bringing on members of the Klan to discuss their views on race relations, welfare, abortion, or child rearing. Usually there'll be representatives from some civil rights organization present to offer an opposing view.

The Klansmen look every inch the pro wrestling "heel." They are invari-   *20* ably overweight and have poor skin and a bad haircut. Watching them sitting there in their Klan robes, shouting racial slurs at their opponents as the audience curses them, I always expect these people to pull out a set of brass knuckles and clobber the "babyface" while the host has his back turned.

More often, though, the villains on talk shows are a little more subtle. The audience seems to value family quite a bit because the most common types of villians on these shows are people who pose a threat to the family: child-deserting wives, cheating husbands, and abusive parents.

One typical show was an episode of "Jenny Jones" where women who date only married men faced off with women whose husbands had left them for other women. The women who dated married men certainly made no attempt to win the audience over. They came in dressed in short skirts or low-cut dresses. They preened; they strutted; they insulted the other guests and the audience members; they bragged about their sexual prowess. "Nature Boy" Buddy Rogers[3] himself could not have worked the crowd better.

Why do such people even show up for these shows? It can't be for the money, since guests receive no more than a plane ticket and a night in a nice hotel. After watching countless shows, I've come to the conclusion that these people really think there is nothing wrong with what they do, and they usually seem quite surprised that the audience isn't on their side.

Is the public's appetite for this sleaze unlimited? Probably not. After all, the carnival came around but once a year. With close to two dozen daytime talk shows competing for viewers, people are bound to grow jaded. Last year, Oprah Winfrey, who already had one of the less sleazy shows, began a policy of toning down tawdry elements. Even her sensational admission to using crack cocaine during the 1980s came in the middle of an "inspirational" program on recovering addicts. The show, which was already the top-rated daytime program, saw its ratings climb. But for those with a taste for the dark side of life, there'll always be a Ricki Lake or a Gordon Elliott.

Engaging the Text

1. In what ways do contemporary television talk shows cater to the "dark side" of the public's need for spectacle as carnivals did in the past? What means does Oliver use to organize his comparison of old-time carnivals with modern-day talk shows? How do the examples he presents illustrate his thesis?

2. What is Oliver's attitude toward the people who watch television shows of this nature? What bond does he create between himself and the audience for whom he is writing?

---

[3] *Buddy Rogers:* A wrestler known for his preening and strutting.

Exploring Your Cultural Perspective

1. What current talk shows illustrate Oliver's thesis? Do others take the high road? If so, do you find them as entertaining? Why or why not? How has the carnival atmosphere invaded other forums (such as "Court TV" on cable)?

2. Would you be more inclined to watch a bizarre spectacle on television than in a carnival sideshow? Explain your answer.

JOHN CHEEVER
The Enormous Radio

Although he wrote five novels, John Cheever (1912–1982) is best known for his deftly constructed short stories of affluent suburban America that frequently appeared in the *New Yorker*. Collections of his works include *The Enormous Radio* (1953), *The Brigadier and the Golf Widow* (1964), and *The Stories of John Cheever* (1978), which won a Pulitzer Prize. The fantastic premise on which the following story is based on has proved to be unusually prophetic, given the electronic invasion of privacy and the tabloid mentality that permeate American life today.

Thinking Critically

As you read, observe how Cheever intrudes on the psyches of his main characters in the same way as they invade the privacy of their neighbors. Note Cheever's use of dialogue and precise details to create an aura of reality that makes us more likely to accept his story's extraordinary premise.

Jim and Irene Westcott were the kind of people who seem to strike that satisfactory average of income, endeavor, and respectability that is reached by the statistical reports in college alumni bulletins. They were the parents of two young children, they had been married nine years, they lived on the twelfth floor of an apartment house near Sutton Place, they went to the theatre on an average of 10.3 times a year, and they hoped someday to live in Westchester. Irene Westcott was a pleasant, rather plain girl with soft brown hair and a wide, fine forehead upon which nothing at all had been written, and in the cold weather she wore a coat of fitch skins dyed to resemble mink. You couldn't say that Jim Westcott looked younger than he was, but you could at least say of him that he seemed to feel younger. He wore his graying hair cut very short, he dressed in the kind of clothes his class had worn at Andover, and his manner was earnest, vehement, and intentionally naïve. The Westcotts differed from their friends, their classmates, and their neighbors only in an interest they shared in serious music. They went to a great many concerts—although they seldom mentioned this to anyone—and they spent a good deal of time listening to music on the radio.

Their radio was an old instrument, sensitive, unpredictable, and beyond repair. Neither of them understood the mechanics of radio—or of any of the other appliances that surrounded them—and when the instrument faltered, Jim would strike the side of the cabinet with his hand. This sometimes helped. One Sunday afternoon, in the middle of a Schubert quartet, the music faded away altogether. Jim struck the cabinet repeatedly, but there was no response; the Schubert was lost to them forever. He promised to buy Irene a new radio, and on Monday when he came home from work he told her that he had got one. He refused to describe it, and said it would be a surprise for her when it came.

The radio was delivered at the kitchen door the following afternoon, and with the assistance of her maid and the handyman Irene uncrated it and brought it into the living room. She was struck at once with the physical ugliness of the large gumwood cabinet. Irene was proud of her living room, she had chosen its furnishings and colors as carefully as she chose her clothes, and now it seemed to her that the new radio stood among her intimate possessions like an aggressive intruder. She was confounded by the number of dials and switches on the instrument panel, and she studied them thoroughly before she put the plug into a wall socket and turned the radio on. The dials flooded with a malevolent green light, and in the distance she heard the music of a piano quintet. The quintet was in the distance for only an instant; it bore down upon her with a speed greater than light and filled the apartment with the noise of music amplified so mightily that it knocked a china ornament from a table to the floor. She rushed to the instrument and reduced the volume. The violent force that was snared in the ugly gumwood cabinet made her uneasy. Her children came home from school then, and she took them to the Park. It was not until later in the afternoon that she was able to return to the radio.

The maid had given the children their suppers and was supervising their baths when Irene turned on the radio, reduced the volume, and sat down to listen to a Mozart quintet that she knew and enjoyed. The music came through clearly. The new instrument had a much purer tone, she thought, than the old one. She decided that tone was most important and that she could conceal the cabinet behind a sofa. But as soon as she had made her peace with the radio, the interference began. A crackling sound like the noise of a burning powder fuse began to accompany the singing of the strings. Beyond the music, there was a rustling that reminded Irene unpleasantly of the sea, and as the quintet progressed, these noises were joined by many others. She tried all the dials and switches but nothing dimmed the interference, and she sat down, disappointed and bewildered, and tried to trace the flight of the melody. The elevator shaft in her building ran beside the living-room wall, and it was the noise of the elevator that gave her a clue to the character of the static. The rattling of the elevator cables and the opening and closing of the elevator doors were reproduced in her loudspeaker, and, realizing that the radio was sensitive to electrical currents of all sorts, she began to discern through the Mozart the ringing of telephone bells, the dialing of phones, and the lamentation of a vacuum cleaner. By listening more carefully, she was able to distinguish doorbells, elevator bells, electric razors, and Waring mixers, whose sounds had been picked up from the apartments that surrounded hers and transmitted through her loudspeaker. The powerful and ugly instrument, with its mistaken sensitivity to discord, was more than she could hope to master, so she turned the thing off and went into the nursery to see her children.

5   When Jim Westcott came home that night, he went to the radio confidently and worked the controls. He had the same sort of experience Irene had had. A man was speaking on the station Jim had chosen, and his voice swung instantly from a distance into a force so powerful that it shook the apartment. Jim turned the volume control and reduced the voice. Then, a minute or two later, the interference began. The ringing of telephones and doorbells set in, joined by the rasp of the elevator doors and the whir of cooking appliances. The character of the noise had changed since Irene had tried the radio earlier; the last of the electric razors was being unplugged, the vacuum cleaners had all been returned to their closets, and the static reflected that change in pace that overtakes the city after the sun goes down. He fiddled with the knobs but couldn't get rid of the noises, so he turned the radio off and told Irene that in the morning he'd call the people who had sold it to him and give them hell.

The following afternoon, when Irene returned to the apartment from a luncheon date, the maid told her that a man had come and fixed the radio. Irene went into the living room before she took off her hat or her furs and tried the instrument. From the loudspeaker came a recording of the "Missouri Waltz." It reminded her of the thin, scratchy music from an old-fashioned phonograph that she sometimes heard across the lake where she spent her summers. She waited until the waltz had finished, expecting an explanation of the recording, but there was none. The music was followed by silence, and then the plaintive and scratchy record was repeated. She turned the dial and got a satisfactory burst of Caucasian music—the thump of bare feet in the dust and the rattle of coin jewelry—but in the background she could hear the ringing of bells and a confusion of voices. Her children came home from school then, and she turned off the radio and went to the nursery.

When Jim came home that night, he was tired, and he took a bath and changed his clothes. Then he joined Irene in the living room. He had just turned on the radio when the maid announced dinner, so he left it on, and he and Irene went to the table.

Jim was too tired to make even a pretense of sociability, and there was nothing about the dinner to hold Irene's interest, so her attention wandered from the food to the deposits of silver polish on the candlesticks and from there to the music in the other room. She listened for a few minutes to a Chopin prelude and then was surprised to hear a man's voice break in. "For Christ's sake, Kathy," he said, "do you always have to play the piano when I get home?" The music stopped abruptly. "It's the only chance I have," a woman said. "I'm at the office all day." "So am I," the man said. He added something obscene about an upright piano, and slammed a door. The passionate and melancholy music began again.

"Did you hear that?" Irene asked.

"What?" Jim was eating his dessert.   *10*

"The radio. A man said something while the music was still going on— something dirty."

"It's probably a play."

"I don't think it *is* a play," Irene said.

They left the table and took their coffee into the living room. Irene asked Jim to try another station. He turned the knob. "Have you seen my garters?" a man asked. "Button me up," a woman said. "Have you seen my garters?" the man said again. "Just button me up and I'll find your garters," the woman said. Jim shifted to another station. "I wish you wouldn't leave apple cores in the ashtrays," a man said. "I hate the smell."

"This is strange," Jim said.   *15*

"Isn't it? Irene said.

Jim turned the knob again. "'On the coast of Coromandel where the early pumpkins blow,'" a woman with a pronounced English accent said, "'in the middle of the woods lived a Yonghy-Bonghy-Bò. Two old chairs, and a half a candle, one old jug without a handle. . . .'"

"My God!" Irene cried. "That's the Sweeneys' nurse."

"'These were all his worldly goods,'" the British voice continued.

"Turn that thing off," Irene said. "Maybe they can hear *us*." Jim switched   *20* the radio off. "That was Miss Armstrong, the Sweeneys' nurse," Irene said. "She must be reading to the little girl. They live in 17-B. I've talked with Miss Armstrong in the Park. I know her voice very well. We must be getting other people's apartments."

"That's impossible," Jim said.

"Well, that was the Sweeneys' nurse," Irene said hotly. "I know her voice. I know it very well. I'm wondering if they can hear us."

Jim turned the switch. First from a distance and then nearer, nearer, as if borne on the wind, came the pure accents of the Sweeneys' nurse again: "'*Lady Jingly! Lady Jingly!*'" she said, "'*sitting where the pumpkins blow, will you come and and be my wife? said the Yonghy-Bonghy-Bó. . . .*'"

Jim went over to the radio and said "Hello" loudly into the speaker.

25   "'*I am tired of living singly*,'" the nurse went on, "'*on this coast so wild and shingly, I'm a-weary of my life; if you'll come and be my wife, quite serene would be my life. . . .*'"

"I guess she can't hear us," Irene said. "Try something else."

Jim turned to another station, and the living room was filled with the uproar of a cocktail party that had overshot its mark. Someone was playing the piano and singing the "Whiffenpoof Song," and the voices that surrounded the piano were vehement and happy. "Eat some more sandwiches," a woman shrieked. There were screams of laughter and a dish of some sort crashed to the floor.

"Those must be the Fullers, in 11-E," Irene said. "I knew they were giving a party this afternoon. I saw her in the liquor store. Isn't this too divine? Try something else. See if you can get those people in 18-C."

The Westcotts overheard that evening a monologue on salmon fishing in Canada, a bridge game, running comments on home movies of what had apparently been a fortnight at Sea Island, and a bitter family quarrel about an overdraft at the bank. They turned off their radio at midnight and went to bed, weak with laughter. Sometime in the night, their son began to call for a glass of water and Irene got one and took it to his room. It was very early. All the lights in the neighborhood were extinguished, and from the boy's window she could see the empty street. She went into the living room and tried the radio. There was some faint coughing, a moan, and then a man spoke. "Are you all right, darling?" he asked. "Yes," a woman said wearily. "Yes, I'm all right, I guess," and then she added with great feeling, "But, you know, Charlie, I don't feel like myself any more. Sometimes there are about fifteen or twenty minutes in the week when I feel like myself. I don't like to go to another doctor, because the doctor's bills are so awful already, but I just don't feel like myself, Charlie. I just never feel like myself." They were not young, Irene thought. She guessed from the timbre of their voices that they were middle-aged. The restrained melancholy of the dialogue and the draft from the bedroom window made her shiver, and she went back to bed.

30   The following morning, Irene cooked breakfast for the family—the maid didn't come up from her room in the basement until ten—braided her daughter's hair, and waited at the door until her children and her husband had been carried away in the elevator. Then she went into the living room and tried the radio. "I don't want to go to school," a child screamed. "I hate school. I won't go to school. I hate school." "You will go to school," an enraged woman said. "We paid eight hundred dollars to get you into that school and you'll go if it kills you." The next number on the dial produced the worn record of the "Missouri Waltz." Irene shifted the control and invaded the privacy of several break-

fast tables. She overheard demonstrations of indigestion, carnal love, abysmal vanity, faith, and despair. Irene's life was nearly as simple and sheltered as it appeared to be, and the forthright and sometimes brutal language that came from the loudspeaker that morning astonished and troubled her. She continued to listen until her maid came in. Then she turned off the radio quickly, since this insight, she realized, was a furtive one.

Irene had a luncheon date with a friend that day, and she left her apartment at a little after twelve. There were a number of women in the elevator when it stopped at her floor. She stared at their handsome and impassive faces, their furs, and the cloth flowers in their hats. Which one of them had been to Sea Island? she wondered. Which one had overdrawn her bank account? The elevator stopped at the tenth floor and a woman with a pair of Skye terriers joined them. Her hair was rigged high on her head and she wore a mink cape. She was humming the "Missouri Waltz."

Irene had two Martinis at lunch, and she looked searchingly at her friend and wondered what her secrets were. They had intended to go shopping after lunch, but Irene excused herself and went home. She told the maid that she was not to be disturbed; then she went into the living room, closed the doors, and switched on the radio. She heard, in the course of the afternoon, the halting conversation of a woman entertaining her aunt, the hysterical conclusion of a luncheon party, and a hostess briefing her maid about some cocktail guests. "Don't give the best Scotch to anyone who hasn't white hair," the hostess said. "See if you can get rid of that liver paste before you pass those hot things, and could you lend me five dollars? I want to tip the elevator man."

As the afternoon waned, the conversations increased in intensity. From where Irene sat, she could see the open sky above the East River. There were hundreds of clouds in the sky, as though the south wind had broken the winter into pieces and were blowing it north, and on her radio she could hear the arrival of cocktail guests and the return of children and businessmen from their schools and offices. "I found a good-sized diamond on the bathroom floor this morning," a woman said. "It must have fallen out of the bracelet Mrs. Dunston was wearing last night." "We'll sell it," a man said. "Take it down to the jeweler on Madison Avenue and sell it. Mrs. Dunston won't know the difference, and we could use a couple of hundred bucks. . . ." "'Oranges and lemons, say the bells of St. Clement's,'" the Sweeneys' nurse sang. "'Halfpence and farthings, say the bells of St. Martin's. When will you pay me? say the bells at old Bailey. . . .'" "It's not a hat," a woman cried, and at her back roared a cocktail party. "It's not a hat, it's a love affair. That's what Walter Florell said. He said it's not a hat, it's a love affair," and then, in a lower voice, the same woman added, "Talk to somebody, for Christ's sake, honey, talk to somebody. If she catches you standing here not talking to anybody, she'll take us off her invitation list, and I love these parties."

The Westcotts were going out for dinner that night, and when Jim came home, Irene was dressing. She seemed sad and vague, and he brought her a drink. They were dining with friends in the neighborhood, and they walked to where they were going. The sky was broad and filled with light. It was one of those splendid spring evenings that excite memory and desire, and the air that touched their hands and faces felt very soft. A Salvation Army band was on the corner playing "Jesus Is Sweeter." Irene drew on her husband's arm and held him there for a minute, to hear the music. "They're really such nice people, aren't they?" she said. "They have such nice faces. Actually, they're so much nicer than a lot of people we know." She took a bill from her purse and walked over and dropped it into the tambourine. There was in her face, when she returned to her husband, a look of radiant melancholy that he was not familiar with. And her conduct at the dinner party that night seemed strange to him, too. She interrupted her hostess rudely and stared at the people across the table from her with an intensity for which she would have punished her children.

35   It was still mild when they walked home from the party, and Irene looked up at the spring stars. "'How far that little candle throws its beams,'" she exclaimed. "'So shines a good deed in a naughty world.'" She waited that night until Jim had fallen asleep, and then went into the living room and turned on the radio.

Jim came home at about six the next night. Emma, the maid, let him in, and he had taken off his hat and was taking off his coat when Irene ran into the hall. Her face was shining with tears and her hair was disordered. "Go up to 16-C, Jim!" she screamed. "Don't take off your coat. Go up to 16-C. Mr. Osborn's beating his wife. They've been quarreling since four o'clock, and now he's hitting her. Go up there and stop him."

From the radio in the living room, Jim heard screams, obscenities, and thuds. "You know you don't have to listen to this sort of thing," he said. He strode into the living room and turned the switch. "It's indecent," he said. "It's like looking in windows. You know you don't have to listen to this sort of thing. You can turn it off."

"Oh, it's so horrible, it's so dreadful," Irene was sobbing. "I've been listening all day, and it's so depressing."

"Well, if it's so depressing, why do you listen to it? I bought this damned radio to give you pleasure," he said. "I paid a great deal of money for it. I thought it might make you happy. I wanted to make you happy."

40   "Don't, don't, don't, don't, quarrel with me," she moaned, and laid her head on his shoulder. "All the others have been quarreling all day. Everybody's been quarreling. They're all worried about money. Mrs. Hutchinson's mother is dying of cancer in Florida and they don't have enough money to send her to the Mayo Clinic. At least, Mr. Hutchinson says they don't have enough money. And some woman in this building is having an affair with the handyman—with

that hideous handyman. It's too disgusting. And Mrs. Melville has heart trouble and Mr. Hendricks is going to lose his job in April and Mrs. Hendricks is horrid about the whole thing and that girl who plays the 'Missouri Waltz' is a whore, a common whore, and the elevator man has tuberculosis and Mr. Osborn has been beating Mrs. Osborn." She wailed, she trembled with grief and checked the stream of tears down her face with the heel of her palm.

"Well, why do you have to listen?" Jim asked again. "Why do you have to listen to this stuff if it makes you so miserable?"

"Oh, don't, don't, don't," she cried. "Life is too terrible, too sordid and awful. But we've never been like that, have we, darling? Have we? I mean, we've always been good and decent and loving to one another, haven't we? And we have two children, two beautiful children. Our lives aren't sordid, are they, darling? Are they?" She flung her arms around his neck and drew his face down to hers. "We're happy, aren't we, darling? We are happy, aren't we?"

"Of course we're happy," he said tiredly. He began to surrender his resentment. "Of course we're happy. I'll have that damned radio fixed or taken away tomorrow." He stroked her soft hair. "My poor girl," he said.

"You love me, don't you?" she asked. "And we're not hypercritical or worried about money or dishonest, are we?"

"No, darling," he said.   *45*

A man came in the morning and fixed the radio. Irene turned it on cautiously and was happy to hear a California-wine commercial and a recording of Beethoven's Ninth Symphony, including Schiller's "Ode to Joy." She kept the radio on all day and nothing untoward came from the speaker.

A Spanish suite was being played when Jim came home. "Is everything all right?" he asked. His face was pale, she thought. They had some cocktails and went in to dinner to the "Anvil Chorus" from *Il Trovatore*. This was followed by Debussey's "La Mer."

"I paid the bill for the radio today," Jim said. "It cost four hundred dollars. I hope you'll get some enjoyment out of it."

"Oh, I'm sure I will," Irene said.

"Four hundred dollars is a good deal more than I can afford," he went on.   *50*
"I wanted to get something you'd enjoy. It's the last extravagance we'll be able to indulge in this year. I see that you haven't paid your clothing bills yet. I saw them on your dressing table." He looked directly at her. "Why did you tell me you'd paid them? Why did you lie to me?"

"I just didn't want you to worry, Jim," she said. She drank some water. "I'll be able to pay my bills out of this month's allowance. There were the slipcovers last month, and that party."

"You've got to learn to handle the money I give you a little more intelligently, Irene," he said. "You've got to understand that we don't have as much money this year as we had last. I had a very sobering talk with Mitchell today.

No one is buying anything. We're spending all our time promoting new issues, and you know how long that takes. I'm not getting any younger, you know. I'm thirty-seven. My hair will be gray next year. I haven't done as well as I'd hoped to do. And I don't suppose things will get any better."

"Yes, dear," she said.

"We've got to start cutting down," Jim said. "We've got to think of the children. To be perfectly frank with you, I worry about money a great deal. I'm not at all sure of the future. No one is. If anything should happen to me, there's the insurance, but that wouldn't go very far today. I've worked awfully hard to give you and the children a comfortable life," he said bitterly. "I don't like to see all my energies, all of my youth, wasted in fur coats and radios and slip-covers and—"

55   "Please, Jim," she said. "Please. They'll hear us."

"*Who'll hear us?* Emma can't hear us."

"The radio."

"Oh, I'm sick!" he shouted. "I'm sick to death of your apprehensiveness. The radio can't hear us. Nobody can hear us. And what if they can hear us? Who cares?"

Irene got up from the table and went into the living room. Jim went to the door and shouted at her from there. "Why are you so Christly all of a sudden? What's turned you overnight into a convent girl? You stole your mother's jewelry before they probated her will. You never gave your sister a cent of that money that was intended for her—not even when she needed it. You made Grace Howland's life miserable, and where was all your piety and your virtue when you went to that abortionist? I'll never forget how cool you were. You packed your bag and went off to have that child murdered as if you were going to Nassau. If you'd had any reasons, if you'd had any good reasons . . . ."

60   Irene stood for a minute before the hideous cabinet, disgraced and sick-ened, but she held her hand on the switch before she extinguished the music and the voices, hoping that the intrument might speak to her kindly, that she might hear the Sweeneys' nurse. Jim continued to shout at her from the door. The voice on the radio was suave and noncommittal. "An early-morning rail-road disaster in Tokyo," the loudspeaker said, "killed twenty-nine people. A fire in a Catholic hospital near Buffalo for the care of blind children was extin-guished early this morning by nuns. The temperature is forty-seven. The humidity is eighty-nine."

Engaging the Text

1. How would you characterize the Westcotts when we first encounter them?

2. How do Irene and her husband change as a result of their experiences with the radio?

3. What is ironic about the way the story ends? What different meanings does the word *enormous* in the title come to have? In what ways has the Internet produced the same voyeuristic involvement in other people's lives that Cheever dramatizes in this story?

Exploring Your Cultural Perspective

1. In what areas of your life have you experienced an infringment on your privacy directly attributable to new electronic capabilities (cell phones, telemarketing, e-mail, medical- and insurance-record databases)? Discuss the implications of the loss of privacy as a feature of everyday life in the twenty-first century.

2. Even today, some people would rather listen to the radio (once the only source of home entertainment) than watch television. Discuss the advantages and disadvantages of both media.

JESSICA HAGEDORN

Asian Women in Film: No Joy, No Luck

Born in the Philippines in 1940, Jessica Hagedorn moved to San Francisco with her family in 1960. She studied music, acting, and martial
arts at the American Conservatory Theatre. Hagedorn founded the
West Coast Gangster Choir and created several dance, radio, and multimedia theater pieces, such as *A Nun's Story* and *Mango Tango*. Her first
full-length fictional work, *Dogeaters* (1990), was nominated for a
National Book Award and explores the influence of American popular
culture in urban Manila in the 1970s. Many of her works, such as *The
Gangster of Love* (1996), refute the stereotyped depiction of Asian
women, as does her anthology *Charlie Chan Is Dead* (1993) and this essay
(which originally appeared in *Ms.* magazine [1994]).

Thinking Critically

*As you read this essay, think about whether you agree with Hagedorn's
observations and claims that Asian women in films have been stereotyped
as either victims or vixens. Observe Hagedorn's tone, attitude toward the
subject, and use of irony in getting her points across.*

---

*Pearl of the Orient. Whore. Geisha. Concubine. Whore. Hostess. Bar Girl. Mama-
san. Whore. China Doll. Tokyo Rose. Whore. Butterfly. Whore. Miss Saigon. Whore.
Dragon Lady. Lotus Blossum. Gook. Whore. Yellow Peril. Whore. Bangkok Bomb-
shell. Whore. Hospitality Girl. Whore. Comfort Woman. Whore. Savage. Whore.
Sultry. Whore. Faceless. Whore. Porcelain. Whore. Demure. Whore. Virgin.
Whore. Mute. Whore. Model Minority. Whore. Victim. Whore. Woman Warrior.
Whore. Mail-Order Bride. Whore. Mother. Wife. Lover. Daughter. Sister.*

As I was growing up in the Philippines in the 1950s, my fertile imagination
was colonized by thoroughly American fantasies. Yellowface variations on
the exotic erotic loomed larger than life on the silver screen. I was mystified
and enthralled by Hollywood's skewed representations of Asian women: sleek,
evil goddesses with slanted eyes and cunning ways, or smiling, sarong-clad

South Seas "maidens" with undulating hips, kinky black hair, and white skin darkened by makeup. Hardly any of the "Asian" characters were played by Asians. White actors like Sidney Toler and Warner Oland played "inscrutable Oriental detective" Charlie Chan with taped eyelids and a singsong, chop suey accent. Jennifer Jones was a Eurasian doctor swept up in a doomed "interracial romance" in *Love Is a Many Splendored Thing.* In my mother's youth, white actor Luise Rainer played the central role of the Patient Chinese Wife in the 1937 film adaptation of Pearl Buck's novel *The Good Earth.* Back then, not many thought to ask why; they were all too busy being grateful to see anyone in the movies remotely like themselves.

Cut to 1960: *The World of Suzie Wong,* another tragic East/West affair. I am now old enough to be impressed. Sexy, sassy Suzie (played by Nancy Kwan) works out of a bar patronized by white sailors, but doesn't seem bothered by any of it. For a hardworking girl turning nightly tricks to support her baby, she manages to parade an astonishing wardrobe in damn near every scene, down to matching handbags and shoes. The sailors are also strictly Hollywood, sanitized and not too menacing. Suzie and all the other prostitutes in this movie are cute, giggling, dancing sex machines with hearts of gold. William Holden plays an earnest, rather prim, Nice Guy painter seeking inspiration in The Other. Of course, Suzie falls madly in love with him. Typically, she tells him, "I not important," and "I'll be with you until you say—Suzie, go away." She also thinks being beaten by a man is a sign of true passion and is terribly disappointed when Mr. Nice Guy refuses to show his true feelings.

Next in Kwan's short-lived but memorable career was the kitschy 1961 musical *Flower Drum Song,* which, like *Suzie Wong,* is a thoroughly American commercial product. The female roles are typical of Hollywood musicals of the times: women are basically airheads, subservient to men. Kwan's counterpart is the Good Chinese Girl, played by Miyoshi Umeki, who was better playing the Loyal Japanese Girl in that other classic Hollywood tale of forbidden love, *Sayonara.* Remember? Umeki was so loyal, she committed double suicide with actor Red Buttons. I instinctively hated *Sayonara* when I first saw it as a child; now I understand why. Contrived tragic resolutions were the only way Hollywood got past the censors in those days. With one or two exceptions, somebody in these movies always had to die to pay for breaking racial and sexual taboos.

Until the recent onslaught of films by both Asian and Asian American film-makers, Asian Pacific women have generally been perceived by Hollywood with a mixture of fascination, fear, and contempt. Most Hollywood movies either trivialize or exoticize us as people of color and as women. Our intelligence is underestimated, our humanity overlooked, and our diverse cultures treated as interchangeable. If we are "good," we are childlike, submissive, silent, and eager for sex (see France Nuyen's glowing performance as Liat in the film version of *South Pacific*) or else we are tragic victim types (see *Casualties of War*, Brian De Palma's graphic 1989 drama set in Vietnam). And if we are not silent, suffering doormats, we are demonized dragon ladies—cunning, deceitful, sexual provocateurs. Give me the demonic any day—Anna May Wong as a villain slithering around in a slinky gown is at least gratifying to watch, neither servile nor passive. And she steals the show from Marlene Dietrich in Josef von Sternberg's *Shanghai Express*. From the 1920s through the '30s, Wong was our only female "star." But even she was trapped in limited roles, in what filmmaker Renee Tajima has called the dragon lady/lotus blossom dichotomy.

Cut to 1985: There is a scene toward the end of the terribly dishonest but weirdly compelling Michael Cimino movie *Year of the Dragon* (cowritten by Oliver Stone) that is one of my favorite twisted movie moments of all time. If you ask a lot of my friends who've seen that movie (especially if they're Asian), it's one of their favorites too. The setting is a crowded Chinatown nightclub. There are two very young and very tough Jade Cobra gang girls in a shootout with Mickey Rourke, in the role of a demented Polish American cop who, in spite of being Mr. Ugly in the flesh—an arrogant, misogynistic bully devoid of any charm—wins the "good" Asian American anchorwoman in the film's absurd and implausible ending. This is a movie with an actual disclaimer as its lead-in, covering its ass in advance in response to anticipated complaints about "stereotypes."

My pleasure in the hard-edged power of the Chinatown gang girls in *Year of the Dragon* is my small revenge, the answer to all those Suzie Wong "I want to be your slave" female characters. The Jade Cobra girls are mere background to the white male foreground/focus of Cimino's movie. But long after the movie has faded into video-rental heaven, the Jade Cobra girls remain defiant, fabulous images in my memory, flaunting tight metallic dresses and spiky cock's-comb hairdos streaked electric red and blue.

> Mickey Rourke looks down with a world-weary pity at the unnamed Jade Cobra girl (Doreen Chan) he's just shot who lies sprawled and bleeding on the street: "You look like you're gonna die, beautiful."
> JADE COBRA GIRL: "Oh yeah? [blood gushing from her mouth] I'm proud of it."
> ROURKE: "You are? You got anything you wanna tell me before you go, sweetheart?"
> JADE COBRA GIRL: "Yeah. [pause] Fuck you."

Cut to 1993: I've been told that like many New Yorkers, I watch movies with the right side of my brain on perpetual overdrive. I admit to being grouchy and overcritical, suspicious of sentiment, and cynical. When a critic like Richard Corliss of *Time* magazine gushes about *The Joy Luck Club* being "a fourfold *Terms of Endearment*," my gut instinct is to run the other way. I resent being told how to feel. I went to see the 1993 eight-handkerchief movie version of Amy Tan's best-seller with a group that included my ten-year-old daughter. I was caught between the sincere desire to be swept up by the turbulent mother-daughter sagas and my own stubborn resistance to being so obviously manipulated by the filmmakers. With every flashback came tragedy. The music soared; the voice-overs were solemn or wistful; tears, tears, and more tears flowed onscreen. Daughters were reverent; mothers carried dark secrets.

I was elated by the grandness and strength of the four mothers and the luminous actors who portrayed them, but I was uneasy with the passivity of the Asian American daughters. They seemed to exist solely as receptors for their mothers' amazing life stories. It's almost as if by assimilating so easily into American society, they had lost all sense of self.

In spite of my resistance, my eyes watered as the desperate mother played   *10* by Kieu Chinh was forced to abandon her twin baby girls on a country road in war-torn China. (Kieu Chinh resembles my own mother and her twin sister, who suffered through the brutal Japanese occupation of the Philippines.) So far in this movie, an infant son had been deliberately drowned, a mother played by the gravely beautiful France Nuyen had gone catatonic with grief, a concubine had cut her flesh open to save her dying mother, an insecure daughter had been oppressed by her boorish Asian American husband, another insecure daugter had been left by her white husband, and so on. . . . The overall effect was numbing as far as I'm concerned, but a man sitting two rows in front of us broke down sobbing. A Chinese Pilipino writer even more grouchy than me later complained, "Must ethnicity only be equated with suffering?"

Because change has been slow, *The Joy Luck Club* carries a lot of cultural baggage. It is big-budget story about Chinese American women, directed by a Chinese American man, cowritten and coproduced by Chinese American women. There's a lot to be thankful for. And its box office success proves that an immigrant narrative told from female perspectives can have mass appeal. But my cynical side tells me that its success might mean only one thing in Hollywood: more weepy epics about Asian American mother-daughter relationships will be planned.

That the film finally got made was significant. By Hollywood standards (think white male; think money, money, money), a movie about Asian Americans even when adapted from a best-seller was a risky proposition. When I asked a producer I know about the film's rumored delays, he simply said, "It's still an *Asian* movie," surprised I had even asked. Equally interesting was director Wayne Wang's initial reluctance to be involved in the project; he told the *New York Times*, "I didn't want to do another Chinese movie."

Maybe he shouldn't have worried so much. After all, according to the media, the nineties are the decade of "Pacific Overtures" and East Asian chic.

Madonna, the pop queen of shameless appropriation, cultivated Japanese high-tech style with her music video "Rain," while Janet Jackson faked kitschy orientalia in hers, titled "If." Critical attention was paid to movies from China, Japan, and Vietnam. But that didn't mean an honest appraisal of women's lives. Even on the art house circuit, filmmakers who should know better took the easy way out. Takehiro Nakajima's 1992 film *Okoge* presents one of the more original film roles for women in recent years. In Japanese, "okoge" means the crust of rice that sticks to the bottom of the rice pot; in perjorative slang, it means fag hag. The way "okoge" is used in the film seems a reappropriation of the term; the portrait Nakajima creates of Sayoko, the so-called fag hag, is clearly an affectionate one. Sayoko is a quirky, self-assured woman in contemporary Tokyo who does voice-overs for cartoons, has a thing for Frida Kahlo paintings, and is drawn to a gentle young gay man named Goh. But the other women's roles are disappointing, stereotypical "hysterical females" and the movie itself turns conventional halfway through. Sayoko sacrifices herself to a macho brute Goh desires, who rapes her as images of Frida Kahlo paintings and her beloved Goh rising from the ocean flash before her. She gives birth to a baby boy and endures a terrible life of poverty with the abusive rapist. This sudden change from spunky survivor to helpless, victimized woman is baffling. Whatever happened to her job? Or that arty little apartment of hers? Didn't her Frida Kahlo obsession teach her anything?

Then there was Tiana Thi Thanh Nga's *From Hollywood to Hanoi*, a self-serving but fascinating documentary. Born in Vietnam to a privileged family that included an uncle who was defense minister in the Thieu government and an idolized father who served as press minister, Nga (a.k.a. Tiana) spent her adolescence in California. A former actor in martial arts movies and fitness teacher ("Karaticize with Tiana"), the vivacious Tiana decided to make a record of her journey back to Vietnam.

15   *From Hollywood to Hanoi* is at times unintentionally very funny. Tiana includes a quick scene of herself dancing with a white man at the Metropole hotel in Hanoi, and breathlessly announces: "That's me doing the tango with Oliver Stone!" Then she listens sympathetically to a horrifying account of the My Lai massacre by one of its few female survivors. In another scene, Tiana cheerfully addresses a food vendor on the streets of Hanoi: "Your hairdo is so pretty." The unimpressed, poker-faced woman gives a brusque, deadpan reply: "You want to eat, or what?" Sometimes it is hard to tell the difference between Tiana Thi Thanh Nga and her Hollywood persona: the real Tiana still seems to be playing one of her B-movie roles, which are mainly fun because they're fantasy. The time was certainly right to explore postwar Vietnam from a Vietnamese woman's perspective; it's too bad this film was done by a Valley Girl.

Nineteen ninety-three also brought Tran Anh Hung's *The Scent of Green Papaya*, a different kind of Vietnamese memento—this is a look back at the peaceful, lush country of the director's childhood memories. The film opens in Saigon, in 1951. A willowy ten-year-old girl named Mui comes to work for a troubled family headed by a melancholy musician and his kind, stoic wife. The men of the bourgeois household are idle, pampered types who take naps while the women do all the work. Mui is a male fantasy: she is a devoted servant, enduring acts of cruel mischief with patience and dignity; as an adult, she barely speaks. She scrubs floors, shines shoes, and cooks with loving care and never a complaint. When she is sent off to work for another wealthy musician, she ends up being impregnated by him. The movie ends as the camera closes in on Mui's contented face. Languid and precious, *The Scent of Green Papaya* is visually haunting, but it suffers from the director's colonial fantasy of women as docile, domestic creatures. Steeped in highbrow nostalgia, it's the arty Vietnamese version of *My Fair Lady* with a wealthy musician as Professor Higgins, teaching Mui to read and write.

And then there is Ang Lee's tepid 1993 hit, *The Wedding Banquet*—a clever culture-clash farce in which traditional Chinese values collide with contemporary American sexual mores. The somewhat formulaic plot goes like this: Wai-Tung, a yuppie landlord, lives with his white lover, Simon, in a chic Manhattan brownstone. Wai-Tung is an only child and his aging parents in Taiwan long for a grandchild to continue the family legacy. Enter Wei-Wei, an artist who lives in a grungy loft owned by Wai-Tung. She slugs tequila straight from the bottle as she paints and flirts boldly with her young, uptight landlord, who brushes her off. "It's my fate. I am always attracted to handsome gay men," she mutters. After this setup, the movie goes downhill, all edges blurred in a cozy nest of happy endings. In a refrain of Sayoko's plight in *Okoge*, a pregnant, suddenly complacent Wei-Wei gives in to family pressures—and never gets her life back.

> *"It takes a man to know what it is to be a real women."*
>
> —SONG LILING in *M. Butterfly*

Ironically, two gender-bending films in which men play men playing women reveal more about the mythology of the prized Asian woman and the superficial trappings of gender than most movies that star real women. The slow-moving *M. Butterfly* presents the ultimate object of Western male desire as the spy/opera diva Song Liling, a Suzie Wong/Lotus Blossom played by actor John Lone with a five o'clock shadow and bobbing Adam's apple. The best and most profound of these forays into cross-dressing is the spectacular melodrama *Farewell My Concubine*, directed by Chen Kaige. Banned in China, *Farewell My Concubine* shared the prize for Best Film at the 1993 Cannes Film Festival with Jane Campion's *The Piano*. Sweeping through 50 years of tumultuous history in China, the story revolves around the lives of two male Beijing Opera stars and the woman who marries one of them. The three characters make an unforgettable triangle, struggling over love, art, friendship, and politics against the bloody backdrop of cultural upheaval. They are as capable of casually betraying each other as they are of selfless, heroic acts. The androgynous Dieyi, doomed to play the same female role of concubine over and over again, is portrayed with great vulnerability, wit, and grace by male Hong Kong pop star Leslie Cheung. Dieyi competes with the prostitute Juxian (Gong Li) for the love of his childhood protector and fellow opera star, Duan Xiaolou (Zhang Fengyi).

Cheung's highly stylized performance as the classic concubine-ready-to-die-for-love in the opera within the movie is all about female artifice. His side-long glances, restrained passion, languid stance, small steps, and delicate, refined gestures say everything about what is considered desirable in Asian women—and are the antithesis of the feisty, outspoken woman played by Gong Li. The characters of Dieyi and Juxian both see suffering as part and parcel of love and life. Juxian matter-of-factly says to Duan Xiaolou before he agrees to marry her: "I'm used to hardship. If you take me in, I'll wait on you hand and foot. If you tire of me, I'll . . . kill myself. No big deal." It's an echo of Suzie Wong's servility, but the context is new. Even with her back to the wall, Juxian is not helpless or whiny. She attempts to manipulate a man while admitting to the harsh reality that is her life.

20 Dieyi and Juxian are the two sides of the truth of women's lives in most Asian countries. Juxian in particular—wife and ex-prostitute—could be seen as a thankless and stereotypical role. But like the characters Gong Li has played in Chinese director Zhang Yimou's films, *Red Sorghum*, *Raise the Red Lantern*, and especially *The Story of Qiu Ju*, Juxian is tough, obstinate, sensual, clever, oafish, beautiful, infuriating, cowardly, heroic, and banal. Above all, she is resilient. Gong Li is one the few Asian Pacific actors whose roles have been drawn with intelligence, honesty, and depth. Nevertheless, the characters she plays are limited by the possibilities that exist for real women in China.

"Let's face it. Women still don't mean shit in China," my friend Meeling reminds me. What she says so bluntly about her culture rings painfully true, but in less obvious fashion for me. In the Philippines, infant girls aren't drowned, nor were their feet bound to make them more desirable. But sons were and are cherished. To this day, men of the bourgeois class are coddled and prized, much like the spoiled men of the elite household in *The Scent of Green Papaya*. We do not have a geisha tradition like Japan, but physical beauty is overtreasured. Our daughters are protected virgins or primed as potential beauty queens. And many of us have bought into the image of the white man as our handsome savior: G.I. Joe.

Buzz magazine recently featured an article entitled "Asian Women/L. A. Men," a report on a popular hangout that caters to white men's fantasies of nubile Thai women. The lines between movies and real life are blurred. Male screenwriters and cinematographers flock to this bar-restaurant, where the waitresses are eager to "audition" for roles. Many of these men have been to Bangkok while working on film crews for Vietnam War movies. They've come back to L.A., but for them, the movie never ends. In this particular fantasy the boys play G.I. Joe on a rescue mission in the urban jungle, saving the whore from herself. "A scene has developed here, a kind of R-rated *Cheers*," author Alan Rifkin writes. "The waitresses audition for sitcoms. The customers date the waitresses or just keep score."

Colonization of the imagination is a two-way street. And being enshrined on a pedestal as someone's Pearl of the Orient fantasy doesn't seem so demeaning, at first; who wouldn't want to be worshipped? Perhaps that's why Asian women are the ultimate wet dream in most Hollywood movies; it's no secret how well we've been taught to play the role, to take care of our men. In Hollywood vehicles, we are objects of desire or derision; we exist to provide sex, color, and texture in what is essentially a white man's world. It is akin to what Toni Morrison calls "the Africanist presence" in literature. She writes: "Just as entertainers, through or by association with blackface, could render permissible topics that otherwise would have been taboo, so American writers were able to employ an imagined Africanist persona to articulate and imaginatively act out the forbidden in American culture." The same analogy could be made for the often titillating presence of Asian women in movies made by white men.

Movies are still the most seductive and powerful of artistic mediums, manipulating us with ease by a powerful combination of sound and image. In many ways, as females and Asians, as audiences or performers, we have learned to settle for less—to accept the fact that we are either decorative, invisible, or one-dimensional. When there are characters who look like us represented in a movie, we have also learned to view between the lines, or to add what is missing. For many of us, this way of watching has always been a necessity. We fill in the gaps. If a female character is presented as a mute, willowy beauty, we convince ourselves she is an ancestral ghost—so smart she doesn't have to speak at all. If she is a whore with a heart of gold, we claim her as a tough feminist icon. If she is a sexless, sanitized, boring nerd, we embrace her as a role model for our daughters, rather than the tragic whore. And if she is presented as an utterly devoted saint suffering nobly in silence, we lie and say she is just like our mothers. Larger than life. Magical and insidious. A movie is never just a movie, after all.

Engaging the Text

1. In what way has the portrayal of Asian women in films changed over the past half-century, according to Hagedorn?

2. Why is Hagedorn unhappy with the representation of Asian women in *The Joy Luck Club* (1993), based on Amy Tan's popular novel? Rent this film, and discuss the validity of Hagedorn's criticism.

Exploring Your Cultural Perspective

1. Hagedorn finds the traditional roles in which Asian women are depicted to be demeaning and offensive. What are some of these stereotypes? Do you view them in the same way? Explain your answer.

2. Do the advertisements and articles in magazines targeted at Asian readers (such as *Transpacific*) depict Asian women in stereotyped ways? Examine a few of these publications, and report your findings to the class.

R. K. NARAYAN
Misguided "Guide"

The prospect of having a film made from one's novel is something most writers anticipate with excitement, especially if they are to be part of the filmmaking process. Yet the transformation of the written word to images on the screen is a precarious journey, as the noted Indian writer R. K. Narayan (1906–2001) soon learned. Narayan had written a series of successful novels (*A Tiger for Malgudi*, 1983; *Talkative Man*, 1986; and *The World of Nagaraj*, 1990) set in the fictional south Indian village of Malgudi. His autobiography, *My Days: A Memoir* (1982), had been awarded the American Academy and Institute of Arts and Letters citation. Now his novel *The Guide* (1958), which had garnered India's highest literary award, was to become a film. The author's growing alarm when film producers changed locations, story line, and characters (over his protests) is recorded in this account from his 1993 collection, *A Writer's Nightmare: Selected Essays (1958–1988)*. His most recent work is *The Mahabarata* (1998).

Thinking Critically
If you had written a memoir or a novel that producers wanted to make into a film, would you accept less money in exchange for full control over the interpretation of your work or give up control for more money?

The letter came by airmail from Los Angeles. "I am a producer and actor from Bombay," it read. "I don't know if my name is familiar to you."

He was too modest. Millions of young men copied his screen image, walking as he did, slinging a folded coat over the shoulder carelessly, buffing up a lock of hair over the right temple, and assuming that the total effect would make the girls sigh with hopeless longing. My young nephews at home were thrilled at the sight of the handwriting of Dev Anand.

The Letter went on to say, "I was in London and came across your novel *The Guide*. I am anxious to make it into a film. I can promise you that I will keep to the spirit and quality of your writing. My plans are to make both a Hindi and an English film of this story." He explained how he had arranged with an American film producer for collaboration. He also described how he had flown from London to New York in search of me, since someone had told him I lived there, and then across the whole continent before he could discover my address. He was ready to come to Mysore if I should indicate the slightest willingness to consider his proposal.

I cabled him an invitation, already catching the fever of hurry characteristic of the film world. He flew from Los Angeles to Bombay to Bangalore, and motored down a hundred miles without losing a moment.

5   A small crowd of autograph-hunters had gathered at the gate of my house in Yadava Giri. He expertly eluded the inquisitive crowd, and we were soon closeted in the dining room, breakfasting on *idli, dosai,* and other South Indian delicacies, my nephews attending on the star in a state of elation. The talk was all about *The Guide* and its cinematic merits. Within an hour we had become so friendly that he could ask without embarrassment, "What price will you demand for your story?" The checkbook was out and the pen was poised over it. I had the impression that if I had suggested that the entire face of the check be covered with closely knit figures, he would have obliged me. But I hemmed and hawed, suggested a slight advance, and told him to go ahead. I was sure that if the picture turned out to be a success he would share with me the glory and the profits. "Oh, certainly," he affirmed, "if the picture, by God's grace, turns out to be a success, we will be on top of the world, and the sky will be the limit!"

The following months were filled with a sense of importance: Long Distance Calls, Urgent Telegrams, Express Letters, sudden arrivals and departures by plane and car. I received constant summonses to be present here or there. "PLEASE COME TO DELHI. SUIT RESERVED AT IMPERIALL HOTEL. URGENTLY NEED YOUR PRESENCE."

Locking away my novel-in-progress, I fly to Delhi. There is the press conference, with introductions, speeches and overflowing conviviality. The American director explains the unique nature of their present effort: for the first time in the history of Indian movie-making, they are going to bring out a hundred-percent-Indian story, with a hundred-percent-Indian cast, and a hundred-percent-Indian setting, for an international audience. And mark this: actually in colour-and-wide-screen-first-time-in-the-history-of-this-country.

A distinguished group of Americans, headed by the Nobel Prize winner Pearl Buck, would produce the film. Again and again I heard the phrase: "Sky is the limit," and the repeated assurances: "We will make the picture just as Narayan has written it, with his co-operation at every stage." Reporters pressed me for a statement. It was impossible to say anything but the pleasantest things in such an atmosphere of overwhelming optimism and good fellowship.

Soon we were assembled in Mysore. They wanted to see the exact spots which had inspired me to write *The Guide*. Could I show them the locations? A photographer, and some others whose business with us I never quite understood, were in the party. We started out in two cars. The American director, Tad Danielewski, explained that he would direct the English version first. He kept discussing with me the finer points of my novel. "I guess your hero is a man of impulsive plans? Self-made, given to daydreaming?" he would ask, and add, before I could muster an answer, "Am I not right?" Of course he had to be right. Once or twice when I attempted to mitigate his impressions, he brushed aside my comments and went on with his own explanation as to what I must have had in mind when I created such-and-such a character.

I began to realize that monologue is the privilege of the film maker, and   10 that it was futile to try butting in with my own observations. But for some obscure reason, they seemed to need my presence, though not my voice. I must be seen and not heard.

We drove about 300 miles that day, during the course of which I showed them the river steps and a little shrine overshadowed by a banyan on the banks of the Kaveri, which was the actual spot around which I wrote *The Guide*. As I had recalled, nothing more needed to be done than put the actors there and start the camera. They uttered little cries of joy at finding a "set" so readily available. In the summer, when the river dried up, they could shoot the drought scenes with equal ease. Then I took them to the tiny town of Nanjangud, with its little streets, its shops selling sweets and toys and ribbons, and a pilgrim crowd bathing in the holy waters of the Kabini, which flowed through the town. The crowd was colourful and lively around the temple, and in a few weeks it would increase a hundredfold when people from the surrounding villages arrived to participate in the annual festival—the sort of crowd described in the last pages of my novel. If the film makers made a note of the date and sent down a cameraman at that time, they could secure the last scene of my novel in an authentic manner and absolutely free of cost.

The producer at once passed an order to his assistant to arrange for an outdoor unit to arrive here at the right time. Then we all posed at the portals of the ancient temple, with arms encircling each other's necks and smiling. This was but the first of innumerable similar scenes in which I found myself posing with the starry folk, crushed in the friendliest embrace.

From Nanjangud we drove up mountains and the forests and photographed our radiant smiles against every possible background. It was a fatiguing business on the whole, but the American director claimed that it was nothing to what he was used to. He generally went 5,000 miles in search of locations, exposing hundreds of rolls of film on the way.

After inspecting jungles, mountains, village streets, hamlets and huts, we reached the base of Gopalaswami Hill in the afternoon, and drove up the five-mile mud track; the cars had to be pushed up the steep hill after encroaching vegetation had been cleared from the path. This was a part of the forest country where at any bend of the road one could anticipate a tiger or a herd of elephants; but, luckily for us, they were out of view today.

15   At the summit I showed them the original of the "Peak House" in my novel, a bungalow built 50 years ago, with glassed-in verandas affording a view of the wildlife at night, and a 2,000-foot drop to a valley beyond. A hundred yards off, a foot-track wound through the undergrowth, leading on to an ancient temple whose walls were crumbling and whose immense timber doors moved on rusty hinges with a groan. Once again I felt that here everything was ready-made for the film. They could shoot in the bright sunlight, and for the indoor scenes they assured me that it would be a simple matter to haul up a generator and lights.

Sitting under a banyan tree and consuming sandwiches and lemonade, we discussed and settled the practical aspects of the expedition: where to locate the base camp and where the advance units consisting of engineers, mechanics, and truck drivers, in charge of the generator and lights. All through the journey back the talk involved schedules and arrangements for shooting the scenes in this part of the country. I was impressed with the ease they displayed in accepting such mighty logistical tasks. Film executives, it seemed to me, could solve mankind's problems on a global scale with the casual confidence of demigods, if only they could take time off their illusory pursuits and notice the serious aspects of existence.

Then came total silence, for many weeks. Finally I discovered that they were busy searching for their locations in Northern India.

This was a shock. I had never visualized my story in that part of India, where costumes, human types and details of daily life are different. They had settled upon Jaipur and Udaipur in Rajaputana, a thousand miles away from my location for the story.

Our next meeting was in Bombay, and I wasted no time in speaking of this problem. "My story takes place in south India, in Malgudi, an imaginary town known to thousands of my readers all over the world," I explained. "It is South India in costume, tone and contents. Although the whole country is one, there are diversities, and one has to be faithful in delineating them. You have to stick to my geography and sociology. Although it is a world of fiction there are certain inner veracities."

20   One of them replied: "We feel it a privilege to be doing your story." This sounded irrelevant as an answer to my statement.

We were sitting under a gaudy umbrella beside a blue swimming pool on Juhu Beach, where the American party was housed in princely suites in a modern hotel. It was hard to believe that we were in India. Most of our discussions took place somewhat amphibiously, on the edge of the swimming pool, in which the director spent a great deal of his time.

This particular discussion was interrupted as a bulky European tourist in swimming briefs fell off the diving plank, hit the bottom and had to be hauled out and rendered first aid. After the atmosphere had cleared, I resumed my speech. They listened with a mixture of respect and condescension, evidently willing to make allowances for an author's whims.

"Please remember," one of them tried to explain, "that we are shooting, for the first time in India, in wide screen and Eastman Colour, and we must shoot where there is spectacle. Hence Jaipur."

"In that case," I had to ask, "Why all that strenuous motoring near my home? Why my story at all, if what you need is a picturesque spectacle?"

I was taken aback when their reply came! "How do you know that Malgudi   25 is where you think it is?"

Somewhat bewildered, I said, with what I hoped was proper humility, "I suppose I know because I have imagined it, created it and have been writing novel after novel set in the area for the last 30 years."

"We are out to expand the notion of Malgudi," one of them explained. "Malgudi will be where we place it, in Kashmir, Rajasthan, Bombay, Delhi, even Ceylon."

I could not share the flexibility of their outlook or the expanse of their vision. It seemed to me that for their purpose a focal point was unnecessary. They appeared to be striving to achieve mere optical effects.

I recalled a talk with Satyajit Ray, the great director, some years earlier, when I met him in Calcutta. He expressed his admiration for *The Guide* but also his doubts as to whether he could ever capture the tone and atmosphere of its background. He had said, "Its roots are so deep in the soil of your part of our country that I doubt if I could do justice to your book, being unfamiliar with its milieu. . . ." Such misgivings did not bother the American director. I noticed that though he was visiting India for the first time, he never paused to ask what was what in this bewildering country.

Finally he solved the whole problem by declaring, "Why should we men-   30 tion where the story takes place? We will avoid the name 'Malgudi.'" Thereafter the director not only avoided the word Malgudi but fell foul of anyone who uttered that sound.

My brother, an artist who has illustrated my stories for 25 years, tried to expound his view. At a dinner in his home in Bombay, he mentioned the forbidden word to the director. Malgudi, he explained, meant a little town, not so picturesque as Jaipur, of a neutral shade, with characters wearing dhoti and jibba when they were not barebodied. The Guide himself was a man of charm, creating history and archeology out of thin air for his clients, and to provide him with solid, concrete monuments to talk about would go against the grain of the tale. The director listened and firmly said, "There is no Malgudi, and that is all there is to it."

But my brother persisted. I became concerned that the controversy threatened to spoil our dinner. The director replied, in a sad tone, that they could as well have planned a picture for black and white and narrow screen if all one wanted was what he contemptuously termed a "Festival Film," while he was planning a million-dollar spectacle to open simultaneously in 2,000 theaters in America. I was getting used to arguments every day over details. My story is about a dancer in a small town, an exponent of the strictly classical tradition of South Indian *Bharat Natyam*. The film makers felt this was inadequate. They therefore engaged an expensive, popular dance director with a troupe of a hundred or more dancers, and converted my heroine's performances into an extravaganza in delirious, fruity colours and costumes. Their dancer was constantly traveling hither and thither in an Air India Boeing no matter how short the distance to be covered. The moviegoer, too, I began to realize, would be whisked all over India. Although he would see none of the countryside in which the novel was set, he would see the latest U.S. Embassy building in New Delhi, Parliament House, the Ashoka Hotel, the Lake Palace, Elephanta Caves and whatnot. Unity of place seemed an unknown concept for a film maker. (Later Mrs. Indira Gandhi, whom I met after she had seen a special showing of the film, asked, "Why should they have dragged the story all over as if it were a travelogue, instead of confining themselves to the simple background of your book?" She added as an afterthought, and in what seemed to me an understatement: "Perhaps they have other considerations.")

The co-operation of many persons was needed in the course of the film making, and anyone whose help was requested had to be given a copy of *The Guide*. Thus there occurred a shortage, and an inevitable black market, in copies of the book. A production executive searched the bookshops in Bombay, and cornered all available copies at any price. He could usually be seen going about like a scholar with a bundle of books under his arm. I was also intrigued by the intense study and pencil-marking that the director was making on his copy of the book; it was as if he were studying it for a doctoral thesis. Not until I had a chance to read his "treatment" did I understand what all his penciling meant: he had been marking off passages and portions that were to be avoided in the film.

When the script came, I read through it with mixed feelings. The director answered my complaints with "I have only exteriorized what you have expressed. It is all in your book."

35   "In which part of my book," I would ask without any hope of an answer.

Or he would say, "I could give you two hundred reasons why this change should be so." I did not feel up to hearing them all. If I still proved truculent he would explain away, "This is only a first draft. We could make any change you want in the final screenplay."

The screenplay was finally presented to me with a great flourish and expressions of fraternal sentiments at a hotel in Bangalore. But I learned at this time that they had already started shooting and had even completed a number of scenes. Whenever I expressed my views, the answer would be either, "Oh, it will all be rectified in the editing," or, "We will deal with it when we decide about the retakes. But please wait until we have a chance to see the rushes." By now a bewildering number of hands were behind the scenes, at laboratories, workshops, carpentries, editing rooms and so forth. It was impossible to keep track of what was going on, or get hold of anyone with a final say. Soon I trained myself to give up all attempts to connect the film with the book of which I happened to be the author.

But I was not sufficiently braced for the shock that came the day when the director insisted upon the production of two tigers to fight and destroy each other over a spotted deer. He wished to establish the destructive animality of two men clashing over one woman: my heroine's husband and lover fighting over her. The director intended a tiger fight to portray the depths of symbolism. It struck me as obvious. Moreover it was not in the story. But he asserted that it was; evidently I had intended the scene without realizing it.

The Indian producer, who was financing the project, groaned at the thought of the tigers. He begged me privately, "Please do something about it. We have no time for tigers; and it will cost a hell of a lot to hire them, just for a passing fancy." I spoke to the director again, but he was insistent. No tiger, no film, and two tigers or none.

Scouts were sent out through the length and breadth of India to explore   *40* the tiger possibilities. They returned to report that only one tiger was available. It belonged to a circus and the circus owner would under no circumstances consent to have the tiger injured or killed. The director decreed, "I want the beast to die, otherwise the scene will have no meaning." They finally found a man in Madras, living in the heart of the city with a full-grown Bengal tiger which he occasionally lent for jungle pictures, after sewing its lips and pulling out its claws.

The director examined a photograph of the tiger, in order to satisfy himself that they were not trying to palm off a pi-dog in tiger clothing, and signed it up. Since a second tiger was not available, he had to settle for its fighting a leopard. It was an easier matter to find a deer for the sacrifice. What they termed a "second unit" was dispatched to Madras to shoot the sequence. Ten days later the unit returned, looking forlorn.

The tiger had shrunk at the sight of the leopard, and the leopard had shown no inclination to maul the deer, whose cries of fright had been so heart-rending that they had paralyzed the technicians. By prodding, kicking and irritating the animals, they had succeeded in producing a spectacle gory enough to make them retch. "The deer was actually lifted and fed into the jaws of the other two," said an assistant cameraman. (This shot passes on the screen, in the finished film, in the winking of an eye as a bloody smudge, to the accompaniment of a lot of wild uproar.)

Presently another crisis developed. The director wanted the hero to kiss the heroine, who of course rejected the suggestion as unbecoming an Indian woman. The director was distraught. The hero, for his part, was willing to obey the director, but he was helpless, since kissing is a co-operative effort. The American director realized that it is against Indian custom to kiss in public; but he insisted that the public in his country would boo if they missed the kiss. I am told that the heroine replied: "There is enough kissing in your country at all times and places, off and on the screen, and your public, I am sure, will flock to a picture where, for a change, no kissing is shown." She stood firm. Finally, the required situation was apparently faked by tricky editing.

Next: trouble at the governmental level. A representation was made to the Ministry dealing with the films, by an influential group, that *The Guide* glorified adultery, and hence was not fit to be presented as a film, since it might degrade Indian womanhood. The dancer in my story, to hear their arguments, has no justification for preferring Raju the Guide to her legally wedded husband. The Ministry summoned the movie principals to Delhi and asked them to explain how they proposed to meet the situation. They promised to revise the film script to the Ministry's satisfaction.

45   In my story the dancer's husband is a preoccupied archaeologist who has no time or inclination for a marital life and is not interested in her artistic aspirations. Raju the Guide exploits the situation and weans her away from her husband. That is all there is to it—in my story. But now a justification had to be found for adultery.

So the archaeological husband was converted into a drunkard and womanizer who kicks out his wife when he discovers that another man has watched her dance in her room and has spoken encouragingly to her. I knew nothing about this drastic change of my characters until I saw the "rushes" some months later. This was the point at which I lamented most over my naivete: the contract that I had signed in blind faith, in the intoxication of cheques bonhomie, and backslapping, empowered them to do whatever they pleased with my story, and I had no recourse.

Near the end of the project I made another discovery: the extent to which movie producers will go to publicize a film. The excessive affability to pressmen, the entertaining of V.I.P.s, the button-holding of ministers and officials in authority, the extravagant advertising campaigns, seem to me to drain off money, energy and ingenuity that might be reserved for the creation of an honest and sensible product.

On one occasion Lord Mountbatten was passing through India, and someone was seized with the sudden idea that he could help make a success of the picture. A banquet was held at Raj Bhavan in his honor, and the Governor of Bombay, Mrs. Vijayalaxmi Pandit, was kind enough to invite us to it. I was home in Mysore as Operation Mountbatten was launched, so telegrams and long-distance telephone calls poured in on me to urge me to come to Bombay at once. I flew in just in time to dress and reach Raj Bhavan. It was red-carpeted, crowded and gorgeous. When dinner was over, leaving the guests aside, our hostess managed to isolate his Lordship and the "Guide"-makers on a side veranda of this noble building. His Lordship sat on a sofa surrounded by us; close to him sat Pearl Buck, who was one of the producers and who, by virtue of her seniority and standing, was to speak for us. As she opened the theme with a brief explanation of the epoch-making effort that was being made in India, in colour and wide-screen, with a hundred-percent-Indian cast, story and background, his Lordship displayed no special emotion. Then came the practical demand: in order that this grand, stupendous achievement might bear fruit, would Lord Mountbatten influence Queen Elizabeth to preside at the world premiere of the film in London in due course?

Lord Mountbatten responded promptly, "I don't think it is possible. Anyway what is the story?"

There was dead silence for a moment, as each looked at the other wonder- *50* ing who was to begin. I was fully aware that they ruled me out; they feared that I might take 80,000 words to narrate the story, as I had in the book. The obvious alternative was Pearl Buck, who was supposed to have written the screenplay.

Time was running out and his Lordship had others to talk to. Pearl Buck began.

"It is the story of a man called Raju. He was a tourist guide. . . ."

"Where does it take place?"

I wanted to shout, "Malgudi, of course," But they were explaining, "We have taken the story through many interesting locations—Jaipur, Udaipur."

"Let me hear the story." *55*

"Raju was a guide," began Pearl Buck again.

"In Jaipur?" asked his Lordship.

"Well, no. Anyway he did not remain a guide because when Rosie came . . ."

"Who is Rosie?"

"A dancer . . . but she changed her name when she became a . . . a . . . *60* dancer. . . ."

"But the guide? What happened to him?"

"I am coming to it. Rosie's husband . . ."

"Rosie is the dancer?"

"Yes, of course . . ." Pearl Buck struggled on, but I was in no mood to extricate her.

Within several minutes Lord Mountbatten said, "Most interesting." His *65* deep bass voice was a delight to the ear, but it also had a ring of finality and discouraged further talk. "Elizabeth's appointments are complicated these days. Anyway her private secretary Lord — must know more about it than I do. I am rather out of touch now. Anyway, perhaps I could ask Philip." He summoned an aide and said. "William, please remind me when we get to London. . . ." Our Producers went home feeling that a definite step had been taken to establish the film in proper quarters. As for myself, I was not so sure.

Elaborate efforts were made to shoot the last scene of the story, in which the saint fasts on the dry river's edge, in hopes of bringing rain, and a huge crowd turns up to witness the spectacle. For this scene the director selected a site at a village called Okla, outside Delhi on the bank of the Jamuna river, which was dry and provided enormous stretches of sand. He had, of course, ruled out the spot we had visited near Mysore, explaining that two coconut trees were visible a mile away on the horizon and might spoil the appearance of unrelieved desert which he wanted. Thirty truckloads of property, carpenters, lumber, painters, artisans and art department personnel arrived at Okla to erect a two-dimensional temple beside a dry river, at a cost of 80,000 rupees. As the director kept demanding, "I must have 100,000 people for a helicopter shot," I thought of the cost: five rupees per head for extras, while both the festival crowd at Nanjangud and the little temple on the river would cost nothing.

The crowd had been mobilized, the sets readied and lights mounted, and all other preparations completed for shooting the scene next morning when, at midnight, news was brought to the chiefs relaxing at the Ashoka Hotel that the Jamuna was rising dangerously as a result of unexpected rains in Simla. All hands were mobilized and they rushed desperately to the location to save the equipment. Wading in knee-deep water, they salvaged a few things. But I believe the two-dimensional temple was carried off in the floods.

Like a colony of ants laboriously building up again, the carpenters and artisans rebuilt, this time at a place in Western India called Limdi, which was reputed to have an annual rainfall of a few droplets. Within one week the last scene was completed, the hero collapsing in harrowing fashion as a result of his penance. The director and technicians paid off the huge crowd and packed up their cameras and sound equipment, and were just leaving the scene when a storm broke—an unknown phenomenon in that part of the country—uprooting and tearing off everything that stood. Those who had lingered had to make their exit with dispatch.

This seemed to me an appropriate conclusion for my story, which, after all, was concerned with the subject of rain, and in which Nature, rather than film makers, acted in consonance with the subject. I remembered that years ago when I was in New York City on my way to sign the contract, before writing *The Guide*, a sudden downpour caught me on Madison Avenue and I entered the Viking Press offices dripping wet. I still treasure a letter from Keith Jennison, who was then my editor. "Somehow I will always, from now on," he wrote, "associate the rainiest days in New York with you. The afternoon we officially became your publishers was wet enough to have made me feel like a fish ever since."

Engaging the Text

1. Why do you think "Bollywood" (the Bombay version of Hollywood) producers changed the locations, story line, and characters of Narayan's novel?

2. What clues alert the reader that Narayan does not spare himself in this satirical look at "Bollywood"? How did Narayan's attitude toward the filming of his novel change over the course of the project?

3. The question of authenticity is at the heart of Narayan's account, but would a film that had strictly adhered to his novel necessarily have been better? Why or why not? Can you cite any great films that have been made from bad novels or any bad films that have been made from great novels? What accounted for the difference in quality in the transition from fiction to film?

Exploring Your Cultural Perspective

1. How does the imaginary landscape and setting of Malgudi provide R. K. Narayan with a vehicle for conveying insights about the real culture? What is the advantage for a writer in using a fictional setting? Why not just set the story in a real place?

2. If you can obtain a film made in "Bollywood," view it, and identify two or three ways in which the cultural values it expresses differ from those in a "Hollywood" picture. (One example might be the means Indian films use to suggest passion.) Discuss your findings.

JACKIE CHAN

A Dirty Job

Jackie Chan was born in Hong Kong in 1954 and was sold by his parents at the age of seven to a theatrical company, where he learned kung fu and singing. Chan's account of his early life, drawn from his autobiography, *I Am Jackie Chan* (1998), documents the emergence of his distinctive style of performing dangerous stunts, which made him a star in Hong Kong cinema. Chan's unique blend of comedy with life-endangering acrobatics changed the nature of kung fu movies and made him an international star.

Thinking Critically

As you read Chan's autobiographical account, observe how humor is integral to the way Chan projects himself and to the characters he plays on screen. If you have ever seen any of his movies, ask yourself how his stunts humanize traditional kung fu films.

In my short career in the movies, I'd already met a lot of famous actors and directors. I was never very impressed; they were pretty, or handsome, or (in the case of the directors) loud and domineering. But none of them could do what I could do: fight, and fly, and fall, and get up and do it again—even if I was broken or hurt. I couldn't really understand what made them so great.

But the senior stuntmen were something else. They were a wild and rugged bunch, living one minute at a time because they knew that every day they spent in their profession could be their last. They smoked, drank, and gambled, spending every penny of each evening's pay by the time the sun rose the next day. Words didn't mean anything to them; if you wanted to make a statement, you did it with your body—jumping higher, tumbling faster, falling farther. With Oh Chang* out of my life, I began to hang out with the senior guys after shooting wrapped. Every night, we'd brush off the dust of the day's work and

---

*An actress who was Chan's former girlfriend.

find ways of laughing at the injuries that we or our brothers had suffered—"we get paid in scars and bruises," one older stuntman told me, only half joking. Of course, every small injury was just a reminder that the next one around the corner could bring the big one that might cripple or kill; and so we drank, and we smoked, and we played, partly to celebrate surviving one more day, partly to forget that when the sun rose again we'd be facing the same giant risks for the same small rewards.

The senior stuntmen had a phrase that described their philosophy, as well as the men who were fearless and crazy enough to follow it: *lung fu mo shi*. It literally meant "dragon tiger"—power on top of power, strength on top of strength, bravery on top of bravery. If you were *lung fu mo shi*, you laughed at life, before swallowing it whole. One way of being *lung fu mo shi* was to do an amazing stunt, earning shouts and applause from the sidelines. An even better way was to try an amazing stunt, fail, and get up smiling, ready to try it again. *"Wah! Lung fu mo shi!"* they'd shout, and you'd know that your drinks would be paid for all night.

For us, especially us junior guys, to be *lung fu mo shi* was the highest compliment we could imagine. And so I threw myself into my work, putting every last bit of energy into proving that I had the spirit of dragons and tigers—impressing stunt coordinators with my willingness to do anything, no matter how boring or how crazy. I'd get to the studio early, and leave with the very last group. I'd volunteer to test difficult stunts for free, to prove that they could be done—and sometimes they could, sometimes they couldn't. I never let anyone see me scream or cry, waiting until I got back home to release all of my pent-up pain. My neighbors would pound on the walls in annoyance as I   5 howled in my apartment alone early in the morning; they never bothered me in person, because they probably thought I was a dangerous lunatic.

One day, we were working on a scene in which the hero of the film was to tumble over a balcony railing backward, spin in midair, and land on his feet, alert and ready to fight. The actor playing the hero was, of course, sitting in the shade, flirting with one of the supporting actresses and drinking tea. It was our job to take the fall.

Most falls of this type were done with the assistance of a thin steel wire, attached to a cloth harness that went underneath the stuntman's clothing. The wire would be run through a pulley tied to a solid anchor—in this case, the railing of the balcony—then fastened to a stout rope, which two or three stuntmen not in the scene would hold on to, their feet planted firmly. This would prevent disaster in case the fall went wrong, allowing them to yank on the wire and stop an out-of-control plummet to the ground.

Today, we were working with a director whom we stuntmen universally considered an idiot. He was a no-talent hack—which didn't make him any worse than a lot of directors working at the time; the problem was that he was a no-talent hack with pretensions toward art.

We'd learned pretty quickly that that was a combination that could get stuntmen killed.

"No wires," shouted the director, his puffy, bearded face turning red. The stunt coordinator, a lean, hollow-cheeked man in his mid-forties, crossed his arms in quiet defiance. My fellow juniors and I thought the coordinator was just about the coolest guy in the world, partly because he never treated us like kids, and partly because he'd stood up time and time again to directors with unrealistic expectations. The night after one epic argument, he treated us to drinks all night at our usual bar.

10   "Even if I wanted to direct, they would never let me, because I have made too many enemies," he confided to us. "But I will give you a word of advice, in case any of you should find yourself in the big chair. If you want the respect of your stunt people, and that is the only way you will make good movies, never ask them to do a stunt that you can't or won't do yourself. If you learn nothing else from me, remember this rule." And then he shouted, *"Kam pai,"* which means, "Empty cup," and so of course, we did.

I still follow that rule today.

I know that some people call me a crazy director, saying I demand the impossible—but I know they're wrong, because every risk I ask my stuntmen to take is one that I've taken before. Somehow, it didn't kill me, and so they understand that—with the luck that stuntmen depend on to survive—it won't kill them.

The director we were working with that day was so fat he could barely walk, much less do stunts. He had no idea how dangerous a fifteen-foot fall could be, even for a trained professional.

"Do you realize that one of my men could be killed doing this stunt?" asked our coordinator, showing remarkable restraint.

15   "That's what they're paid for," retorted the director. "If you use wires in this scene, the fall will look like a puppet dropping to the ground. Unacceptable!"

The director even refused to lay out a padded mat or a stack of cardboard boxes to cushion the fall, wanting to shoot the scene from a wide angle in a single cut.

"Ridiculous," said our coordinator. "You want this stunt done that way, you do it yourself. None of my men will volunteer to take that kind of risk."

Throughout the dialogue, I was considering the setup for the stunt. The main problem with the fall was that it took place backward. You couldn't see where you would land, or figure out how far you were from the ground. But it was all a matter of timing—counting out the moments in your head before twisting your body to avoid a messy impact.

I could do this stunt, I decided. I could, and I would.

20   "Excuse me," I blurted. "I'd like to try the fall."

The stunt coordinator looked at me with a stony expression, then pulled me aside.

"Are you trying to make me look foolish?" he said angrily.

"No," I said, sticking out my chin. "You're right. The director is an idiot. You don't want to risk any of your experienced people on this stunt, because you need them. But I'm nobody, and if I don't do something like this, I'll always be nobody. If I fail, then the director knows you were right. If I succeed, I'll say that it was because you told me exactly what to do—and he'll know better than to challenge you again."

The stunt coordinator looked at me with narrowed eyes. "Yuen Lo," he said, "you're a clever boy. Don't make the mistake of trying to be too clever for your own good."

Then he turned back to the director and threw up his hands. "All right,"   25 he said. "There's actually someone stupid enough to try this stunt your way. I've just done my best to tell him how to do it without killing himself. Maybe if he's lucky, he'll just be crippled for life."

And then he walked up to the director until his face was just inches away, close enough to feel the heat of his breath. "And you," he said, his voice flat and dangerous. "You cross me up again, and all of us walk off this set. I don't give a damn about your reputation, your big ideas, or your ego. We risk our lives because we are stuntmen, and that is what we do. Not because you piss in our direction."

The director turned purple, and then pale. Not a single stuntman moved or made a noise. Finally, he nodded, and waved his flabby hand at the camerman.

I felt the coordinator's touch on my shoulder. "Good luck," he said. "Keep your body loose, be ready to roll as soon as you hit the ground. And whatever you do, don't land on your head or back. I don't mind taking you to the hospital, but I don't want to take you to the cemetery."

And then I was pulling on my costume, while a makeup girl dabbed rouge on my cheeks and streaks of fake blood across my brow. I climbed the stairs to the balcony and looked down at the crowd below. Every eye was on me, and the camera was ready to roll. But at that moment, the only eyes I cared about were the eyes of my fellow stuntmen, watching me do something foolish and fantastic.

Lung fu mo shi, I thought. It was time to prove myself. The actor playing   30 the villain who would knock me over the railing joined me, staring at me and shaking his head in disbelief. I shrugged and smiled at him, then raised my hand to show I was ready.

"Action!" shouted the director.

"Rolling!" answered the cameraman.

And then, as the fake kick from the villain nearly brushed my nose, I vaulted backward over the railing, counted quickly in my head, and arched my back, twisting my body smoothly through the air. I saw a flash of ground as my head came up and I got my legs underneath me, just in time to catch the ground with my feet. I stumbled a bit, giving a small stutter step as I pulled myself upright.

Success! The director cut the camera and actually pulled himself up and out of his chair. The stunt coordinator trotted over to where I was standing, as my brothers shouted my name. He slapped me on the back, grinning broadly.
35 "You'll be a stuntman yet," he said.

Maybe it was cocky, but cocky was what being a stuntman was all about. "I almost lost my footing on the landing," I said. "Let me try it again—I'll get it perfect this time."

He laughed, squeezing my arms until they ached. "Try it again?" he bellowed. "Did you hear that, men? Once is not enough for the boy. *Lung fu mo shi!*"

And my stunt brothers echoed the phrase: *"Lung fu mo shi!"*

That night, the stuntmen gave me a new nickname: Double Boy. "Once ain't enough for Double! Better try again!" they laughed.

"He wants to work twice as hard, he has to drink twice as much, right?" said the stunt coordinator. "One more round, Double. *Kam pai!*"
40 That night, for the first time since I left the school, and the first time since I'd lost Oh Chang, I felt like I'd found a place where I belonged. I was with family.

I was home.

Engaging the Text

1. How would you describe Jackie Chan's career in the movies before the incident he describes occurred? What sort of relationship existed between stuntmen and other actors and the director?

2. Why was the stunt Chan performed so dangerous? What does his readiness to do it again tell us about him? Why was it so important for Chan to distinguish himself before his fellow stuntmen?

3. The prevailing class system in Hong Kong movies elevated the stars but relegated stuntmen to marginal status. How important was this fact in motivating Chan to show what he could do? If you have never seen a movie of this kind, would Chan's account make you want to do so? Explain your answer.

Exploring Your Cultural Perspective

1. Did Chan's account alter your view of the kung fu acrobatics that have become so much a part of action films? View one of Chan's films (*Rumble in*

FIGURE 7.7

the *Bronx* [1996] and *Who Am I?* [1997] are typical), and discuss how seeing Chan perform the stunts helps you understand this excerpt from his autobiography. For an account of Chan's life, visit the official Web site at <http://www.jackiechan.com>. Chan's development from cult hero to mainstream icon is covered in *Jackie Chan: Inside the Dragon* by Clyde Gentry III (1997).

2. What explains the growing American preoccupation with dangerous leisure pursuits, such as white-water rafting, rock climbing, and paragliding? What is the riskiest "stunt" you have ever performed? What was the result? Would you do it again? Why or why not?

3. Does the film still (Figure 7.7) of a typical Chan stunt (from *Project A*, reissued in 2000) encourage you to see the movie? Why or why not?

JESSE W. NASH
Confucius and the VCR

VCRs have become a common fixture in U.S. homes, but the role they play for immigrants is often different from what it is for native-born Americans. In the following essay, Jesse W. Nash describes the unique place that videotaped movies made in Taiwan and Hong Kong occupy in the lives of Vietnamese immigrants. Nash teaches religious studies at Loyola University in New Orleans and has written *Romance, Gender, and Religion in a Vietnamese American Community: Tales of God and Beautiful Women* (with Elizabeth Trinh Nguyen, 1995). This essay originally appeared in the May 1988 issue of *Natural History*.

Thinking Critically

Underline and annotate the passages in which Nash develops his thesis about the role Confucian values play in the films that are so popular with Vietnamese immigrants. In what ways do foreign films convey a different sense of social order than do U.S.-made movies?

Vietnamese immigrants in the United States are intensely curious about almost all movies or television shows, aptly referring to themselves as "movie addicts." The TV set and videocassette recorder have become common features of their homes and are the focus of much conversation concerning what it means to be an American and what it means to be Vietnamese in the United States.

American television and movies worry many Vietnamese, especially parents and elders, who see them as glorifying the individual and his or her war with the family, social institutions, the community, and even the state. Reflecting the individualism of American culture, conflict resolution typically occurs at the expense of the family or community (except in situation comedies usually panned as being "saccharine" or "unrealistic" by the television critics). American movies and television, many Vietnamese assert, are most effective in imagining worlds of mistrust, promoting self-righteous rebellion, and legitimizing the desires of the individual.

The antiauthorianism of much of Ameican television and movies disturbs Vietnamese, but there are also offerings they commend, such as "The Cosby Show," which explores and promotes values they themselves prize: familial loyalty, togetherness, and a resolution of conflicts within the established social structures. Such shows, I've been told, remind the Vietnamese of their Confucian education and heritage.

Because the language of the immigrant community is still primarily Vietnamese, movies on videotapes imported from Taiwan and Hong Kong and dubbed in Vietnamese form a significant portion of the entertainment diet. The movies most favored are long, multitape epics that run from five to more than twenty hours. These include contemporary crime stories, soap operas, and romantic comedies, but the clear favorites are the medieval-military-romance cum kung fu extravaganzas.

There is a steady stream of customers at the various local shops that rent 5 imported videotapes. Neighbors, friends, and relatives compare notes on favorite films and stars. Posters and pocket photos of heroes and heroines are eagerly bought. Entire families will sit through the night eating up the latest kung fu romance, their reddened eyes a testimony of devotion to the genre and quality of the film.

Atop nearly every TV set in the community rests a tape. While babysitting, grandmothers and aunts will place toddlers in front of the tube and play a Chinese film. (Depending on the time of day, little boys will cut in to watch "The Transformers," "Thundercats," or "G.I. Joe.") Young women confess that they would like to visit Hong Kong, where their favorite movies are made and their favorite stars live. Young men with a definite tendency to hesitancy and the doldrums are not so much reacting to a harsh social and familial atmosphere as modeling their behavior on the beloved melancholic hero of the Chinese movie. Older, more mature men are not immune to the wiles of the films either. I have observed formerly impassive faces creased with emotion and dampened by tears during the viewing of a particularly sad movie, the dialogue of which is punctuated by sniffling sounds and a periodic blowing of noses.

The plots of these films are complicated and try the patience of outside audiences to whom I have introduced these films. Their broad outline can best be described as a series of concentric circles of conflict. At the outer edge, there is a general global conflict, such as a war between the Chinese and the Mongols (the latter sure to bring heated boos from the audience). Moving toward the center, the scope of the conflict—but not its intensity—narrows to two families or two different kung fu schools. Judging either side is a difficult endeavor; the conflict is not merely a matter of an obvious good versus an obvious evil, as in American movies. Conflict is inherent in the human desire to form groups, whether the group is a family unit or a kung fu school. And beneath this umbrella of intergroup conflict, there is intragroup conflict. This kind of conflict is generally romantically induced when someone falls in love with a member of an opposing family or school.

While Western media are filled with conflict, they have nothing over the conflict-fraught Chinese film. Take, for example, *The Mighty Sword* (Than Chau Kiem Khach). Bac Phi, the hero, is a promising kung fu artist, whose master has high hopes of elevating him to take his own place upon retirement. To belong to a kung fu school is to belong to a family, with all that that entails in Oriental culture. The master is the father, and the other members are brothers and sisters. The school's members generally marry members of other schools to form alliances. As in any real family, there is considerable conflict and dissent, but the ideal of remaining faithful and obedient to the master is stressed.

Bac Phi's troubles begin when he helps a damsel, Lady Tuyet, who is being besieged by ruffians. She herself is an incredibly gifted kung fu fighter and, as fate would have it, perhaps the most beautiful woman in the world. They immediately fall in love—love at first sight being the rule in the world of Chinese film.

10   In the film one gets a feel for the Chinese and, by derivation, the Vietnamese way of romance. The hero and heroine do not touch; most certainly, they do not fondle or kiss. With a particularly sad melody in the background, they look into each other's eyes. The viewers all sigh and point; they know that the two are in love by "reading their eyes." Traditionally in Vietnam, lovers communicated with their eyes. Folklore, proverbs, and songs all depict a romance of the eyes: "Like a knife cutting the yellow betel leaf,/His eyes glance, her eyes dart back and forth." The stage is set for what appears to be a romance made in Heaven. Our two lovers vow to marry and to love each other forever.

After this moment, the meaning of the sad melody becomes apparent. The hero and heroine have pledged their love in ignorance of certain facts ruling the social reality around them. The lovers learn that their two schools are mortal enemies. Bac Phi's school and master are held to be responsible for the murder of Tuyet's father, and neither Bac Phi's master nor Tuyet's mother will countenance the marriage. The intragroup relationships of both lovers are strained. Tuyet and her mother are at odds and come to blows. Bac Phi's relationship with his best friend is strained, and he learns that his master is planning to have him marry another girl.

At this point in American television and movies, we would expect an easy solution to the problem. (To the dismay of the audience, I counseled "Elope!") The Chinese and Vietnamese solution is much more complicated. To decide between Tuyet and his school is not a simple matter, and characteristically for the Chinese hero, Bac Phi is paralyzed by the situation, torn between his lover and his quasi family, his desire and his duty. He becomes lovesick and pines away for Tuyet but never decides once and for all to choose her over his school.

To make matters worse, there are forces behind the scenes manipulating all involved as if they were puppets. Unseen powers are seeking to deepen the rift between Bac Phi's school and that of Tuyet. These powers attempt to undermine Bac Phi's love for and trust in Tuyet by posing one of their own as Tuyet and having him/her murder one of Bac Phi's schoolmates. An already impossible situation is raised to the nth degree. Bac Phi, because of his position in his school, must now avenge the death.

The conflict and its resolution are characteristic of the Vietnamese community. When I asked why the couple simply didn't run away and elope, the Vietnamese audience laughed. "That is the American way," I was told. "But we have a Confucian tradition." The Vietnamese were trained in Confucian values at school and at home. Confucianism, in a Vietnamese context, is a tradition of loyalty to one's family, superiors, and prior obligations. "We were always taught to love our parents more than life itself," one woman observed. "Parents were more important than the man or woman you loved."

The conflict would not actually be resolved by Bac Phi and Tuyet eloping   15
and abandoning the social units to which they belong. As the Vietnamese themselves ask, "Could Tuyet trust Bac Phi if he were to fudge on his obligations to the school?" If Bac Phi will sever the bonds of previously established relationships, such as those with friends and superiors, what guarantee does Tuyet have that, when she has lost her figure and taken on wrinkles, he won't abandon her and chase after a younger, more nubile woman? There is a logic of trust in the films and the community that forbids them to take advantage of a simplistic formula, namely, "If you want it, go for it." The Vietnamese, ever moralistic, will ask, "Is it right for you to want it?"

The conflict, in the case of *The Mighty Sword*, is eventually resolved by the defeat of the powers behind the scenes, by a change of heart and character on the part of Tuyet's mother and Bac Phi's master, and by the two lovers working to break the endless cycle of revenge and misunderstanding. The conflict is resolved within the social structures, not by their destruction. Despite the mazelike layers of deceit, fear, and manipulation, the movie ends affirming the ultimate worthwhileness of living in society, of being a social animal and not merely a lover.

Unlike most American television shows and movies, the Chinese hero does not always get the girl. A happy ending cannot be predicted. Although most Vietnamese I have talked to prefer a happy ending to their Chinese films, they appreciate and approve of the ethical message of a melancholic ending. "Love doesn't conquer all," one viewer told me, tears in his eyes. "Sometimes we have to pay for our mistakes. Sometimes we don't get what we want just because we want it." One woman recommended a particularly touching Chinese soap opera to me. "It has a very sad ending. It is very beautiful. It is very Confucian." She explained that the movie, which I later watched with a lump in my jaded throat, tried to teach that romance must be accompanied by ethics. One cannot simply be a lover. One also has to be a good son or daughter and citizen.

In America, where films and television shows tend to glorify the individual and romance, the Chinese films the Vietnamese adore reaffirm traditional values and help educate their children in the art of being Confucian. Traditional Vietnamese Confucianism has sneaked in through the back door, so to speak, through the VCR. American pluralism and technology have made this possible. They also may have let in a Trojan horse that promises to offer a venerable critique of certain American values. The Vietnamese may do American culture a favor by offering a countervision of what it means to be a social animal, and not merely an animal.

Engaging the Text

1. What important role do videotapes of Chinese movies play in the U.S. Vietnamese community? In what significant ways do Chinese films differ from their U.S. counterparts? What do these differences reveal about the two cultures?

2. How do the conflicts embodied in the film *The Mighty Sword* and the methods by which these conflicts are resolved reveal distinct Vietnamese cultural values?

3. In what sense is the title "Confucius and the VCR" effective in alerting the reader to the connections between Eastern and Western values that Nash discusses?

Exploring Your Cultural Perspective

1. Do you agree with Nash's conclusion: "The Vietnamese may do American culture a favor by offering a countervision of what it means to be a social animal, and not merely an animal"? Is Nash's interpretation of American values as portrayed on U.S. television accurate? Why or why not?

2. Can you think of a foreign film that plays the same role for Americans that the Chinese films do among the Vietnamese? When you watch movies in a foreign language, do you prefer them to be subtitled or dubbed into English? Explain your preference.

CONNECTING THE TEXTS

1. In what ways are singers and movie stars transformed into cultural symbols according to Greil Marcus (in "Dead Elvis") and Sandra Tsing Loh (in "The Return of Doris Day")? What different places do Elvis and Doris Day occupy in the national psyche?

2. How does the "good girl"/"bad girl" dichotomy analyzed by Sandra Tsing Loh in "The Return of Doris Day" operate in John Cheever's story "The Enormous Radio"?

3. Indian cinema, as described by R. K. Narayan in "Misguided 'Guide,'" has its own cultural version of the "good girl" archetype. How does it compare with that described by Sandra Tsing Loh in "The Return of Doris Day"? What values unique to Indian culture does it project?

4. To what extent has the carnival-sideshow atmosphere of daytime talk shows, as described by Charles Oliver in "Freak Parade," infiltrated TV news broadcasts, as discussed by Neil Postman and Steve Powers in "TV News as Entertainment"?

5. Many Jackie Chan movies (see "A Dirty Job") portray Asian women in nonstereotyped ways. After reading both Chan's and Jessica Hagedorn's ("Asian Women in Film: No Joy, No Luck") essays and viewing one of Chan's films, write a synthesis essay exploring this topic.

6. In what ways do Jackie Chan's account ("A Dirty Job") and R. K. Narayan's narrative "Misguided 'Guide'" provide a behind-the-scenes glimpse of filmmaking in Hong Kong and in Bombay? In what sense are the effects so popular with audiences really carefully constructed illusions?

7. In what way do the readings by Jackie Chan ("A Dirty Job") and Jesse W. Nash ("Confucius and the VCR") provide complementary perspectives on the making and marketing of kung fu films from Hong Kong and Taiwan?

8. In what ways do the kinds of films Jessica Hagedorn (in "Asian Women in Film: No Joy, No Luck") discusses, featuring Asian characters but made for U.S. audiences, differ from their Taiwanese counterparts as described by Jesse Nash (in "Confucius and the VCR")?

9. To what extent do Doris Day movies (described by Sandra Tsing Loh) represent the same traditional values to American audiences that the made-in-Hong Kong films do for Vietnamese immigrants (as described by Jesse W. Nash in "Confucius and the VCR")?

10. Discuss the role that spectacle plays in Indian films (described by R. K. Narayan in "Misguided 'Guide'") and in U.S. TV news broadcasts (discussed by Neil Postman and Steve Powers in "TV News as Entertainment").

11. How does the theme of vicarious enjoyment of other people's troubles define both the Westcotts in John Cheever's story "The Enormous Radio" and audiences for television talk shows, as Charles Oliver describes them in "Freak Parade"?

12. Is Elvis's ascension to icon status, as discussed by Greil Marcus in "Dead Elvis," due to the same kind of voyeuristic involvement that John Cheever depicts in his story "The Enormous Radio"? What are the similarities and differences?

WRITING ABOUT ENTERTAINMENT

1. What role does television occupy in your life? Do you feel that its effect is more beneficial than harmful? Why or why not? Analyze the extent to which your schedule revolves around your favorite programs. What are they, and why do you like them?

2. Who are your favorite comedians? What is noteworthy about the way they use language to be witty, satiric, humorous, or ironic? Describe one of these comics' routines in detail, and discuss why you find it funny?

3. What is your favorite hobby or amusement? Discuss the social dimension of this activity or event, describe its intrinsic appeal for you, and speculate how it might appear to the proverbial "visitor from Mars." You might consider magic (either as a performer or a spectator at a magic show), making home videos, photography, cat shows, dog shows, car shows, horse racing, car racing, swap meets, scuba diving, playing in a band, singing in a choir or a barbershop quartet, or any other fun activity that has a social dimension. Collecting stamps, coins, comic books, or memoribilia or any other activity that has a social dimension would also make an appropriate topic.

4. What elements make a game enjoyable to you? (The game can be a board game like *Monopoly, Pictionary,* or *Trivial Pursuit* or an electronic game, including those on CD-ROM or PlayStation. Many games can be found at <http://www.happypuppy.com> and <http://www.gamekingdom.net/html/pax>.) What identifiable social values underlie the game, even if it is set in a fantasy environment? What do fantasy role-playing games suggest about contemporary culture?

5. The TV series *Survivor,* along with other reality-based programs, is quite popular. What social values does this show promote, and, most important, what explains its popularity in today's society?

6. Since its inception, MTV has evolved into a unique cultural phenomenon. Do you watch this channel? Analyze one of its programs or features (for example, *Spring Break*), exploring what it says about contemporary culture.

7. Rap music often expresses social criticism, albeit in a form some audiences find offensive. Analyze the lyrics of any rap song: discuss the message it communicates as well as the manner in which it conveys its message (through gestures, music, and clothing).

Hodgkiss quieted the crowd with his
mathematical proof that there is, indeed,
no business like show business.

FIGURE 7.8

8. What educational, travel, adventure, or history shows do you watch for entertainment? What techniques do these factual shows use to enliven potentially dull content? (See Dave Blazek's cartoon, Figure 7.8.) For example, how do wildlife documentaries create story lines through selectively edited sequences?

9. If you are a fan of soap operas, explain their appeal in a few paragraphs. What notable differences exist between daytime and nighttime soap operas? What might account for them?

10. What kinds of plays do you like? In a short essay, select a few favorites, and describe why you found them enjoyable. Compare the experience of watching a live drama with that of seeing a televised or a film version. Have you ever worked as part of a theater group: either as a performer or behind the scenes? Describe your experiences.

11. Science fiction films explore the dark underside of new technologies just as the public becomes aware of them. In the 1950s it was nuclear power (*The Incredible Shrinking Man* [1957]); in the 1980s and 1990s it was genetic engineering (*The Fly* [1986], *Jurassic Park* [1993]); in 2000 it was biotechnology (*The Matrix* [1999]). Select one of these or another relevant film, and in a short essay analyze how it explores important social concerns. A good place to start your research on the Web is Science Fiction Gallery at <http://www.euro.net/mark-space/index.html>.

FIGURE 7.9

12. Dancing is a popular form of entertainment in many countries. Research the history of any dance (waltz, Viennese waltz, fox-trot, cha-cha, swing, rumba, mambo, bolero, salsa, merengue, samba, quickstep, tango), and explore the unique cultural associations it embodies. You'll find information at <http://www.bb-entertainers.co.uk/dance_style/ballroom_dancing_links.htm>. What social values do the picture of the world-class dancers Lora and Danny Villavicencio and the accompanying text (Figure 7.9) express?

CHAPTER 8

It's All in the Game

Sports and games have a profound importance in all societies. Through them,
cultures enact rites that confirm their collective identity. In the sports that a
society embraces we can discern the hidden cultural assumptions and desires
that motivate its people. Carl Sagan in "Game: The Prehistoric Origin of
Sports" speculates that competitive sports and games are "symbolic conflicts,
thinly disguised" that can be traced back to prehistoric hunting and gathering
skills and as such, satisfy "an almost forgotten craving for the hunt."

SPORTS AS HUMAN DRAMA

For most fans, having something at stake, even if only for the duration of a
game, is an important, and for some addictive, diversion from everyday life.
Fans' identification with a team (or a coach), as in the much publicized firing
of Bobby Knight (after twenty-nine years as the coach of Indiana University's
winning basketball team, in September 2000), can become the most important
event in a fan's life. Sports are intrinsically dramatic and appeal to people for
the same reasons that theater does: we see the very stuff of drama—conflict,
victory, and defeat—and can vicariously participate in the game.

For example, the boxing ring has always served as an arena for the expression of primal human drama. Joyce Carol Oates in "On Boxing" tells us that as

early as 900 BC in Greece, fighters whose fists were covered with leather thongs (sometimes embedded with metal spikes) fought to the death. Roman gladiatorial combats were promoted and advertised much as boxing matches are today. The unleashing of primal emotions in ways that were not sanctioned in everyday life explains the passions of fans who crowded into the Roman amphitheaters to see these bloody contests. Their reactions were not so different from those of today's fans. For example, riots at soccer games are not uncommon occurrences in many countries; attacks on officials and fellow fans (such as the hockey-dad killing in Massachusetts in 2000) have unfortunately become more frequent at sporting events all over the world.

The role of sports as a catharsis for sublimated aggression underlies its universal appeal, but the forms sports take (some quite bizarre from our perspective) vary from culture to culture. For example, although cockfighting (as discussed by Clifford Geertz in "The Balinese Cockfight") is now illegal in Bali, it was immensely popular for centuries as an arena for venting masculine aggression through ritual in the same way that boxing functions in our culture. Both cockfighting and boxing are clearly male-centered domains from which women are largely excluded as participants. Even though cockfighting is the quintessential expression of Balinese society, the role of sports in the United States is more complex. In America, as well as in Bali, sports were once a pastime acceptable only for men. This has changed in the United States today as women now participate in many competitive sports.

THE MEANING OF SPORTS

Each sport reflects a distinctive cultural mythology, replete with its own stylized behaviors, rules, and ethos that reflect different facets of a given society. For example, football and baseball express different sides of the American character. Baseball is pastoral and leisurely; football (with its emphasis on conquest of territory, formations, and ritualized violence) is aggressive and quasi-military. Soccer in Latin America and Europe and hockey in Canada may serve a function similar to that of football in the United States.

Although we in the United States see sports in terms of competition, some other cultures view conflict resolution rather than competition as the goal of sports. In one such culture, that of the Mbuti Pygmies in the Congo, as reported by Colin Turnbull in *The Mbuti Pygmies: Change and Adaptation* (1983): "The adults begin to play a special form of 'tug of war' that is clearly ritual rather than a game. All the men are on one side, the women on the other. At first it looks like a game, but quickly it becomes clear that the objective is for *neither* side to win." When one side gains an advantage, a member goes over to the losing side to even things up. Because cooperation and equality are the prime values of Mbuti culture and men and women are valued equally, it is natural for them to evolve games that embody the principle of opposition without hostility.

A noncompetitive trend may be emerging in American sports as well. Increasing numbers of people have left the ballparks to risk life and limb hanging from the sides of cliffs, paragliding, white-water rafting, and extreme skiing. The growing popularity of these and other high-risk sports may be a reaction to our culture's obsession with safety measures (seat belts, guardrails, safety helmets) designed to reduce risk. The same trend can be seen in the newly emerging category of "anti sports," as typified by the X games (extreme sports such as skateboarding, in-line skating, snowboarding, sky surfing, and street luge) at the expense of more traditional competitive team sports, such as football and baseball.

The French semiologist Roland Barthes (1915–1980) observed that what often appears to be natural and ordinary may be part of a highly sophisticated constructed mythology. Barthes examined both boxing and wrestling from this perspective in *Mythologies* (trans. 1972) and discovered that boxing served quite a different function in French society than did wrestling. Each sport has its distinctive symbolism. Boxers stoically endure pain, whereas wrestlers suffer extravagantly with theatrical displays of agony. Boxers always fight as themselves, whereas wrestlers fight as larger-than-life heroes or villains attired in elaborate costumes. Everyone knows that wrestling is a contrived performance, and not a true contest, yet people enjoy it as a staged conflict between good and evil. In America, it is immensely popular and is watched by an estimated 34 million people each week. Barthes's unique insight—that the meaning of a particular sport can be best understood in relationship to the values, beliefs, and symbols of the surrounding culture—also explains why the same games take on different meanings when they are played in various countries.

SPORTS OUTSIDE THE UNITED STATES

Baseball was brought to Japan in the 1800s by an American educator and is now played on both amateur and professional levels there. Although traditional sports such as judo, kendo (fencing using bamboo poles), and karate continue to be popular (as is sumo wrestling as a spectator sport), baseball has become a national pastime. Yet the way in which it is played in Japan reflects the values of Japanese culture. The imported American players (or *gaigin*) are expected to suppress their identity as stars ("the nail that stands up is hammered down") and to not outshine other members of the team. Players in Japan do not offer their talents to the highest bidder or market their name for commercial purposes. In short, individualism is as out of place in baseball as it is in a Japanese company. The team, like the company, becomes a lifelong employer that serves as an extended family. By contrast, American baseball takes pride in its role as a model of diversity (with players from all over the world) and encourages players to become stars. The biggest stars become cultural icons whose influence extends far beyond the boundaries of sports.

In Cuba, however, baseball serves quite a different function, according to Roberto Gonzalez Echevarria in "First Pitch." Since it was introduced in the 1860s, it has been Cuba's national game. When Fidel Castro took control in 1959, baseball and its many talented players were drawn into the political struggle with the United States. The Cuban League was reorganized to demonstrate that communism could produce superior athletes. The rigorous training methods produced such stars as the Yankee pitcher Orlando Hernandez ("El Duque"), who in 1997 risked his life to reach the United States. In Cuba, baseball became another venue (in the same way the Olympics did during the Cold War) for proving the superiority of one political system over another.

SPORTS AND RACE

As thinly disguised symbolic conflicts, sports reflect not only political agendas and national loyalties (witness the Olympics' role in enhancing a nation's self-esteem) but class distinctions and racial conflicts as well. The histories of boxing and basketball serve as a subtext to the history of race relations in America because of the role that minorities have played in these sports in the twentieth century. Joe Louis's winning defense of his heavyweight championship against a white contender in the early 1930s was an event of unparalleled importance to the black community of that era, as Maya Angelou tells us in "Champion of the World." His victory symbolized a triumph over oppressive social forces and racism. The persistence of racial stereotyping can be seen in the symbolic resonance of Tiger Woods's victories. In 1997, he became the first player of African or Asian heritage to win a major golf championship (the Masters Tournament), and in 2000 he won the British Open to complete golf's Grand Slam. Sports often serve as surrogate arenas for the playing out of unresolved social conflicts.

Like golf, tennis was once considered the domain of white athletes. It was only in 1968 that the U.S. Open admitted unrecognized players and Arthur Ashe became the first black player to win this tournament, a particularly significant event given the racially charged climate of that year. Ashe went on to become the first black player to win at Wimbledon in 1975. Ashe's startling claim (in "The Burden of Race") that "race is for me a more onerous burden than AIDS" is especially significant. Ashe's victory was as momentous as Joe Louis's had been forty years earlier. It was even more important than those of Tiger Woods and the Williams sisters today because black athletes—no matter what their sport—are readily accepted now in ways they were not in 1975. Although Ashe was battling AIDS (contracted through a blood transfusion), he was even more concerned about the limitations placed on him in his role as a famous black athlete.

SPORTS AS A BUSINESS

Business interests have always exercised great influence on sports events. A notable example occurred during the 1992 Olympics. Members of the "Dream Team" representing the United States in the basketball competition draped U.S. flags over their team uniforms during the medal ceremony because, although Reebok was the official sponsor of the Olympic team, many of the individual players were sponsored by Nike and didn't want to give Reebok the publicity.

The commercialization of sports guarantees that a winning performance will be rewarded with lucrative endorsement contracts. For example, Mia Hamm was voted the most marketable female athlete in the country (by the *Sports Business Daily*), and Nike immediately put her name on a building at its corporate headquarters (see Bonnie De Simone's "Mia Hamm: Grateful for Her Gifts"). Of course, the ultimate shared objective of sports and business is appearing on a Wheaties box, as Tiger Woods did in July 2000. Tiger is also sponsored by Nike and wears a complete Nike ensemble whenever he competes. In September 2000 he signed a $100 million contract with Nike Golf division.

Even the slightest possibility of participating in the Olympics, with its lure of multimillion-dollar endorsements, explains the American obsession with gymnastics and figure skating. Joan Ryan in "Little Girls in Pretty Boxes" investigated the treatment of young Olympic hopefuls by their families and at the hands of their tyrannical coaches. Girls are routinely urged to starve themselves to stave off puberty and maintain the "ideal body shape" to fulfill the public's fantasy (conditioned by the Barbie doll myth) of what an ice skater should look like.

With such prevailing cultural values, it is no surprise that *USA Today* (March 2000) reported that the body mass index (BMI) of Miss Americas has been dropping steadily over the past twenty years. Today, winners of this pageant have the same BMI the World Health Organization uses to identify malnourishment in Third World countries. The same cultural forces that motivate Miss Americas and supermodels (for example, Kate Moss) also motivate gymnasts and skaters to "be thin and win."

Another unhealthy consequence of the cultural emphasis on winning at all costs is the distorted idea that successful athletes are above the law (the O. J. Simpson syndrome). A widely publicized incident took place in Glen Ridge, New Jersey, in 1989. A group of the town's most popular high school athletes lured a retarded girl into a basement and raped her. Later, they were all but exonerated by the community and the justice system. The willingness of this wealthy suburban town to overlook crimes committed by their winning team—hence, the title of Bernard Lefkowitz's 1997 award-winning exposé, *Our Guys*—took precedence over any sense of morality.

WOMEN IN SPORTS

The idea that certain sports are for women whereas others are for men has changed considerably. As recently as 1996, in Spain, a country where machismo thrives, Cristina Sanchez became the first woman in Europe to achieve renown as a professional matador. The great athlete Martina Navratilova created a new standard for women's tennis when she came to the United States from the Czech Republic.

It was only in 1972 that the United States approved Title IX, which introduced gender equity into college sports and immeasurably improved women's sports opportunities. The change in climate paved the way for the success of athletes like Cynthia Cooper, who led the Women's National Basketball Association's Houston Comets to two consecutive championships and has inspired many women to follow her example. The emergence of women's team sports such as soccer speaks volumes about the changing attitude toward women in sports. In "Mia Hamm: Grateful for Her Gifts" Bonnie De Simone offers unique insights into the motivations and character of an athlete who is arguably the best female soccer player in the world.

Even the traditional male sport of fly-fishing (angling with a rod, line, and hook) is now enjoyed by women. In "A River Ran over Me," Lin Sutherland tells an amusing story of a woman whose seventy-two-year-old mother views fly-fishing as akin to religion.

As you read through each of the selections in this chapter, consider how the sports and games in which a culture engages often reveal far more about it than do the officially designated organizations and systems (for example, courts, politics, education) that are meant to serve as its idealized projections.

CARL SAGAN

Game: The Prehistoric Origin of Sports

Carl Sagan (1934–1996), a modern-day Renaissance man, was professor of astronomy at Cornell University and served as director of the Laboratory of Planetary Studies. He was awarded the NASA medal for exceptional scientific achievement in 1972 (after his hypotheses were validated by data from the Mars Mariner expedition). He wrote many distinguished books, including *Dragons of Eden*, which received the Pulitzer Prize in 1977, and *Cosmos* (1980), to accompany his widely acclaimed television series of the same name. His last book was *The Demon-Haunted World: Science as a Candle in the Dark* (1996). Sagan was a fascinating figure whose many interests included being the sports editor of his high school newspaper, captain of a championship intramural basketball team in college, and a lifelong fan of the New York Knicks. In this essay, which first appeared in *Parade* magazine (September 1987), Sagan traces the worldwide passion for sports back to the skills our hunter-gatherer forebearers needed to survive.

Thinking Critically

As you read Sagan's analysis, you might consider how the games children play incorporate many of the skills (stalking, throwing, teamwork) that our ancestors needed for survival.

We can't help ourselves. On Sunday afternoons and Monday nights in the fall of each year, we abandon everything to watch small moving images of 22 men—running into one another, falling down, picking themselves up and kicking an elongated object made from the skin of an animal. Every now and then, both the players and the sedentary spectators are moved to rapture or despair by the progress of the play. All over America, people (mainly men), transfixed before glass screens, cheer or mutter in unison. Put this way, it sounds stupid. But once you get the hang of it, it's hard to resist, and I speak from experience.

Athletes run, jump, hit, slide, throw, kick, tackle—and there's a thrill in seeing humans do it so well. They wrestle each other to the ground. They're keen on grabbing or clubbing or kicking a fast-moving brown or white thing. In some games, they try to herd the thing toward what's called a "goal"; in other games, the players run away and then return "home." Teamwork is almost everything, and we admire how the parts fit together to make a jubilant whole.

But these are not the skills most of us use to earn our daily bread. Why should we feel compelled to watch people run or hit? Why is this need transcultural? (Ancient Egyptians, Persians, Greeks, Romans, Mayans and Aztecs also played ball. "Polo" is Tibetan.)

There are sports stars who make 10 times the annual salary of the President; who are themselves, after retirement, elected to high office. They are national heroes. Why, exactly? There is something here transcending the diversity of political, social and economic systems. Something ancient is calling.

5   Most major sports are associated with a nation or a city, and they carry with them elements of patriotism and civic pride. Our team represents *us*—where we live, our people—against those other guys from some different place, populated by unfamiliar, maybe hostile people. (True, most of "our" players are not *really* from here. They're mercenaries and with clear conscience regularly defect from opposing cities for suitable emolument: A Pittsburgh Pirate is reformed into a California Angel; A San Diego Padre is raised to a St. Louis Cardinal; a Golden State Warrior is crowned a Sacramento King. Occasionally, a whole team picks up and migrates to another city.)

Competitive sports are symbolic conflicts, thinly disguised. This is hardly a new insight. The Cherokees called their ancient form of lacrosse "the little brother of war." Or here is Max Rafferty, former California Superintendent of Public Instruction, who, after denouncing critics of college football as "kooks, crumbums, commies, hairy loudmouthed beatniks," goes on to state, "Football is war without killing . . . Football players . . . possess a clear, bright, fighting spirit which is America itself." (That's worth mulling over.) An often-quoted sentiment of the late coach Vince Lombardi is that the only thing that counts is winning. Former Washington Redskins' coach George Allen put it this way: "Losing is like death."

Indeed, we talk of winning and losing a war as naturally as we do of winning and losing a game. In a televised U.S. Army recruitment ad, we see the aftermath of an armored warfare exercise in which one tank destroys another; in the tag line, the victorious tank commander says, "When we win, the whole team wins, the whole tank wins—not one person." The connection between sports and combat is made quite clear. Sports fans (the word is short for "fanatics") have been known to commit assault and battery, and sometimes murder, when taunted about a losing team; or when prevented from cheering on a winning team; or when they feel an injustice has been committed by the referees.

The British prime minister was obliged in 1985 to denounce the rowdy, drunken behavior of British soccer fans who attacked an Italian contingent for having the effrontery to root for their own team. Dozens were killed when the stands collapsed. In 1969, after three hard-fought soccer games, Salvadoran tanks crossed the Honduran border, and Salvadoran bombers attacked Honduran ports and military bases. In this "Soccer War," the casualties numbered in the thousands.

Afghani tribesmen played polo with the severed heads of former adversaries. And 600 years ago, in what is now Mexico City, there was a ball court where gorgeously attired nobles watched uniformed teams compete. The captain of the losing team was beheaded, and the skulls of earlier losing captains were displayed on racks—an inducement possibly even more compelling than winning one for the Gipper.

Suppose you're idly flipping the dial on your television set, and you come   10
upon some competition in which you have no particular emotional investment—say off-season volleyball between Burma and Thailand. How do you decide which team to root for? But wait a minute: Why root for either? Why not just enjoy the game? Most of us have trouble with this detached posture. We want to take part in the contest, to feel ourselves a member of a team. The feeling simply sweeps us away, and there we are rooting, "Go, Burma!" Initially, our loyalties may oscillate, first urging on one team and then the other. Sometimes we root for the underdog. Other times, shamefully, we even switch our allegiance from loser to winner as the outcome becomes clear. (When there is a succession of losing seasons, fan loyalties tend to drift elsewhere.) What we are looking for is victory without effort. We want to be swept into something like a small, safe, successful war.

The earliest known organized athletic events date back 3500 years to preclassical Greece. During the original Olympic Games, an armistice put all wars among Greek city-states on hold. The games were more important than the wars. The men performed nude; no women spectators were allowed. By the eighth century B.C., the Olympic Games consisted of running (*lots* of running), jumping, throwing things (including javelins) and wrestling (sometimes to the death). While none of these events was a team sport, they were clearly central to modern team sports.

They were also central to low-technology hunting. Hunting is traditionally considered a sport, as long as you don't eat what you catch—a proviso much easier for the rich to comply with than the poor. From the earliest pharaohs, hunting has been associated with military aristocracies. Oscar Wilde's aphorism about English fox hunting, "the unspeakable in full pursuit of the uneatable," makes a similar dual point. The forerunners of football, soccer, hockey and kindred sports were so-called "rabble games," recognized as substitutes for hunting—because young men who worked for a living were barred from the hunt.

TEAMS AND TOTEMS

Teams associated with cities have names, and so do hunter-gatherer groups worldwide. The names are sometimes called totems. Below (at far right) are some from the !Kung San people of Botswana. Of course there are differences. It's hard to imagine an American sports team named the Diarrheas ("Gimme a 'D' . . ."). Or even the Big Talkers. And one in which the players are called the Owners would probably cause some consternation in the front office.

USA BASKETBALL	USA FOOTBALL	JAPANESE BASEBALL	NORTH AMERICAN BASEBALL	!KUNG NAMED GROUPS
Hawks	Cardinals	Hawks	Blue Jays	Ant Bears
Bucks	Eagles	Swallows	Cardinals	Elephants
Bulls	Falcons	Carp	Orioles	Giraffes
Mavericks	Seahawks	Buffaloes	Cubs	Impalas
Bullets	Bears	Lions	Tigers	Jackals
Clippers	Bengals	Tigers	Astros	Rhinos
Nets	Broncos	Whales	Athletics	Steenboks
Pistons	Chargers	Braves	Braves	Wildcats
Rockets	Colts	Ham Fighters	Brewers	Ants
Spurs	Dolphins	Dragons	Dodgers	Lice
Supersonics	Lions	Giants	Expos	Scorpions
Cavaliers	Rams	Orions	Indians	Tortoises
Celtics	Jets		Mariners	Bitter Melons
Jazz	Bills		Mets	Long Roots
Kings	Buccaneers		Phillies	Medicine Roots
Knickerbockers	Chiefs		Pirates	Carrying Yokes
Lakers	Cowboys		Rangers	Cutters
Pacers	49'ers		Royals	Big Talkers
76'ers	Oilers		Twins	Cold Ones
Trail Blazers	Packers		Yankees	Diarrheas
Warriors	Patriots		Red Sox	Dirty Fighters
Nuggets	Raiders		White Sox	Fighters
Suns	Redskins		Angels	Owners
	Steelers		Giants	Penises
	Vikings		Padres	Short Feet
	Giants		Reds	
	Saints			
	Browns			

So, perhaps team sports are not just stylized echoes of ancient wars. Perhaps they also satisfy an almost-forgotten craving for the hunt. Since our passions for sports run so deep and are so broadly distributed, they are likely to be hard-wired into us—not in our brains but in our genes. The 10,000 years since the invention of agriculture is not nearly enough time for such predispositions to have evolved. If we want to understand them, we must go much further back.

The human species is hundreds of thousands of years old. We have led a sedentary existence—based on farming and domestication of animals—for only the last 3 percent of that period, during which is all our history. In the first 97 percent of our tenure on Earth, almost everything that is characteristically human came into being. We can learn something about those times from the few surviving hunter-gatherer communities uncorrupted by civilization.

We wander. With our little ones and all our belongings on our backs, we *15* wander—following the game, seeking the waterholes. We set up camp for a while, then move on. In providing food for the group, the men mainly hunt, the women mainly gather. Meat and potatoes. A typical itinerant band, mainly an extended family of relatives and in-laws, numbers a few dozen; although annually many hundreds of us, with the same language and culture, gather— for religious ceremonies, to trade, to arrange marriages, to tell stories. There are many stories about the hunt.

I'm focusing here on the hunters, who are men. But women have significant social, economic and cultural power. They gather the essential staples— nuts, fruits, tubers, roots—as well as medicinal herbs, hunt small animals and provide strategic intelligence on large animal movements. Men do some gathering as well, and considerable "housework" (even though we have no houses). But hunting—only for food, never for sport—is the lifelong occupation of every able-bodied male.

Preadolescent boys stalk birds and small mammals with bows and arrows. By adulthood they have become experts in weapons-procurement; in stalking, killing and butchering the prey; and in carrying the cuts of meat back to camp. The first successful kill of a large mammal marks a young man's coming of age. In his initiation, ceremonial incisions are made on his chest or arms and an herb is rubbed into the cuts so that, when healed, a patterned tattoo results. It's like campaign ribbons—one look at his chest, and you know something of his combat experience.

From a jumble of hoofprints, we can accurately tell how many animals passed; the species, sexes and ages; whether any are lame; how long since they passed; and how far away they are likely to be. Some young animals can be caught by open-field tackles; others with slingshots or boomerangs, or just by throwing rocks accurately and hard. Animals that have not yet learned to fear man can be approached boldly and clubbed to death. At greater distances, for warier prey, we hurl spears or shoot poisoned arrows. Sometimes we're lucky and, by a carefully coordinated rush, can drive a herd of animals into an ambush or off a cliff.

Teamwork among the hunters is essential. If we are not to frighten the quarry, we must communicate by sign language. For the same reason, we need to have our emotions under control; both fear and exultation are dangerous. We are ambivalent about the prey. We respect the animals, recognize our kinship, identify with them. But if we reflect too closely on their intelligence or devotion to their young, if we feel pity for them, our dedication to the hunt will slacken; we will bring home less food, and again our band may be endangered. We are obliged to put an emotional distance between us and them.

20   So contemplate this: For a million years, our male ancestors are scampering about, throwing rocks at pigeons, running after baby antelopes and wrestling them to the ground, forming a single line of shouting, running hunters and trying to terrify a herd of startled wart hogs upwind. Imagine that their lives depend on hunting skills and teamwork. And good hunters were also good warriors. Then, after a long while—a few thousand centuries, say—a natural predisposition for both hunting and teamwork will inhabit many newborn boys. Why? Because incompetent or unenthusiastic hunters leave fewer offspring. I don't think how to chip a spearpoint out of stone or how to feather an arrow is in our genes. That's taught or figured out. But a zest for the chase—I bet that *is* hard-wired. Natural selection helped mold our ancestors into superb hunters.

The clearest evidence of the success of the hunter-gatherer lifestyle is the simple fact that it extended to six continents and lasted a million years. After 40,000 generations in which the killing of animals was our hedge against starvation, those inclinations must still be in us. We hunger to put them to use, even vicariously. Team sports provide a way.

Some part of our being longs to join a small band of brothers on a daring and intrepid quest. The traditional manly virtues—taciturnity, resourcefulness, modesty, consistency, deep knowledge of animals, love of the outdoors—were all adaptive behavior in hunter-gatherer times. We still admire these traits, although we've almost forgotten why.

Besides sports, there are few outlets available. In our adolescent males, we can still recognize the young hunter, the aspirant warrior—leaping across apartment rooftops; riding, helmetless, on a motorcycle; making trouble for the winning team at a post-game celebration. In the absence of a steadying hand, those old instincts may go a little askew (although our murder rate is about the same as among the !Kung San, the present-day hunter-gatherer people of Botswana). We try to ensure that any residual zest for killing does not spill over onto humans. We don't always succeed.

I think of how powerful those hunting instincts are, and I worry. I worry that Monday-night football is insufficient outlet for the modern hunter-gatherer, decked out in his overalls or uniform or three-piece suit. I think of that ancient legacy about not expressing our feelings, about keeping an emotional distance from those we kill, and it takes some of the fun out of the game.

25   Hunter-gatherers generally posed no danger to themselves: because their economies tended to be healthy (many had more free time than we do); because, as nomads, they had few possessions, almost no theft and little envy; because greed and arrogance were considered to be not only social evils but also pretty close to

mental illnesses; because women had real political power and tended to be a sta-bilizing and mitigating influence before the boys started going for their poisoned arrows; and because, when serious crimes were committed—murder, say—the band collectively rendered judgment and punishment. Hunter-gatherers orga-nized egalitarian democracies. They had no chiefs. There was no political or cor-porate hierarchy to dream of climbing. There was no one to revolt against.

So, if we're stranded a few hundred centuries from when we long to be—if (through no fault of our own) we find ourselves, in an age of nuclear weapons, with Pleistocene emotions but without Pleistocene social safeguards—perhaps we can be excused for a little Monday-night football.

FOR FURTHER READING

A good anecdotal summary of professional sports and its admirers is *Fans!* by Michael Roberts (New Republic Book Co., 1976). A classic study of hunter-gatherer society is *The !Kung San* by Richard Borshay Lee (Cambridge U. Press, 1979). Most of the hunter-gatherer customs mentioned in this article apply to the !Kung and to many other nonmarginal hunter-gatherer cultures worldwide—before they were destroyed by civilization.

Engaging the Text

1. In what ways have the terminology and ethos of competitive sports perme-ated nonsporting activities, such as politics? Can you give some examples?

2. In Sagan's view, what explains the similarity between the kinds of skills our hunter-gatherer forebears developed to survive and the games we play? Might these skills be useful in other areas of life, such as the workplace?

3. What function does the comparative chart of team names in different cul-tures serve in Sagan's discussion? What do you know about the origins of the nicknames used for your school's sports teams?

Exploring Your Cultural Perspective

1. How does paintball, in which participants wear camouflage and other mock Army gear and hunt opposing teams with guns that fire nonlethal but painful projectiles filled with paint, illustrate Sagan's thesis? You can find the official online magazine for paintball at <http://www.paintballsportsinc. com>. Alternatively, analyze the iconography of a popular video game to see whether it illustrates Sagan's thesis.

2. Describe a sport (such as water skiing) or game to which Carl Sagan's hypothesis might not apply. What values does the sport or game embody?

JOYCE CAROL OATES

On Boxing

Joyce Carol Oates was born in Lockport, New York, in 1938 and was raised on her grandparents' farm in Erie County. She received the National Book Award in 1970 for her novel *them*. An extraordinarily prolific author, Oates has written countless essays, novels, poems, plays, short works of fiction, reviews, and nonfiction pieces on topics ranging from D. H. Lawrence to boxing. Her latest works include *Broke Heart Blues* (1999); *Solstice: A Novel* (2000); *Blonde*, a fictionalized account of Marilyn Monroe (2000); *Faithless: Tales of Transgression* (2001); and *Middle Age: A Romance* (2001). Oates has taught writing and literature at Princeton University since 1978. "On Boxing," drawn from her book of the same name (1994), tackles the difficult question of why "our most dramatically 'self-destructive' sport" has proved so enduring.

Thinking Critically

Before you read this piece, imagine what a boxing match would be like if there were no referee and no rules. Notice the function that the historical context plays in Oates's analysis.

Boxing is the sport to which all other sports aspire.
> —GEORGE FOREMAN, former heavyweight champion of the world

At least in theory and by way of tradition boxing is a sport. But what *is* sport?—and why is a man, *in* sport, not the man he is or is expected to be at other times?

Consider the history of gladiatorial combat as the Romans practiced it, or caused it to be practiced, from approximately 265 B.C. to its abolishment by Theodoric in A.D. 500. In the ancient world, among part-civilized nations, it was customary after a battle to sacrifice prisoners of war in honor of commanders who had been killed. It also became customary to sacrifice slaves at the funerals of all persons of importance. But then—for what reason?—for amusement, or for the sake of "sport"?—the condemned slaves were given arms and urged to defend themselves by killing the men who were ordered to kill them. Out of this evolution of brute sacrifice into something approaching a recognizable sporting contest the notorious phenomenon of Roman gladiatorial combat—death as mass amusement—gradually arose. Surely there is nothing quite like it in world history.

At first the contests were performed at the funeral pyre or near the sepulcher, but, with the passage of time, as interest in the fighting detached itself from its ostensibly religious context, matches were moved to the Forum, then to the Circus and amphitheaters. Contractors emerged to train the slaves, men of rank and political importance began to keep "families" of gladiators, upcoming fights were promoted and advertised as sporting contests are today, shows lasting as long as three days increased in number and popularity. Not the mere sacrifice of helpless individuals but the "sport" of the contest excited spectators, for, though the instinct to fight and to kill is surely qualified by one's personal courage, the instinct to watch others fight and kill is evidently inborn. When the boxing fan shouts, "Kill him! Kill him!" he is betraying no peculiar individual pathology or quirk but asserting his common humanity and his kinship, however distant, with the thousands upon thousands of spectators who crowded into the Roman amphitheaters to see gladiators fight to the death. That such contests for mass amusement endured not for a few years or even decades but for centuries should arrest our attention.

According to Petronius the gladiators took the following oath: "We swear, after the dictation of Eumolpus, to suffer death by fire, bonds, stripes, and the sword; and whatever else Eumolpus may command, as true gladiators we bind ourselves body and mind to our master's service." Their courage became legendary. Cicero referred to it as a model for all Roman citizens—that one should be willing to suffer nobly in the defense of the Commonwealth. In general, gladiators were slaves and condemned criminals who could hope to prolong their lives or even, if they were champions, to gain freedom; but impoverished freemen often fought as well. With the passage of time, paralleling and surely contributing to what we see as the decadence of Rome, even men of rank volunteered to compete publicly. (Under Nero, that most notorious of Roman emperors, such wild exhibitions flourished. It is estimated that during his reign from A.D. 54 to 68 as many as one thousand aristocrats performed as gladiators in one way or another, in fights fair, handicapped, or fixed. At times even women of rank competed—which matches were no doubt particularly noteworthy.) So drawn to these violent sports were Roman aristocrats that the Emperor Augustus was finally moved to issue an edict forbidding them to train as gladiators.

The origins of gladiatorial boxing are specifically Greek. According to tradition a ruler named Thesus (circa 900 B.C.) was entertained by the spectacle of two matched fighters, seated, facing each other, hammering each other to   5 death with their fists. Eventually the men fought on their feet and covered their fists with leather thongs; then with leather thongs covered with sharp metal spikes—the cestus. A ring of some kind, probably a circle, became a neutral space to which an injured boxer might temporarily retreat. When the Romans cultivated the sport it became extremely popular: one legendary cestus-champion was said to have killed 1,425 opponents. Winning gladiators were widely celebrated as "kings of athletes" and heroes for all. By confirming in the public arena the bloody mortality of other men they established for themselves, as champions always do, a kind of immortality.

So it happens that the wealthier and more advanced a society, the more fanatic its interest in certain kinds of sport. Civilization's trajectory is to curve back upon itself—naturally? helplessly?—like the mythical snake biting its own tail and to take up with passion the outward signs and gestures of "savagery." While it is plausible that emotionally effete men and women may require ever more extreme experiences to arouse them, it is perhaps the case too that the desire is not merely to *mimic* but, magically, to *be* brute, primitive, instinctive, and therefore innocent. One might then be a person for whom the contest is not mere self-destructive play but life itself; and the world, not in spectacular and irrevocable decline, but new, fresh, vital, terrifying and exhilarating by turns, a place of wonders. It is the lost ancestral self that is sought, however futilely. Like those dream-remnants of childhood that year by year continue to elude us but are never abandoned, still less despised, for that reason.

Roman gladiatorial combat was abolished under the Christian emperors Constantine and Theodoric, and its practice discontinued forever. Boxing as we know it in the United States derives solely from English bare-knuckle prize-fighting of the eighteenth century and from an entirely different conception of sport.

The first recorded account of a bare-knuckle fight in England—between "a gentleman's footman and a butcher"—is dated 1681 and appeared in a publication called the *London Protestant Mercury*. This species of fight, in which maiming and death were not the point, was known as a "Prize Fight" or the "Prize Ring," and was public entertainment of an itinerant nature, frequently attached to village fairs. The Prize Ring was a movable space created by spectators who formed a loose circle by holding a length of rope; the Prize Fight was a voluntary contest between two men, usually a "champion" and a "challenger," unrefereed but governed by rudimentary rules of fair play. The challenge to fight was put to a crowd by a fighter and his accomplices and if any man wanted to accept he tossed his hat into the ring—hence the political expression with its overtone of bellicosity—and the fight was on. Bets were commonly placed on which man would knock the other down first or draw "first blood." Foul play was actively discouraged by the crowd; the fighters shook hands after the fight. "The Noble Art," as prizefighting was called, began as a low-life species of entertainment but was in time enthusiastically supported by sporting members of the aristocracy and the upper classes.

England's earliest bare-knuckle champion was a man named James Figg who won the honor in 1719. The last of the bare-knuckle champions was the American heavyweight John L. Sullivan whose career—from approximately 1882 to 1892—overlapped both bare-knuckle fighting and gloved boxing as established under the rules of the Marquis of Queensberry which are observed, with some elaboration, to the present time. The most significant changes were two: the introduction of leather gloves (mainly to protect the hand, not the face—a man's knuckles are easily broken) and the third man in the ring, the referee, whose privilege it is to stop the fight at his own discretion, if he thinks a boxer has no chance of winning or cannot defend himself against his opponent. With the introduction of the referee the crudeness of "The Noble Art" passes over into the relative sophistication of boxing.

The "third man in the ring," usually anonymous so far as the crowd is concerned, appears to many observers no more than an observer himself, even an intruder; a ghostly presence as fluid in motion and quick-footed as the boxers themselves (indeed, he is frequently an ex-boxer). But so central to the drama of boxing is the referee that the spectacle of two men fighting each other unsupervised in an elevated ring would seem hellish, if not obscene—life rather than art. The referee makes boxing possible. 10

The referee is our intermediary in the fight. He is our moral conscience extracted from us as spectators so that, for the duration of the fight, "conscience" need not be a factor in our experience; nor need it be a factor in the boxers' behavior. (Asked if boxers are ever sorry for having hurt their opponents, Carmen Basilio replied: "Sorry? Are you kidding? Boxers are never sorry.") Which is not to say that boxers are always and forever without conscience: all boxers are different, and behave differently at different times. But there are occasions when a boxer who is trapped in the ropes and unable to fall to the canvas while being struck repeatedly is in danger of being killed unless the referee intervenes—the attacking boxer has been trained not to stop his attack while his opponent is still technically standing. In the rapidly escalating intensity of the fight only the referee remains neutral and objective.

Though the referee's role is highly demanding and it has been estimated that there are perhaps no more than a dozen really skilled referees in the world, it seems necessary in the drama of the fight that the referee himself possesses no dramatic identity: referees' names are rarely remembered after a fight except by seasoned boxing fans. Yet, paradoxically, the referee's participation is crucial. He cannot control what happens in the ring but he can control to a degree *that* it happens—he is responsible for the fight if not for the individual fighters' performances. In a match in which boxing skills and not merely fighting are predominant the referee's role can be merely functional, but in a fiercely contested match it is of incalculable importance. The referee holds the power of life and death at certain times since his decision to terminate a fight, or to allow it to continue, can determine a boxer's fate. (One should know that a well-aimed punch with a heavyweight's full weight behind it can have the equivalent force of ten thousand pounds—a blow that must be absorbed by the brain in its jelly sac.) In the infamous Benny Paret–Emile Griffith fight of March 1962 the referee Ruby Goldstein was said to have stood paralyzed as Griffith trapped Paret in the ropes, striking him as many as eighteen times in the head. (Paret died ten days later.) Boxers are trained not to quit. If knocked down, they try to get up to continue the fight, even if they can hardly defend themselves. The primary rule of the ring—to defend oneself at all times—is both a parody and a distillation of life.

In the past—well into the 1950s—it was not customary for a referee to interfere with a fight, however brutal and one-sided. A boxer who kept struggling to his feet after having been knocked down, or, like the intransigent Jake LaMotta in his sixth and final fight with Sugar Ray Robinson in 1951, refused to fall to the canvas though he could no longer defend himself and had become a human punching bag, was simply left to his fate. The will of the crowd—and overwhelmingly it *is* the will of the crowd—that one man defeat the other totally and irrevocably, was honored. Hence the bloody "great" fights of boxing's history—Dempsey's triumph over Willard, for instance—inconceivable today.

It should be understood that "boxing" and "fighting," though always combined in the greatest of boxers, can be entirely different and even unrelated activities. Amateur boxers are trained to win their matches on points; professionals usually try for knockouts. (Not that professionals are more violent than amateurs but why trust judges?—and the knockout is dramatically spectacular.) If boxing is frequently, in the lighter weights especially, a highly complex and refined skill, belonging solely to civilization, fighting belongs to something predating civilization, the instinct not merely to defend oneself—for how has the masculine ego ever been assuaged by so minimal a response to threat?—but to attack another and to force him into absolute submission. This accounts for the electrifying effect upon a typical fight crowd when fighting suddenly emerges out of boxing—when, for instance, a boxer's face begins to bleed and the fight seems to enter a new and more dangerous phase. The flash of red is the visible sign of the fight's authenticity in the eyes of many spectators and boxers are justified in being proud, as many are, of their facial scars.

15   If the "violence" of boxing seems at times to flow from the crowd, to be a heightened expression of the crowd's delirium—rarely transmitted by television, by the way—the many restraints and subtleties of boxing are possible because of the "third man in the ring," a counter of sorts to the inchoate wash

of emotion beyond the ropes and the ring apron: our conscience, as I've indicated, extracted from us, and granted an absolute authority.

Engaging the Text

1. How does Oates's historical survey provide a context in which to understand the evolution of boxing as a unique cultural phenomenon?

2. Oates speculates on the role that savage sports play at certain points in the life cycle of a civilization. Do you find her analysis credible? Why or why not?

3. Although usually an invisible figure, the referee, according to Oates, is an essential element in a boxing match. What kind of power does this figure exercise, and why is his presence indispensable?

Exploring Your Cultural Perspective

1. What do you think George Foreman meant when he said that "boxing is the sport to which all other sports aspire"? Do you agree? Why or why not? You might wish to rent the film *Gladiator* (2000) and compare the ways in which boxing exhibits characteristics of gladiatorial combat.

2. Recently, women have started boxing. One of the best-known women boxers is Muhammad Ali's daughter Laila Ali. Do you think boxing is a sport for women? Why or why not?

CLIFFORD GEERTZ
The Balinese Cockfight

According to anthropologist Clifford Geertz, for those who can interpret the signs, a culture's preference for a particular sport offers revealing clues about its underlying values. The Balinese mania for cockfighting displays a unique world view, charged with gods and demons, that
projects the very essence of masculinity in its elaborate ritual. This essay,
based on the author's extensive field work, is from *The Interpretation of
Culture* (1973). Geertz's recent publications include *Works and Lives: The
Anthropologist as Author* (1992) and *Available Light: Anthropological Reflections on Philosophical Topics* (2000).

Thinking Critically
*Notice how Geertz interprets the meaning of cockfighting in terms of Bali-
nese cultural values. In Bali, cockfighting is considered just as normal as
horse racing or dog racing is in the United States, yet most North Americans would find it difficult to define cockfighting as a sport. What **ethno-
centric** biases (belief in the superiority of one's own culture) are at work?*

Bali, mainly because it is Bali, is a well-studied place. Its mythology, art, ritual,
social organization, patterns of child rearing, forms of law, even styles of trance,
have all been microscopically examined for traces of that elusive substance Jane
Belo called "The Balinese Temper."[1] But, aside from a few passing remarks,
the cockfight has barely been noticed, although as a popular obsession of consuming power it is at least as important a revelation of what being a Balinese
"is really like" as these more celebrated phenomena.[2] As much of America surfaces in a ball park, on a golf links, at a race track, or around a poker table,
much of Bali surfaces in a cock ring. <u>For it is only apparently cocks that are</u>
<u>fighting there. Actually, it is men</u>.

✝ To anyone who has been in Bali any length of time, the deep psychological
identification of Balinese men with their cocks is unmistakable. The double
entendre here is deliberate. It works in exactly the same way in Balinese as it
does in English, even to producing the same tired jokes, strained puns, and

uninventive obscenities. Bateson and Mead have even suggested that, in line with Balinese conception of the body as a set of separately animated parts, cocks are viewed as detachable, self-operating penises, ambulant genitals with a life of their own.[3] And while I do not have the kind of unconscious material either to confirm or disconfirm this intriguing notion, the fact that they are masculine symbols par excellence is about as indubitable, and to the Balinese about as evident, as the fact that water runs downhill.

The language of everyday moralism is shot through, on the male side of it, with roosterish imagery. *Sabung*, the word for cock (and one which appears in inscriptions as early as A.D. 922), is used metaphorically to mean "hero," "warrior," "champion," "man of parts," "political candidate," "bachelor," "dandy," "lady-killer," or "tough guy." A pompous man whose behavior presumes above his station is compared to a tailless cock who struts about as though he had a large, spectacular one. A desperate man who makes a last, irrational effort to extricate himself from an impossible situation is likened to a dying cock who makes one final lunge at his tormentor to drag him along to a common destruction. A stingy man, who promises much, gives little, and begrudges that, is compared to a cock which, held by the tail, leaps at another without in fact engaging him. A marriageable young man still shy with the opposite sex or someone in a new job anxious to make a good impression is called "a fighting cock caged for the first time."[4] Court trials, wars, political contests, inheritance disputes, and street arguments are all compared to cockfights.[5] Even the very island itself is perceived from its shape as a small, proud cock, poised, neck extended, back taut, tail raised, in external challenge to large, feckless, shapeless Java.[6]

But the intimacy of men with their cocks is more than metaphorical. Balinese men, or anyway a large majority of Balinese men, spend an enormous amount of time with their favorites, grooming them, feeding them, discussing them, trying them out against one another, or just gazing at them with a mixture of rapt admiration and dreamy self-absorption. Whenever you see a group of Balinese men squatting idly in the council shed or along the road in their hips down, shoulders forward, knees up fashion, half or more of them will have a rooster in his hands, holding it between his thighs, bouncing it gently up and down to strengthen its legs, ruffling its feathers with abstract sensuality, pushing it out against a neighbor's rooster to rouse its spirit, withdrawing it toward his loins to calm it again. Now and then, to get a feel for another bird, a man will fiddle this way with someone else's cock for a while, but usually by moving around to squat in place behind it, rather than just having it passed across to him as though it were merely an animal.

In the houseyard, the high-walled enclosures where the people live, fighting cocks are kept in wicker cages, moved frequently about so as to maintain the optimum balance of sun and shade. They are fed a special diet, which varies somewhat according to individual theories but which is mostly maize, sifted for impurities with far more care than it is when mere humans are going to eat it, and offered to the animal kernel by kernel. Red pepper is stuffed down their beaks and up their anuses to give them spirit. They are bathed in the same ceremonial preparation of tepid water, medicinal herbs, flowers, and onions in which infants are bathed, and for a prize cock just about as often. Their combs are cropped, their plumage dressed, their spurs trimmed, and their legs massaged, and they are inspected for flaws with the squinted concentration of a diamond merchant. A man who has a passion for cocks, an enthusiast in the literal sense of the term, can spend most of his life with them, and even those, the overwhelming majority, whose passion though intense has not entirely run away with them, can and do spend what seems not only to an outsider, but also to themselves, an inordinate amount of time with them. "I am cock crazy," my landlord, a quite ordinary *aficionado* by Balinese standards, used to moan as he went to move another cage, give another bath, or conduct another feeding. "We're all cock crazy."

The madness has some less visible dimensions, however, because although it is true that cocks are symbolic expressions or magnifications of their owner's self, the narcissistic male ego writ out in Aesopian terms, they are also expressions—and rather more immediate ones—of what the Balinese regard as the direct inversion, aesthetically, morally, and metaphysically, of human status: animality.

The Balinese revulsion against any behavior regarded as animal-like can hardly be overstressed. Babies are not allowed to crawl for that reason. Incest, though hardly approved, is a much less horrifying crime than bestiality. (The appropriate punishment for the second is death by drowning, for the first being forced to live like an animal.)[7] Most demons are represented—in sculpture, dance, ritual, myth—in some real or fantastic animal form. The main puberty rite consists in filing the child's teeth so they will not look like animal fangs. Not only defecation but eating is regarded as a disgusting, almost obscene activity, to be conducted hurriedly and privately, because of its association with animality. Even falling down or any form of clumsiness is considered to be bad for these reasons. Aside from cocks and a few domestic animals—oxen, ducks—of no emotional significance, the Balinese are aversive to animals and treat their large number of dogs not merely callously but with a phobic cruelty. In identifying with his cock. the Balinese man is identifying not just with his ideal self, or even his penis, but also, and at the same time, with what he most fears, hates, and ambivalence being what it is, is fascinated by—"The Powers of Darkness."

The connection of cocks and cockfighting with such Powers, with the animalistic demons that threaten constantly to invade the small, cleared-off space in which the Balinese have so carefully built their lives and devour its inhabitants, is quite explicit. A cockfight, any cockfight, is in the first instance a blood sacrifice offered, with the appropriate chants and oblations, to the demons in order to pacify their ravenous, cannibal hunger. No temple festival should be conducted until one is made. (If it is omitted, someone will inevitably fall into a trance and command with the voice of an angered spirit that the oversight be immediately corrected.) Collective responses to natural evils—illness, crop failure, volcanic eruptions—almost always involve them. And that famous holiday in Bali, "The Day of Silence" (*Njepi*), when everyone sits silent and immobile all day long in order to avoid contact with a sudden influx of demons chased momentarily out of hell, is preceded the previous day by large-scale cockfights (in this case legal) in almost every village on the island.

In the cockfight, man and beast, good and evil, ego and id, the creative power of aroused masculinity and the destructive power of loosened animality fuse in a bloody drama of hatred, cruelty, violence, and death. It is little wonder that when, as is the invariable rule, the owner of the winning cock takes the carcass of the loser—often torn limb from limb by its enraged owner—home to eat, he does so with a mixture of social embarrassment, moral satisfaction, aesthetic disgust, and cannibal joy. Or that a man who has lost an important fight is sometimes driven to wreck his family shrines and curse the gods, an act of metaphysical (and social) suicide. Or that in seeking earthly analogues for heaven and hell the Balinese compare the former to the mood of a man whose cock has just won, the latter to that of a man whose cock has just lost.

Notes

1. J. Belo, "The Balinese Temper," in *Traditional Balinese Culture*, ed. J. Belo (New York: Books Demand UMI, 1970) (originally published in 1935), pp. 85–110.
2. The best discussion of cockfighting is again Bateson and Mead's *Balinese Character*, pp. 24–25, 140; but it, too, is general and abbreviated.
3. Ibid., pp. 25–26. The cockfight is unusual within Balinese culture in being a single-sex public activity from which the other sex is totally and expressly excluded. Sexual differentiation is culturally extremely played down in Bali and most activities, formal and informal, involve the participation of men and women on equal ground, commonly as linked couples. From religion, to politics, to economics, to kinship, to dress, Bali is a rather "unisex" society, a fact both its customs and its symbolism clearly express. Even in contexts where women do not in fact play much of a role—music, painting, certain agricultural activities—their absence, which is only relative in any case, is more a mere matter of fact than socially enforced. To this general pattern, the cockfight, entirely of, by, and for men (women—at least *Balinese* women—do not even watch), is the most striking exception.
4. C. Hooykaas, *The Lay of the Jaya Prana* (London, 1958), p. 39. The lay has a stanza (no. 17) which the reluctant bridegroom uses. Jaya Prana, the subject of a Balinese Uriah myth, responds to the lord who has offered him the loveliest of six hundred servant girls: "Godly King, my Lord and Master / I beg you, give me leave to go /

such things are not yet in my mind; / like a fighting cock encaged / indeed I am on my mettle / I am alone / as yet the flame has not been fanned."

5. For these, see V. E. Korn, *Het Adatrecht van Bali*, 2d ed. (The Hague, 1932), index under *toh*.

6. There is indeed a legend to the effect that the separation of Java and Bali is due to the action of a powerful Javanese religious figure who wished to protect himself against a Balinese culture hero (the ancestor of two Ksatria castes) who was a passionate cock-fighting gambler. See C. Hooykaas, *Agama Tirtha* (Amsterdam, 1964), p. 184.

7. An incestuous couple is forced to wear pig yokes over their necks and crawl to a pig trough and eat with their mouths there. On this, see J. Belo, "Customs Pertaining to Twins in Bali," in *Traditional Balinese Culture*, ed. J. Belo, p. 49; on the abhorrence of animality generally, Bateson and Mead, *Balinese Character*, p. 22.

Engaging the Text

1. In what respects do Balinese men identify with fighting cocks? What details illustrate the extent of this identification?

2. Geertz assumes that you can learn as much about a culture from its sports and games as from its more official institutions. In a short essay, support or challenge his claim. Compare and contrast Balinese cockfighting with American baseball or football.

3. In view of the Balinese attitude toward "animal-like" behavior, how might cockfighting be understood as a kind of "safety valve" for venting aggression?

Exploring Your Cultural Perspective

1. Extend Geertz's argument into the realm of animals used as team mascots or emblems. (For example, the custom of throwing an octopus onto the ice before Detroit Red Wings hockey games started in the 1952 Stanley Cup playoffs after the Red Wings swept the series with eight wins—corresponding to the eight tentacles of the octopus. See <http://detroit.freenet.org/redwings/history/octopus.html>.)

2. In your opinion, is cockfighting more primitive than dog racing or horse racing? If you answer yes, consider that horses and dogs are routinely given performance-enhancing and pain-killing drugs so that they can run and are sometimes destroyed when they fail to perform. In a short essay, compare the way animals are used in sports in the United States and in Bali, emphasizing underlying cultural values.

ROBERTO GONZALEZ ECHEVARRIA

First Pitch

Roberto Gonzalez Echevarria was born and raised in Cuba and is Sterling Professor of Hispanic and Comparative Literature at Yale University. He is the author and editor of numerous books, including *The Oxford Book of Latin American Short Stories* (1999). A former semipro catcher, he plays for the Madison Ravens of the Connecticut Senior Baseball League. In this chapter from *The Pride of Havana: A History of Cuban Baseball* (1999), Echevarria explores the paradox that Cuba defines itself politically in opposition to the United States but shares our love for baseball.

Thinking Critically

One of the tasks Echevarria sets for himself is to explain how baseball was transformed, after Castro came to power, from the game he remembered as a child. To follow his line of thought, underline the passages where Echevarria recovers the essence of authentic Cuban baseball.

Alonso de Ojeda, one of the first conquistadors to rush to the Caribbean in the wake of Columbus, was a man of great physical strength and skill. Lore has it that one of his favorite feats was to stand at the base of the Giralda Tower in Seville, which is a full 250 feet high, and hurl an orange clear over the statue on top of it. Almost 500 years later, in 1965, Pedro Ramos, a Cuban pitcher with the Yankees at the time, tried to reach the ceiling of the Houston Astrodome (208 feet) with a baseball before the first game ever played there. Ojeda's stunt uncannily anticipated that throwing a round object would become a passion of the variegated progeny he and others were to leave in the Caribbean. It is among the first things a boy learns in the region.

In the provinces of Cuba I grew up throwing stones at cans, bottles, trees, fruits, and animals. Some of my friends routinely killed birds by picking them off trees with stones. Their accuracy or *puntería* was, as I recall it now, truly remarkable. A good deal of worth was attached to how well one could throw, and how far. We often engaged in battles using the entire cornucopia of tropical fruits or mudballs, which when laced with a stone caused real damage. We could throw even before a baseball entered our lives. And it did early. Middle- and upper-class boys could expect baseball equipment as Christmas gifts, particularly because the professional baseball season coincided with the holidays. Baseball was literally in the air, broadcast by several radio stations throughout the island, and later by television. Poorer boys made their own balls and bats using various materials, or got their hands on equipment in a variety of ways (including, of course, stealing it). We played baseball, which in Cuba is familiarly known as *pelota* or ball, all year. But we were in a baseball frenzy during the winter because of the professional season, which polarized us mostly into Habanistas (followers of the Habana Leones or Lions), whose color was red, and Almendaristas (followers of the Almendares Alacranes or Scorpions), whose color was blue. There was a smattering of followers of Marianao (the Tigers), who wore orange and black, and of Cienfuegos (the Elephants), who wore green. I should confess from the start that I was, that I still am, an Habanista.

As young boys we played anywhere: in open fields, in roads and city streets, in schoolyards. We also played in a variety of ways to adjust to the number of players available, the size of the field, and the time available. We sometimes played to a given number of runs, or more conventionally to a set number of innings. I have played hundreds of games with only two bases and home plate, and quite a few with only one base and home. It was slow-pitch, *a la floja*, for the most part, and the number of bases off a hit depended on the kind of field. Equipment was apportioned according to ownership, ability, and position. The first baseman, not to mention the catcher, had to have a glove to catch the throws if we were playing *a la dura*, or hardball. Outfielders often had no glove. We used many kinds of balls; some we made ourselves wrapping twine around a small rubber ball and covering the finished product with adhesive tape. But we often had a real baseball, which we called *pelotas poli*, "poli" being a deformation of Spalding, which was the most popular brand early in Cuban baseball. By my time the ball we coveted was the Wilson, used by the professional league, which I will always call here the Cuban League. Although we played mostly pickup games, we took them seriously, particularly if they attracted a crowd of idlers and passersby. I remember games in which the spectators (a taxi driver taking a break and a few loafers) placed bets, adding to the pressure. At school we divided into several squads and later joined neighborhood teams.

Adult supervision at this stage was minimal or nonexistent. We organized the games, later the teams, with undisguised ruthlessness. If one was afraid of the ball, could not field, or struck out often, these weaknesses were brought up loudly and without mercy whenever it came time to choose up sides or to make up a team. It was survival of the fittest all the way. We did not learn baseball the way kids do in Little League. We were like artisans learning a craft: We watched and imitated others with more skill. We had no special drills and no formal instruction. One just had to learn to do things the right way. An older boy might tell you if you did something wrong, but most likely he would make fun of you.

Nobody gave a thought to baseball being American or Cuban. We revered 5 the great players we heard about and whose pictures we saw in newspapers and magazines, no matter what their nationality or race. The pickup games we played and the neighborhood teams we organized may have been poor in supervision and equipment, but they were rich in experience: On a good week I might get fifty at-bats, whereas many a kid in the U.S. Little League comes to the plate two or three times in the same period. Later we moved up in baseball through different channels. Some might make the school teams and then move up to the Juveniles (under-twenty league), and later the amateurs, the teams in what I will always call here the Amateur League. Others might play for a sugarmill team, or one sponsored by a store or factory in a semipro league. Race would then enter into the picture. But childhood baseball in the Cuba of the fifties and earlier was truly a child's world, stratified by skill, strength, and bravado, not by color or class. This was the world I left behind with the advent of the revolution in 1959, when we came as exiles to Tampa, Florida. It remains pristine and self-enclosed in my memory, along with recollections of the Cuban League and my beloved Habana Lions (I will write Habana when referring to the baseball club).

This book is an attempt to recover those feelings and memories, inevitably filtered through the mind of the literature professor I have become in the interim. I have tried not to disguise the clash between personal memories and the academic discourse that has allowed me to fully evoke them. I have often hesitated to continue my research for fear that learning too much about Cuban baseball would destroy the pleasure of my intimate reminiscences. Yet I cannot still the voice that learned to write history in libraries, graduate seminars, professional conventions, and teaching undergraduate classes. Hence I have tried as best as I can to get it right, by going to the newspapers, talking to participants, and reconstructing a cultural and socioeconomic context. I have attempted to write a history of Cuban baseball from its inception in the 1860s to the present, trying to figure out, using the full array of my intellectual equipment, the significance of the game in the nation's culture. This is the part of baseball about which I had no interest or clue as a child but that beckoned now as a mystery, a huge historical irony to be analyzed: that my country's political evolution, fueled by intense anti-Americanism, had continued to embrace the most American of games as its own. But I have not left myself, or the child I was, out of this research project, as one often pretends to do in academic writing. On the contrary, I have tried to weave my personal memories as a witness and participant (both as player and as fan) into the narrative.

The dialogue between the professor and the child is not the only one at the center of this book; a more intense debate within myself has been about whether to write it in English or Spanish. In English there is a certain style of writing about Latin American baseball that involves much condescension and humor of questionable taste. The differences of attitude, rituals, and customs are portrayed by sportswriters who think themselves quite free of prejudice, as being funny, or as instances of the zany spirit of Latin people. All this is written from an implicitly supercilious position that assumes that in the United States there is an order in what is, after all, Organized Baseball, that would not allow for any shenanigans. I believe that in most cases the writers or broadcasters who are most guilty of this are simply covering up their own ignorance and sense of uncanniness at seeing a game they consider theirs played by strangers. Writing in English, I sometimes feared, would inevitably contaminate my discourse with this built-in racism. Another apprehension was to write too much in an effort to correct the distortions of Cuban, and by extension Latin American, baseball in the United States. In a polemic, one's emphases can be dictated by the opponent's biases, and this in itself can lead to distortions. Spanish beckoned because I could write for my own audience, without need for explanations. The solution was to write in both. There are pages of this book that I first wrote in Spanish and later translated into English to avoid a certain point of view imposed by the language in which one first thinks of something. I realized that I was also an American baseball fan and that I had to let both the Cuban and the American sides of me speak.

I have written a book that I hope will correct some of the views Americans and others have of Cuban baseball. To me, the most vexing example of how lightly and condescendingly the history of Latin baseball is dealt with in the United States involves a story about Fidel Castro that I would like to set straight here once and for all. Every time I mentioned that I was writing a book about Cuban baseball, the first thing Americans said had to do with Fidel's (which is how we Cubans call him, never "Castro") alleged prowess in the sport, and the irony that, had he been signed by the Senators or the Giants, there would have been no Cuban Revolution. This story even worked itself into a book by eminent historian John M. Merriman, one of my closest friends and batterymate in the Yale Intramural Baseball League. The whole thing is a fabrication by an American journalist whose name is now lost, and it is never told in Cuba because everyone would know it to be false. Let it be known here that Fidel Castro was never scouted by any major-league team, and is not known to have enjoyed the kind of success in baseball that could have brought a scout's attention to him. In a country where sports coverage was broad and thorough, in a city such as Havana with a half-dozen major newspapers (plus dozens of minor ones) and with organized leagues at all levels, there is no record that Fidel Castro ever played, much less starred, on any team. No one has produced even one team picture with Fidel Castro in it. I have found the box score of an intramural game played between the Law and the Business Schools at the University of Havana where a certain F. Castro pitched and lost, 5–4, in late November 1946; this is likely to be the only published box score in which the future dictator appears (*El Mundo*, November 28, 1946). Cubans know that Fidel Castro was no ballplayer, though he dressed himself in the uniform of a spurious, tongue-in-cheek team called Barbudos (Bearded Ones) after he came to power in 1959 and played a few exhibition games. There was no doubt then about his making any team in Cuba. Given a whole country to toy with, Fidel Castro realized the dream of most middle-aged Cuban men by pulling on a uniform and "playing" a few innings.

Even well-meaning writers distort Cuban and Latin American baseball when they plea for the acceptance of its exuberant, flashy, and carefree style of play, which they often liken to their (also faulty) understanding of Latin music and dance. In other words, they argue in favor of allowing the Latin players to live up to American stereotypes about them. The fact is that Cuban (and most Latin) baseball has always been conservative, highly strategic, and has frowned on flamboyant players, who are derisively called *postalitas*. The word means "little post card," I presume because it is thought that the player is posturing, as if posing for a picture. As the reader will discover here, Cuba's style of "inside" baseball, consisting of bunting, slapping a grounder past a charging infielder, almost no base-stealing, and patience at the plate was derived from the pioneers of Negro Leagues baseball, who had much influence in Cuba during the early part of the twentieth century. With exceptions, Cuban players have been small, not the slugger type; hence the game adopted a patient strategy, and there was even a snobbish disdain for the home-run mentality. Pitching, because of the general lack of overpowering speed, depends on guile, junk, and much control. Given the pervasiveness of betting at all levels of Cuban baseball throughout history (to the present), it has never been prudent to jeopardize somebody else's money by being reckless. Like baseball everywhere, Cuban baseball is not lacking in amusing anecdotes, so there is no need for fabrication. I have told or retold some of these, but my aim has been to stick to the truth, or as close to it as I can get by going to the written record and oral sources.

Another reason for writing the book, a powerful incentive for someone   *10* like me trained in philology and literary criticism, was to undo some of the abuse visited on the names of Cuban ballplayers over the years by American sportswriters, broadcasters, and even sports historians. Three kinds of errors mar the historical record. First, the American press has simply misspelled the names of countless Cuban (and other Latin) ballplayers. I have seen Cristóbal Torriente's rather elegant name appear as Cristebal Torrienti, to take just one example. Second, the names of Cuban players have often been truncated by

American teammates, or even the front offices of the teams they played for, perhaps because Americans find long names pretentious. In Spanish it is common practice (even a legal requirement) to have two surnames, as I do; the first is my father's, González; the second, my mother's maiden name, Echevarría. In informal situations it is the second surname that would be dropped. Thus the late Cuban infielder Hiraldo Sablón Ruiz was known as "Hiraldo Sablón" by his countrymen. Americans, however, bewildered Cuban fans by referring to him as "Chico Ruiz," adding insult to injury by giving him a generic nickname.

The nicknames given to Latin players are the third kind of offense, in this case both to historical accuracy and to their dignity. They have typically combined ignorance and condescension. "Chico" or "chica" is one way Cubans (and other Spanish speakers) might familiarly call for each other's attention, somewhat like "buddy" or "mac" in American idiom. Naming a player "Chico" because one of his teammates used the word would be like calling the Yankee star "Buddy" Mantle because someone said, "Way to go, buddy!" when he hit a homer. Yet this nickname has stuck to many Latin American athletes, from Chico Fernández, known in Cuba by his rather serious name Humberto Fernández, to the Panamanian Chico Salmón, and to countless others. There was even a "Chica." Other nicknames infantilize athletes: Orestes Miñoso, with his proud classical name, became "Minnie" Minoso in the United States; Edmundo Amorós, "Sandy" Amoros; while that patriarch of Cuban baseball Miguel Angel González was reduced to "Mike" Gonzalez (or worse, Gonzales). The list of indignities, the worst of which was perhaps calling Luis Tiant "El Tiante," could go on and on. In this book I have preserved the names of all players in the original Spanish form (as they were known in Cuba, or other Latin country of origin), but included in parentheses, the first time he is mentioned or when relevant, the nickname in the United States. I could not have written a whole book referring to Orestes Miñoso as "Minnie."

But the most powerful reason to write the book was to preserve and exalt the memory of Cuban, Latin American, and American players who played in Cuba and performed feats worthy of remembrance. This is the epic side of my work, and the reason for the Homeric lists that sometimes appear in it. Given the recent history of Cuba, including the diaspora and the separation of Cubans inside and outside the island, preservation of a common memory such as baseball is an important, even urgent endeavor. In Cuba itself, the effort to bolster the achievements of the revolution have led to an erasure of our baseball memory, a sort of cultural lobotomy. Foreign historians of Cuban sports have often bought into the idea that Cuba's sports history begins in 1959 and mouth the propaganda churned out by bureaucrats and ideologues. But the fact is that Cuba has a rich sports history and that the country's emphasis on sports is something derived from its proximity to the United States. While touting its achievements and triumphs, the current Cuban regime has really profited from the strength of Cuban sports before 1959, and the importance Cubans attach to sports, particularly to baseball. The regime, as in the arts (ballet, literature, painting, music), has really been invested in Cuba's strengths as far back as the nineteenth century. Rather than a break, as they claim, Cuba's achievements in these areas after 1959 are really continuities and retentions. My aim is to preserve the common memory.

Engaging the Text

1. What role did baseball play in Echevarria's life while he was growing up in Cuba?

2. How does Echevarria feel about the Castro regime and its impact on baseball?

3. What kinds of distortions did Echevarria hope to correct about Cuban baseball by writing *The Pride of Havana*?

Exploring Your Cultural Perspective

1. Explore the way in which prominent Latino baseball players (for example, Sammy Sosa from the Dominican Republic, Orlando Hernandez [El Duque] from Cuba) have been marketed as cultural icons. Keep in mind that twenty-four percent of all major league baseball players are Latino.

2. Using the Olympic Games as an example, how relevant is Echevarria's claim that sports get drawn into the struggle between political ideologies? In what ways do vested interests and underlying agendas operate in the international sports arena?

MAYA ANGELOU
Champion of the World

Certain sports figures and events take on symbolic importance when they dramatize the hopes and dreams of an entire community. Such was the case when Joe Louis (the "Brown Bomber") defeated a white contender to retain his world heavyweight championship in the 1930s. The poet and novelist Maya Angelou recreates the electrifying impact of Louis's victory on her family, friends, and neighbors and describes its monumental implications for African Americans of that era. Born in 1928, Angelou was raised in the segregated South. The following recollection is drawn from her autobiography, *I Know Why the Caged Bird Sings* (1969). Her most recent work is *Still I Rise* (2001).

Thinking Critically
As you read, notice how Angelou integrates many speaking voices into her account and how they dramatize the urgency with which African Americans at the time viewed Louis's victory. What sports figure or event has taken on a larger-than-life quality today?

The last inch of space was filled, yet people continued to wedge themselves along the walls of the Store. Uncle Willie had turned the radio up to its last notch so that youngsters on the porch wouldn't miss a word. Women sat on kitchen chairs, dining-room chairs, stools, and upturned wooden boxes. Small children and babies perched on every lap available and men leaned on the shelves or on each other.

The apprehensive mood was shot through with shafts of gaiety, as a black sky is streaked with lightning.

"I ain't worried 'bout this fight. Joe's gonna whip that cracker like it's open season."

"He gone whip him till that white boy call him Momma."

5   At last the talking finished and the string-along songs about razor blades were over and the fight began.

"A quick jab to the head." In the Store the crowd grunted. "A left to the head and a right and another left." One of the listeners cackled like a hen and was quieted.

"They're in a clinch, Louis is trying to fight his way out."

Some bitter comedian on the porch said, "That white man don't mind hugging that niggah now, I betcha."

"The referee is moving in to break them up, but Louis finally pushed the contender away and it's an uppercut to the chin. The contender is hanging on, now he's backing away. Louis catches him with a short left to the jaw."

A tide of murmuring assent poured out the door and into the yard.   *10*

"Another left and another left. Louis is saving that mighty right . . ." The mutter in the Store had grown into a baby roar and it was pierced by the clang of a bell and the announcer's "That's the bell for round three, ladies and gentlemen."

As I pushed my way into the Store I wondered if the announcer gave any thought to the fact that he was addressing as "ladies and gentlemen" all the Negroes around the world who sat sweating and praying, glued to their "Master's voice."

There were only a few calls for RC Colas, Dr. Peppers, and Hires root beer. The real festivities would begin after the fight. Then even the old Christian ladies who taught their children and tried themselves to practice turning the other cheek would buy soft drinks, and if the Brown Bomber's victory was a particularly bloody one they would order peanut patties and Baby Ruths, also.

Bailey and I laid coins on top of the cash register. Uncle Willie didn't allow us to ring up sales during a fight. It was too noisy and might shake up the atmosphere. When the gong rang for the next round we pushed through the near-sacred quiet to the herd of children outside.

"He's got Louis against the ropes and now it's a left to the body and a right   *15* to the ribs. Another right to the body, it looks like it was low . . . Yes, ladies and gentlemen, the referee is signaling but the contender keeps raining the blows on Louis. It's another to the body, and it looks like Louis is going down."

My race groaned. It was our people falling. It was another lynching, yet another Black man hanging on a tree. One more woman ambushed and raped. A Black boy whipped and maimed. It was hounds on the trail of a man running through slimy swamps. It was a white woman slapping her maid for being forgetful.

The men in the Store stood away from the walls and at attention. Women greedily clutched the babes on their laps while on the porch the shufflings and smiles, flirtings and pinching of a few minutes before were gone. This might be the end of the world. If Joe lost we were back in slavery and beyond help. It would all be true, the accusations that we were lower types of human beings. Only a little higher than apes. True that we were stupid and ugly and lazy and dirty and, unlucky and worst of all, that God Himself hated us and ordained us to be hewers of wood and drawers of water, forever, and ever, world without end.

We didn't breathe. We didn't hope. We waited.

"He's off the ropes, ladies and gentlemen. He's moving towards the center of the ring." There was no time to be relieved. The worst might still happen.

20 "And now it looks like Joe is mad. He's caught Carnera with a left hook to the head and a right to the head. It's a left jab to the body and another left to the head. There's a left cross and a right to the head. The contender's right eye is bleeding and he can't seem to keep his block up. Louis is penetrating every block. The referee is moving in, but Louis sends a left to the body and it's an uppercut to the chin and the contender is dropping. He's on the canvas, ladies and gentlemen."

Babies slid to the floor as women stood up and men leaned toward the radio.

"Here's the referee. He's counting. One, two, three, four, five, six, seven . . . Is the contender trying to get up again?"

All the men in the store shouted, "NO."

"—eight, nine, ten." There were a few sounds from the audience, but they seemed to be holding themselves in against tremendous pressure.

25 "The fight is all over, ladies and gentlemen. Let's get the microphone over to the referee . . . Here he is. He's got the Brown Bomber's hand, he's holding it up . . . Here he is . . ."

Then the voice, husky and familiar, came to wash over us—"The winnah, and still heavyweight champeen of the world . . . Joe Louis."

Champion of the world. A Black boy. Some Black mother's son.

He was the strongest man in the world. People drank Coca-Colas like ambrosia and ate candy bars like Christmas. Some of the men went behind the Store and poured white lightning in their soft-drink bottles, and a few of the bigger boys followed them. Those who were not chased away came back blowing their breath in front of themselves like proud smokers.

It would take an hour or more before people would leave the Store and head home. Those who lived too far had made arrangements to stay in town. It wouldn't do for a Black man and his family to be caught on a lonely country road on a night when Joe Louis had proved that we were the strongest people in the world.

Engaging the Text

1. In what sense did the sporting event Angelou describes represent much more than who would win a boxing match? What was at stake, according to Angelou, given the state of race relations in the segregated South in the 1930s?

2. Angelou was quite young when these events occurred. How does she combine an adult's sophisticated knowledge of the past with childhood memories?

3. How does Angelou's narrative suggest the enormous, even desperate, identification that communities can have with their sports heroes? What insight does Angelou's essay offer into why Joe Louis became an icon of popular culture?

Exploring Your Cultural Perspective

1. What criteria could be used to evaluate whether a great fighter of one era is equal to or better than one of another era? For example, how might you compare the relative strengths of Joe Louis and Jack Johnson, "Sugar" Ray Robinson, Muhammad Ali, or any contemporary fighter?

2. The black athlete has always borne the additional burden (as Angelou points out) of being a standard bearer for collective achievement. Has this expectation influenced the way in which the media have covered the less-than-praiseworthy actions of some athletes, such as Mike Tyson's biting of Evander Holyfield's ear during their 1997 fight?

ARTHUR ASHE

The Burden of Race

When Arthur Ashe defeated Jimmy Connors in 1975 to win the Wimbledon singles title, he became the first black man to win the world's most prestigious grass-court tournament. A chronicle of Ashe's life includes other notable firsts, such as being the first African American player named to the U.S. Davis Cup team in 1963 and the first black to win the U.S. Open in 1968 (a tournament now played in the Arthur Ashe Stadium in Forest Hills, New York). He also became the first black pro to play in South Africa's championships in 1973, when the country was still under apartheid. What makes these victories so poignant is that, during double-bypass surgery in 1983, Ashe received blood contaminated with HIV and died ten years later from AIDS. This essay, taken from his memoir, *Days of Grace* (1993, written with Arnold Rampersad), contains Ashe's thoughtful reflections on the psychic toll of racism.

Thinking Critically

Ashe uses an event in his own life to raise the larger issue of the political and psychological consequences of racism. Notice how Ashe moves between telling his story and reflecting on the meaning of his experiences. To what extent have such sports as tennis and golf changed in terms of race since Ashe wrote this in 1993?

I had spent more than an hour talking in my office at home with a reporter for *People* magazine. Her editor had sent her to do a story about me and how I was coping with AIDS. The reporter's questions had been probing and yet respectful of my right to privacy. Now, our interview over, I was escorting her to the door. As she slipped on her coat, she fell silent. I could see that she was groping for the right words to express her sympathy for me before she left.

"Mr. Ashe, I guess this must be the heaviest burden you have ever had to bear, isn't it?" she asked finally.

I thought for a moment, but only a moment. "No, it isn't. It's a burden, all right. But AIDS isn't the heaviest burden I have had to bear."

"Is there something worse? Your heart attack?"

I didn't want to detain her, but I let the door close with both of us still inside. "You're not going to believe this," I said to her, "but being black is the greatest burden I've had to bear."

"You can't mean that."

"No question about it. Race has always been my biggest burden. Having to live as a minority in America. Even now it continues to feel like an extra weight tied around me."

I can still recall the surprise and perhaps even the hurt on her face. I may even have surprised myself, because I simply had never thought of comparing the two conditions before. However, I stand by my remark. Race is for me a more onerous burden than AIDS. My disease is the result of biological factors over which we, thus far, have had no control. Racism, however, is entirely made by people, and therefore it hurts and inconveniences infinitely more.

Since our interview (skillfully presented as a first-person account by me) appeared in *People* in June 1992, many people have commented on my remark. A radio station in Chicago aimed primarily at blacks conducted a lively debate on its merits on the air. Most African Americans have little trouble understanding and accepting my statement, but other people have been baffled by it. Even Donald Dell, my close friend of more than thirty years, was puzzled. In fact, he was so troubled that he telephoned me in the middle of the night from Hamburg, Germany, to ask if I had been misquoted. No, I told him, I had been quoted correctly. Some people have asked me flatly, what could *you*, Arthur Ashe, possibly have to complain about? Do you want more money or fame than you already have? Isn't AIDS inevitably fatal? What can be worse than death?

The novelist Henry James suggested somewhere that it is a complex fate being an American. I think it is a far more complex fate being an African American. I also sometimes think that this indeed may be one of those fates that are worse than death.

I do not want to be misunderstood. I do not mean to appear fatalistic, self-pitying, cynical, or maudlin. Proud to be an American, I am also proud to be an African American. I delight in the accomplishments of fellow citizens of my color. When one considers the odds against which we have labored, we have achieved much. I believe in life and hope and love, and I turn my back on death until I must face my end in all its finality. I am an optimist, not a pessimist. Still, a pall of sadness hangs over my life and the lives of almost all African Americans because of what we as a people have experienced historically in America, and what we as individuals experience each and every day. Whether one is a welfare recipient trapped in some blighted "housing project" in the inner city or a former Wimbledon champion who is easily recognized on the streets and whose home is a luxurious apartment in one of the wealthiest districts of Manhattan, the sadness is still there.

In some respects, I am a prisoner of the past. A long time ago, I made peace with the state of Virginia and the South. While I, like other blacks, was once barred from free association with whites, I returned time and time again, under the new rule of desegregation, to work with whites in my hometown and across the South. But segregation had achieved by that time what it was intended to achieve: It left me a marked man, forever aware of a shadow of contempt that lies across my identity and my sense of self-esteem. Subtly the shadow falls on my reputation, the way I know I am perceived; the mere memory of it darkens my most sunny days. I believe that the same is true for almost every African American of the slightest sensitivity and intelligence. Again, I don't want to overstate the case. I think of myself, and others think of me, as supremely self-confident. I know objectively that it is almost impossible for someone to be as successful as I have been as an athlete and to lack self-assurance. Still, I also know that the shadow is always there; only death will free me, and blacks like me, from its pall.

The shadow fell across me recently on one of the brightest days, literally and metaphorically, of my life. On 30 August 1992, the day before the U.S. Open, the USTA and I together hosted an afternoon of tennis at the National Tennis Center in Flushing Meadows, New York. The event was a benefit for the Arthur Ashe Foundation for the Defeat of AIDS. Before the start, I was nervous. Would the invited stars (McEnroe, Graf, Navratilova, et al.) show up? Would they cooperate with us, or be difficult to manage? And, on the eve of a Grand Slam tournament, would fans pay to see light-hearted tennis? The answers were all a resounding yes (just over ten thousand fans turned out). With CBS televising the event live and Aetna having provided the air time, a profit was assured. The sun shone brightly, the humidity was mild, and the temperature hovered in the low 80s.

What could mar such a day? The shadow of race, and my sensitivity, or perhaps hypersensitivity, to its nuances. Sharing the main stadium box with Jeanne, Camera, and me, at my invitation, were Stan Smith, his wife Marjory, and their daughter Austin. The two little girls were happy to see one another. During Wimbledon in June, they had renewed their friendship when we all stayed near each other in London. Now Austin, seven years old, had brought Camera a present. She had come with twin dolls, one for herself, one for Camera. A thoughtful gesture on Austin's part, and on her parents' part, no doubt. The Smiths are fine, religious people. Then I noticed that Camera was playing with her doll above the railing of the box, in full view of the attentive network television cameras. The doll was the problem; or rather, the fact that the doll was conspicuously a blond. Camera owns dolls of all colors, nationalities, and ethnic varieties. But she was now on national television playing with a blond doll. Suddenly I heard voices in my head, the voices of irate listeners to a call-in show on some "black format" radio station. I imagined insistent, clamorous callers attacking Camera, Jeanne, and me:

"Can you believe the doll Arthur Ashe's daughter was holding up at the AIDS   15
benefit? Wasn't that a shame?"

"Is that brother sick or what? Somebody ought to teach that poor child about her true black self!"

"What kind of role model is Arthur Ashe if he allows his daughter to be brain-washed in that way?"

"Doesn't the brother understand *that he is corrupting his child's mind with notions about the superiority of the white woman? I tell you, I thought we were long past that!"*

The voices became louder in my head. Despite the low humidity, I began to squirm in my seat. What should I do? Should I say, To hell with what some people might think? I know that Camera likes her blond dolls, black dolls, brown dolls, Asian dolls, Indian dolls just about equally; I know that for a fact, because I have watched her closely. I have searched for signs of racial partiality in her, indications that she may be dissatisfied with herself, with her own color. I have seen none. But I cannot dismiss the voices. I try always to live practically, and I do not wish to hear such comments on the radio. On the other hand, I do not want Austin's gift to be sullied by an ungracious response. Finally, I act.

"Jeanne," I whisper, "we have to do something."   20

"About what?" she whispers back.

"That doll. We have to get Camera to put that doll down."

Jeanne takes one look at Camera and the doll and she understands immediately. Quietly, cleverly, she makes the dolls disappear. Neither Camera nor Austin is aware of anything unusual happening. Smoothly, Jeanne has moved them on to some other distraction.

I am unaware if Margie Smith has noticed us, but I believe I owe her an explanation. I get up and go around to her seat. Softly I tell her why the dolls have disappeared. Margie is startled, dumbfounded.

"Gosh, Arthur, I never thought about that. I never *ever* thought about any-   25
thing like that!"

"You don't have to think about it," I explain. "But it happens to us, in similar situations, all the time."

"All the time?" She is pensive now.

"All the time. It's perfectly understandable. And it certainly is not your fault. You were doing what comes naturally. But for us, the dolls make for a bit of a problem. All for the wrong reasons. It shouldn't be this way, but it is."

I return to my seat, but not to the elation I had felt before I saw that blond doll in Camera's hand. I feel myself becoming more and more angry. I am angry at the force that made me act, the force of racism in all its complexity, as it spreads into the world and creates defensiveness and intolerance among the very people harmed by racism. I am also angry with myself. I am angry with myself because I have just acted out of pure practicality, not out of morality. The moral act would have been to let Camera have her fun, because she was innocent of any wrongdoing. Instead, I had tampered with her innocence, her basic human right to act impulsively, to accept a gift from a friend in the same beautiful spirit in which it was given.

30   Deeply embarrassed now, I am ashamed at what I have done. I have made Camera adjust her behavior merely because of the likelihood that some people in the African American community would react to her innocence foolishly and perhaps even maliciously. I know I am not misreading the situation. I would have had telephone calls that very evening about the unsuitability of Camera's doll. Am I being a hypocrite? Yes, definitely, up to a point. I have allowed myself to give in to those people who say we must avoid even the slightest semblance of "Eurocentric" influence. But I also know what stands behind the entire situation. Racism ultimately created the state in which defensiveness and hypocrisy are our almost instinctive responses, and innocence and generosity are invitations to trouble.

      This incident almost ruined the day for me. That night, when Jeanne and I talked about the excitement of the afternoon, and the money that would go to AIDS research and education because of the event, we nevertheless ended up talking mostly about the incident of the dolls. We also talked about perhaps its most ironic aspect. In 1954, when the Supreme Court ruled against school segregation in *Brown v. Board of Education*, some of the most persuasive testimony came from the psychologist Dr. Kenneth Clark concerning his research on black children and their pathetic preference for white dolls over black. In 1992, the dolls are still a problem.

      Once again, the shadow of race had fallen on me.

Engaging the Text

1. What expectations did Ashe have for the event on August 30, 1992? Why was it an especially important day for him?

2. What does Ashe's reaction to the incident with the doll (which was quickly resolved) tell you about him? Why was it important to Ashe to forestall criticism that he was overreacting?

Exploring Your Cultural Perspective

1. Ashe refers to the testimony of Dr. Kenneth Clark on the low self-esteem of black children produced by segregated schools. Research the 1954 *Brown*

v. Board of Education Supreme Court decision for more information on Clark's testimony. What role did black children's playing with white dolls assume in the decision to integrate public schools?

2. Why was seeing his young daughter playing with a blonde doll so disturbing to Ashe? How does the no-win situation in which he found himself help explain his statement that "race is for me a more onerous burden than AIDS"?

BONNIE DE SIMONE

Mia Hamm: Grateful for Her Gifts

Mia Hamm was born in Selma, Alabama, in 1972—fittingly, the year in which Title IX, requiring gender equity in sports in any educational institution that receives federal funds, was approved. Mia Hamm's remarkable achievements include being one of only a few players to score 100 goals in soccer, being named U.S. Soccer's Female Athlete of the Year for three consecutive years (1994–1996), and being a member of the Gold Medal–winning U.S. Women's National Team at the 1996 Olympic Games. This article by Bonnie De Simone (reprinted from *Women's Soccer: The Game and the World Cup*, edited by Jim Trecker and Charles Miers [1999]) provides an unusual behind-the-scenes look at the athlete who is generally considered the best female soccer player in the world.

Thinking Critically
When you read, keep in mind that girls who play soccer (7.2 million in 1998) are now the norm. In what other sports do girls regularly compete? In which sports do boys and girls compete together?

She has given her sport a face.

A heart-shaped face.

A game face.

Mia Hamm has nothing left to prove, yet she plays on. She is only 27 years old. That's easy to forget, because she has always been there. Women's soccer, like a slow-motion film of a tulip opening, has bloomed out of adolescence into adulthood right along with her.

5   Hamm has helped win every title there is to win: in college, at the world level, at the Goodwill Games, in the Olympic Games. She will almost certainly finish her career as the world's all-time leading scorer, which is a bit like saying that Secretariat was a few lengths better than the other horses, or that Michael Jordan sure could jump. Hamm has set the bar so high that it is hard to imagine anyone else clearing it.

Only once has Hamm been part of a team that failed to meet expectations: in 1995 when the U.S. women, the defending champions, finished third at the World Cup in Sweden. It wasn't for lack of effort by Hamm, who was later voted team MVP. In one match, with goalkeeper Briana Scurry ejected and no more subs left, Hamm pulled on the big splayed gloves and marched resolutely into the net. She did not, of course, allow a goal.

So there is, after all, one more mission. To regain the World Cup trophy, at home. The response would most likely be different than it was eight years ago, when resounding silence greeted the National Team on its return from winning the inaugural World Championship in China.

Now, the United States is Mia Hamm's personal version of "Cheers." Everybody knows her name. Nike put it on a building at corporate headquarters. Pert used it to sell shampoo. Hamm was voted the most marketable female athlete in the country last year by *The Sports Business Daily*, finishing ahead of figure skaters Michelle Kwan and Tara Lipinski and tennis star Venus Williams. *People* magazine put her among its 50 Most Beautiful.

Mia-mania reigns after nearly every U.S. National Team match, when hundreds of grade-school sopranos sing her name from the sidelines, pleading for autographs. She obliges, over and over. Ambassadorships are supposed to be soft jobs, but Hamm and her teammates are evidence to the contrary.

"We're going to sign for as long as it takes," Hamm said after a match last   *10* June. "Every time we step on the field we know the responsibility we have. We take it very seriously."

She speaks softly. There is a layer of Texas and the Carolinas in her voice and perhaps even a latent hint of Italy, where her father Bill, a retired Air Force colonel, was stationed when she was a little girl.

Being a public figure is somewhat of a discipline for Hamm, a keenly private person. But passion and discipline describe her both on and off the field. To understand what drives her, you first have to understand the experiences that have taught her how precious and temporal life's gifts can be.

Her grandfather and her uncle, a government geologist, were killed in a plane crash on an expedition in Alaska the very week that Hamm made her first appearance for the U.S. team in 1987. She was just 15, the youngest player, male or female, ever to wear a national team uniform.

Hamm went on to glory at the University of North Carolina, where she scored 103 goals and helped win four NCAA titles, taking a year off in midstream to help win the 1991 World Championship.

Shortly before the 1996 Olympic Games, Hamm was rocked again when   *15* Navy Admiral Jeremy Boorda, a close family friend for whom Bill Hamm once served as chief advisor, took his own life.

Hamm grieved, then set her focus back on the Olympic Games. She was hobbled by a sprained ankle for much of the tournament but still contributed her share and more, setting up the winning goal in the gold-medal game against China. The 76,489 fans who watched that match in Athens, Georgia, constituted the largest crowd ever to witness a women's sporting event.

After the match, Hamm sought out her family and fell into the arms of her brother, Garrett, her original athletic idol. As it turned out, it would be the last triumph they celebrated together.

Hamm, the third of four girls, distinctly recalls the day she got an older brother. New and strange toys multiplied in the closet: baseballs and gloves, footballs, skateboards. Garrett Hamm was a Vietnam War child, shy and insecure from having lived with three different families by the time the Hamms adopted him at age eight.

Yet he was completely confident with a ball in his hands or at his feet. And when tiny, dainty Mia, named for her mother's favorite dance instructor, followed him to his touch football games, he picked her for his team when no one else would and sent her out on the post pattern.

20   "She was his secret weapon," said Hamm's mother, Stephanie. "He knew what great hands she had and how fast she was."

Mia followed Garrett into soccer, too, and it will forever be her sorrow that he had to quit while she kept playing.

Garrett Hamm struggled for years with the consequences of a rare blood disorder that forced him to give up the sports he loved. He died at the age of 28 on April 16, 1997, when a fungal infection overtook his weakened immune system two months after he underwent a bone marrow transplant. He left behind a wife and a toddler son.

At the time of the transplant, Mia made the difficult decision to go public to try to raise money for her brother's medical expenses. "I knew that with the financial situation that he was in, it was going to be a struggle," she said. "I was given a gift, and I was willing to do anything to help that. I remember thinking, 'I don't care if I have to beg.' And it was amazing, the response I got." A benefit game between the National Team and a group of college all-stars netted $50,000. The match, now used to promote awareness of the National Bone Marrow Registry, has become an annual tradition called The Garrett Game.

When Garrett died, the National Team was preparing for a belated six-game victory tour to celebrate its Olympic success. Mia requested a leave of absence for the first two matches. She and her family buried Garrett in a quiet ceremony in Wichita Falls, Texas.

25   Two weeks later, Mia was back, running on the diagonal, ponytail snapping smartly behind her like the colors of a depleted, but still-defiant, brigade. With the pure act of movement, she saluted her brother. In a torrential downpour in Milwaukee, she scored twice and made one assist in the first 16 minutes she was on the field.

She made her point. She always does. She is determined to use the gifts of a healthy body and a healthy spirit to their utmost. In a way, she will always play for two. "When Garrett passed away, there was no bitterness," Hamm said. "He didn't want us to feel guilty. He knew we'd be sad, but he would want us to remember him most by going out and doing the things that he couldn't do and the things we love to do. I'd give up all this in a heartbeat to have him back, just to give him one more day or one more week. But I know Garrett wouldn't want that."

Throughout Hamm's soccer journey, her teammates have hiked right alongside, never a deferential step behind. They keep her grounded, eliminating the static that can overwhelm an athlete of her stature. They challenge her, they needle her, and several of them are so spectacular in their own right that they keep Hamm from being constantly double-teamed.

After Hamm became just the third player ever to score 100 goals last September in a U.S. Women's Cup match in Rochester, New York, she made a characteristically modest statement. "The crowd was great, and it was a lot of fun, but it was even better because I could share it with my teammates," she said. "I wouldn't have scored any goals without them, and it's a credit to this team that we can have moments like this."

Her humility is no act. Hamm is one of the least spoiled superstars of the modern age. Yet there's an obvious irony: She has spoiled us forever. Her artistry has become habitual, expected. How many times has she split defenders on the run, or appeared magically in the one spot on the field where no opponent thought to go?

We tend to take her skills for granted.   30

She doesn't.

We shouldn't.

Engaging the Text

1. The keynote of De Simone's account of Mia Hamm is the unusual humility and reserve the soccer star displays. What does this emphasis imply about other U.S. superstars?

2. How does knowing about the tragedies in Hamm's life add to the reader's understanding of her?

3. De Simone establishes Hamm as a public icon by referring to her marketability, affiliation with Nike, and elevation by *People* magazine. What do these connections imply about the way icons are constructed?

Exploring Your Cultural Perspective

1. For a cross-cultural perspective, look into the impact of Egypt's Sara Mohammed in putting women's soccer on the map in a country where

Arabic tradition creates special challenges for women playing sports. A good starting point is the Women's Soccer Foundation Web site at <http://www.womensoccer.org>.

2. In an essay, discuss the phenomenon of women's team sports (such as soccer, basketball, softball, volleyball) and its impact on North American culture's traditional emphasis on stars. You might include the growing role played by organized team sports (soccer and softball, for example) in the lives of middle-class suburban girls.

JOAN RYAN

Little Girls in Pretty Boxes

With its precision acrobatics that combine elements of dancing and gymnastics with raw strength and courage, ice skating has become one of today's most popular sports. Joan Ryan, an award-winning columnist for the *San Francisco Chronicle*, has investigated the behind-the-scenes pressures applied to young female athletes. Ryan has won eleven Associated Press Sports Editors Awards. Her 1995 book, *Little Girls in Pretty Boxes: The Making and Breaking of Elite Gymnasts and Figure Skaters*, was made into a movie by Lifetime television. Ryan has also written (with Tara Vanderveer) *Shooting from the Outside: How a Coach and Her Olympic Team Transform Women's Basketball* (1997).

Thinking Critically

As you read, underline the key points in Ryan's essay to better understand how her analysis of ice skaters and gymnasts supports her thesis. Write your responses to her points in the margins (including questions and points on which you agree or disagree).

Though Nancy Kerrigan was twenty-four when she won the silver medal at the 1994 Olympics—old by skating standards—she had the slight body of a teenage fashion model. Her coach Evy Scotvold told Kerrigan she could succeed only if she prevented nature from taking its course. "As soon as it's a woman's body, it's over," he says. "When they have lovely figures like the girl on the street, they're probably too heavy [for skating]. The older you get trying to do children's athletics, the thinner you must be."

Scotvold weighed his skaters at least once a week and forgave neither puberty nor body type for a skater's being anything but rail thin. When Kerrigan put on a few pounds in 1993 at age twenty-three, for example, she told Scotvold her body was going through its natural maturing process. Nonsense, Scotvold said. Rigorous self-discipline can beat back nature. Keep the weight down and your body won't change. "You can make Twiggies out of anybody," he says.

In truth, the perfect skater is a combination of Twiggy and Barbie, thin enough to perform the difficult jumps and desirable enough to fit skating's cover-girl image. Dating back to Sonja Henie in the 1920s, when she introduced dazzling fur-trimmed costumes, skaters have fed the cultural fantasy of the ideal female: young, beautiful, refined, glamorous, wholesomely sexy and, of course, thin. Creating a skating star, like creating a movie star, is as much an exercise in politics and public relations as it is in coaching and training. "It's a packaging process, very much so," Scotvold says. "You're trying to create a princess of the ice . . . You try to make sure they know they have to behave, have good manners and be well-dressed. They know they will be watched on and off the ice."

"Image," as another coach bluntly puts it, "is everything." Four-time U.S. champion Linda Fratianne once hired a special coach to teach her how to smile while she skated. Off-ice training often includes "mirror time," when skaters practice the facial expressions they'll use in their programs. In skating no aesthetic detail goes unnoticed, on or off the ice. "The judges would see you in the hotel lobby and you had to look perfect," recalls one Olympian. "Everything counts. You do your hair and makeup even in practice during Nationals. If you had a hole in your tights—oh my God!"

5   "Hair and weight are everything in this sport," says ice dancer Susie Wynne, only slightly exaggerating.

One Olympic skater, who has requested anonymity, recalls days on end when she ate one can of asparagus and a frozen diet dinner and drank a dozen cups of coffee and diet Coke in a quest to fit her coach's image of the perfect skating body. She had seen what happened when her sister gained weight. The coach pulled the scale into the lobby of the rink, where girls were putting on their skates. The coach summoned the Olympian's sister and made the mortified young girl stand on the scale and announce her weight. "If you were skating better at a hundred and five pounds but looked better at a hundred, your coach wanted you to be a hundred," the Olympian says. For weeks before a competition, skaters would starve themselves, holding on to the thought of bingeing when they finished competing. "We lived for food," says one. "It's so funny to watch a group of skaters after they finish a competition. As soon as we got off the ice, we headed right for Mrs. Fields [cookie stand]. We'd eat until we felt sick. You'd be disgusted if you saw it."

Skaters who didn't throw up regularly understand why others, like Susie Wynne, did. "Even if you know something's not good for you," says one skater, "you don't think long-term. You think *now*: 'I need to lose five pounds.'" Wynne began vomiting at age nineteen when she gained weight during the off-season. To appease her angry coach, Wynne began throwing up before his daily 7 A.M. weigh-in. Then she threw up after every meal. Once, when Wynne's weight was still too high for her coach's liking, he told her to lose

10 pounds by week's end or he wasn't taking her to the national championships. Wynne stopped eating, threw up, took laxatives, tried everything. She lost the weight, and her coach was happy. He never asked how she did it.

By then Wynne knew she had a problem. She was losing control. Food became the focus of her life off the ice. She had stopped eating in front of people but binged in private. She would eat an entire pizza in a sitting, then vomit. She hated what she was doing, but she couldn't tell anyone. Her parents would have pulled her out of the sport. Her coach, she felt, didn't want to know. Oblivious to her turmoil, he kept weighing her every day. "It became overwhelming," Wynne recalls.

She found herself in church one day, listening to a priest's sermon about turning one's burdens over to God. "Take it away," Wynne prayed. "Here, God. I can't deal with it."

Soon afterward she found a support group for bulimics, hired a nutritionist and began running every day. Most important, she left her coach. "Nobody," she told her new coach, "is weighing me in. If anybody talks to me about weight, I'm leaving." 10

Twenty-nine, married and still competing in 1994, she wants to shake every young skater she hears fretting about her weight. Today's skaters, she says, are no smarter than she was. The same dramas keep playing out over and over again. "Now I don't weigh myself. Why should I let that thing control my life? Why should I let that little number tell me if I'm going to have a good day or a bad day?"

But the message in skating is clear: Be thin and win. When thirteen-year-old Michelle Kwan stood on the podium to accept her silver medal at the 1994 U.S. Figure Skating Championships, one skating observer cracked, "Sure she can do it now, but wait till she gets older and her body changes."

One of Michelle's coaches, Evelyn Kramer, overheard the remark and seethed, nearly spitting her words, "It's a whole image sport. It's bullshit."

Kramer is a maverick among skating's coaches. She's loud, earthy, irreverent—the anti-princess. She once told quiet and feminine Caryn Kadavy she ought to give her coach a nice "fuck you" every now and then. "I've been told," Kramer says in her unfiltered Brooklyn accent, "I'm vulgar." She holds a master's degree in psychology—earning her the nickname Rink Shrink—so she knows something about the complicated interplay between weight and self-esteem. She says every female skater she's ever known, with the exception of Kadavy, has had eating disorders. She knows a Russian ice dancer who had her teeth capped because they had been eroded by the acid in her vomit. She knows of an Olympic medalist who began pulling her hair out as she battled bulimia.

Kramer herself, now in her fifties, says she still can't shake her own preoc- 15 cupation with weight and food, which she developed as a young skater. She ate herself out of the sport as a teenager, secretly consuming whole boxes of candy because her coach and her parents harangued her so incessantly about weight. Her mother put a lock on the kitchen door. "I still talk about my body all the time. My weight is up and down. <u>I'm obsessed with food. I think about it all the time.</u> If I hadn't been in a sport like this while my body was going through puberty, I wouldn't have been so preoccupied with it. Nobody told me what was going on. I felt it was my fault my body changed. I was told I had no self-control. The change is emotional as well as physical, and the emotional feelings manifest themselves in food."

When her daughter, Jessica, began skating, she sent her to a nutritionist to avoid a repeat of her own childhood pain. Yet Kramer found herself inflicting other abuses. "Look at all these girls your age and they're doing more," Kramer would snap at Jessica. "All I care about," answered Jessica, "is what I do."

Kramer confesses to having pinched her, punched her and screamed at her. "I'd say hateful things, all because of skating. I don't feel like I was living through her. It wasn't that. I think it was because there is nothing like seeing your own kid go out there. No higher high, no scarier scare."

She finally realized that history was repeating itself. The craving for success that had driven her own mother to lock the kitchen door had seized Kramer too. She would do anything to push her daughter to win. Skating for the joy of it, as Jessica wanted, went against everything Kramer had learned in life. Winning was the only truly respected virtue. And in skating, there is no simpler indicator of success than body type.

The inevitable evolution of the sport's appetite for ever thinner, ever younger skaters was on display at the 1994 U.S. Championships in the shape of Michelle Kwan, an eighth grader from Mary P. Henck Intermediate School in Torrance, California. She was in third place after the technical program, and ten rows of reporters in the press room of the Joe Louis Arena in Detroit wanted to know what music would accompany her long program. She leaned hesitantly toward the microphone, her eyebrows arching and her mouth twisting sheepishly like a child who hadn't read the homework assignment. "Ummm," she stammered, shrugging and giggling and looking at her coach, Frank Carroll, seated beside her.

20   "*Man from Snowy River*," Carroll told her.

"*Man from Snowy River*," Kwan repeated into the microphone. "And . . ." Kwan giggled again and looked at Carroll once more. She had been rehearsing to this music every day for months. She had no idea what it was.

"*East of Eden*," Carroll prompted.

If Kwan's success at the 1994 U.S. Championships at the age of thirteen left any doubts that ladies' figure skating had become, like gymnastics, a sport for children, the Olympics a month later removed them. Flanking American Nancy Kerrigan on the winners' podium in Lillehammer were two wispy sixteen-year-olds, Oksana Baiul and Chen Lu, neither of whom weighed more than 95 pounds or stood more than 5 feet 1 inch tall.

Size informs every step of a skater's career. At one competition press conference, coach Kathy Casey fielded a question about the progress of her skater, sixteen-year-old Nicole Bobek. Casey didn't hesitate with her answer: "She's learned to handle her growth, and she lost a little weight." End of answer. She mentioned nothing about Bobek's learning new jumps or becoming more graceful.

Coaches become so attuned to their skaters' bodies they can usually detect 25 even the slightest weight gain. When Alex McGowan coached national champion and Olympic medalist Debi Thomas, he knew by watching the height of her jumps if she had gained a few pounds. His current pupil, fifteen-year-old Lisa Talbot, went home to the Midwest for three days during Christmas and when she returned to McGowan in California, he took one look at her and said, "You put on two pounds." She had.

"I always say to them, 'You never see a fat ballerina at the ballet,'" McGowan says.

Though weight and appearance have always counted in figure skating, the sport rewards the lighter skaters more richly than ever because scores now depend so much on acrobatic triple jumps. School figures—the torturously boring exercise of tracing figures in the ice—used to count for 60 percent of a skater's total score, with the technical and free-skate programs making up the rest. Mastering school figures took years, thus skewing competitions in favor of older skaters. Skating dropped school figures from elite competition in 1990; now the two-minute-and-forty-second technical program counts for 33.3 percent and the four-minute free-skate program for 66.7 percent. Triple jumps separate the great long programs from the merely good. Sonja Henie's most difficult jump when she won three consecutive Olympic gold medals from 1928 to 1936 was a single Axel, a jump with one-and-a-half revolutions in the air. Dorothy Hamill won the Olympic gold in 1976 with a double Axel as her flashiest jump. Now a strong long program includes five or six triple jumps, even from the juniors. Kwan won the 1993 U.S. Olympic Festival at age thirteen by landing six clean triples.

Making the jumps means staying light and thin. The less weight a skater has to haul into the air, the better her prospects of completing the jump. Tonya Harding, with her thick, pear-shaped body, seemed to contradict the weight maxim because her jumps were the strength of her skating. She was the only American female ever to land the three-and-a-half-revolution triple Axel. But she landed the triple Axel consistently only when her weight was low. After winning the 1991 U.S. Championships with the triple Axel, she landed only one more in competition for the remainder of her career, at the 1991 Skate America in Oakland.

Though skating doesn't see the traumatic injuries that plague gymnastics, the increasingly difficult skills demanded by the sport have brought their share of stress fractures, broken bones and torn muscles, which is why many in skating would like to see the jumps deemphasized. "I keep saying it's not necessary,

that triples aren't everything," says Joan Burns, a top U.S. judge from California. "There are four elements to figure skating: jumps, spins, footwork and
choreography. They all have to be good, not just the jumps."

30   Nevertheless, skating's new archetype, as represented by Kwan, is small,
thin and prepubescent, strong enough to launch into the air but light enough
to soar high, spin quickly and land softly. When Kwan glided effortlessly across
the ice at the 1994 national championships in Detroit, she drew longing
glances from older and larger skaters.

One competitor, however, watched Kwan with knowing eyes. Twenty-
eight-year-old Elaine Zayak had been in Kwan's shoes once—young, small and
extraordinarily gifted. Like Kwan, Zayak was the rising star in a country hungry for its next pixie icon. Then something doomed her career. She grew up.

Zayak won the 1981 U.S. Championships at age fifteen and had no doubts
about winning it again the following year and the year after that. She was
bulletproof. No one could jump the way she could. She finished second at the
1981 World Figure Skating Championships, a remarkable achievement for one
so young. She was going to be the best there ever was. She dropped out of
ninth grade to train seven days a week, six hours a day. A New Jersey girl who
had lost half her foot in a lawnmower accident as a toddler, Elaine was the toast
of nearby New York City. The reporters there loved this unlikely skating
queen. She talked like a truck-stop waitress, spewing double negatives, laughing from her belly, sharing every notion that crossed her mind.

But at the 1982 U.S. Championships she fell three times and finished third.
While the failure rattled Elaine's coaches and parents, it nearly paralyzed
Elaine. She was scared to return to the ice, especially at the upcoming World
Championships. What if she embarrassed herself again? What if everybody
laughed at her? The pressure and fear closed in on her. In her hotel room the
day and night before the competition, she cried for hours on end. "Don't make
me do this," she pleaded to her parents. "Don't make me go out there and make
a fool of myself again."

Elaine's mother cried with her. "Just try," her mother said. "If you don't at
least try, you won't be happy." Her father, exasperated, retreated to the hotel bar.

35   "Okay, Mom," Elaine finally conceded. "But no matter what happens,
whether I skate well or not, this is it, all right? I don't want to compete anymore."

"Okay."

Elaine won, but the euphoria touched her like a breeze, light and fleeting,
barely felt. She was relieved more than anything. Now maybe everybody would
get off her back. But even her mother joined the chorus: "How can you quit *now?*"

After the World Championships, Elaine returned to school—but for just
two hours a day, from eight to ten every morning. It was a joke. She wasn't
learning or working toward anything. "But so what," she thought. She had
contracts worth $300,000 to skate in ice shows. She had her own fully loaded

sports car. Her hometown erected a sign at the edge of town: PARAMUS, HOME OF WORLD CHAMPION ELAINE ZAYAK. Life had handed this daughter of a tavern owner one of the grandest jewels in the figure skating crown. Dorothy Hamill, Peggy Fleming, Sonja Henie. Elaine Zayak's name would be chiseled alongside theirs on the exclusive list of world champions.

But now Elaine wanted out of competitive skating. After doing ice shows for two months, she took off with some friends to Florida and didn't train for two more. She had been skating since she was a toddler as therapy for her partially severed foot and by age ten was training six hours a day, traveling two and a half hours round-trip from New Jersey to a rink on Long Island. At sixteen she was tired. Tired of the United States Figure Skating Association telling her what she could and couldn't say in interviews. Tired of judges calling her parents to suggest she see a dermatologist for a patch of acne on her face—and, by the way, she ought to wear more pink. Tired of hearing about how her parents scrimped to pay the $25,000-a-year tab for her skating.

More than anything, she was tired of everyone harping about her weight. *40* Elaine never looked like a ballerina. She was never going to be Peggy Fleming or Carol Heiss no matter how much she dieted. To make matters worse, she had begun menstruating the year before. Before puberty, girls have 10 to 15 percent more body fat than boys; after puberty, girls have 50 percent more. Elaine was feeling the change. By the time she returned from Florida in early summer, she had gained 15 pounds. No longer the girlish sprite, she found herself in the midst of a whirling battle with her coaches, her parents and her own body. Now more than ever, she wanted to quit. Her parents, upset she was throwing away everything for which she and they had worked so hard, grounded her. "It was basically, 'You don't have a say in this,'" Elaine recalls. "They felt I couldn't make my own decisions." They took away her new car— and Elaine's father infuriated her by driving it himself. Angry and frustrated and feeling that without skating even her own family had no respect for her, she stormed out of the house one night with no clear idea where to go. She ended up at the home of a classmate she barely knew and stayed for a week without telling her parents where she was. "I really didn't even want to hang out with my friends. I didn't know what I wanted to do," Elaine says.

One night Elaine and her friend missed their ten-thirty curfew and the girl's parents locked them out. The world figure skating champion huddled in a New Jersey backyard all night, sleeping on the grass like a vagabond.

Inevitably, her parents and coaches wore her down and she returned to the rink. It was already August. The competitive season would begin in October. And her weight had climbed to 125 pounds. "I felt like I was normal size," she recalls. "To me, it just didn't look like I was fourteen or fifteen anymore . . . You gain weight in those years even if you're not eating much. You gain weight because you're physically becoming a woman. My father didn't understand that. He goes, 'That's bullshit.'"

Elaine couldn't open the refrigerator door without her parents quizzing her. She tried Weight Watchers and Diet Center. She biked. She hired a nutritionist. Her coaches weighed her every week, exhorting her to lose more. But the weight wouldn't come off. Desperate, Elaine tried amphetamines, given to her by a classmate. She succeeded only in making herself sick.

So she conceded the battle. What else could she do that she wasn't doing? She began to eat in secret. The more she was told not to eat, the more she ate. In her mind she was claiming control for the first time in her life. Her sport, like gymnastics, was all about control: coaches' control, parents' control, physical control, emotional control. Her coaches could order her back into training, her parents could take away her car, they could forbid her to date—they could dictate everything in her life, but they couldn't dictate what she ate. She would eat whatever she pleased. Eating was a rebellion, but it was also a refuge. As world champion, she knew she was expected to win every competition through the 1984 Olympics, still two years away. Food became a drug, dulling her anxieties.

45   Because she couldn't eat at home, she stuffed herself at convenience stores and delicatessens. Once, when she tried to buy a bagel and cream cheese at the deli near the rink, the man behind the counter wouldn't serve her. "Coaches' orders," the man said. Elaine's coaches had instructed him not to sell her anything but tea and coffee. Humiliated, she drove to the 7-Eleven down the road, bought a pint of ice cream and ate it in the parking lot.

Marylynn Gelderman shudders as she recalls how she and Peter Burrows coached Elaine. "Elaine was our first Olympian. I was very young, and we were a very hungry school. Here was one of the most talented people ever to hit skating, and she's eating and growing. So you panic. I think now that I look back on it, I would never do that again. I would handle it very differently." Gelderman doesn't weigh her skaters anymore. Instead, she emphasizes how much easier they can jump and spin when they're smaller and lighter. "Those who want to lose weight, will." She shrugs. "Those who don't, won't."

Elaine tried throwing up after she ate, but she couldn't. By late September, with competitions a month away, Elaine panicked. The extra pounds were straining her right foot, which bore more than its share of weight to compensate for the half-severed left foot. A friend, a Harvard-educated former skater, told Elaine she had lost 10 pounds in one week with diet pills. Elaine flew up to Boston for the day without telling her parents and visited the friend's doctor, who prescribed the pills. What the woman, then a coach in Boston, didn't tell Elaine was that the pills were on the United States Olympic Committee's list of banned substances.

"It was very hush-hush," Elaine remembers. "Nobody knew about it. My mother would just die if she knew I was doing drugs. It's not something you want people to know about, especially if you're national and world champion."

Tipped off by Elaine's dramatic mood swings, Gelderman found out about the pills and pitched a fit. "You won't make the Olympic team if you get tested!" she told the skater. "Get rid of them!" Elaine first waited until she lost 10 pounds.

But plagued by nagging leg and ankle injuries and doomed by her wom- *50* anly figure, she would never again be the skater who won the World Championships seven months earlier. The press, once so gushing, wrote that she was fat and washed up. "Look what kind of world champion you turned out to be," her father said to her one day. Elaine stopped talking to him. She never won another national title, finishing second in 1983 and third in 1984. She finished sixth at the 1984 Olympics. In the ice shows afterward, she skated in the supporting cast—no Olympic medal, no starring role. She tried going to Monmouth College in New Jersey and she worked in a deli for a while. She tried coaching. Nothing stuck. With only a high school degree, she found few opportunities.

"This sport is so unforgiving," says ABC's Jurina Ribbens. "Finish second and all of a sudden you're a has-been. They don't look at the long term. They should have let Elaine finish third or fourth for a while, then allow her to come back at her own pace. There's too much emphasis on winning and winning young."

Engaging the Text

1. What impact do stringent rules have on the lives of competitive female figure skaters?

2. Although this chapter from Ryan's 1995 book is presented as an objective report, her attitude toward the subject is clear. What do you think she hoped to achieve by writing this book?

3. Many of the athletes Ryan mentions are familiar to the public. What insight does Ryan's behind-the-scenes account give you into the pressures that drive these female stars?

Exploring Your Cultural Perspective

1. Image and weight are all-important in the lives of skaters and gymnasts. To what extent does their situation reflect an important theme in American culture? Are these athletes so highly valued because they represent an unattainable ideal?

2. In a short essay, discuss the social consequences of female gymnasts and skaters who, as icons, unwittingly encourage young girls to become anorexic and/or bulimic.

LIN SUTHERLAND

A River Ran over Me

With the success of the book and film *A River Ran through It* (1992), fly-fishing has attained unprecedented popularity in recent years. Lin Sutherland is an award-winning writer who specializes in travel and humor. Her articles and stories have been published in *Field and Stream, Outdoor Photographer, Women's Day,* and numerous other magazines. She is a contributor to *Uncommon Waters: Women Write about Fly Fishing* (1994) and *The Little Book of Fishing* (1994). Sutherland has just completed a memoir about her unconventional family called *KinSHIP HAPPENS.* "A River Ran over Me" first appeared in *A Different Angle: Fly Fishing Stories by Women,* edited by Holly Morris (1995).

Thinking Critically

"If fishing is a religion, then fly-fishing is high church," according to NBC's Tom Brokaw. As you read Sutherland's story, consider how the author interweaves religious metaphors to describe the unique pleasures of fly-fishing.

Fly fishing is beyond sport, skill, and even obsession. It's a religion, and my baptism into the faith was on the Gunnison River in Colorado. I thought I was merely going to learn something new and different. I didn't anticipate the dogma, the intricate litany, the saints, the tithing, the penance. Nor did I anticipate my mother would become the Joan of Arc of fly fishing.

It started out innocently enough. I chose to take my first stab at fly fishing with Mama because she was a Bass Master of the First Order, the Blood Bait Queen of my youth. But at the age of seventy-two, Mama discovered fly fishing, and as usual, she took something complicated and learned it in about three weeks. Face it, for a woman who took eleven years of Latin in Charleston, South Carolina, anything is easy.

At first she had been skeptical.

"Buncha little snots," she'd remark about fly fishermen. "Effete elitist purists," she'd add.

Then one day she was forced to stop at a little specialty angling shop   *5*
instead of her usual Live Bait Marina. It was the kind of place that displays fly
fishing *ensembles*—and the only reason she went in there was to look for a particular fishing book.

Mama stood there in the front of the store with her calico mane flying and
took in the woven creels, leather belts, fifty-dollar floppy fishing hats and six-
hundred-dollar graphite rods.

"HEY!" she shouted. "What kind of foo foo fish shop is this?"

Several customers looked around at her and a pony-tailed young man
wearing a very expensive fly fishing shirt with a little fly and hook embroidered
on its breast pocket rushed forward.

"Yes, Ma'am? May I help you?" he asked.

"Where the hell are your foo foo fish books, young man?" She looked him   *10*
up and down, then jabbed his chest with one big-knuckled forefinger.

"Young man, you have feathers embroidered on your chest. Just what does
that mean?"

He stammered and opened his mouth.

"Never mind!" she interrupted. "I don't want to know. . . . Hey, here it is—"
She reached behind a polished wood counter and pulled out the book she sought.

To make a long story short, Mama and the young man got into a conversation, most of which consisted of her railing about how none of her daughters
could fish worth a plugged nickel. The young man turned out to be John
Tavenner, a well-respected fly fishing guide from Santa Fe who pulls trout regularly out of the Rio Grande, which hardly anyone could consider a trout
stream. He showed my mother boxes of thousands of flies he'd carefully constructed out of chicken necks, hare's ears, and the like. He was twenty-eight
but had started fly fishing with his father at the age of twelve.

As happens often to those who meet my mother, Tavenner became   *15*
intrigued. Mama has a blunt exterior, but you never doubt she's a lady. A Southern lady, at that. Her piercing china-blue eyes shine with intelligence and interest . . . she simply exudes life. The two began to talk fishing, and it wasn't long
before Tavenner invited her to attend one of his fly fishing clinics. And that was
that. She was the best he'd ever instructed, he told me later. She had the knack.

Working relentlessly, Mama became an expert in about four months, then
a total convert. There is nothing worse than a convert, you know, and the next
summer she all but forced me to join her and Tavenner at the bottom end of
the Black Canyon of the Gunnison River known for its gold-medal waters. We
camped in a delightful overhang of cliffs, where the river was crystal clear and
lively and the rapids abundant.

On our first day out, I watched Tavenner land and release one rainbow
trout after another. He approached fly fishing as kind of a cross between religion and reincarnation.

"You need to become the fish," he explained excitedly to me. "You visualize what the *fish* wants, not what you want. You let your intuitive side override the thinking part of your brain."

"Right-brained fishing?" I inquired.

20 He considered a moment. "Yes. You're triggering their fish archetypes which have evolved over generations to strike at a certain object. So you have to be intuitive to anticipate what they want. Thinking is a slowing-down process. Action and reaction. That's why it's spiritual."

"So what's the first commandment?" I asked.

"Presentation," he replied. "Presentation is everything."

"Ah," I nodded knowingly, not having the faintest clue what he meant. But I learned.

The Gunnison happens to be perfect for trout. It is not just one river, but a series of them layered into a single, sometimes chaotic unit. At the bottom is the river of sand, then there is the river of water above, and above that a river of air. Within those three are the rivers of life: the snails, insects, snakes, frogs, cephalopods, nutria, beaver, otter, and then the eagles and ospreys that swoop down to snatch the top of the water food chain, the trout.

25 Trout, as everyone knows, are wily, skitterish and fine-tasting. They are the highest predator in the river, except for the fly fishermen, who attempt to imitate what the trout are eating, often at great trouble and expense, and talk about the "hatches" as if they were Saint's Days. It so happened that the Gunnison had just seen one of the biggest hatches of stone flies, and as a result the trout had "shoulders." Anyway, that's what Mama told me.

"How can a trout have shoulders?" I asked. "They don't even have necks."

"They're hogs," she replied. "Fat and sassy." Mama goes for only two kinds of fish—hogs and lunkers. These are leftover terms from her bass days, and they're self-explanatory.

Of course, fly fishing has a language of its own—a litany as oblique as any service in Latin. Tavenner was well-versed in the arcane terminology. He spoke to us of P.M.D., which at first I assumed was some kind of insect P.M.S., a femme fly in a nasty mood. It turned out to be a Pale Morning Dun. I was relieved P.M.S. had not invaded the bug world.

Later he announced that he was going out nymphing and invited us to come along. Visions of young things flitting through the wild Colorado woods, with Tavenner, his ponytail flapping, in hot pursuit raced through my mind.

30 "I'll be using a common nymph," he added, as if in explanation. Dang it, I thought, *there's vulgar ones.* Then he talked about the prince. I thought the prince would probably be the one after the nymphs, but no, this guy's made of green hare's ear, imitating an emerging caddis. Only a trout would go for a green hairy fake prince, I thought. No, wait a minute—I've dated a few of those myself.

"Of course, we could use the Girdle Bitch," Mama suggested helpfully.

"What!" I exclaimed, summoning from the past nightmarish visions of my large aunts with too-tight corsets under their cotton dresses spraddled over lawn chairs in the shade after too much pecan pie at our family reunions. Seeing my expression, Mama explained that a Girdle Bitch was just another fly—a Bitch Creek Nymph with Spandex legs. Even the explanations were surreal.

"A lot of people don't tie Girdle Bitches with Spandex legs, but I do," Mama said proudly. "They're ugly—but I've caught fish on them."

I took her word for it.

Naturally, I made all the first-timer faux pas on our initial foray to the river.   *35*
In fact, the list of my sins is excruciatingly extensive:

1. I called the custom-built, monographed, nine-foot, lightweight, five-hundred-dollar graphite fly rod Tavenner let me use "a pole." "Lemme see that pole," I said cheerfully. His face contorted in pain.

2. I asked Tavenner why he didn't have "a bigger bobber." "That's a strike indicator," he informed me, his voice dripping disgust.

3. I put my arms inside my chest-waders. (I was trying to pull up my socks.)

4. I fell over in the rushing water with both my arms inside my chest-   *40*
waders. I needn't tell you how bad a mistake *that* was. The river ran over me. Baptized me. In the name of the Mother, the Sun, and the Holy Float. It would have drowned me, too, if Tavenner hadn't caught me as I washed downstream and dragged me to shore by my suspenders.

5. I hooked my hair, my leg, my backside. Mama and Tavenner moved several hundred paces upriver from me.

6. I fished with moss. "Clean the moss off your fly every second cast, why don't you, honey?" suggested Mama in a kindly fashion, after noticing my half-hour's moss-casting.

7. I forgot to look at the strike indicator. I was too occupied watching my mother jerking in hogs and lunkers repeatedly. Suddenly, I had a strike myself, but the fish was gone in a flash when I didn't set the hook.

8. When we rafted downstream to fish the riffles, I actually succeeded in hooking *and landing* a rainbow trout, but got so excited I fell out of the boat—onto my fish. It swished a lot under me. Scared me. Scared the fish, too, no doubt. I could be the only fisherman who has ever squashed her fish in the water.

But for all these transgressions and more, I did penance. All fly fishermen   *45*
do, whether they sin or not. Standing in freezing water for long periods of

time: that's the flagellation part of the religion. When I got to where I enjoyed it, I began to worry.

Mama, however, had risen to a higher plane—Cardinal status at least, if not exactly Joan of Arc. She had cut an intriguing figure out on the river, constantly moving with the smooth, fluid motion of an expert caster. It was meditational. Every once in a while the rhythm would be interrupted with an abrupt yelp, which meant she'd caught another lunker with shoulders.

All this spirituality hadn't been free, of course. Like all sects, this one included tithing. Why, one rooster neck for making flies is forty dollars, and one packet of green hare's ear hair, twelve bucks. And when you add to it the state-of-the-art graphite rods, reels, vests, waders, hats, bags, nets, and so on, it makes you gasp.

Yet the most unique item Tavenner had sold to my mother, which she wore around her neck like a vestment and never removed, was the least expensive. This was the fisherman's tool lanyard, a tool originally used for bait rigging while fishing offshore, but adapted for fly fishermen. It's particularly advantageous for deep-river waders and floaters because all the tools you need are visible and securely fastened on a lanyard around your neck, handier than having to dig through a tackle box or vest.

The typical setup includes a Swiss army knife or small scissors to cut line, hemostats to remove hooks, small needlenose pliers to debarb hooks, a leader straightener, a leader sink, silicone floatant, a hook file, and finally, a stomach pump.

50 This last item was a revelation. I've seen some pretty outrageous things done in the name of sport, like whacking off bull parts in Spain, but trout stomach pumping has to be at the top. With the first trout Mama caught, she, without warning, began to suck all the insides out of the thing.

"What are you *doing to that fish*?" I shouted, making her leap in alarm.

"Pumping out the little bugger's belly," she replied nonchalantly. "You have to see what they're eating, you know," she added instructively.

I *hadn't* known that. "There must be a better way," I insisted.

She examined the green stuff in the tube. "Shoot, nothing but moss," she muttered and dropped the dripping mess onto her shirt front, where the stain spread.

55 "Think I'll get another cup of coffee," I gagged.

You can renounce all these worldly goods and take your fly fishing back to its simplest state, as the ascetics do in any religion. For instance, Tavenner told us about a client he'd once guided on the river who fished with spines from the barrel cactus with a fly tied on. This man, Tavenner said, had explored the length and breadth of fly fishing and discovered its pure, natural form.

"That's the largest wad of horse crap I ever heard," Mama exclaimed, staring at Tavenner. She was about to say something else, but just then one of those

Amazing But True Fish Things happened. I got a strike, a good one. All of us turned our attention to the end of my line. The fish dived straight down, then shot straight up, hit the water, and flew several feet into the air. It was so fast, I couldn't keep the tension on my line. The huge rainbow coiled high in the air for a moment, glistening, poised, droplets of water spraying outward and catching the sun. Then, facing its hunter, the fish turned and spat the fly out in my face. It was well-timed and altogether amazing. I heard Mama laugh.

"That fish has been in this game before," she remarked drolly.

"That fish just made my trip," I sighed lightly with satisfaction. Gazing at the rippling water, I reflected, "It's funny, but in all my years of fishing, the ones I remember most are the big ones I've lost."

And somehow, that seemed a perfect benediction for the day.   *60*

Engaging the Text

1. What aspects of Sutherland's story suggest that she intends it to be a light-hearted satire of her mother's obsession with fly-fishing?

2. How would you characterize the narrator's relationship with her mother and the way it changes as a result of the experiences the story describes?

3. In what sense is this story intended to revise the premise that although fly-fishing was traditionally considered a male sport (akin to a rite of passage for young men), it is now an acceptable activity for women?

Exploring Your Cultural Perspective

1. Watch Robert Redford's 1992 film *A River Runs through It,* and relate the serious and satiric elements in Lin Sutherland's story to the film.

2. Is fly-fishing marketed differently to women than it is to men? You might wish to visit Women's Flyfishing at <http://www.halcyon.com/wffn/>, as well as more traditional fly-fishing Web sites.

CONNECTING THE TEXTS

1. In what areas do Carl Sagan's and Joyce Carol Oates's views of the origin of sports and their function in society overlap?

2. What is the connection between the use of animal names for teams (as classified by Carl Sagan in "Game: The Prehistoric Origin of Sports") and the Balinese obsession with fighting cocks, as described by Clifford Geertz in "The Balinese Cockfight"? In a few paragraphs, discuss the symbolism of naming teams after animals.

3. What insights do Roberto Gonzalez Echevarria in "First Pitch" and Carl Sagan in "Game: The Prehistoric Origin of Sports" offer in the way sports become politicized?

4. To what extent do competitive sports in the West, as described by Carl Sagan in "Game: The Prehistoric Origin of Sports," play the same role that the cockfight does in Bali, as described by Clifford Geertz?

5. How does boxing, as described by Joyce Carol Oates in "On Boxing," serve as a vehicle for sublimated male aggression in ways comparable to the purposes of the Balinese cockfight, as described by Clifford Geertz?

6. Compared with Arthur Ashe's dilemma about his daughter's doll (in "The Burden of Race"), Maya Angelou's account of the meaning of Joe Louis's victory (in "Champion of the World") is a tale from a simpler time. What do these two accounts suggest about changes in U.S. culture since the 1930s? Discuss the forms that racism takes in sports today.

7. In his day, Arthur Ashe ("The Burden of Race") was a role model for African Americans, much as Mia Hamm has been for young women (see Bonnie De Simone's essay). Discuss how the public perception of sports figures has changed in terms of the importance given to race or sex.

8. Women's soccer is becoming an important part of the culture of many countries. To what extent has Mia Hamm served as a catalyst for women today (see Bonnie De Simone's essay) as Joe Louis did for African Americans in the 1930s, as described by Maya Angelou in "Champion of the World"?

9. To what extent do highly trained gymnasts and skaters fulfill the same function for their coaches and parents (as described by Joan Ryan in "Little Girls in Pretty Boxes") as the roosters do in Balinese cockfights (as described by Clifford Geertz in "The Balinese Cockfight")?

10. The girls in Joan Ryan's essay "Little Girls in Pretty Boxes" are described as having to conform to rigid gender roles in order to compete. Compare the issue of gender stereotyping as it is presented in Ryan's account and in Lin Sutherland's story "A River Ran over Me."

11. Implicit in Lin Sutherland's story "A River Ran over Me" is the premise that a sport can become an obsession with quasi-religious overtones. How does her insight overlap with Clifford Geertz's analysis of the role of cockfighting as ritual in Balinese culture?

12. How do the rituals of fly-fishing (in which the fish is often put back once it has been caught) as described by Lin Sutherland connect with the hunting-gathering origin of sports discussed by Carl Sagan in "Game: The Prehistoric Origin of Sports"? In your opinion, why is fly-fishing acceptable to everyone, whereas hunting is not, at least to certain segments of the population? What cultural biases are at work?

FIGURE 8.1

WRITING ABOUT SPORTS

1. Analyze the cultural significance of any of the following sports: cricket (West Indies or England), hurling (Ireland), kendo (fencing with bamboo poles, Japan), squash (Pakistan), jai alai and stone-lifting (Basque region), ice hockey and lacrosse (Canada), rugby (England), polo (Argentina), soccer (Italy and worldwide; what does Figure 8.1 say about the popularity of soccer?).

2. Carl Sagan believes that "competitive sports are symbolic conflicts, thinly disguised." Based on this insight, what would a sport of the future look like? One possibility is the fictional blood sport known as "roller ball" featured in the 1975 movie of the same title with James Caan. Roller ball combines motorcycling, football, jai alai, the roller derby, and hand-to-hand combat. The protagonist in *Roller Ball* embodies the last vestiges of individualism in a quasi-totalitarian world of the future. Analyze *Roller Ball* in light of Sagan's insights.

3. Does your college or university depend on sports programs to increase enrollments and boost alumni contributions? Should a new football stadium cost twice as much as a new library? Why or why not?

4. Is part of the appeal of a sport all the gear required to participate? If you want to scuba dive, for example, you need masks, snorkels, regulators, tanks, buoyancy jackets, weights, fins, wet suits, lights, knives, compasses, diving watches, and whistles.

FIGURE 8.2

Select a sport, and describe the gear it requires and the symbolic meanings that gear communicates (for example, nondivers who wear diving watches).

5. Analyze how sports are reported on television or radio, and examine the connotations of the verbs used to describe the outcomes of sporting events. Discuss the way in which emotionally charged language is designed to affect the audience's perceptions. Why does the rhetoric of sports reporting differ from that used to report the weather or other aspects of the news? For example, how do the volume level, style of delivery, and film clips suggest that this segment is more important than other parts of the broadcast?

6. What benefits does a fan receive by proclaiming allegiance to a team through caps, T-shirts, sweatshirts, and other items emblazoned with the team's insignia?

7. To what extent have performance-enhancing drugs or steroids become an important component of sports in North American society? In your opinion, are athletes coerced into taking these drugs to remain competitive? Why or why not?

8. How do Eastern forms of exercise (such as tai chi or yoga) differ from traditional Western exercise, such as aerobics, push-ups, jumping jacks, or sit-ups? Analyze how

FIGURE 8.3

the objectives and methods of Eastern kinds of exercise differ from their Western counterparts.

9. In films about boxing, such as *Rocky* (1976), *Raging Bull* (1980), *When We Were Kings* (1996), and *The Hurricane* (1999), boxing becomes a metaphor for the individual's struggle against a corrupt society. In an essay, discuss what any boxing-related film reveals about the underside of society.

10. Metaphors drawn from sports have become part of everyday usage. Pick one of the following phrases and discuss the difference between its literal meaning and its metaphorical use:

- *Baseball:* cover all the bases, go to bat for, batting a thousand, hit a home run
- *Boxing:* ring someone's bell, take it on the chin, down and out
- *Football:* punt, Monday-morning quarterback, blitz
- *Bullfighting:* see red, take the bull by the horns
- *Soccer:* get a kick out of, keep the ball rolling, on the ball

11. What do Figures 8.2 and 8.3 suggest about the star power of women in traditional male sports?

12. Critics object to the staged nature of professional wrestling matches. Write an essay in which you support or challenge the claim that professional wrestling can hardly be considered a sport because it lacks sportsmanship, honor, and the pure competition that have traditionally been associated with sports. As part of your essay, research the evolution of a professional wrestler, such as Stone Cold Steve Austin or Jesse Ventura, who went on to become the governor of Minnesota on the independent ticket.

CHAPTER 9

Worldly Goods

> *Modern man, if he dared to be articulate about his concept of heaven,*
> *would describe a vision which would look like the biggest department store*
> *in the world . . . he would wander around open mouthed in this heaven of*
> *gadgets and commodities, provided only that there were ever more and*
> *newer things to buy, and perhaps that his neighbors were just a little less*
> *privileged than he.*
>
> —ERICH FROMM (1900–1980, U.S. psychologist), *The Sane Society*

As a society, Americans display an endless appetite for material goods. Conspicuous accumulation of possessions is an indispensable aspect of the American Dream, a curious feature of a self-proclaimed egalitarian society. Unlike in traditional cultures in which one's place is unambiguously established by birth, caste, or class, it is possible in American society for people to establish their social identity through what they buy, wear, and own. Today, any American with enough cash or a credit card (first introduced in the 1950s) can purchase the requisite markers of social status and communicate an aura of importance and prestige. Whether they can afford to or not, everyone now can participate in the consumer culture. Competition and acquisition have become the salient features of American society, and the term *shopaholic* has been coined to define a new addiction.

Living in a society where people are encouraged to feel good about themselves based on their ability to buy things has a downside. For every habitué of shopping malls, mail-order catalogs, and television shopping channels who is caught up in the fantasy of consumption, there are countless others who live on the margin. The advent of the Internet in the 1990s served to broaden the opportunity for the "haves" to participate fully and easily in our consumer culture. But the gap between the haves and the have-nots has carried over into the electronic marketplace, where it has been called the digital gap—the divide between those who are wired and those who are not. Information itself has become a commodity, the newest status symbol, available only to those who can afford the connection.

ADVERTISING

In "The Culture of Consumerism," Juliet B. Schor describes how expectations stimulated by advertising and the media have intensified competitive consumption. Schor claims that people now look to the media's depiction of the rich and famous as a model (however inappropriate) for their own decisions as to what to buy. We no longer wish simply to keep up with the Joneses but overspend in the quest to possess the luxury items once owned only by the rich.

This new social phenomenon (of trying to measure up to an idealized group whose incomes vastly exceed our own) has created a new science of marketing called clustering. Clusters, as Schor describes them, are "groups of people who share values, orientations, and, most important, *lifestyles.*" Michael J. Weiss has studied this shift in *The Clustered World* (1998); he identified similar patterns of consumption within sixty-two clusters with such names as "Boomers and Babies," "Golden Ponders," "Pools and Patios," "Asian Heights," "Money and Brains," "Latino America," and "Shot Guns and Pick-Ups." In the last group, for example, Weiss notes that

> it is not unusual to find adults who have never flown in an airplane, never
> seen a first-run movie, never sniffed the cloying aromas of a trendy
> French bistro. Residents still sew their own bedroom quilts and fill their
> freezers with fish and game from hunting trips. (265)

As consumers, says Weiss, this cluster favors Spam, Diet Rite cola, and chewing tobacco; reads *Guns and Ammo* and *Motor Trend;* watches *The Young and the Restless, Geraldo Rivera,* and *Baywatch;* listens to Rush Limbaugh; and drives U.S.-made pickup trucks. A status symbol is a new four-wheel-drive truck with a CD player and a gun rack. Cluster analysis suggests that the growing cultural gap between this group and other clusters represents an increasing polarization in U.S. society.

Cluster-based marketing is now used by corporate, nonprofit, and political groups who target audiences (as do direct-mailers) to discover the best prospects for their products and services. Mapping consumption patterns throughout the United States and around the world reveals a globalization of cultures in which people often have more in common with members of the same cluster group *in other countries* than with their neighbors.

In "The Hard Sell: Advertising in America," Bill Bryson discusses how advertisers tap into and exploit the national mandate for consumption in ways that are profoundly ingenious. The same methods George Eastman hit upon to sell his cameras more than a hundred years ago are still being used today. The single most important technique for creating a distinctive image for a product (whether a brand of soap, a financial service, or a type of gasoline) involves transferring positive attributes to the product itself. Advertisers promise that their products or services will deliver otherwise-unattainable satisfactions to those who buy them. Bryson points out that ads for internationally marketed products can misfire when companies fail to research how brand names will translate into other languages. The unanticipated effects can range from the harmless and amusing to the insulting, obscene, and costly ("Fresca" in Mexican slang means lesbian, "Pinto" in Portuguese slang equals "small male appendage," "Nova" in Spanish translates as "it doesn't go"). In 1997, Nike had to recall millions of pairs of sneakers because the logo on the shoes (which was intended to depict flames) was almost identical with the Arabic script for "Allah."

SHOPPING

The advertising and availability of goods and services began well before 1900, but it was in the twentieth century that shopping came into its own, especially in the most distinctive American creation, the shopping mall. Shopping malls combine elements of traditional marketplace, town square, and amusement arcade in a temperature-controlled environment.

The modern shopping mall, according to Richard Keller Simon in "The Shopping Mall and the Formal Garden," uses features of garden design and architecture of the past to commodify moments from history in a self-enclosed environment designed to focus the shopper's energies on a single objective: consuming. We can visit a late-Victorian colonial outfitter (Banana Republic), revisit the rise of science in the sixteenth century at the Nature Company, or get a snack in an ersatz French bistro. The advent of e-shopping in virtual malls now allows consumers to visit the Web sites of these stores to make purchases without ever leaving home.

CULTURAL ARTIFACTS

The mythic dimension of consumerism has long been symbolized by the Barbie doll. We can appreciate the irony of Rabbi Susan Schnur's discovery (related in "Barbie Does Yom Kippur") that the girls in her congregation had brought their most valued possession, Barbie, to the synagogue during the holiest day of the year. The contrast between adults fasting and praying while the younger generation compared Barbie dolls was most disconcerting.

The fax and the cellular phone, along with other electronic artifacts, have become symbols of technological progress that enchant the masses. Umberto Eco (in "How Not to Use the Fax Machine and the Cellular Phone") satirizes the self-congratulatory tone of the middle class, enamored by gadgets symbolizing the good life, to which everyone is encouraged to aspire. He relishes playfully demythologizing these ubiquitous gizmos. These gadgets ultimately become what George Carlin describes as "stuff" in "A Place for Your Stuff." Carlin satirizes the end result of falling prey to the acquisitive impulse—the goods, objects, and junk that we have accumulated. Carlin's breezy tone softens his targeted criticism of modern life ("so you keep gettin' more and more stuff, and puttin' it in different places").

The U.S. Patent Office (with more than 250,000 applications each year) bears witness to the flood of products that promise the consumer a better life. We take for granted telephones (invented in 1896), radios (1901), airplanes (1903), television (1925), antibiotics (1928), photocopiers (1938), jet engines (1939), computers (1945), VCRs (1951), lasers (1960), the Internet (1969), and gene splicing (1980). Everything on this list has been or may be useful in our daily lives. But consider the surplus "stuff" in our drawers and basements that more accurately chronicles changes in social tastes and fashions. These artifacts tell us as much about our culture as do the historically important items. Where are our CB radios, mood rings, Cabbage Patch and Troll dolls, Pet Rocks, Nehru jackets, granny glasses, hula hoops, and Silly Putty? At some point, the "stuff" we acquire becomes the "dirt" we can't wait to discard—to make room for newer and better stuff.

Terence McLaughlin in "Dirt: A Social History as Seen through the Uses and Abuses of Dirt" analyzes the psychological and cultural factors that determine what we perceive of as "dirt." The difference between "stuff" and "dirt" varies from culture to culture but has one constant feature: fear of contamination by our fellow human beings (litter in the countryside can spoil our picnic, whereas pinecones do not).

CONSUMING IN OTHER CULTURES

Our sense of attachment to our personal belongings is so profoundly conditioned by our culture that it may surprise us to discover that people in other cultures have different ideas about their possessions. When Edward T. Hall was traveling in Japan, he was alarmed to discover that the hotel management had moved his belongings to a different room without telling him in advance. When the same thing happened at hotels in different cities, Hall became curious as to why the Japanese felt free to move his property without asking his permission. He found in these inexplicable events the key (reported in "Hidden Culture") to unlock unique Japanese attitudes and assumptions about privacy, personal belongings, and social acceptance.

Raymonde Carroll, in "Sex, Money, and Success," discovered another difference in cultural assumptions about worldly goods when she realized that Americans were ill at ease hearing the French converse about their sexual exploits, just as the French found the American tendency to harp on money and business in poor taste. Carroll investigated why money (rather than sexual conquests) or sex (rather than money) was chosen by each culture as the vehicle for establishing social status.

In many societies, the reciprocal exchange of possessions creates a social bond based on mutual obligation. The different forms this practice can take depends on the medium of exchange in a given culture. When David R. Counts moved to Papua New Guinea with his family, he discovered that the money he had brought was useless: he had to exchange goods—tobacco, cooking oil, and chewing gum—for food. If you have ever received a gift that placed you under an obligation you later found burdensome, you can understand why Counts found it difficult (as he tells us in "Too Many Bananas") to adjust to an unfamiliar barter system based on food (often too much and the wrong kind).

Just as food provides the social glue that holds the community together in New Guinea, rings, necklaces, bracelets, watches, and other expensive ornaments are the outward signs of friendship and belonging that bond a group of working-class men in Italy. Alberto Moravia describes this bond in his story, "Jewellery."

As capitalism inundates cultures around the world with more and more goods and reinforces the American philosophy that shopping and consuming is a sacred rite (and right), the pace of acquisition is escalating worldwide. Whether these material possessions make us any happier is something for each of us to consider.

JULIET B. SCHOR
The Culture of Consumerism

In a culture where spending has come to define the way people determine how happy they are, it is no wonder that Americans save less than do their peers in other countries—and work more. In the following excerpt from *The Overspent American* (1998), Juliet Schor explains why we no longer compare ourselves with the proverbial Joneses and instead aspire to the lifestyles of the rich and famous. Schor is a director of women's studies and professor of economics at Harvard. Her 1992 book, *The Overworked American*, was acclaimed by the *New York Times* as one of the ten best of that year.

Thinking Critically

To help you follow Schor's line of thought, underline passages that present research findings, expert opinions, and the results of surveys. Observe how Schor uses these as evidence to support her thesis that for America's middle class, "spending becomes you."

In 1996 a best-selling book entitled *The Millionaire Next Door* caused a minor sensation. In contrast to the popular perception of millionaire lifestyles, this book reveals that most millionaires live frugal lives—buying used cars, purchasing their suits at JC Penney, and shopping for bargains. These very wealthy people feel no need to let the world know they can afford to live much better than their neighbor.

Millions of other Americans, on the other hand, have a different relationship with spending. What they acquire and own is tightly bound to their personal identity. Driving a certain type of car, wearing particular designer labels, living in a certain kind of home, and ordering the right bottle of wine create and support a particular image of themselves to present to the world.

This is not to say that most Americans make consumer purchases solely to fool others about who they really are. It is not easy to say that we are a nation of crass status-seekers. Or that people who purchase more than they need are simply demonstrating a base materialism, in the sense of valuing material possessions above all else. But it is to say that, unlike the millionaires next door, who are not driven to use their wealth to create an attractive image of themselves, many of us are continually comparing our own lifestyle and possessions to those of a select group of people we respect and want to be like, people whose sense of what's important in life seems close to our own.

This aspect of our spending is not new—competitive acquisition has long been an American institution. At the turn of the century, the rich consumed conspicuously. In the early post–World War II decades, Americans spent to keep up with the Joneses, using their possessions to make the statement that they were not failing in their careers. But in recent decades, the culture of spending has changed and intensified. In the old days, our neighbors set the standard for what we had to have. They may have earned a little more, or a little less, but their incomes and ours were in the same ballpark. Their house down the block, worth roughly the same as ours, confirmed this. Today the neighbors are no longer the focus of comparison. How could they be? We may not even know them, much less which restaurants they patronize, where they vacation, and how much they spent for their living room couch.

For reasons that will become clear, the comparisons we make are no longer 5 restricted to those in our own general earnings category, or even to those one rung above us on the ladder. Today a person is more likely to be making comparisons with, or choose as a "reference group," people whose incomes are three, four, or five times his or her own. The result is that millions of us have become participants in a national culture of upscale spending. I call it the new consumerism.

Part of what's new is that lifestyle aspirations are now formed by different points of reference. For many of us, the neighborhood has been replaced by a community of coworkers, people we work alongside and colleagues in our own and related professions. And while our real-life friends still matter, they have been joined by our media "friends." (This is true both figuratively and literally—the television show *Friends* is a good example of an influential media referent.) We watch the way television families live, we read about the lifestyles of celebrities and other public figures we admire, and we consciously and unconsciously assimilate this information. It affects us.

So far so good. We are in a wider world, so we like to know that we are stacking up well against a wider population group than the people on the block. No harm in that. But as new reference groups form, they are less likely to comprise people who all earn approximately the same amount of money. And therein lies the problem. When a person who earns $75,000 a year compares herself to someone earning $90,000, the comparison is sustainable. It creates some tension, even a striving to do a bit better, to be more successful in a career. But when a reference group includes people who pull down six or even seven-figure incomes, that's trouble. When poet-waiters earning $18,000 a year, teachers earning $30,000, and editors and publishers earning six-figure incomes all aspire to be part of one urban literary referent group, which exerts pressure to drink the same brand of bottled water and wine, wear similar urban literary clothes, and appoint apartments with urban literary furniture, those at the lower economic end of the reference group find themselves in an untenable situation. Even if we choose not to emulate those who spend ostentatiously, consumer aspirations can be a serious reach.

Advertising and the media have played an important part in stretching out reference groups vertically. When twenty-somethings can't afford much more than a utilitarian studio but think they should have a New York apartment to match the ones they see on *Friends*, they are setting unattainable consumption goals for themselves, with dissatisfaction as a predictable result. When the children of affluent suburban and impoverished inner-city households both want the same Tommy Hilfiger logo emblazoned on their chests and the top-of-the-line Swoosh on their feet, it's a potential disaster. One solution to these problems emerged on the talk-show circuit recently, championed by a pair of young urban "entry-level" earners: live the *faux* life, consuming *as if* you had a big bank balance. Their strategies? Use your expense account for private entertainment, date bankers, and sneak into snazzy parties without an invitation. Haven't got the wardrobe for it? No matter. Charge expensive clothes, wear them with the tags on, and return them the morning after. Apparently the upscale life is now so worth living that deception, cheating, and theft are a small price to pay for it.

These are the more dramatic examples. Millions of us face less stark but problematic comparisons every day. People in one-earner families find themselves trying to live the lifestyle of their two-paycheck friends. Parents of modest means struggle to pay for the private schooling that others in their reference group have established as the right thing to do for their children.

10   Additional problems are created by the accelerating pace of product innovation. To gain broader distribution for the plethora of new products, manufacturers have gone to lifestyle marketing, targeting their pitches of upscale items at rich and nonrich alike. Gourmet cereal, a luxurious latte, or bathroom fixtures that make a statement, the right statement, are offered to people almost everywhere on the economic spectrum. In fact, through the magic of plastic, anyone can buy designer anything, at the trendiest retail shop. Or at outlet prices. That's the new consumerism. And its siren call is hard to resist.

The new consumerism is also built on relentless ratcheting up of standards. If you move into a house with a fifties kitchen, the presumption is that you will eventually have it redone, because that's a standard that has now been established. If you didn't have air conditioning in your old car, the presumption is that when you replace it, the new one will have it. If you haven't been to Europe, the presumption is that you will get there, because you deserve to get there. And so on. In addition to the proliferation of new products (computers, cell phones, faxes, and other microelectronics), there is a continual upgrading of old ones—autos and appliances—and a shift to customized, more expensive versions, all leading to a general expansion of the list of things we have to have. The 1929 home I just moved into has a closet too shallow to fit a hanger. So the clothes face forward. The real estate agents suggested I solve the "problem" by turning the study off the bedroom into a walk-in. (Why read when you could be buying clothes?) What we want grows into what we *need*, at a sometimes dizzying rate. While politicians continue to tout the middle class as the heart and soul of American society, for far too many of us being solidly middle-class is no longer good enough.

Oddly, it doesn't seem as if we're spending wastefully, or even lavishly. Rather, many of us feel we're just making it, barely able to stay even. But what's remarkable is that this feeling is not restricted to families of limited income. It's a generalized feeling, one that exists at all levels. Twenty-seven percent of all households making more than $100,000 a year say they cannot afford to buy everything they really need. Nearly 20 percent say they "spend nearly all their income on the basic necessities of life." In the $50,000–100,000 range, 39 percent and one-third feel this way, respectively. Overall, half the population of the richest country in the world say they cannot afford everything they really need. And it's not just the poorer half.

This book is about why: About why so many middle-class Americans feel materially dissatisfied. Why they walk around with ever-present mental "wish lists" of things to buy or get. How even a six-figure income can seem inadequate, and why this country saves less than virtually any other nation in the world. It is about the ways in which, for America's middle classes, "spending

TABLE 1.1 How Much Is Enough?

Percentage Agreeing with Statement, by Income

STATEMENT	<$10,000	10,001–25,000	25,001–35,000	35,001–50,000	50,001–75,000	75,001–100,000	>100,000
I cannot afford to buy everything I really need	64	62	50	43	42	39	27
I spend nearly all of my money on the basic necessities of life	69	64	62	46	35	33	19

SOURCE: Author's calculations from Merck Family Fund poll (February 1995).

becomes you," about how it flatters, enhances, and defines people in often wonderful ways, but also about how it takes over their lives. My analysis is based on new research showing that the need to spend whatever it takes to keep current within a chosen reference group—which may include members of widely disparate resources—drives much purchasing behavior. It analyzes how standards of belonging socially have changed in recent decades, and how this change has introduced Americans to highly intensified spending pressures.

And finally, it is about a growing backlash to the consumption culture, a movement of people who are downshifting—by working less, earning less, and living their consumer lives much more deliberately.

SPENDING AND SOCIAL COMPARISON

15   I am hardly the first person to have argued that consumption has a comparative, or even competitive character. Ideas of this sort have a long history within economics, sociology, and other disciplines. In *The Wealth of Nations*, Adam Smith observed that even a "creditable day-laborer would be ashamed to appear in publick without a linen shirt" and that leather shoes had become a "necessary of life" in eighteenth-century England. The most influential work on the subject, however, has been Thorstein Veblen's *Theory of the Leisure Class*. Veblen argued that in affluent societies, spending becomes the vehicle through which people establish social position. The conspicuous display of wealth and leisure is the marker that reveals a man's income to the outside world. (Wives, by the way, were seen by Veblen as largely ornamental, useful to display a man's finest purchases—clothes, furs, and jewels.) The rich spent conspicuously as a kind of personal advertisement, to secure a place in the social hierarchy. Everyone below stood watching and, to the extent possible, emulating those one notch higher. Consumption was a trickle-down process.

The phenomenon that Veblen identified and described, conspicuous consumption by the rich and nouveaux riches, was not new even in his own time. Spending to establish a social position has a long history. Seventeenth- and eighteenth-century Italian nobles built opulent palaces with beautiful facades and, within those facades, placed tiles engraved with the words *Pro Invidia* (To Be Envied). For centuries, aristocrats passed laws to forbid the nouveaux riches from copying their clothing styles. At the turn of the century, the wealthy published the menus of their dinner parties in the newspapers, And fifty years ago, American social climbers bought fake "ancestor portraits" to hang in their libraries.

Veblen's story made a lot of sense for the upper-crust, turn-of-the-century urban world of his day. But by the 1920s, new developments were afoot. Because productivity and output were growing so rapidly, more and more people had entered the comfortable middle classes and begun to enjoy substantial discretionary spending. And this mass prosperity eventually engendered a new socioeconomic phenomenon—a mass keeping-up process that led to convergence among consumers' acquisitions goals and purchasing patterns.

The advent of mass production in the 1920s made possible an outpouring of identical consumer goods that nearly everybody wanted—and were better able to afford, thanks to declining prices. By the fifties, the Smiths had to have the Joneses' fully automatic washing machine, vacuum cleaner, and, most of all, the shiny new Chevrolet parked in the driveway. The story of this period was that people looked to their own neighborhoods for their spending cues, and the neighbors grew more and more alike in what they had. Like compared with like and strove to become even more alike.

This phenomenon was chronicled by James Duesenberry, a Harvard economist writing just after the Second World War. Duesenberry updated Veblen's trickle-down perspective in his classic discussion of "keeping up with the Joneses." In contrast to Veblen's Vanderbilts, Duesenberry's 1950s Joneses were middle-class and they lived next door, in suburban USA. Rather than seeking to best their neighbors, Duesenberry's Smiths mainly wanted to be like them. Although the ad writers urged people to be the first on the block to own a product, the greater fear in most consumers' minds during this period was that if they didn't get cracking, they might be the last to get on board.

In addition to Veblen and Duesenberry, a number of distinguished economists have emphasized these social and comparative processes in their classic accounts of consumer culture—among them, John Kenneth Galbraith, Fred Hirsch, Tibor Scitovsky, Richard Easterlin, Amartya Sen, Clair Brown, and Robert Frank. Among the most important of their messages is that consumer satisfaction, and dissatisfaction, depend less on what a person has in an absolute sense than on socially formed aspirations and expectations. Indeed, the very term "standard of living" suggests the point: the standard is a social norm. 20

By the 1970s, social trends were once again altering the nature of comparative consumption. Most obvious was the entrance of large numbers of married women into the labor force. As the workplace replaced the coffee klatch and the backyard barbecue as locations of social contact, workplace conversation became the source of information on who went where for vacation, who was having a deck put on the house, and whether the kids were going to dance class, summer camp, or karate lessons. But in the workplace, most employees are exposed to spending habits of people across a wider economic spectrum, particularly those employees who work in white-collar settings. They have meetings with people who wear expensive suits or "real" Swiss watches. They may work with their boss, or their boss's boss, every day and find out a lot about what they and their families have.

There were also ripple effects on women who didn't have jobs. When many people lived in one-earner households, incomes throughout the neighborhood tended to be close to each other. As many families earned two paychecks, however, mothers who stayed at home or worked part-time found themselves competing with neighbors who could much more easily afford pricey restaurants, piano lessons, and two new cars. Finally, as Robert Frank and Philip Cook have argued, there has been a shift to a "winner-take-all" society: rewards within occupations have become more unequally distributed. As a group of extremely high earners emerged within occupation after occupation, they provided a visible, and very elevated, point of comparison for those who weren't capturing a disproportionate share of the earnings of the group.

Daily exposure to an economically diverse set of people is one reason Americans began engaging in more upward comparison. A shift in advertising patterns is another. Traditionally advertisers had targeted their market by earnings, using one medium or another depending on the income group they were trying to reach. They still do this. But now the huge audiences delivered by television make it the best medium for reaching just about *every* financial group. While *Forbes* readers have a much higher median income than television viewers, it's possible to reach more wealthy people on television than in the pages of any magazine, no matter how targeted its readership. A major sports event or an *ER* episode is likely to deliver more millionaires *and* more laborers than a medium aimed solely at either group. That's why you'll find ads for Lincoln town cars, Mercedes-Benz sports cars, and $50,000 all-terrain vehicles on the Super Bowl telecast. In the process, painters who earn $25,000 a year are being exposed to buying pressures never intended for them, and middle-class housewives look at products once found only in the homes of the wealthy.

Beginning in the 1970s, expert observers were declaring the death of the "belonging" process that had driven much competitive consumption and arguing that the establishment of an individual identity—rather than staying current with the Joneses—was becoming the name of the game. The new trend was to consume in a personal style, with products that signaled your individuality, your personal sense of taste and distinction. But, of course, you had to be different in the right way. The trick was to create a unique image through what you had and wore—and what you did not have and would not be seen dead in.

25   While the observers had identified a new stage in consumer culture, they were right only to a point. People may no longer have wanted to be just like all others in their socioeconomic class, but their need to measure up within some idealized group survived. What emerged as the new standards of comparison, however, were groups that had no direct counterparts in previous times. Marketers call them clusters—groups of people who share values, orientations, and, most important, *lifestyles.* Clusters are much smaller than traditional hori-

zontal economic strata or classes and can thereby satisfy the need for greater individuality in consumption patterns. "Yuppie" was only the most notorious of these lifestyle cluster groups. There are also middle Americans, twenty-somethings, upscale urban Asians, top one-percenters, and senior sun-seekers. We have radical feminists, comfortable capitalists, young market lions, environmentalists. Whatever.

Ironically, the shift to individuality produced its own brand of localized conformity. [. . .] Apparently lots of people began wanting the same "individual identity-creating" products. But this predictability, while perhaps a bit absurd, brought with it no *particular* financial problem. Seventies consumerism was manageable. The real problems started in the 1980s as an economic shift sent seismic shocks through the nation's consumer mentality. Competitive spending intensified. In a very big way.

TABLE 1.2 The Good Life Goes Upscale

Percentage Identifying Item as a Part of "The Good Life"

	1975	1991
Vacation home	19	35
Swimming pool	14	29
Color TV	46	55
Second color TV	10	28
Travel abroad	30	39
Really nice clothes	36	44
Car	71	75
Second car	30	41
Home you own	85	87
A lot of money	38	55
A job that pays much more than average	45	60
Happy marriage	84	77
One or more children	74	73
Interesting job	69	63
Job that contributes to the welfare of society	38	38
Percentage who think they have a very good chance of achieving the "good life"	35	23

SOURCE: Roper Center, University of Connecticut; published in *American Enterprise* (May–June 1993), p. 87.

TABLE 1.3 The Expanding Definition of "Necessities"

Percentage Indicating Item Is a Necessity

	1973	*1991*	*1996*
Second television	3	15	10
Dishwasher	10	24	13
VCR	—*	18	13
Basic cable service	—	26	17
Remote control for TV or VCR	—	23	—
Answering machine	—	20	26
Home computer	—	11	26
Microwave	—	44	32
Second automobile	20	27	37
Auto air conditioning	13	42	41
Home air conditioning	26	47	51
Television	57	74	59
Clothes dryer	54	74	62
Clothes washer	88	82	86
Automobile	90	85	93
Cellular phone	—	5	—
Housekeeper	—	4	—

*Item did not exist, was not widely in use, or was not asked about in 1973.
SOURCE: Roper Center, University of Connecticut; 1973 and 1991 data published in *American Enterprise* (May–June 1993), p. 89.

WHEN $18,000 FEELS LUXURIOUS: JEFF LUTZ

Some Americans are pursuing another path. Want less. Live more simply. Slow down and get in touch with nature. A growing "voluntary simplicity" movement is rejecting the standard path of work and spend. This is a committed, self-conscious group of people who believe that spending less does not reduce their quality of life and may even raise it. Their experience is that *less* (spending) is *more* (time, meaning, peace of mind, financial security, ecological responsibility, physical health, friendship, appreciation of what they do spend). Seattle, long a laid-back, nature-oriented city, is home not only to Boeing and Microsoft but also to many of these individuals. I spent nearly a week there in the summer of 1996, meeting people who were living on less than $20,000 a year. Jeff Lutz was one of them.

After graduating from a small college back east, Jeff and his girlfriend Liza moved to Seattle, where they inhabit a nice, spacious old house in a middle-class neighborhood. They share a place with one friend; their rent is $312 per person. Jeff is self-employed as a medical and legal interpreter and is putting a lot of effort into "growing" his business. Nicely dressed and groomed, he doesn't look too different from other twenty-five-year-old graduates of the prep school and college he attended. But he is. Living on about $10,000 a year, he says he has basically everything he wants and will be content to live at this level of material comfort for the rest of his life. Youthful naïveté? Perhaps. But maybe not.

Lutz grew up in Mexico. His mother, a writer and social activist, went to Mexico with her parents, refugees from Franco's civil war. His father was a lawyer from New York. Family role models helped form his commitment to a frugal lifestyle, "My great-grandfather, who escaped czarist jail in Lithuania, lived in Mexico with one lightbulb and a record player. He had three photos behind his bed. One was Tolstoy, and one was Gandhi, and one was Pious XXIII."

As a teenager, Lutz went to a private school in western Massachusetts. 30 There he began to feel like "part of a herd being prodded along to do one thing after the next in semiconscious wakefulness. You go to elementary school, and then you go to junior high, and then you go to high school, and then you go to college in order to get a job, in order to compete with other people in higher salaries, in order to have more stuff. I saw really clearly in high school just where it was leading." At that point, he made up his mind about two things. First, "I needed to find a way to not be in a nine-to-five-until-I-died treadmill. I had a vision of life being much, much more than spending most of my life in a job that was somebody else's agenda." Second, "I wanted to learn how human beings could live more lightly on the earth."

His experiences in Mexico motivated these sentiments. "I spent a week with some Mazotec Indians in the mountains. And some of these kids my age, one of them had a Washington Redskins jersey. I mean, Spanish is their second language; they spoke Mazoteca, and yet they were listening to Michael Jackson and they wanted to buy my sunglasses and they wanted to buy my watch. And they wanted me to bring more sunglasses and watches so that they could resell them to their friends. It was very clear that our culture was sort of surrounding other cultures through the media. I grew up watching *The Love Boat* dubbed in Spanish."

In college, he designed his own major in environmental studies. But unlike many young people who begin their work lives enthusiastically believing they can combine improving the world with making a good salary, Lutz never really considered that path. "The things I was interested in were pretty outside the box." Near the end of his college years, he came across an article by Joe Dominguez, the creator of a nine-step program of "financial independence."

Dominguez's program, contained in his best-selling book (with collaborator Vicki Robin) *Your Money or Your Life*, promises freedom from the grind of the working world, not through getting rich but by downsizing desire. Dominguez and Robin believe Americans have been trained to equate more stuff with more happiness. But that is true only up to a point, a point they feel most of us have passed. Doing it their way, you don't need to save a million dollars to retire, but just one, two, or three hundred thousand.

The program involves meticulously tracking all spending. And not just tracking it but scrutinizing it, by comparing the value of whatever you want to buy with the time it takes to earn the money for it. That calculation involves determining your real hourly wage, by taking into account all the hours you work and subtracting all job-related expenses, including the cost of your job wardrobe and takeout food because you're too tired to cook. Equipped with your real wage rate, you can figure out whether a new couch is worth three weeks of work, whether four nights in the Bahamas justify a month of earning, or whether you want to stick with the morning latte (even those half-hours add up). People who follow the program find that when they ask these questions, they spend less. Much less.

Jeff was getting close to financial independence, which entailed earning enough to spend between $800 and $1,200 per month, including health insurance. He says he does not feel materially deprived, and he is careful to point out that voluntary simplicity is not poverty. While he decided against the lattes, he does own a car and a computer, goes out to eat between one and three times a month, rents videos, has friends over for dinner, and buys his clothes both new and used. His furniture is an eclectic mix—nothing fancy, but nothing shabby either. He is convinced that "a higher standard of living will not make me happier. And I'm very clear internally. It's not a belief I picked up from somewhere." It's "something that I've gained an awareness about."

Engaging the Text

1. Why, in Schor's view, have Americans since the 1970s come to define the "good life" as requiring luxuries that are now seen as "necessities"? Did Schor succeed in making you take a closer look at your assumptions about the possessions you need to live the good life?

2. What role has the media played in changing people's conceptions of what they deserve to have and should want? Have media messages and images had this effect on you?

3. The experience of Jeff Lutz provides a dramatic contrast to what most Americans feel they need. Would you ever choose such a lifestyle? Why or why not?

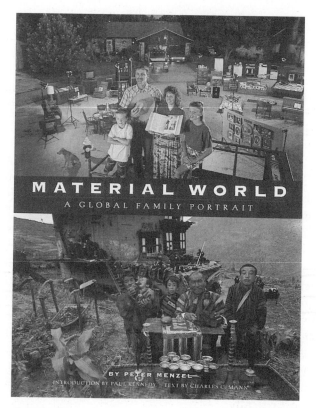

FIGURE 9.1

Exploring Your Cultural Perspective

1. Examine the comparative statistics that Schor provides in Tables 1.2 and 1.3. Which patterns of consumption most nearly approximate your own? An interesting exercise might be to inventory your possessions in two categories: what you absolutely need and what you have bought for no apparent reason. Draw on Schor's analysis, and discuss the validity of her thesis in terms of what you and your friends buy.

2. To what extent do you subscribe to the notion that you are what you buy? Are you the sum total of your possessions? If not, what aspects of your identity are not attached to the things you own? Consider the pictures from the book *Material World: A Global Family Portrait* in Figure 9.1. The author asked families all around the world to pose with all of their possessions. If all of your possessions were displayed in the same way, what would they say about you?

BILL BRYSON
The Hard Sell: Advertising in America

Advertisers use ingenuity and skill, and spend untold amounts of money, to market their products. Yet, although we see on average 38,000 or so commercials on television each year, we know very little about the marketing strategies advertisers use to sell their products in magazines and newspapers, and on television, radio, and the Internet. Bill Bryson's investigation into advertising reveals that since its inception one hundred years ago, advertisers have sought to create distinctive images for their products by tapping into consumer's needs and desires. This selection first appeared in *Made in America: An Informal History of the English Language in the United States*. (1994). Bryson has also written *A Walk in the Woods* (1998) and *In a Sunburned Country* (2000).

Thinking Critically
As you read this selection, consider the various techniques American advertisers use to get us to buy their products. Because Bryson does not provide visuals with his analysis, you might look at the ads in current magazines to discover whether what he says is still true. Has an ad ever encouraged you to buy something that you did not really need?

In 1885, a young man named George Eastman formed the Eastman Dry Plate and Film Company in Rochester, New York. It was rather a bold thing to do. Aged just thirty-one, Eastman was a junior clerk in a bank on a comfortable but modest salary of $15 a week. He had no background in business. But he was passionately devoted to photography and had become increasingly gripped with the conviction that anyone who could develop a simple, untechnical camera, as opposed to the cumbersome, outsized, fussily complex contrivances then on the market, stood to make a fortune.

Eastman worked tirelessly for three years to perfect his invention, supporting himself in the meantime by making dry plates for commercial photographers, and in June 1888 produced a camera that was positively dazzling in its simplicity: a plain black box just six and a half inches long by three and a quarter inches wide, with a button on the side and a key for advancing the film. Eastman called his device the *Detective Camera*. Detectives were all the thing—Sherlock Holmes was just taking off with American readers—and the name implied that it was so small and simple that it could be used unnoticed, as a detective might.

The camera had no viewfinder and no way of focusing. The *photographer* or *photographist* (it took a while for the first word to become the established one) simply held the camera in front of him, pressed a button on the side, and hoped for the best. Each roll a hundred pictures. When a roll was fully exposed, the anxious owner sent the entire camera to Rochester for developing. Eventually he received the camera back, freshly loaded with film, and—assuming all had gone well—one hundred small circular pictures, two and a half inches in diameter.

Often all didn't go well. The film Eastman used at first was made of paper, which tore easily and had to be carefully stripped of its emulsion before the exposures could be developed. It wasn't until the invention of celluloid roll film by a sixty-five-year-old Episcopal minister named Hannibal Goodwin in Newark, New Jersey—this truly was the age of the amateur inventor—that amateur photography became a reliable undertaking. Goodwin didn't call his invention *film* but *photographic pellicule*, and, as was usual, spent years fighting costly legal battles with Eastman without ever securing the recognition or financial payoff he deserved—though eventually, years after Goodwin's death, Eastman was ordered to pay $5 million to the company that inherited the patent.

In September 1888, Eastman changed the name of the camera to *Kodak*—   5
an odd choice, since it was meaningless, and in 1888 no one gave meaningless names to products, especially successful products. Since British patent applications at the time demanded full explanation of trade and brand names, we know how Eastman arrived at his inspired name. He crisply summarized his reasoning in his patent application: "First. It is short. Second. It is not capable of mispronunciation. Third. It does not resemble anything in the art and cannot be associated with anything in the art except the Kodak." Four years later the whole enterprise was renamed the Eastman Kodak Company.

Despite the considerable expense involved—a Kodak camera sold for $25, and each roll of film cost $10, including developing—by 1895, over 100,000 Kodaks had been sold and Eastman was a seriously wealthy man. A lifelong bachelor, he lived with his mother in a thirty-seven-room mansion with twelve bathrooms. Soon people everywhere were talking about snapshots, originally a British shooting term for a hastily executed shot. Its photographic sense was coined by the English astronomer Sir John Herschel, who also gave the world the terms *positive* and *negative* in their photographic senses.

From the outset, Eastman developed three crucial strategies that have been the hallmarks of virtually every successful consumer goods company since. First, he went for the mass market, reasoning that it was better to make a little money each from a lot of people rather than a lot of money from a few. He also showed a tireless, obsessive dedication to making his products better and cheaper. In the 1890s, such an approach was widely perceived as insane. If you had a successful product you milked it for all it was worth. If competitors came along with something better, you bought them out or tried to squash them with lengthy patent fights or other bullying tactics. What you certainly did not do was create new products that made your existing lines obsolescent. Eastman did. Throughout the late 1890s, Kodak introduced a series of increasingly cheaper, niftier cameras—the Bull's Eye model of 1896, which cost just $12, and the famous slimline Folding Pocket Kodak of 1898, before finally in 1900 producing his eureka model: the little box Brownie, priced at just $1 and with film at 15 cents a reel (though with only six exposures per reel).

Above all, what set Eastman apart was the breathtaking lavishness of his advertising. In 1899 alone, he spent $750,000, an unheard-of sum, on advertising. Moreover, it was *good* advertising: crisp, catchy, reassuringly trustworthy. "You press a button—we do the rest" ran the company's first slogan, thus making a virtue of its shortcomings. Never mind that you couldn't load or unload the film yourself. Kodak would do it for you. In 1905, it followed with another classic slogan: "If It Isn't an Eastman, It Isn't a Kodak."

Kodak's success did not escape other businessmen, who also began to see virtue in the idea of steady product refinement and improvement. AT&T and Westinghouse, among others, set up research laboratories with the idea of creating a stream of new products, even at the risk of displacing old ones. Above all, everyone everywhere began to advertise.

10   Advertising was already a well-established phenomenon by the turn of the twentieth century. Newspapers had begun carrying ads as far back as the early 1700s, and magazines soon followed. (Benjamin Franklin has the distinction of having run the first magazine ad, seeking the whereabouts of a runaway slave, in 1741.) By 1850, the country had its first *advertising agency*, the American Newspaper Advertising Agency, though its function was to buy advertising space rather than come up with creative campaigns. The first advertising agency in the modern sense was N. W. Ayer & Sons of Philadelphia, established in 1869. *To advertise* originally carried the sense of to broadcast or disseminate news. Thus a nineteenth-century newspaper that called itself the *Advertiser* meant that it had lots of news, not lots of ads. By the early 1800s the term had been stretched to accommodate the idea of spreading the news of the availability of certain goods or services. A newspaper notice that read "Jos. Parker, Hatter" was essentially announcing that if anyone was in the market for hats, Jos. Parker had them. In the sense of persuading members of the pub-

lic to acquire items they might not otherwise think of buying—items they didn't know they needed—advertising is a phenomenon of the modern age.

By the 1890s, advertising was appearing everywhere—in newspapers and magazines, on *billboards* (an Americanism dating from 1850), on the sides of buildings, on passing streetcars, on paper bags, even on matchbooks, which were invented in 1892 and were being extensively used as an advertising medium within three years.

Very early on, advertisers discovered the importance of a good slogan. Many of our more venerable slogans are older than you might think. Ivory Soap's "99 44/100 percent pure" dates from 1879. Schlitz has been calling itself "the beer that made Milwaukee famous" since 1895, and Heinz's "57 varieties" followed a year later. Morton Salt's "When it rains, it pours" dates from 1911, the American Florist Association's "Say it with flowers" was first used in 1912, and the "good to the last drop" of Maxwell House coffee, named for the Maxwell House Hotel in Nashville, where it was first served, has been with us since 1907. (The slogan is said to have originated with Teddy Roosevelt, who pronounced the coffee "good to the last drop," prompting one wit to ask, "So what's wrong with the last drop?")

Sometimes slogans took a little working on. Coca-Cola described itself as "the drink that makes a pause refreshing" before realizing, in 1929, that "the pause that refreshes" was rather more succinct and memorable. A slogan could make all the difference to a product's success. After advertising its soap as an efficacious way of dealing with "conspicuous nose pores," Woodbury's Facial Soap came up with the slogan "The skin you love to touch" and won the hearts of millions. The great thing about a slogan was that it didn't have to be accurate to be effective. Heinz never actually had exactly "57 varieties" of anything. The catchphrase arose simply because H. J. Heinz, the company's founder, decided he liked the sound of the number. Undeterred by considerations of verity, he had the slogan slapped on every one of the products he produced, already in 1896 far more than fifty-seven. For a time the company tried to arrange its products into fifty-seven arbitrary clusters, but in 1969 it gave up the ruse altogether and abandoned the slogan.

Early in the 1900s, advertisers discovered another perennial feature of marketing—the *giveaway*, as it was called almost from the start. Consumers soon became acquainted with the irresistibly tempting notion that if they bought a particular product they could expect a reward—the chance to receive a prize, a free book (almost always ostensibly dedicated to the general improvement of one's well-being but invariably a thinly disguised plug for the manufacturer's range of products), a free sample, or a rebate in the form of a shiny dime, or be otherwise endowed with some gratifying bagatelle. Typical of the genre was a turn-of-the-century tome called *The Vital Question Cook Book*, which was promoted as an aid to livelier meals, but which proved upon receipt to contain 112 pages of recipes all involving the use of Shredded Wheat. Many of these had a certain air of desperation about them, notably the "Shredded Wheat Biscuit Jellied Apple Sandwich" and the "Creamed Spinach on Shredded Wheat Biscuit Toast." Almost all involved nothing more than spooning some everyday food on a piece of shredded wheat and giving it an inflated name. Nonetheless the company distributed no fewer than four million copies of *The Vital Question Cook Book* to eager consumers.

15   The great breakthrough in twentieth-century advertising, however, came with the identification and exploitation of the American consumer's Achilles' heel: anxiety. One of the first to master the form was King Gillette, inventor of the first safety razor and one of the most relentless advertisers of the early 1900s. Most of the early ads featured Gillette himself, who with his fussy toothbrush mustache and well-oiled hair looked more like a caricature of a Parisian waiter than a captain of industry. After starting with a few jaunty words about the ease and convenience of the safety razor—"Compact? Rather!"—he plunged the reader into the heart of the matter: "When you use my razor you are exempt from the dangers that men often encounter who allow their faces to come in contact with brush, soap, and barbershop accessories used on other people."

Here was an entirely new approach to selling goods. Gillette's ads were in effect telling you that not only did there exist a product that you never previously suspected you needed, but if you *didn't* use it you would very possibly attract a crop of facial diseases you never knew existed. The combination proved irresistible. Though the Gillette razor retailed for a hefty $5—half the average workingman's weekly pay—it sold by the millions, and King Gillette became a very wealthy man. (Though only for a time, alas. Like many others of his era, he grew obsessed with the idea of the perfectibility of mankind and expended so much of his energies writing books of convoluted philosophy with titles like *The Human Drift* that he eventually lost control of his company and most of his fortune.)

By the 1920s, advertisers had so refined the art that a consumer could scarcely pick up a magazine without being bombarded with unsettling questions: "Do You Make These Mistakes in English?"; "Will Your Hair Stand Close Inspection?"; "When Your Guests Are Gone—Are You Sorry You Ever Invited Them?" (because, that is, you lack social polish); "Did Nature fail to put roses in your cheeks?"; "Will There be a Victrola in Your Home This Christmas?"[1] The 1920s truly were the Age of Anxiety. One ad pictured a former golf champion, "now only a wistful onlooker," whose career had gone sour because he had neglected his teeth. Scott Tissues mounted a campaign show-

---

[1] The most famous 1920s ad of them all didn't pose a question, but it did play on the reader's anxiety: "They Laughed When I Sat Down, but When I Started to Play . . .". It was originated by the U.S. School of Music in 1925.

ing a forlorn-looking businessman sitting on a park bench beneath the bold caption "A Serious Business Handicap—These Troubles That Come from Harsh Toilet Tissue." Below the picture the text explained: "65% of all men and women over 40 are suffering from some form of rectal trouble, estimates a prominent specialist connected with one of New York's largest hospitals. 'And one of the contributing causes,' he states, 'is inferior toilet tissue.'" There was almost nothing that one couldn't become uneasy about. One ad even asked: "Can You Buy a Radio Safely?" Distressed bowels were the most frequent target. The makers of Sal Hepatica warned: "We rush to meetings, we dash to parties. We are on the go all day long. We exercise too little, and we eat too much. And, in consequence, we impair our bodily functions—often we retain food within us too long. And when that occurs, poisons are set up— *Auto-Intoxication begins.*"

In addition to the dread of auto-intoxication, the American consumer faced a gauntlet of other newly minted maladies—*pyorrhea, halitosis* (coined as a medical term in 1874, but popularized by Listerine beginning in 1922 with the slogan "Even your best friend won't tell you"), *athlete's foot* (a term invented by the makers of Absorbine Jr. in 1928), *dead cuticles, scabby toes, iron-poor blood, vitamin deficiency* (*vitamins* had been coined in 1912, but the word didn't enter the general vocabulary until the 1920s, when advertisers realized it sounded worryingly scientific), *fallen stomach, tobacco breath*, and *psoriasis*, though Americans would have to wait until the next decade for the scientific identification of the gravest of personal disorders—*body odor*, a term invented in 1933 by the makers of Lifebuoy soap and so terrifying in its social consequences that it was soon abbreviated to a whispered *B.O.*

The white-coated technicians of American laboratories had not only identified these new conditions, but—miraculously, it seemed—simultaneously come up with cures for them. Among the products that were invented or rose to greatness in this busy, neurotic decade were *Cutex* (for those deceased cuticles), *Vick's VapoRub, Geritol, Serutan* ("Natures spelled backwards," as the voiceover always said with somewhat bewildering reassurance, as if spelling a product's name backward conferred some medicinal benefit), *Noxema* (for which read: "knocks eczema"), *Preparation H, Murine* eyedrops, and *Dr. Scholl's Foot Aids.*[2] It truly was an age of miracles—one in which you could even cure a smoker's cough by smoking, so long as it was Old Golds you smoked, because, as the slogan proudly if somewhat untruthfully boasted, they contained "Not a cough in a carload." (As late as 1953, L&M cigarettes were advertised as "just what the doctor ordered!")

---

[2]And yes, there really was a Dr. Scholl. His name was William Scholl, he was a real doctor, genuinely dedicated to the well-being of feet, and they are still very proud of him in his hometown of LaPorte, Indiana.

20   By 1927, advertising was a $1.5-billion-a-year industry in the United States, and advertising people were held in such awe that they were asked not only to mastermind campaigns but even to name the products. An ad man named Henry N. McKinney, for instance, named *Keds* shoes, *Karo* syrup, *Meadow Gold* butter, and *Uneeda Biscuits.*

Product names tended to cluster around certain sounds. Breakfast cereals often ended in *-ies (Wheaties, Rice Krispies, Frosties);* washing powders and detergents tended to be gravely monosyllabic *(Lux, Fab, Tide, Duz).* It is often possible to tell the era of a product's development by its termination. Thus products dating from the 1920s and early 1930s often ended in *-ex (Pyrex, Cutex, Kleenex, Windex),* while those ending in *-master (Mixmaster, Toastmaster)* generally betray a late-1930s or early-1940s genesis. The development of *Glo-Coat* floor wax in 1932 also heralded the beginning of American business's strange and long-standing infatuation with illiterate spellings, a trend that continued with *ReaLemon* juice in 1935, *Reddi-Wip* whipped cream in 1947, and many hundreds of others since, from *Tastee-Freez* drive-ins to *Toys 'Я' Us,* along with countless others with a *Kwik, E-Z,* or *U* (as in *While-U-Wait*) embedded in their titles. The late 1940s saw the birth of a brief vogue for endings in *-matic,* so that car manufacturers offered vehicles with *Seat-O-Matic* levers and *Cruise-O-Matic* transmissions, and even fitted sheets came with *Ezy-Matic* corners. Some companies became associated with certain types of names. Du Pont, for instance, had a special fondness for words ending in *-on.* The practice began with *nylon*—a name that was concocted out of thin air and owes nothing to its chemical properties—and was followed with *Rayon, Dacron, Orlon,* and *Teflon,* among many others. In recent years the company has moved on to what might be called its *Star Trek* phase with such compounds as *Tyvek, Kevlar, Sontara, Cordura, Nomex,* and *Zemorain.*

Such names have more than passing importance to their owners. If American business has given us a large dose of anxiety in its ceaseless quest for a healthier *bottom line* (a term dating from the 1930s, though not part of mainstream English until the 1970s), we may draw some comfort from the thought that business has suffered a great deal of collective anxiety over protecting the names of its products.

A certain cruel paradox prevails in the matter of preserving brand names. Every business naturally wants to create a product that will dominate its market. But if that product so dominates the market that the brand name becomes indistinguishable in the public mind from the product itself—when people begin to ask for a *thermos* rather than a "Thermos brand vacuum flask"—then the term has become generic and the owner faces loss of its trademark protection. That is why advertisements and labels so often carry faintly paranoid-sounding lines like "Tabasco is the registered trademark for the brand of pepper sauce made by McIlhenny Co." and why companies like Coca-Cola suffer palpitations when they see a passage like this (from John Steinbeck's *The Wayward Bus*):

> "Got any coke?" another character asked.
> "No," said the proprietor. "Few bottles of Pepsi-Cola. Haven't had any coke for a month. . . . It's the same stuff. You can't tell them apart."

An understandable measure of confusion exists concerning the distinction between patents and trademarks and between trademarks and trade names. A *patent* protects the name of the product and its method of manufacture for seventeen years. Thus from 1895 to 1912, no one but the Shredded Wheat Company could make shredded wheat. But because patents require manufacturers to divulge the secrets of their products—and thus make them available to rivals to copy when the patent runs out—companies sometimes choose not to seek their protection. *Coca-Cola*, for one, has never been patented. A *trademark* is effectively the name of a product, its *brand name*. A *trade name* is the name of the manufacturer. So *Ford* is a trade name, *Taurus* a trademark. Trademarks apply not just to names, but also to logos, drawings, and other symbols and depictions. The MGM lion, for instance, is a trademark. Unlike patents, trademark protection goes on forever, or at least as long as the manufacturer can protect it.

For a long time, it was felt that this permanence gave the holder an unfair   25
advantage. In consequence, America did not enact its first trademark law until 1870, almost a century after Britain, and then it was declared unconstitutional by the Supreme Court. Lasting trademark protection did not begin for American companies until 1881. Today, more than a million trademarks have been issued in the United States and the number is rising by about thirty thousand a year.

A good trademark is almost incalculably valuable. Invincible-seeming brand names do occasionally falter and fade. *Pepsodent, Rinso, Chase & Sanborn, Sal Hepatica, Vitalis, Brylcreem,* and *Burma-Shave* all once stood on the commanding heights of consumer recognition but are now defunct or have sunk to the status of what the trade calls "ghost brands"—products that are still produced but little promoted and largely forgotten. For the most part, however, once a product establishes a dominant position in a market, it is exceedingly difficult to depose it. In nineteen of twenty-two product categories, the company that owned the leading American brand in 1925 still has it today—*Nabisco* in cookies, *Kellogg's* in breakfast cereals, *Kodak* in film, *Sherwin Williams* in paint, *Del Monte* in canned fruit, *Wrigley's* in chewing gum, *Singer* in sewing machines, *Ivory* in soap, *Campbell's* in soup, *Gillette* in razors. Few really successful brand names of today were not just as familiar to your grandparents or even great-grandparents, and a well-established brand name has a sort of self-perpetuating power. As *The Economist* has noted: "In the category of food blenders, consumers were still ranking General Electric second twenty years after the company had stopped making them."

An established brand name is so valuable that only about 5 percent of the sixteen thousand or so new products introduced in America each year bear all-new brand names. The others are variants on an existing product—*Tide with Bleach, Tropicana Twister Light Fruit Juices,* and so on. Among some types of product a certain glut is evident. At last count there were 220 types of branded breakfast cereal in America. In 1993, according to an international business survey, the world's most valuable brand was *Marlboro,* with a value estimated at $40 billion, slightly ahead of *Coca-Cola.* Among the other top ten brands were *Intel, Kellogg's, Budweiser, Pepsi, Gillette,* and *Pampers. Nescafé* and *Bacardi* were the only foreign brands to make the top ten, underlining American dominance.

Huge amounts of effort go into choosing brand names. General Foods reviewed 2,800 names before deciding on *Dreamwhip.* (To put this in proportion, try to think of just ten names for an artificial whipped cream.) Ford considered more than twenty thousand possible car names before finally settling on *Edsel* (which proves that such care doesn't always pay), and Standard Oil a similar number of names before it opted for *Exxon.* Sometimes, however, the most successful names are the result of a moment's whimsy. *Betty Crocker* came in a flash to an executive of the Washburn Crosby Company (later absorbed by General Mills), who chose *Betty* because he thought it sounded wholesome and sincere and *Crocker* in memory of a beloved fellow executive who had recently died. At first the name was used only to sign letters responding to customers' requests for advice or information, but by the 1950s, Betty Crocker's smiling, confident face was appearing on more than fifty types of food product, and her loyal followers could buy her recipe books and even visit her "kitchen" at the General Foods headquarters.

Great efforts also go into finding out why people buy the brands they do. Advertisers and market researchers bandy about terms like *conjoint analysis technique, personal drive patterns, Gaussian distributions, fractals,* and other such arcana in their quest to winnow out every subliminal quirk in our buying habits. They know, for instance, that 40 percent of all people who move to a new address will also change their brand of toothpaste, that the average supermarket shopper makes fourteen impulse decisions in each visit, that 62 percent of shoppers will pay a premium for mayonnaise even when they think a cheaper brand is just as good, but that only 24 percent will show the same largely irrational loyalty to frozen vegetables.

30   To preserve a brand name involves a certain fussy attention to linguistic and orthographic details. To begin with, the name is normally expected to be treated not as a noun but as a proper adjective—that is, the names should be followed by an explanation of what it does: *Kleenex facial tissues, Q-Tip cotton swabs, Jell-O brand gelatin dessert, Sanka brand decaffeinated coffee.* Some types of

products—notably cars—are granted an exemption, which explains why General Motors does not have to advertise *Cadillac self-propelled automobiles* or the like. In all cases, the name may not explicitly describe the product's function, though it may hint at what it does. Thus *Coppertone* is acceptable; *Coppertan* would not be.

The situation is more than a little bizarre. Having done all they can to make their products household words, manufacturers must then in their advertisements do all in their power to imply that they aren't. Before trademark law was clarified, advertisers positively encouraged the public to treat their products as generics. Kodak invited consumers to "Kodak as you go," turning the brand name into a dangerously ambiguous verb. It would never do that now. The American Thermos Product Company went so far as to boast, "Thermos is a household word," to its considerable cost. Donald F. Duncan, Inc., the original manufacturer of the *Yo-Yo*, lost its trademark protection partly because it was amazingly casual about capitalization in its own promotional literature. "In case you don't know what a yo-yo is . . ." one of its advertisements went, suggesting that in commercial terms Duncan didn't. Duncan also made the elemental error of declaring, "If It Isn't a Duncan, It Isn't a Yo-Yo," which on the face of it would seem a reasonable claim, but was in fact held by the courts to be inviting the reader to consider the product generic. Kodak had long since stopped saying "If it isn't an Eastman, it isn't a Kodak."

Because of the confusion, and occasional lack of fastidiousness on the part of their owners, many dozens of products have lost their trademark protection, among them *aspirin, linoleum, yo-yo, thermos, cellophane, milk of magnesia, mimeograph, lanolin, celluloid, dry ice, escalator, shredded wheat, kerosene,* and *zipper.* All were once proudly capitalized and worth a fortune.

On July 1, 1941, the New York television station WNBT-TV interrupted its normal viewing to show, without comment, a Bulova watch ticking. For sixty seconds the watch ticked away mysteriously, then the picture faded and the normal programming resumed. It wasn't much, but it was the first television *commercial.*

Both the word and the idea were already well established. The first commercial—the term was used from the very beginning—had been broadcast by radio station WEAF in New York on August 28, 1922. It lasted for either ten or fifteen minutes, depending on which source you credit. Commercial radio was not an immediate hit. In its first two months, WEAF sold only $550 worth of airtime. But by the mid-1920s, sponsors were not only flocking to buy airtime but naming their programs after their products—*The Lucky Strike Hour, The A&P Gypsies, The Lux Radio Theater,* and so on. Such was the obsequiousness of the radio networks that by the early 1930s, many were allowing the sponsors to take complete artistic and production control for the programs.

Many of the most popular shows were actually written by the advertising agencies, and the agencies naturally seldom missed an opportunity to work a favorable mention of the sponsor's products into the scripts.

35   With the rise of television in the 1950s, the practices of the radio era were effortlessly transferred to the new medium. Advertisers inserted their names into the program title—*Texaco Star Theater, Gillette Cavalcade of Sports, Chesterfield Sound-Off Time, The U.S. Steel Hour, Kraft Television Theater, The Chevy Show, The Alcoa Hour, The Ford Star Revue, Dick Clark's Beechnut Show,* and the arresting hybrid *The Lux-Schlitz Playhouse,* which seemed to suggest a cozy symbiosis between soapflakes and beer. The commercial dominance of program titles reached a kind of hysterical peak with a program officially called *Your Kaiser Dealer Presents Kaiser-Frazer "Adventures in Mystery" Starring Betty Furness in "Byline."* Sponsors didn't write the programs any longer, but they did impose a firm control on the contents, most notoriously during a 1959 *Playhouse 90* broadcast of *Judgment at Nuremberg,* when the sponsor, the American Gas Association, managed to have all references to gas ovens and the gassing of Jews removed from the script.

Where commercial products of the late 1940s had scientific-sounding names, those of the 1950s relied increasingly on secret ingredients. Gleem toothpaste contained a mysterious piece of alchemy called *GL-70.*[3] There was never the slightest hint of what GL-70 was, but it would, according to the advertising, not only rout odor-causing bacteria but "wipe out their enzymes!"

A kind of creeping illiteracy invaded advertising, too, to the dismay of many. When Winston began advertising its cigarettes with the slogan "Winston tastes good like a cigarette should," nationally syndicated columnists like Sydney J. Harris wrote anguished essays on what the world was coming to—every educated person knew it should be "as a cigarette should"—but the die was cast. By 1958, Ford was advertising that you could "travel smooth" in a Thunderbird Sunliner and the maker of Ace Combs was urging buyers to "comb it handsome"—a trend that continues today with "pantihose that fits you real comfortable" and other grammatical manglings too numerous and dispiriting to dwell on.

We may smile at the advertising ruses of the 1920s—frightening people with the threat of "fallen stomach" and "scabby toes"—but in fact such creative manipulation still goes on, albeit at a slightly more sophisticated level. *The New York Times Magazine* reported in 1990 how an advertising copywriter had been told to come up with some impressive labels for a putative hand

---

[3]For purposes of research, I wrote to Procter & Gamble, Gleem's manufacturer, asking what GL-70 was, but the public relations department evidently thought it eccentric of me to wonder what I had been putting in my mouth all through childhood and declined to reply.

cream. She invented the arresting and healthful-sounding term *oxygenating moisturizers* and wrote accompanying copy with reference to "tiny bubbles of oxygen that release moisture into your skin." This done, the advertising was turned over to the company's research and development department, which was instructed to come up with a product that matched the copy.

If we fall for such commercial manipulation, we have no one to blame but ourselves. When Kentucky Fried Chicken introduced "Extra Crispy" chicken to sell alongside its "Original" chicken, and sold it at the same price, sales were disappointing. But when its advertising agency persuaded it to promote "Extra Crispy" as a premium brand and to put the price up, sales soared. Much of the same sort of verbal hypnosis was put to work for the benefit of the fur industry. Dyed muskrat makes a perfectly good fur, for those who enjoy cladding themselves in dead animals, but the name clearly lacks stylishness. The solution was to change the name to *Hudson seal.* Never mind that the material contained not a strand of seal fur. It sounded good, and sales skyrocketed.

Truth has seldom been a particularly visible feature of American advertising. In the early 1970s, Chevrolet ran a series of ads for the Chevelle boasting that the car had "109 advantages to keep it from becoming old before its time." When looked into, it turned out that these 109 vaunted features included such items as rearview mirrors, backup lights, balanced wheels, and many other components that were considered pretty well basic to any car. Never mind; sales soared. At about the same time, Ford, not to be outdone, introduced a "limited edition" Mercury Monarch at $250 below the normal list price. It achieved this, it turned out, by taking $250 worth of equipment off the standard Monarch. 40

And has all this deviousness led to a tightening of the rules concerning what is allowable in advertising? Hardly. In 1986, as William Lutz relates in *Doublespeak,* the insurance company John Hancock launched an ad campaign in which "real people in real situations" discussed their financial predicaments with remarkable candor. When a journalist asked to speak to these real people, a company spokesman conceded that they were actors and "in that sense they are not real people."

During the 1982 presidential campaign, the Republican National Committee ran a television advertisement praising President Reagan for providing cost-of-living pay increases to federal workers "in spite of those sticks-in-the-mud who tried to keep him from doing what we elected him to do." When it was pointed out that the increases had in fact been mandated by law since 1975 and that Reagan had in any case three times tried to block them, a Republican official responded: "Since when is a commercial supposed to be accurate?" Quite.

In linguistic terms, perhaps the most interesting challenge facing advertisers today is that of selling products in an increasingly multicultural society.

Spanish is a particular problem, not just because it is spoken over such a widely scattered area but also because it is spoken in so many different forms. Brown sugar is *azucar negra* in New York, *azucar prieta* in Miami, *azucar morena* in much of Texas, and *azucar pardo* pretty much everywhere else—and that's just one word. Much the same bewildering multiplicity applies to many others. In consequence, embarrassments are all but inevitable.

In mainstream Spanish, *bichos* means *insects*, but in Puerto Rico it means *testicles*, so when a pesticide maker promised to bring death to the *bichos*, Puerto Rican consumers were at least bemused, if not alarmed. Much the same happened when a maker of bread referred to its product as *un bollo de pan* and discovered that to Spanish-speaking Miamians of Cuban extraction that means a woman's private parts. And when Perdue Chickens translated its slogan "It takes a tough man to make a tender chicken" into Spanish, it came out as the slightly less macho "It takes a sexually excited man to make a chick sensual."

45   Never mind. Sales soared.

Engaging the Text

1. How did the methods George Eastman invented to sell cameras become the model advertisers used to sell everything for the next hundred years?

2. What is the difference between a trademark and a brand name? Why don't companies wish their brand names to become household words? Which current products (for example, Kleenex) and processes (for example, Xerox) originated as brand names?

3. Analyze an advertisement that displays evidence of what Bill Bryson calls "creeping illiteracy": unconventional spelling, incomplete sentences, or grammatical errors. To what extent do you find the ad to be manipulative or deceptive?

Exploring Your Cultural Perspective

1. The psychological manipulation of the consumer is an important theme in Bryson's analysis. What role does the "exploitation of the American consumer's Achilles' heel: anxiety" play in getting people to buy things they don't really need? What recent ad using scare tactics convinced you to buy something (such as insurance or snow tires)?

2. Have you ever tried to sell something (a product, a service, or your skills)? What words or graphics did you use? What image of your product were you trying to convey?

RICHARD KELLER SIMON

The Shopping Mall and the Formal Garden

A clear sign that malls are a vital feature of modern culture can be inferred from the fact that the largest mall in the world, located in Bloomington, Minnesota, has had more visitors than Disney World. Richard Keller Simon has looked at the function of the mall from a new perspective. Simon describes how the modern shopping mall incorporates and updates garden designs of the past to create a self-enclosed world devoted to consumption. Simon is professor of English and director of the humanities program at California Polytechnic State University, San Luis Obispo. He is the author of *The Labyrinth of the Comic* (1986) and *Trash Culture: Popular Culture and the Great Tradition* (1999), in which this selection first appeared.

Thinking Critically

Consider Simon's statement that "visitors learn the meanings of consumer society at the mall." Simon looks at the mall as a text to be read and interprets its concealed meanings by referring to formal gardens of the past. While you read, think how you might apply the same critical methods to other large architectural structures, such as stadiums, railway stations, and airports.

The contemporary shopping mall is a great formal garden of American culture, a commercial space that shares fundamental characteristics with many of the great garden styles of Western history. Set apart from the rest of the world as a place of earthly delight like the medieval walled garden; filled with fountains, statuary, and ingeniously devised machinery like the Italian Renaissance garden; designed on grandiose and symmetrical principles like this seventeenth-century French garden; made up of the fragments of cultural and architectural history like the eighteenth-century irregular English garden; and set aside for the public like the nineteenth-century American park, the mall is the next phase of this garden history, a synthesis of all these styles that have come before. But it is now joined with the shopping street, or at least a sanitized and standardized version of one, something never before allowed within the garden. In this latest version of the earthly paradise, people live on the goods of the consumer economy peacefully, pleasurably, and even with sophisticated complexity, for although their pleasure comes from buying and everything is set up to facilitate that pleasure, the garden itself is no simple place. Nordstrom has come to Eden. There were dangers and temptations in the very first garden, of course, and the delights dangled before us have been equally powerful. We have moved from the knowledge of good and evil to the joys of shopping.

Visitors learn the meanings of consumer society at the mall, not only in the choices they make in their purchases but also in the symbol systems they walk through, just as visitors to those earlier gardens were invited to learn about the meanings of their own times from the pastoral adventures presented to them. Like the formal garden, the shopping mall is a construct of promenades, walls, vistas, mounts, labyrinths, fountains, statues, archways, trees, grottoes, theaters, flowering plants and shrubs, trellises, and assorted reproductions from architectural history, all artfully arranged. Some of these features, such as the mount, have undergone technological or economic modification. The mount—the manmade earthworks designed to present a vista of the garden to the visitor and typically reached by path or staircase—was a standard part of garden design from the Middle Ages to the eighteenth century. This has been replaced by the escalator, which rises at key points in the enclosed central parts of the mall, where it presents a similar vista of the space to the visitor, who is now lifted dramatically from the floor below by unseen forces without any effort on his or her part. And this, in its turn, is only the modification of a standard feature from Italian Renaissance gardens, the elaborate hydraulic machinery or automata that engineers had devised to move statues about in striking dramatic tableaux. Now in the mall it is the visitors who are moved about by the escalators, becoming themselves the actors in a tableau we might title "modern shopping." Combining the mount with the automata, the mall then encloses this machinery in two or three stories of space, topped with skylights. The result is something like Houston's Galleria Mall, a massive, three-story, enclosed mall topped with skylights. This, in turn, is an updated version of Henry VIII's great garden at Hampton Court, where a mount was topped by a three-story glass arbor surrounded by figures of the king's beasts and royal crown. We have dispensed with the beasts and crown; joggers now run on the roof of the Galleria. But the mount in the king's garden allowed the visitor to look both inside and outside of his garden; the escalator within the enclosed mall of the Galleria, by contrast, only allows the visitor to look at the inside space.

Similarly, the labyrinth—the maze of pathways or hedges that confounded the visitor's attempts to find an easy way out and was a favorite device of Renaissance gardens—is now the cleverly laid out pattern of aisles with department stores, which can be designed to discourage the visitor's easy exit. Shoppers simply cannot find a way out. A decade ago Bloomingdale's in the Willow Grove Mall in suburban Philadelphia received so many complaints from irate shoppers lost in its mazes that finally small, discreet exit signs were posted. What might have originated in the mazes of the early Christian Church, which penitents traveled on their knees while praying at particular points, was first moved outside into the garden, where it was secularized, and has now become thoroughly commodified, a journey in which purchases have replaced prayers. Buy enough and we will let you out.

Played against the maze and labyrinth in the Renaissance garden were the axial and radial avenues that began as extensions of hallways of the palace and ended in suitably grand natural vistas. Played against the department store maze in the mall are the axial and radial avenues that begin as extensions of hallways of one anchor department store and end in the grand vistas of the entrances to other anchor department stores.

The kitchen garden, that area of the formal garden closest to the house   5 and set aside for the production of food, has become the food court, that area of the mall set aside for the consumption of food. The statues—the assorted imitations of Greek and Roman models, portraits of contemporary royalty, or stylized representations of the ancient virtues—have become mannequins decked out in fashionable clothing, the generalized imitations of consumers in their most beautiful, heroic, and changeable poses, portraits of contemporary anonymous life that we should see as stylized representations of the modern virtues: pose, flexibility, nubility, interchangeability, emotional absence. The generalized faces on the statues are now the empty faces of the mannequins. And the various architectural antiquities that became a feature of eighteenth-century English irregular gardens—the miscellaneous copies of Greek temples, Gothic ruins, Japanese pagodas, Roman triumphal arches, and Italian grottoes—are now represented not so much by the miscellaneous architectural reproductions that appear seasonally in the mall, as in the Easter Bunny's cottage or Santa's Workshop, but much more profoundly by many of the stores themselves, which present idealized versions of architectural and cultural history to the consumer: the Victorian lingerie shop, the high modernist fur salon, the nineteenth-century Western goods store, the Mexican restaurant, the country store designed as a red barn, the dark bar designed as a grotto. Also present in smaller details—in the grand staircase, the wall of mirrors, the plush carpeting, the man playing the white grand piano—are echoes of the 1930s movie set; in the merry-go-round, the popcorn cart, and the clown with balloons, the echoes of funland. The eighteenth-century garden included such historical reproductions in an effort to make sense of its past and to accommodate its cultural inheritances to new situations. One can say the same about the mall's inclusion of historical recollections. If we judge this to be playful and parodic, then we can also call the space postmodern, but if it is only a nostalgic recovery of history, we cannot. This can be a tricky thing. The mall's appropriation of history into idealized spaces of consumption can be a nostalgia or parody, or both at the same time.

The Stanford Shopping Center near Palo Alto presents such a parodic and nostalgic bricolage of cultural and architectural history: Crabtree and Evelyn with its images of eighteenth-century life; Laura Ashley with its images of Romantic and early Victorian life; Victoria's Secret, the late Victorian whorehouse with overtones of French fashion; Banana Republic, the late Victorian colonial outfitter; the Disney Store with its images of 1940s art; and The Nature Company, closest to the sixteenth century and the rise of science in its stock of simple instruments and decor of simple observations of nature. One walks through the images of history just as one did in the formal garden, but now they can be appropriated through the act of consuming. One buys images but learns "history." It is a clean, neat, middle-class version of history without the homeless of a downtown big city, and thus a retreat from the frenzy of urban life and of contemporary history, which is exactly what the formal garden was designed to be. To one side is an alley devoted to food: a lavishly idealized greengrocer, a pseudo-Italian coffee bar, and Max's Opera Café, a reproduction of a grand nineteenth-century cafe in Vienna—but what one finds when one wanders inside is not real or ersatz Vienna, but a glorified Jewish deli. Here the history of central Europe is rewritten as it might have been.

In one Renaissance garden a grotto dedicated to Venus and voluptuous pleasure was juxtaposed with one dedicated to Diana and virtuous pleasure. In another a Temple of Ancient Virtue was contrasted with one representing Modern Virtue. In a similar manner the visitor to the modern garden at Stanford is presented with choices between Victoria's Secret, the shop of voluptuous pleasure, and Westminster Lace, the shop of virtuous pleasure and chastity, but he or she does not have to choose between the Temple of Modern Virtue, the modern shopping center itself, or the Temple of Ancient Virtue, the remnants of the gardens of the past, because the mall artfully combines both.

We are almost at an end of our catalogue of garden elements. In fact, the only standard feature of garden design not present in the modern mall, either in original or in modified form, is the hermitage ruin, a favorite eighteenth-century architectural device designed to allow the visitor to pretend to be a hermit, to be alone and to meditate. There are only two places where a visitor can be alone in the mall: in the lavatories and in the clothing store changing room, but even there one can find surveillance cameras. Meditation and isolation are not virtues encouraged by the modern garden because, interestingly enough, given the opportunity, too many consumers will not meditate there at all, but try to steal whenever they can.

The shopping mall is, of course, quite an imperfect paradise, but the fault does not lie so much with the garden as with the shopping street it has come to assimilate. It is true that there are very few trees in these postmodern gardens, and those that do appear are typically confined in antipastoral concrete planters, but such subordination of nature has occurred before in garden history. Plants were incidental to the Renaissance garden, where visitors instead were expected to direct their attention to the grottoes, fountains, and various mechanical automata.

By bringing the mundane world of commerce into the garden, along with its 10 attendant ills, the mall appears to be inverting the fundamental purposes of many of those earlier gardens as places of repose and contemplation, of escape from the mundane world. Conspicuous consumption has replaced quiet repose. But many of the great styles of garden history have been practical, if not precisely in this way, for example, the *ferme ornée* or eighteenth-century ornamented working farm with its fields, kitchen gardens, orchards, and pastures placed beside the more decorative and formal elements of the garden. These were gardens that had their practical commercial aspects. But although the mall is a far more commercial place than the practical garden, the shift has not so much destroyed the garden—for most of history a space set aside for the rich—as adapted it to new social and economic realities, and it thus can be seen as the appropriate garden for a consumer-oriented culture. In the formal gardens of the past, where nature was rearranged to fit the aesthetic taste of the period, one walked through the landscape contemplating the vistas and approaching the beautiful. In the shopping mall, where nature is similarly rearranged to fit the commercial needs of the period, one walks through the landscape, now contemplating not the vistas of nature, which have been completely blocked out, but rather the vistas presented by the entrances to the anchor department stores, and now approaching not the beautiful but rather the commodities by means of which one can become beautiful. These are practical times. The aristocrat who walked down the path of the garden admired the flowers and smelled their scents; the consumer who walks down the path of the shopping mall buys the flower scents in bottles and then smells like the flower or the musk ox. The focus has shifted from the individual in reverie facing an artificial version of nature to the individual in excitement facing a garden of consumer products. In the eighteenth century the visitor to the garden was expected to feel the elevation of his or her soul. It is unlikely that the visitor to the modern mall has a comparable experience.

Engaging the Text

1. How does the modern shopping mall incorporate features of gardens of the past for a single-minded purpose: consumption? What are some of these features, and what function do they serve?

2. Why is it significant that, of all past garden features, only the hermitage (the place in which to be alone to meditate) is not included in the modern shopping mall?

Exploring Your Cultural Perspective

1. In what ways have past historical eras been re-presented in commercialized forms within the confines of particular stores in the mall? What are some sample "worlds" of the past that one can enter in the mall? How is the fantasy dimension of these stores designed to stimulate consumer purchases? Do they work this way for you?

2. Do you like spending time in shopping malls? Do you actually shop, or do you hang out and meet friends? Analyze how the layout of a mall or department store you frequent is designed to encourage consumption.

RABBI SUSAN SCHNUR

Barbie Does Yom Kippur

In this essay, which originally appeared in *The Barbie Chronicles: A Living Doll Turns Forty*, edited by Yona Zeldis McDonough (1999), Rabbi Susan Schnur draws on personal experience to raise the broader issue of materialism's intrusion into the spiritual world. Rabbi Schnur is a clinical psychologist at Princeton University and the editor of *Lilith* magazine, a Jewish-feminist quarterly.

Thinking Critically

Before you read this selection, think about the experiences you might have had with Barbie. Consider how she both influences and reflects popular culture—as a beloved icon or as a notorious little piece of plastic.

Some years ago, when I was fresh out of seminary and installed in my first pulpit, I nourished a number of stupid ideas about synagogue life—not the least of which was the idea that kids should do whatever they want during religious services. That's right, *whatever they want*. I based this ridiculous notion on my own childhood congregational experience—years and years of weekly shulgoing, during which time I never so much as *once* cracked open a prayerbook. What I did do, however, *religiously*—what a whole loose-knit bunch of us kids did every Sabbath at synagogue, *religiously*, was smash each other with the sanctuary's swinging doors, hold shrieking matches in the stairwells, toss all the fur coats in the cloakroom into one huge pile and bury ourselves, crawl under and over bathroom stalls in strict monastic sequences, terrify each other in the industrial kitchen's enormous walk-in freezer, and play checkers on the parquet floor of the elegant shul vestibule with *yahrtzeit* glasses purloined from the custodial closet.

Years after these anarchic Sabbaths, when, as a grown-up, I would occasionally bump into an old shul-crony, we would immediately rush into blabbing contentedly about those long-ago long-shadowed tumbleweed Saturdays—orthodox, of course, in their own scrupulous fashion—and we'd marvel about how our luxurious *Shabbos* antics had translated for us, for all of us—effortlessly, cozily—into a bedrock love of religion.

Thus it was with complete confidence that I headed into my first Yom Kippur as a full-fledged rabbi, inviting children to bring whatever they wanted to the season's long penitential services: Barbies, Lotto, He-Men, comic books, *Pat the Bunny*. That year's haunting Kol Nidre service, I remember, felt particularly spiritual and introspective: lights low, Torahs held aloft by ancient *zeidehs* (grandpas) whose davvening (praying) was mood-alteringly Yiddish-inflected, the feel in the sanctuary lean, the medieval chant spellbinding, almost primevally genetic . . . when *kaboom!!!*, an ear-splitting volley of machine-gun fire hit the room, and I wheeled around to see my own rotten child, age four, gunning down all the Jews in the sanctuary with his man-sized, Toys "Я" Us weapon. My husband yanked the kid out the door, and the room became abruptly, tensely silent. There *is* historic precedent, after all, for Jews being shot, burned, beaten, raped, starved, frozen, et cetera, in locked Ashkenazy shuls during the Days of Awe. Why wasn't this kid playing red-light, green-light in his fuzzy-wuzzy socks on the wall-to-wall Berber like a *good* little recreant? What happened to checkers?

But heavy-duty weaponry, it turned out, was not the only arsenal being built up that Yom Kippur. While the boys stockpiled their counterphobic fantasy objects—that is, those items of play that children gravitate toward in order to master their anxieties about someday being full grown-ups who run the world, who win—the girls were amassing theirs, in the form of Barbies, those beautiful women with "female power" who the girls hoped one day to become. By the next morning at shul, there were dozens of Barbies in attendance; leggy Trojan horses in the High Holiday wings, they were virginal, masochistic, eager to offer themselves sacrificially on the Yom Kippur altar.

5   Barbie's formal religious debut, however, did not occur until the near-end of the holy day, at the twilight—at which dust-motey hour the sanctuary is no longer a roomful of individuals praying but rather a single fossil organism that breathes, a palliation of survivors, a lump of gatekeepers against the silence of the universe, glazed guardians of the human promise to *be* in this world. Those of us who lasted twenty-five hours had stood, sat, bowed, chanted, ritually beaten our breasts with our fists, and intoned hour after endless hour—tired, thirsty, very bored, hungry, irritable, malodorous—until finally dusk began to hint at our reward: Catharsis, Renewal, Virtue, Serenity, Purity, Love.

Suddenly, though, as we lugubriously cranked out the final "Our Father, our King, we have sinned before Thee," dragging the syllables so that our crowning prayer would coincide with the achingly slow filibuster of the dying sun, we heard a stampeding racket above our heads, painfully reminiscent of the awfulness of the previous night's shrill gunfire. Wasting not a second, I ran out the door, up the Hebrew-school steps, and there, in flagrante delicto, I caught sight of dozens of girls, little girls, very little girls—the oldest, maybe eleven—barreling up and down the hall holding Barbies. They were racing, up and back, up and back, clutching Barbies.

"Let me guess," I said to the girls breathlessly, hushing them and gathering them around. "Barbie's exercising." They nodded. "Why?" I continued rhetorically, still panting. "Because, let me guess, she fasted for Yom Kippur." They nodded again.

"Barbie is exercising off some last-minute pounds before she breaks the fast by bingeing on all the food they're setting up downstairs. You smell it?" They nodded. "Am I right?" "Yeah." *Our rabbi knows everything!* I imagined them thinking. I considered, in my own head, the nature of epiphany. Was my discernment of the meaning of the girls' play a theosophical insight sent to me by the Lord God Himself, King of the Bathroom Scales, deeply male Ruler of the Universe, Who loves virgins and nonvirgins alike, so long as they all stand naked before Him, genuflecting to better read the little numbers, praying for the miracle of the lost half pound, surrendering themselves before His all-critical Power? This God, I thought problematically, *loves* complicitous girls who are preoccupied by self-loathing and utterly stupid tiny meaningless things. No, I think, my quick take on the meaning of Barbie's weight-reduction marathon was not a religious epiphany at all, but rather a reflexive lurch toward warped bulimic logic, derived from a combination, in this circumstance, of the previous night's gendered shoot-out and my own plummeting heart. Downstairs we were fasting for moral redemption, and upstairs we were fasting for Ken.

Suddenly, the girls started a spontaneous chant—Barbie's Kol Nidre, I guess—holding the dolls, modern iconic war goddesses, at flat chest-height, and militarily marching them down the hall: "I/Lost/the *Most*/Weight. I/Lost/the *Most*/Weight. . . ."

"Look," I said to them in summary, crouching to their level to impart a final piece of resigned rabbinic wisdom. "If you're going to run around, take off your shoes."

As I headed back down to the chapel in my white *kittel*, the special garment that is the color of mercy, worn only on the Day of Atonement, I heard a precocious five-year-old avouch nasally, "My Barbie *wins*."

It was this kid—*this kid*—who I credit finally with ruining my entire spiritual year.

There are many ways to understand the role Barbie played that Day of Atonement, but what struck me then was that *my* childhood synagogue impieties felt worlds apart from that of these kids'. *Our* actings-out had to do with the absolute safety and all-encompassing coherence of our religious, liberal, white, middle-class, American, 1950s lives—exemplified by the Sabbath but present *every* day. On *Shabbos*, parking our parents (and their parents, and virtually every grown-up we knew) with God as babysitter, we had the *preconditions* for running amok, for our unruly intoxications at the margins. Our palimpsest was *simpler* than met the eye; Barbie's, though, is more complicated.

Barbie, Toys "Я" Us machine guns—these are "charged objects," contaminative; they represent the dog-eat-dog world, the obsessively competitive culture that synagogues and mosques and churches strive to keep *out*. Barbie expresses the dilemmas of our desires, the sustained dissonance in our lives between the spiritual and the materialistic, the emotional gridlock inherent in our culture of relentless individualism. Barbie is a concretization of what the critic Walter Lippmann called, as far back as 1929, "the acids of modernity"; she strands us in narcissism, self-esteem struggles, the empty victories of consumerism. The kiddy-instigated pollutions at my latter-day shul (not my childhood one) involved gendered mastery exercises around the dialectical themes of domination/control, violence/beauty, sexuality/power, love/envy, aggression toward the self and toward the other.

15   In my childhood shul, our developmental task felt quite different: We kids used the synagogue the way babies use parents' laps: to be rocked, soothed, reassured, to be filled up with love and emotional security, to be steeped in the predictable *because* it is developmentally empowering.

Then again, these interpretations are all, perhaps, beside the point. I could as easily say that the theme of Yom Kippur *is* "the acids of modernity," *is* contamination, since the liturgy is all about the construction of contrasts: pure vs. impure, obedience vs. rebellion, order vs. disorder, Life vs. Death. To quote the seminal High Holiday prayer,

> On Rosh Hashana the decree is inscribed and on Yom Kippur it is sealed, who shall live and who shall die, who shall perish by fire and who by water, who by sword and who by beast, who by hunger and who by thirst, who shall have rest and who shall go wandering, who shall be tranquil and who shall be disturbed. . . .

The penitential season is one of purification, a realigning of everything that is out of whack, a killing off of what's "bad." This is why the Israelite priests took the famous ur-scapegoat and drove it into the wilderness with all the people's sins on its head, to chase out all that was impure, to cleanse. The word *kippur* itself means "purge"—to purge ourselves of anxieties and dissatisfactions, to choose a new course in life, to purify. Maybe even binge and purge—one of Barbie's specialties.

Perhaps the girls running laps with their Barbies at synagogue, exercising addictively, fasting, were pointing out the hypocrisies of religious life—that our penance doesn't really change us, that our "fasts" are feel-good catharses that fail to generalize into our real lives, that fasts only set up binges, penitence only sets up the next reactive round of guilty indulgences.

It could be that we need *more* Barbies and war toys at our religious services in order to mock our prayers, to shove into our faces the entrenched hear-no-evil/see-no-evil ethos that religious life secretly sanctions. As we read (on Yom Kippur) from the prophet Isaiah, "Is such the fast I desire, a day for people to starve their bodies? No. *This* is the fast I desire: to loose the fetters of injustice." Or maybe, if I had been speedier of mind at Barbie's anorectic Yom Kippur debut, I could have gathered up all the dolls and all the plastic weapons, put all our community's sins upon them, and driven them into the wilderness with great ceremony, or burned them, or thrown them off a cliff, or put them in the recycling bin and thought about that. How to restore Eden. Next year in Jerusalem. All that stuff.

As I sit at my desk finishing up this essay, my son, now tall and sixteen,   20 reads over my shoulder. "I think you have it wrong, Ma," he concludes. "You know that Chassidic story about the illiterate shepherd boy who comes to synagogue on Yom Kippur but he doesn't know how to pray? Finally, he just takes out his shepherd's flute in synagogue and blows it as hard as he can, and the people freak out because it's forbidden to play instruments on the most holy day of the year. But the rabbi says, 'This boy's prayer, more than ours, will *certainly* reach Heaven, because he prays from the gut.'

"I remember that incident in shul when I was four," he continues, "and Dad came from nowhere and yanked me out to the parking lot. Maybe I was praying with that machine gun. Maybe we pray with our violence; we pray with our anorexia. We pray." He shrugs.

"That's lovely," I say to my wonderful son who once gunned down a roomful of worshipers. And I put it in my essay.

Engaging the Text

1. What is the significance of Yom Kippur? What kinds of activities are customary on this holiday?

2. Schnur recalls how she and her friends behaved in the synagogue when they were young and is disturbed by the behavior of the current generation. What upsets her?

3. How does Schnur use the contrast between spiritual and secular reasons for fasting to point out the encroachment of consumer culture into religion?

Exploring Your Cultural Perspective

1. Barbie's defenders see her as a constructive influence on young girls, whereas her detractors claim she disempowers women. What cultural values does Barbie communicate? Do the roles she enacts (including surgeon, astronaut, UNICEF ambassador, and candidate for president, in 2000) override her impact as an image of narcissistic self-indulgence? Present your views in a short essay. A relevant Web site is <http://www.barbie.com>.

2. Barbie has been marketed in almost every conceivable costume or outfit with innumerable accessories, yet a Barbie dressed in religious garb would clearly be offensive. Or would she? If so, why?

UMBERTO ECO

How Not to Use the Fax Machine
and the Cellular Phone

Umberto Eco is a professor of **semiotics** (the study of sign systems) at the University of Bologna. Born in 1932, he is the author of several novels, including *Foucault's Pendulum* (1989), *The Name of the Rose* (1994), and *The Island of the Day Before* (1995), as well as numerous collections of essays. The *Boston Phoenix* has described Eco as "Roland Barthes by way of Woody Allen. Eco takes delight in the absurd, the surreal, and the wildly fanciful." This selection is drawn from *How to Travel with a Salmon* (1995). A recent work is *Kant and the Platypus: Essays on Language and Cognition* (1999).

Thinking Critically

Notice that Eco uses artifacts of daily life to interpret modern culture. Keep in mind that he finds it ironic that our gadgets have acquired cult status. How would you react if you were told that for one week you would be denied access to your electronic gadgets: fax machine, Palm Pilot, cellular phone? What would you do?

The fax machine is truly a great invention. For anyone still unfamiliar with it, the fax works like this: you insert a letter, you dial the number of the addressee, and in the space of a few minutes the letter has reached its destination. And the machine isn't just for letters: it can send drawings, plans, photographs, pages of complicated figures impossible to dictate over the telephone. If the letter is going to Australia, the cost of the transmission is no more than that of an intercontinental call of the same duration. If the letter is being sent from Milan to Saronno, it costs no more than a directly dialed call. And bear in mind that a call from Milan to Paris, in the evening hours, costs about a thousand lire. In a country like ours, where the postal system, by definition, doesn't work, the fax machine solves all your problems. Another thing many people don't know is that you can buy a fax for your bedroom, or a portable version for travel, at a reasonable price. Somewhere between a million five and two million lire. A considerable amount for a toy, but a bargain if your work requires you to correspond with many people in many different cities.

Unfortunately, there is one inexorable law of technology, and it is this: when revolutionary inventions become widely accessible, they cease to be accessible. Technology is inherently democratic, because it promises the same services to all; but it works only if the rich are alone in using it. When the poor also adopt technology, it stops working. A train used to take two hours to go from A to B; then the motor car arrived, which could cover the same distance in one hour. For this reason cars were very expensive. But as soon as the masses could afford to buy them, the roads became jammed, and the trains started to move faster. Consider how absurd it is for the authorities constantly to urge people to use public transport, in the age of the automobile; but with public transport, by consenting not to belong to the elite, you get where you're going before members of the elite do.

In the case of the automobile, before the point of total collapse was reached, many decades went by. The fax machine, more democratic (in fact, it costs much less than a car), achieved collapse in less than a year. At this point it is faster to send something through the mail. Actually, the fax encourages such postal communications. In the old days, if you lived in Medicine Hat, and you had a son in Brisbane, you wrote him once a week and you telephoned him once a month. Now, with the fax, you can send him, in no time, the snapshot of his newborn niece. The temptation is irresistible. Furthermore, the world is inhabited by people, in an ever-increasing number, who want to tell you something that is of no interest to you: how to choose a smarter investment, how to purchase a given object, how to make them happy by sending them a check, how to fulfill yourself completely by taking part in a conference that will improve your professional status. All of these people, the moment they discover you have a fax, and unfortunately there are now fax directories, will trample one another underfoot in their haste to send you, at modest expense, unrequested messages.

As a result, you will approach your fax machine every morning and find it swamped with messages that have accumulated during the night. Naturally, you throw them away without having read them. But suppose someone close to you wants to inform you that you have inherited ten million dollars from an uncle in America, but on condition that you visit a notary before eight o'clock: if the well-meaning friend finds the line busy, you don't receive the information in time. If someone *has* to get in touch with you, then, he has to do so by mail. The fax is becoming the medium of trivial messages, just as the automobile has become the means of slow travel, for those who have time to waste and want to spend long hours in gridlocked traffic, listening to Mozart or Dire Straits.

Finally, the fax introduces a new element into the dynamics of nuisance.   5
Until today, the bore, if he wanted to irritate you, paid (for the phone call, the postage stamp, the taxi to bring him to your doorbell). But now you contribute to the expense, because you're the one who buys the fax paper.

How can you react? I have already had letterhead printed with the warning "Unsolicited faxes are automatically destroyed," but I don't think that's enough. If you want my advice, I'd suggest keeping your fax disconnected. If someone has to send you something, he has to call you first and ask you to connect the machine. Of course, this can overload the telephone line. It would be best for the person who has to send a fax to write you first. Then you can answer, "Send your message via fax Monday at 5.05.27 P.M., Greenwich mean time, when I will connect the machine for precisely four minutes and thirty-six seconds."

It is easy to take cheap shots at the owners of cellular phones. But before doing so, you should determine to which of the five following categories they belong.

First come the handicapped. Even if their handicap is not visible, they are obliged to keep in constant contact with their doctor or the 24-hour medical service. All praise, then, to the technology that has placed this beneficent instrument at their service. Second come those who, for serious professional reasons, are required to be on call in case of emergency (fire chiefs, general practitioners, organ-transplant specialists always awaiting a fresh corpse, or President Bush, because if he is ever unavailable, the world falls into the hands of Quayle). For them the portable phone is a harsh fact of life, endured, but hardly enjoyed. Third, adulterers. Finally, for the first time in their lives, they are able to receive messages from their secret lover without the risk that family members, secretaries, or malicious colleagues will intercept the call. It suffices that the number be known only to him and her (or to him and him, or to her and her: I can't think of any other possible combinations). All three categories listed above are entitled to our respect. Indeed, for the first two we are willing to be disturbed even while dining in a restaurant, or during a funeral; and adulterers are very discreet, as a rule.

Two other categories remain. These, in contrast, spell trouble (for us and for themselves as well). The first comprises those persons who are unable to go anywhere unless they have the possibility of chattering about frivolous matters with the friends and relations they have just left. It is hard to make them understand why they shouldn't do it. And finally, if they cannot resist the compulsion to interact, if they cannot enjoy their moments of solitude and become interested in what they themselves are doing at that moment, if they cannot avoid displaying their vacuity and, indeed, make it their trademark, their emblem, well, the problem must be left to the psychologist. They irk us, but we must understand their terrible inner emptiness, be grateful we are not as they are, and forgive them—without, however, gloating over our own superior natures, and thus yielding to the sins of spiritual pride and lack of charity. Recognize them as your suffering neighbor, and turn the other ear.

10   In the last category (which includes, on the bottom rung of the social ladder, the purchasers of fake portable phones) are those people who wish to show in public that they are greatly in demand, especially for complex business discussions. Their conversations, which we are obliged to overhear in airports, restaurants, or trains, always involve monetary transactions, missing shipments of metal sections, an unpaid bill for a crate of neckties, and other things that, the speaker believes, are very Rockefellerian.

Now, helping to perpetuate the system of class distinctions is an atrocious mechanism ensuring that, thanks to some atavistic proletarian defect, the nouveau riche, even when he earns enormous sums, won't know how to use a fish knife or will hang a plush monkey in the rear window of his Ferrari or put a San Gennaro on the dashboard of his private jet, or (when speaking his native Italian) use English words like "management." Therefore he will not be invited by the Duchesse de Guermantes (and he will rack his brain trying to figure out why not; after all, he has a yacht so long it could almost serve as a bridge across the English Channel).

What these people don't realize is that Rockefeller doesn't need a portable telephone; he has a spacious room full of secretaries so efficient that at the very worst, if his grandfather is dying, the chauffeur comes and whispers something in his ear. The man with power is the man who is not required to answer every call; on the contrary, he is always—as the saying goes—in a meeting. Even at the lowest managerial level, the two symbols of success are a key to the executive washroom and a secretary who asks, "Would you care to leave a message?"

So anyone who flaunts a portable phone as a symbol of power is, on the contrary, announcing to all and sundry his desperate, subaltern position, in which he is obliged to snap to attention, even when making love, if the CEO happens to telephone; he has to pursue creditors day and night to keep his head above water; and he is persecuted by the bank, even at his daughter's First Holy Communion, because of an overdraft. The fact that he uses, ostentatiously, his cellular phone is proof that he doesn't know these things, and it is the confirmation of his social banishment, beyond appeal.

Engaging the Text

1. What does Eco mean when he states that "when the poor also adopt technology, it stops working." Is he merely being ironic, or is there some truth to his observation?

2. Given Eco's viewpoint about technology, do you think his tone is appropriate? Why or why not?

Exploring Your Cultural Perspective

1. Cellular phones have altered people's everyday behavior in profound ways. In some places, such as public meetings, theaters, and restaurants, the use of cell phones is being discouraged. Should the use of cell phones be restricted, or should people be free to use them whenever they want? Explain your answer.

2. In what ways has the cellular phone become a fetish in modern society? What does it signify? Do you own one? If so, how often do you use it and for what purposes?

3. How has the anthrax scare changed the way we communicate?

GEORGE CARLIN
A Place for Your Stuff

George Carlin's social criticism, presented in the guise of stand-up comedy, has made him one of the most successful performers over the past forty years. He was awarded the Lifetime Achievement Award in 2001 at the 15th Annual American Comedy Awards. In this classic monologue, reprinted from *Braindroppings* (1997), Carlin looks at our love-hate relationship with our possessions. Carlin's hilarious monologue will strike many people as being right on target. His latest work is *Napalm and Silly Putty* (2001).

Thinking Critically
Notice how Carlin uses irony and exaggeration to get his point across. Consider how many times you use the word stuff *(or hear it) in the course of a day.*

Hi! How are ya? You got your stuff with you? I'll bet you do. Guys have stuff in their pockets; women have stuff in their purses. Of course, some women have pockets, and some guys have purses. That's okay. There's all different ways of carryin' your stuff.

Then there's all the stuff you have in your car. You got stuff in the trunk. Lotta different stuff: spare tire, jack, tools, old blanket, extra pair of sneakers. Just in case you wind up barefoot on the highway some night.

And you've got other stuff in your car. In the glove box. Stuff you might need in a hurry: flashlight, map, sunglasses, automatic weapon. You know. Just in case you wind up barefoot on the highway some night.

So stuff is important. You gotta take care of your stuff. You gotta have a *place* for your stuff. Everybody's gotta have a place for their stuff. That's what life is all about, tryin' to find a place for your stuff! That's all your house is: a place to keep your stuff. If you didn't have so much stuff, you wouldn't *need* a house. You could just walk around all the time.

5   A house is just a pile of stuff with a cover on it. You can see that when you're taking off in an airplane. You look down and see all the little piles of

stuff. Everybody's got his own little pile of stuff. And they lock it up! That's right! When you leave your house, you gotta lock it up. Wouldn't want somebody to come by and *take* some of your stuff. 'Cause they always take the *good* stuff! They don't bother with that crap you're saving. Ain't nobody interested in your fourth-grade arithmetic papers. *National Geographics*, commemorative plates, your prize collection of Navajo underwear; they're not interested. They just want the good stuff; the shiny stuff; the electronic stuff.

So when you get right down to it, your house is nothing more than a place to keep your stuff . . . while you go out and get . . . *more stuff.* 'Cause that's what this country is all about. Tryin' to get more stuff. Stuff you don't want, stuff you don't need, stuff that's poorly made, stuff that's overpriced. Even stuff you can't afford! Gotta keep on getting' more stuff. Otherwise someone else might wind up with more stuff. Can't let that happen. Gotta have the most stuff.

So you keep getting' more and more stuff, and puttin' it in different places. In the closets, in the attic, in the basement, in the garage. And there might even be some stuff you left at your parents' house: baseball cards, comic books, photographs, souvenirs. Actually, your parents threw that stuff out long ago.

So now you got a houseful of stuff. And, even though you might like your house, you gotta move. Gotta get a bigger house. Why? Too much stuff! And that means you gotta move all your stuff. Or maybe, put some of your stuff in storage. Storage! Imagine that. There's a whole industry based on keepin' an eye on other people's stuff.

Or maybe you could sell some of your stuff. Have a yard sale, have a garage sale! Some people drive around all weekend just lookin' for garage sales. They don't have enough of their own stuff, they wanna buy other people's stuff.

Or you could take your stuff to the swap meet, the flea market, the rummage sale, or the auction. There's a lotta ways to get rid of stuff. You can even give your stuff away. The Salvation Army and Goodwill will actually come to your house and pick up your stuff and give it to people who don't have much stuff. It's part of what economists call the Redistribution of Stuff. 10

OK, enough about your stuff. Let's talk about other people's stuff. Have you ever noticed when you visit someone else's house, you never quite feel at home? You know why? No room for your stuff! Somebody *else's* stuff is all over the place. And what crummy stuff it is! "God! Where'd they get *this* stuff?"

And you know how sometimes when you're visiting someone, you unexpectedly have to stay overnight? It gets real late, and you decide to stay over? So they put you in a bedroom they don't use too often . . . because Grandma died in it eleven years ago! And they haven't moved any of her stuff? Not even the vaporizer?

Or whatever room they put you in, there's usually a dresser or a nightstand, and there's never any room on it for your stuff. Someone else's shit is on the dresser! Have you noticed that their stuff is shit, and your shit is stuff?

"Get this shit off of here, so I can put my stuff down!" Crap is also a form of stuff. Crap is the stuff that belongs to the person you just broke up with. "When are you comin' over here to pick up the rest of your crap?"

Now, let's talk about traveling. Sometimes you go on vacation, and you gotta take some of your stuff. Mostly stuff to wear. But which stuff should you take? Can't take all your stuff. Just the stuff you really like; the stuff that fits you well that month. In effect, on vacation, you take a smaller, "second version" of your stuff.

15   Let's say you go to Honolulu for two weeks. You gotta take two big suitcases of stuff. Two weeks, two big suitcases. That's the stuff you check onto the plane. But you also got your carry-on stuff, plus the stuff you bought in the airport. So now you're all set to go. You got stuff in the overhead rack, stuff under the seat, stuff in the seat pocket, and stuff in your lap. And let's not forget the stuff you're gonna steal from the airline: silverware, soap, blanket, toilet paper, salt and pepper shakers. Too bad those headsets won't work at home.

And so you fly to Honolulu, and you claim your stuff—if the airline didn't drop it in the ocean—and you go to the hotel, and the first thing you do is put away your stuff. There's lots of places in a hotel to put your stuff.

"I'll put some stuff in here, you put some stuff in there. Hey, don't put your stuff in *there*! That's my stuff! Here's another place! Put some stuff in here. And there's another place! Hey, you know what? We've got more places than we've got stuff! We're gonna hafta go out and buy . . . *more stuff!!!*"

Finally you put away all your stuff, but you don't quite feel at ease, because you're a long way from home. Still, you sense that you must be OK, because you do have some of your stuff with you. And so you relax in Honolulu on that basis. That's when your friend from Maui calls and says, "Hey, why don't you come over to Maui for the weekend and spend a couple of nights over here?"

Oh no! Now whaddya bring? Can't bring all this stuff. You gotta bring an even *smaller* version of your stuff. Just enough stuff for a weekend on Maui. The "third version" of your stuff.

20   And, as you're flyin' over to Maui, you realize that you're really spread out now: You've got stuff all over the world!! Stuff at home, stuff in the garage, stuff at your parents' house (maybe), stuff in storage, stuff in Honolulu, and stuff on the plane. Supply lines are getting longer and harder to maintain!

Finally you get to your friends' place on Maui, and they give you a little room to sleep in, and there's a nightstand. Not much room on it for your stuff, but it's OK because you don't have much stuff now. You got your 8 x 10 autographed picture of Drew Carey, a large can of gorgonzola-flavored Cheez Whiz, a small, unopened packet of brown confetti, a relief map of Corsica, and a family-size jar of peppermint-flavored, petrified egg whites. And you know that even though you're a long way from home, you must be OK because you do have a good supply of peppermint-flavored, petrified egg whites. And so you begin to relax in Maui on that basis. That's when your friend says, "Hey, I think tonight we'll go over to the other side of the island and visit my sister. Maybe spend the night over there."

Oh no! Now whaddya bring? Right! You gotta bring an even smaller version. The "fourth version" of your stuff. Just the stuff you *know* you're gonna need: Money, keys, comb, wallet, lighter, hankie, pen, cigarettes, contraceptives, Vaseline, whips, chains, whistles, dildos, and a book. Just the stuff you *hope* you're gonna need. Actually, your friend's sister probably has her own dildos.

By the way, if you go to the beach while you're visiting the sister, you're gonna have to bring—that's right—an even smaller version of your stuff: the "fifth version." Cigarettes and wallet. That's it. You can always borrow someone's suntan lotion. And then suppose, while you're there on the beach, you decide to walk over to the refreshment stand to get a hot dog? That's right, my friend! Number six! The most important version of your stuff: your wallet! Your wallet contains the only stuff you really can't do without.

Well, by the time you get home you're pretty fed up with your stuff and all the problems it creates. And so about a week later, you clean out the closet, the attic, the basement, the garage, the storage locker, and all the other places you keep your stuff, and you get things down to manageable proportions. Just the right amount of stuff to lead a simple and uncomplicated life. And that's when the phone rings. It's a lawyer. It seems your aunt has died . . . and left you all her stuff. Oh no! Now whaddya do? Right. You do the only thing you can do. The honorable thing. You tell the lawyer to stuff it.

Engaging the Text

1. How much of everyday life is devoted to "stuff" (buying it, keeping it, repairing it, trading it, loaning it, returning it)? According to Carlin, what factors explain why people have very different views about their own stuff than about other people's stuff?

2. Carlin's breezy, sarcastic tone is what you might expect in a comic monologue, but it is also appropriate given his thesis. What point does he make about our culture? Do you agree with him? Why or why not?

3. In Carlin's hypothetical example about taking a vacation, why is the final collection of "stuff" brought to Maui particularly effective in illustrating the capricious nature of what we designate as important stuff?

Exploring Your Cultural Perspective

1. Consider the contents of your most cluttered drawer or closet as they might appear to an archeologist of the future analyzing the artifacts of a past

FIGURE 9.2

civilization. What would the archeologist conclude about aspects of our culture from these items? Speculate about the function and significance of any of these items as if you did not know what purpose it had served.

2. How do Americans dispose of their unwanted "stuff"? Give it away? Recycle it? Sell it at flea markets? Does this "stuff" have value to someone else?

3. How does Figure 9.2 depict what Carlin describes? For more on "stuff" and other observations by Carlin, see his Web site at <http://www.laugh.com>.

TERENCE MCLAUGHLIN

Dirt: A Social History as Seen through the Uses and Abuses of Dirt

At what point, exactly, does the "stuff" you can't wait to acquire become the dirt you can't wait to discard? This is the question Terence McLaughlin, a member of the Royal Institute of Chemistry in Great Britain and an authority on the problems of pollution, addresses. McLaughlin analyzes how the concept of dirt is related to a given society's view of contamination and varies with the context. This essay first appeared in McLaughlin's 1971 book of the same name.

Thinking Critically

Observe how McLaughlin draws ideas, interpretations, and information from a broad range of literary, historical, and psychological sources. As you read, think about whether his claims are credible. To better understand McLaughlin's concept of the variable nature of dirt, consider whether you would eat food past its expiration date.

Dirt is evidence of the imperfections of life, a constant reminder of change and decay. It is the dark side of all human activities—human, because it is only in our judgements that things are dirty: there is no such material as absolute dirt. Earth, in the garden, is a valuable support and nourishment for plants, and gardeners often run it through their fingers lovingly; earth on the carpet is dirt. A pile of dung, to the dungbeetle, is food and shelter for a large family; a pile of dung to the Public Health Inspector, is a Nuisance. Soup in a plate, before we eat it, is food; the traces that we leave on the plate imperceptibly become dirt. Lipstick on a girl's lips may make her boy-friend more anxious to touch them with his own lips; lipstick on a cup will probably make him refuse to touch it.

Because of this relativity, because dirt can be almost anything that we choose to call dirt, it has often been defined as "matter out of place." This fits the "earth (garden)/earth (carpet)" difference quite well, but it is not really very useful as a definition. A sock on the grand piano or a book in a pile of plates may be untidy, and they are certainly out of place, but they are not necessarily dirty. To be dirt, the material has to be hard to remove and unpleasant. If you sit on the beach, particularly if you bathe, sand will stick to you, but not many people would classify this as *dirt*, mainly because it brushes off so easily. However, if, as often happens the sand is covered with oil, tar, or sewage, and this sticks to you, it is definitely dirt.

Sartre, in his major philosophical work on Existentialism, *L'Etre et le Neant*,[1] presents a long discussion on the nature of sliminess or stickiness which has quite a lot to do with our ideas of dirt. He points out that quite small children who presumably have not yet learned any notions of cleanliness, and cannot yet be worried by germs, still tend to recognize that slimy things are unpleasant. It is because slimy things are clinging that we dislike them—they hold on to us even when we should like to let them go, and like an unpleasant traveling companion or an obscene telephone caller, seem to be trying to involve us in themselves. "If an object which I hold in my hands is solid," says Sartre, "I can let go when I please. . . . Yet here is the slimy reversing the terms . . . I open my hands, I want to let go of the slimy material and it sticks to me, it draws me, it sucks me. Its mode of being is neither the reassuring inertia of the solid nor a dynamism like that in water which is exhausted in fleeing from me. It is a soft yielding action, a moist and feminine sucking, it *lives* obscurely under my fingers. . . ."

This is the feeling of *pollution*, the kind of experience where something dirty has attached itself to us and we cannot get rid of the traces, however hard we try. Ritual defilement is one aspect of this feeling, and one which provides an enormous field of study for anthropologists (when they are not engaged in their favourite activity of reviling one another), but powerful irrational feelings of defilement exist in the most sophisticated societies. Try serving soup in a chamber-pot. However clean it may be, and however much a certain type of guest may find it "amusing," there will be a very real uneasiness about the juxtaposition. There are some kinds of dirt that we treat, in practice, as irremovable—as in the case of the old lady who was unlucky enough to drop her false teeth down the lavatory, where they were flushed into the sewer. When a search failed to find them, she heaved a sigh of relief. "I would never have fancied them again," she said, and most people would agree.

5   Even things which in themselves are clean, but can be associated with dirt, tend to be suspect. Vance Packard, in *The Hidden Persuaders*,[2] quotes the sad story of a company who tried to boost their sales of soup mix by offering free nylon stockings. The scheme was a complete fiasco. ". . . people seeing the offer were offended. Subconsciously they associated feet and soup and were alienated because they didn't like the idea of feet being in their soup." Faced by such reactions from industrialized society, we are in a better position to

understand such primitive taboos as the fact that, for instance, a woman of the Lele tribe who is menstruating must not cook for her husband or even poke the fire that is used for cooking.

Sartre, in his analysis, goes on to discuss the fear and disgust inspired by slimy things. When we touch them, they not only cling to us, but the boundary line between ourselves and the slime is blurred—if we dip our fingers in oil or honey (Sartre's favourite exemplar—it is difficult to tell whether he likes honey or dislikes it so intensely as to have a fixation about it) it hangs in strings from our fingers, our hands seem to be dissolving in it: "To touch slime is to risk being dissolved in sliminess. Now this dissolution by itself is frightening enough . . . but it is still more frightening in that the metamorphosis is not just into a *thing* (bad as that would be) but into slime. . . ."

There is a feeling of helplessness when you are faced by something slimy: the real horror to some of eating oysters is that, once the *thing* is in your mouth, there is no way of avoiding eating all of it. Other food of a strange character may be sampled in nibbles or sips, and if it is too distasteful you can stop; oysters take over the situation as the dominant partner. The same applies to the raw herrings beloved by the Dutch. Unfortunately for our peace of mind, most of the products of the human body are slimy—saliva, mucus, excrement, pus, semen, blood, lymph—and even honest sweat gets sticky by evaporation. "If I can fervently drink his tears," wrote Genet,[3] "Why not so the limpid drop on the end of his nose?" And the answer is quite clear. The drop on the end of his nose is slimy. We do not wish to be associated so closely and so permanently with other human beings. Their various slimy secretions will pollute us, will bring us into a closer and more permanent relationship with them than we should wish.

Of course, our own secretions are different. We have learned to live with them. We do not object to our own saliva, for instance, but the idea of someone else's saliva touching us is usually repellant, just as we do not like to think of cooks tasting the food which we are going to eat. Brahmins[4] carry this even further, and do not like their own saliva to touch their skin: if a Brahmin accidentally touches his fingers to his lips he must bathe or at least change his clothes, and this means that he has to eat by effectively throwing the food into his mouth. Spitting on other people is a sign of great loathing, and being spat on is extremely humiliating and disgusting, despite the fact that the saliva is mostly water. There was an old music-hall joke about a man called away from a public-house bar, leaving a glass on the counter; to protect his drink he put up a little notice saying, "I have spat in this beer." When he returned the drink was still there, but there was an addition to the notice: "So have I."

We are tolerant of our own bodily functions and smells, like Mr. Bloom in *Ulysses*[5] reading *Tidbits* in the outside privy—"He read on, seated calm above his own rising smell"—and the Icelanders have a coarse but accurate proverb, that every man likes the smell of his own farts, but too much evidence of other people's bodily function is "dirty."

10   We can extend some tolerance to the people we love, because the sense of close contact and lasting association is not then a matter of pollution. Lovers can share a cup or a bath with one another, and not worry about the close contact that this implies, but we do not extend this tolerance to the rest of humanity. Indeed, the whole act of sexual intercourse, without the tolerance induced by love and respect, would be hopelessly polluting and grotesque. Those who find it difficult to reconcile themselves to human contact often consider lovemaking a disgusting affair, like the lady who wrote to the *Bristol Evening Post* some years ago:

> Sex used to be treated with decent reticence—now it is discussed openly. This sort of thing can do immense harm. The moral standards accepted as "normal" by most young people today are a case in point.
>   Why our all-wise Creator should have chosen such a distasteful—even disgusting—means of reproducing humanity is a thing that I, personally, have never been able to understand.

Where the tolerance stops is a matter of taste. Those couples whose desire to "merge" into one another is greater than their innate or acquired fear of pollution may resort to practices that appear "dirty" to other people. Krafft-Ebing[6] in the *Psychopathia Sexualis*, deals with the curious deviation of *coprolegny*, where people derive sexual pleasure from licking or touching the bodily secretions of others, including excrement. Bizarre as this habit may seem . . . dirt is an entirely relative concept, and . . . there is no limit to the strangeness of people's attitudes to it. Coprophilia, the love of filth, can take all forms, from Aubrey Beardsley's[7] joking reference to it in *Under the Hill* and *Venus and Tannhauser*, where it seems to be introduced out of a scholarly wish to include *everything*, to a complete acceptance and even enjoyment of living conditions and bodily habits that seem disgusting.

On this crowded planet, it is very difficult to get away from contact with other people, and the traces they leave behind. In the countryside, if we settle down to rest or picnic, we do not consider pine cones, dead sticks, leaves, pebbles, earth, or anything else *natural* strewn over the ground as dirt, or even as litter, and we are not likely to be very worried even by rabbit droppings and other traces of animal life, but paper bags, beer cans, and other signs of human life make us annoyed, and human excrement left in the open will probably make us look for another place to sit. It is the human traces that we object to, because we fear contamination, a kind of magical power that these traces might exert on us if we happened to touch them or even smell them. We dislike the feeling that these unknown people who have been in the place before us may somehow infect us with their own diseases and shortcomings, and their lives may be permanently entwined with ours, just as the Thieves in Circle VIII of the *Inferno*[8] lose their individual likenesses and are constantly melting one into another. This is not just a fear of germs, for the feelings date from pre-Pasteur days, and are shared, or even intensified, in primitive societies where no notions of the germ theory exist. "And this shall be his uncleanness in his issue whether his flesh run with his issue, or his flesh be stopped from his issue, it is his uncleanness. Every bed, whereon he lieth that hath the issue, is unclean: and every thing, whereon he sitteth, shall be unclean. And whosoever toucheth his bed shall wash his clothes, and bathe himself in water, and be unclean until the even. . . ." And so on in *Leviticus* chapters xi to xv, in passages that the well-known Biblical interpreter Nathan Micklem[9] has called "the least attractive in the whole Bible. To the modern reader there is much in them that is meaningless or repulsive." Of course we know now that such regulations helped to prevent the spread of infectious diseases, and that the orthodox Jews who followed these hygienic laws managed to survive plague periods and other epidemics better than the mass of the population, but the founders of the law were working only on instinct and the formalization of instinct that we call ritual. The Jewish hygienic rules may be stricter than many other systems, but they are not different in kind. An orthodox Jew's abstention from pork is no more logical or illogical than his Christian neighbour's abstention from dog or cat; both feelings are deeply held, and have nothing to do with the habits of the animals themselves. Those writers who try to explain away such customs as the results of semi-scientific investigation often say that Jews abstain from pork because the pig is dirty, or because pork is more liable to *Salmonella* infection than other meat. Both statements are true, but if these were the only reasons, Jews and Christians should be eating cats, who have very clean habits, or guinea-pigs, who keep themselves free from vermin. The purely hygienic laws, about leprosy, skin diseases, menstruation, and discharges from the body, are not based on bacteriology, they are based on avoidance of defilement by other people.

We are all jealous of our "one-ness," our individuality, and we resent and fear any situation that forces us to become intimate, in the real sense of the word, with another person against our will. Contamination by other people is what we really fear about dirt: Sartre says in *Huis Clos*[10] that Hell is other people. Dirt is also other people.

Notes

1. In English, this major work of the French Existentialist philosopher Jean Paul Sartre (1905–1980) was translated as *Being and Nothingness*.—Ed.

2. This 1957 work investigates techniques that advertisers use to manipulate the public into buying products.—Ed.
3. The French playwright and novelist (1910–).—Ed.
4. The highest caste in Hindu society.—Ed.
5. A groundbreaking novel (published in 1922) by Irish novelist, poet, and playwright James Joyce (1882–1941).—Ed.
6. Richard von Krafft-Ebing (1840–1902) was one of the earliest investigators of deviant sexual behavior.—Ed.
7. Aubrey Beardsley (1872–1898) was an English artist and writer.—Ed.
8. The region designated as Hell in Dante Alighieri's (1265–1321) epic allegory, *Divine Comedy*.—Ed.
9. A noted professor of theology at Oxford University (1888–1977).
10. Jean Paul Sartre's play *No Exit* (1944).—Ed.

Engaging the Text

1. McLaughlin's innovative definition of dirt starts from the conventional view that dirt is "matter out of place." How does he enlarge this concept by showing the importance of cultural beliefs about pollution and contamination? Which examples are particularly persuasive in illustrating his analysis?

2. How would you characterize McLaughlin's tone and attitude toward his subject? Can you find evidence of his background as a chemist? McLaughlin's analysis draws on a psychological theory of dirt (based on the ego's fear of dissolution) and applies it to the traditional customs of various religions, such as Hinduism and Judaism. How successful is his synthesis? Write a few paragraphs in which you support or challenge his argument.

3. McLaughlin asserts that the fear of dirt is actually a fear of being contaminated by others. How do science fiction films or television shows routinely use the fear of contamination or defilement as a theme? In fact, couldn't it be said that science fiction as a genre wouldn't exist without the fear of the contaminating alien, or "other"? Why or why not?

Exploring Your Cultural Perspective

1. Discuss some other examples that illustrate how attitudes toward dirt are based on cultural expectations. For example, would you retrieve discarded clothing, food, books, furniture, Christmas ornaments, toys, gadgets? What do you throw out at the end of a semester that someone else might find valuable?

2. In a short essay, explore any aspect of the social history of doing laundry in America and other countries (see the pictures in Figure 9.3). You might wish to include the culture of laundromats, the history of washing machines and

Haiti

Thailand

Ethiopia

South Africa

Israel

Guatemala

China

FIGURE 9.3

(continued)

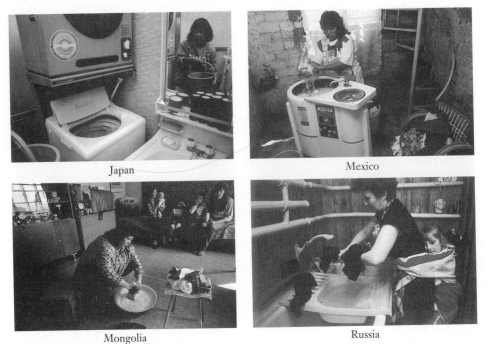

Japan

Mexico

Mongolia

Russia

FIGURE 9.3 *(continued)*

the empires built on them and related products, and the crucial role played by immigrants. Take a spin through this fascinating subject by reading the essay "It All Comes Out in the Wash" by Chiori Santiago in the September 1997 issue of *Smithsonian* magazine.

EDWARD T. HALL

Hidden Culture

Imagine that you have just checked into a hotel, unpacked your belongings, and left your room. On your return, you discover that the hotel management has moved your possessions to a different room. How would you feel? When this happened repeatedly to the American anthropologist Edward T. Hall throughout Japan, initial anger gave way to curiosity. What cultural assumptions could be responsible for such a curious event? The answer can be found in the following essay from Hall's book *Beyond Culture* (1981).

Thinking Critically

As you read Hall's piece, observe how he takes an anthropological, or comparative cultural, approach to his own experiences to understand the hidden logic that governs behavior in Japan.

A few years ago, I became involved in a sequence of events in Japan that completely mystified me, and only later did I learn how an overt act seen from the vantage point of one's own culture can have an entirely different meaning when looked at in the context of the foreign culture. I had been staying at a hotel in downtown Tokyo that had European as well as Japanese-type rooms. The clientele included a few Europeans but was predominantly Japanese. I had been a guest for about ten days and was returning to my room in the middle of an afternoon. Asking for my key at the desk, I took the elevator to my floor. Entering the room, I immediately sensed that something was wrong. Out of place. Different. I was in the wrong room! Someone else's things were distributed around the head of the bed and the table. Somebody else's toilet articles (those of a Japanese male) were in the bathroom. My first thoughts were, "What if I am discovered here? How do I explain my presence to a Japanese who may not even speak English?"

I was close to panic as I realized how incredibly territorial we in the West are. I checked my key again. Yes, it really was mine. Clearly they had moved somebody else into my room. But where was my room now? And where were my belongings? Baffled and mystified, I took the elevator to the lobby. Why hadn't they told me at the desk, instead of letting me risk embarrassment and loss of face by being caught in somebody else's room? Why had they moved me in the first place? It was a nice room and, being sensitive to spaces and how they work, I was loath to give it up. After all, I had told them I would be in the hotel for almost a month. Why this business of moving me around like someone who has been squeezed in without a reservation? Nothing made sense.

At the desk I was told by the clerk, as he sucked in his breath in deference (and embarrassment?) that indeed they had moved me. My particular room had been reserved in advance by somebody else. I was given the key to my new room and discovered that all my personal effects were distributed around the new room almost as though I had done it myself. This produced a fleeting and strange feeling that maybe I wasn't myself. How could somebody else do all those hundred and one little things just the way I did?

Three days later, I was moved again, but this time I was prepared. There was no shock, just the simple realization that I had been moved and that it would now be doubly difficult for friends who had my old room number to reach me. *Tant pis*, I was in Japan. One thing did puzzle me. Earlier, when I had stayed at Frank Lloyd Wright's Imperial Hotel for several weeks, nothing like this had ever happened. What was different? What had changed? Eventually I got used to being moved and would even ask on my return each day whether I was still in the same room.

5   Later, at Hakone, a seaside resort where I was visiting with friends, the first thing that happened was that we were asked to disrobe. We were given *okatas*, and our clothes were taken from us by the maid. (For those who have not visited Japan, the okata is a cotton print kimono.) We later learned, when we ventured out in the streets, that it was possible to recognize other guests from our hotel because we had all been equipped with identical okatas. (Each hotel had its own characteristic, clearly recognizable pattern.) Also, I noted that it was polite to wave or nod to these strangers from the same hotel.

Following Hakone, we visited Kyoto, site of many famous temples and palaces, and the ancient capital of Japan.

There we were fortunate enough to stay in a wonderful little country inn on the side of a hill overlooking the town. Kyoto is much more traditional and less industrialized than Tokyo. After we had been there about a week and had thoroughly settled into our new Japanese surroundings, we returned one night to be met at the door by an apologetic manager who was stammering something. I knew immediately that we had been moved, so I said, "You had to move us. Please don't let this bother you, because we understand. Just show us to our new rooms and it will be all right." Our interpreter explained as we started to go through the door that we weren't in that hotel any longer but had been moved to *another* hotel. What a blow! Again, without warning. We wondered what the new hotel would be like, and with our descent into the town our hearts sank further. Finally, when we could descend no more, the taxi took off into a part of the city we hadn't seen before. No Europeans here! The streets got narrower and narrower until we turned into a side street that could barely accommodate the tiny Japanese taxi into which we were squeezed. Clearly this was a hotel of another class. I found that, by then, I was getting a little paranoid, which is easy enough to do in a foreign land, and said to myself, "They must think we are very low-status people indeed to treat us this way."

As it turned out, the neighborhood, in fact the whole district, showed us an entirely different side of life from what we had seen before, much more interesting and authentic. True, we did have some communication problems, because no one was used to dealing with foreigners, but few of them were serious.

Yet, the whole matter of being moved like a piece of derelict luggage puzzled me. In the United States, the person who gets moved is often the lowest-ranking individual. This principle applies to all organizations, including the Army. Whether you can be moved or not is a function of your status, your performance, and your value to the organization. To move someone without telling him is almost worse than an insult, because it means he is below the point at which feelings matter. In these circumstances, moves can be unsettling and damaging to the ego. In addition, moves themselves are often accompanied by great anxiety, whether an entire organization or a small part of an organization moves. What makes people anxious is that the move usually presages organizational changes that have been coordinated with the move. Naturally, everyone wants to see how he comes out vis-à-vis everyone else. I have seen important men refuse to move into an office that was six inches smaller than someone else's of the same rank. While I have heard some American executives say they wouldn't employ such a person, the fact is that in actual practice, unless there is some compensating feature, the significance of space as a communication is so powerful that no employee in his right mind would allow his boss to give him a spatial demotion—unless of course he had already reached his crest and was on the way down.

These spatial messages are not simply conventions in the United States— *10* unless you consider the size of your salary check a mere convention, or where your name appears on the masthead of a journal. Ranking is seldom a matter that people take lightly, particularly in a highly mobile society like that in the United States. Each culture and each country has its own language of space, which is just as unique as the spoken language, frequently more so. In England, for example, there are no offices for the members of Parliament. In the United States, our congressmen and senators proliferate their offices and their office buildings and simply would not tolerate a no-office situation. Constituents, associates, colleagues, and lobbyists would not respond properly. In England, status is internalized; it has its manifestations and markers—the upper-class received English accent, for example. We in the United States, a relatively new country, externalize status. The American in England has some trouble placing people in the social system, while the English can place each other quite accurately by reading ranking cues, but in general tend to look down on the importance that Americans attach to space. It is very easy and very natural to look at things from one's own point of view and to read an event as though it were the same all over the world.

I knew that my emotions on being moved out of my room in Tokyo were of the gut type and quite strong. There was nothing intellectual about my initial response. Although I am a professional observer of cultural patterns, I had no notion of the meaning attached to being moved from hotel to hotel in Kyoto. I was well aware of the strong significance of moving in my own culture, going back to the time when the new baby displaces older children, right up to the world of business, where a complex dance is performed every time the organization moves to new quarters.

What was happening to me in Japan as I rode up and down elevators with various keys gripped in my hand was that I was reacting with the cultural part of my brain—the old, mammalian brain. Although my new brain, my symbolic brain—the neocortex—was saying something else, my mammalian brain kept repeating, "You are being treated shabbily." My neocortex was trying to fathom what was happening. Needless to say, neither part of the brain had been programmed to provide me with the answer in Japanese culture. I did have to put up a strong fight with myself to keep from interpreting what was going on as though the Japanese were the same as I. This is the conventional and most common response and one that is often found even among anthropologists. Any time you hear someone say, "Why *they* are no different than the folks back home—they are just like I am," even though you may understand the reasons behind these remarks you also know that the speaker is living in a single-context world (his own) and is incapable of describing either his world or the foreign one.

The "they are just like the folks back home" syndrome is one of the most persistent and widely held misconceptions of the Western world, if not the whole world. There is very little any outsider can do about this, because it expresses views that are very close to the core of the personality. Simply talking about "cultural differences" and how we must respect them is a hollow cliché. And in fact, intellectualizing isn't much more helpful either, at least at first. The logic of the man who won't move into an office that is six inches smaller than his rival's is *cultural* logic; it works at a lower, more basic level in the brain, a part of the brain that synthesizes but does not verbalize. The response is a total response that is difficult to explain to someone who doesn't already understand, because it is so dependent on context for correct interpretation. To do so, one must explain the entire system; otherwise, the man's behavior makes little sense. He may even appear to be acting childishly—which he most definitely is not.

It was my preoccupation with my own cultural mold that explained why I was puzzled for years about the significance of being moved around in Japanese hotels. The answer finally came after further experiences in Japan and many discussions with Japanese friends. In Japan, one has to "belong" or he has no identity. When a man joins a company, he does just that—joins himself to the corporate body—and there is even a ceremony marking the occasion. Normally, he is hired for life, and the company plays a much more paternalistic role than in the United States. There are company songs, and the whole company meets frequently (usually at least once a week) for purposes of maintaining corporate identity and morale.

As a tourist (either European or Japanese) when you go on a tour, you *join* 15 that tour and follow your guide everywhere as a group. She leads you with a little flag that she holds up for all to see. Such behavior strikes Americans as sheeplike; not so the Japanese. The reader may say that this pattern holds in Europe, because there people join Cook's tours and the American Express tours, which is true. Yet there is a big difference. I remember a very attractive young American woman who was traveling with the same group I was with in Japan. At first she was charmed and captivated, until she had spent several days visiting shrines and monuments. At this point, she observed that she could not take the regimentation of Japanese life. Clearly, she was picking up clues, such as the fact that our Japanese group, when it moved, marched in a phalanx rather than moving as a motley mob with stragglers. There was much more discipline in these sightseeing groups than the average Westerner is either used to or willing to accept.

It was my lack of understanding of the full impact of what it means to belong to a high-context culture that caused me to misread hotel behavior at Hakone. I should have known that I was in the grip of a pattern difference and that the significance of all guests being garbed in the same okata meant more than that an opportunistic management used the guests to advertise the hotel. The answer to my puzzle was revealed when a Japanese friend explained what it means to be a guest in a hotel. As soon as you register at the desk, you are no longer an outsider; instead, for the duration of your stay you are a member of a large, mobile family. *You belong.* The fact that I was moved was tangible evidence that I was being treated as a family member—a relationship in which one can afford to be "relaxed and informal and not stand on ceremony." This is a very highly prized state in Japan, which offsets the official properness that is so common in public. Instead of putting me down, they were treating me as a member of the family. Needless to say, the large, luxury hotels that cater to Americans, like Wright's Imperial Hotel, have discovered that Americans do tenaciously stand on ceremony and want to be treated as they are at home in the States. Americans don't like to be moved around; it makes them anxious. Therefore, the Japanese in these establishments have learned not to treat them as family members.

Engaging the Text

1. What events, inexplicable from Hall's point of view, prompt him to investigate the Japanese's concept of social acceptance?

2. In what ways do Japanese attitudes about personal space and possessions differ from those of Americans? What cultural assumptions are at work when guests at a hotel are given *okatas* (cotton robes) to wear when out in public?

3. How does Hall expand his analysis to include differences in behavior between Japanese and American tour groups and a comparison of the importance of spacious offices in the United States and England? How does Hall use each of these examples to support his hypothesis? Does his theory make sense? Why or why not?

Exploring Your Cultural Perspective

1. How important is it to you to have your own space? When you were growing up, did you have your own room or share one? How did you show the boundaries of your space? To what extent do you think your attitude toward personal space is culturally conditioned?

2. Belonging to a group confers identity in Japan. How, in America, does advertising encourage the same sense of belonging to a group through the purchase of similar consumer goods?

RAYMONDE CARROLL
Sex, Money, and Success

Why is bragging about sexual conquests as much a status symbol for the French as boasting about business success is for Americans? Raymonde Carroll has investigated this question and provides some surprising answers. Born in Tunisia, Carroll was educated in France and the United States. She was trained as an anthropologist and studied the culture of Micronesia while living for three years on the Pacific atoll Nukuoro. She presently teaches in the Department of Romance Languages at Oberlin College. This selection is drawn from her book, *Cultural Misunderstandings: The French-American Experience* (translated by Carol Volk, 1988).

Thinking Critically

Consider how Carroll integrates the speaking voices of both the French and the Americans into her analysis. Why are sexual conquests and money two time-honored indicators by which people measure personal success?

Money. For a French person, the face of an American could easily be replaced by a dollar sign. A sign of "incurable materialism," of arrogance, of power, of "vulgar," unrefined pleasure . . . the list goes on. I have never read a book about Americans, including those written with sympathy, which did not speak of the "almighty dollar"; I have never had or heard a conversation about Americans which did not mention money.

Foreigners often discover with "horror" or "repulsion" that "everything in the United States is a matter of money." Indeed, one need only read the newspapers to find constant references to the price of things. Thus, a fire is not a news item but an entity (natural or criminal), the dimensions of which are calculated by what it has destroyed—for example, ". . . a house worth two hundred *thousand* dollars . . ." In fact, if it is at all possible to attach a price to something, as approximate as it may be, that price will surely be mentioned. Thus, a French woman became indignant toward her American brother-in-law:

"He showed us the engagement ring he had just bought, and he just had to give us all the details about the deal he got in buying the diamond. . . . Talk about romantic!" I cannot even count the number of informants who had similar stories to tell ("I was admiring the magnificent antique pieces in his living room, and do you know what he did? He gave me the price of each piece, with all kinds of details I hadn't asked for. I felt truly uncomfortable . . . really . . ."). Many French informants claimed to be shocked by the "constant showing off," the "lack of taste typical of nouveaux riches" and added, some not in so many words, "As for me, you know, I am truly repulsed by money."

On the other side, many Americans expressed surprise at the frequency with which French people spoke about money, only to say that "they weren't interested in it" ("so why talk about it?"), or at the frequency with which they say "it's too expensive" about all types of things. Some find the French to be "cheap" ("They always let you pay") or "hypocritical" ("Why, then, do the French sell arms to just anyone?"), too respectful of money to trifle with it, or too petty to take risks. The list of adjectives hurled from either side on this topic seems particularly long.

Yet a brief examination of certain ethnographic details left me puzzled. For instance, what is the American article, about the forest fire that destroyed the row of two-hundred-thousand-dollar homes in California, really saying? Living in the United States, I know that a house worth two hundred thousand dollars in California is far from a palace; on the contrary. Thus, if I took the price quoted literally, I would misinterpret the article as meaning that the fire had destroyed a row of quite ordinary houses—in which case the mention of the "price" is uninformative, uninteresting, and useless. Therefore, what this article conveys, by talking about hundreds of thousands of dollars, is the fact that the fire destroyed very valuable homes. This meaning is also conveyed by the use of the word "homes," which connotes individuality and uniqueness, rather than "houses," which suggests plain buildings. The mention of the price, therefore, carries meaning of a different nature: I think that this "price" serves only as a common point of reference; it does not represent the true monetary values but a symbolic value which can be grasped immediately by anyone reading this article. A French equivalent would be a reference to the period ("from the seventeenth century") with no mention of the state of the building.

5 Similarly, it is difficult to take the example of the engagement ring literally ("I'm a tightwad"; "I'm not romantic"); it is more comprehensible if we interpret it as a message with a different meaning. For the American in question, having obtained a discount in no way altered the true value of the diamond or the symbolic value of the gesture; this "feat" probably made the gesture even more significant because of the time and attention devoted to it (the worst gift is the one that demands no effort) and probably earned him the admiration and appreciation of his fiancée.

The study of cases in which money is mentioned would require an entire book. . . . I will content myself merely with raising the question here and will indicate the general orientation of my interpretation.

The striking thing is that money is charged with a multiplicity of meanings in American culture, that it has attained a level of abstraction difficult to imagine elsewhere. Money represents both good and bad, dependence and independence, idealism and materialism, and the list of opposites can go on indefinitely, depending on whom one speaks to. It is power, it is weakness, seduction, oppression, liberation, a pure gamble, a high-risk sport; a sign of intelligence, a sign of love, a sign of scorn; able to be tamed, more dangerous than fire; it brings people together, it separates them, it is constructive, it is destructive; it is reassuring, it is anxiety-producing; it is enchanting, dazzling, frightening; it accumulates slowly or comes in a windfall; it is displayed, it is invisible; it is solid, it evaporates. It is everything and nothing, it is sheer magic, it exists and does not exist at the same time; it is a mystery. The subject provokes hatred, scorn, or impassioned defense from Americans themselves, who are constantly questioning themselves on the topic.

I believe that one association remains incontestable, no matter how much resentment it provokes. Money symbolizes success. It is not enough to have money to be admired, but quite the contrary; there is no excuse for the playboy who squanders an inherited fortune. To earn money, a lot of money, and to spend it, is to give the most concrete, the most visible sign that one has been able to realize one's potential, that one has not wasted the "opportunities" offered by one's parents or by society, and that one always seeks to move on, not to stagnate, to take up the challenge presented in the premises shaping the education of children. . . .

As a result, money has become a common denominator. It is supposed to be accessible to all, independent of one's origins. And if it creates classes, it also allows free access to those classes to whoever wants to enter. (Let's not forget that we are talking here about "local verities," about cultural premises, and not about social realities.) Money is therefore the great equalizer, in the sense that the highest social class is, in principle, open to everyone, and that while those who are born into this social class have definite advantages, they must nonetheless deserve to remain there, must "prove themselves." And the newspapers are filled with enough stories of poor people turned millionaires to reinforce this conviction.

From this perspective, it is understandable that one does not hide one's success but displays it, shows it off. By making my humble origins known, by displaying my success, I am not trying to humiliate others (although it is possible that I, personally, am a real "stinker"), but I am showing others that it is possible, I am encouraging emulation through example, I am reaffirming a cultural truth: "if I can do it, you can do it." Hence the constant copresence of dreams

10

and success, that is to say, the constant reaffirmation that the impossible is possible, and that attaining the dream depends solely on me. The logical, and ironic, conclusion to all this is the essentially idealistic significance of money in American culture, which does not exclude its "materialistic" utilization.

I do not believe that the misunderstanding between the French and Americans concerning money can be resolved by performing a parallel analysis of the meaning of money in French culture, not because money is not a concern for the French, but because I believe that what Americans express through money is expressed by the French in another domain.

From this brief analysis, I will reiterate three points. The first is that money in America serves as a common point of reference, a shortcut for communication, a means of defining a context that is recognizable by all and comprehensible no matter what one's financial situation may be. The second is that it is not in bad taste to recount one's triumphs, one's success in this domain, whether it is a matter of having obtained a half-price diamond or of having accumulated a veritable fortune, insofar as this in no way implies that I wish to put down others, that I am conceited, and so on, characteristics which depend not on money but on my personality. And the third is that money is accessible to all, makes possible upward mobility, that is to say, access to any class.

To the extent that these three points I just made are not "true" for French culture—and that they might in fact provoke "real repulsion"—one must look in a realm other than that of money for what carries the same message. . . .

The repulsion with which many French people react to the "bad taste" of Americans who "brag about their wealth," "show off their money," and so on closely resembles the disgust with which many Americans speak of the "bad taste," the "vulgarity" of French people who "brag about their sexual exploits," "are proud of their sexual successes," which is a subject reserved by Americans for the "uncivilized" world of locker rooms, for the special and forced intimacy of these dressing rooms for athletes. (Although the expression "locker-room talk" traditionally evokes male conversation, it is just as applicable today to female locker-room talk.) The repugnance on the part of "tasteful" Americans to speak in public about their successes with men or women or their sexual "conquests" is interpreted, among the French, as additional proof of American "puritanism," whereas the French "modesty" concerning public conversations about money would tend to be interpreted by Americans as a type of French "puritanism."

15   This reciprocal accusation of "bad taste" led me to wonder if what was true for financial successes and conquests in American culture was not true for seduction, for amorous conquests, for sexual successes in French culture.

While it is not looked on favorably, in France, to show off one's money or titles, one may speak of one's amorous conquests without shocking anyone (unless one does it to belittle others with one's superiority, to insult them, etc., in which case it is not the subject that is important but the manner in which a particular person makes use of it). We have, in France, a great deal of indulgence and admiration for the "irresistible" man or woman, for "charmers" large and small of both cases. <u>Seduction is an art which is learned and perfected.</u>

Like money for Americans, amorous seduction is charged with a multiplicity of contradictory meanings for the French, depending on the person to whom one is speaking and the moment one raises the topic. Nonetheless, if a (French) newspaper article defines a particular person as *séduisante*, the term does not refer to indisputable characteristics but to a category recognizable by all, to a common point of reference, to a comprehensible descriptive shortcut. (It is interesting to note that the American translation of *séduisante* would be "attractive," a word which, as opposed to the French, evokes identifiable and predictable characteristics. The word *seductive*—not an adequate translation— evokes manipulation and the negative connotations attached to taking advantage of naiveté.)

Seduction, as I have said, is an art for the French. <u>It is not enough to be handsome or beautiful to seduce</u>; a certain <u>intelligence</u> and <u>expertise</u> are necessary, which can only be acquired through a long apprenticeship, even if this apprenticeship begins in the most tender infancy. (Thus, an ad for baby clothing, a double spread in the French version of the magazine *Parents*, shows the perfect outfit for the "heartbreak girl" and for the "playboy"; <u>this is an indication of the extent to which this quality is desirable</u>, since I assume the ad is geared toward the parents who provide for and teach these babies, and not toward the babies themselves.) It is therefore "normal" for me to be proud of my successes, for me to continually take up the challenge of new conquests, for me never to rest on my laurels, for me not to waste my talent. It is therefore not in "bad taste" to talk about it (bad taste and seduction are, in a sense, mutually exclusive in French). What is more, I can "freely" share my secrets and my "reflections" on the subject of men or women—a topic I have thoroughly mastered.

Like money for Americans, <u>seduction for the French may be the only true class equalizer.</u> In fact, one of the greatest powers of amorous seduction is precisely the fact that it permits the transgression of class divisions. The French myths of the "kept woman," of the attractiveness of the *midinette* (a big-city shopgirl or office clerk, who is supposed to be very sentimental), of the seductive powers of "P'tit Louis" (a "hunk," a good dancer, from the working class), and the innumerable seducers of both sexes in French novels, songs, and films are sufficient proof.

The interest of a parallel such as the one I have just established is that it *20* shows how astonishingly similar meanings can be expressed in areas which seem to be completely unrelated. Yet the greatest attraction of cultural analysis, for me, is the possibility of replacing a dull exchange of invectives with an exploration that is, at the very least, fascinating—a true feast to which I hereby invite you.

Engaging the Text

1. What culturally based misunderstandings do the French and Americans have about each other in terms of money and sex?

2. How is the approach Carroll takes that of an anthropologist who is interested in why success is measured in such different ways in France and the United States?

3. The playboy (womanizer) in France is regarded very differently from his American counterpart. What differences in cultural values between the two countries explain this perception?

Exploring Your Cultural Perspective

1. Write a short essay in which you support or challenge Carroll's claim by exploring the way in which the subjects of money and sex are treated in a range of magazines. In what ways do magazines devoted to money (such as *Money* and *Forbes*) focus on business success in the same way that magazines devoted to sex (such as *Playboy*) commodify seduction?

2. Carroll asserts that seduction in France and money in America signify social mobility. Write a short rebuttal to Carroll's argument in which you give equal importance to race and ethnicity as indicators of social class.

DAVID R. COUNTS

Too Many Bananas

Suppose you lived in a society where food, rather than money, was the only medium of exchange used to "pay" for goods. David R. Counts and his family faced this predicament when they moved to Papua New Guinea (the world's second largest island, located in the Pacific Ocean). In this excerpt from *The Humbled Anthropologist: Tales from the Pacific* (1990), Counts relates the exasperating, often humorous, underlying rules of reciprocity in Papua. In 1992, Counts and his wife, Dorothy, began research on the nomadic life of recreational vehicle owners (RVers) in the United States, which resulted in their book *Over the Next Hill: RVing Seniors in North America* (1996).

Thinking Critically

Counts's essay is divided into three sections. Take a moment after reading each section to write a brief summary of the new information in that part about the role of food in a barter society.

NO WATERMELON AT ALL

The woman came all the way through the village, walking between the two rows of houses facing each other between the beach and the bush, to the very last house standing on a little spit of land at the mouth of the Kaini River. She was carrying a watermelon on her head, and the house she came to was the government "rest house," maintained by the villagers for the occasional use of visiting officials. Though my wife and I were graduate students, not officials, and had asked for permission to stay in the village for the coming year, we were living in the rest house while the debate went on about where a house would be built for us. When the woman offered to sell us the watermelon for two shillings, we happily agreed, and the kids were delighted at the prospect of watermelon after yet another meal of rice and bully beef. The money changed hands and the seller left to return to her village, a couple of miles along the coast to the east.

It seemed only seconds later that the woman was back, reluctantly accompanying Kolia, the man who had already made it clear to us that he was the leader of the village. Kolia had no English, and at that time, three or four days into our first stay in Kandoka Village on the island of New Britain in Papua New Guinea, we had very little Tok Pisin. Language difficulties notwithstanding, Kolia managed to make his message clear: The woman had been outrageously wrong to sell us the watermelon for two shillings and we were to return it to her and reclaim our money immediately. When we tried to explain that we thought the price to be fair and were happy with the bargain, Kolia explained again and finally made it clear that we had missed the point. The problem wasn't that we had paid too much; it was that we had paid at all. Here he was, a leader, responsible for us while we were living in his village, and we had shamed him. How would it look if he let guests in his village *buy* food? If we wanted watermelons, or bananas, or anything else, all that was necessary was to let him know. He told us that it would be all right for us to give little gifts to people who brought food to us (and they surely would), but *no one* was to sell food to us. If anyone were to try—like this woman from Lauvore—then we should refuse. There would be plenty of watermelons without us buying them.

The woman left with her watermelon, disgruntled, and we were left with our two shillings. But we had learned the first lesson of many about living in Kandoka. We didn't pay money for food again that whole year, and we did get lots of food brought to us . . . but we never got another watermelon. That one was the last of the season.

LESSON 1: *In a society where food is shared or gifted as part of social life, you may not buy it with money.*

TOO MANY BANANAS

5   In the couple of months that followed the watermelon incident, we managed to become at least marginally competent in Tok Pisin, to negotiate the construction of a house on what we hoped was neutral ground, and to settle into the routine of our fieldwork. As our village leader had predicted, plenty of food was brought to us. Indeed, seldom did a day pass without something coming in—some sweet potatoes, a few taro, a papaya, the occasional pineapple, or some bananas—lots of bananas.

We had learned our lesson about the money, though, so we never even offered to buy the things that were brought, but instead made gifts, usually of tobacco to the adults or chewing gum to the children. Nor were we so gauche as to haggle with a giver over how much of a return gift was appropriate, though the two of us sometimes conferred as to whether what had been brought was a "two-stick" or a "three-stick" stalk, bundle, or whatever. A "stick" of tobacco was a single large leaf, soaked in rum and then twisted into a ropelike form. This, wrapped in half a sheet of newsprint (torn for use as cigarette paper), sold in the local trade stores for a shilling. Nearly all of the adults in the village smoked a great deal, and they seldom had much cash, so our stocks of twist tobacco and stacks of the Sydney *Morning Herald* (all, unfortunately, the same day's issue) were seen as a real boon to those who preferred "stick" to the locally grown product.

We had established a pattern with respect to the gifts of food. When a donor appeared at our veranda we would offer our thanks and talk with them for a few minutes (usually about our children, who seemed to hold a real fascination for the villagers and for whom most of the gifts were intended) and then we would inquire whether they could use some tobacco. It was almost never refused, though occasionally a small bottle of kerosene, a box of matches, some laundry soap, a cup of rice, or a tin of meat would be requested instead of (or even in addition to) the tobacco. Everyone, even Kolia, seemed to think this arrangement had worked out well.

Now, what must be kept in mind is that while we were following their rules—or seemed to be—we were *really still buying food*. In fact we kept a running account of what came in and what we "paid" for it. Tobacco as currency got a little complicated, but since the exchange rate was one stick to one shilling, it was not too much trouble as long as everyone was happy, and meanwhile we could account for the expenditure of "informant fees" and "household expenses." Another thing to keep in mind is that not only did we continue to think in terms of our buying the food that was brought, we thought of them as *selling it*. While it was true they never quoted us a price, they also never asked us if we needed or wanted whatever they had brought. It seemed clear to us that when an adult needed a stick of tobacco, or a child wanted some chewing gum (we had enormous quantities of small packets of Wrigley's for just such eventualities) they would find something surplus to their own needs and bring it along to our "store" and get what they wanted.

By late November 1966, just before the rainy season set in, the bananas were coming into flush, and whereas earlier we had received banana gifts by the "hand" (six or eight bananas in a cluster cut from the stalk), donors now began to bring bananas, "for the children," by the *stalk!* The Kaliai among whom we were living are not exactly specialists in banana cultivation—they only recognize about thirty varieties, while some of their neighbors have more than twice that many—but the kinds they produce differ considerably from each other in size, shape, and taste, so we were not dismayed when we had more than one stalk hanging on our veranda. The stalks ripen a bit at the time, and having some variety was nice. Still, by the time our accumulation had reached *four* complete stalks, the delights of variety had begun to pale a bit. The fruits were ripening progressively and it was clear that even if we and the kids ate nothing but bananas for the next week, some would still fall from the stalk onto the floor in a state of gross overripeness. This was the situation as, late one afternoon, a woman came bringing yet another stalk of bananas up the steps of the house.

10   Several factors determined our reaction to her approach: one was that there was literally no way we could possibly use the bananas. We hadn't quite reached the point of being crowded off our veranda by the stalks of fruit, but it was close. Another factor was that we were tired of playing the gift game. We had acquiesced in playing it—no one was permitted to sell us anything, and in turn we only gave things away, refusing under any circumstances to sell tobacco (or anything else) for money. But there had to be a limit. From our perspective what was at issue was that the woman wanted something and she had come to trade for it. Further, what she had brought to trade was something we neither wanted nor could use, and it should have been obvious to her. So we decided to bite the bullet.

The woman, Rogi, climbed the stairs to the veranda, took the stalk from where it was balanced on top of her head, and laid it on the floor with the word, "Here are some bananas for the children." Dorothy and I sat near her on the floor and thanked her for her thought but explained, "You know, we really have too many bananas—we can't use these; maybe you ought to give them to some-one else. . . ." The woman looked mystified, then brightened and explained that she didn't want anything for them, she wasn't short of tobacco or any-thing. They were just a gift for the kids. Then she just sat there, and we sat there, and the bananas sat there, and we tried again. "Look," I said, pointing up to them and counting, "we've got four stalks already hanging here on the veranda—there are too many for us to eat now. Some are rotting already. Even if we eat only bananas, we can't keep up with what's here!"

Rogi's only response was to insist that these were a gift, and that she didn't want anything for them, so we tried yet another tack: "Don't *your* children like bananas?" When she admitted that they did, and that she had none at her house, we suggested that she should take them there. Finally, still puzzled, but convinced we weren't going to keep the bananas, she replaced them on her head, went down the stairs, and made her way back through the village toward her house.

As before, it seemed only moments before Kolia was making his way up the stairs, but this time he hadn't brought the woman in tow. "What was wrong with those bananas? Were they no good?" he demanded. We explained that there was nothing wrong with the bananas at all, but that we simply couldn't use them and it seemed foolish to take them when we had so many and Rogi's own children had none. We obviously didn't make ourselves clear because

Kolia then took up the same refrain that Rogi had—he insisted that we shouldn't be worried about taking the bananas, because they were a gift for the children and Rogi hadn't wanted anything for them. There was no reason, he added, to send her away with them—she would be ashamed. I'm afraid we must have seemed as if we were hard of hearing or thought he was, for our only response was to repeat our reasons. We went through it again—there they hung, one, two, three, *four* stalks of bananas, rapidly ripening and already far beyond our capacity to eat—we just weren't ready to accept any more and let them rot (and, we added to ourselves, pay for them with tobacco, to boot).

Kolia finally realized that we were neither hard of hearing nor intentionally offensive, but merely ignorant. He stared at us for a few minutes, thinking, and then asked: "Don't you frequently have visitors during the day and evening?" We nodded. Then he asked, "Don't you usually offer them cigarettes and coffee or milo?" Again, we nodded. "Did it ever occur to you to suppose," he said, "that your visitors might be hungry?" It was at this point in the conversation, as we recall, that we began to see the depth of the pit we had dug for ourselves. We nodded, hesitantly. His last words to us before he went down the stairs and stalked away were just what we were by that time afraid they might be. "When your guests are hungry, *feed them bananas!*"

LESSON 2: *Never refuse a gift, and never fail to return a gift. If you cannot use* *15*
it, you can always give it away to someone else—there is no such thing as too much—there are never too many bananas.

NOT ENOUGH PINEAPPLES

During the fifteen years between that first visit in 1966 and our residence there in 1981 we had returned to live in Kandoka village twice during the 1970s, and though there were a great many changes in the village, and indeed for all of Papua New Guinea during that time, we continued to live according to the lessons of reciprocity learned during those first months in the field. We bought no food for money and refused no gifts, but shared our surplus. As our family grew, we continued to be accompanied by our younger children. Our place in the village came to be something like that of educated Kaliai who worked far away in New Guinea. Our friends expected us to come "home" when we had leave, but knew that our work kept us away for long periods of time. They also credited us with knowing much more about the rules of their way of life than was our due. And we sometimes shared the delusion that we understood life in the village, but even fifteen years was not long enough to relieve the need for lessons in learning to live within the rules of gift exchange.

In the last paragraph I used the word *friends* to describe the villagers intentionally, but of course they were not all our friends. Over the years some really had become friends, others were acquaintances, others remained consultants or informants to whom we turned when we needed information. Still others, unfortunately, we did not like at all. We tried never to make an issue of these distinctions, of course, and to be evenhanded and generous to all, as they were to us. Although we almost never actually refused requests that were made of us, over the long term our reciprocity in the village was balanced. More was given to those who helped us the most, while we gave assistance or donations of small items even to those who were not close or helpful.

One elderly woman in particular was a trial for us. Sara was the eldest of a group of siblings and her younger brother and sister were both generous, informative, and delightful persons. Her younger sister, Makila, was a particularly close friend and consultant, and in deference to that friendship we felt awkward in dealing with the elder sister.

Sara was neither a friend nor an informant, but she had been, since she returned to live in the village at the time of our second trip in 1971, a constant (if minor) drain on our resources. She never asked for much at a time. A bar of soap, a box of matches, a bottle of kerosene, a cup of rice, some onions, a stick or two of tobacco, or some other small item was usually all that was at issue, but whenever she came around it was always to ask for something—or to let us know that when we left, we should give her some of the furnishings from the house. Too, unlike almost everyone else in the village, when she came, she was always empty-handed. We ate no taro from her gardens, and the kids chewed none of her sugarcane. In short, she was, as far as we could tell, a really grasping, selfish old woman—and we were not the only victims of her greed.

20   Having long before learned the lesson of the bananas, one day we had a stalk that was ripening so fast we couldn't keep up with it, so I pulled a few for our own use (we only had one stalk at the time) and walked down through the village to Ben's house, where his five children were playing. I sat down on his steps to talk, telling him that I intended to give the fruit to his kids. They never got them. Sara saw us from across the open plaza of the village and came rushing over, shouting, "My bananas!" Then she grabbed the stalk and went off gorging herself with them. Ben and I just looked at each other.

Finally it got to the point where it seemed to us that we had to do something. Ten years of being used was long enough. So there came the afternoon when Sara showed up to get some tobacco—again. But this time, when we gave her the two sticks she had demanded, we confronted her.

First, we noted the many times she had come to get things. We didn't mind sharing things, we explained. After all, we had plenty of tobacco and soap and rice and such, and most of it was there so that we could help our friends as they helped us, with folktales, information, or even gifts of food. The problem was that she kept coming to get things, but never came to talk, or to tell stories, or to bring some little something that the kids might like. Sara didn't argue—she agreed. "Look," we suggested, "it doesn't have to be much, and we don't mind giving you things—but you can help us. The kids like pineapples, and we don't have any—the next time you need something, bring something—like maybe a pineapple." Obviously somewhat embarrassed, she took her tobacco and left, saying that she would bring something soon. We were really pleased with ourselves. It had been a very difficult thing to do, but it was done, and we were convinced that either she would start bringing things or not come. It was as if a burden had lifted from our shoulders.

It worked. Only a couple of days passed before Sara was back, bringing her bottle to get it filled with kerosene. But this time, she came carrying the biggest, most beautiful pineapple we had seen the entire time we had been there. We had a friendly talk, filled her kerosene container, and hung the pineapple up on the veranda to ripen just a little further. A few days later we cut and ate it, and whether the satisfaction it gave came from the fruit or from its source would be hard to say, but it was delicious. That, we assumed, was the end of that irritant.

We were wrong, of course. The next afternoon, Mary, one of our best friends for years (and no relation to Sara), dropped by for a visit. As we talked, her eyes scanned the veranda. Finally she asked whether we hadn't had a pineapple there yesterday. We said we had, but that we had already eaten it. She commented that it had been a really nice-looking one, and we told her that it had been the best we had eaten in months. Then, after a pause, she asked, "Who brought it to you?" We smiled as we said, "Sara!" because Mary would appreciate our coup—she had commented many times in the past on the fact that Sara only *got* from us and never gave. She was silent for a moment, and then she said, "Well, I'm glad you enjoyed it—my father was waiting until it was fully ripe to harvest it for you, but when it went missing I thought maybe it was the one you had here. I'm glad to see you got it. I thought maybe a thief had eaten it in the bush."

LESSON 3: *Where reciprocity is the rule and gifts are the idiom, you cannot demand a gift, just as you cannot refuse a request.* 25

It says a great deal about the kindness and patience of the Kaliai people that they have been willing to be our hosts for all these years despite our blunders and lack of good manners. They have taught us a lot, and these three lessons are certainly not the least important things we learned.

Engaging the Text

1. When Counts was rebuffed after offering money for a watermelon, what did he learn about the importance of reciprocity in Papua New Guinea?

2. What additional insights did Counts gain from the incident of "too many bananas"? To what extent did Sara's unusual behavior change Counts's attitude toward the system of reciprocity?

3. Does the way Counts presents his findings—as a series of three problems—make an effective pattern of organization? Why or why not? When viewed collectively, what did the three lessons Counts describes teach him about the culture of Papua New Guinea? To what extent did this experience alter his view of himself as an anthropologist?

Exploring Your Cultural Perspective

1. How does the principle of reciprocity function in the United States on holidays in similar fashion to its operation year-round in Papua New Guinea? For example, have you ever received a gift that you suspected the giver had gotten from someone else and was simply passing along to fulfill an obligation? If so, what did you do with the gift?

2. In the United States, the closely knit culture of the Amish (a North American Protestant group of Mennonite origin) offers an interesting comparison with the community in Papua New Guinea that Counts describes. The cultural ties that unite the Amish as a farming community promote mutual assistance, an avoidance of technology, and a market economy based more on the exchange value of labor than on money. You can find a number of sites on the Internet about Amish communities in Pennsylvania, Ohio, and Indiana. In a short essay, compare the two cultures, and note the lessons modern commercial society might learn from them.

ALBERTO MORAVIA
Jewellery

Have you ever wondered why jewelry becomes an object of desire for so many people? To what extent is its mystique based on cultural values? The Italian writer Alberto Moravia (1907–1990) addresses this issue in his short story "Jewellery" (the spelling is Moravia's), translated by Angus Davidson, which originally appeared in *Roman Tales* (1956). He focuses on the symbolic role that jewelry serves in enhancing self-worth in male-dominated Italian culture. Moravia completed his first novel, *The Time of Indifference* (1929), before he was twenty and published it at his own expense. Ten of his novels and several collections of his short stores have been translated into English. His novel *Two Women* (1957) was made into the 1961 Academy Award–winning film starring Sophia Loren. Moravia's last work was his autobiography, *Life* (1990).

Thinking Critically

As you read this story, notice how jewelry acts as a catalyst that brings a group of friends together—and drives them apart.

You can be quite sure that, when a woman finds her way into a group of men friends, that group, without the slightest doubt, is bound to disintegrate and each member of it to go off on his own account. That year we formed a group of young men who were all in the closest sympathy with each other, always united, always in agreement, always together. We were all of us earning a very good living, Tore with his garage, the two Modesti brothers with their meat-broker's business, Pippo Morganti with his pork-butcher's shop, Rinaldo with his bar, and I with a varied assortment of things: at that moment I was dealing in resin and products allied to it. Although we were all under thirty, none of us weighed less than twelve or thirteen stone: we all knew how to wield a knife and fork. During the day we were at work; but from seven o'clock onwards we were always together, first at Rinaldo's bar in the Corso Vittorio, and then in a restaurant with a garden in the neighbourhood of the Chiesa Nuova. We spent

Sundays together, of course: either at the stadium watching football matches, or on expeditions to the Castelli Romani, or, in the warm weather, at Ostia or Ladispoli. There were six of us, yet it might be said that we were one single person. So, supposing that one of us was smitten by a caprice, the other five were soon smitten too. With regard to jewellery, it was Tore who started it: he came one evening to the restaurant wearing a wristwatch of massive gold, with a plaited gold strap nearly an inch wide. We asked him who had given it to him. "The Director of the Bank of Italy," he said, by which he meant that he had bought it with his own money. Then he slipped it off and showed it to us: it was a watch of a well-known make, double-cased and with a second hand, and, together with its stiff plaited strap, it weighed goodness knows how much. It made a great impression upon us. "An investment," said somebody. But Tore replied: "What d'you mean, an investment? I like wearing it on my wrist, that's all." When we met next day at the usual restaurant, Morganti already had a wristwatch of his own, with a gold strap too, but not such a heavy one. Then it was the turn of the Modesti brothers who each bought one—larger ones than Tore's and with plaited straps that were less solid but broader. As for Rinaldo and me, as we both liked Tore's watch, we asked him where he had got it and then went together to a good shop in the Corso and each bought one.

It was now May, and often in the evenings we used to go to Monte Mario, to the inn there, to drink wine and eat fresh beans and sheep's milk cheese. One evening Tore put out his hand to help himself to beans and we all saw a ring on his finger, a massive ring containing a diamond of no very great size but a fine one nevertheless. "My goodness!" we exclaimed. "Now look here," he said roughly, "you're not to imitate me, you pack of monkeys. . . . I bought this so as to be different." However, he took it off and we passed it round: it was really a very fine diamond, limpid, perfect. But Tore is a big, rather soft-looking chap, with a flat, flabby face, two little pig-like eyes, a nose that looks as if it were made of butter and a mouth like a purse with broken hinges. With that ring on his small, fat finger and that watch on his stumpy wrist, he looked almost like a woman. The diamond ring, as he wished, was not copied. However, we each of us bought a nice ring for ourselves. The Modesti brothers had two similar rings made both of red gold but with different stones in them, one green and one blue; Rinaldo bought himself a ring of a more or less antique style, pierced and carved, with a brown cameo containing a little white figure of a nude woman; Morganti, always anxious to cut a dash, acquired one actually made of platinum, with a black stone; while I myself, being more conventional, contented myself with a ring which had a square setting and a flat yellow stone upon which I had my initials cut, so that I could use it for sealing parcels. After the rings came cigarette-cases. It was Tore, as usual, who began it, by producing a long, flat case—made of gold, of course—with crossed lines incised on it, and snapping it open under our noses; and then everyone imitated him, some in one way and some in another. After the cigarette-cases, we all indulged our own whims: somebody bought a bracelet with a medal, to wear on his other wrist; somebody else a pressure-controlled fountain pen; somebody else a little chain with a cross and a medallion of the Madonna to hang round his neck; and somebody else a cigarette-lighter. Tore, vainest of all, acquired three more rings; and now he looked more like a woman than ever, especially when he took off his jacket and appeared in a short-sleeved shirt, displaying his big, soft arms and hands covered with rings.

We were all laden with jewellery now; and I don't know why, but it was just at that moment that things began to go wrong. It didn't amount to much—a little teasing, a few rather caustic remarks, a few sharp retorts. And then one evening Rinaldo, who owned the bar, arrived at our usual restaurant with a girl, his new cashier. Her name was Lucrezia and she was perhaps not yet even twenty, but she was as fully developed as a woman of thirty. Her skin was white as milk, her eyes black, large, steady and expressionless, her mouth red, her hair black. She looked indeed like a statue, especially as she always remained still and composed and hardly spoke at all. Rinaldo confided to us that he had found her by means of a commercial advertisement, and he said he knew nothing about her, not even whether she had a family or whom she lived with. She was just the right person, he added, for the cash-desk: a girl like that attracted clients by her good looks and then, by her serious demeanour, kept them at a distance; a plain girl fails to attract; and a pretty but forthcoming one does no work and creates disorder. The presence of Lucrezia that evening caused considerable constraint among us: we sat very upright the whole time, with our jackets on, talking in a reserved manner without any jokes or coarse words and eating very politely; even Tore tried to eat his fruit with a knife and fork, without much success however. Next day we all rushed to the bar to see her at her duties. She was sitting on a tiny stool, her hips—which were already too broad for her age—bulging over its sides: and her haughty bosom was almost pressing against the keys of the cash-register. We all stood there open-mouthed as we watched her calmly, precisely, unhurriedly distributing price-dockets, continually pressing down the keys of the machine without even looking at them, her eyes fixed straight ahead of her in the direction of the bar counter. She notified the barman, each time, in a quiet, impersonal voice: "Two coffees. . . . One bitter. . . . One orangeade. . . . One beer." She never smiled, she never looked at the customer; and certainly there were some who went up very close to her in the hope of being looked at. She was dressed with propriety, but like the poor girl that she was: in a simple, sleeveless white dress. But clean, fresh, well ironed. *She* wore no jewellery, not even ear-rings, although the lobes of her ears had been pierced. We, of course, when we saw how pretty she was, started making jokes, encouraged by Rinaldo, who was proud of her. But she, after the first few jokes, said: "We shall meet at the restaurant this evening, shan't we? So leave me in peace now. . . . I don't like being disturbed while I'm working." Tore, to whom these words were addressed because he was the most prying and ill-mannered, said with feigned surprise: "I say, I'm sorry . . . we're only poor people, and we didn't know we had to do with a princess. . . . I'm sorry . . . we didn't mean any offence." She replied, drily: "I'm not a princess but a poor girl who works for her living . . . and I'm not offended. . . . One coffee and one bitter." And so we went away feeling rather humiliated.

In the evening we all met, as usual, at the restaurant. Rinaldo and Lucrezia were the last to arrive; and we immediately ordered our dinner. For a short time, while we were waiting for our food, there was again a feeling of constraint; then the proprietor brought in a big dish of chicken *alla romana*, already cut up, with tomato sauce and red peppers. We all looked at each other, and Tore, interpreting our common feeling, exclaimed: "You know what I say? When I eat I like to feel free . . . do as I do and you'll feel better." As he spoke he seized hold of a leg of chicken and, lifting it to his mouth with his two ring-covered hands, started to devour it. This was the signal; after a moment of hesitation we all began eating with our hands—all except Rinaldo and, of course, Lucrezia who nibbled delicately at a little piece of breast. After the first moment we recovered ourselves and went back, in every possible respect, to our old noisy ways. We talked as we ate and ate as we talked; we gulped down brimming glasses of wine with our mouths full; we slouched back in our chairs; we told our usual racy stories. In fact, perhaps out of defiance, we behaved worse than usual; and I don't remember ever having eaten so much, and with so much enjoyment, as I did that evening. When we had finished dinner, Tore loosened the buckle of his trouser-band and uttered a profound belch, which would have shaken the ceiling if it hadn't happened that we were out of doors, under a pergola. "Ugh, I feel better," he declared. He took a toothpick and, as he always did, started prodding at his teeth, all of them, one by one, and then all over again; and finally, with the toothpick stuck into the corner of his mouth, he told us a really indecent story. At this, Lucrezia rose to her feet and said: "Rinaldo, I feel tired. . . . If you don't mind, will you take me home now?" We all exchanged meaning glances: she had been Rinaldo's cashier for barely two days and already she was talking to him familiarly and calling him by his Christian name. A commercial advertisement in the paper, indeed! They went out and, the moment they had gone, Tore gave another belch and said: "About time too . . . I'd had enough. . . . Did you see the haughtiness of it? And him following behind as good as gold . . . as meek as a lamb! As for that commercial advertisement—matrimonial advertisement, I should say!"

5   For two or three days the same scenes were repeated: Lucrezia eating composedly and silently; the rest of us trying to pretend she wasn't there; Rinaldo divided between Lucrezia and us and not knowing what line to take. But there was something brewing, we all felt that. The girl—still waters run deep—gave

no sign, but all the time she was wanting Rinaldo to choose between herself and us. At last, one evening, for no precise reason—perhaps because it was hot and, as one knows, heat gets on people's nerves—Rinaldo, half-way through dinner, made an attack upon us, in this way: "This is the last time I'm coming to eat with you." We were all astonished, and Tore asked: "Oh, is that really so? And may we ask why?" "Because I don't like you." "You don't like us? Well, I'm sure we're all very sorry for that—really terribly sorry." "You're a bunch of swine, that's what you are." "Now be careful what you say, but . . . are you crazy?" "Yes, you're a bunch of swine; I say it and I repeat it. . . . Eating with you makes me feel sick." By this time we were all red in the face with anger, and some of us had jumped up from the table. "It's you," said Tore, "who's the biggest swine of all. Who gave you the right to judge us? Haven't we always been all together? Haven't we always done the same things?" "You be quiet," Rinaldo said to him; "with all that jewellery on you, you look like one of those women—you know who I mean. . . . All you need is some scent. . . . I say, haven't you ever thought of putting on some scent?" This blow was aimed at all of us; and, realizing the source from which it came, we all looked at Lucrezia: but she, hypocritically, kept on pulling Rinaldo by the sleeve and urging him to stop and come away. Then Tore said: "You've got jewellery too . . . you've got a watch and a ring and a bracelet . . . just as much as anyone else." Rinaldo was beside himself now. "But you know what I'm going to do?" he cried. "I'm taking them all off and giving them to her. . . . Come on, take them, Lucrezia, I'm giving them to you." As he spoke, he slipped off his ring, his bracelet, his wristwatch, pulled his cigarette-case out of his pocket and threw the whole lot into the girl's lap. "None of the rest of you," he said insultingly, "would ever do that . . . you *couldn't* do it." "Go to hell," said Tore; but you could see, now, that he was ashamed of having all those rings on his fingers. "Rinaldo," said Lucrezia calmly, "take your things and let's go." She gathered all the things Rinaldo had given her into a heap and put them into his pocket. Rinaldo, however, owing to some kind of grudge that he had against us, continued to abuse us even while allowing Lucrezia to drag him away. "You're a bunch of swine, I tell you. . . . Why don't you learn how to eat; why don't you learn how to live. . . . Swine!" "Idiot!" shouted Tore, mad with rage. "Imbecile! . . . You've allowed yourself to be led away by that other idiot who's standing beside you!" If you could have seen Rinaldo! He jumped right over the table and seized hold of Tore by the collar of his shirt. We had to pull them apart.

That evening, after they had gone, we did not breathe a word and we all left after a few minutes. Next evening we met again, but now our old gaiety was gone. We noticed, on this occasion, that several of the rings had vanished and some of the watches too. After two evenings we none of us had any jewellery left, and we were duller than ever. A week went by and then, with one excuse and another, we ceased to meet at all. It was all finished, and, as one knows, when things are finished they don't begin again: no one likes warmed-up soup. Later on I heard that Rinaldo had married Lucrezia; I was told that, at the church, she was more thickly covered with jewellery than a statue of the Madonna. And Tore? I saw him at his garage a short time ago. He had a ring on his finger, but it was not of gold and it had no diamond in it: it was one of those silver rings that mechanics wear.

Engaging the Text

1. How would you characterize the relationship among the six friends before Lucrezia arrives? What unites them, and what role does jewelry play in their friendship?

2. What attracts Rinaldo to Lucrezia, and how does his relationship with his friends change after he meets her? In your opinion, why does the friendship among the men dissolve?

3. Why is it significant that Lucrezia at first has no jewelry and then at the end of the story is "more thickly covered with jewellery than a statue of the Madonna"? In what sense is Lucrezia herself the ultimate jewel?

Exploring Your Cultural Perspective

1. In Moravia's story, jewelry serves as a way to measure friendship and love. Do you own any jewelry that you value because of its unique associations? How did you come to have it, and why does it have special meaning for you?

2. The slogan "a diamond is forever" has played an indispensable role in the DeBeer's marketing campaign for more than fifty years. Look for one of DeBeer's ads, and analyze how it attempts to transform the desire for diamonds into a basic human need. In what way has DeBeer's marketed diamonds so that they are seen as the supreme expression of love at key moments in life (engagements, anniversaries, birthdays, graduations)? Analyze the reasons for the success of this ad campaign and the central place diamonds occupy as highly valued objects in many cultures. You can find more specific information on DeBeer's at <http://www.debeers.com>.

CONNECTING THE TEXTS

1. Draw on the essays by Juliet B. Schor ("The Culture of Consumerism") and Bill Bryson ("The Hard Sell: Advertising in America") to analyze how advertising slogans communicate the message of upward mobility.

2. In light of Bill Bryson's analysis in "The Hard Sell: Advertising in America," take a look at current ad campaigns for the kinds of gadgets that Umberto Eco satirizes in "How Not to Use the Fax Machine and the Cellular Phone." What do these ads really promise?

3. How does shopping on the Internet create a virtual mall that draws on the advertising techniques described by Bill Bryson in "The Hard Sell: Advertising in America" and the features of the mall described by Richard Keller Simon in "The Shopping Mall and the Formal Garden"?

4. What do Rabbi Susan Schnur (in "Barbie Does Yom Kippur") and Juliet B. Schor (in "The Culture of Consumerism") have to say about the underlying competitive nature of consumer culture? Do you agree or disagree with their analyses? Explain your answer in a synthesis essay.

5. In "How Not to Use the Fax Machine and the Cellular Phone," Umberto Eco implies that gadgets now are a way of proclaiming one's social status and are in essence a new form of self-advertising. Compare this assertion with the more traditional means of self-promotion discussed by Raymonde Carroll in "Sex, Money, and Success."

6. Compare the ritual of detachment from one's "stuff" at Yom Kippur (see Rabbi Susan Schnur's "Barbie Does Yom Kippur") with George Carlin's observations about accumulation of "stuff" in "A Place for Your Stuff." Draw on both readings in a short synthesis essay that expresses your views on material possessions.

7. In what way does George Carlin's monologue "A Place for Your Stuff" bring Terence McLaughlin's theoretical discussion (in "Dirt: A Social History as Seen through the Uses and Abuses of Dirt") down to earth? What similar points do the two writers make, and how do they express them?

8. The cost of a product usually includes elaborate packaging that adds to its allure but is soon discarded as "dirt," as defined by Terence McLaughlin in his piece of the same name. In what ways does American culture (see Juliet Schor's "The Culture of Consumerism") encourage this kind of wastefulness?

9. Americans' identification with their stuff is a theme in Edward T. Hall's "Hidden Culture" and in George Carlin's monologue "A Place for Your Stuff." How do an anthropologist and a comedian approach the same topic from different perspectives?

10. Has greed come to define Americans (see Juliet B. Schor's analysis in "The Culture of Consumerism"), making them more like Sara in David Counts's "Too Many Bananas"? Why or why not?

11. In what way does Lucrezia boost Rinaldo's status in Alberto Moravia's story "Jewellery" (so that he no longer needs his jewelry) in the same way that sex and money

demonstrate personal success in France and America, respectively, according to Raymonde Carroll in "Sex, Money, and Success"?

12. What common skepticism do Alberto Moravia (in "Jewellery") and Umberto Eco (in "How Not to Use the Fax Machine and the Cellular Phone") share about material goods that serve as status symbols?

WRITING ABOUT CONSUMERISM

1. Describe an invention that would make the world a better place (even if the principle upon which it is based, such as anti-gravity, does not yet exist). Alternatively, choose a real invention (for example, the photocopier, the laser, or the Sony Walkman) and discuss how it changed society. A survey of the one hundred greatest inventions of the past can be found in the Millennium edition of *Popular Science* and on the magazine's Web site at <http://www.popsci.com>.

2. What do popular toys reflect about contemporary culture? In the past, Cabbage Patch dolls, Beanie Babies, Tickle Me Elmo, *Star Wars* action figures, talking Teletubbies, Furbys, Pokémon, and countless others have captured childrens' imaginations and their parent's wallets. For an entertaining read on this subject, consult Daniel Harris's *Cute, Quaint, Hungry and Romantic: The Aesthetics of Consumerism* (Basic Books, 2000).

3. The $200 billion teenagers spend annually (on clothes and such gizmos as PlayStations, joysticks, boomboxes, stereo systems, cell phones, pagers, and CD players) makes it vitally important for advertisers to identify what is currently deemed to be "cool." Describe something that you consider cool, and write your own ad for it.

4. To discover what possession you value most, imagine that the place where you live is on fire and you can save only one inanimate object. What would it be, and what does your choice reveal about what is important to you?

5. In many cultures around the world the custom of "potlatch," or the ritual destruction of material goods, is believed to attract abundance. What rituals function this way in America? For example, would you rather spend more than you can afford on an elaborate wedding (that could magically attract abundance) or have a less costly wedding? Or would you simply elope and save your cash? Explain your answer in terms of your personal and cultural values.

6. Describe an object, memento, talisman, or gift that you value because of its associations with a parent, grandparent, or other relative. Relate its history and the meaning it has for you.

7. Analyze the worldly goods component of the promotional materials intended to attract students to your college or university. To what extent do they employ appeals similar to those described by Anne Matthews in the following excerpt from *Bright College Years* (1997)?

> Food is a recurring motif. Sushi bars, waffle bars, made to order omelettes and fireside snack lounges crowd the catalogues. . . . The University of Central Florida is even more direct: ". . . Disney World and great beaches are an hour away." "When a little retail therapy is in order," admits Franklin and Marshall, "shop till you drop at the nearby malls' 190 stores."

More examples of promotional material can be found at <http://www.clas.ufl.edu/CLAS/american-universities.html>.

8. Are you a walking billboard—providing free advertising for designers and their logos? Is the designer's name important to you when you purchase an item?

9. Objects that we once took for granted as part of everyday life may have vanished, but they continue to evoke nostalgia. This is true of vinyl records, typewriters, rotary-dial telephones, manual car windows, slide rules, hula hoops, mood rings, carbon paper, girdles, men's garters, and many other items. Other things, such as hotel keys, are just beginning to disappear. Select an item that is an icon of late-twentieth-century life, and describe the nostalgic and cultural meanings it embodies. What items do you already feel nostalgic about because they are on their way out? Discuss the significance of collecting things from the past in an increasingly throwaway culture. Does the cartoon in Figure 9.4 make a valid point?

10. In his essay "My Wood" (from *Abinger Harvest,* 1936), the English novelist E. M. Forster describes the following as effects of owning property: a sense of importance ("my wood makes me feel heavy"), greed ("it makes me feel it ought to be larger"), embellishment ("property makes its owner feel he ought to do something to it"), and selfishness ("I shall wall in and fence out until I really taste the sweets of property"). Has owning property (a car, stereo, or computer) changed you in this way? Describe your experiences.

11. What can you infer about a culture's attitudes toward material possessions by the fact that it buries its dead (with elaborate caskets, floral tributes, and carved monuments) rather than cremates them? What similarities (and differences) can you discover between contemporary American practices attending death and those of the ancient Egyptians or modern-day Hindus in Varanasi? Use sources from the library and the Internet to help you answer this question.

12. People in other countries enjoy seeing the abundance of material goods in U.S. movies as much as they do the characters and the plot. Watch an American-made

"YOU DON'T CLICK 'QUIT'...YOU JUST SHUT IT."

FIGURE 9.4

movie, paying close attention to the way the film serves as a showcase for many products. Write a few paragraphs on the significance of the setting in the film you select.

13. The ability to buy things online (including bidding for goods on ebay.com and priceline.com) has radically reshaped the nature of consumerism. How has this new form of shopping capitalized on a competitive, auctionlike atmosphere that encourages ill-considered purchases?

Writing across Themes: Essay Suggestions

CHAPTER 2

1. Draw on the information on the dynamics of mass-merchandising that Bill Bryson provides in "What's Cooking?: Eating in America" (Chapter 2) and "The Hard Sell: Advertising in America" (Chapter 9), and, in a synthesis essay, develop a thesis that expresses your reaction to his essays. What do Bryson's two essays have in common, and how are they different?

2. Summarize the specific features that create the controlled environments found in a McDonald's franchise (see Conrad P. Kottak's "Rituals at McDonald's" in Chapter 2) and in a Moroccan harem (see Fatima Mernissi's "The French Harem" in Chapter 4). In an essay, address the question of why control is so important to the success of these two very different institutions.

3. How do the essays by Diane Ackerman ("The Social Sense" in Chapter 2) and Terence McLaughlin ("Dirt: A Social History as Seen through the Uses and Abuses of Dirt" in Chapter 9) illustrate how cultural forces determine what a given society finds palatable or unpalatable? In an essay, analyze how the authors interpret similar data differently and employ different emphases to suit their purposes.

4. In an essay, discuss Margaret Visser's description of the evolution of table manners (in "Fingers" in Chapter 2) as an example of how a society conditions its members' concepts of cleanliness and pollution, as analyzed by Terence McLaughlin in "Dirt: A Social History as Seen through the Uses and Abuses of Dirt" (Chapter 9).

5. Evaluate the evidence that Susan Bordo ("Never Just Pictures" in Chapter 4) presents to illustrate and support her assertions. Does her indictment of

the masochism she observes in women who starve to be thin suggest that Puritanism, as defined by Octavio Paz ("Hygiene and Repression" in Chapter 2), still prevails in North America? In an essay, discuss the different emphases each author places on the role of self-denial.

6. In what ways do Garrett Hongo (in "Who among You Knows the Essence of Garlic?" in Chapter 2) and Luis Alberto Urrea (in "Nobody's Son" in Chapter 5) take an ironic stance toward the stereotyping of minorities in mainstream North American culture? As part of your analysis, evaluate whether each author's tone enhances or detracts from the effectiveness of his piece.

7. In an essay, discuss the differences between consumer psychology in Eastern Europe, as described by Slavenka Drakulić ("Pizza in Warsaw, Torte in Prague" in Chapter 2), and in the United States, as discussed by Juliet B. Schor ("The Culture of Consumerism" in Chapter 9). Is the need to designate certain items as "luxuries" an impulse that transcends political systems?

CHAPTER 3

8. In an essay, compare and contrast the intensive training regimens described by Joan Ryan in "Little Girls in Pretty Boxes" (Chapter 8) with the forms of self-mutilation described by Germaine Greer in "One Man's Mutilation Is Another Man's Beautification" (Chapter 3).

9. Drawing on the articles by Alison Lurie ("The Language of Clothes," Chapter 3) and Greil Marcus ("Dead Elvis," Chapter 7) and the official Elvis Web site at <http://www.elvispresley.com>, write a synthesis essay that explores the social meanings of the distinctive outfits Elvis wore. What links do his various costumes have with myths, legends, and popular music?

10. In an essay, discuss whether the jeans and black leather described by Farid Chenoune (Chapter 3) serve the same purpose for white males as the "cool pose" does for black males, as described by Richard Majors and Janet Mancini Billson (Chapter 4).

11. Is Dodie Kazanjian ("The Kelly Bag as Icon," Chapter 3) a prisoner of the acquisitive and competitive forces that Juliet B. Schor describes in "The Culture of Consumerism" (Chapter 9)? In a synthesis essay, explain your answer.

12. In what sense does the geisha in Japanese culture, described in Liza Dalby's "Kimono" (Chapter 3), embody both the "good girl" and the "bad girl" archetypes that Sandra Tsing Loh describes in "The Return of Doris Day" (Chapter 7)?

13. Mita's concept of herself as a woman changes with the clothes she wears as she moves from India to the United States (in Chitra Banerjee Divakaruni's "Clothes" in Chapter 3). How does her changing self-concept suggest that

gender roles are culturally constructed, as discussed by Brian Pronger in "Sexual Mythologies" (Chapter 4)? Explain your answer in an essay.

CHAPTER 4

14. According to Brian Pronger in "Sexual Mythologies" (Chapter 4), gender operates as a de facto class system that reinforces inequities in power between men and women. To what extent does the depiction of Asian women by Jessica Hagedorn in "Asian Women in Film: No Joy, No Luck" (Chapter 7) illustrate this sexual mythology? Explain your answer in an essay.

15. Discuss how Marge Piercy's poem "Barbie Doll" (Chapter 4) and Rabbi Susan Schnur's essay "Barbie Does Yom Kippur" (Chapter 9) use the Barbie doll as a vehicle for social criticism. Write a synthesis essay in which you support or challenge the claims of these two writers. For up-to-date information on Barbie, visit her official Web site at <http://www.barbie.com>.

16. Bragging is a component of the "cool pose" discussed by Richard Majors and Janet Mancini Billson (Chapter 4) and of the self-promotion described by Raymonde Carroll in "Sex, Money, and Success" (Chapter 9). In an essay, compare these different forms of boasting and how culture influences them.

CHAPTER 5

17. In what ways do the accounts of Barbara Mellix ("From Outside, In" in Chapter 5) and Arthur Ashe ("The Burden of Race" in Chapter 8) reveal the stresses of being an African American in mainstream white culture? Explain your answer in an essay.

18. How do John Agard ("Listen mr oxford don" in Chapter 5) and Umberto Eco ("How Not to Use the Fax Machine and the Cellular Phone" in Chapter 9) use sarcasm and humor to puncture cultural myths?

19. What do Luis Alberto Urrea ("Nobody's Son" in Chapter 5) and Roberto Gonzalez Echevarria ("First Pitch" in Chapter 8) say about how the use of language in mainstream North America stereotypes Hispanics? Explain your answer in an essay.

20. Kyoko Mori ("Polite Lies" in Chapter 5) and David R. Counts ("Too Many Bananas" in Chapter 9) are frustrated by the rituals of courtesy in Japan and Papua New Guinea. What cultural functions do these rituals serve? Do North Americans have any rituals of courtesy? Explain your answer in an essay.

21. Amy Tan in "The Language of Discretion" (Chapter 5) reveals a very different side of Asian women than the one Jessica Hagedorn criticizes in

"Asian Women in Film: No Joy, No Luck" (Chapter 7). Create a dialogue between Tan and Hagedorn in which each expresses her point of view.

22. Do you agree that freakishness has come to be a quality associated with Internet chat rooms, as Gary Chapman believes ("Flamers: Cranks, Fetishists, and Monomaniacs" in Chapter 5), and daytime TV talk shows, according to Charles Oliver ("Freak Parade" in Chapter 7)? In an essay, compare and contrast the two types of media.

23. In what ways do Anthony Burgess's story "A Clockwork Orange" (Chapter 5) and Farid Chenoune's article "Jeans and Black Leather: Gangs Don a Second Skin" (Chapter 3) focus on the way in which language and clothes can represent deviance? Explain your answer in an essay.

CHAPTER 6

24. The function of mannequins in presenting idealized body types (described by Richard Keller Simon in "The Shopping Mall and the Formal Garden" in Chapter 9) offers an interesting perspective on issues discussed by Lennard J. Davis in "Visualizing the Disabled Body" (Chapter 6). Discuss the ideal versus the real as a theme in modern culture.

25. Why would someone who looked like Lucy Grealy ("Autobiography of a Face" in Chapter 6) never be asked to appear on television (even if she were willing)? What are society's limits for freakishness, despite the spectacles on daytime TV talk shows (as discussed by Charles Oliver in "Freak Parade" in Chapter 7)? In your opinion, why are only certain forms of freakishness culturally sanctioned—and therefore marketable—whereas others are not?

26. The psychology of intolerance can express itself through the most basic senses of taste and smell. How do these senses operate in Constance Classen's analysis "The Odour of the Other" (Chapter 6) and in Octavio Paz's essay "Hygiene and Repression" (Chapter 2)? In an essay, compare and contrast the two approaches Classen and Paz take to the subject.

27. In what ways do Americans display the same kind of cultural imperialism toward Cuba (as discussed by Roberto Gonzalez Echevarria in "First Pitch," Chapter 8) that Western Europeans do toward the Balkans (as dramatized in Milorad Pavić's story "The Wedgwood Tea Set," Chapter 6)? Explain your answer in an essay.

CHAPTER 7

28. Both Elvis (see Greil Marcus's "Dead Elvis" in Chapter 7) and Joe Louis (see Maya Angelou's "Champion of the World" in Chapter 8) have be-

come icons because each changed the concept of what it means to be an American. In an essay, compare and contrast what these two men meant to their fans.

29. To what extent have commercialism and pandering to the audience, as discussed by Neil Postman and Steve Powers in "TV News as Entertainment" (Chapter 7), come to define the coverage of gymnasts and figure skaters at the Olympics, according to Joan Ryan in "Little Girls in Pretty Boxes" (Chapter 8)? Explain your answer in an essay.

30. In what way is the passivity that Jessica Hagedorn finds so objectionable in the film portrayal of Asian women ("Asian Women in Film: No Joy, No Luck" in Chapter 7) also a component of the female stereotype discussed by Brian Pronger in "Sexual Mythologies" (Chapter 4)? What insights do both authors provide into how gender roles perpetuate class inequities? Explain your answer in an essay.

31. R. K. Narayan's attitude toward the bastardization of his novel ("Misguided 'Guide'" in Chapter 7) is simultaneously funny and serious, as is Rabbi Susan Schnur's reaction to the usurpation of Yom Kippur services by Barbie ("Barbie Does Yom Kippur" in Chapter 9). In an essay, explore the theme of how popular culture displaces what is authentic that these two works share.

32. In an essay, analyze how John Cheever's story "The Enormous Radio" (Chapter 7) can be understood as a parable about the excesses of consumerism in ways that reflect Juliet B. Schor's observations in "The Culture of Consumerism" (Chapter 9)?

CHAPTER 8

33. After reading Carl Sagan's article "Game: The Prehistoric Origin of Sports" (Chapter 8) and Neil Postman and Steve Powers's "TV News as Entertainment" (Chapter 7), in an essay analyze the emotional connotations of the language (especially violent metaphors) used by any local or national sports commentator to report a sports event.

34. How do conflicting political ideologies redefine commonplace things such as sports and food in the essays by Roberto Gonzalez Echevarria ("First Pitch" in Chapter 8) and Slavenka Drakulić ("Pizza in Warsaw, Torte in Prague" in Chapter 2)? Explain your answer in an essay.

35. In what sense does the role of Joe Louis as a symbol of racial pride in the 1930s, as Maya Angelou describes him in "Champion of the World" in Chapter 8, illuminate the importance of the "cool pose," as discussed by Richard Majors and Janet Mancini Billson in Chapter 4? Explain your answer in an essay.

36. Deborah Tannen's concept of being "marked" (see "There Is No Unmarked Woman" in Chapter 3) provides an interesting approach to the racial predicament Arthur Ashe confronts in "The Burden of Race" (Chapter 8). In an essay, discuss how this concept operates in the arenas of race and gender.

37. To what extent does the iconography of the Barbie doll in Marge Piercy's poem in Chapter 4 support Joan Ryan's argument in "Little Girls in Pretty Boxes" (Chapter 8)? Explain your answer in an essay.

38. In an essay, compare and contrast the relationships between the mothers and daughters in Lin Sutherland's story "A River Ran over Me" (Chapter 8) and in Amy Tan's account "The Language of Discretion" (Chapter 5).

39. How have the realms of religion and business begun to overlap in contemporary U.S. culture, as described by Conrad P. Kottak in "Rituals at McDonald's" (Chapter 2) and by Rabbi Susan Schnur in "Barbie Does Yom Kippur" (Chapter 9)? Explain your answer in an essay.

40. In what ways do material possessions come to symbolize one's status in society, or lack thereof, in George Carlin's satire "A Place for Your Stuff" (Chapter 9) and in Milorad Pavić's story "The Wedgwood Tea Set (Chapter 6)? Explain your answer in an essay.

41. How does Terence McLaughlin's analysis of the meanings attributed to dirt in different societies (Chapter 9) offer insight into the way religions differentiate what is clean from what is unclean, as discussed by Dinitia Smith in "Did a Barnyard Schism Lead to a Religious One?" (Chapter 2)? Explain your answer in an essay.

42. In an essay, compare and contrast the symbolism of the Kelly bag as a sign of exclusivity (see Dodie Kazanjian's "The Kelly Bag as Icon" in Chapter 3) with the Japanese *okata*, as described by Edward T. Hall in "Hidden Culture" (Chapter 9).

43. What the French and Americans find unseemly about each other's culture (see "Sex, Money, and Success" by Raymonde Carroll in Chapter 9) overlaps Octavio Paz's critique of North Americans from the Mexican perspective (see "Hygiene and Repression" in Chapter 2). Write a synthesis essay in which you support or challenge Carroll's and Paz's claims. Be sure to include your own view in your essay.

44. Discuss the symbolic role food plays in the different societies described by David R. Counts ("Too Many Bananas" in Chapter 9) and Slavenka Drakulić ("Pizza in Warsaw, Torte in Prague" in Chapter 2).

Appendix: Documenting Sources in MLA Style

Students in the humanities (such as English and history) follow the guidelines published by the Modern Language Association (MLA) on how to document and punctuate quotations. Students in the social sciences (such as psychology and sociology) use the style manual of the American Psychological Association (APA), and those in the life sciences follow the style recommended by the Council of Science Editors (CSE). The format for the MLA style of citation, which is used in this book, is fully described in the *MLA Handbook for Writers of Research Papers*, 5th ed. (New York: Modern Language Association of America, 1999), and answers to frequently asked questions appear on the MLA Web site <http://www.mla.org>.

In essence, the MLA system of documentation has two complementary parts. Parenthetical in-text citations signal the source of a quotation, paraphrase, or summary in your paper. These in-text citations correspond to a list of works cited that appears at the end of the paper and provides full publication information.

IN-TEXT CITATIONS

If you identify the source of a quotation or a paraphrase in your text, you do not have to repeat the name in a parenthetical citation. Simply include the page number inside parentheses at the end of the quotation or paraphrase.

Source with One Author

Margaret Visser informs us that "left hands are very commonly disqualified from touching food at dinner" (4).

Source with Two or Three Authors

Social scientists who have investigated the reasons why African American males adopt the "cool pose" claim: "It enhances manhood, commands respect, vents bitterness and anger, establishes a sense of control, expresses artistry, accentuates the self, and provides a form of amusement" (Billson and Majors 9).

An Indirect Source

For novelist Stephanie Grant, her anorexia was about "living without longing of any kind" (qtd. in Bordo 112).

LIST OF WORKS CITED

At the end of your paper, on a separate page, include all sources quoted, paraphrased, or summarized in your paper. Begin each entry on a separate line. Alphabetize the list by the author's last name, and provide full publishing information. Don't forget to indicate the date you accessed any online sources. If the entry uses more than one line, indent all subsequent lines 1/2 inch from the left margin. Double-space all lines.

Book by One Author

Visser, Margaret. <u>The Rituals of Dinner</u>. New York: Penguin, 1991.

Book by Two or More Authors

Billson, Janet Mancini, and Richard Majors. <u>Cool Pose: The Dilemmas of Black Manhood in America</u>. New York: Lexington Books, 1992.

Note that only the first author's name is reversed.

Work in an Anthology

Dalby, Liza. "Kimono." <u>Every Day, Everywhere: Global Perspectives on Popular Culture</u>. Ed. Stuart Hirschberg and Terry Hirschberg. San Francisco, CA: McGraw-Hill 2002.

Article in a Weekly Magazine

Sagan, Carl. "Game: The Prehistoric Origin of Sports." <u>Parade</u> 13 Sept. 1987: 22–26.

Article in a Monthly Magazine

Dirie, Waris. "The Tragedy of Female Circumcision." <u>Marie Claire</u> Mar. 1996: 64+.

A plus sign shows that the article is not printed on consecutive pages; if it were, a page range would be given: 64–70, for example.

Article in a Journal

Mellix, Barbara. "From Outside, In." <u>Georgia Review</u> 41 (1987): 128–39.

Film or Videotape

<u>Rumble in the Bronx</u>. Dir. Stanley Tong. Perf. Jackie Chan, Anita Mui, Francoise Yip. New Line Cinema, 1995.

If the work of a particular person is the reason for the entry, it can start with the person's name, as do entries for print sources.

Television Program

<u>3rd Rock from the Sun</u>. Perf. John Lithgow. NBC, New York. 22 June 2000.

Personal Interview

Radziewicz, Josie Mendez. Personal interview. 17 Mar. 2000.

Electronic Sources

Web source documentation contains the same information as that for traditional print sources, such as author, title of document, and date of publication. However, entries for electronic sources also need to include the date of access and the URL enclosed in angle brackets < >. (If a URL will not fit on one line, break it only after a slash or a period.) Below are guidelines for documenting some kinds of electronic sources: you can find suggestions for other sources on the MLA Web site <http://www.mla.org>.

E-mail
Pepin, Jacques. "Lemon Cake." E-mail to the author. 2 Dec. 2000.

Article in an Online Reference Book
"Barthes, Roland." Encyclopaedia Britannica Online. Vers. 99.1. 1994–2000. Encyclopaedia Britannica. 19 June 2000 <http://search.eb.com/bol/ topic?eu=13685&sctn=1&pm=1>.

Article in an Online Journal
Caesar, Terry. "In and Out of Elevators in Japan." Journal of Mundane Behavior 1.1 (2000): 6 pars. 12 Mar. 2000 <http://www. mundanebehavior.org/issues/v1n1/caesar.htm>.

If the pages or paragraphs are numbered, include that information. The abbreviation for *pages* is *pp.*, and the abbreviation for *paragraphs* is *pars.*

Article in an Online Magazine
Ollivier, Debra S. "Mothers Who Think: Les birds et les bees." Salon 12 May 1998. 19 June 2000 <http://www.salon.com/mwt/feature/1998/05/ 12feature2.html>.

Web Site
EyeWire Studios. Home page. Apr. 1999. 19 Aug. 1999 <http://www.eyewire.com>.

Glossary

agenda A prioritized plan or outline for action; an underlying plan or program that has an ideological intent, as in "the writer's agenda."

allusion In a literary work, a brief reference to a real or fictional person, place, thing, or event that the writer expects the reader to recognize.

analogy The likening of one thing to another based on similarities between certain of their observable features, despite obvious differences between the things; assumes that the things share unobservable qualities as well.

archetype A theme, image, universal character type (such as the hero), or narrative pattern (such as the quest) found in literature, mythology, and popular culture that embodies recurrent features of the human experience; a perfect example.

argument The process of reasoning and providing evidence about controversial issues; a statement or fact presented in support of a point.

assumption An idea or belief that is taken for granted.

attitude A writer's emotional stance toward a subject.

audience The group of spectators, listeners, viewers, or readers that a performance or written work reaches.

bias A preconceived, unsubstantiated, and generally negative outlook or opinion about a person or group.

causal analysis A method of analysis that seeks to discover why something happened or will happen.

characterization The writer's creation and revelation of a fictional personality through descriptions of the character's appearance, actions, thoughts, and feelings.

class Persons or things grouped together because of their common attributes, characteristics, qualities, or traits. People who are at the same economic level, or social class (working class, middle class, upper class), often share similar political viewpoints and social values.

classification/division A method of sorting, grouping, collecting, and analyzing things by categories based on features shared by all members of a class or group. Division involves breaking down a whole into separate parts or sorting a group of items into nonoverlapping categories.

cliché A timeworn expression that has, through overuse, lost its power to evoke concrete images. Examples include "gentle as a lamb," "smart as a whip," "hard as nails," and "pleased as punch."

code A system of signs that represent specific meanings. To decode the meaning of a sign is to discover what it means within the system to which it belongs.

community A social group whose members share common characteristics (they live in a specific area) or interests.

comparison/contrast A rhetorical technique for pointing out similarities or differences; writers may use a point-by-point or a subject-by-subject approach.

connotation The associative meanings of a word as distinct from its explicit or primary meaning, its **denotation**; the emotional overtones of a word or phrase. The word *fireplace*, for example, might connote feelings of warmth, hospitality, and comfort, whereas it denotes the portion of a chimney in which fuel is burned.

consumer culture A society that uses more goods and services than it produces; one that links its members' self-worth to their ability to consume products and services.

context The set of circumstances that surrounds an event or a situation; in the field of **semiotics**, the total environment within which a sign is interpreted.

cross-cultural analysis Comparison of one society's ways of living, which its people have evolved over time and transmitted from one generation to the next, with those of other societies.

cultural sign Any significant cultural feature whose meaning has been assigned by the culture's inhabitants.

cultural studies An academic discipline that investigates how the meanings or connotations of ordinary phenomena in everyday life were constructed.

culture The entire way of life (all the practices and institutions) developed, preserved, and transmitted by a given group of people; also, the repository of knowledge that current members of a group pass among themselves and to future generations. A society can include numerous cultures. A **multicultural** society incorporates cultures having diverse ethnic, racial, and religious identifications and viewpoints.

definition Specification of the basic nature of a phenomenon, idea, or thing. A dictionary definition places the subject being defined in the class to which it belongs and identifies features that differentiate it from other things in its class.

denotation The explicit, primary, or literal meaning of a word, as distinct from its associative meanings, or **connotations.**

description Writing that reports how a person, place, or thing is perceived by the senses. *Objective* description recreates the appearance of objects, events, scenes, or people. *Subjective* description emphasizes the writer's feelings and reactions to a subject.

dialogue A conversation between two or more persons or between characters in a literary work.

discourse The conventions governing an exchange of ideas within an academic or professional field of study (such as law, theater arts, or medicine).

dominant culture Within a society, the majority group whose values, beliefs, and viewpoints are considered to represent those of the larger society and are seen as "natural" and "correct"; also called the mainstream culture.

dominant ideology The belief system of the dominant culture (group in power) in a society; the language and ideas that represent this group's way of seeing, interpreting, and controlling what happens in the society and that are used in intellectual discussions within the society.

doublespeak Language used to distort and manipulate rather than to communicate.

ethnocentrism Belief in the inherent superiority of one's own group and culture.

ethos The moral element on which an argument can be based.

euphemism An inoffensive, indirect, or agreeable expression used instead of a word or phrase perceived as socially unacceptable or unnecessarily harsh—for example, "private parts" for sex organs, "disadvantaged" for poor, "full-figured" for fat. From the Greek word meaning "to speak well of."

Eurocentrism A world view that holds the values, traditions, and beliefs of European culture to be the norm (and superior to others).

evidence Support for a claim; includes expert testimony, statistics, cases (real, hypothetical, or analogical), and facts.

examples Specific incidents that illustrate, document, or substantiate a writer's **thesis**.

exemplification *See* **illustration.**

fad *See* **trend.**

figurative language Language characterized by use of such figures of speech as hyperbole, **irony, metaphor,** personification, and **simile;** language that creates effective images by going beyond literal meanings to suggest fresh associations and comparisons.

gender Society's ideas of what it means to be male or female, of the appropriate roles for each sex to play. It is distinguished from sex, the biological fact of being male or female.

genre A specific type of literary work—essay, short story, novel, poem, or play—that has defined characteristics of form, technique, or content.

high culture   The most valued artistic and intellectual accomplishments of a people: classical music, fine arts, drama, opera, literature, sculpture, and painting. Generally attracts a limited audience.

icon   An image within a culture that is widely recognizable—as, for example, Michael Jordan is within professional sports and as Mercedes is as an icon of wealth and prestige.

ideology   A society's underlying values, beliefs, and interests, which shape its actions and interpretations in accordance with a preset agenda.

illustration (exemplification)   Use of one or more examples to explain, elucidate, or corroborate.

image   How one chooses to project oneself to others, through behavior, speech, clothing, and other body accoutrements. Body piercings and tattoos, for example, convey an image whose meaning others are intended to decode, or **read.**

irony   The use of words to convey a meaning different from—and usually opposite to—their actual meaning.

jargon   A specialized language used by people in the same profession or social group as a shorthand means of communication.

logos   Rational principles on which an argument can be based.

marked   A term adapted from linguistics that indicates the extent to which everything about someone's appearance and behavior is socially construed to convey information.

mass media   All forms of communication, including newspapers, magazines, radio, television, film, and the Internet, that serve as a vehicle for disseminating information and entertainment within a culture.

metaphor   A figure of speech that likens two fundamentally different things by ascribing the qualities of one to the other and by linking different meanings (such as abstract and concrete, literal and figurative) without the use of the words *like* or *as*—for example, "couch potato" as a metaphor for someone who spends lots of time watching television.

multiculturalism   Acceptance by the mainstream, or dominant, culture in a society of the ethnic, racial, and religious identifications and viewpoints of diverse subcultures. In American education, recognition and acknowledgment of the contributions of non-European cultures within what was previously a Eurocentric curriculum.

myth   An assumption, belief, or value within a culture's larger view of the world. A social construct that is meaningful only within a given society.

mythology   The assumptions, beliefs, and values that comprise a specific culture's view of the world.

narration A true or made-up story that relates events and/or experiences. Narrations tell what happened, when it happened, and to whom; relate events from a consistent point of view; organize a story with a clear beginning, middle, and end; and use events and incidents to dramatize important moments in the action.

natural signs vs. social signs Signs that occur naturally (such as animal cries) compared with signs designed for communication within cultures (such as human speech).

norm A concept that began in the nineteenth century with the application of the Bell curve dictating statistical distribution. In some cultures, deviations from the norm are considered abnormal and are seen as **the other.**

objectivity A point of view in which a writer emphasizes independently observable characteristics of objects, people, events, or scenes. Compare **subjectivity.**

occasion The specific set of circumstances the writer must consider when creating a piece—for example, whether the product is to be a dinner speech at a local fundraiser, a journal article for an academic audience, or a fictional short story for a literary magazine.

other, the In societies in which the concept of the **norm** is operative, those whose characteristics deviate from that norm—for example, those with disabilities.

pathos Expressive elements, capable of swaying an audience, on which an argument can be based.

persona Literally, "actor's mask;" the way in which the writer chooses to project himself or herself as the narrator.

persuasion Convincing another to accept a claim through the combined effects of ethos (the audience's confidence in the speaker's character), logos (appeals to reason), and pathos (the audience's emotional needs and values).

point of view The writer's (narrator's) relationship to the events he or she describes in an essay or a story. A writer can relate a story using the first-person (I) or the third-person (he, she, they) point of view.

popular culture Those aspects of a culture—chiefly, the artifacts and icons displayed in its forms of entertainment, consumer goods, and means of communication—that have mass appeal.

post-modernism A movement underlying contemporary music, art, literature, architecture, and philosophy that emphasizes the audience's interaction with the material and role as cultural mediator of norms and values.

propaganda Information or ideas spread methodically to promote or harm a cause, person, group, or nation.

protagonist The main character in a literary work.

purpose The writer's objective; also, the goals of the four types of prose writing: narration (to tell or relate), description (to represent or delineate), exposition (to explain or clarify), and argument (to persuade).

racist language Discriminatory labeling that stigmatizes a race or an ethnic group.

read In the language of **semiotics,** to decipher the latent social meanings governing the way people dress, what they eat, how they socialize and speak, and other cultural phenomena.

rhetorical situation The context in and for which a writer creates a piece; the author's purpose for writing in relation to the audience, the occasion, and the topic.

satire Use of irony, wit, and exaggeration to ridicule people and social institutions.

semiotics The study of linguistic, cultural, and behavioral sign systems.

sign A word, object, image, form of behavior, or anything whose meaning is conditioned by and can be interpreted according to an underlying code. For example, within the system of medical symptoms, the classical sign of fever is a flushed countenance. *See also* **code, system.**

signifier/signified According to the linguist Ferdinand de Saussure, a linguistic sign is made up of a signifier (the sound of the word and its appearance when written—i.e., the word *cat*) and the signified (the mental concept of "catness" that the word *cat* evokes). The signifier and the signified are inseparable, but their connection is also arbitrary: the signifier *chat* (French), *schatz* (German), and *cat* (English) all indicate "catness."

simile A figure of speech that makes a direct comparison between two unlike things using the word *like* or *as*—for example, "Passengers were crammed into the train like sardines in a can." Compare **metaphor.**

society Human beings collectively; a structured system of human organization for large-scale community living that normally furnishes continuity, security, and a group identity.

speaker The voice the reader hears in a poem, story, or novel that relates events from a consistent point of view.

stereotype An oversimplified view, often pejorative, held by one group about another group or its members.

subculture A group that has distinctive economic, ethnic, or other traits that distinguish it from the dominant group (dominant or mainstream culture) within a society.

subjectivity A point of view in which a writer communicates personal feelings about scenes, objects, or events and encourages readers to empathize with the expressed feelings.

symbol Something concrete (like an object, person, place, or event) that stands for or represents something abstract (like an idea, quality, concept, or condition). For example, the staff (caduceus) carried by Mercury, the messenger of the Roman gods, is the universal symbol of the medical profession.

symbolic sign vs. iconic sign A symbolic sign relates to its object through convention alone (i.e., the word *flag* is arbitrarily assigned to a cloth of specific colors), whereas an iconic sign resembles the object it represents (i.e., a photograph of a pear resembles the real fruit).

system The larger context in which a sign functions and is imbued with meaning. Fashion is a sign system, with its own codes, conventions, and taboos.

taboo A act or item a society forbids its members to engage in or use, to distinguish itself from other cultures; a socially constructed concept. For example, the Islamic ban on alcohol distinguishes followers of Mohammed from members of other religions; Jewish dietary (kosher) laws include taboos on pork, shellfish, and mixing meat and dairy.

text In **semiotics,** any network of signs that can be interpreted ("**read**"), whether communicated through language, pictures, behavior, music, architecture, cuisine, or fashion, among other modes.

theme An important underlying idea, either stated or implied, in fiction or nonfiction writing.

thesis The position the writer develops or supports (often expressed in a single sentence) in his or her piece.

tone The writer's attitude toward the subject, expressed in style and word choice; the voice the writer chooses to project—for example, serious, lighthearted, concerned—to relate to readers.

topic The subject a writer addresses, as distinct from the writer's **thesis** (opinion) about the subject.

transition A signal word or phrase that connects two sentences, paragraphs, or sections of an essay to produce coherence. Can include pronoun references, parallel clauses, conjunctions, restatements of key ideas, and expressions such as "furthermore," "moreover," "by contrast," "therefore," "consequently," "accordingly," and "thus."

trend (fad) A temporary fashion or manner of conduct that is embraced enthusiastically by a culture but that has little staying power. Compare **icon.**

values Moral or ethical principles or beliefs that express standards or criteria for judging actions right or wrong, good or bad, acceptable or unacceptable, appropriate or unseemly.

virtual reality A simulated but almost lifelike environment generated by a computer.

voice The distinctive qualities that define the speaker in a literary work (usually a poem).

Rhetorical Contents

Contents by Academic Discipline

SEMIOTIC ANALYSIS/CULTURAL STUDIES

SOCIOLOGY/ANTHROPOLOGY

WOMEN'S STUDIES

Acknowledgments

TEXT CREDITS

DIANE ACKERMAN, "The Social Sense," from *A Natural History of the Senses* by Diane Ackerman. Copyright © 1990 by Diane Ackerman. Reprinted by permission of Random House, Inc.

JOHN AGARD, "Listen mr oxford don," from *Mangoes and Bullets* by John Agard, Pluto Press, 1985. By kind permission of John Agard, c/o Caroline Sheldon Literary Agency.

MAYA ANGELOU, *Champion of the World*. Copyright © 1997 by Maya Angelou. Reprinted by permission of Random House, Inc.

ARTHUR ASHE AND ARNOLD RAMPERSAD, "The Burden of Race," from *Days of Grace*. Copyright © 1993 by Jeanne Moutoussamy-Ashe and Arnold Rampersad. Reprinted by permission of Alfred A. Knopf, a division of Random House, Inc.

PAUL BARBER, "The Real Vampire." With permission from *Natural History*, October 1990. Copyright © 1990 the American Museum of Natural History.

SUSAN BORDO, "Never Just Pictures," from *Twilight Zones: The Hidden Life of Cultural Images from Plato to O.J.* by Susan Bordo. Copyright © 1997 The Regents of the University of California. Reprinted by permission.

BILL BRYSON, "The Hard Sell: Advertising in America" and "What's Cooking? Eating in America," from *Made in America* by Bill Bryson. Copyright © 1995 by Bill Bryson. Reprinted by permission of HarperCollins Publishers, Inc.

ANTHONY BURGESS, from *A Clockwork Orange*. Copyright © 1962, 1989, renewed 1990 by Anthony Burgess. Used by permission of W. W. Norton & Company, Inc.

GUANLONG CAO, "Chopsticks," from *The Attic: A Memoir of a Chinese Boyhood* by Guanlong Cao. Copyright © 1996 The Regents of the University of California. Reprinted by permission.

GEORGE CARLIN, "A Place for Your Stuff," from *Brain Droppings* by George Carlin. Copyright © 1997 by Comedy Concepts, Inc. Reprinted by permission of Hyperion.

RAYMONDE CARROLL, "Sex, Money, and Success," from *Cultural Misunderstandings: The French-American Experience* by Raymonde Carroll, The University of Chicago

Press, 1988. Copyright © 1988 The University of Chicago Press. Reprinted by permission.

JACKIE CHAN, "A Dirty Job," from *I Am Jackie Chan.* Copyright © 1998 by Ballantine Publishing Group, a division of Random House, Inc. Reprinted by permission of the publisher.

GARY CHAPMAN, "Flamers: Cranks, Fetishists, and Monomaniacs," from *The New Republic*, 212, No. 15, April 10, 1995. Copyright © 1995 The New Republic, Inc. Reprinted by permission of The New Republic.

JOHN CHEEVER, "The Enormous Radio," from *The Stories of John Cheever.* Copyright © 1947 by John Cheever. Reprinted by permission of Alfred A. Knopf, a division of Random House, Inc.

FARID CHENOUNE, "Jeans and Black Leather: Gangs Don a Second Skin," from *A History of Men's Fashion*, translated by Deke Dusinberre. Paris: Flammarion. Reprinted by permission of Flammarion, BNP Paris St Germain des Pres: No. Flammarion 00027504043, Cele RFB 20.

CONSTANCE CLASSEN, "The Odour of the Other," from *Worlds of Sense* by Constance Classen. Reprinted by permission of Routledge, U.K.

JUDITH ORTIZ COFER, "The Myth of the Latin Woman: I Just Met a Girl Named María," from *The Latin Deli: Prose and Poetry* by Judith Ortiz Cofer, University of Georgia Press, 1993. Reprinted by permission of the publisher.

DAVID COUNTS, "Too Many Bananas, Not Enough Pineapples, and No Watermelon at All: Three Object Lessons in Living with Reciprocity," from *The Humbled Anthropologist: Tales from the Pacific*, Philip R. deVita, ed., Wadsworth, 1990, pp. 18–24. Reprinted with permission from the author.

LIZA DALBY, "Kimono," from *Geisha*, University of California Press, 1988, pp. 281–90. Copyright © 1983, 1998. Liza Dalby. Reprinted by permission.

LENNARD J. DAVIS, "Visualizing the Disabled Body," from *Enforcing Normalcy* by Lennard J. Davis, W. W. Norton, 1995. Reprinted by permission from Verso.

GINO DEL GUERCIO, "The Secrets of Haiti's Living Dead," *Harvard Magazine* (January/February 1986). Courtesy of Gino Del Guercio.

BONNIE DE SIMONE, "Mia Hamm: Grateful for Her Gifts," from *Women's Soccer, the Game and the World Cup.* Reprinted by permission of the author.

WARIS DIRIE AND LAURA ZIV, "The Tragedy of Female Circumcision," from *Marie Claire*, March 1996. Reprinted with permission from the publisher.

CHITRA DIVAKARUNI, "Clothes," from *Arranged Marriage* by Chitra Divakaruni. Copyright © 1995 by Chitra Divakaruni. Used by permission of Doubleday, a division of Random House, Inc.

SLAVENKA DRAKULIĆ, "Pizza in Warsaw, Torte in Prague," from *How We Survived Communism and Even Laughed* by Slavenka Drakulić. Copyright © 1991 by Slavenka Drakulić. Used by permission of W. W. Norton & Company, Inc.

UMBERTO ECO, "How Not to Use the Fax Machine" and "How Not to Use the Cellular Phone," from *How to Travel with a Salmon and Other Essays* by Umberto Eco. Copyright © Gruppo Editoriale Fabbri, Bompiani, Sonzogno, etas S.p.A., English translation by William Weaver, copyright © 1994 by Harcourt, Inc. Reprinted by permission of Harcourt, Inc.

ELIZABETH FERNEA AND ROBERT FERNEA, "A Look behind the Veil," in *Human Nature Magazine*, Volume 2, Number 1. Copyright © 1979 by Human Nature, Inc. Reprinted by permission of the publisher.

ANNE TAYLOR FLEMING, "Sperm in a Jar," *The New York Times Magazine*, June 12, 1994. Reprinted with permission from the author.

CLIFFORD GEERTZ, "Deep Play: Notes on the Balinese Cockfight," from *Myth, Symbol, and Culture* by Clifford Geertz. Copyright © 1971 by the American Academy of Arts and Sciences. Used by permission of W. W. Norton & Company, Inc.

ROBERTO GONZALEZ ECHEVARRIA, "First Pitch," from *Pride of Havana: A History of Cuban Baseball.* Copyright © 1999 by Roberto Gonzalez Echevarria. Used by permission of Oxford University Press, Inc.

TEMPLE GRANDIN, *Thinking in Pictures.* Copyright © 1995 by Temple Grandin. Used by permission of Doubleday, a division of Random House, Inc.

LUCY GREALY, *Autobiography of a Face.* Copyright © 1994 by Lucy Grealy. Reprinted by permission of Houghton Mifflin Co. All rights reserved.

GERMAINE GREER, "One Man's Mutilation Is Another Man's Beautification," from *The Madwoman's Underclothes* by Germaine Greer. Copyright © 1986 by Germaine Greer. Reprinted by permission of Grove/Atlantic, Inc.

JESSICA HAGEDORN, "Asian Women in Film: No Joy, No Luck," in *Ms.*, January/February 1994. Reprinted with permission from Harold Schmidt Literary Agency.

EDWARD T. HALL, "Hidden Culture," from *Beyond Culture* by Edward T. Hall. Copyright © 1976, 1981 by Edward T. Hall. Used by permission of Doubleday, a division of Random House, Inc.

GARRETT HONGO, "Who among You Knows the Essence of Garlic?" from *Yellow Light* by Garrett Hongo, Wesleyan University Press, 1982. Reprinted with permission from the publisher.

DODIE KAZANJIAN, "The Kelly Bag as Icon," from *Icons: The Absolute of Style* by Dodie Kazanjian, pp. 26–30. Copyright © 1995 by Dodie Kazanjian. Reprinted by permission of St. Martin's Press, LLC.

GINA KOLATA, "A Clone Is Born," from *Clone*, HarperCollins, 1998, pp. 1–21. Copyright © 1998 by Gina Kolata. Reprinted by permission of HarperCollins Publishers, Inc.

CONRAD P. KOTTAK, "Rituals at McDonald's," with permission from *Natural History*, January 1978. Copyright © 1978 the American Museum of Natural History.

SANDRA TSING LOH, "The Return of Doris Day," in *Buzz*, September 1995. Copyright © 1995 by Sandra Tsing Loh. Reprinted by permission of International Creative Management, Inc.

ALISON LURIE, *The Language of Clothes.* Copyright © 1981 by Alison Lurie. Reprinted by permission of Melanie Jackson Agency, L.L.C.

RICHARD MAJORS AND JANET MANCINI BILLSON, "Cool Pose," from *Cool Pose: The Dilemmas of Black Manhood.* Copyright © 1992 Lexington Books. Reprinted by permission of Jossey-Bass, Inc., a subsidiary of John Wiley & Sons, Inc.

GREIL MARCUS, "1981: Elvis: The Ashtray," from *Dead Elvis*, Harvard University Press, 1991. Copyright © 1991 by Greil Marcus. Reprinted by permission of The Wendy Weil Agency, Inc.

WILLIAM MAXWELL, "The Pilgrimage," from *Over the River and Other Stories* by William Maxwell. Copyright © 1953 by William Maxwell. Reprinted by permission of Alfred A. Knopf, a division of Random House, Inc.

TERENCE MCLAUGHLIN, *Dirt: A Social History as Seen through the Uses and Abuses of Dirt*, Stein and Day, 1971.

BARBARA MELLIX, "From Outside, In" originally appeared in *The Georgia Review*, Volume XLI, No. 2 (Summer 1987). Copyright © 1987 by The University of Georgia/

© 1987 by Barbara Mellix. Reprinted by permission of Barbara Mellix and *The Georgia Review*.

FATIMA MERNISSI, "The French Harem," from *Dreams of Trespass: Tales of a Harem Girlhood* by Fatima Mernissi. Copyright © 1994 by Fatima Mernissi. Reprinted by permission of Perseus Books Publishers, a member of Perseus Books, L.L.C.

PAUL MONETTE, "Borrowed Time," from *Borrowed Time: An AIDS Memoir*. Copyright © 1988 by Paul Monette. Reprinted by permission of Harcourt, Inc.

ALBERTO MORAVIA, "Gioielli" ("Jewellery"), from *Racconti Romani (Roman Tales)* by Alberto Moravia, translated by Angus Davidson. Copyright © 1954 R.C.S. Libri SpA–Milano Bompiani. Reprinted with permission.

KYOKO MORI, *Polite Lies: On Being a Woman Caught between Cultures*. Copyright © 1997 by Kyoko Mori. Reprinted by permission of Henry Holt and Company, L.L.C.

R. K. NARAYAN, "Misguided 'Guide,'" from *A Writer's Nightmare: Selected Essays 1958–88* by R. K. Narayan.

JESSE W. NASH, "Confucius and the VCR," with permission from *Natural History*, May 1988. Copyright © 1988 the American Museum of Natural History.

JOYCE CAROL OATES, *On Boxing*. Copyright © 1994 by Ontario Review, Inc. Reprinted with permission of John Hawkins & Associates, Inc.

CHARLES OLIVER, "Freak Parade," reprinted with permission from the April 1995 issue of *Reason Magazine*. Copyright © 1998 by the Reason Foundation, 3415 S. Sepulveda Blvd., Suite 400, Los Angeles, CA 90034. <www.reason.com>.

GARETH PALMER, "Bruce Springsteen and Masculinity," from *Sexing the Groove*, Sheila Whiteley, ed., Routledge, U.K., 1997. Reprinted by permission of the publisher.

MILORAD PAVIĆ, "The Wedgwood Tea Set," translated by Darka Topali, from *The Prince of Fire: An Anthology of Contemporary Serbian Short Stories*, Radmila J. Gorup and Nadezda Obradovic, eds. Reprinted by permission of the University of Pittsburgh Press.

OCTAVIO PAZ, "Hygiene and Repression," from "At Table and in Bed" in *Convergences, Essays on Art and Literature* by Octavio Paz. Copyright © 1973 by Editorial Joaquin Moritz, S. A., copyright © 1984, 1983, 1979 by Editorial Siex Barral, S. A., copyright © 1984, 1983, 1979 by Octavio Paz; English translation by Helen Lange, copyright © 1987 by Harcourt, Inc. Reprinted by permission of Harcourt, Inc.

MARGE PIERCY, "Barbie Doll," from *Circles on the Water* by Marge Piercy. Copyright © 1982 by Marge Piercy. Reprinted by permission of Alfred A. Knopf, a division of Random House, Inc.

NEIL POSTMAN AND STEVE POWERS, "TV News as Entertainment," from *How to Watch TV News* by Neil Postman and Steve Powers. Copyright © 1992 by Neil Postman and Steve Powers. Used by permission of Viking Penguin, a division of Penguin Putnam, Inc.

BRIAN PRONGER, "Sexual Mythologies," from *The Arena of Masculinity: Sports, Homosexuality, and the Meaning of Sex* by Brian Pronger. Copyright © 1990 by Brian Pronger. Reprinted by permission of St. Martin's Press.

MONIQUE PROULX, "Sans Coeur et Sans Reproche" ("Feint of Heart"), translation by Sheila Fischman, from *Intimate Strangers*, originally published in *Sans Coeur et Sans Reproche* (Montreal, Quebec/Amerique, 1983). Reprinted with permission from the author.

BERNARD RUDOFSKY, *The Unfashionable Human Body*. Copyright © 1971 by Bernard Rudofsky. Used by permission of Doubleday, a division of Random House, Inc.

JOAN RYAN, *Little Girls in Pretty Boxes* by Joan Ryan. Copyright © 1995 by Joan Ryan. Used by permission of Doubleday, a division of Random House, Inc.

CARL SAGAN, "Game: The Prehistoric Origin of Sports," *Parade Magazine*, September 13, 1987. Copyright © 1987 by Carl Sagan, copyright © 1996 by the Estate of Carl Sagan. Originally published in *Parade Magazine*.

LUC SANTE, "Lingua Franca," from *The Anchor Essay Annual: Best of 1998*, edited by Phillip Lopate, Anchor/Doubleday, 1998. Copyright © 1997 Luc Sante. Reprinted with permission from the Joy Harris Literary Agency.

RABBI SUSAN SCHNUR, "Barbie Does Yom Kippur," from *The Barbie Chronicles: A Living Doll Turns Forty*, Yona Zeldis McDonough, ed., Touchstone, 1999, pp. 145–51. Reprinted with permission from the author.

JULIET B. SCHOR, "The Culture of Consumerism," from *The Overspent American* by Juliet B. Schor. Copyright © 1998 by Juliet B. Schor. Reprinted by permission of Basic Books, a member of Perseus Books, L.L.C.

RICHARD KELLER SIMON, "The Shopping Mall and the Formal Garden," from *Trash Culture: Popular Culture and the Great Tradition* by Richard Keller Simon. Copyright © 1999 The Regents of the University of California. Reprinted by permission.

DINITIA SMITH, "Did a Barnyard Schism Lead to a Religious One?" *The New York Times*, March 14, 1998. Copyright © 1998 by the New York Times Co. Reprinted by permission.

BRUCE SPRINGSTEEN, "Streets of Philadelphia," copyright © 1993 by Bruce Springsteen (ASCAP). Reprinted by permission. Excerpts from "Thunder Road," copyright © 1975 by Bruce Springsteen (ASCAP). Reprinted by permission. Excerpts from "Walk Like A Man," copyright © 1987 by Bruce Springsteen (ASCAP). Reprinted by permission. Excerpts from "Adam Raised a Cain," copyright © 1978 by Bruce Springsteen (ASCAP). Reprinted by permission. Excerpts from "Independence Day," copyright © 1980 by Bruce Springsteen (ASCAP). Reprinted by permission. Excerpts from "Living Proof," copyright © 1992 by Bruce Springsteen (ASCAP). Reprinted by permission. Excerpts from "Cautious Man," copyright © 1987 by Bruce Springsteen (ASCAP). Reprinted by permission. Excerpts from "Brilliant Disguise," copyright © 1987 by Bruce Springsteen (ASCAP). Reprinted by permission. Excerpts from "Candy's Room," copyright © 1978 by Bruce Springsteen (ASCAP). Reprinted by permission. Excerpts from "Tunnel of Love," copyright © 1987 by Bruce Springsteen (ASCAP). Reprinted by permission. Excerpts from "Darkness on the Edge of Town," copyright © 1978 by Bruce Springsteen (ASCAP). Reprinted by permission. Excerpts from "Man's Job," copyright © 1992 by Bruce Springsteen (ASCAP). Reprinted by permission.

VALERIE STEELE AND JOHN S. MAJOR, *China Chic: East Meets West*, Yale University Press, 1999, pp. 37–44. Copyright © 1999 by Yale University Press. Reprinted by permission.

LIN SUTHERLAND, "A River Ran over Me," from *A Different Angle: Fly Fishing Stories by Women*, Holly Morris, ed. Copyright © 1995 Lin Sutherland. Reprinted by permission of Seal Press.

AMY TAN, "The Language of Discretion," from *The State of Language*, edited by C. Ricks and L. Michaels, University of California Press, 1990, pp. 25–32. Copyright © 1990 by Amy Tan. Reprinted by permission of Amy Tan and the Sandra Dijkstra Literary Agency.

DEBORAH TANNEN, "There Is No Unmarked Woman," *The New York Times Magazine*, June 20, 1993. Copyright © 1993 Deborah Tannen. Reprinted by permission of the author. This article was originally titled "Marked Women, Unmarked Men."

LUIS ALBERTO URREA, "Nobody's Son," from *Across the Wire: Life and Hard Times on the Mexican Border* by Luis Alberto Urrea. Copyright © 1993 by Luis Alberto Urrea.

MARGARET VISSER, "Fingers," from *The Rituals of Dinner* by Margaret Visser, Harper Perennial Canada, HarperCollins Publishers, Ltd. Reprinted with permission from the publisher.

PHOTO CREDITS

Chapter 1 P. 52, "Repelling Water," L. L. Bean, Inc., Spring 2001; p. 53, courtesy Toyota and Saatchi & Saatchi. **Chapter 2** P. 71, © Dick Luria; p. 80, © Bettmann/Corbis; p. 81, © Richard T. Nowitz/Corbis; pp. 94T, © Alán Gallegos/AG Photograph; p. 94B, © Timepix; p. 96, © Gerd Ludwig; pp. 138, 139, from *Last Dinner on the Titanic: Menus & Recipes from the Legendary Liner*, ed. Dana McCauley, Rick Archbold, Walter Lord, © 1997 Hyperion; p. 140, © Lake County Museum/Corbis. **Chapter 3** P. 176T, © Lonny Kalfus/International Stock Photography; p. 176B, © Jeffrey Aaronson/Network Aspen; p. 199, © Herman LeRoy Emmet/True Blue Pictures; p. 217, © Jeremy Horner/Corbis. **Chapter 4** P. 248, © Mitchell Gerber/Corbis; p. 258, © Neal Preston/Corbis. **Chapter 5** P. 364, © Alan Wnuk, Novato, CA; p. 365, © Neil Farrin. **Chapter 6** P. 404, © CBS Photo Archive; p. 448, courtesy Adirondack Museum, Blue Mountain Lake, NY; photo by James Swedeberg Photography; p. 449B, courtesy the artist and Metro Pictures. **Chapter 7** P. 465, courtesy Mobilization.com; p. 473, © Bettmann/Corbis; p. 474TL, © Neal Preston/Corbis; p. 474TM, © Reuters/Remy LeMorvan/Hulton/Archive/Liaison Agency, Inc.; p. 474TR, © Neal Preston/Corbis; p. 474BL, © Neal Preston/Corbis; p. 474BM, © Neal Preston/Corbis; p. 474BR, © Neal Preston/Corbis; p. 482, © Reuters NewMedia, Inc./Corbis; p. 483, © AFP/Corbis; p. 525, courtesy Colin Geddes; p. 534, © 2000 Cooking Light® Magazine, dancers © Steven Freeman, background © Chuck Pefley/Stone. **Chapter 8** P. 597, © Richard Hamilton Smith/Corbis; p. 598, © AFP/Corbis; p. 599, © Reuters NewMedia Inc./Corbis. **Chapter 9** P. 617, © Peter Menzel/Material World; p. 652, © Peter Krogh; p. 659TL, © Joanna Pinneo/Material World; p. 659TR, © Maggie Steber/Material World; p. 659MR, © Melissa Farlow/Material World; p. 659BL, © Melissa Farlow/Material World; p. 659BR, © Lori Grinker/Material World; p. 660TL, © Annie Griffiths Belt/Material World; p. 660TR, © Lynn Johnson/Material World; p. 660ML, © Karen Kasmauski/Material World; p. 660MR, © Stephanie Maze/Material World; p. 660BL, © Lynn Johnson/Material World; p. 660BR, © Lynn Johnson/Material World.

Index of Authors and Titles